THE JEWISH PEOPLE

AN ILLUSTRATED HISTORY

Yohanan Aharoni
Michael Avi-Yonah • Shmuel Safrai
Anson F. Rainey • Ze'ev Safrai
Haim Beinart • Evyatar Friesel
Sergio Dellapergola

Edited by Shmuel Ahituv

continuum

NEW YORK • LONDON

2006

The Continuum International Publishing Group Inc
80 Maiden Lane, New York, NY 10038

The Continuum International Publishing Group Ltd
The Tower Building, 11 York Road, London SE1 7NX

www.continuumbooks.com

Previously published as:
Historical Atlas of the Jewish People

Portions of this volume have been previously published as:
The Macmillan Bible Atlas
Carta's Atlas of the Period of the Second Temple, Mishnah and Talmud
Atlas of Medieval Jewish History
Atlas of Modern Jewish History

Managing editor: Barbara Laurel Ball
Cartography: Carta, Jerusalem
Map scans: Tsahi Ben-Ami

Library of Congress Cataloging-in-Publication Data
Aharnoi, Yohanan, 1919–1976
Historical atlas of the Jewish people / Yohanan Aharoni . . . [et al.]; edited by
Shmuel Ahituv.
p. cm.
Includes index.
ISBN 0-8264-1470-2 (alk. paper); Paperback ISBN 0-8264-1886-4 (alk. paper)
1. Jews–History. 2. Jews–History–Mape. 3. Jews–Palestine–History–Maps. 4.
Jews–Israel–History–Maps. 5. Jews—Europe–History–Maps. 6. Jews–
Middles East–History–Maps. 7. Bible. O.T.–Geography–Maps. I. Ahituv,
Shmuel. II. Title
DS116.A54 2003
990`.04924`00223–dc21

2002035184

FOREWORD

DESCRIBING the history of the Jewish people is not an easy task. Their history goes back almost four millennia and it spans five continents.

A people whose emergence is shrouded in the mists of myth and legends, some of which extend to even later periods, Jews through the ages have lived and adapted themselves to different regimes. Mostly independent or at least autonomous during the first and second commonwealths, they were then subjugated by pagan empires, who treated them much as they did other populations with their different religions. They suffered exile but also return.

Before and during the Middle Ages and depending on the political-economic framework and social fabric of the period, Jews were sometimes tolerated by Christian and Muslim rulers but restricted and persecuted at other times.

The advent of the modern era witnessed the Jews' struggle for emancipation and their desire to participate in the modern state as equal citizens on the same footing as their Christian compatriots. However, in most countries the Jews encountered prejudice, enmity and exclusion from professions and society at large, despite, or maybe because of, their attempts at integration and assimilation and their success in many fields of endeavor.

In time, antisemitism, both open and concealed, led to recurring persecution and eventually paved the way for the Holocaust. This same period of distress and pain also witnessed—some will say miraculously—the revival of Jewish consciousness and aspirations for independence. Seven decades of Zionist effort found ever more resonance among the Jewish people and culminated in the establishment in May 1948 of the State of Israel, which then had a population of just 600,000 souls.

No single scholar can encompass such a vast and varied history and this unique atlas is the result of the combined efforts of its authors. It grew out of decades of research and teaching by the participants. Each author deals with a distinctive period and his individual style has been retained here. Among the foremost authorities in their fields, they went to great pains to document the historical events against their geographical background so that texts could be enhanced by visual means, showing migrations, movements of ideas, formations of institutions, and more.

The framework for this atlas was provided in somewhat different form by the historical-atlas series published earlier in separate volumes by Carta in English, Hebrew and other languages. This volume has been updated and revised with maps adapted to fit the present format and style. The final section with the latest figures on world Jewish populations and forecasts to the year 2050 make it that much more valuable to scholars and students alike.

It should be noted that the bibliographies and sources absent here appear in the atlases listed on the opposite page.

Lastly, thanks are due to all the many friends and colleagues who aided us in many instances and to the editors, cartographers and artists at Carta who enlivened the text with their maps, graphs and illustrations—particularly to Tsahi Ben-Ami, Lorraine Kessel and Vladimir Shestakovsky who adapted the maps and graphs for this edition.

Shmuel Ahituv

TABLE OF CONTENTS

I. **ANCIENT TIMES** 1
A. **The Conquest and Settlement**
   The Tradition of Abraham's Migration 2
      Abraham and Isaac in the Land of Canaan 3
      Jacob and His Sons 4
   The Exodus and Wandering in the Wilderness 5
      Egypt of the Exodus 5
   The Penetration into Transjordan 7
   The Narrative of the Conquest of the Land of Canaan 8
   Conquests in the South 9
      The Battle of Gibeon 10
      Conquest of Southern Shephelah Districts (and Central Hill Country)
      (latter half of 12th cent. BCE) 11
   The War of Deborah and the Battle of the Waters of Merom 12
      The War of Deborah—The Deployment of Forces (12th cent. BCE) 13
      The War of Deborah—The Battle 13
      The Death of Sisera 14
      The Battle of the Waters of Merom 15
   The Limits of Israelite Control (12th–11th cent. BCE) 16
   The Twelve Tribes 19
      The Borders of the Tribal Territories (12th–11th cent. BCE) 20
   The Judges According to Their Tribes (12th–11th cent. BCE) 21
B. **The United Monarchy**
   The Kingdom of Saul (c 1035–1017 BCE) 23
   The Kingdom of David (c 1000–970 BCE) 25
   The Kingdom of David and Solomon (c 1000–930 BCE) 25
      The Israelite Hegemony During the Reigns of David and Solomon (c. 1000–930 BCE).... 26
   The Building and Expansion of Jerusalem (mid-10th cent. BCE) 27
C. **Israel and Judah**
   The Division of the Kingdom (931 BCE) 28
   The Wars Between Israel and Judah 30
      Abijah's Conquest (c 911 BCE) 30
      Baasha's Attack on Asa (c. 895 BCE) 31
      Ahab's Wars with Aram (855–853 BCE) 32
   The Battle of Qarqar (853 BCE) 33
   Israel and Judah in the Days of Jeroboam II and Uzziah (mid-8th cent. BCE) 35
      The Cities of the Prophets (9th–7th cent. BCE) 35
   The Campaign of Rezin and Pekah Against Judah (735 BCE) 37
   The Assyrian Campaigns (734–712 BCE) 39
      The Campaigns of Tiglath-pileser III (734–732 BCE) 40
      The Campaigns of Shalmaneser V and Sargon II to Palestine (724–712 BCE) 41
   Sennacherib's Reconquest of Phoenicia (701 BCE) 42
      Sennacherib in Philistia and Judah (701 BCE) 43
D. **The Kingdom of Judah**
   Judah and Her Neighbors During the Reign of Manasseh (701–642 BCE) 44
   The Kingdom of Josiah (628–609 BCE) 46
   The Districts of Judah 48
   The Closing Years of the Kingdom of Judah (599–586 BCE) 50
   The Exile from Judah (597–582 BCE) 51
   The Flight to Egypt (c 586 BCE) 51
   Judah Under Babylonian Rule (early 6th cent. BCE) 52
   The Return to Zion (538–445 BCE) 53
   Post-Exilic Jerusalem (c 440 BCE) 54

The Province of Yehud (c 440 BCE) 54
E. The Hellenistic Period
Alexander the Great in Palestine (332–331 BCE) 56
The Jewish Diaspora (3rd–1st cent. BCE) 58
   The Jewish Diaspora in Babylonia, Asia Minor and Greece 58
   The Jewish Diaspora in the Ptolemaic Kingdom 59
F. The Maccabess
The Beginnings of the Maccabean Revolt (167 BCE)............................... 60
The Battle of Beth-zur and the Rededication of the Temple (165 BCE)........................... 61
The Expansion of Judea in the Days of Jonathan (152–142 BCE) 62
Jerusalem of the Maccabees (164–141 BCE) 63
The Kingdom of Alexander Janneus (103–76 BCE) 64
G. The Roman Conquest
Pompey's Campaign in Palestine (63 BCE) 66
Pompey's Territorial Arrangements (63–55 BCE) 67
   Pompey's Territorial Arrangements 68
The Parthian Invasion and the Escape of Herod (40 BCE)......................... 69
The Growth of Herod's Kingdom (40–4 BCE) 70
Herod's Building in Jerusalem 70
The Division of Herod's Kingdom (4 BCE–6 CE)..................................... 73
The Early Procurators of Judea (6–41 CE) 74
The Essenes.. 76
H. In the Time of Jesus
The Journeys of Jesus (5 BCE–30 CE) 77
Around the Sea of Galilee 78
Jesus' Last Journey to Jerusalem.. 80
The Jewish Diaspora in the Time of Jesus 81
I. The First Revolt Against the Romans
The Kingdom of Agrippa I (37–44 CE) 82
The Kingdom of Agrippa II (44–66 CE) 83
The Outbreak of the First Revolt Against Rome...................................... 84
The Siege of Jerusalem in the Year 70 CE 86
The Fall of Masada (73 CE) 88
The Sages of Jabneh 89
The Land of Israel After the First Revolt (70–131 CE) 90
J. The Second Revolt Against the Romans
Jewish Revolts in the Diaspora (115–117 CE)... 93
   The Jewish Revolt in Cyrenaica and Egypt (116 CE) 93
   Trajan's Campaign in the East; Cyprus Revolt and "the War of Quietus" (115–117 CE). 94
The Beginnings of the Bar Kokhba Revolt (131–132 CE) 94
The Third and Fourth Years of the Bar Kokhba Revolt (133–134 CE)............ 97
The Siege of Bethther (135 CE) 98
The Decrees of Hadrian (135 CE) 99
Aelia Capitolina (135–324 CE) 100
K. Renewal of Jewish Settlement in Palestine
The Wanderings of the Sanhedrin (after 70 CE) 101
The Twenty-four Priestly Divisions 101
The Jewish Settlement After 140 CE... 102
The Jewish Diaspora in the Time of Antoninus Pius (138–161 CE) 103
The Boundaries of the Land According to *Halakhah* 105
The Urbanization of the Land (63–330 CE)... 106
Migration Routes from Babylonia to Eretz Israel 108
L. The Talmudic Sages
The Third- and Fourth-Generation *Tannaim* (115–175 CE)........................ 109
The First Generation of *Amoraim* (225–260 CE) 110
The Second Generation of *Amoraim* (260–290 CE) 111

The Third Generation of *Amoraim* (280–320 CE) 113
The Fourth- and Fifth-Generation *Amoraim* (320–400 CE) 114
Julian's Attempt to Rebuild the Temple (362–363 CE) 115
The First Generation of Babylonian *Amoraim* (200–254 CE)......................115
The Second Generation of Babylonian *Amoraim* (254–299 CE) 117
The Third Generation of Babylonian *Amoraim* (299–330 CE)......................118
The Fourth Generation of Babylonian *Amoraim* (330–352 CE).....................119
The Fifth and Sixth Generations of Babylonian *Amoraim* (352–376 CE) 119
The Political Division of Palestine in the Byzantine Period 120
The Jewish Diaspora in the Fifth Century..122

II. THE MIDDLE AGES 123
A. From the Barbarian Invasion of Europe Until the Crusades
The Barbarian Invasions of Europe (5th cent.)..124
The Dispersion of the Jews (mid-6th cent.)..126
Synagogues in Palestine (2nd–6th cent.) 128
The Himyar Kingdom and Its War with the Ethiopians (6th cent.) 130
Wars Between Persia and Byzantium (609–629)..132
    The Persian Invasion of Palestine (614–618) 133
The Jews in the Arabian Peninsula (beginning of the 7th cent.) 133
    Muhammad's Wars Against the Jews (623–629) 135
    The City of Medina 135
Arabian Conquest and the Rise of Islam (622–721) 136
Visigothic Spain (7th cent.) 138
The Jews in Italy During the Papacy of Gregory I (the Great) (590–604) 139
Charlemagne's Empire..141
    Boundaries of the Divided Carolingian Empire (843) 143
The Khazars and Pressure form the Christian States (8th–10th cent.) 144
    The Khazars..146
The Radhanite Merchants..147
Italy in the Framework of Byzantium and the Holy Roman Empire (9th–10th cent.).......150
    The Norman Invasion of Southern Italy 152
The Ahimaaz Scroll of Genealogies..152
Religious Ferment and Sects in Judaism (until the 12th cent.) 153
The Gaonate in Babylonia..155
Bonds Between Babylonia, Eretz Israel and the Diaspora 160
The Geonim of Eretz Israel; and Aliyah to Eretz Israel 162
The Jews of North Africa (12th–15th cent.)..165
    Tunisia 165
    Egypt 167
    Morocco 167
Muslim Spain: Economy and Centers of Jewish Settlement (10th–12th cent.)...................168
Reconquista: The Reconquest (until the mid-12th cent.) 170
Jewish Communities in Ashkenaz (up to 1096)..173
The Massacres of 1096: "Gezerot Tatnu" (4856) 175
The First Crusade (1096–1099) 177
    The Crusader Kingdom of Eretz Israel 178
    The Capture of Jerusalem (7 June–15 July 1099) 179
From Crusade to Crusades 179
    The Crusades..180
    The City of Norwich..182
B. Until the Black Death
Blood Libels 184
The Travels of Benjamin of Tudela (1160–1173)..185
    In Italy, Greece and Turkey..187
    In the Holy Land 187

In the Near East 187
Jewish Communities in the Holy Land (12th–14th cent.) 188
   Immigration to the Holy Land (12th cent.)...189
   Immigration to the Holy Land (13th–early 14th cent.) 190
The Jews of Italy (13th cent.) 192
Jewish Communities in Spain and the Reconquest (13th and 14th cent.) 193
The Collecta Organization 197
Spiritual Creativity: The Tosafists 198
The Spread of the Kabbalah 202
The Maimonidean Controversy 204
Hebrew Manuscripts of Ashkenaz, France and Spain..207
The Jews of England up to the Expulsion 209
The Jewish Communities of France (13th cent.) 211
Persecutions in Ashkenaz (13th and 14th cent.)..213
   Massacres in the Rhine Districts...215
The Pastoureaux and "Lepers" Massacres (1320–1321) 216
The Black Death (1348)..217

C. Until the Expulsion from Spain
Destruction of the Jewish Community of France (14th cent.) 219
The Beginning of Jewish Settlement in Poland 220
The Jews of Spain up to the Massacres of 1391..222
   The Jewish Quarter in Toledo 223
Jewish Settlement in Portugal (13th and 14th cent.) 225
The Mongol Invasions of Palestine..226
   The Mongol Empire 227
Immigration to the Holy Land (14th and 15th cent.)..228
The Beginnings of the Ottoman Empire 230
The Fall of Constantine 232
Commerce in the Mediterranean Basin (14th–15th cent.) 232
The Jews of Germany in the Shadow of Expulsions and Massacres (14th and 15h cent.)..234
   Centers of Dissemination of Hatred of the Jews..236
The Jews of Switzerland (13th–15th cent.) 237
The Jews of Spain on the Eve of the Expulsion (15th cent.) 238
   Spanish Jewish Communities..239
   The Kingdom of Aragón at the Time of Alfonso V 240
   Violent Attacks Against the Conversos of Córdoba 241
   The Conquest of Granada (1 January 1492) 242
The Jewish Communities in Italy (14th–16th cent.) 244
   The City of Rome 247
Jewish Demographic Changes (from the 13th cent. until the Expulsion from Spain) 248
   Jewish Populations in Europe..252
   The Expulsion Order..254
Expulsion from Spain (31 March 1492)...256
Jewish Exodus from Spain and Portugal (1492–1497)..257
   Routes Taken by Jews Expelled from Spain 260
   The Wanderings of R. Judah Hayyat..260

D. Until the Chmielnicki Massacres and Shabbatean Movement
The Ottoman Empire at the Height of Its Expansion (until 1683) 261
   The Jews of the Balkan Peninsula (16th cent.) 263
Immigration to the Holy Land (16th and 17th cent.)..264
   Palestine Under Ottoman Rule (16th cent.) 265
   Emissaries from the Holy Land to the Diaspora (15th–16th cent.) 267
   Jewish Communities in North Africa and in the Egyptian Delta (15th–16th cent.)........267
Kabbalists and Kabbalistic Centers (16th and 17th cent.) 268
Jewish Printers and Admission of Jews to Universities (15th–16th cent.) 270
Universities..271

The Jews of Italy (16th and 17th cent.) 272
   The Jewish Ghetto in Venice 274
The Travels of David Reuveni (16th cent.) 274
The Emigration of Conversos from Portugal and Their Dispersion; The Readmission
of Jews to England (16th and 17th cent.) 276
   Area of Jewish Settlement in the City of London 279
   Jewish Communities in Holland (17th cent.) 279
Jewish Settlement in America and the Far East (16th and 17th cent.) 280
   Jewish Settlement in America (17th cent.)...280
   Jewish Settlement in India (16th and 17th cent.)..................................281
Inquisition Tribunals (15th–17th cent.) 282
   In Spain and Portugal..283
   In Italy 283
The Jews of Germany During the Reformation......................................286
   The Jews of Silesia, Moravia and Bohemia (16th cent.) 287
   The Thirty Years' War (1618–1648)..288
The Jews of Hungary Under Turkish and Austrian Rule 288
The Jews of Eastern Europe (until the 1650s) 290
The Jews of Poland Within the Council of Four Lands (17th cent.) 292
The Chmielnicki Massacres (1648–1649)..295
Shabbetai Zevi—Activities and Travels 297
   The Travels of Nathan of Gaza 299
   Leaders of the Shabbatean Movement After the Death of Shabbetai Zevi 300

III. MODERN TIMES 301
A. Jewish Demography
Modern Times in Jewish History 302
Migratory Directions: The Middle Ages to the Modern Period 304
Jewish Migrations (19th and 20th cent.)..305
   Jewish Migrations Within Europe 306
   Intercontinental Migrations of the Jews 307
The Jewish People in the Nineteenth Century 308
The Jewish People on the Eve of World War II 309
B. European Jewry Until World War I
The Spanish-Portuguese Jews in Europe and in the Americas (17th and 18th cent.) 312
   The Beginning of Jewish Settlement in the Americas............................313
   Economic Activities of Spanish-Portuguese Jews (17th and 18th cent.)....................314
The Court Jews in Central Europe (17th and 18th cent.) 315
The Jews in Poland and Lithuania Before the Eighteenth-Century Partitions ... .318
   Partitions of Poland...319
   Poland and Lithuania (18th cent.)...320
The Jews in the Russian Empire (late 19th cent.)...................................322
The Jews in the Hapsburg Empire (late 18th cent.) 324
The Jews in Austria-Hungary (early 20th cent.).....................................326
The Jews in France (18th and 19th cent.) 327
   The Jews in Alsace-Lorraine (late 18th cent.).....................................328
   The Consistories (19th cent.) 329
C. Major Themes in Modern Jewish History
Jewish Entrepreneurs (19th and 20th cent.)...330
   Jewish Entrepreneurs in the United States 331
The Legal Situation of the Jews Until World War I.................................332
The Legal Situation of the Jews in Muslim Countries 334
Jewish Enlightenment (*Haskalah*) in Europe (18th and 19th cent.) 335
Shabbateanism, Frankism, and Early Hasidism......................................338
Hasidism: Beginnings and Expansion..340
Religious Tendencies in Modern Judaism 340

Religious Trends and Institutions Among European Jews 346
Orthodoxy (*Haredut*) in Eastern Europe 348
The Great Yeshivas in Eastern Europe and the *Musar* Movement 348
The Hasidic Movement (19th cent.) 350
The Religious Organization of American Jewry (mid-19th and early 20th cent.) 350
  Reform and Conservative Congregations in the United States (early 20th cent.) 352
Modern Antisemitism: Ideological Sources 353
  Antisemitic Parties and Organizations in Europe (late 19th and early 20th cent.) 355
  The "Hep-Hep" Disturbances (1819) 356
  Anti-Jewish Riots During the Revolutions of 1848 357
  Anti-Jewish Riots in Russia (1881–1906) 358
  Blood Libels (19th and 20th cent.) 360
Judaic Studies (19th and 20th cent.) 361
  Judaic Studies in Europe and in Palestine/Israel 362
  Judaic Studies in North America 363
Languages of the Jews 364
The Roots of Jewish Nationalism (late 19th cent.) 366
Jewish Nationalism: Ideological and Organizational Tendencies 367
Jewish Socialism: The Bund 369
  The Rise of the Bund and Its Spread in the Pale of Settlement 369
Zionism: Ideological Components 370
  The Beginning of the Zionist Movement 372
  The Structure of the World Zionist Organization (1929) 373
  The Political Composition of Zionist Congresses (1921–1939) 375
Jewish Student Organizations and Youth Movements 376
  Jewish Student Organizations in Europe 378
  Jewish Student Organizations in the United States 379

D. Muslim Countries
The Jews in Muslim Countries 380
The Jews in Morocco 381
The Jews in Algeria 383
The Jews in Tunisia 384
The Jews in Libya 385
The Jews in Egypt 385
The Jews in the Ottoman Empire and Turkey 387
  The Jews in Constantinople (Istanbul) 388
  The Jews in Salonika 389
The Karaites 390
The Ethiopian Jews 391
The Jews in Iraq 392
The Jews in Kurdistan 393
The Jews in Iran 394
The Jews in Afghanistan 396
The Jews in Yemen 396
The Jews in India 398
The Jews in the Far East 400

E. European Jewry in the Interwar Years
The Jews in East Central Europe 401
The Jews in Eastern Europe After World War I 402
  Pogroms in Russia and Poland (1917–1921) 403
  Jewish Delegations at the Paris Peace Conference (1919) 403
  Equal Rights and Minority Rights After World War I 404
The Jews in Poland (1921–1931) 404
  Historical Subgroups in Polish Jewry 404
  The Jews in Warsaw 407
The Jews in the Baltic States in the Interwar Years 407

The Jews in the Soviet Union (1920s and 1930s) 409
  The Caucasian "Mountain Jews" and the Jews in Georgia 410
  The Jews in Bukhara...410
  The Jewish Autonomous Region in Birobidzhan 411
The Jews in Czechoslovakia in the Interwar Years........................411
The Jews in Hungary in the Interwar Years.............................412
The Jews in Romania in the Interwar Years 413
The Jews in Southeastern Europe (early 20th cent.) 415
The Jews in Western Europe in the 1930s..............................416
The Jews in Germany: 1925 418
Jewish Emgration from Germany During the Nazi Period 420

F. European Jewry: 1940 ff.
The Holocaust: 1939 to 1945..421
  Jewish Reactions and Resistance................................424
  The Warsaw Ghetto Uprising...................................425
  Auschwitz 426
  The Escape from Europe (*Briha*)..............................427
  The Outcome of the Holocaust: 1951...........................428
  The Extermination of European Jews, by Countries................428
European Jewry (late 20th cent.)....................................429
The Jews in the Soviet Union (late 20th cent.) 430

G. The New Centers of Jewry
Palestine in the Nineteenth Century..................................432
Jewish Immigration to Palestine/Israel 433
  Early Jewish Immigrations (*Aliyot*) to Palestine................434
  Jewish Immigration (*Aliyah*) to Israel After 1948...............434
The Boundaries of Palestine 435
Toward the Establishment of the Jewish State in Palestine (1940–1948) 436
The Wars Fought by Israel 437
The Jews in Canada...439
The Development of American Jewry (1878 ff.)........................440
  Jewish Immigration to the United States (19th and 20th cent.) 441
  American Jewry in the 1920s...................................442
  The Socioeconomic Development of American Jewry................444
  The Jewish Labor Movement in the United States................444
  Jewish Institutions in Manhattan Until 1914....................445
The Jews in Latin America (19th and 20th cent.)......................446
  The Jews in Argentina..447
The Jews in South Africa...448
The Jews in Australia and New Zealand 449

H. A Changing World Jewry: Late 20th to Early 21st Centuries 450
Jewish Population Since World War II 451
Geographical Distribution 452
  The Jewish People in 2002 452
  The Jews in the Former Soviet Union...........................455
Core and Enlarged Jewish Populations 456
The Jews in the World System.......................................457
The Jews in Major Urban Areas.....................................458
  Jewish Centers in the United States, 2002......................459
International Migration of the Jews 460
Ideological and Other Determinants of *Aliyah* 462
Jewish Marriages, Births and Deaths................................464
Major Brands of Jewish Identification 466
Jewish Population Projections 467

Index 470

I
ANCIENT TIMES

Rembrandt's Abraham and the Angels.

A. THE CONQUEST AND SETTLEMENT

THE TRADITION OF ABRAHAM'S MIGRATION

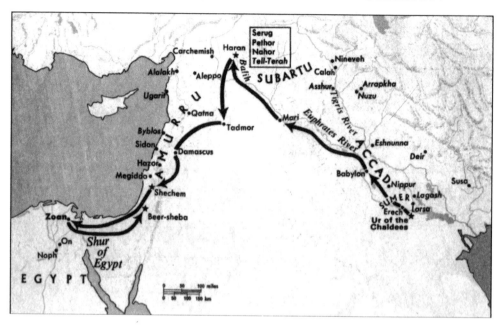

THE narrative about the migration of the patriarchal ancestor of the Israelite nation emphasizes their origin in Mesopotamia and their subsequent association with Egypt, the two great riverine cultures of the ancient Near East. Ur of the Chaldees was the venerable city of the moon god Sin in southern Mesopotamia, Sumer. It had once controlled a vast commercial empire in the late third millennium BCE. The Chaldees, however, are the former nomadic people who settled there in the early Iron Age and achieved supremacy with their capital at Babylon, during the seventh century BCE. Haran was at the principal crossroads of commerce in Upper Mesopotamia. Several of the patriarchal relatives are actually the patronyms of known cities in that vicinity; Haran and Nahor appear in the Mari letters of the eighteenth century BCE while Tell Terah and Serug are known from later Assyrian sources.

"The Canaanite was then in the land" but Amorites lived at Hebron, said to have been founded seven years before Zoan in Egypt. Zoan was the new capital of the delta, founded after the channels near Pr-Rameses were no longer usable, probably during the eleventh century BCE. Other ethnic groups encountered in Canaan were the Midianites (Ishmaelites) and the Philistines. The latter first appear in the eastern Mediterranean as leaders of the invasion by Aegean peoples in the eighth year of Rameses III (1174 BCE). The Ishmaelites were present in the steppe lands up to the tenth century BCE.

The Patriarchs came into the country from Transjordan and confined their migratory movements in Cisjordan to the watershed route through the hill country, from Shechem via Beth-el to Hebron. They also sojourned in the Negeb, that is, Beer-sheba and vicinity. Their livelihood was based on the herd-

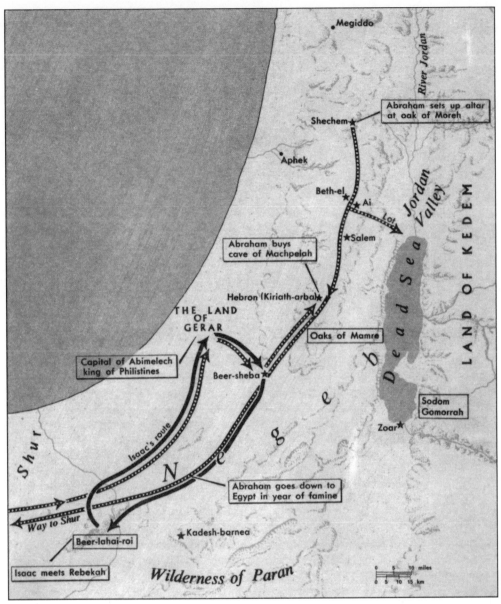

ABRAHAM AND ISAAC IN THE LAND OF CANAAN

ing of small cattle and their movements were primarily for the seasonal utilization of local pasturage. They sought to live in symbiosis with certain urban centers, namely Shechem and Gerar, and probably also Beth-el and Hebron. From Beer-sheba they made journeys into the Sinai steppe "between Kadesh and Shur," reminiscent of the Shasu from Edom in Mount Seir who sought pasturage in the eastern Delta of Egypt. Narratives about a sojourn in the land of Gerar feature both Abraham and Isaac. The latter obtained urban living accommodations and invested in grain production but was forced back to Beer-

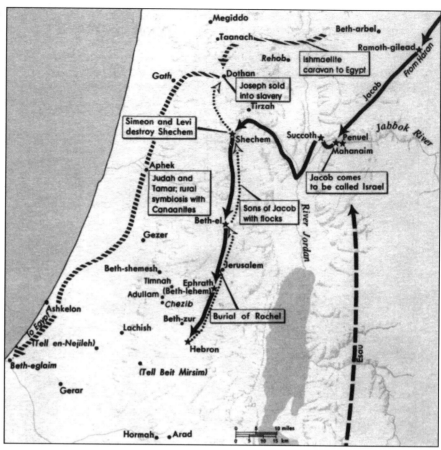

Map labels:
- Megiddo
- Beth-arbel
- Taanach
- Ramoth-gilead
- Rehob
- Ishmaelite caravan to Egypt
- From Haran
- Gath
- Dothan
- Joseph sold into slavery
- Jacob
- Tirzah
- Succoth
- Penuel
- Jabbok River
- Simeon and Levi destroy Shechem
- Shechem
- Mahanaim
- Aphek
- Jacob comes to be called Israel
- Judah and Tamar; rural symbiosis with Canaanites
- Sons of Jacob with flocks
- Beth-el
- River Jordan
- Gezer
- Beth-shemesh
- Jerusalem
- Timnah
- Ephrath (Beth-lehem)
- Adullam
- Chezib
- Ashkelon
- Beth-zur
- Burial of Rachel
- To Egypt
- Lachish
- (Tell en-Nejileh)
- Esau
- Beth-eglaim
- Hebron
- (Tell Beit Mirsim)
- Gerar
- Hormah
- Arad
- 10 miles / 15 km

sheba by the jealousy of the local residents. Beer-sheba seems to be on the periphery of the territory ruled by Abimelech, king of Gerar. The Patriarchs could live there without clashing with the people of Gerar, but the king preferred to legalize the relationship by means of treaties (covenants). During times of drought and famine, the Patriarchs sought respite by going to Egypt.

In the later phase of the patriarchal narratives, that pertaining to Jacob and his sons, the action is restricted almost entirely to the central hill country. Esau is now living in Mount Seir. Peaceful symbiosis with sheep-raising Canaanites is reflected in the story of Judah and Tamar which takes place in the northern Shephelah near the junction of the Vale of Elah with the geographical "trough" separating the Shephelah from the hill country of Judah. Unlike the Abrahamic account, Jacob's entrance into Canaan via Transjordan is clearly defined. While Jacob's entourage derives from the Haran region, their contacts with the outside world after settling in Canaan are with Egypt. Joseph is sold to a caravan passing through the Valley of Dothan (on the southern route from the Jezreel Valley to the Sharon Plain as defined by Thutmose III). Jacob's sons make trips to Egypt and finally the patriarch himself migrates to the Land of Goshen in the eastern delta.

JACOB and his sons were allowed to settle in a choice portion of "the land of Rameses" (Gen. 47:11) called "the land of Goshen." The city of Rameses (Egyptian "the House of Rameses") was built on the former site of the Hyksos capital, Avaris. It served as the northern capital for the pharaohs of the nineteenth and twentieth dynasties. By the end of the twelfth century BCE the branch of Nile beside Rameses had silted up, forcing the pharaohs of the twenty-first dynasty to build a new capital at Zoan (Tanis). They plundered the ruins of Rameses and brought many statues, stelae and other ornamented architectural pieces to their new city. The pharaohs of the twenty-second dynasty established a second delta capital at Bubastis and also brought in statues and other pieces from the ruins of Rameses. During the fourth century BCE, the worship of a deified Rameses was practiced at both Zoan and Bubastis, while the gateway city to Egypt had become Pelusium. This led late Jewish writers to identify Zoan with Rameses (Ps. 78:12, 78:43) or with Pithom (the Targum) and Pelusium with Rameses (Targum; Josephus). The translators of the Greek Septuagint equated Pithom with Heliopolis (biblical On) and the Goshen/Land of Rameses area as the Wadi Tumeilat.

Egyptian inscriptions point to Pithom (Egyptian Pr-Atum) as the site at the western end of an ancient overflow lake in the Wadi Tumeilat. Biblical Succoth is the name associated with watering pools farther west of Pithom, towards the modern Timsah lake. The land of Goshen was the plain between Rameses and Pithom. The Shihor was evidently an elongated lake or pond lying alongside the course of the ancient eastern branch of the Nile between Baal-zephon (Daphne) and Pelusium. The "Reed Sea" was the large marshy area that once existed to the southeast of

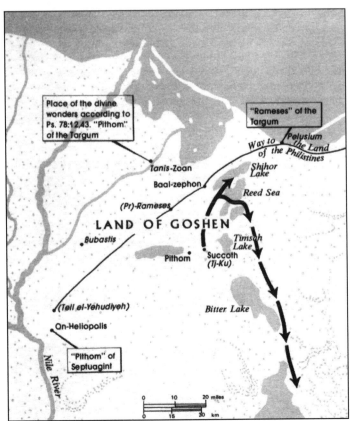

EGYPT OF THE
EXODUS

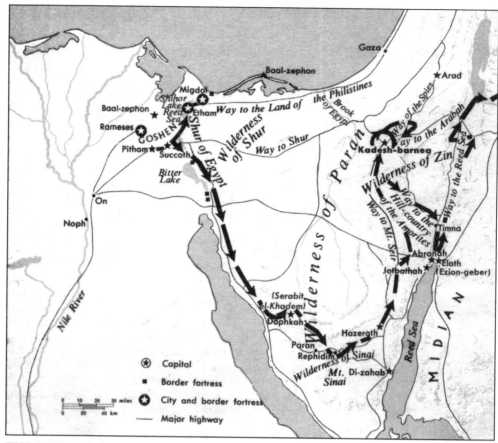

THE EXODUS AND WANDERING IN THE WILDERNESS

Baal-zephon. Between these two bodies of water passed the "Way of Horus," the route taken by New Kingdom pharaohs (incarnates of Horus) on their military campaigns to Canaan and Syria. The Bible calls it "the Way to the Land of the Philistines" (Exod. 13:17).

Brickmaking (tomb painting at Thebes, fifteenth century BCE).

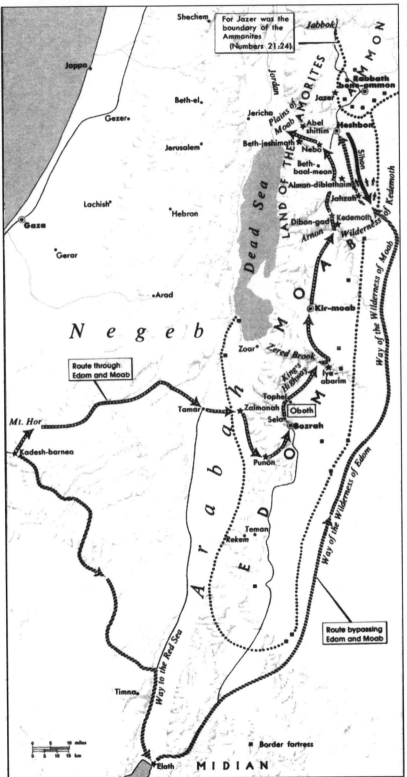

Shechem

For Jazer was the
boundary of the
Ammonites
(Numbers 21:24)

Jabbok

Joppa

AMMON

Rabbath
bene-ammon

Jazer

Beth-el

Jordan

Jericho

AMORITES

Plains of Moab

Abel
shittim

Heshbon

Jerusalem

Beth-jeshimoth

Sihon

Nebo

Dead Sea

Beth-
baal-meon

Almon-diblathaim

LAND OF THE

Lachish

Hebron

Jahzah

Kedemoth

Gaza

Dibon-gad

Way of the Wilderness of Kedemoth

Gerar

Arnon

Wilderness of Kedemoth

Arad

M

O

Kir-moab

B

N e g e b

A

Zoar

Zered Brook

King's Highway

Way of the Wilderness of Moab

Route through
Edom and Moab

Iye-
abarim

Tophel

Tamar

Zalmonah

Oboth

Mt. Hor

Sela

Bozrah

Kadesh-barnea

Punon

O

A r a b a h

Way of the Wilderness of Edom

E

Teman

D

Rekem

O

M

Route bypassing
Edom and Moab

Way to the Red Sea

Timna

0   5   10 miles

0 5 10 15 km

■ Border fortress

Elath **M I D I A N**

7

THE Israelite conquest began in eastern Transjordan, beyond the borders of the Land of Canaan. In this sparsely settled region, there were extensive lands for pasturage (Num. 32:1–4). Peoples related to the Israelites had already settled in the southern parts of Transjordan, soon forming organized kingdoms—Edom, Moab, and Ammon. The Amorite kingdom of Heshbon was located between Moab and Ammon; its ruler, Sihon, warred against Moab's first king and conquered the entire plateau of Moab to the Arnon River (Num. 21:26). Moses exploited this political situation by asking the Kings of Moab and Edom to grant the Israelites passage through their lands on the King's Highway, to reach the territory of Sihon (Num. 20:14–21; Judg. 11:17); when refused this permission, Moses turned southward to Elath, avoiding Edom and Moab, and then penetrated Sihon's kingdom from the eastern desert (the wilderness of Kedemoth). Since that time, the Arnon has been considered the traditional border between the Israelite tribes and Moab, even though Moab never accepted the fact and took every opportunity to regain

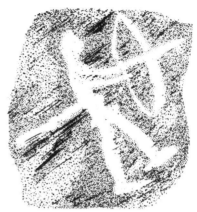

Archer (graffito in Negeb).

control over "the plain," north of the Arnon.

In contrast, the picture revealed by the list of desert stations shows a direct route, passing through the heart of Edom and Moab to "the plains of Moab" opposite Jericho (Num. 33:37–49). Many scholars are of the opinion that this list reflects a tradition of an older wave of immigration by several tribes, prior to the setting up of the Transjordanian kingdoms. The biblical traditions concerning the camp at Abel-shittim and the fierce war against the Midianites are connected with this movement.

THE NARRATIVE OF THE CONQUEST OF THE LAND OF CANAAN

THE conquest of the Land of Canaan begins with the crossing of the river Jordan; the first spot reached by the tribes was Gilgal, east of Jericho (Josh. 4:19). Gilgal was evidently the first place sanctified in the Land of Canaan, serving for a time as the center of the Israelite tribes; it was not by chance that Saul, the first Israelite king, was crowned there (1 Sam. 11:15).

Related to Gilgal are the stories of the conquests of Jericho and Ai. These stories contain many legendary shadings and historically they are enveloped in obscurity. The conquest of Jericho and Ai in this period has received no archaeological confirmation. At Ai this question is especially difficult, for the city seems to have been utterly destroyed a thousand years before the time of Joshua.

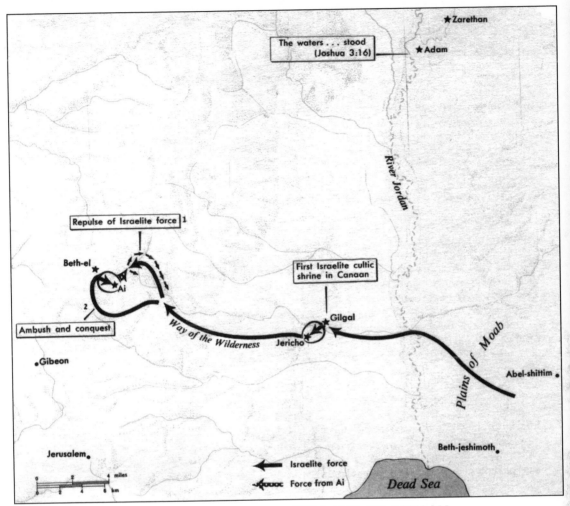

THE NARRATIVE OF THE CONQUEST OF THE LAND OF CANAAN

Some scholars are of the opinion that, in the biblical narrative, Ai was substituted for nearby Beth-el; others assume that the source of the story of the conquest of Ai is a popular legend, surrounding the sanctuary at Gilgal, and was intended to explain the ruined cities dotting the landscape in this area. On the other hand, the conquest of Beth-el, described in Judges 1:22–26, has been substantiated by archaeological excavations.

CONQUESTS IN THE SOUTH

IN reconstructing the Israelite occupation of the land, it must be remembered that only selected events are described in the Bible. There were probably many other conflicts between the Israelites and the indigenous population which have been lost or at best survive only as vague allusions in the record. Furthermore, there were some areas where the tribes managed to settle down without con-

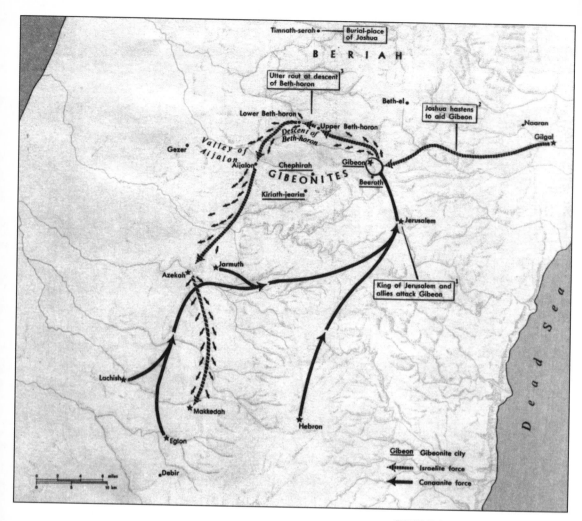

THE BATTLE OF GIBEON

quering the adjacent Canaanite cities. On the other hand, the Book of Joshua ascribes the entire process to a lightning campaign conducted by all the tribes together under the leadership of one man, Joshua son of Nun. Even the Transjordanian tribes are said to have crossed over to Cisjordan to help their brothers in the conquest. This tendency is most obvious with regard to the conquest of Hebron and Debir, which was first ascribed to Caleb and Kenaz (Josh. 15:13–19; Judg. 1:12–15), then to Judah (Judg. 1:10–11), and finally to Joshua and the entire people of Israel (Josh.

10:36–39). Joshua himself belonged to the clan of Beriah which lived in the hills of Beth-el between Naaran and Beth-horon (1 Chron 7:23–28). Joshua's principle activities were probably originally restricted to that central hill country, especially the victory at Gibeon. While the Book of Joshua presents this unified picture of the conquest, the victories gained by individual tribes, or local groups of tribes, is stressed in the Book of Judges. Activities in the central and southern regions are portrayed in the Book of Joshua under three stages:

1. *The battle of Gibeon.* Here the

Israelites rallied around Joshua to come to the aid of the Gibeonites, a Hivite enclave living in four towns on the plateau northwest of Jerusalem. The king of Jerusalem called up his allies to punish the Gibeonites for making a covenant with Israel. He saw this as a threat to his control over the main approach route from the coastal plain to the hill country, via Beth-horon. The Canaanite forces were routed as they sought to retreat down the Beth-horon road. Their flight southward "as far as Azekah and as far as Makkedah" (Josh. 10:11) serves as a link with the subsequent campaign in the southern Shephelah.

2. *The invasion by the southern tribes.* Judah is credited with a victory over the Canaanite king Adoni-bezek at a place called Bezek. Although the identification is not certain, it is thought that this Bezek is identical with the Bezek of 1 Samuel 11:8. The subsequent reference to the conquest of Jerusalem by Judah (Judg. 1:8) is probably an editorial retrospect concerning David's conquest of the city. While Judah and Simeon may have entered the Judean hill country from the north, the subsidiary tribes of the Calebites and the Kenazzites probably did penetrate from the south, conquering Hebron and Debir. The Kenites settled around Arad in the Negeb, having come via "the city of Palms," perhaps Tamar in the Arabah rather than Jericho (Judg. 1:16). The Simeonites originally managed to settle in five Shephelah and Negeb sites, Etam, En-rimmon, Tochen, Ether,

CONQUEST OF SOUTHERN SHEPHELAH DISTRICTS (AND CENTRAL HILL COUNTRY) LATTER HALF OF 12TH CENTURY BCE

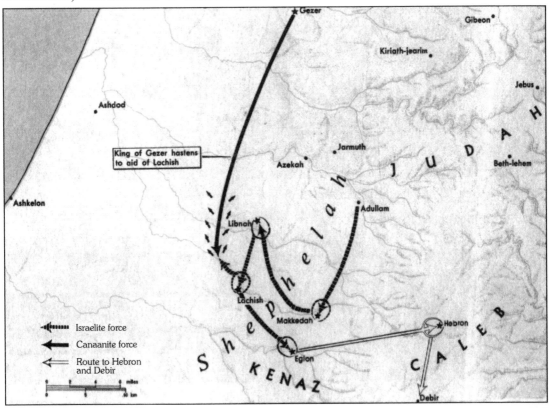

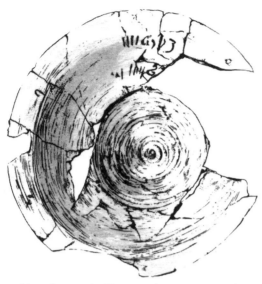

List of taxes in Egyptian hieratic script from Lachish (end of Canaanite period).

three known districts in the Shephelah, the northern one, from the Valley of Sorek to the Vale of Elah (Josh. 15:33–36), was evidently occupied peacefully, without any serious conflicts (cf. Gen. 38). The conquest of the cities in the central and southern districts seems to follow a circuit based on the connection with the previous narrative (the Canaanite retreat after the battle of Gibeon) and the ensuing narrative (the conquest of Hebron and Debir in the hill country). Thus, the sequence starts with Makkedah and the capture of the fugitive Canaanite kings and leads to the ascent to Hebron and Debir.

A metal object bearing the cartouche of pharaoh Rameses III found near the gate at Lachish indicates that that Canaanite city was under Egyptian control until at least the mid-twelfth century BCE. The votive bowl with a hieratic inscription found there previously must refer to the reign of Rameses III. Therefore, the Israelite conquest of that area could have taken place in the latter half of the twelfth century BCE.

and Ashan (1 Chron. 4:31–32) and shared with Judah in the conquest of Hormah (Judg. 1:17).

3. *The conquest of the southern Shephelah.* This was probably the latest stage in the occupation of the greater Judean territory. It is noteworthy that of the

THE WAR OF DEBORAH AND THE BATTLE OF THE WATERS OF MEROM

The Bible records two major conflicts between the Israelite tribes and the Canaanites of the cities in Galilee: the battle of the waters of Merom (Josh. 11:1–15) and the battle of Deborah (Judg. 4 and 5). In both accounts, the leader of the Canaanite league is Jabin, king of Hazor. Thus, they are both related to the same chronological period. Deborah's victory is said to have brought about the decline of Jabin (Judg. 4:24) while the battle of the waters of Merom culminates in the utter destruction of Hazor (Josh. 11:10–11). Using that as a criterion, scholars have suggested that Deborah's victory preceded that of the Merom battle; it would follow that the order of the two events became reversed when the Merom victory was assigned to Joshua by the later author of the Book of Joshua. Others hold that the reference to Jabin in the narrative of Deborah's victory is a later addition and that the original leader of the Canaanite coalition in Judges 4 and 5 was Sisera. However, Sisera is never called a king, nor does he have a specific city of his own. There is no city by the name of Harosheth-

THE WAR OF DEBORAH—
THE DEPLOYMENT OF FORCES
12TH CENTURY BCE

Canaanite charioteer wounded by arrow. Decoration on chariot of Thutmose IV.

- ◄•••••• Israelite force
- ◄——— Canaanite force
- ⊣•••••••• Israelite volunteers
- ⊠ Canaanite chariot camp
- ▨ Area of continuous Israelite settlement

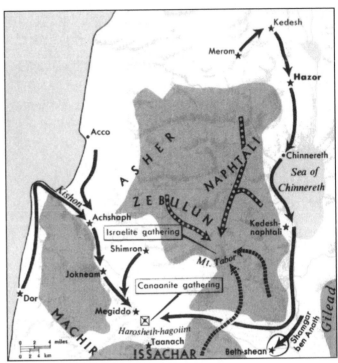

Kedesh
Merom ★
Hazor ★
Acco •
ASHER
NAPHTALI
ZEBULUN
• Chinnereth
Sea of Chinnereth
Kishon
Achshaph •
Israelite gathering
Kedesh-naphtali ★
Shimron ★
Mt. Tabor
Jokneam ★
Canaanite gathering
• Dor
MACHIR
Megiddo ★ ⊠
Gilead
Harosheth-hagoiim
Taanach ★
Shamgar ben Anath
ISSACHAR
Beth-shean ★

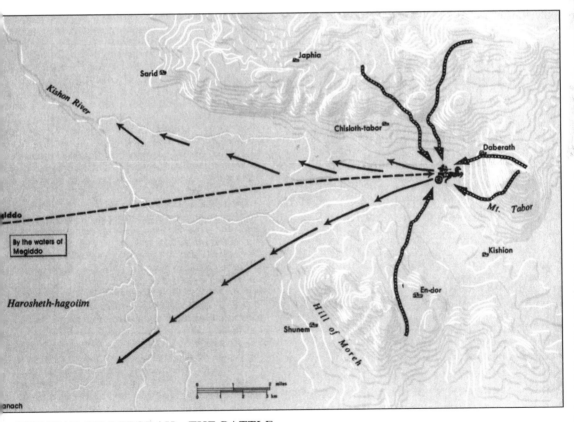

Japhia
Sarid
Kishon River
Chisloth-tabor
Daberath
Mt. Tabor
Megiddo
By the waters of Megiddo
Kishion
Harosheth-hagoiim
En-dor
Hill of Moreh
Shunem
Taanach

THE WAR OF DEBORAH—THE BATTLE

13

hagoiim in any extra-biblical sources and attempts to find its name in the Arabic toponymy of the Jezreel Valley have been futile. In fact, Harosheth-hagoiim is apparently identical with Galil-hagoiim (Isa. 9:1 [Heb. 8:23]) and is to be derived from the root meaning "to plow." Harosheth means "cultivated land" and refers to the

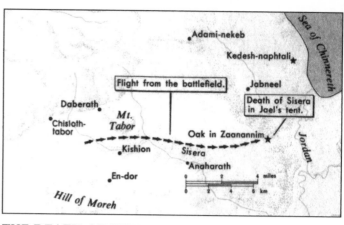

THE DEATH OF SISERA

rich farm area on the southern side of the Jezreel Valley; since the time of Thutmose III it had been known as royal domain, cultivated for the benefit of an overlord. It was Sisera's job to protect the interests of his master, the king of Hazor in this highly profitable center for agriculture. Harosheth-hagoiim of the prose account (Judg. 4:2, 4:13, 4:16) is synonymous with "at Taanach by the waters of Megiddo" of the poetic version (Judg. 5:19).

The battle of Deborah is one of the few such narratives which can be reconstructed geographically in considerable detail; the prose and poetic versions complement one another. The conflict is said to have been preceded by the deeds of Shamgar the son of Anath who, inspired by Jael, the wife of Heber the Kenite, smote the Philistines (Judg. 3:31). Perhaps this echoes a clash with the Philistine garrison at Beth-shean (1 Sam. 31:10, 31:12). The situation had reached an impasse in which security along the roads was severely threatened (compare the danger of traveling through the 'Aruna Pass for fear of the wild tribesmen as depicted in Papyrus Anastasi I). The tensions between the Israelite tribes living in the hills and the Canaanite

city-states, who controlled most of the good farm land and water sources, erupted into open conflict; the tribesmen were assembled by Barak and brought to Mount Tabor by night. This holy mountain marked the juncture of the tribal territories of Zebulun, Naphtali and Issachar (Deut. 33:18–19). The largest contingent came from Zebulun and Naphtali with volunteers from Issachar and the three tribes in Mount Ephraim. Issachar was evidently living mainly along the southern edge of the Jezreel Valley in subservience to the Canaanites who imposed corvée labor on them (Gen. 49:14–15). They had not yet been settled on the plateau east of the Hill of Moreh. Machir was still dwelling in the northern part of Mount Ephraim, just south of the Jezreel Valley; later Machir moved to Transjordan where it came to be reckoned as a branch of the Manasseh tribe. Kedesh in Naphtali, the birthplace of Barak, the son of Abinoam, is not the Canaanite Kedesh in Upper Galilee (Josh. 20:7; 21:32; 1 Chron. 6:61) but rather Khirbet Kedish, an extensive Israelite site overlooking the Sea of Chinnereth, only a few hours' walk from Mount Tabor.

The names of the individual Canaanite

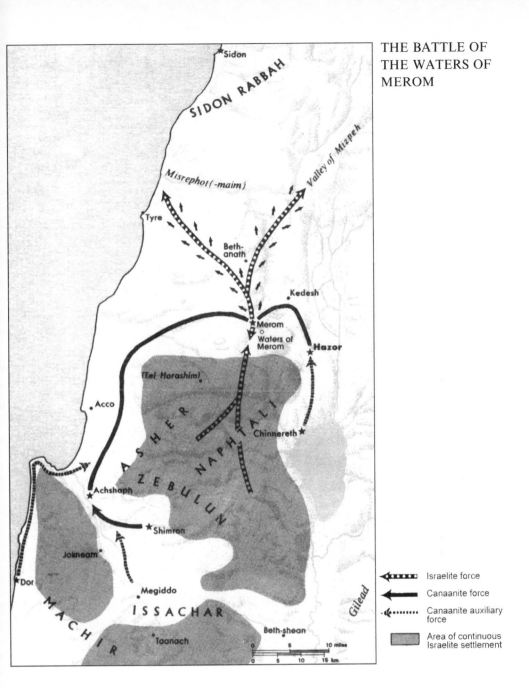

THE BATTLE OF
THE WATERS OF
MEROM

kings involved are not enumerated in
Judges but they may have been preserved
in the list of conquered Canaanite cities
in Joshua 12. Sisera gathered the Canaanite chariotry at Harosheth-hagoiim,
and after crossing the upper reaches of
the Kishon stream, proceeded toward
Mount Tabor. The Canaanites were

confident that with the mobility of their
chariots they could intimidate the foot
troops from the Israelite tribes and soon
have them scattered before a rain of
arrows. On the day chosen for the
confrontation, it began to rain and the
chariots bogged down in the mud of the
valley floor. This gave the advantage to

the Israelite warriors who charged down the mountainside on foot, gaining momentum and courage as they ran. The Kishon, becoming swollen by the rains, hindered the escape of the Canaanite warriors who had abandoned their chariots and were fleeing on foot. They had gone to the battle expecting to receive great rewards upon their victorious return to "Taanach by the waters of Megiddo" but they got no "spoil of silver" there; instead, they were swept away by the torrent of the Kishon.

Sisera had also abandoned his chariot, but instead of fleeing towards his own headquarters in Harosheth-hagoiim (probably Megiddo itself though that town is never mentioned in the narrative), he struck for the Jordan Valley via the hills of Lower Galilee. Thus, he came to the settlement of Heber the Kenite. Heber's family were descendants of Hobab, the father-in-law of Moses, and ancestor of the Kenites who had settled in the wilderness of Arad (Judg. 1:16). The encampment located at Allon (Oak of) Zaanannim, on the southern border Naphtali's territory (Josh. 19:33), was probably a cult center (compare Allon [=Oak of] Moreh, near Shechem; Gen. 12:6). Jael, the wife of Heber, was probably a renowned prophetess, familiar to both Canaanites and Israelites. Sisera was evidently seeking refuge in her sanctuary. Instead, he met his death at her hands.

Only four Canaanite cities are mentioned in the narrative about the conflict at the waters of Merom. The Madon and Shimron of the Hebrew version are ghost words; the Greek Septuagint translation, based on a superior Hebrew text, proves that the originals were Maron (= Merom) and Simeon (known as Shim'on in the Egyptian sources; and compare 2 Chron. 16:9, 34:6). The Canaanites had gathered at the waters of Meron/Merom (the name is preserved in Marun er-Ras), a central point in Upper Galilee. The non-biblical references (Egyptian and Assyrian) to Meron/Merom also suggest a location in this area. The line of the Canaanite retreat, "as far as Great Sidon and Misrephoth-maim and east as far as the valley of Mizpeh" (Josh. 10:8) confirms that the battle took place in Upper Galilee. The original clans involved were probably those of Naphtali and perhaps of Asher, whose initial settlements were in the high mountainous area of southern Upper Galilee as demonstrated by archaeological surveys.

The leader of this campaign is ascribed by the Book of Joshua to Joshua himself, who is also credited with the destruction of Canaanite Hazor. Archaeological excavations have revealed the wholesale destruction of the Canaanite city, but the exact date of this event cannot be determined by material remains alone. Nor is there any archaeological proof for the identity of the attackers.

THE LIMITS OF ISRAELITE CONTROL
12TH TO 11TH CENTURIES BCE

By the twelfth century BCE the principle rival peoples in Palestine were becoming well established in their respective areas: the Canaanites continued to dwell in the northern valleys and plains, the Philis- tines (with other "sea peoples"?) in the southern coastal plain, and the tribes of Israel in the hill country. The biblical tradition confirms that Israelites were unable to dislodge the Canaanites and

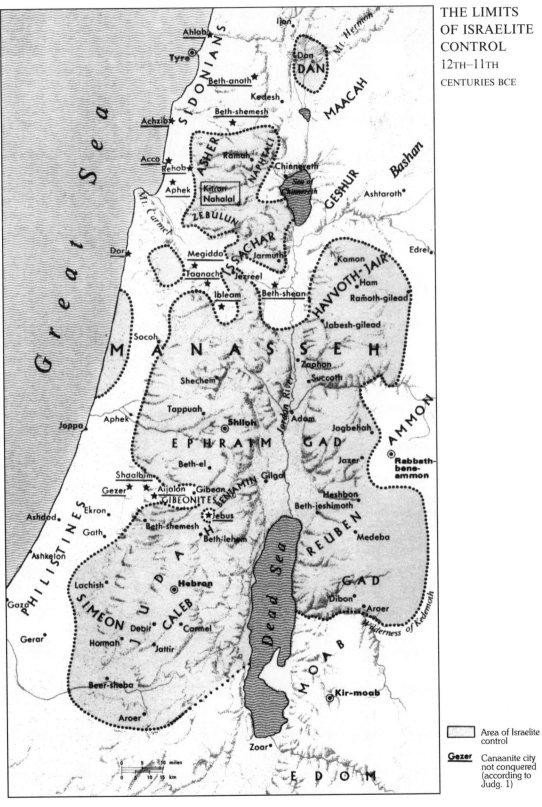

THE LIMITS
OF ISRAELITE
CONTROL
12TH–11TH
CENTURIES BCE

Great Sea

Ijon
Ahlab
Tyre
DAN
Dan
Beth-anath
MAACAH
Kedesh
Mt Hermon
Achzib
Beth-shemesh
ASHER
Ramah
NAPHTALI
Acco
Rehob
Chinnereth
Bashan
Aphek
Kitron
Nahalal
Sea of
Chinnereth
GESHUR
Ashtaroth
ZEBULUN
Mt Carmel
ISSACHAR
Edrei
Dor
Megiddo
Jarmuth
Kamon
HAVVOTH-JAIR
Taanach
Jezreel
Ham
Ibleam
Beth-shean
Ramoth-gilead
Jabesh-gilead
MANASSEH
Socoh
Zaphon
Shechem
Succoth
Tappuah
Joppa
Aphek
Shiloh
Adam
Jogbehah
AMMON
EPHRAIM
GAD
Jazer
Rabbath-
bene-
ammon
Beth-el
Shaalbim
Gilgal
Gezer
Aijalon
Gibeon
GIBEONITES
BENJAMIN
Heshbon
Ekron
Jebus
Beth-jeshimoth
Ashdod
Beth-shemesh
Gath
Beth-lehem
REUBEN
Medeba
Ashkelon
Dead Sea
Jordan River
GAD
Gaza
Lachish
Hebron
Dibon
Gerar
SIMEON
CALEB
Aroer
Debir
Carmel
Wilderness of Kedemoth
Hormah
Jattir
MOAB
Beer-sheba
Aroer
Kir-moab
PHILISTINES
JUDAH
Zoar
EDOM

0   5   10 miles
0   5   10   15 km

Area of Israelite
control

Gezer Canaanite city
not conquered
(according to
Judg. 1)

17

Beth-anath (relief of Rameses II at Thebes).

Amorites in the lowland areas, for they had "chariots of iron" (Josh. 17:18). A list of the areas where the non-Israelites continued to dwell is given in Judges 1 and similar allusions appear here and there in the Book of Joshua (Josh. 15:63, 17:11–13). Judges 1:18–19 (LXX) confirms that Judah did not subdue the Philistines. Judges 1:27–35 lists the unconquered areas according to tribe. The main surviving Canaanite enclaves were in the Valley of Jezreel, and along the Phoenician coast. The Asherites gained acceptance among the Phoenicians (Sidonians), apparently as client farmers for a society whose manpower was heavily committed to maritime activities (Judg. 1:31–32). No tradition exists about the conquest of Shechem, whose situation may have been like Gezer (Judg. 1:19), a Canaanite population living in symbiosis with the Israelites. Jebus-Jerusalem, Gezer and the Amorite towns that resisted the Danites were in the center of the country. Very early traditions reveal that the Ephraimites came into early contact with the indigenous population of the area where the Danites were driven out (1 Chron. 7:20–24; Judg. 1:35). Some clans from Benjamin also migrated to the same area (1 Chron. 8:12–13; 2 Sam. 4:3–4).

Recent archaeological surveys in the hill country areas confirm the arrival of pastoralists who began their settlement along the fringes of the steppe land, east of the watershed. Gradually they expanded and established settlements in the areas of mixed agriculture and eventually moved into the western hill zones where it became necessary to develop terraces and plant orchards and vineyards. Thus, originally pastoral groups became transformed into a thoroughly sedentary society with varied subsistence strategies. The tribal groups that settled in Upper Galilee went through a similar process; their material culture reflects a certain cultural symbiosis with the Phoenicians on the coast below.

All of this data confirms the new population revolution brought about in the twelfth and eleventh centuries. In the Late Bronze Age the main concentrations of population were in the plains; the hill country areas were largely uninhabited, providing refuge for 'apiru outlaws and for the Shosu pastoralists. The latter became more and more numerous and adopted sedentary ways of life, perhaps because of a decline in the overall Canaanite agricultural productivity.

The dichotomy between Canaanites on the plains and Israelites in the hills characterizes the narratives throughout the books of Judges and Samuel.

THE TWELVE TRIBES

THE description of the tribal territories in Joshua 13–19 is comprised of some detailed border descriptions and of lists of towns for the respective tribes. The town lists are assumed by most scholars to date to a period of centralized administration during the monarchy. This is especially relevant for the extensive lists of Judah which are organized into regions and districts. The border descriptions are only partial. The map on the following page shows that detailed descriptions are given for only a few of the tribes. Those accounts that do exist consist of recognizable boundary points given in geographical order. The course of the border can be traced by means of the descriptive verbs used in the delineations. Comparison of parallel passages giving the same border, such as the mutual boundary of Benjamin with Judah and Ephraim, show that the original text must have been much more detailed than the abridged versions preserved in the Book of Joshua. One finds careful recording of small details only in crucial areas, such as the boundary passing around Jerusalem. The zones where definite borders are not given correspond roughly to those areas where the Israelites had not actually penetrated during the initial stages of the settlement process (as depicted in Judg. 1).

The tribes of Issachar, Dan, Simeon and the Transjordanian tribes have only town lists coupled with some general topographical designations. The Judean border is not really that of the tribe; the northern segment corresponds to that of Benjamin while the southern is evidently the political border of the Judean monarchy (also applied to the description of Canaan). The northwestern extension of the border of Judah (beyond Beth-shemesh) was actually the border between Philistia and the kingdom of Israel. The Asherite border is also related to the national Israelite boundary during the monarchy (compare 2 Sam. 24:5–7).

The only tribes with border descriptions are Benjamin, Manasseh, Ephraim, Zebulun, Asher and Naphtali, the same tribes mentioned as those who failed to conquer the Canaanite enclaves (Judg. 1:22–38). There is also an intriguing correlation with the Solomonic districts described in 1 Kings 4. For the districts defined by tribal names in the Solomonic list, we have borders in Joshua 13–19; for those Solomonic districts defined by town lists (corresponding to the lists of unconquered towns in Judg. 1) there is a lack of border descriptions in Joshua.

THE BORDERS
OF THE
TRIBAL
TERRITORIES
12TH–11TH
CENTURIES BCE

Great Sea

Ahlab
Tyre
Hosa
Kanah
Hammon
A S H E R
Achzib
Abdon
Beth-emek
Acco
Rehob
Neiel
Cabul
Aphek

Ijon
Abel-beth-maacha
Dan
Beth-anath
Kedesh
Yiron
Beth-shemesh
N A P H T A L I
Ramah
Chinnereth
Sea of
Chinnereth

Mt. Carmel
Valley of Iphtahel
ZEBULUN
Helkath
Joknean
Sarid
Shunem
Dor
Megiddo

Heleph
Japhia
Mt. Tabor
Jabneel

Mt. Bashan
Ashtaroth
Edrei
HAVVOTH-JAIR
Lo-debar
Jarmuth

Taanach
Ibleam
Beth-shean

M A N A S S E H

Tirzah
Shechem
Michmethath
Janoah
Tappuah
Kanah Brook

Zaphon
Succoth
Mahanaim
Taanath-shiloh
Shiloh
Ramath-mizpeh

G i l e a d

River Jordan

A M M O N
Rabbath-bene-
ammon

E P H R A I M

Betonim
Jazer

Beth-el
Lower Beth-horon
Shaalbim
Gezer
Aijalon
Kiriath-jearim
B E N J A M I N
Jebus
Jericho
Beth-hoglah

Beth-nimrah
Beth-horam
Heshbon
Mephaath
Beth-jeshimoth
Beth-peor
Kiriathaim
Medebaland

Ashdod
Ekron
Gath
Beth-shemesh
PHILISTINES

Beth-baal-meon
Zereth-shahar
Jahzah

Tableland

Hebron

J U D A H

Dead Sea

Arnon River

Dibon
Kedemoth
Aroer

M O A B

Kir-moab

0   5   10 miles
0 5 10 15 km

.... Tribal border
●●●●●●●● Political border in days of David

The most prominent cult center for the northern tribes seems to have been Shiloh. During the period of the judges, the bond between these northern tribes and those of the south was rather tenuous. Judah, Simeon and the neighboring groups (Calebites, Kenazzites, Kenites, Jerachmeelites) did not take part in any common war venture (such as the battles of Deborah and Gideon). It is possible that at least the non-Judean tribes in the south looked to Hebron as an important cult center. However, it is not at all certain that there were any official "leagues" of tribes, either in the north or in the south, prior to the years of conflict between David and Eshbaal (Ishbosheth).

Mesopotamian border marker, c. 12th century BCE.

THE JUDGES ACCORDING TO THEIR TRIBES
12TH TO 11TH CENTURIES BCE

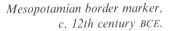

The Book of Judges was intended to give due credit to the various tribal heroes of the pre-monarchial age. On the other hand, the book stressed the shortcomings of even the most renowned of the judges, or deliverers. Subtle stress is placed on the fact that life is much better under the monarchy. At the beginning of the book, in chapter 1, the list of unconquered cities is annotated by the references to forced labor which was later imposed on the Canaanite population. The administration of such an institution as forced labor was only possible during the reigns of David and Solomon. The two accounts at the end of the Book of Judges are more explicit. Social anarchy and moral depravity, especially at the ancestral home of Saul, were rampant in the age when "There was no king in Israel; every man did what was right in his own eyes."

Besides the great Judges of deliverance, the Book of Judges also mentions several "minor Judges" (Judg. 10:1–5, 12:8–15), who judged the people from their native cities. Their wealth is usually emphasized in the Scriptures, and no tradition concerning wars under their leadership has come down to us. In times of peace, their authority was quite limited. Five "minor Judges" are given and it may be more than incidental that the total number of judges mentioned in the Book of Judges is twelve, a judge for each tribe. It is doubtful whether these were the only "minor Judges"; their names may have been chosen on the basis of their tribal affiliations, in order to provide each tribe with a judge, even if not a deliverer.

Tyre⊙

Dan•

Kedesh•

A S H E R

N A P H T A L I

Ashtaroth•

Acco•

| Shamgar son of Anath | 3

Z E B U L U N

Kedesh-naphtali★

| Barak son of Abinoam | 4

| Elon | 10

Kamon★

Megiddo•

I S S A C H A R

| Jair the Gileadite | 7   Ramoth-gilead•

Beth-shean•

M A N A S S E H

| Tola son of Puah of Issachar | 6

Shamir★   Zaphon★

| Gideon son of Joash | 5

Ophrah★ | Jephtah the Gileadite | 8

Pirathon★   •Shechem   •Succoth

| Abdon son of Hillel | 11

G A D

•Adam

R i v e r   J o r d a n

Joppa•

Shiloh⊙

Jazer•

E P H R A I M

Rabbath-bene-ammon⊙

Beth-el•

| Ehud son of Gera | 2   Gilgal•

B E N J A M I N

•Heshbon

Ashdod•

D A N

★Zorah   •Jebus

| Samson | 12   •Beth-lehem

Ashkelon•

| Ibzan | 9

R E U B E N

J U D A H

•Gaza | Othniel son of Kenaz | 1   •Hebron   •Dibon

D e a d   S e a

★Debir

S I M E O N   •Arad

Beer-sheba•   ⊙Kir-moab

Aroer•

Zoar•

THE JUDGES ACCORDING TO THEIR TRIBES

B. THE UNITED MONARCHY

THE KINGDOM OF SAUL C. 1035 TO 1017 BCE

SAUL was the last of the judges and the first of Israel's kings. Saul not only delivered Israel from the Philistine yoke, but also warred upon all the other surrounding enemies, and he "delivered Israel out of the hands of those who plundered them" (1 Sam. 14:48). In the account of the reign of Saul's son Eshbaal (Ishbosheth—2 Sam. 2:9), the regions of his kingdom are listed as the five areas of "all Israel." These are the regions of dense Israelite settlement: Gilead in Transjordan; the Geshurites (incorrectly transmitted as Ashurites) in Galilee; the plain of Jezreel (named after the major city of Issachar); Ephraim in the central hill country, and Benjamin. To these must be added Judah, over which Saul had also extended his rule, but which fell to David "in the days of Eshbaal."

The mention of Jezreel in this passage probably reflects the status of the tribe of Issachar, who had settled in the town of Jezreel and who had been serving the Canaanites as corvée laborers (Gen. 49:14–15). The major towns along the sides of the great Valley were probably still maintaining their Canaanite character under nominal Philistine hegemony (like Beth-shean). Saul had died trying to dislodge the Philistines from this area. There must have been some degree of symbiosis between the Canaanites in these towns and the Israelites in the surrounding villages throughout the late twelfth and eleventh centuries BCE.

The borders of the kingdom of Israel in the days of Saul were those of the Israelite settlement (1 Sam. 13:19). He made no attempt to impose his rule over

Philistine noble, faience plaque of time of Rameses III, Medinet Habu.

the various Canaanite enclaves; even pagan Jebus, very close to his capital, was never conquered by him. The task of uniting the entire Holy Land under a single Israelite king was left to his successor, David.

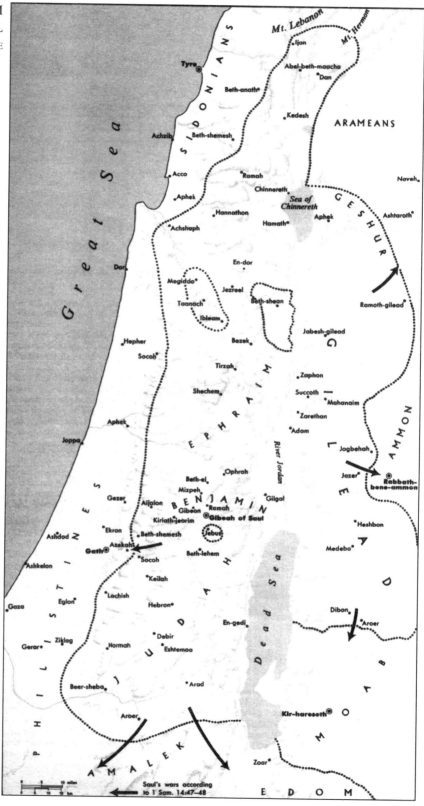

Great Sea

Mt. Lebanon

Mt. Hermon

Ijon

Tyre

Abel-beth-maacha

Dan

Beth-anath

Kedesh

ARAMEANS

Achzib

Beth-shemesh

Acco

Ramah

Naveh

Chinnereth

GESHUR

Aphek

Sea of
Chinnereth

Ashtaroth

Hannathon

Hamath

Aphek

Achshaph

En-dor

Dor

Megiddo

Jezreel

Ramoth-gilead

Taanach

Beth-shean

Ibleam

G

Bezek

Jabesh-gilead

Hepher

Socoh

Tirzah

Zaphon

Shechem

Succoth

Mahanaim

Zarethan

Aphek

Adam

E
P
H
R
A
I
M

River Jordan

Joppa

Jogbehah

AMMON

Ophrah

Jazer

Rabbath-
bene-ammon

Beth-el

Mizpeh

B E N J A M I N

Gilgal

Gezer

Gibeon

Ramah

Aijalon

Gibeah of Saul

Heshbon

Kiriath-jearim

Ekron

Ashdod

Beth-shemesh

Jebus

Medeba

Azekah

Gath

Socoh

Beth-lehem

Dead Sea

Ashkelon

Keilah

Dibon

Aroer

Gaza

Eglon

Lachish

Hebron

En-gedi

Ziklag

Gerar

Debir

Eshtemoa

J
U
D
A
H

Hormah

Beer-sheba

Arad

Kir-hareseth

O

Aroer

A
M
A
L
E
K

Zoar

M
O
A
B

Saul's wars according
to 1 Sam. 14:47–48

E D O M

P
H
I
L
I
S
T
I
N
E
S

G
I
L
E
A
D

THE KINGDOM
OF DAVID
c. 1000–970 BCE

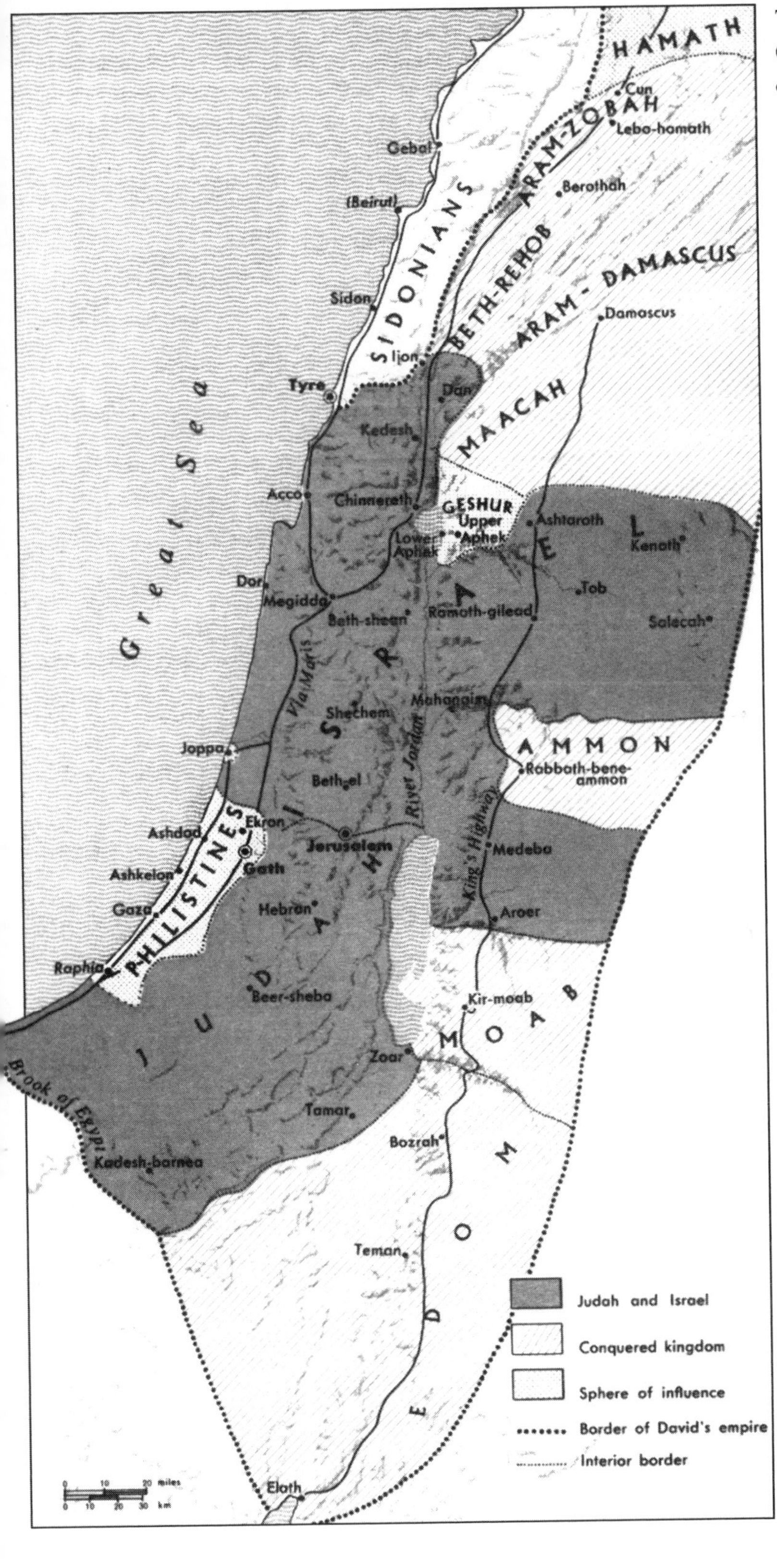

HAMATH

Cun
Lebo-hamath

Gebal

ARAM-ZOBAH

Berothah

(Beirut)

BETH-REHOB

ARAM - DAMASCUS

Sidon

Damascus

Ijon

SIDONIANS

Tyre

Dan

Kedesh

MAACAH

Acco

Chinnereth

GESHUR
Upper
Aphek

Ashtaroth

Kenath

Dor

Lower
Aphek

Megiddo

Beth-shean

Ramoth-gilead

Tob

Salecah

G I L E A D

I S R A E L

Via Maris

Shechem

Mahanaim

River Jordan

Joppa

Beth-el

AMMON

Rabboth-bene-
ammon

Great Sea

Ashdod

Ekron

Jerusalem

PHILISTINES

Gath

Medeba

King's Highway

Ashkelon

Gaza

Hebron

Aroer

J U D A H

Raphia

Beer-sheba

Kir-moab

Zoar

M O A B

Brook of Egypt

Tamar

Bozrah

Kadesh-barnea

E D O M

Teman

	Judah and Israel
	Conquered kingdom
	Sphere of influence
••••••	Border of David's empire
·–·–·	Interior border

Eloth

0 10 20 miles
0 10 20 30 km

THE KINGDOM OF DAVID AND SOLOMON
C. 1000 TO 930 BCE

THE kingdom of Israel reached the height of its military and political power under David. The larger kingdoms in the Ancient East were at their nadir, leaving a vacuum in the western part of the "Fertile Crescent." In David, Israel found a brilliant and far-sighted military and political leader, able to exploit the prevailing situation. Following the encounter with Aram-zobah, Israel became the major power in Syria and Palestine. The extent of the Israelite empire under David and Solomon is revealed by the passage concerning Solomon: "For he had dominion over all the region west of the Euphrates from Tiphsah to Gaza, over all the kings west of the Euphrates" (1 Kings 4:24). In the Hebrew, "west of the Euphrates" is "the other side of the river," the name used by the peoples of Mesopotamia for this area. Thus the influence of David and Solomon spread from Tiphsah on the Great Bend of the Euphrates to Philistine Gaza on the southern border of the Land of Canaan.

This was an administratively complex empire, three main elements being discernible within it: the Israelite population; conquered kingdoms; and vassal kings. At the center of the empire stood the tribes of Israel and Judah, to which were appended the Canaanite-Amorite regions brought under David's control. Around these lay the conquered and tributary kingdoms: Edom, Moab, Ammon, Aram-damascus, and Aram-zobah. Israelite governors were appointed over

some of these territories, as in Edom and Damascus (2 Sam. 8:6, 8:14), while in others members of the local royal house ruled, under the tutelage of the king of Israel. These latter were actually governors, as in Ammon. One of the notables of Transjordan, who had come to David's aid during the rebellion of Absalom—Shobi the son of Nahash of Rabbath-bene-ammon (2 Sam. 17:27)—was probably the son of the king of Ammon who died before his kingdom was conquered by David (1 Chron. 19:1). The third element, the vassal kings, had been forced, in one way or another, to accept David's hegemony; they included Philistia and various kingdoms in north-

THE ISRAELITE HEGEMONY
DURING THE REIGNS OF
DAVID AND SOLOMON
C. 1000–930 BCE

ern Transjordan, such as Geshur, whose king was the grandfather of Absalom (2 Sam. 3:3, 13:37). The relationship with Toi king of Hamath (2 Sam. 8:10) and Hiram king of Tyre was probably of a similar nature (2 Sam. 5:11).

THE BUILDING AND EXPANSION OF JERUSALEM
MID-10TH CENTURY BCE

SOLOMON extended the limits of Jerusalem, fortifying and embellishing it as befitting the capital of a powerful state. The temple, which took seven years to build, was overshadowed by the royal palace, which took thirteen. The two buildings represented the two leading institutions of the realm, the Aaronic/Levitical religious organization and the monarchy. Each depended upon the other to govern the nation; each had large holdings of land and resources throughout the country.

The threshing floor purchased by David and its hill were converted into a citadel, extending the effective area of the city northward. The technical improvements included massive retaining walls, a sample of which was uncovered in the excavations above the Gihon spring.

On the adjacent hills to the southeast, there were diplomatic missions from Solomon's political allies (as exemplified by his royal marriages, 1 Kings 1:11). Each diplomatic compound had its own shrine for worship of the national deities

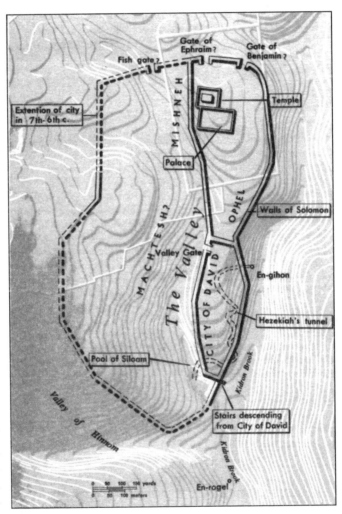

(1 Kings 11:4–8; 2 Kings 23:13). The wives of Solomon's many political marriages could make offerings at a shrine of their home deity. In his later years Solomon also joined with them in their worship.

C. ISRAEL AND JUDAH

THE DIVISION OF THE KINGDOM 931 BCE

THE deep-seated differences between the northern tribes of Israel and the southern alliance of Judah (with Caleb, Kenaz, etc.) were never truly resolved under David and Solomon. The heavy burden of the corvée rankled the people of the north, particularly those of the House of Joseph. Solomon's son, Rehoboam, failed to realize the gravity of their dissatisfaction. His succession in Jerusalem was acknowledged without apparent dissent, but he had to go to Shechem for ratification of his kingship by the tribes of the north. The latter had chosen as their spokesman the recently returned political exile, Jeroboam (who had formerly been in charge of the corvée work carried out by the House of Joseph).

The economic crisis brought about by the external troubles during the latter years of Solomon's reign had made life even more difficult for the citizens of Israel. When Rehoboam haughtily rejected their demands for an easing of their burdens, he foolishly sent an unpopular bureaucrat, Adoniram, to intimidate them. Adoniram was in charge of the hated levy, the forced labor imposed on the formerly non-Israelite enclaves. No wonder that the Israelites expressed their displeasure by stoning him to death! Rehoboam hastened to return to Jerusalem but was dissuaded by the prophet Shemaiah from trying to use armed force against the northern rebels.

The population of Benjamin was closely linked with Jerusalem; there were crown lands, Levitical cities and the Gibeonites did special service at the temple. So Benjamin remained part of the Davidic kingdom.

Damascus and Edom had recently revolted, Ezion-geber was threatened if not lost already; the other neighboring countries were doubtlessly glad to break their ties with the weakened kingdoms of Israel and Judah. The Israelite monopoly over trade and commerce was broken.

Jeroboam I began to organize his new government. Shechem was chosen as the first northern capital and a Transjordan headquarters was set up at Penuel (1 Kings 12:25). Royal worship centers were established at Beth-el and Dan, two places with long cultic traditions, one at the southern and the other at the northern extremity of his realm (1 Kings 12:29–30). Other local shrines were also staffed with non-Levitical priests. Shiloh and Tirzah are mentioned (1 Kings 14:4, 14:17).

Phoenician ship, relief from palace of Sargon II at Khorsabad.

THE DIVISION
OF THE
KINGDOM
931 BCE

Then Jeroboam built Shechem ... and he went out from there and built Penuel
(1 Kings 12:25)

Royal sanctuary

Sidon

Damascus

Tyre

Dan

ARAM-DAMASCUS

Hazor

GESHUR

Acco

Ashtaroth

Dor

Megiddo

Ramoth-gilead

Coronation of Jeroboam over Israel

Tirzah

I
S
R
A
E
L

Shechem

Penuel

Joppa

Zeredah
Shiloh

AMMON

Royal sanctuary

Beth-el

Rabbath-bene-
ammon

Gibbethon

Gezer

Gath

Jerusalem

Gaza

Hebron

J
U
D
A
H

Dibo

Raphia

Arad

M O A B

Beer-sheba

Kir-moab

Tamar

Bozrah

J
U
D
A
H

Kadesh-barnea

E
G
Y
P
T

Teman

E
D
O
M

Great Sea

P
H
I
L
I
S
T
I
N
E
S

S
I
D
O
N
I
A
N
S

Elath

0   10   20 miles
0   10   20   30 km

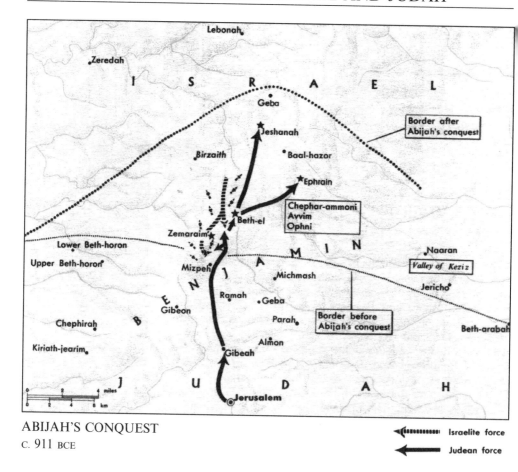

ABIJAH'S CONQUEST
C. 911 BCE

◄▬▬▬▬▬ Israelite force

◄▬▬▬ Judean force

A STATE of belligerence between Judah and Israel continued throughout the reigns of Rehoboam, Abijah and Asa, kings of Judah, and the dynasties of Jeroboam and Baasha in Israel. After Shishak's campaign, both kingdoms were doubtless exhausted; the first open conflict we hear about took place in the short reign of Abijah (913–911/910 BCE). After a bitter confrontation at Zemaraim the Israelites retreated, leaving the towns of Beth-el, Jeshanah and Ephrain (Ophrah) at the mercy of the Judeans. Abijah thus pushed the border between the two nations north of Beth-el, probably encompassing the district of Benjamin north of the "official" tribal border as reflected in the tribal town list (Josh. 18:22–24).

Jeroboam I died shortly after this crushing defeat and was succeeded by his son Nadab who soon found himself at war with the Philistines. He was assassinated by Baasha son of Ahijah while he and the Israelite army were besieging Gibbethon (1 Kings 15:27; 909 BCE). Meanwhile, Abijah had also gone to his fate and had been succeeded by his son Asa (911/910 BCE). Baasha evidently did not pursue the war with Philistia; he may have maintained a belligerent stance toward Judah but probably found it necessary to concern himself with internal affairs. Asa thus enjoyed a decade of peace (c. 909–899 BCE) in which to rebuild the strength of Judah (2 Chron. 13:23–14:7).

That peace was shattered by the invasion of Zerah the Cushite with an army of Cushites. Zerah was probably an Arabian leader from the northern Hejaz (cf. Gen. 10:7; Hab. 3:7; 2 Chron. 21:16) (ruled 904–890 BCE). He may have been invited by the Philistines to attack Judah. He may have begun by destroying some of the newly rebuilt Judean fortresses in the Negeb, such as Beer-sheba. When he tried to penetrate the Shephelah of Judah, Asa routed his forces in the valley "north of Mareshah" (following the Greek version). The army of Judah pursued the enemy back through the western Negeb; there they ravaged and plundered the sedentary population in the towns and the pastoralists in their tent camps, "throughout the vicinity of Gerar" (2 Chron. 14:13–14). In the wake of this victory, Asa capitalized on the national spirit to reform the religious institutions and to strengthen the central temple cult which supported the monarchy. His national convocation took place in 896 BCE, his fifteenth year (2 Chron. 15:10), that is the thirty-fifth year of the separate Judean monarchy (ibid., 15:19).

The respite in hostilities between Israel and Judah was rudely interrupted in Asa's sixteenth year, 895 BCE, the thirty-sixth year of the Judean monarchy (2 Chron. 16:1), when Baasha invaded the Benjaminite territory and established a strong point at Ramah. By seizing the junction between the watershed trunk

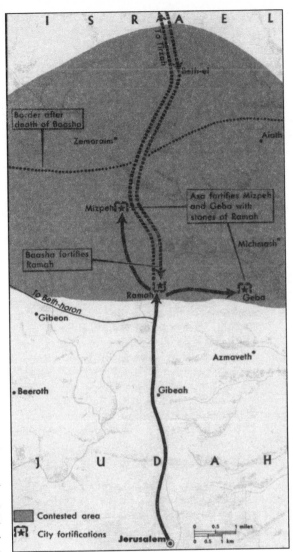

BAASHA'S ATTACK ON ASA
c. 895 BCE

road and the Beth-horon road, Baasha was able to cut Jerusalem off from its most important road link with the coastal plain (1 Kings 15:17; 2 Chron. 16:1). Asa preferred a political maneuver rather than risk another military confrontation with his northern neighbor. He sent a large bribe to Ben-hadad I (a dynastic name), "the king of Aram enthroned in Damascus." The latter invaded northern Israel and occupied most, if not all, of eastern Galilee (1 Kings 15:20; 2 Chron. 16:4).

Baasha withdrew from Ramah and returned to his headquarters at Tirzah. Asa brought out his people and dismantled the fortifications Baasha had built and used the building materials to fortify Mizpeh, on the main trunk road to Beth-el, and Geba, facing the second-ary eastern road that skirts the steppe land. It would appear that most of Abijah's territorial gains in the hill country of Ephraim were relinquished at this time. A logical border between Israel and Judah was established between Mizpeh and Beth-el; to the west some territory may have remained in dispute (cf. 2 Chron. 25:13).

AHAB'S WARS WITH ARAM 855 TO 853 BCE

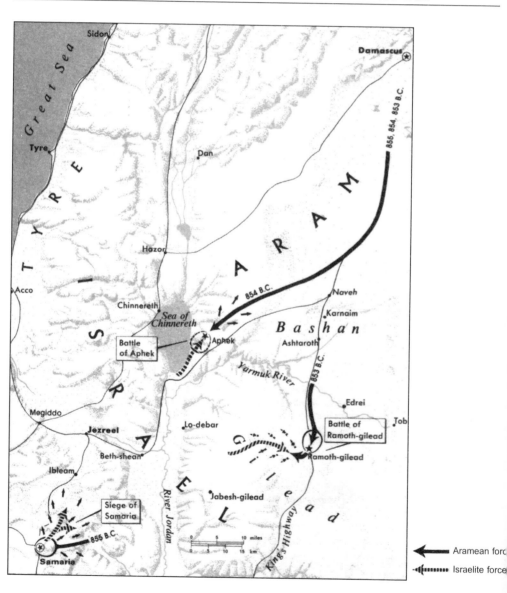

AHAB pushed ahead with the program launched by his father. The clash of interests with Aram-Damascus was inevitable. The Arameans took the initiative by invading Israel and besieging Samaria itself but their feudal social structure, a league of vassal kings, made it impossible to exercise a unified command; the kinglets were routed in a surprise attack as they lounged in their pavilions (1 Kings 20:1–22). As a result, the king of Damascus reorganized his kingdom and replaced the kings with governors. However, the initiative had passed to Ahab, who carried the battle to Aphek on the heights above Chinnereth. His decisive victory won him political and trade concessions from the Aramean (1 Kings 20:23–43). There followed a three-year armistice between the two countries during which time all the states of the Levant banded together to face the invasion by Shalmaneser III at Qarqar. Afterwards Damascus issued another challenge to Israel and Ahab appealed to Jehoshaphat to help him. Jehoshaphat agreed and appointed his son, Jehoram, as co-regent to protect the succession (2 Kings 1:17, 3:1, 8:16). The battle was drawn at Ramoth-gilead; Ahab lost his life and Damascus gained the upper hand in Transjordan (2 Kings 22:1–40; 2 Chron. 18:2–34).

THE BATTLE OF QARQAR 853 BCE

THE states of the Levant were rudely shaken by the resurgence of Assyrian might in the ninth century BCE. About 1100 BCE Tiglath-pileser I, king of Assyria, had reached the "Upper Sea" (the Mediterranean), but under his successors Assyria again reverted to a minor status. Asshurnasirpal II (883–859 BCE) inaugurated a new expansionist policy. His armies reached Syria and the coastal cities of Phoenicia—Arvad, Byblos, Tyre and Sidon, and extorted heavy tribute. His son, Shalmaneser III (859–824 BCE), continued this aggressive policy; in his first year his army reached the Amanus Mountains.

The campaign of his sixth year (853 BCE) saw him march forth from Nineveh to the ford of the Euphrates near Pethor, which he crossed in flood tide. He continued via Aleppo to the territory subservient to the king of Hamath, capturing and plundering. This time the Levantine states had ceased their local quarrels (1 Kings 22:1) and had banded together to stop the invader. They met him in battle at Qarqar on the Orontes and dealt the Assyrian army a heavy blow. Though Shalmaneser III claimed a victory, he did not return to this area for another four years.

The only detailed report of this battle is a provincial Assyrian stele the text of which is replete with mistakes. The list of the Levantine allies is probably quite authentic but the number of chariots and infantry supposedly brought by each are highly exaggerated. The 500 men from Byblos, the thousand men from Egypt, and the ten chariots from Irqanata may be correct (also the 30 chariots from Siannu, etc.). But the thousands of chariots and troops assigned to Hadad-ezer, Irhuleni, Ahab and others are patently false. This inscription should not be taken as evidence of some mighty chariot force at Ahab's disposal. In reality, he probably had about twenty chariots; compare the chariot forces of Irqanata and Siannu. Judah does not

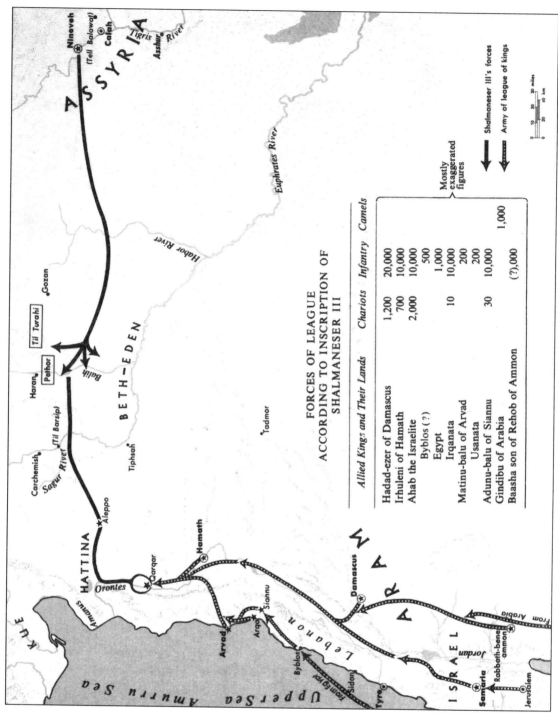

FORCES OF LEAGUE ACCORDING TO INSCRIPTION OF SHALMANESER III

Allied Kings and Their Lands	Chariots	Infantry	Camels
Hadad-ezer of Damascus	1,200	20,000	
Irhuleni of Hamath	700	10,000	
Ahab the Israelite	2,000	10,000	
Byblos (?)		500	
Egypt		1,000	
Irqanata	10	10,000	
Matinu-balu of Arvad		200	
Usanata		200	
Adunu-balu of Siannu	30	10,000	
Gindibu of Arabia			1,000
Baasha son of Rehob of Ammon		(?),000	

Mostly exaggerated figures

→ Shalmaneser III's forces

→ Army of league of kings

THE BATTLE
OF QARQAR
853 BCE

King of Assyria at head of army, bronze relief of Shalmaneser III from Tell Balawat.

seem to have taken part unless her forces are subsumed under those of Ahab.

Throughout the ninth century, the Assyrian army was making adventurous forays into Syria and other areas, far from their home bases. They were constantly facing a difficult logistic problem. Only by successfully plundering hapless cities and their surrounding countryside could they keep up their momentum. There was always a chance that a well-supplied city could survive unscathed.

After the Assyrian army withdrew, the local states began once again to engage in their local wars. Such was the case between Damascus and Israel. Within a few months at most, Ahab was slain on the field of battle at Ramoth-gilead.

ISRAEL AND JUDAH IN THE DAYS OF JEROBOAM II AND UZZIAH MID-8TH CENTURY BCE

THE kingdoms of Israel and Judah achieved their last zenith of real prosperity and power during the second quarter of the eighth century BCE. Together they once again dominated the major arteries of world commerce across the southern arm of the Fertile Crescent. The success of Jeroboam II was acclaimed by Jonah, son of Amittai, a prophet from Gath-hepher in Galilee (2 Kings 14:25). The prophetic schools of the ninth century continued to flourish in the eighth; their critique of ethical and moral affairs was directed at both the international and the internal scene. Amos, from Tekoa, issued his pronouncements at Beth-el, the royal cult center of Israel (Amos 7:10–17). In the name of the Lord of Israel he proclaimed judgment on Israel's principal enemies: Damascus for its aggressions in Gilead (Amos 1:3–5), Philistia (Gaza, Ashdod, Ashkelon, Ekron) for helping

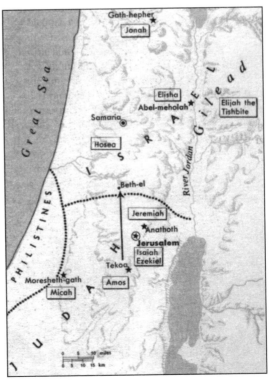

THE CITIES OF THE PROPHETS
9TH TO 7TH CENTURIES BCE

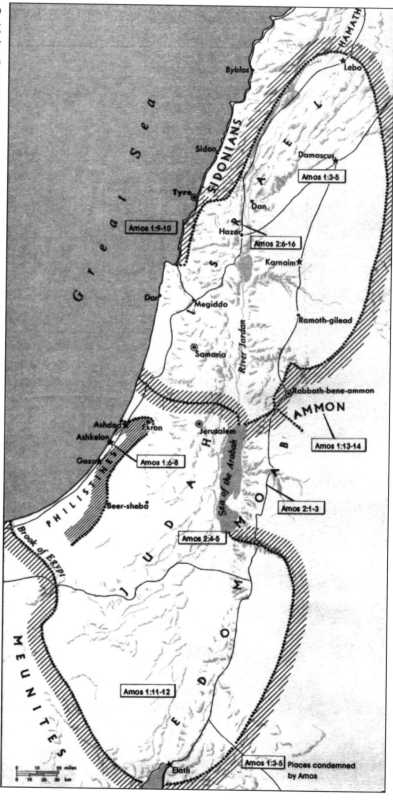

ISRAEL AND
JUDAH IN THE
DAYS OF
JEROBOAM II AND
UZZIAH
MID-8TH
CENTURY BCE

Byblos

Lebo

Great Sea

SIDONIANS

Sidon

Damascus

Amos 1:3-5

Tyre

Dan

I S R A E L

Amos 1:9-10

Hazor

Amos 2:6-16

Karnaim

Megiddo

Dor

Ramoth-gilead

River Jordan

Samaria

Rabbath-bene-ammon

Ashdod   Ekron

AMMON

Ashkelon

Jerusalem

Amos 1:13-14

Gaza

J U D A H

Amos 1:6-8

Sea of the Arabah

M O A B

Amos 2:1-3

Beer-sheba

P H I L I S T I N E S

Amos 2:4-5

Brook of EGYPT

E D O M

Amos 1:11-12

M E U N I T E S

0   10   20 miles
0   10   20   30 km

Elath

Amos 1:3-5 Places condemned
by Amos

the Edomites to enslave Judeans (vs. 6–8), Tyre for sharing in that enterprise (vs. 9–10), Edom for his cruelty against the Judeans (vs. 11–12), Ammon for its atrocities in Gilead (vs. 13–14), and Moab for desecrating the bones of a rival king (2:1–3). Then Amos turned his wrath upon Judah for not keeping the Law of the Lord (vs. 4–5), and upon Israel for gross violations of social justice (vs. 6–16).

Amos saw that the defense of walled cities (as practiced by Samaria and Damascus in the ninth century) would not succeed against a determined conqueror like Tiglath-pileser III, who would advance inexorably from province to province, never mounting a major campaign without adequate logistic support from an Assyrian governor close by (Amos 3:11).

Hosea, whose city is unknown, reveals a deep love for the countryside of Samaria alongside an abhorrence for its religious corruption.

THE CAMPAIGN OF REZIN AND PEKAH AGAINST JUDAH 735 BCE

THE Kingdom of Israel began its disintegration with the assassination of Zechariah, son of Jeroboam II, after only six months in office (752 BCE). His successor, Shallum, lasted only one month (2 Kings 15:8–14). Menahem, the new usurper, reigned in Samaria for ten years and was followed by his son, Pekahiah for two more years (752–742/741 BCE; 2 Kings 15:17–26). Meanwhile, Pekah the son of Remaliah, began a twenty-year rule in Gilead (see Hosea 5:3–5); he apparently had a presumed reconciliation with Pekahiah but assassinated him and took power over all of Israel for another eight years (740–732 BCE; 2 Kings 15:25–31). Jotham had taken advantage of the divided rule in the north to exert Judean military power against the king of Ammon, thus gaining a foothold in Transjordan.

However, Tiglath-pileser III renewed Assyria's expansionist policy. Unlike most of his predecessors, he was not satisfied with the submission of local kings and the payment of tribute; rather he initiated the annexation of conquered territories, reducing them to provinces under Assyrian governors. Opposition to Assyrian permanent rule was squelched by exiling the upper classes and resettling deportees from some other part of the empire. Tiglath-pileser III avoided long campaigns far from his supply bases. The newly appointed governors provided logistic support for the Assyrian army when it pushed out in the next step of conquest.

In 743 BCE Tiglath-pileser III was faced by a coalition of western states surprisingly led by Azariah of Judah. The effort was unsuccessful and Menahem of Israel paid tribute to the Assyrians (2 Kings 15:19–20). The heavy burden that this payment imposed on the nobility of Israel may have engendered the unrest that led Pekah to power in Samaria three years later. While Tiglath-pileser III was engaged elsewhere, especially in Urartu (Ararat), Pekah made an alliance with Rezin, king of Damascus. They hoped to organize a strong united front against the Assyrians. Jotham apparently shared his late father's anti-Assyrian bias but the leadership in Jerusalem did not. After sixteen years of reign, Jotham was effectually deposed in favor of his son, Ahaz (735 BCE), who refused to join Pekah and Rezin against Tiglath-pileser III. Jotham actually lived to his twentieth year (732/731 BCE; 2 Kings 15:30).

Pekah and Rezin immediately declared war on Ahaz in an attempt to depose him in favor of a certain Tabal (probably Tabel, from a Judean noble family recently settled in Transjordan, ancestors of the later Tobiads). Rezin assisted the Edomites in the reconquest of Elath (2 Kings 16:6) and the Edomites attacked Judah from the south (2 Chron. 28:17). Meanwhile, the Philistines invaded the northern Shephelah of Judah and occupied many towns on the key approaches to the hill country (2 Chron. 28:5–15). Pekah was unable to force his will upon Jerusalem and the prisoners taken during his foray were returned (2 Kings 16:5b; 2 Chron. 28:17–19; Isaiah 7:1–6). Ahaz promptly turned to Tiglath-pileser III for help.

THE CAMPAIGN OF
REZIN AND PEKAH
AGAINST JUDAH

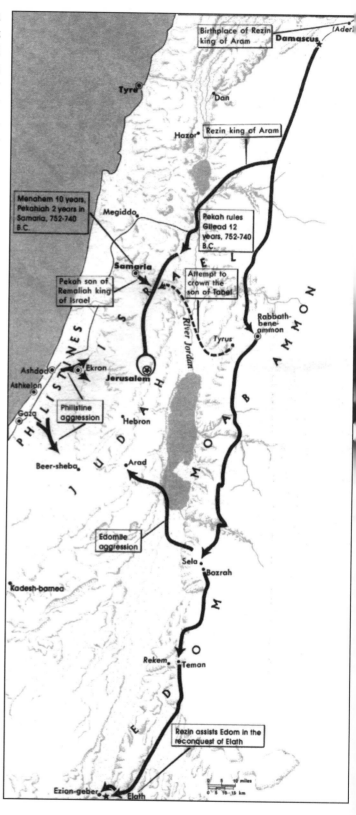

TIGLATH-PILESER III responded with alacrity. The dates of his campaigns in the southern Levant are determined in accordance with his annals and the Eponym Chronicle. In 734 BCE he marched against Philistia. Since the northern Shephelah had recently fallen into Philistine hands, the siege of Gezer depicted on one of Tiglath-pileser's reliefs must have taken place during this campaign. Gaza was conquered next after its king, Hanun, had fled to Egypt. The Assyrian army proceeded into northern Sinai where the Meunites were also forced to submit; a garrison was left at the Brook of Egypt. The kings of Palestine were cut off from any possible help on the part of the Egyptians.

The following year, 733 BCE, saw the invasion of northern Israel. The main course of the campaign can be deduced from 2 Kings 15:29. Tiglath-pileser III launched the attack from the Lebanese Beqa' Valley, first taking Ijon and Abel-beth-maacha. Then he turned westward across Upper Galilee to Janoah, in the foothills above Tyre. Thus he assured his lines of communication with Tyre. Marching back across Upper Galilee, he conquered Kedesh. Yiron and Merom appear in an Assyrian list of prisoners from this campaign, so they were evidently taken at this time. He could now concentrate on the siege of Hazor without fear of harassment from Upper Galilee. Forces were sent into Gilead and to "Galilee, all the land of Naphtali." Isaiah describes these territories, the first to fall under a conqueror's heel, as "The way of the sea, the land beyond Jordan, and Galilee of the nations." Biblical semantics require that "way of the sea" be a route leading to the sea; this fits perfectly the road from Abel-beth-maacha to Janoah. Gilead is, of course, the "land beyond Jordan," and "Galilee of the nations" is literally the "Region of the goiim," mainly the Jezreel Valley (the equivalent of Harosheth-ha-goiim in Judges 4:2).

Damascus was now completely isolated. The following year, 732 BCE, saw its downfall before the victorious army of Tiglath-pileser III. An Assyrian relief from Calah shows the exile of inhabitants from Ashtaroth, chief city of Bashan, one of the cities taken at this time.

In the wake of this crushing defeat, Pekah was assassinated by Hoshea, son of Elah (732 BCE). Tiglath-pileser III says that he appointed Hoshea as king of Israel and received a heavy payment of tribute from him. This was also the twentieth, and last, year of Jotham (2 Kings 15:30); Ahaz's sole reign of sixteen years is reckoned from this date (2 Kings 16:2; 2 Chron. 28:1).

Exile of inhabitants of Ashtaroth, relief from palace of Tiglath-pileser III at Calah.

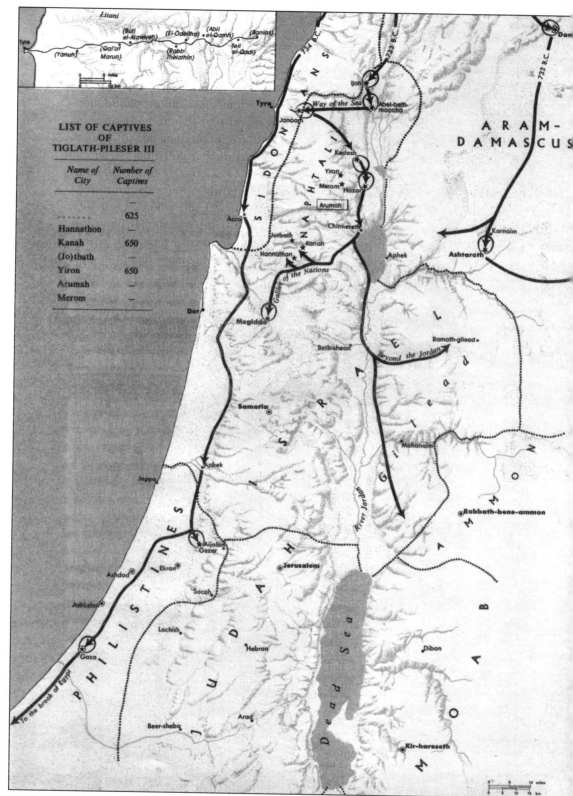

LIST OF CAPTIVES
OF
TIGLATH-PILESER III

Name of City	Number of Captives
	—
......	625
Hannathon	—
Kanah	650
(Jo)tbath	—
Yiron	650
Arumah	—
Merom	—

THE CAMPAIGNS OF TIGLATH-PILESER III 734–732 BCE

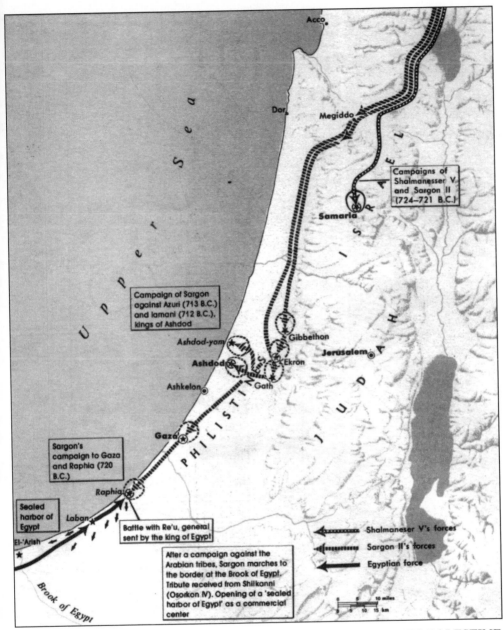

Campaigns of
Shalmaneser V
and Sargon II
(724–721 B.C.)

Campaign of Sargon
against Azuri (713 B.C.)
and Iamani (712 B.C.),
kings of Ashdod

Sargon's
campaign to Gaza
and Raphia (720
B.C.)

Sealed
harbor of
Egypt

Battle with Re'u, general
sent by the king of Egypt

After a campaign against the
Arabian tribes, Sargon marches to
the border at the Brook of Egypt.
Tribute received from Shilkanni
(Osorkon IV). Opening of a 'sealed
harbor of Egypt' as a commercial
center

Shalmaneser V's forces

Sargon II's forces

Egyptian force

THE CAMPAIGNS OF SHALMANESER V AND SARGON II TO PALESTINE
724–712 BCE

WITH the death of Tiglath-pileser III in 727 BCE, his successor, Shalmaneser V, found it necessary to campaign in the west. Hoshea paid his tribute when the Assyrian threat approached (2 Kings 17:3). However, Hoshea turned to "So, king of Egypt" (Osorkon IV or "Tef-nakhte" ruler of Sais) for help and ceased paying his tribute to Shalmaneser. The Assyrian king arrested Hoshea and launched his attack on the disloyal kingdom of Samaria in Hoshea's seventh year

(725/724 BCE). The city succumbed to the siege in Hoshea's ninth year (723/722 BCE), and its population was taken into exile. Shalmaneser V died shortly thereafter and was succeeded by Sargon II. Years later, Sargon's scribes assigned the conquest of Samaria to their master.

Conquest of Ekron, relief from palace of Sargon II at Khorsabad.

SENNACHERIB'S RECONQUEST OF PHOENICIA 701 BCE

SENNACHERIB, now on his third military campaign, arrived with his army in 701 BCE. The first objective was conquest of the Phoenician coast; the rebellious leader, Luli (Elulaios) of Sidon, fled to Iadana (Cyprus) where he met his death. Ethobaal was appointed in his place. The fall of the Phoenician cities inspired fear in many of Hezekiah's erstwhile allies; they rushed to Acco to pay their tribute and renew their allegiance to Sennacherib (see map below).

Sennacherib then marched against Philistia and Judah. Joppa and its hinterland towns, occupied by the rebellious Sidqia of Ashkelon, were taken, thus assuring logistic support by sea from Phoenicia. Here the Assyrian scribes mention two logically, but not chronologically, related events, namely the deposing of Sidqia and the defeat of the Egyptian-Cushite army that had come to the aid of Sidqia and Hezekiah. The biblical chronology of events shows that the battle at Eltekeh came after the fall of Lachish and during the siege of Libnah (2 Kings 19:9; Isaiah 37:9). The next conquest was Timnah in the Sorek Valley; Ekron was thus cut off from immediate support by Hezekiah. Ekron was taken and the rebels punished by impalement. A fragmentary "Letter to the god (Asshur)" reporting the king's victory supplements the account in Sennacherib's Annals. Its reference to the capture of Azekah, a lofty Judean fortress, is followed by a Philistine town taken over by Hezekiah, most likely Gath. The seizure of Azekah would leave

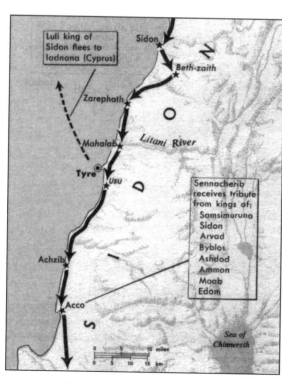

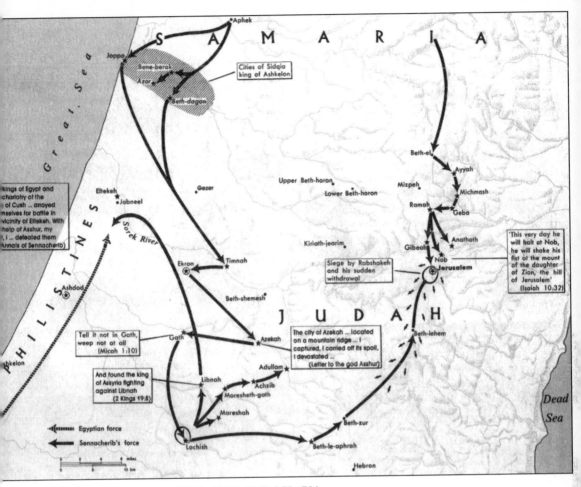

The map contains the following labels:

- Great Sea
- Aphek
- Joppa
- S A M A R I A
- Bene-berak
- Azor
- Beth-dagon
- Cities of Sidqia king of Ashkelon
- Beth-el
- Ayyah
- Michmash
- Mizpeh
- Ramah
- Geba
- Upper Beth-horon
- Lower Beth-horon
- Gezer
- Eltekeh
- Jabneel
- kings of Egypt and chariotry of the ... of Cush ... arrayed ...nselves for battle in vicinity of Eltekeh. With help of Asshur, my ...I ... defeated them (Annals of Sennacherib)
- Kiriath-jearim
- Gibeah
- Anathoth
- Nob
- Jerusalem
- 'This very day he will halt at Nob, he will shake his fist at the mount of the daughter of Zion, the hill of Jerusalem' (Isaiah 10:32)
- Ekron
- Timnah
- Siege by Rabshakeh and his sudden withdrawal
- Ashdod
- P H I L I S T I N E S
- Sorek River
- Beth-shemesh
- J U D A H
- Beth-lehem
- Tell it not in Gath, weep not at all (Micah 1:10)
- Gath
- Azekah
- The city of Azekah ... located on a mountain ridge ... I captured, I carried off its spoil, I devastated ... (Letter to the god Asshur)
- Adullam
- Ashkelon
- Libnah
- Achzib
- Moresheth-gath
- And found the king of Assyria fighting against Libnah (2 Kings 19:8)
- Mareshah
- Beth-zur
- Dead Sea
- Egyptian force
- Sennacherib's force
- Lachish
- Beth-le-aphrah
- Hebron

SENNACHERIB IN PHILISTIA AND JUDAH 701 BCE

Gath unprotected. The two main approaches to Judah from the west were now blocked. Lachish, the largest city conquered on this campaign would have been next, followed by Libnah. Micah's dirge over the towns of the Shephelah suggests the fate of other towns in the area (Mic. 1:8–16). Isaiah defines the march of a hostile force from the north to threaten Jerusalem (Isaiah 10:28–32). Sennacherib claims the capture of forty-six walled cities and their surrounding villages. Excavations have found remains of severe destruction at this time at Lachish, Beer-sheba, Arad, Debir, Beth-shemesh and elsewhere. It was a blow from which Judah never fully recovered. But Jerusalem was saved. After defeating the Egyptians, led by Shabako's younger brother, Tirhaka (Taharka), the Assyrian army was smitten—in biblical terms by "the Angel of the Lord." Sennacherib accepted Hezekiah's promise of heavy tribute payments and withdrew.

D. THE KINGDOM OF JUDAH

JUDAH AND HER NEIGHBORS DURING THE REIGN OF MANASSEH 701 TO 642 BCE

JUDAH'S territory was greatly reduced by Sennacherib as punishment for leading the revolt. The towns and areas in question were given to the loyal kings of Gaza, Ashdod and Ekron.

Hezekiah may have enjoyed a certain notoriety because of his deliverance from Sennacherib (2 Chron. 32:23), but he continued to pay a heavy indemnity to the Assyrians. Meanwhile, because of his recent illness, he appointed his son, Manasseh, co-regent as soon as the latter became twelve years of age (2 Kings 21:1; 2 Chron. 33:1; 697 BCE). In Egypt, the Cushite Taharka (biblical Tirhaka) came to the throne in 690 BCE and engaged in an active policy of interference in Asia. The Phoenicians leaned strongly to the Egyptian side. When Esarhaddon became king of Assyria after the assassination of Sennacherib (681 BCE), he was soon faced with a rebellion by Tyre and Sidon (679 BCE). That year he assured his control of the southern coast by seizing the town of Arza at the "border of the Brook of Egypt." Two years later, Esarhaddon conquered Sidon and ended its hegemony in Phoenicia. A treaty was made with Baal, king of Tyre, in which the Assyrian towns along the coast were given to Tyre, down to the border of Philistia; Dor and Acco were included.

During that same year (677 BCE), the rulers of twelve states of the Land of Hatti—Beyond the River, provided corvée labor to cut and deliver trees from Lebanon to Esarhaddon's new palace being built at Nineveh.

Manasseh was now sole ruler of Judah with its heavy economic burdens. He turned to his neighbors, especially to Tyre, now Assyria's favored state, which meant reintroduction of all the Canaanite cult practices that Hezekiah had removed, including worship of Baal, Asherah and the host of heaven. Thus, he is compared with Ahab of Israel (2 Kings 21:3). The many foreign cults, Sidonian, Moabite and Ammonite, represented diplomatic and economic as well as religious links with the neighboring states; their shrines (and embassies) were located "east of Jerusalem, to the south of the mount of corruption" (2 Kings 23:13). These religious forms were not required by Assyria; the imperial god Asshur was not even worshipped in Jerusalem. The Assyrians did not generally make a policy of forcing their vassals to worship the Assyrian gods.

During the years after 676 BCE, Esarhaddon was engaged in military and diplomatic efforts toward the Arabians. A hostile Arabian leader was deposed and a man loyal to Assyrian interests was installed. The Assyrian monarch intended to invade Egypt; for this he needed Arab support. In return they enjoyed control of the caravan routes. From the first successful invasion of Esarhaddon (671 BCE) to Asshurbanipal's conquest of No-amon (664/663 BCE), the Levantine states, including Judah, were involved in the war effort. Manasseh, along with his neighbors, sent troops to Egypt (667 BCE).

Judah's fortunes changed radically after the great civil war that rocked the Assyrian empire. Shamash-shum-ukin, Asshurbanipal's younger brother, was

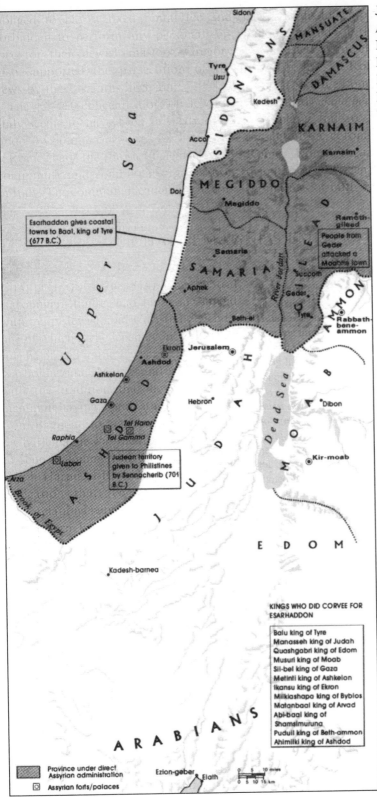

JUDAH
AND HER
NEIGHBORS
DURING THE
REIGN OF
MANASSEH
701–642 BCE

Sidon

MANSUATE

Tyre
Usu

DAMASCUS

Kedesh

KARNAIM

S I D O N I A N S

Karnaim

Acco

M E G I D D O

Dor

Megiddo

Ramoth-gilead

Esarhaddon gives coastal
towns to Baal, king of Tyre
(677 B.C.)

People from
Geder
attacked a
Moabite town

U p p e r   S e a

Samaria

S A M A R I A

Succoth

G I L E A D

Aphek

Geder

Tyre

River Jordan

A M M O N

Beth-el

Rabbath-
bene-
ammon

Ekron

Jerusalem

Ashdod

Ashkelon

A S H D O D

Gaza

Hebron

J U D A H

Dead Sea

Dibon

M O A B

Tel Haror
Tel Gamma

Raphia

Judean territory
given to Philistines
by Sennacherib (701
B.C.)

Labon

Kir-moab

Arza

Brook of Egypt

E D O M

Kadesh-barnea

KINGS WHO DID CORVEE FOR
ESARHADDON

A R A B I A N S

Balu king of Tyre
Manasseh king of Judah
Quashgabri king of Edom
Musuri king of Moab
Sil-bel king of Gaza
Metinti king of Ashkelon
Ikansu king of Ekron
Milkiashapa king of Byblos
Matanbaal king of Arvad
Abi-baal king of
Shamsimuruna
Puduil king of Beth-ammon
Ahimilki king of Ashdod

Province under direct
Assyrian administration

Assyrian forts/palaces

Ezion-geber
Elath

0 5   10 miles
0 5 10 15 km

not content to be king of Babylon only; he challenged his brother's imperial throne (652 BCE). The Tyrians and the Arabians supported Babylon. An Arabian army was caught and demolished by the Assyrians as it tried to enter the Euphrates Valley (650 BCE). Babylon fell and its young king died in 648 BCE. While reorganizing Babylonia, Asshurbanipal had the western leaders brought there for interrogation. Manasseh was among them; he managed to convince the Assyrian king of his loyalty and was returned to Judah with permission (and probably funds) to rebuild Jerusalem and to reestablish the fortified cities of Judah (2 Chron. 33:11–17). Later on, Asshurbanipal carried out an extensive campaign against the Arabians (644/643 BCE); on the return march he also attacked Usu and Acco as punishment for Tyre's support of his erstwhile brother.

Manasseh died in 642 BCE, leaving his successors with an opportunity to capitalize on this extraordinary turn of events.

THE KINGDOM OF JOSIAH 628 TO 609 BCE

AMON son of Manasseh reigned only two years (642–640 BCE) before he was slain in a palace plot. The "people of the land," that is the landed nobility, executed the regicides and crowned the eight-year-old Josiah as king (2 Kings 21:23–22:1; 2 Chron. 33:24–34:1). At age fourteen he was already a father (634 BCE); Jehoiakim was born to him by Zebidah, daughter of Pedaiah from Rumah in Lower Galilee (2 Kings 23:36; 2 Chron. 36:5). Two years later Hamutal, daughter of Jeremiah from Libnah, bore him Jehoahaz. In this, his eighth year (632 BCE), he began to seek "the god of David his father" (2 Chron. 34:3), under the influence of his father-in-law from the priestly city of Libnah in the Shephelah.

News of Asshurbanipal's retirement (in 630 BCE) may have inspired Josiah to launch his campaign against all the cult places rivaling Jerusalem, not only in Judah but also in "the towns of Manasseh and Ephraim and Simeon and as far as Naphtali in the hill country" (2 Chron. 34:6). Simeon is the city of Zebulun on the Jezreel Plain called Shimron in the

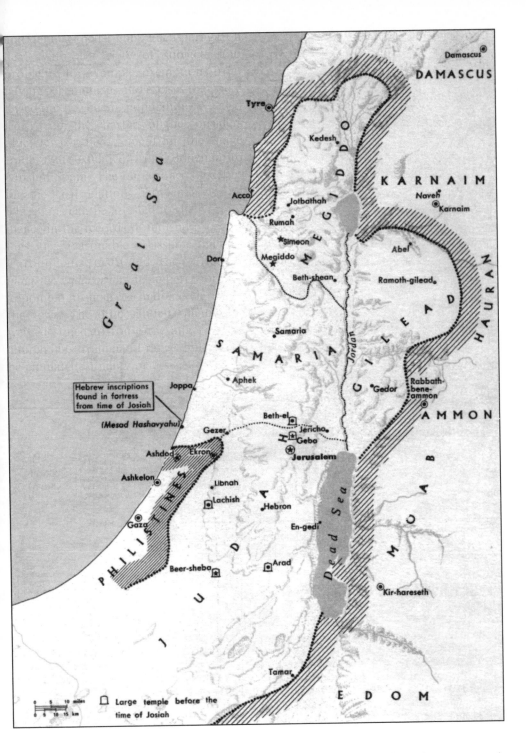

Book of Joshua (Josh. 11:1, 19:15) but
known as Shim'on in the Execration
Texts, the list of Thutmose III, and the
Amarna Letters. Its name in the Second
Temple period was Simonia as attested
by Josephus and Talmudic sources. It
was the leading Israelite town in the
Jezreel Valley after Megiddo became an

Hebrew letter from Mesad Hashavyahu.

governors were apparently unable to oppose him. In the year of Asshurbanipal's death (627 BCE), Jeremiah began his twenty-three years of prophecy (Jer. 1:2, 25:1–3) and by the time Nabopolassar was firmly established in Babylon (623 BCE), the kingdom of Judah was ready to seal its covenant of independence. Josiah's great covenant ceremony and national reform was inaugurated in 622 BCE (2 Kings 22:3–24:28; 2 Chron. 34:8–35:39). Only the Jerusalem-oriented cadre of priests and Levites was allowed to function (2 Kings 23:9).

The chance find of a small fort on the shore north of Ashdod-yam brought to light some inscriptions in good Judean Hebrew script and language, proving that Josiah's authority had been extended to the seacoast. Just how firm was his control over "all of Israel" is uncertain but he seems to have been well on the way to reestablishing the Israelite kingdom with Jerusalem as the capital.

Assyrian headquarters. Even Megiddo was abandoned by the Assyrians by 609 BCE when Josiah chose to do battle there with Neco II.

Josiah was following the example of Hezekiah in drawing the northern Israelites back to Jerusalem. The Assyrian

THE DISTRICTS OF JUDAH

THE settlement pattern of Judah is reflected in great detail by Joshua 15:20–63. That passage is the most detailed geographical text preserved in the Bible. The date of the original document incorporated by the author of Joshua is disputed. The references to administrative reorganization by Jehoshaphat (2 Chron. 17:1–13) and his appointment of royal sons as local governors (21:3) have led some to suggest that the roster of Judean towns was compiled in the mid-ninth century. Others favor an eighth- or seventh-century date. In any case the roster is defective as it stands; key towns like Beth-shemesh and Adoraim are missing along with other known settlements from

the genealogies of Judah, Caleb and Simeon (1 Chron. 2–4). An entire district is missing from the Hebrew text but can be partially supplied from the Greek version (Josh. 15:59a).

The Joshua list is based on strictly topographical, rather than kinship principles. Comparison with the geographical distribution of clans and families in "Greater Judah" (1 Chron. 2–4) reveals that the pattern of kinship settlement is only partially commensurate with the topographical divisions of Joshua 15:20–63. Here the four principal ecological zones of Judah, namely the Negeb, the Shephelah, the Hill Country and the Steppe ("Wilderness"), are the organizational basis for the list. The towns are

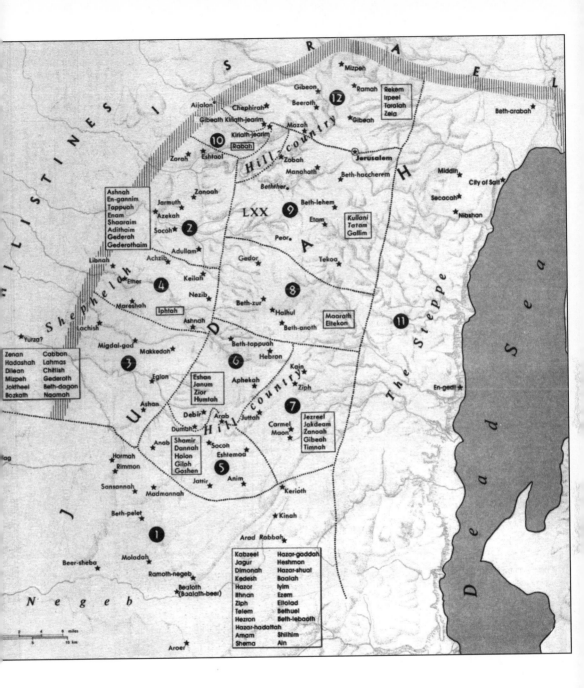

grouped into geographical clusters indicated by subtotals; the Negeb and the Steppe each have a subtotal. The Shephelah has three subtotals corresponding to three districts; the Hill Country has six (counting the district preserved in the Greek). This total of eleven may be supplemented by the southernmost dis-trict of Benjamin, which had remained under Judean control. Levitical cities are not distinguished. In the Shephelah and the southern Hill Country, the district boundaries correspond to watersheds between wadi systems. In district 2 the roster runs clockwise around the district; in district 4 it is counterclockwise.

THE CLOSING YEARS OF THE KINGDOM OF JUDAH
599 TO 586 BCE

NEBUCHADNEZZAR (Nebuchad-rezzar) stayed in Babylon in 600 BCE; in 599 Babylonian troops attacked the Arabians while local Chaldean, Aramean (or Edom-ite?), Moabite, and Ammonite troops were sent to harass Judah (2 Kings 24:2). The Babylonian army was sent to besiege "the city of Judah" (Jerusalem) in 598 BCE. They set out from Babylon in Kislev (17 Dec. 598 to 15 Jan. 597); meanwhile, Jehoiakim had already died on 21 Marheshvan (8 Dec.) 598 BCE and his young son, Jehoiachin, assumed the throne under the tutelage of his mother, Nehushta. The Edo-mites, and perhaps others, at-tacked Judah from the south, "the cities of the Negeb are closed and there is no one to open" (Jer. 13:19). The Babylonian army laid siege to Jerusalem and Nebu-chadnezzar arrived shortly there-after; on 2 Adar (Sat., 16 March) 597 BCE the city was taken. A little over a month later, on 10 Nisan (22 April) 597 BCE, Neb-uchadnezzar sent orders to bring Jehoiachin and his entourage as prisoners to Babylon. Zedekiah, another son of Josiah, was appointed king (2 Kings 24:10–17; 2 Chron. 36:10a, 36:6b–7, 36:10b).

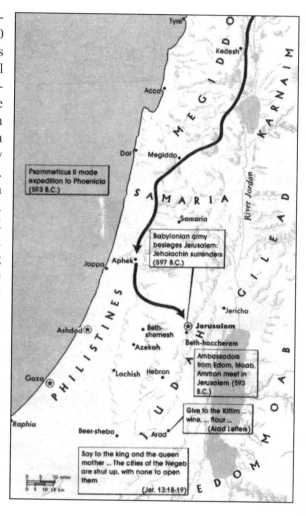

The Chaldean army was sent once again to the Levant in 596 BCE; in 595 the king had to crush a rebellion in Babylon itself. The next two years saw him back in the west. Egypt was appar-ently stirring up diplomatic ferment; ambassadors from Edom, Moab and Ammon were conferring in Jerusalem (Jer. 27:3, 27:12, 28:1) and Psammeticus II, successor of Neco, made a trip to Phoenicia. Zedekiah was taken to Baby-lon (Jer. 51:1) but managed to convince Nebuchadnezzar of his loyalty. He re-turned to Jerusalem and his government remained loyal to Babylon for a time. Kittim, probably Cypriote mercenaries in Chaldean service, patrolled the Negeb and received supplies from Judean for-tresses such as Arad.

THE EXILE FROM JUDAH 597 TO 582 BCE

THE epilogue to the Book of Jeremiah gives what seem to be fairly accurate figures for three stages of exile from Judah (Jer. 52:28–30). They took place in 597, 586 and 582 BCE. The latter seems to have been carried out during Nebuchadnezzar's campaign in the west against "Coele Syria" and the Moabites and Ammonites (Josephus, *Antiq.*, X, 181–182). Neo-Babylonian cuneiform tablets, especially the archive of the banking house of Murashu at Nippur, contain many references to Judeans as well as other exiled peoples.

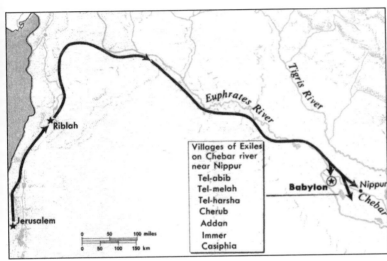

Villages of Exiles
on Chebar river
near Nippur
Tel-abib
Tel-melah
Tel-harsha
Cherub
Addan
Immer
Casiphia

This is the number of the people whom Nebuchadrezzar [Nebuchadnezzar] carried away captive: in the seventh year, three thousand and twenty-three Jews; in the eighteenth year of Nebuchadrezzar he carried away captive from Jerusalem eight hundred and thirty-two persons; in the twenty-third year of Nebuchadrezzar, Nebuzaradan the captain of the guard carried away captive of the Jews seven hundred and forty-five persons; all persons were four thousand and six hundred.

(Jeremiah 52:28–30)

THE FLIGHT TO EGYPT C. 586 BCE

GEDALIAH son of Ahikam, the former "Steward of the royal palace," was appointed governor of Judah by the Babylonians. He made his headquarters at Mizpah (Mizpeh). Other Judeans who had fled to neighboring countries such as Moab, Ammon and Edom, gathered to him there. Ishmael, son of Nethaniah, of the royal house, was incited by Baalis, king of the Ammonites, to assassinate Gedaliah. This deed was perpetrated in the seventh month (October, 586 BCE). Afterwards, a band of leading Judeans chose flight to Egypt for fear of Babylonian reprisals. They settled in Tahpanes (where Baal-zephon was worshipped) and eventually entered service as mercenaries. Their one attested colony is at Yeb (Elephantine) where family and community documents in Aramaic have been found.

Stone window railing, from the palace of Jehoiakim at Ramat Rahel.

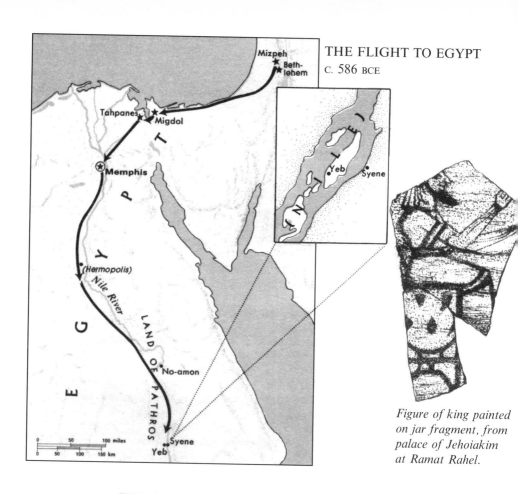

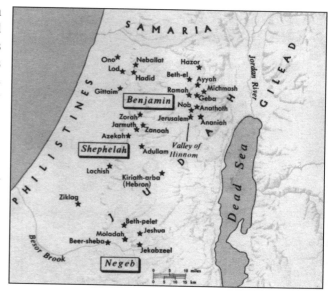

Figure of king painted on jar fragment, from palace of Jehoiakim at Ramat Rahel.

JUDAH UNDER BABYLONIAN RULE
EARLY 6TH CENTURY BCE

THE destruction was harsh and cruel and overlooked none of the important cities of Judah. Some of the lands and destroyed settlements were quickly occupied by the "residue of the people" (Jer. 40:10), causing much resentment among the captive exiles (Ez. 33:21–27).

The central highlands of Judah, however, were denuded of their populations, and the Babylonians did not bring new settlers here to fill the void. These areas were gradually seized by the Edomites—who were crowded by the pressure of Arabian tribes—and the southern Judean hills to the region of Beth-zur now became "Idumea."

Judean settlements remained mainly in the outlying regions, some of which probably became detached from Judah already in 597 BCE. These were included in the list of the "residue of Israel" preserved in Nehemiah 11:20–36, which records mostly sites in Benjamin, the Negeb, and the Shephelah on the border of Philistia.

THE RETURN TO ZION 538 TO 445 BCE

CYRUS the Great won the allegiance of his subject peoples by tolerance of their religious and national feelings. Upon entering Babylon he issued a decree permitting the return of cult statues to their home temples (Nabonidus had dragged them into the capital). A similar decree from his first year of reign (over the empire) is preserved in the Bible (2 Chron. 36:22–23; Ezra 1:1–5) granting permission for Jews to return home and to rebuild the temple in Jerusalem. The first wave of returnees, led by Sheshbazzar (probably Shenazzar, son of Jehoiakim, 1 Chron. 3:18), arrived in 538 BCE. The altar was set up and in the second year the foundations were laid (Ezra 5:14 [Heb. 17]), but due to opposition from the neighboring peoples, the temple was not built until the reign of Darius I. In his second year (520 BCE), Darius ordered that the work be completed. The temple was finished in his sixth year on the 3rd of Adar (13 March, 515 BCE).

Though contacts with Babylonian Jewry were frequent (e.g., Zech. 5:9), the returnees were relatively few. More came with Ezra in the seventh year of Artaxerxes I (458 BCE; Ezra 7:7). The Law of the Lord was certified by the Persian king as the official code of the Jewish community in the satrapy "Beyond the River" (Ezra 7:25–26).

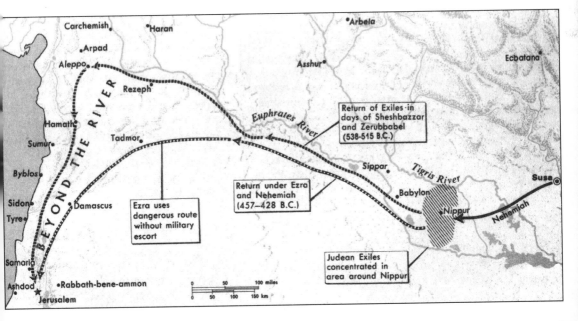

THE Jews who had come from Artaxerxes in the mid-fifth century (Ezra 4:12, 7:7) took steps to refortify Jerusalem, doubtless in the face of the tumultuous events of that time, e.g., the rebellion of the satrap Megabyzus. The local officials and regional leaders protested to the Persian king and were ordered to halt the construction (Ezra 4:21–22). This state of affairs was reported to Nehemiah (Neh. 1:3) who got an appointment as governor of Judea with authority to fortify Jerusalem. The narrative of his nocturnal inspection of the walls (Neh. 2:12–15) and his account of the construction teams (Neh. 3:1–32) depict the gates, the towers and many buildings adjacent to the city wall. Archaeological research has shown that the post-exilic city was considerably smaller than in the days of the monarchy. Only the eastern spur was occupied and the walls were higher up the slope.

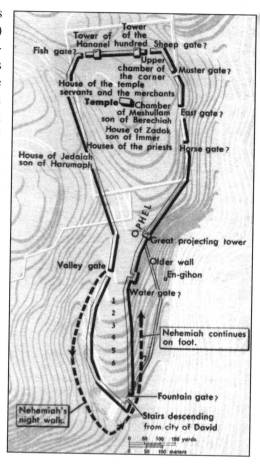

1 Upper house of the king	5 Ascent to the armory
2 House of Azariah	6 House of the mighty men
3 House of Benjamin and Hasshub	7 Artificial pool
4 House of Eliashib the high priest	8 Sepulchres of David

THE PROVINCE OF YEHUD C. 440 BCE

JEWISH communities in the post-exilic period fall into two categories, those within the Judean province known officially by the Aramaic name, Yehud, and those living outside it (Neh. 4:12). Ezra was sent to enforce the Law as the binding code for all the Jews in the province Beyond the River (Ezra 4:25–26). The Jerusalem leaders were strict about who should participate in building the temple (Ezra 4:1–3) but Nehemiah recognized settlements in Kiriath-arba (Hebron), the Negeb, the Shephelah, and the "Plain of Ono" (Neh. 11:25–36). In the list of returnees (Ezra 2:1–34; Neh. 7:6–38) many towns are recorded, some of which can hardly have been in Yehud. Society was comprised of three groups: Israel, priests and Levites (Ezra 9:1), the former including people from Judah, Benjamin, Ephraim and Manasseh; Shilonites; and Netophathites (1 Chron. 9:1–16).

The list of those who rebuilt the city's defenses mentions geographic communities (Neh. 3:1–32). Certain men in this roster bore the title "officer of (half) the work crew (*pelekh*) of (place)." The

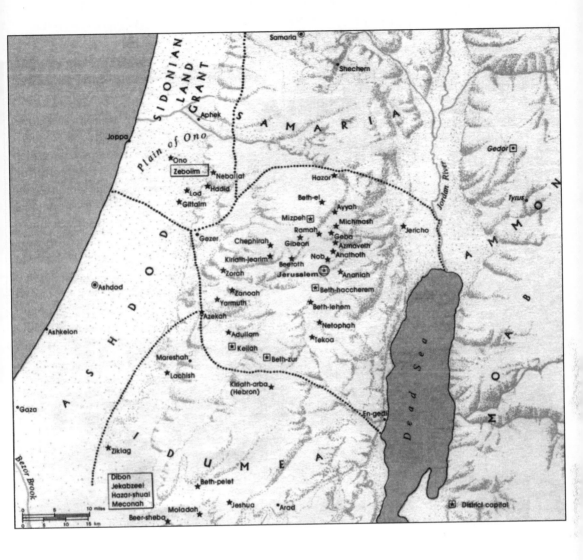

distribution of these towns may be compared to that of the official "Yehud" seal impressions, found on jar handles from Mizpah in the north, Jericho in the east, En-gedi in the south and Gezer in the west. The jars represent the official wine industry; other seals mention "Mozah," or governor with his title, *pahwa*. The settlement pattern from the Hellenistic age confirms this picture; below Beth-zur the Edomites (Idumeans) have come in.

Nehemiah refused to meet with the other governors on the "Plain of Ono" (Neh. 6:2–3) because it was at that time part of the land grant awarded to Eshmunazer, king of Sidon, by Artaxerxes II, "Dor and Joppe, the rich grain lands in the territory of Sharon." In spite of its Jewish population, it would have been an ideal venue for an assassination plot against the governor of Yehud.

Inscription "Yehud" in seal impression, Persian period.

55

E. THE HELLENISTIC PERIOD

ALEXANDER THE GREAT IN PALESTINE 332 TO 331 BCE

AFTER the surrender of Tyre in 332 BCE, Alexander proceeded along the coast toward Egypt. While he was still besieging Tyre, Syrian and Palestinian delegations arrived, offering peaceful submission.

According to tradition, Sanballat, sa-trap of Samaria, and his army of 8,000 men, joined Alexander; the king, however, placed little trust in reinforcements of this kind. There was, however, some resistance, and Alexander sent cavalry units into the mountains of Lebanon to suppress rebellious tribes. Acco, the royal fortress in northern Palestine, surrendered without a fight and the army advanced south, most probably along the coast, to Strato's Tower. Here it was undoubtedly forced to swerve east, for the coastal area was at that time still covered by swamps and sand dunes. From Lod the Macedonian army probably turned again to the coast, there to accept the surrender of Azotus and Ascalon. At Gaza the eunuch Batis, commander of the fortress, aided by Arab mercenaries, refused to surrender and Alexander once more started a siege. The fierce resistance of Gaza can be explained by the apprehension of its citizens and their Nabatean allies, who feared the domination of their Greek competitors in this important port city, their outlet to the Mediterranean. Alexander captured Gaza in September, 332 BCE, after a siege of two months, by means of earthworks and siege machinery brought from Tyre. Most male captives were killed on the spot; the women and children were sold into slavery. The city was repopulated with people from the neighboring areas. While the siege was still in progress, Greek cavalry proceeded against the Nabateans. It is possible that troops were also sent to Lachish, the capital of the province of Idumea.

With Gaza fell the last obstacle on Alexander's way to Egypt, where he wintered in 332/331 BCE. He crossed Palestine once more on his return to Tyre. Two traditions are connected with this journey: Samaritan allegiance to the Greeks was, according to some sources, short-lived, and they rose against their governor Andromachus and burned him alive. In revenge, Alexander destroyed Samaria and, on its lands, settled Macedonian veterans. According to another

Alexander the Great, from a mosaic found at Pompeii.

version, it was not Alexander but the regent Perdiccas who founded this colony. However, archaeological evidence proves that the city was destroyed at about that time. In a cave in Wadi Daliah papyrus documents were found belonging to refugees from Samaria. They took refuge here from the advancing Macedonian army and brought with them their personal documents. The Macedonians had trapped them there and smothered them by building fires at the mouth of the cave. The Macedonian colony in Samaria resulted in the revival of Shechem as a Samaritan center for future generations. The Macedonians seem to have penetrated as far inland as Jericho, and it can be presumed that some troops, and maybe the king himself, forayed into the interior. These units then rejoined the main force, which must have marched along the coastal road, probably at Acco.

Of a more legendary nature is the story of Alexander's visit to Jerusalem and his meeting with the high priest Jaddua. Josephus ascribes this to the time of the siege of Gaza (*Antiq.* 11:325–339). Talmudic sources repeat this tradition, but refer it to the high priest Simon the Just.

Dium and Gerasa, two cities beyond the Jordan, were thought to have been founded by Alexander, but this story also lacks foundation.

THE small land of Judea could not feed its entire population. Already in the Hellenistic period we find, side-by-side with the ancient forms of population movement (exile and military colonies), the emigration of individual families attracted by the material prosperity of the surrounding world. Thus there appear in Egypt, in addition to the military colonies of Pelusium-Migdol, Daphne, Elephantine and Cyrene, many Jews who earned their bread by farming or government service. They were concentrated in Alexandria the capital and in the Arsinoite District (Fayum), which had been resettled through the initiative of the Ptolemies. Many others lived in Thebes (Diospolis Magna), in Upper Egypt and its vicinity. Evidence exists of Jewish settlements throughout Egypt. Of special interest is the temple built by Onias, the deposed high priest, at Leontopolis in the Delta in the second century BCE, known in Talmudic literature as the "House of Onias." It stood until after the destruction of the Second Temple, but it too was destroyed soon after. In the hundreds of papyri discovered in ancient Egyptian

Epitaph mentioning the "all-highest god" found at Rhenea near Delos.

cities there is information about the Jewish population and its organizational structure.

While the relative abundance of papyri found in Egypt enables us to reconstruct the map of Jewish settlement there with reasonable detail, there are few sources for the Jews in other parts of the Hellenistic world. The Diaspora there falls into three groups: the early Babylonian exiles, agricultural-military settlements established by the Seleucids in Asia Minor—mainly in Caria, Pamphylia and Phrygia—and isolated communities in the commercial centers of Greece and Asia Minor. These are known mainly from 1 Maccabees 15:22–23.

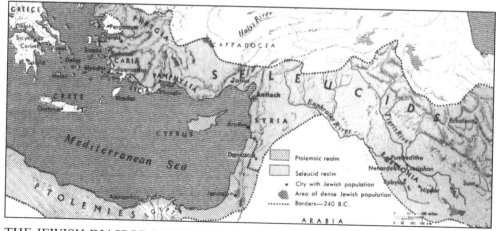

THE JEWISH DIASPORA IN BABYLONIA, ASIA MINOR AND GREECE

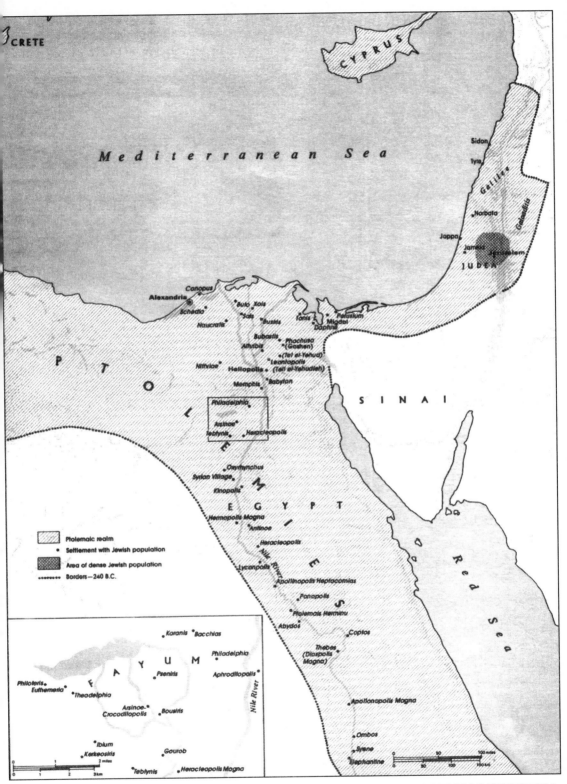

CRETE

CYPRUS

Mediterranean Sea

Sidon

Tyre

Galilee

Gaulanitis

Narbata

Joppa

Jamnia

Jerusalem

JUDEA

Canopus

Alexandria

Buto Xois

Schedia

Sais

Naucratis

Busiris

Tanis

Pelusium

Migdol

Daphne

Bubastis

Athribis

Phachusa

(Goshen)

(Tel el-Yehud)

Nithriae

Leontopolis

Heliopolis

(Tell el-Yehudieh)

Memphis   Babylon

Philadelphia

Arsinoe

Teblynis   Heracleopolis

P   T   O   L   E   M   E

S   I   N   A   I

Oxyrrhynchus

Syrian Village

Kinopolis

E   G   Y   P   T

Hermopolis Magna

Antinoe

Heracleopolis

Lycopolis

Apollinopolis Heptacomias

Panopolis

Ptolemais Hermiu

Abydos

Coptos

Thebes

(Diospolis

Magna)

Nile River

Red Sea

Apollonopolis Magna

Ombos

Syene

Elephantine

▨ Ptolemaic realm

• Settlement with Jewish population

▩ Area of dense Jewish population

······ Borders—240 B.C.

Koranis *Bacchias*

F   A   Y   U   M

Philadelphia

Pseniris

Aphrodilopolis

Philoteris

Euthemeria

Theadelphia

Arsinoe-

Crocodilopolis

Bousiris

Nile River

Ibium

Kerkeosiris

Gourob

Teblynis   Heracleopolis Magna

THE JEWISH DIASPORA IN THE PTOLEMAIC KINGDOM

F. THE MACCABEES

THE BEGINNINGS OF THE MACCABEAN REVOLT
167 BCE

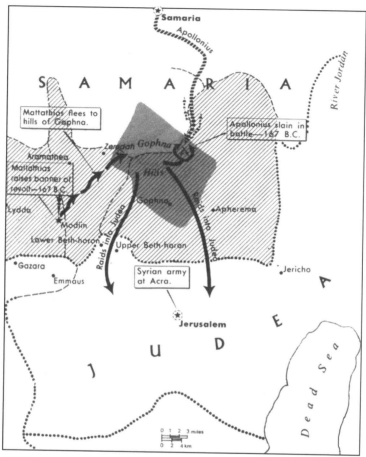

Area transferred from Judea to Samaria

Antiochus IV, from bronze statue.

in history: worship of God was forbidden and the Jews were forced to sacrifice to other gods. The Hellenists built a fortress, the "Acra," to secure their position in Jerusalem, and next to it a new city, in the Greek style.

The persecution led to a revolt that broke out not in Jerusalem, but in the Jewish townlet of Modiin, in the district of Lydda. Some of the leaders came from neighboring villages, such as Yose ben Joezer of Zeredah, leader of the Hasidim, pious Jews who rallied to the defense of the Law. Mattathias, priest of the Hasmonean family, and his sons refused to obey the royal order to sacrifice to Zeus. Mattathias killed a Jew who was about to obey the order, as well as the king's representative, and destroyed the altar there. Modiin itself

ANTIOCHUS IV and his advisers, heeding the more extreme of the Hellenized Jews, believed that the majority of the Jewish nation was ready to accept Greek culture. Being impatient with the slow progress of Hellenization, Antiochus decided to turn the House of God into a Greek temple of Zeus or Dionysius, whom he equated with the God of Israel. The strong resistance of the people led to the first known instance of religious persecution

was close to Lydda, the district capital, and thus exposed to reprisals. Mattathias and his sons fled, probably to the mountains "around Samaria" (Gophna). There they were joined by the Hasidim. From their refuge Mattathias and his men went forth, overturned the altars of the foreign gods, and roused the Jewish villages against the Hellenizers living in Jerusalem under the protection of the Seleucid army. Apollonius, commander of the troops at Samaria and governor of the region near Gophna, went out to crush the rebellion. Judas Maccabeus, who had assumed command on the death of his father Mattathias, attacked the royal troops, probably at the ascent of Lebonah, and destroyed them. Apollonius was killed in the fighting and Judas took his sword "and fought with it thereafter" (1 Macc. 3:12). In response, the Seleucid authorities removed the regions of Lydda and Gophna from Judea and annexed them to Samaria.

THE BATTLE OF BETH-ZUR AND THE REDEDICATION OF THE TEMPLE 165 BCE

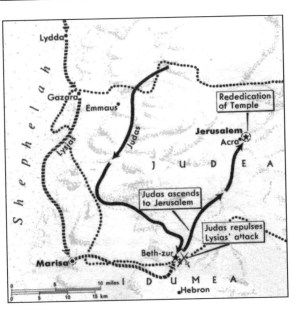

LYSIAS made one last attempt against the Jews. He chose the route along the watershed in Idumea, rather than endangering his forces in the narrow passes and on the steep ascents, which thrice had been the undoing of the Seleucid army. The new campaign passed along the coast to Marisa, inhabited at the time by Hellenized Sidonians and Idumeans— enemies of the Jews. From Marisa they marched with ease and arrived opposite Beth-zur, the border fortress of Judea.

The Maccabean, who surely used his interior lines of communication to follow the movements of the enemy, went forth from Beth-zur to face the invader and succeeded in repulsing the attack. Lysias retreated and Judas and his men, rejoicing, went up to Jerusalem. The fortress of Acra was still in the hands of their enemies, but the Temple Mount was regained by the Jews. Judas and his men now cleansed the temple and repaired it after the long period of neglect. The service of God was restored after having been interrupted for three and one-half years, and they lit the lamps of the menorah to light up the temple.

Thus, the feast of Hanukkah was observed for the first time on the twenty-fifth of Kislev, 165 BCE. Judas fortified Mount Zion (the "Mount of the Temple") and Beth-zur, "that the people might have a fortress against Idumea."

THE EXPANSION OF JUDEA IN THE DAYS OF JONATHAN 152 TO 142 BCE

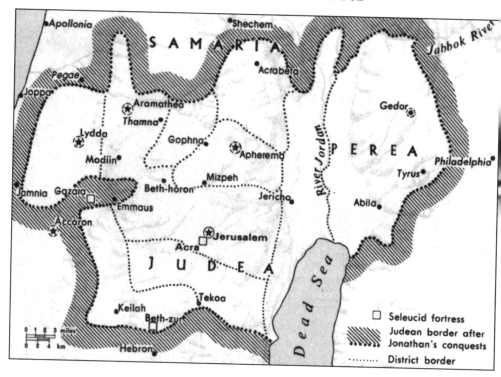

JONATHAN the Hasmonean exploited the decline of Seleucid rule to raise the prestige of Judea. When Demetrius I learned that Alexander Balas, who claimed to be the son of Antiochus IV, had invaded Ptolemais, he felt endangered and granted Jonathan the privileges of a royally appointed commander. He permitted the Hasmonean to recruit an army and to forge weapons. He also returned the Jewish hostages held in the Acra. These concessions enabled Jonathan to establish himself in Jerusalem and repair the fortifications of the Temple Mount. Except for the Acra and Beth-zur, Jonathan was the de facto ruler of Judea.

Alexander Balas, who also wanted Jonathan's support, appointed him high priest. Jonathan wore the finery of this office for the first time during the feast of Tabernacles in the year 152 BCE. Deme-

trius in turn tempted Jonathan by offering him the three districts with Jewish populations, still under the administration of Samaria. Jonathan, however, supported Alexander, the weaker of the two rivals; and Alexander defeated Demetrius I in 150 BCE.

At a meeting in Ptolemais between Alexander and Ptolemy VI in the same year, Jonathan was also present and the Syrian king granted him the title "Strategos and Meridarches" (commander and governor) of Judea. After Jonathan had overcome the forces of Demetrius II in the battle of Jamnia, Alexander gave him the district of Accaron as an estate (147 BCE). Demetrius II then also realized that it was preferable to have Jonathan as a friend rather than an enemy and approved the transfer of three districts (Lydda, Aramathea, and Apherema) from Samaria to Judea. When Tryphon, regent for Antiochus VI, rose against Demetrius II, he too wished to remain in the good graces of Jonathan and, in 144 BCE, endorsed his annexation of the "four districts." From the phrasing of the endorsement we can infer that Jonathan had meanwhile added the Perea—Jewish "Transjordan"—a legacy from the Tobiads, to his dominions: it is possible that the fourth district was Accaron or Acrabeta.

JERUSALEM OF THE MACCABEES 164 TO 141 BCE

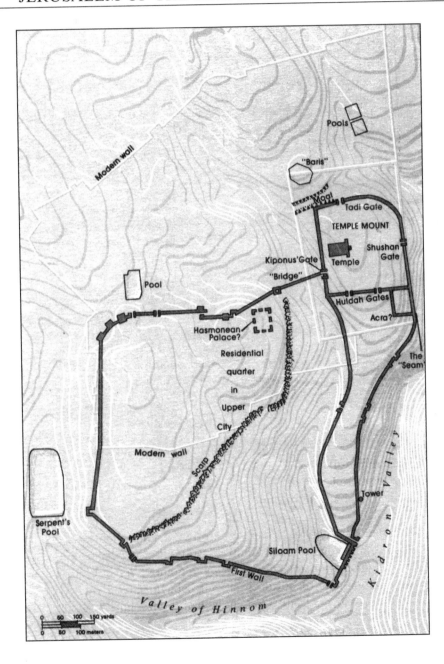

At the beginning of Hellenization, the more "progressive" citizens felt that the old city on the eastern hill, surrounded by ancient walls (restored by Nehemiah, and again in the days of Antiochus III), was hardly fit to be the new "Antiochia." They probably decided to build a city in the Hippodamic tradition: straight streets intersecting at right angles. They started to construct this city on the western hill between the Valley of Hinnom and the Tyropoeon Valley. A hillock at the eastern end of this new Hellenistic city, protected by a small valley to the west, served as its fortress. In the Maccabean period it was called Acra—not to be confused with the old Acra, the citadel (Baris) of the days of Nehemiah, which was situated north of the Temple Mount.

With the capture by Judas Maccabeus of the Temple Mount and the renewal of worship in the Temple, in 164 BCE, the city was divided into two parts, a division which lasted till 141 BCE. The Macca-beans held Mount Zion in the days of Judas, and again in the days of Jonathan and Simon—always in opposition to the Hellenizers' fortress. By raising a siege wall, the "Caphenatha," and rebuilding a quarter named after it, Jonathan and Simon tried to cut off the garrison of the Acra from the market place (the Hellenistic "Agora") and to force its surrender through starvation.

After the final conquest of the Acra in 141 BCE, the Jews razed the part of the fortress commanding the Temple (*Antiq.* 13:217). The Maccabeans, now lords of the entire city, built a wall around the western hill, constructed a bridge across the Tyropoeon Valley, between the Temple Mount and the western hill, and built a palace for themselves on the ruins of the Acra. They also strengthened the "Citadel" by adding towers, one of which was called Strato's Tower in the days of Aristobulus I.

THE KINGDOM OF ALEXANDER JANNEUS
103 TO 76 BCE

Aristobulus' successor, his brother Alexander Janneus (103–76 BCE), completed the conquest of almost the whole of the Land of Israel. Although generally unlucky in the field, he succeeded through his perseverance in a series of campaigns, and added to the Maccabean domains Dora and Strato's Tower, together with the Carmel cape; Gaza and her satellite towns down to Rhinocorura on the Brook of Egypt; the lands surrounding the Dead Sea; and most of the lands east of the Jordan from Panias at the source of the river southward—only Philadelphia remained unconquered. Alexander also succeeded in staving off various enemies—Ptolemy

A song for the welfare of Jonathan the King (Alexander Janneus).

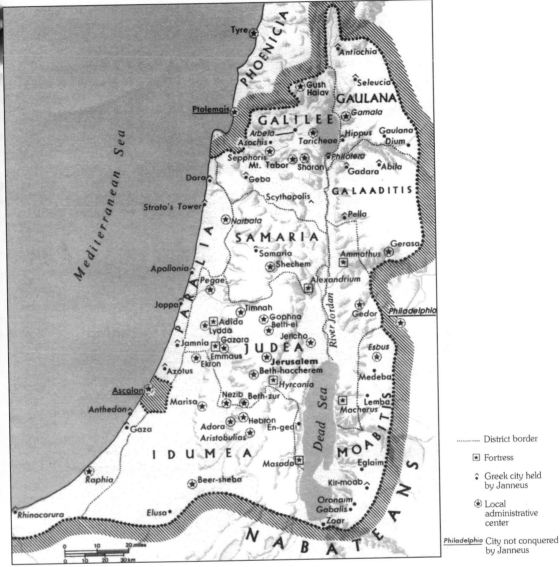

THE KINGDOM OF ALEXANDER JANNEUS

Map legend:

.... District border

⊡ Fortress

♦ Greek city held by Janneus

✳ Local administrative center

Philadelphia City not conquered by Janneus

Lathyrus, king of Cyprus; the Seleucids Demetrius III and Antiochus XII; and the Nabatean kings. He was less successful in the interior; dissension between the ruling dynasty and its Sadducee followers, and the Pharisees (who first rose under Hyrcanus) waxed under Janneus into a rebellion, subsequently suppressed with great cruelty. Under Janneus, the Maccabean state reached its apogee.

Coin of Alexander Janneus.

G. THE ROMAN CONQUEST

POMPEY'S CAMPAIGN IN PALESTINE 63 BCE

AFTER Janneus' death (76 BCE), his widow Alexandra reigned till 67 BCE. Upon her death, civil war broke out between her sons, Hyrcanus II and Aristobulus II. The former was weaker and, prompted by Antipater the Idumean (the evil genius of the Hasmonean dynasty), called Aretas, the Nabatean king, to his aid. The invaders besieged Jerusalem, but the Romans finally intervened.

Rome had gradually annexed the entire Hellenistic East after defeating the Seleucids. From 88 to 64 BCE she fought Mithradates, king of Pontus, her most dangerous enemy in the East. In 64 BCE, Pompey, who finally defeated Mithradates, came to Damascus, annexed the Seleucid kingdom (which then became the province of Syria) and turned his attention toward Judea.

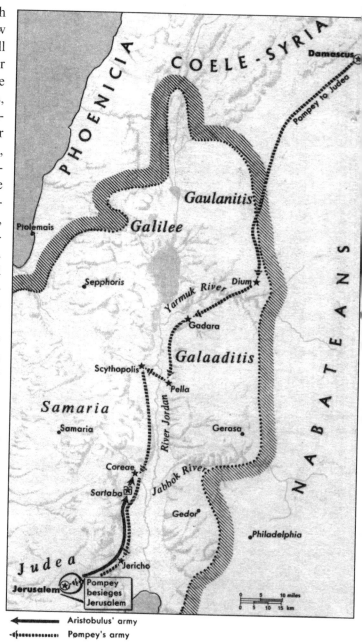

Aristobulus' army

Pompey's army

At first he sent Scaurus, one of his commanders, to Judea and ordered a truce. Aretas and Hyrcanus retreated (on their way back they were soundly defeated by Aristobulus at Papyron near the Jordan). Pompey next ordered the two rivals to appear before him; seeing that Hyrcanus was the weaker personality of the two, he chose him to rule over the Jews. Aristobulus retired to the fastness of Alexandrium, overlooking the Jordan Valley. Pompey followed him with his army, passing Dium (and probably also Gadara), Pella, and Scythopolis. At Coreae the Roman army entered Judea proper. Aristobulus negotiated from weakness and finally surrendered. Pompey then advanced to Jericho, where he learned that Aristobulus' adherents refused to surrender the capital; thereupon the Roman army—now in high spirits, for at Jericho news had arrived of the death of Mithradates of

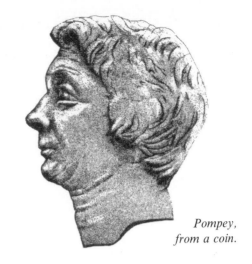

Pompey, from a coin.

Pontus, Pompey's old foe—marched upon the Holy City.

POMPEY'S TERRITORIAL ARRANGEMENTS 63 TO 55 BCE

THE arrangements of Pompey after the conquest, completed by Gabinius (proconsul of Syria in 57–55 BCE) were relatively easy on the Nabateans, harder on the Itureans, and very harsh on the Jewish state. Pompey "liberated" the Greek and Hellenized cities occupied by the Jews since the days of Hyrcanus and subjugated their rural populations to these Greek cities. Thus, there again rose autonomous units (under the supervision of the Roman proconsul in Syria) such as: Gaza, Azotus, Jamnia, Joppa, Apollonia, Arethusa (Aphek), Strato's Tower, and Dora on the coast; in the interior, Marisa, Sebaste, and Scythopolis. Beyond the Jordan, Gadara, Hippus, Abila, Dium, Pella, and Gerasa were "reestablished." The Jews kept Judea proper, the eastern part of Idumea, Perea, and Galilee. The Samaritans became independent, and the plain of Esdraelon was detached from Galilee. Esbus was returned to the Nabateans who, except for being removed from Damascus, hardly

Coin of Mattathias Antigonus.

suffered any diminution of the area under their control. The area of Lake Semechonitis, Panias, and Gaulanitis were given to the Itureans, but they lost their possessions on the Mediterranean coast.

Pompey joined the majority of the cities beyond the Jordan into a "League of Ten Cities"—the Decapolis, including also Scythopolis west of the Jordan, to minimize the danger of their being isolated. The Carmel was returned to Ptolemais. The Jews held on to those areas that were densely populated by them, except Joppa and its neighborhood and the plain of Esdraelon.

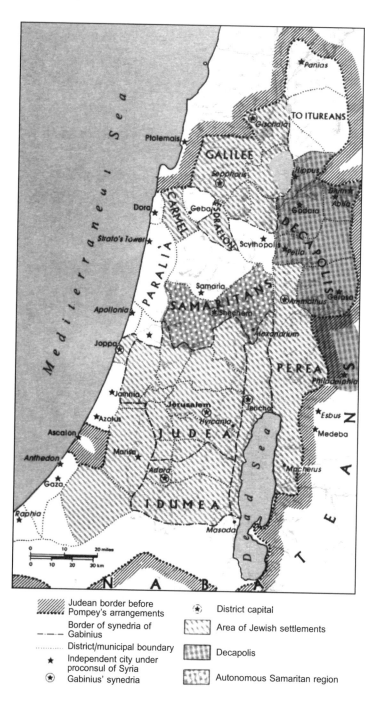

POMPEY'S TERRITORIAL ARRANGEMENTS

his family were exiled to Rome.

During the rule of Gabinius, an attempt was made to split the Jewish State into five synedria (districts), a tactic applied by the Romans in Macedonia. The seats of the synedria were in Sepphoris (Galilee), Ammathus (Perea), Jericho, Jerusalem, and Adora (eastern Idumea). But the unity of the people could not be destroyed by such means, and the synedria were dissolved after a short time.

Judea profited from the civil war between Pompey and Julius Caesar. When Caesar emerged victorious, he pursued Pompey to Egypt and there became entangled in fighting at Alexandria. In the ensuing events, Antipater was of great assistance to the relieving army of Mithradates of Pergamum and was duly rewarded by Caesar.

Hyrcanus II was appointed ethnarch by Caesar, and Antipater as the effective administrator of the State. In appreciation of the help he had received from the Jews, Julius Caesar returned to them Joppa and the plain of Esdraelon. From then on Antipater was the actual ruler of the land. He appointed Phasael, his firstborn, as governor over Jerusalem, and his younger son Herod, who was yet a boy, as governor of Galilee.

Map legend:
- Judean border before Pompey's arrangements
- Border of synedria of Gabinius
- District/municipal boundary
- ★ Independent city under proconsul of Syria
- ⊛ Gabinius' synedria
- ⊛ District capital
- Area of Jewish settlements
- Decapolis
- Autonomous Samaritan region

In all the Greek cities reestablished by Pompey and Gabinius, the populations exiled by the Maccabeans were returned. Hyrcanus II again became high priest in Jerusalem, but administration was entrusted to Antipater. Aristobulus II and his family were exiled to Rome.

68

THE PARTHIAN INVASION AND THE ESCAPE OF
HEROD 40 BCE

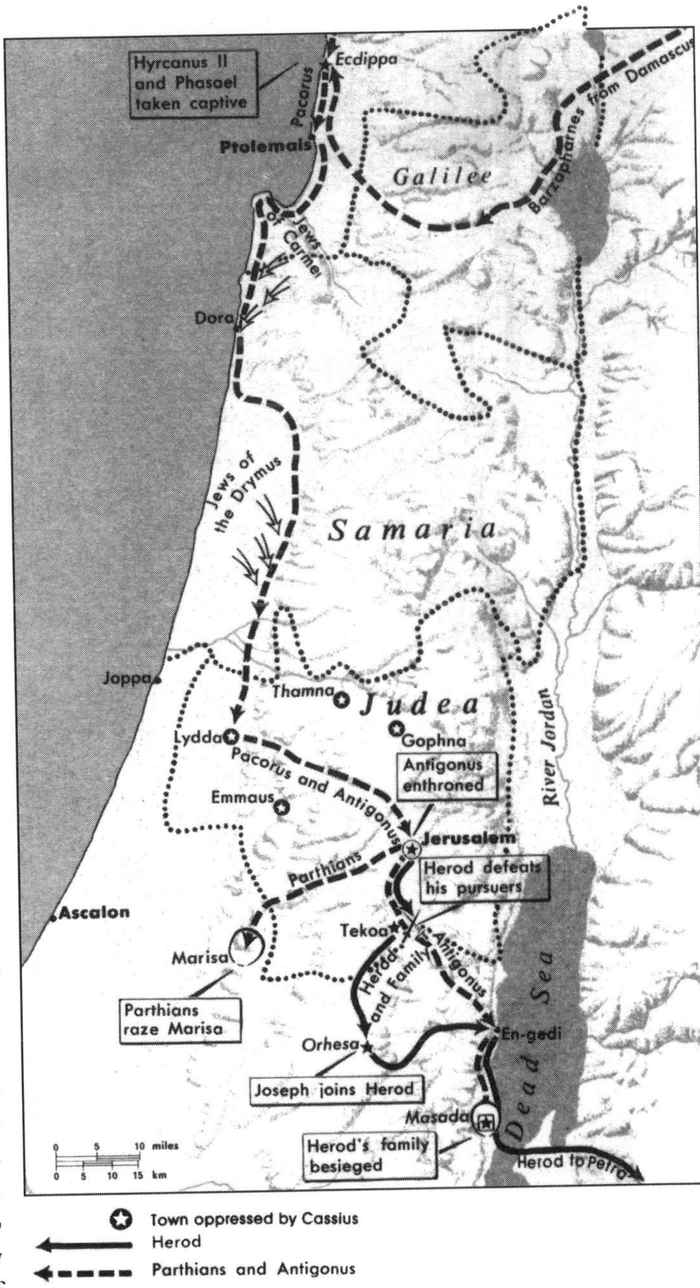

THE assassination of Julius Caesar in Rome (44 BCE) caused the renewal of the civil war, but Antipater and his sons succeeded in keeping the reins of government by submitting to the various Roman rulers. One of these was Cassius, proconsul of Syria, who tyrannized the population of Judea. He sold into slavery the inhabitants of Lydda, Thamna, Gophna, and Emmaus, and razed their towns when they were late in paying taxes. In 43 BCE, Antipater was murdered by one of his opponents, but Herod avenged his father, and suppressed the unrest; and he, together with his brother Phasael, was appointed ruler over all Judea (42 BCE).

When the Parthians invaded Syria two years later, they were joined by Antigonus (Mattathias), the son of Aristobulus II. He accompanied Pacorus, son of Ordes king of the Parthians, along the coast; simultaneously the satrap Barzapharnes invaded Galilee from Damascus. When Pacorus came up to Jerusalem, he was joined by the Jews of Carmel and of the Drymus (the great forest in the Sharon plain). In Jerusalem, the people revolted against Phasael and Herod, who were forced to open the gates to the Parthians. Phasael submitted to Barzapharnes, but was imprisoned near Ecdippa, together with Hyrcanus II; he committed suicide in captivity, and Hyrcanus was maimed to make him unfit

Map labels: Hyrcanus II and Phasael taken captive; Ecdippa; Pacorus; Barzapharnes from Damascus; Ptolemais; Galilee; Jews of Carmel; Dora; Samaria; Jews of the Drymus; Joppa; Thamna; Judea; Lydda; Gophna; Antigonus enthroned; Pacorus and Antigonus; Emmaus; Jerusalem; Herod defeats his pursuers; Parthians; Ascalon; Tekoa; Antigonus; Marisa; Herod and Family; Dead Sea; River Jordan; Parthians raze Marisa; Orhesa; En-gedi; Joseph joins Herod; Masada; Herod's family besieged; Herod to Petra

0 5 10 miles
0 5 10 15 km

⊕ Town oppressed by Cassius
◄ Herod
◄--- Parthians and Antigonus

69

Julius Caesar.

daughter of Alexander and granddaughter of Aristobulus) fled south. At Tekoa, where the fortress Herodium was later to rise, he overcame his pursuers and continued on his way to Idumea. He was joined by his brother Joseph at Orhesa, and together they proceeded to Masada, where Herod's family was later besieged by Antigonus. Herod himself crossed the Dead Sea and went to the Nabateans. When Malchus II, king of the Arabs, refused to come to his aid, Herod continued to Alexandria in Egypt and thence to Rome. The siege of Masada was meanwhile carried on in a most lethargic manner; at one time the defenders were saved from thirst only by a sudden cloud-burst. The Parthians, allies of Antigonus, returned beyond the Euphrates after invading Judea.

for the priesthood. Mattathias Antigonus was thereupon crowned in Jerusalem.

Herod and his family (including his betrothed, Mariamme the Hasmonean,

THE GROWTH OF HEROD'S KINGDOM 40 TO 4 BCE

HEROD maintained his position under Cleopatra, and when the battle of Actium (31 BCE) made Octavian—now the emperor Augustus—undisputed master of the Roman world, Herod quickly gained the favor of his new overlord. He was confirmed in his kingdom, to which Augustus in 30 BCE added Gaza and the coastal cities (except Ascalon and Dora) as well as Gadara and Hippus. In 23 BCE, Herod received the task of pacifying the unruly Batanea, Trachonitis, and Auranitis, and in 20 BCE, Panias and Gaulanitis were placed under his rule. By then Herod's kingdom had reached its greatest extent.

Apart from the conquest of his own kingdom Herod made only one conquest by arms: having in 32 BCE defeated the Nabateans in the field, he annexed Esbus and settled veterans there.

HEROD'S BUILDING IN JERUSALEM

Herod's love of pomp, his wish to immortalize his name, to secure his rule, and to appease the hostile population and provide it with work—these were the main motives for fortifying and embellishing Jerusalem. His revenues derived from trade and from taxes allowed him to build a magnificent palace in the northwestern corner of the Upper City; it was guarded on the north by three strong towers that he named Phasael (after his brother), Mariamme (in honor of his

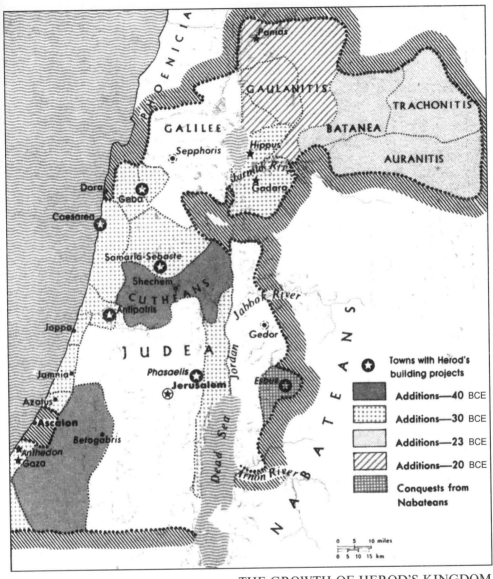

THE GROWTH OF HEROD'S KINGDOM
40–4 BCE

wife), and Hippicus (after his friend). He also built a theater in the part of the city inhabited by wealthy Hellenizers, and strengthened the North Gate in the Second Wall. South of the Temple Mount he built a stadium, probably in the Tyropoean Valley.

Herod was even more active on the Temple Mount: doubling the area of the Temple esplanade, he girdled it with walls

Coin of
Herod the Great.

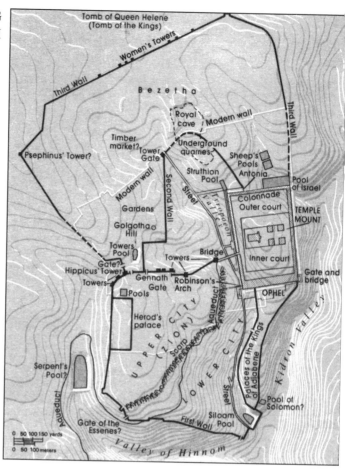

and porticoes. Its most prominent feature was the "royal portico" (basilica) in the south of the square. The king also rebuilt the Temple proper and to secure control over the Temple rebuilt the old Baris, at the northwestern corner of the Temple Mount, into a huge fortress, which he called "Antonia" in honor of Mark Antony.

Herod was also active as a builder outside his capital: he founded the harbor city of Caesarea in place of Strato's Tower and rebuilt Samaria, calling the new city "Sebaste" in honor of the emperor Augustus. He also built at Geba, Phasaelis and Antipatris. He built fortresses at Herodium and near Jericho, and entirely reconstructed Macherus and

Masada on the two opposing shores of the Dead Sea.

Reconstruction of Herod's Temple.

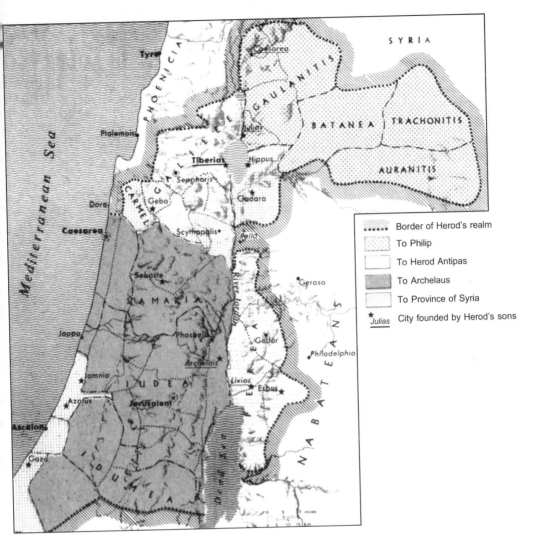

THE DIVISION OF HEROD'S KINGDOM 4 BCE TO 6 CE

AFTER much hesitation, the emperor Augustus decided in 4 BCE to divide Herod's kingdom among his three surviving sons, as recommended by the dead king. Archelaus, the son of Malthace the Samaritan, was appointed ethnarch ("ruler of the nation") over Judea, Idumea, and Samaria. The cities of Caesarea and Sebaste were included in his domain, which included Jews and non-Jews in about equal proportions. Herod Antipas, the second son, received two purely Jewish, but widely separated, areas:

Galilee and Perea (Jewish Transjordan). The third son, Herod Philip, was endowed with the newly settled lands of the Gaulanitis, Batanea, Trachonitis and Auranitis, as well as Caesarea Panias. Most of his subjects were probably non-Jews, but as the Jews in his lands had been settled by Herod the Great, they were loyal to the dynasty. Salome, Herod's sister, was given Jamnia and Azotus, and Phasaelis in the Jordan Valley. The cities of Gaza, Gadara, and Hippus, which had borne Herod's rule with much dissatisfaction, were attached to the province of Syria.

All of Herod's sons tried to emulate their father in building cities; Archelaus even called a new settlement in his own name: Archelais. Antipas built Tiberias (named in honor of the emperor Tiberius) and Livias (in honor of the emperor's mother). Philip added to Caesarea Panias, which was from this time called Caesarea Philippi, and built Julias (also in honor of Livia) near Bethsaida.

Archelaus had a short and turbulent reign and was banished in 6 CE, his lands being handed over to a Roman procura-

Coin of Herod Antipas, struck at Tiberias.

tor. Herod Antipas remained till 39 CE. Only Philip died in possession of his tetrarchy, in 34 CE.

THE EARLY PROCURATORS OF JUDEA 6 TO 41 CE

WHEN Archelaus was deposed, Judea passed under the direct rule of the Caesars. However, out of lack of foresight the emperors did not properly assess the importance of Judea, and assigned the region to low-ranking officers, either a prefect (*praefectus*) or a procurator. Although given the right to try criminals, these governors did not hold high official status, and even freed slaves were sometimes assigned these positions. The procurators were not given command over the legions, but the auxiliary troops from Ascalon and Sebaste—longstanding enemies of the Jews—were under their authority. The prefect of Judea was under the supervision of the governor of Syria, a former consul and the commander of four legions. Because he sat in Antioch, some distance away, his armies, when needed, were usually late in coming.

The procurators of Judea had their headquarters in Caesarea, and went up with their troops to Jerusalem only in hours of need, especially during the three pilgrimages, when the easily incited multitudes would gather in the city. The Romans did, however, take great care to respect the religious sentiments of the Jews. For example, Gentiles, even soldiers, who trespassed onto the Temple court would be sentenced to death, and the legionnaires were careful not to carry their cultic emblems with them when traveling through Judea. The procurators of Judea were partly financed by the collection of taxes and customs at the borders of their region.

The early prefects were seven in number: the first was the Roman equestrian

Coin of Pontius Pilate.

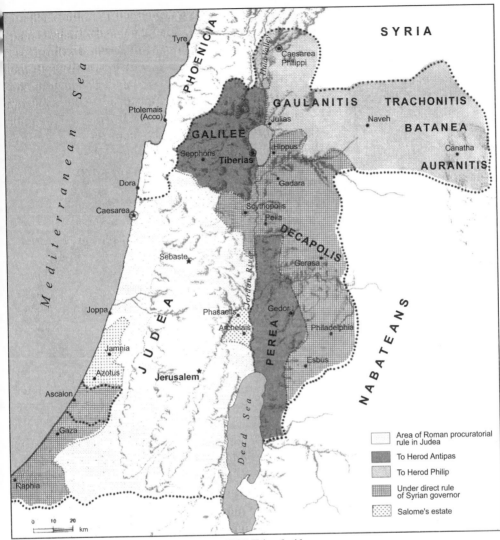

THE EARLY PROCURATORS OF JUDEA 6–41 CE

Coponius, after whom one of the Temple gates was named. Two others, Valerius Gratus and Pontius Pilate, governed for ten years each. Pilate is the best known of the prefects, because the activities and trial of Jesus took place under his rule (26–36 CE).

The province of Judea also included the estates of Salome which upon her death (10 CE) she bequeathed to Livia, wife of Augustus and mother of Tiberius. When Livia died, these estates were inherited by her son Tiberius and turned into imperial estates, assigned to a special procurator. The rest of Judea underwent few changes during this period. Herod's son Philip died in 34 CE and his lands were put under the administration of the Syrian governor, although Herod Antipas— "that fox" as he was termed in the Gospels (Luke 13:32)—knew how to hold his ground. The political situation described in the map was the background to events in Christian tradition, whose influence on human history has been enormous.

THE ESSENES

TOWARD the end of the Second Temple period sectarianism with its attendant rivalries and antagonisms was on the rise. Josephus lists three major sects: the Pharisees, the Sadducees and the Essenes. In addition there were the Zealots who were not a religious sect but held nationalistic religious views which were also held by some Pharisees and Essenes. We learn of the Pharisees mainly from the Oral Law which was handed down and recorded during the second and third centuries CE. We know somewhat more about the Essenes due to contemporary finds discovered in the Judean desert during the late 1950s and 1960s. The Essenes apparently developed their creed and teachings in the days of Hasmonean rule. During the reign of Janneus they isolated themselves from the rest of the population; many adherents and their leader, possibly the founder of the sect himself, the "Teacher of Righteousness," took voluntary refuge in the Judean desert. Living in the desert, with its messianic inspirations, the Essenes were cut off from the world around them and devoted themselves to a fundamental and ascetic existence. Part of their writings have survived to the present day owing to the hot and dry desert climate. From their scrolls we can deduce much about their way of life and culture. The term Essenes refers to many different sects and offshoots, and the scholars themselves are in dispute as to whether all the documents found in the Judean desert caves belonged to the Essenes. It appears that at least part of them belonged to the Pharisees; some of the Essene groups were indeed very similar to the Pharisees.

In general, the Essenes did not not attach great importance to the Oral Law.

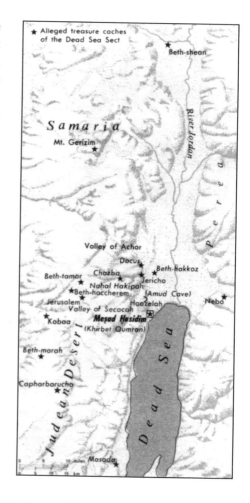

Their teachings contained addenda to and interpretations of the Written Law, but nothing in these writings points to a belief that their leaders had the authority to interpret or change the holy writ.

The Essene sect was messianic in nature, and their fervent belief in the coming of the Messiah is evidenced in many of their writings. At first theirs was an active and political messianism; later it became less strident. In the Revolt against Rome the Essenes sided with the rebels and as a result their centers (Khirbet Qumran) in the Judean desert were destroyed by the Romans.

H. In the Time of Jesus

THE JOURNEYS OF JESUS 5 BCE TO 30 CE

THE end of the Second Temple period witnessed great spiritual turmoil among the people. The masses could not see the reasons for the declining fortunes of the Hasmoneans nor the loss of their freedom, and they viewed their subservience to Rome as part of the "pre-messianic tribulations." The feeling that the "end of the world was near" caused many to seek repentance, preachers abounded and various sects arose. This spiritual ferment formed the backdrop to the Christian traditions about the life and activities of Jesus. According to these traditions, Jesus was born in Bethlehem in the last days of Herod (5 BCE). When Herod plotted Jesus' death, the family—Jesus, his mother Mary and her husband, Joseph, a carpenter and resident of Nazareth in the Galilee—escaped to Egypt. After Herod's death, the family returned to Nazareth.

Jesus grew up in Nazareth and lived there continuously for some twenty years. He went up to Jerusalem several times. In about 27 CE a preacher by the name of John called on the people to repent, baptizing his followers in the river Jordan to expiate their sins. Jesus, too, was among those baptized. After a solitary sojourn in the desert of Jericho, Jesus returned to Nazareth. The Gospels ascribe his first miracle (at Cana, where he turned water into wine during a wedding feast) to this same period. The people of Nazareth refused to believe in Jesus and tried to kill him. He left the city to dwell in Capernaum, on the shores of the Sea of Galilee, which became the focus of most of his activities. Beyond this region he also traveled to the Phoenician cities of Tyre and Sidon, and also to Caesarea Philippi and the cities of the Decapolis. Once, on his return from Jerusalem, Jesus met a Samaritan woman near Sychar, in the vicinity of Jacob's Well, near Shechem.

Finally, Jesus made a pilgrimage to

Route traditionally traveled by Jesus

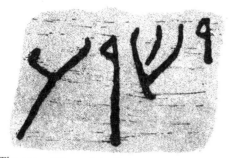

The name "Jesus," in Hebrew on an ossuary.

Jerusalem for the Passover festival by way of "Jewish Transjordan" (Perea), a route taken by Jews who, for various reasons, wished to bypass the land of the Cutheans. Jesus made his way from Transjordan to Jericho, and from there went up to Jerusalem. Upon entering the city, he was received with great joy by the people. He dwelt for a while in the house of Annas, on the Mount of Olives, whence he would descend to the Temple courts to preach to the people. On the eve of Passover, he officiated at a Seder (festive supper) that was held in the house of a wealthy resident. That same night Jesus was arrested in Gethsemane, brought before the Sanhedrin, and accused of blasphemy. The Jewish authorities referred his trial to the Roman procurator, Pontius Pilate, who had Jesus sentenced for rebellion (as "King of the Jews") and ordered him to be crucified. According to Christian tradi-

tion, Joseph of Arimathaea (a *bouleutes*— a "member of the council"—in Jerusalem who was one of those looking for the heavenly kingdom) secured permission from Pilate to remove the body of Jesus from the cross, and bury it in a tomb he had hewn for himself. Christian belief has it that Jesus was resurrected on the third day after his crucifixion, appeared several times before his disciples—in the vicinity of Emmaus, in Jerusalem, and on the shores of the Sea of Galilee—and finally ascended to heaven from the summit of the Mount of Olives.

There remained in Jerusalem a small Christian community which began to preach, first to the Jews in both Israel and the Diaspora, but when they refused to believe in Jesus, the Christians addressed their preaching to the other nations of the world. This change was chiefly due to Saul of Tarsus, a disciple of Rabban Gamaliel and a Pharisee who adopted the name Paul and became a Christian apostle. This act of Paul's transformed Christianity into a major force in history. The fusion of the Jewish belief in a messiah who would come to establish the reign of justice in the world with the Hellenistic concept of a god incarnate on earth, attracted the Gentiles but was not accepted by the Jews. In the second century CE, Judaism and Christianity parted their ways forever.

AROUND THE SEA OF GALILEE

APART from several journeys, Jesus' entire activity before his final departure for Jerusalem was concentrated around the Sea of Galilee (Matthew 15:29; Mark 1:16, 6:31), also called Lake Gennesaret (Luke 5:1) and Lake Tiberias (John 6:1, 21:1), and usually just "the sea" in the Gospels. Gennesaret seems to be an

earlier name, for it replaces the biblical "Sea of Chinnereth" (Numbers 34:11), because the city of Gennesaret was located on the site of Chinnereth (Tell Ureime). "Sea of Tiberias" is clearly posterior to the foundation of that city in 18–19 CE. The first Apostles were fishermen; sometimes Jesus taught while

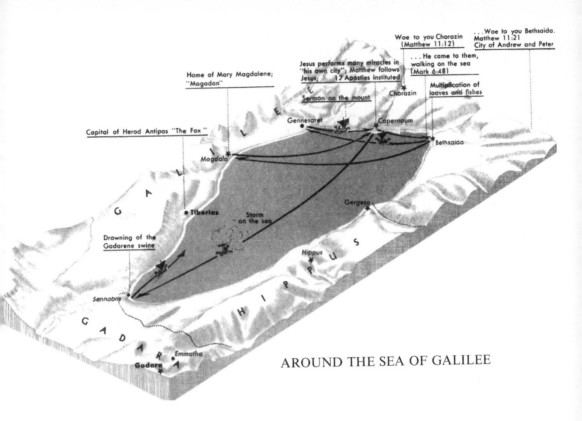

Woe to you Chorazin
(Matthew 11:12)

...Woe to you Bethsaida.
Matthew 11:21
City of Andrew and Peter

Jesus performs many miracles in
"his own city"; Matthew follows
Jesus;   17 Apostles instituted

...He came to them,
walking on the sea
(Mark 6:48)

Home of Mary Magdalene;
"Magadan"

Sermon on the mount

Multiplication of
loaves and fishes

Chorazin

Gennesaret

Capernaum

Bethsaida

Capital of Herod Antipas "The Fox"

Magdala

Gergesa

G A L I L E E

G

Tiberias

Storm
on the sea

Hippus

Drowning of the
Gadarene swine

H I P P U S

Sennabris

G A D A R A

Emmatha

Gadara

AROUND THE SEA OF GALILEE

standing in a boat, with the crowds listening on the shore. The Sermon on the Mount was delivered according to tradition near Capernaum (Matthew 8:1 and 5); the site is said to be located on the height just behind Capernaum. Only occasionally did Jesus upbraid the cities that refused to repent ("Woe to you Chorazin, woe to you Bethsaida, Capernaum shall be brought down to Hades" —Matthew 11:21–23; Luke 10:13–15).

On the Sea of Galilee there are frequent storms. During one such storm, Jesus slept while sailing across to the Gadarenes (Mark 5:35–41; Matthew 8:23–27; Luke 8:22–24) and upon his awakening the sea was suddenly becalmed. The location of the incident of the "Gadarene swine" has been much disputed (the usual version "Gerasene" is quite impossible, for there was no territory of Gerasa on the lake shore); the two possibilities are "Gergesene"—pointing to Gergesa

(Kursi) on the eastern shore of the lake in the territory of Hippus—and "Gadarene;" Gadara might have possessed a stretch of the shore that lay between the river Jordan and Kefar-zemah. The shore there is steep; thus the plunging of the herd of swine into the waters of the lake is plausible. The inhabitants of Gadara, being Gentiles, did not share Jewish scruples regarding the raising of swine. In any event, the name Gergesa appears in an ancient Jewish source as the name of a village east of the Jordan River and is thus evidence that a village by this name existed. In the sixth century a large monastery was founded in the area.

Other events recorded in the Gospels pertaining to the Sea of Galilee and its surroundings are the Multiplication of Loaves and Fishes at a lonely spot near the town of Bethsaida, the story of Jesus' walking on the water, and Peter's attempt to follow his example (Mark 6:45–51;

Matthew 15:22–23; and John 6:15–21). Other journeys of Jesus include a visit to "Magadan" ("Dalmanutha", in Mark 8:10); in both cases we should read Magdala, the most important town on the sea shore after Tiberias, and famous for its fish-curing industry. This locality was the home of Mary Magdalene, who followed Jesus to Jerusalem; she was one of a group of women "who had been healed of evil spirits and infirmities...who provided for him out of their means" (Luke 8:2–3).

JESUS' LAST JOURNEY TO JERUSALEM

WHEN the days drew near for him "to be received up" (Luke 9:51), at the end of his stay in Galilee, Jesus began to foretell of his fate in Jerusalem to his disciples, "and they were greatly distressed" (Matthew 17:23).

We may possibly insert into the story of Jesus' last journey to Jerusalem the incident mentioned in Luke 9:52–56. Perhaps Jesus intended to take the shorter route to Jerusalem by way of Samaria but, as the people would not receive him, he turned eastward and went through Perea, the "Judea beyond the Jordan." From there, he and his disciples crossed the Jordan and continued by way of Jericho, where he stayed at the house of Zacchaeus, a chief tax-collector (probably of the imperial estates in the Jordan Valley, inherited by the emperor from the Herodian dynasty). Two blind beggars were healed outside the town. Then Jesus continues along the pilgrim road, which went up to the Mount of Olives and so to Bethphage on the mount and to Bethany, where he stayed at the house of Martha and Mary, the sisters of Lazarus.

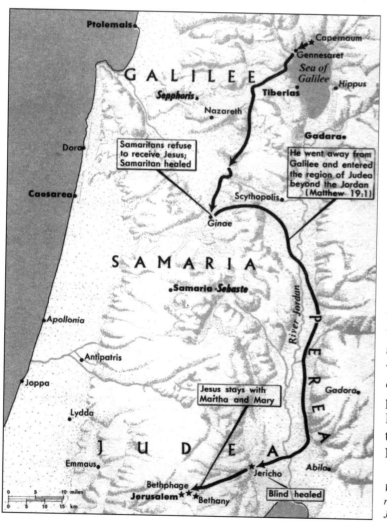

When the days drew near for him to be received up, he set his face to go to Jerusalem. (Luke 9:51)

80

THE JEWISH DIASPORA IN THE TIME OF JESUS

AT the beginning of the Christian era, the Jewish communities were mainly concentrated in the Eastern, Greek-speaking half of the Roman Empire. Two outlying areas were central Italy, where Jews had been brought as slaves after Pompey's campaign and where conditions became favorable under Julius Caesar, and Babylonia, where the communities grew strong under Parthian rule. But the bulk of the Jewish Diaspora was still confined to the Greek world. There the Jewish communities were centered around the synagogue, with full internal autonomy, their own archons and elders, communicating with each other and with Jerusalem. This state of affairs goes far to explain the context of Paul's missionary activity. The communities were on the whole prosperous, but dependent on Gentile authorities and anxious to preserve good relations with them.

I. THE FIRST REVOLT AGAINST THE ROMANS

THE KINGDOM OF AGRIPPA I 37 TO 44 CE

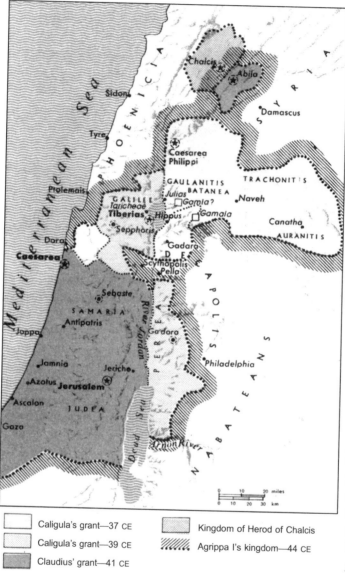

Caligula's grant—37 CE

Caligula's grant—39 CE

Claudius' grant—41 CE

Kingdom of Herod of Chalcis

Agrippa I's kingdom—44 CE

youth, passed mostly at Rome, he became the favorite of Gaius Caesar (Caligula), the successor of Tiberius as emperor. In 37 CE Caligula endowed him with Philip's tetrarchy and, in 39 CE when Antipas had fallen out of the emperor's favor, with that of his other uncle. Caligula was assassinated at Rome in 41 CE. Agrippa, who was then on a visit to the imperial capital, rendered such services to the emperor Claudius, on his accession, that the grateful ruler gave him the lands of Archelaus. Thus Agrippa united under his hand almost the whole of his grandfather's kingdom. Once established in Jerusalem, Agrippa became the favorite of the people by his strict observance of Jewish laws: his reign was regarded as the last peak in the Second Temple period, before disaster overcame the nation. As part of his orthodox policy, Agrippa was severe with the Christians in his domain. Agrippa I died suddenly at Caesarea during a performance in the theater.

AGRIPPA was the grandson of King Herod and the son of Aristobulus, whose mother was Mariamme, the last of the Hasmoneans. After an adventurous

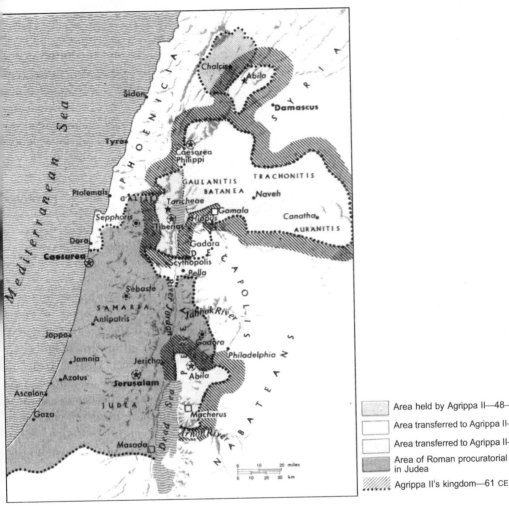

Area held by Agrippa II—48–53 CE

Area transferred to Agrippa II—53 CE

Area transferred to Agrippa II—61 CE

Area of Roman procuratorial rule in Judea

Agrippa II's kingdom—61 CE

ON his death Agrippa I left only an adolescent son; the emperor Claudius therefore decided to return Judea to the rule of Roman procurators. Four years later, however, he granted Agrippa II the land of Chalcis in Lebanon, and in 53 CE exchanged this area for Abila (near Damascus) and the tetrarchy of Philip (Gaulanitis, Batanea, Trachonitis, Auranitis, and Caesarea Philippi). Under Nero, Agrippa II also received Tiberias and Taricheae, as well as Abila in Perea, with its surrounding villages. The revolt against the Romans prevented Agrippa II from enlarging his kingdom, as did his father before him, but he remained in power until his death (about 95 CE).

Among the procurators ruling Judea after 44 CE were Tiberius Alexander (scion of a patrician Jewish family from Egypt, a nephew of Philo, who had forsaken his religion, and joined the Romans) and Felix, a slave freed by Claudius. Felix, and after him Albinus (62–64 CE) and Gessius Florus (64–66 CE), were corrupt and cruel, and by their acts helped spark the revolt.

THE OUTBREAK OF THE FIRST REVOLT AGAINST ROME

FEARING the recurrence of Caligula's attempt to desecrate the Temple by putting up his statue there and inspired by messianic hopes, the majority of Pharisees joined the Zealots, who had been fighting Rome relentlessly since the days of Herod; thus the revolt of the people against Rome became general. After a clash at Caesarea between Jews and Greeks, the Jews were forced to leave Caesarea for Narbata. When news of this reached Jerusalem, riots broke out there too; the appearance of the hated procurator, Gessius Florus, together with his soldiers, only served to fan the flames. Agrippa II tried to calm the people but his efforts came to nought.

Menahem, son of Judas the Galilean, arrived in Jerusalem with his men, after he had secured Masada with its stores of arms. Eleazar, son of Ananias, one of the chief officials in the Temple, with the support of a few "teachers" who were close to the Pharisees, ordered the sacrifice for the emperor to cease, thereby giving the signal for open revolt. One by one, the strongholds of Jerusalem were captured and in the month of August the entire city was in the hands of the Jews. Though Menahem was put to death by his aristocratic rivals among the Jews, the revolt continued. The Jews captured the fortresses of Cyprus and Macherus and the rebellion spread throughout the entire country. Jews attacked the Greek cities in the vicinity of Judea, these in turn revenging themselves on the Jews living in their midst. Most cruel were the inhabitants of Scythopolis, who repulsed the Zealot attack with the help of their Jewish fellow citizens, whom they later treacherously slaughtered in cold blood. Only the people of Gerasa, among all the cities, protected the lives of its Jewish citizens.

Hearing of the outbreak at Jerusalem, the governor of Syria, Cestius Gallus, who was in general charge of the affairs of Judea, decided to intervene (for the local procurator had no legionary troops at his disposal). Taking with him the Twelfth Legion Fulminata ("the Thundering One"), he marched along the coast until he reached Antipatris. Several forays were made by the Romans to intimidate the rebels of Galilee and Joppa. Advancing by way of Lydda, Beth-horon, and Gabaon, Gallus arrived in Jerusalem. He even penetrated into the city, but faltered before the walls of the Temple. As the winter had already begun, he decided to retreat. During the descent the Romans were attacked in the pass of Beth-horon and suffered disastrous losses. The Twelfth Legion lost its eagle, and all its siege equipment, which afterward did good service to Jerusalem. The Romans finally disengaged themselves, but their defeat turned the revolt into a full-scale rebellion. Freed from the imminent menace of Roman intervention, the rebels set up a government in Jerusalem, struck silver coins, and divided the country into seven military districts, each with its own commander. The most exposed post, the command of Galilee, was given to a young priest, Joseph, the son of Mattathias (the future historian, Josephus Flavius), who lacked all military experience.

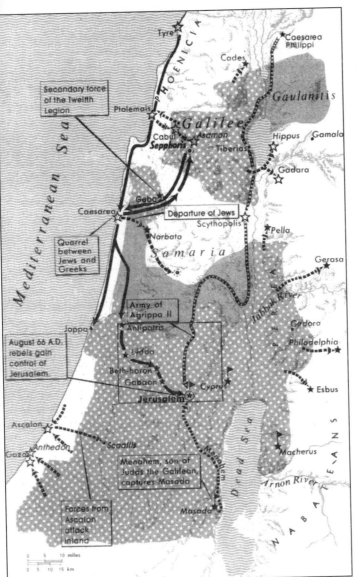

Secondary force
of the Twelfth
Legion

Departure of Jews

Quarrel
between
Jews and
Greeks

Army of
Agrippa II

August 66 A.D.
rebels gain
control of
Jerusalem.

Forces from
Ascalon
attack
inland

Menahem, son of
Judas the Galilean,
captures Masada

Tyre
Caesarea
Philippi
Cades
Gaulanitis
Ptolemais
Galilee
Cabul   Asamon
Sepphoris   Tiberias
Hippus   Gamala
Geba
Gadara
Caesarea
Scythopolis
Pella
Narbata
Samaria
Gerasa
Mediterranean Sea
Joppa
Antipatris
Gadora
Philadelphia
Lydda
Beth-horon
Gabaon   Cypros
Jerusalem
Esbus
Ascalon
Scaaltis
Anthedon
Gaza
Macherus
Arnon River
Dead Sea
Masada
N A B A T A E A N S
Tabbok River

0   5   10 miles
0   5 10 15 km

Roman legionary eagle.

THE OUTBREAK OF
THE FIRST REVOLT
AGAINST ROME

⚑ Jewish rebel conquests

☆ City in which Jews were attacked

◄┅┅┅┅ Jewish forces

◄┅┅┅┅ Agrippa II's army

◄━━━━ Gallus' army

▦ Area in revolt

▓ Area in partial revolt

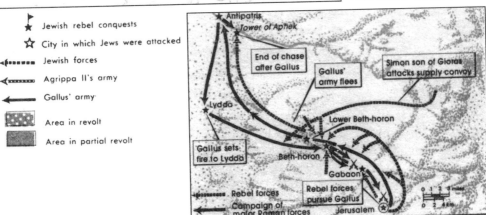

Antipatris
Tower of Aphek

End of chase
after Gallus

Gallus'
army flees

Simon son of Giorat
attacks supply convoy

Lydda

Lower Beth-horon

Gallus sets
fire to Lydda

Beth-horon

Gabaon

Rebel forces
pursue Gallus

Jerusalem

0 1 2 3 miles
0   4 km

┅┅┅┅┅ Rebel forces

━━━━ Campaign of
major Roman forces

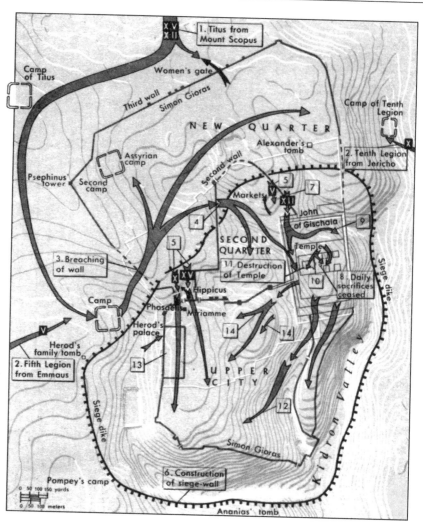

WITH the approach of the Romans, conflicts among the Zealots finally ceased; their commanders, Simon the son of Gioras (Simeon Bar Giora) and John of Gischala, divided between them responsibility for the defense of the city. Simon was to guard the section running from the northeastern corner of the wall to the Pool of Siloam, while John was assigned the eastern wall. At a later stage, Simon defended the Upper City and John the Temple itself. Their combined armies did not exceed 25,000 men; against them were drawn up four legions (the Fifth, Tenth, Twelfth and Fourteenth), and a great number of auxiliaries, about 80,000 men in all.

After preliminary skirmishes in the orchards just outside the Gate of Women (no. 1 in the map), the Romans set up their main camp in the west and a secondary one (that of the Tenth Legion) on the Mount of Olives (2). They breached the third wall about May 25th (3) and, about May 30th, the second wall (4); the main camp was then transferred

Triumphal parade with Temple vessels—Arch of Titus, Rome.

inside the city. About June 16th, the Romans launched an all-out attack on the towers north of Herod's palace and on the fortress of Antonia (5). Great damage was inflicted by the defenders on the siege machinery and dikes, and the assault was fended off.

Titus ordered a siege-wall to be thrown around the city (early in July) to starve out the defenders (6); the results were soon apparent, for much food had gone up in flames during the internecine strife among the Zealot factions. The Romans renewed their onslaught from July 20th to 22nd (7). Simon the son of Gioras held fast, but the fortress of Antonia, under the command of John of Gischala, was taken and razed. On August 6th, the perpetual sacrifice ceased in the Temple (8), and the porticoes were burned between August 15th and 17th (9). After a ramp had been raised against the inner wall, the Temple itself was entered (10) and burned on the ninth of Ab (about August 28th) (11).

On August 30th, the Romans captured the Lower City (12). Even then, the defenders of the Upper City did not surrender. But after another month of effort the Romans succeeded in capturing the Upper City and Herod's palace (13–14), and only then did resistance cease. By decree of Titus, all the people of Jerusalem were taken captive and its buildings were leveled to the ground. Only the three towers around which the Tenth Legion had camped were left standing, and the ruins of Jerusalem and its region were placed under the surveillance of this legion.

Roman battering ram.

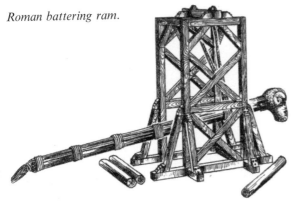

MASADA was built atop a rock, its sheer cliffs rising out of the deep ravines surrounding it. The Roman siege-force was divided between the lower camp (B) and the upper camp (F), which also contained the headquarters. The problem facing the Romans was how to get their siege-towers up to the walls of the fortress, at the top of the cliffs. They first built a siege-wall around the whole of the rock, except for the impassable areas. The wall, which was equipped with catapults, completely isolated the defenders, yet there was little prospect of vanquishing them quickly by starving them out, for there were abundant stores of food and water inside.

Flavius Silva chose a site to the west of Masada, where there is a low saddle between the two surrounding ravines,

View of Masada, looking south.

and began a ramp from the so-called White Rock (Leuke) up to the defenders' wall, a height of 300 cubits (according to Josephus; in actuality, it is only 260 feet). At 200 cubits the Romans raised a platform of wood and iron, 50 cubits tall; on this they placed a siege-tower reaching a further 60 cubits, its top thus standing about 20 feet above the walls of Masada. The wall was breached with the aid of an iron battering ram on May 1st, 73 CE. The defenders hastily put up a barricade of wood which the Romans tried to burn down; at first they had the wind against them, but later in the day it changed and the barricade caught fire and burned.

With victory assured, the Romans put off their final assault until the next day, but the 960 defenders of Masada—men, women and children—the last vestiges of open defiance against Rome in the first Jewish war, committed suicide during the night.

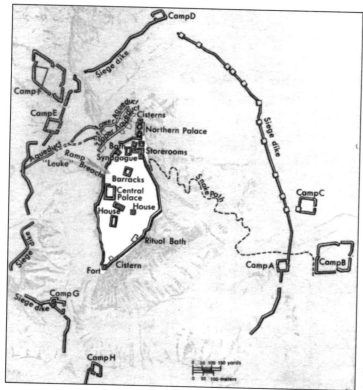

WHILE Jerusalem was still under siege, the moderate faction of the Pharisees whose numbers increased with the de-cline of the Zealots) succeeded in smug-gling their leader, Rabban Johanan ben Zakkai, out of the besieged city. The

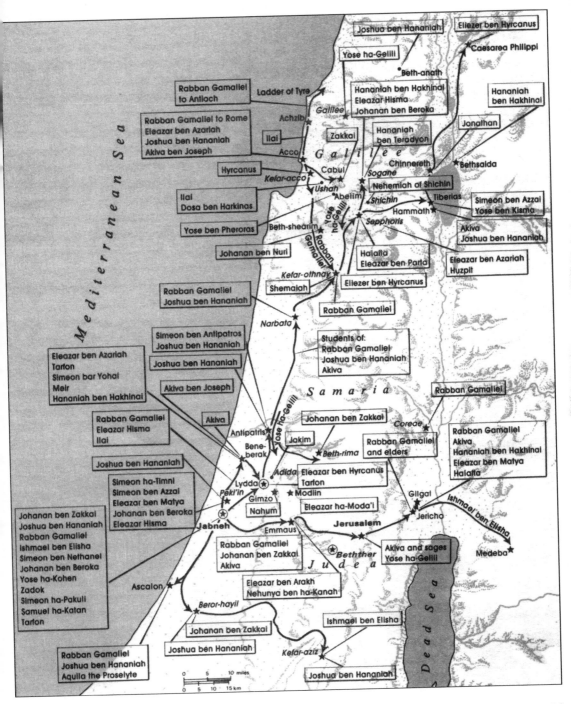

Roman authorities eventually allowed the Pharisee leader to teach Torah in Jabneh, where he had been banished and at first held prisoner. A spiritual center was consequently established, and with the destruction of the Temple and the annihilation or dispersion of the priesthood and the Sadducees, Jabneh in effect became the new administrative center of the Jewish people. Here the Sanhedrin was reconstituted, under R. Johanan, and the Hebrew calendar was intercalated. Institutions arose and frameworks were established to administer the people's lives without a temple or political independence. When Rabban Gamaliel b. R. Simeon, a follower of the School of Hillel, received the presidency in Jabneh, R. Johanan moved to Beror-hayil.

A number of *batei midrash* (lit., "houses of study") were built in and around Jabneh, such as the one at Lydda, where R. Eleazar b. Hyrcanus and R. Tarfon resided. The *beth midrash* in Bene-berak was particularly successful; Rabbi Akiva—the sage who rose to be the nation's leader early in the second century—taught there. Only R. Eleazar b. Arakh, who parted from his colleagues to live in Emmaus, is reputed to have "forgotten his learning." Another sage, R. Ishmael b. Elisha, went to live in "the south," at Kefar-aziz, but kept in contact with the others.

The sages went from town to town on matters of Torah and community issues. A frequent traveler was R. Gamaliel, who went on missions to Antioch via Narbata, Kefar-othnay, Acco, Achzib and the Ladder of Tyre. In 95–96 CE he left for Rome accompanied by the leading sages of Jabneh. Many scholars went up to Jerusalem to mourn its destruction. Some visited the reputed site of the stones at Gilgal; they also sojourned in Ascalon and Emmaus, Acco and Tiberias. Their activities also led them eastward, beyond the river Jordan: R. Ishmael set up a *mikveh* (ritual bath) for the people of Medeba. Numerous, too, are the traditions surrounding the travels of the sages to various communities in the Diaspora.

In Jabneh a practice was instituted to distinguish the heretics (mainly Judeo-Christians) from the community of Israel by inserting a "blessing" against Christians and other heretics in the *Amidah* (the "Eighteen Benedictions"). The sages of Jabneh also interpreted and introduced many halakhic laws, and amended *takkanot* (regulations) therein, so as to fill the gap that was left in the lives of the Jewish people when Jerusalem and its Temple were destroyed. The sages of Jabneh thus demonstrated that there was an alternative to the Temple, and the Jewish nation did not disintegrate in the aftermath of the destruction.

THE LAND OF ISRAEL AFTER THE FIRST REVOLT
70 TO 131 CE

DESPITE the fierceness of the Romans' war against the Jews from 66 to 73 CE, it was not a war of annihilation. Vespasian as a rule abided by the old Roman maxim: "fight the proud, spare the meek." Even towns that were twice destroyed, such as Joppa, rose up again with the cessation of hostilities. A sparse settlement also remained amid the ruins of Jerusalem, near the camp of the Tenth Roman Legion. The map of the Jewish towns and villages known to us after the

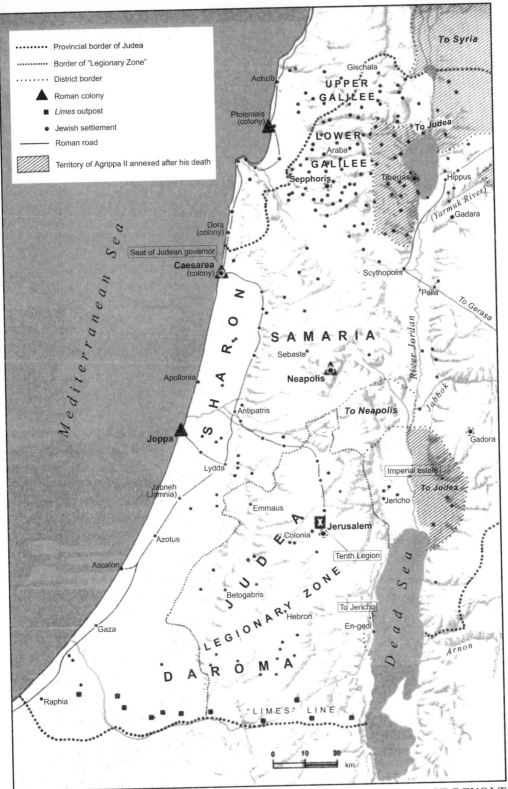

Legend

- ●●●●● Provincial border of Judea
- ●●●●● Border of "Legionary Zone"
- ●●●●● District border
- ▲ Roman colony
- ■ *Limes* outpost
- ● Jewish settlement
- — Roman road
- ▨ Territory of Agrippa II annexed after his death

Mediterranean Sea

To Syria

Gischala

Achzib

UPPER GALILEE

Ptolemais (colony) ▲

To Judea

LOWER GALILEE

Araba

Sepphoris

Tiberias

Hippus

(Yarmuk River)

Gadara

Dora (colony)

Seat of Judean governor

Caesarea (colony) ▲

Scythopolis

River Jordan

Pella

To Gerasa

S H A R O N

S A M A R I A

Sebaste

Neapolis ▲

Jabbok

Apollonia

Antipatris

To Neapolis

Gadora

Joppa ▲

Imperial estate

To Judea

Lydda

Jericho

Jabneh (Jamnia)

Emmaus

J U D E A

Colonia

Jerusalem ⊠

Azotus

Tenth Legion

Ascalon

Betogabris

L E G I O N A R Y   Z O N E

To Jericho

Dead Sea

Hebron

En-gedi

Gaza

Arnon

D A R O M A

"L I M E S"   L I N E

Raphia

0 10 20 km

THE LAND OF ISRAEL AFTER THE FIRST REVOLT

91

Seal emblem of the Tenth Roman Legion—a ship and a boar—engraved on a roof tile found in Jerusalem.

Romans turned it into an area where legions were stationed and expropriated much land, although the Jewish landowners, for the most part, were allowed to remain on their property as tenants. The orchards in the Jordan Valley and in En-gedi (which were then annexed to the Jericho district) were kept by the royal treasury, thereby protecting the Jewish farmers who knew how to tend the valuable trees. Already in the final days of Claudius, Ptolemais was granted the rights of a Roman colony and soldiers who had been released from several legions settled there.

The Flavian emperors continued in the same tradition: Vespasian granted colonial rights to Caesarea and later to Joppa. He established a new city in place of the village Mabarta, between Mount Ebal and Mount Gerizim, and named it Neapolis (present-day Nablus). This city received as part of its domain the land of the Cutheans as well as the district of Akrabeta, which was separated from Judea. The provincial governor resided in Caesarea and the legion under his command camped in Jerusalem. In order to ease communication between the civil center and the army, a branch off the coastal road was built from Antipatris to Jerusalem. The coastal road itself was a vital artery in the Roman military-political system—a line of communication between Alexandria and Antioch. It began to be laid in the days of Nero, and was apparently completed at the time of the revolt. Another road connected Damascus with Gadara–Scythopolis and the other cities of the Decapolis. As a precautionary measure, the Romans developed a fortified boundary line (*limes*), which already existed along the brook of Besor, between the Mediterranean and Dead seas, in the time of Herod.

destruction of the Temple (it should be noted that the evidence concerning these places is largely a matter of chance and does not reflect the true picture of Jewish settlement as a whole) shows that the Galilee was densely populated, Judea fairly so (mainly in the southern part), and the coastal region, the Jordan Valley and Transjordan were also moderately populated. The fact that Judea witnessed the outbreak of a second great revolt after only sixty years attests to the staying power of the Jews in their land.

The long drawn-out campaign in Judea taught the Roman authorities a lesson concerning the nature of the land and the character of its citizens. Judea was thus elevated to a province ruled by a former *praetor* and stationed with a legion. The boundaries of the new province encompassed the coastal cities and those of the Decapolis, and after the death of Agrippa II, his realm (apart from Caesarea Philippi, Batanea, Trachonitis, and Auranitis) became part of Judea. Thus, shortly before the name "Judea" finally disappeared from the political map, it had spread over a very wide area. On the other hand, many changes were made within the limited area of Judea: the

J. The Second Revolt Against the Romans

THE REVOLTS IN THE DIASPORA 115 TO 117 CE

DURING Trajan's campaign in the east, a Jewish revolt broke out in Cyrenaica under the leadership of Lucuas ("Andreas" in Greek), whose supporters saw him as the King-Messiah. The rebels captured the city of Cyrene, destroyed its temples and bathhouse, and damaged the road linking the city to the port of Apollonia. From Cyrenaica they turned to Egypt. The capital Alexandria withstood their attack with the help of the local Greeks who gathered in its defense. However, the Jews living in the Nile Delta also decided to join the rebels, and the revolt turned into a full-scale war that lasted some two years. The battles spread to Athribis in the Delta, along the Nile River, and to the Fayum district. Battles were also fought in the districts of Heracleopolis, Oxyrrhynchus, Kinopolis, Hermopolis, Lycopolis, and Thebes. Despite the recruitment of Egyptian farmers and civil servants, the authorities failed to suppress the rebellion. Finally the Roman commander Turbo was dispatched with new legions, and defeated the Jews near Memphis. In this savage struggle almost all Egyptian Jewry except in Alexandria was destroyed and the results of the war were felt well into the late second century.

Cyprus was another arena of bloody battles between Jews and non-Jews, with both sides suffering heavy losses. In the end the rulers won, and Cypriot Jewry ceased to exist for hundreds of years.

The outbreaks both in Cyrenaica and Cyprus occurred while the emperor and his elite troops were engaged in an arduous campaign in the east. Trajan conquered Armenia in 114–115, and Mesopotamia in 115 with its fortifications at Edessa, Nisibis and Singara. In 116 Trajan continued his campaign to Adiabene (where the province of Assyria was established), and continued down along the river Tigris. He captured the Parthian capital of Ctesiphon and reached Mesene and the port of Spasinu Charax on the Persian Gulf. However, in 117, a general revolt broke out against the Roman army. The Jews of Babylonia and Adiabene joined in the hostilities against the Romans. Although the rebel-

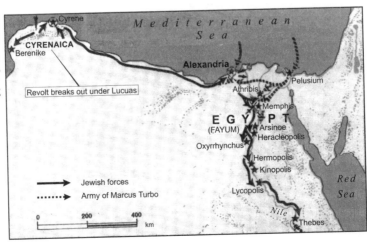

THE JEWISH REVOLT IN CYRENAICA AND EGYPT 116 CE

Revolt breaks out under Lucuas

Jewish forces
Army of Marcus Turbo

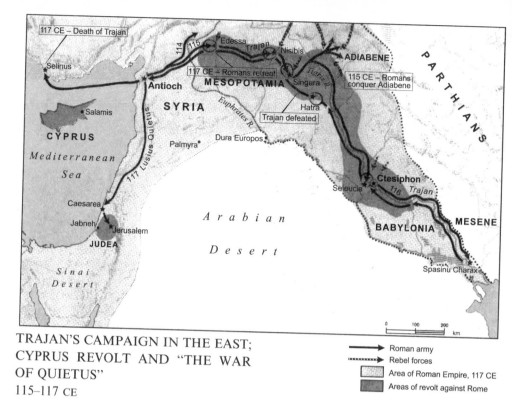

TRAJAN'S CAMPAIGN IN THE EAST;
CYPRUS REVOLT AND "THE WAR
OF QUIETUS"
115–117 CE

→ Roman army
⇢ Rebel forces
▢ Area of Roman Empire, 117 CE
▦ Areas of revolt against Rome

lious cities of Seleucia, Nisibis and Edessa were reconquered by Trajan's commanders, Trajan himself was defeated at Hatra and returned to Antioch. There he appointed the general Lusius Quietus, of Moorish origin, ruler of Judea, ordering him to go there and crush the Jews, who were stirred up by the events in the neighboring lands. The actions of this savage ruler are recorded in talmudic sources as "the war of Quietus." He brought with him the Sixth Legion, which was stationed at Kefar-othnay (present-day Lejjun-Legio), near Megiddo; from this time on the governors of Judea had the status formerly held by consuls. Trajan died in September 117 at Selinus in Cilicia. His successor, Hadrian, relinquished all the conquered lands beyond the Euphrates, thereby temporarily restoring peace to the eastern border.

THE BEGINNINGS OF THE BAR KOKHBA REVOLT
131 TO 132 CE

NEWS of Hadrian's plan to found a Roman colony in the city of Jerusalem which would have included the usual pagan temples—thus thwarting all hope of reconstructing the Temple—stirred anew the spirit of the struggle against Rome. The Jews had learned a lesson from the First Revolt, in which proper preparation and unity were lacking. This time they chose the most suitable moment, at a time when the emperor was far from Judea. They prepared fortified positions in the countryside, so as not to be trapped again in fortresses. Pre-

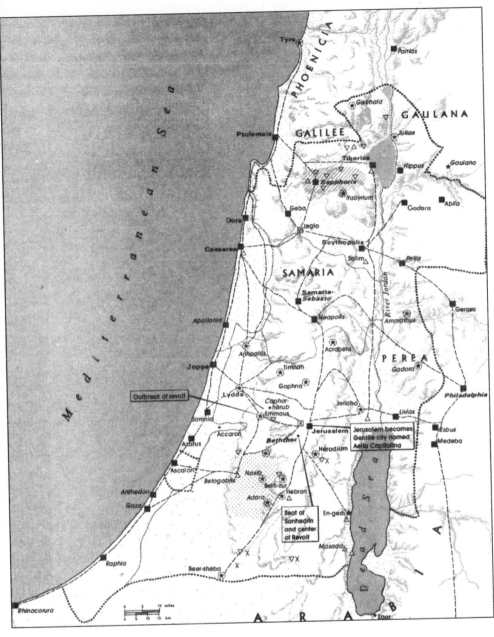

Tyre ⊛

Panias ■

⚝ Gischala

G A U L A N A

GALILEE

Ptolemais ■

△ Julias

▽ △

Tiberias ■

Hippus ■   ⭑ Gaulana

▽ Sepphoris ▽

Itabyrium △

Gadara ■   Abila ■

Geba ●

Dora ■   Legio ●

Scythopolis ■

Salim △   Pella ⭑

Caesarea ■

S A M A R I A   River Jordan

Samaria-Sebaste ■

Gerasa ■

Apollonia ■   Neapolis ■

Ammathus ⊛

⊛ Antipatris   Acrabeta ⊛

P E R E A

Joppa ■   Timnah ●

Gadora ⊛

Gophna ⊛

[Outbreak of revolt]   Lydda ■   Philadelphia ■

Caphar-harub ●

Jericho ⊛   Livias ⊛

Jamnia ■   Emmaus ●

Accaron ●   ⊠ Jerusalem   [Jerusalem becomes Gentile city named Aelia Capitolina]   Esbus ■

Azotus ■   Bethther ⭑   Herodium ⊛   Medeba ■

Ascalon ■   ▽ Nasib   ▽ X

Belogabris ●   Beth-zur ⭑

Anthedon ●   Adora ⊛   △ Hebron

En-gedi ⭑   D e a d   S e a

Gaza ■   [Seat of Sanhedrin and center of Revolt]

Masada ▽   △

▽ X

Raphia ■   Beer-sheba ⊛   X   ▽ X

0   5   10 miles

0   5   10   15 km

A   R   A   B   I   A

Rhinocorura ●   Zoar ●

P H O E N I C I A

- - - - Roman road
·········· Provincial border
•••••••• Border
□ Headquarters of the Legion
△ Roman army camp
■ Polis
● Settlement
⊛ Rural administrative capital
▽ Hiding complex
X Jewish fortress
▦ Concentration of hiding places
▨ Scattered hiding places

parations also included hundreds of underground hiding systems in the Judean plains and some in the Galilee. These underground systems were quarried into the rock exploiting existing caves and caverns. They made ready quantities of arms and mobilized all possible inhabitants. A unified command was set up and it remained in control

Coin of
Bar Kokhba.

from the beginning of the Revolt to its end.

The Bar Kokhba Revolt lacks a chronicler such as Josephus was for the First Revolt, and we are forced to glean our information from various talmudic and other sources, and from documents and other archaeological finds from the caves in the Judean Desert. The documents reveal that Bar Kokhba (Bar Kosiba) was the same man as "Simeon Prince of Israel" mentioned on Jewish coins from the time of the Revolt, and that his full title was "Simeon son of Kosiba Prince of Israel." It may be assumed that this Simeon, who was regarded as the "Messiah," was descended from the Davidic line.

The Revolt broke out in the fall of 131 CE, evidently at Caphar-harub, near Modiin. The careful preparations bore fruit: the people of Judea rallied around Jerusalem, where the Tenth Legion was stationed. The Revolt included all of Judea down to the Coastal Plain. There is evidence that some Samaritans joined the Bar Kokhba rebels, and there are also indications that Gentiles, mainly from among the oppressed local inhabitants, also found their way to the rebel camp and joined the "brotherhood" of warriors. The new leader, who was supported by the Sanhedrin, and mainly by Rabbi Akiva, saw his government as the sole legal authority in the land; those who

opposed him, such as Christians of Jewish extraction who obviously could not see Bar Kokhba as the "Messiah," were persecuted by the rebel authorities.

The suddenness of the outbreak and the defensive preparations of the rebels were such that the Roman governor, Tinneius Rufus, had no alternative but to order the evacuation of Jerusalem. The Tenth Legion and the non-Jewish inhabitants left for Caesarea, and the Jews once again took control of their ancient capital. An orderly administration was set up and a new reckoning of the calendar was instituted. The first year of the Revolt (131–132 CE) was declared "The Year One of the Redemption of Israel," and the following years "Year… of the Redemption" or "of the Freedom of Israel." Documents found in the Judean Desert caves reveal the efficiency of the new land registry and the leasing of former imperial lands. District commanders were appointed and the new government issued silver and bronze coinage, struck over imperial Roman and provincial city coins.

Upon the success of his uprising in Judea, Bar Kokhba attempted to extend the Revolt to the Galilee. The damage to Sepphoris and to the few hiding tunnels found in the Galilee bears witness to rebellious activity and preparations. Olive groves were uprooted. However, it is clear that most of the Jews of Galilee did not join the rebels. The Romans made every effort to suppress the Revolt, which they regarded as highly dangerous. The proconsul Julius Severus was called from Britain to Palestine. Besides the two legions already stationed in Judea (the Sixth and the Tenth), forces were brought from Syria, Arabia, Moesia on the Danube, and Egypt, in addition to smaller cavalry and infantry units from Panonia, Rhetia and other lands. Pressure was put on Bar Kokhba and his followers from every quarter.

Julius Severus decided to advance slowly, to conquer position after position and village after village, in order to keep up pressure on the rebels. The reason behind this course is evident from the fate of the Twenty-second Legion, that had dared rashly to advance into the interior and was completely wiped out; from this time onward its name disappears from the Roman army list.

THE THIRD AND FOURTH YEARS OF THE BAR KOKHBA REVOLT 133 TO 134 CE

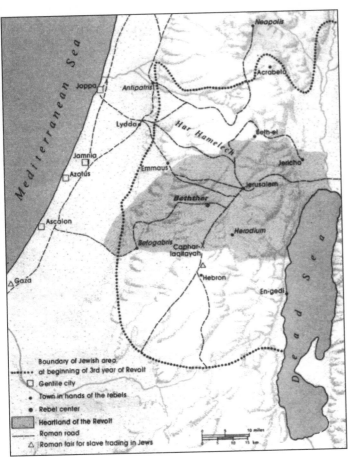

AFTER the initial successes of the rebels, the military situation changed rapidly. The Romans assembled a large army in Judea and began the conquest of Palestine. We have little information on the battles proper. Both sides appear to have steered clear of frontal confrontations and were reluctant to engage in decisive battles. Instead, the Romans besieged dozens of smaller villages and persistently reduced the areas held by the rebels. Following each conquest the Romans annihilated the rebellious communities. Sources from this period ascribe the atrocities to one Rufus.

In the third year of the Bar Kokhba Revolt Julius Severus took command of all Roman expeditionary forces. At this time it seems that all of Palestine was in the hands of the Romans except for Judea (as witnessed by coins from the third year of the rebellion found in the Shephelah and Judean mountains). An important battle was apparently fought at Emmaus (maybe the battle in which Horbat Eqed was captured). To commemorate this victory the town was called Nicopolis—city of victory. After this battle, to seal off the rebellious population, the Romans erected barriers at Emmaus, Capharlaqitiyah and Beth-el or Bethlehem. In the third year of the rebellion the Romans took the remaining part of Judea including the last stronghold, Bethther.

The fighting was very heavy: the historian Dio Cassius tells us that during the Bar Kokhba Revolt the Romans captured fifty fortresses, destroyed 985 villages, and slaughtered more than a million persons. However, the Roman army also suffered great losses, so much so that at the end of the war Hadrian was obliged in his address to the Senate, to refrain from using the normal formula "The Emperor and the Army are well."

In spite of heavy losses, Bar Kokhba and his followers kept up their high spirits. From documents dated the "Year Three" of the Revolt, and even of the "Year Four" (the latest document is dated to the month of Marheshvan Year Four), it is apparent that civilian and economic life went on as usual. In Bar Kokhba's letters to his commanders, we

Bar Kokhba Letter from the Judean Desert.

can still feel, along with the tension, the care of his staff concerning the fulfilling of religious commandments: along with orders for the confiscation of foodstuffs, for the transport of supplies from the port of En-gedi, and for the suppression of opposition elements, we read instructions for the gathering of lulabs and ethrogs for the Feast of Tabernacles.

THE SIEGE OF BETHTHER 135 CE

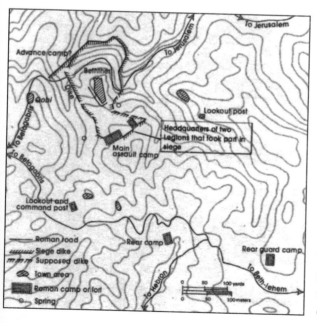

IN the fourth year of the Revolt (spring 135 CE), Bar Kokhba and his army were driven into the fortress of Bethther (southwest of Jerusalem), to which Severus and his legions promptly laid siege. (Hadrian had in the meanwhile left Judea, upon the restoration of Roman control in Jerusalem.) The fortress is situated on a hill overlooking a deep canyon and was protected by a fosse on the south. The position was quite strong, though it lacked a sure water supply. The Romans surrounded it with a siege-wall and, later in the siege, crossed the fosse by means of a siege dam. At the end of summer 135, the Romans had breached the wall and slaughtered the surviving defenders, including Bar Kokhba.

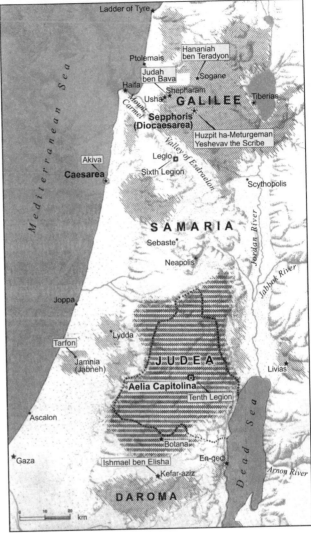

WITH the suppression of the Revolt a period of persecutions began, which Jewish sources term "the Religious Persecution" (*Ha-Shmad*). The plan of the Roman government was to completely eradicate all Jewish settlement in Judea and to blur the Jews' national identity in the rest of the land. Hadrian ordered the expulsion of all Jews who remained in Judea, thus emptying the region of most of its inhabitants. When the battles began, many Jews had already escaped, to such a degree that the Mediterranean ports were crowded with refugees. Those who were taken prisoner by the Roman army were sold in two large slave markets, one in Botana (north of Hebron) and the other in Gaza. The number of prisoners-of-war was so large that the price of slaves decreased in all the markets of the empire. Hadrian ensured the reinstatement of Aelia Capitolina (Jerusalem) and settled the city and its environs with foreigners, mainly Arabians and Syrians. Entry to the city was forbidden to the circumcised, including Christians of Jewish origin.

Judea was left with only rural settlements, in "Daroma" ("the South"), from En-gedi to Gerar, in the lowlands of Jamnia and Lydda, and in the Jordan Valley, from En-gedi to Livias. From this time forth, the Galilee became the main refuge of Palestinian Jewry. But even there a foreign image was imposed on the city councils of Tiberias and Sepphoris, the latter city being renamed "Diocaesarea." Hadrian aspired to destroy all memory of the defeated people and ordered that the name of Judea be changed to "Syria Palaestina."

The leaders who had supported Bar Kokhba were put to death. Among them were the "Ten Martyrs," headed by

Rabbi Akiva, who died a martyr's death in Caesarea. R. Yeshevav the Scribe and R. Huzpit ha-Meturgeman ("the Translator") apparently fled to Sepphoris, but the authorities caught up with them there, as they did with R. Hananiah b. Teradyon, in Sogane. To weaken the

Jews' self-image, the Romans forbade the performance of numerous commandments such as circumcision, and congregating in the synagogue. The Romans also prohibited rabbinical ordination, i.e., passing full judicial authority from one generation of sages to another. The authorities threatened to destroy any town which tolerated this practice. Nonetheless, R. Judah b. Bava martyred himself by ordaining five students of R. Akiva between Shepharam and Usha, thereby ensuring the continuation of this judicial system. Many sages of this generation, such as R. Simeon bar Yohai, went into hiding. Others, like R. Meir and R. Yose, fled the country for a time. Nevertheless, the existence of a Diaspora Jewry that remained scattered in places either unaffected or outside the boundaries of the empire, nullified Hadrian's decrees to some extent.

AELIA CAPITOLINA 135 TO 324 CE

WHEN the Roman governor Tinneius Rufus "plowed up the Temple Mount," as the Talmud said, he was actually conducting a traditional Roman ceremony—that of founding a new city—whereby the founder or governor would plow a furrow (pomerium) along the site of the city's future walls. The city founded by Hadrian, upon the ruins of Jerusalem, was called "Aelia," after the emperor (Aelius Hadrianus), and "Capitolina," after the three Capitoline gods (Jupiter, Juno, Minerva).

The city was typically planned on the model of a Roman army camp, square in shape with two streets intersecting at the center. In this case, however, for practical reasons, the plan deviated somewhat from the usual layout. A square with a column at its center was built near the northern gate. Branching off the square were the two colonnaded main streets. One led to the forum (marketplace), where a temple to Aphrodite stood nearby, and continued along the side of the Roman legionary camp that lay in the shadow of what remained of Herod's towers. The second street ran past the public bathhouses, where a side street led to the eastern gate. Above this side street a triumphal arch was built to mark the site of the Antonia fortress. On the Temple Mount platform (the "Quadra") stood the temple to Jupiter and in front of it, a statue of Hadrian on horseback. A second triumphal arch stood at the city's northern entrance. Here pilgrims would arrive from the coastal areas, from Caesarea or Joppa. To this day, this city plan can be recognized in the structure of Jerusalem's Old City.

K. Renewal of Jewish Settlement in Palestine

THE WANDERINGS OF THE SANHEDRIN AFTER 70 CE

AFTER being exiled from Jerusalem, the Sanhedrin first resided in Jabneh. Following the religious persecutions by Hadrian, it moved to the Galilean town of Usha and, according to one theory, based on the Babylonian Talmud (*Rosh Hashana* 31b), returned temporarily to Jabneh, but was forced to return to Galilee. The seat of the Sanhedrin then moved from Usha to Shepharam, and from there to Beth-shearim. R. Judah ha-Nasi ("the Prince"), during the last days of his presidency, transferred it to Sepphoris. Finally, in the days of Judah ha-Nasi's grandson, R. Judah Nesiah, the Sanhedrin moved to Tiberias, where it remained until its dissolution. However, even afterward its members continued to function in Tiberias under other names (e.g., *rashei ha-perek*, or academy lecturers), until Jerusalem again became the religious center after the Arab conquest.

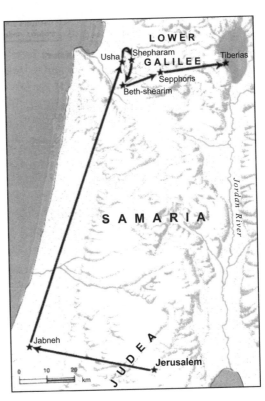

THE TWENTY-FOUR PRIESTLY DIVISIONS

AFTER the Bar Kokhba Revolt, twenty-four divisions (*mishmarot*) of priests (1 Chron. 24:7–18) who persisted in guarding their social unity, settled in various towns and villages in the Galilee. The list of these places, hinted at in the Jerusalem Talmud, was inscribed in synagogue inscriptions and preserved in its entirety in *piyyutim* (liturgical poems). The nation apparently wished to memorize the order of the divisions—which also in a way served as a calendar—in anticipation of the resumption of their duties in the Temple, the rebuilding of which was

משמרת אתתהעשרה אליש יבכדזן קנה
משמרת שתהעשרה יקים פשחורי עצת
משמרת שלושעשרה חופהבית מעון
משמרת ארבע עשרה ישבאב פיתשיחין
משמרת חמש עשרה בלעריה בלגדזיונית
משמרת שש עשרה אמרכבפרנמרה
משמרת שבעשרה חזיר ג...
משמרת שמונה עשרה הפיצץ...
משמרת תשע עשרה פתחיהאכלב עלב
משמרת עשרים יחזקאל בי צלא וזוא
משמרת אחד ועשרים יכין כפר יוחנה
משמרת שנים ועשרים גמול ביתחביה
משמרת שלושה ועשרים דליהזגתען צלמין
משמרת ארבעה עשרה מעזיהחממאת ...

Fragments and reconstruction of inscription listing the 24 priestly courses, from mosaic floor of synagogue found at Caesarea.

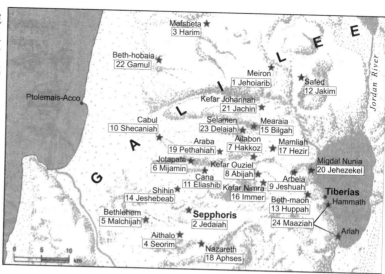

Mafsheta ★
3 Harim

Beth-hobaia ★
22 Gamul

Meiron ★
1 Jehoiarib

Safed ★
12 Jakim

Ptolemais-Acco

Kefar Johannah
21 Jachin ★

Cabul
10 Shecaniah ★

Selamen
23 Delaiah ★

Mearaia
15 Bilgah ★

Araba
19 Pethahiah ★

Ailabon
7 Hakkoz ★

Mamliah
17 Hezir ★

Jotapata ★
6 Mijamin

Kefar Ouziel ★
8 Abijah ★

Migdal Nunia
20 Jehezekel ★

Cana
11 Eliashib

Kefar Nimra
16 Immer ★

Arbela
9 Jeshuah ★

Tiberias

Shihin ★
14 Jeshebeab

Beth-maon
13 Huppah ★

Hammath

Bethlehem
5 Malchijah ★

Sepphoris
2 Jedaiah ★

24 Maaziah ★

Ariah

Aithalo ★
4 Seorim

Nazareth ★
18 Aphses

G A L I L E E

Jordan River

0   5   10
km

expected at any time. Until the First Crusade, it was the custom in Palestinian synagogues, every Sabbath, to mention the priestly watch of the week, to recite the relevant *piyyut* and to offer a prayer for the priests to resume their duties.

THE JEWISH SETTLEMENT AFTER 140 CE

HADRIAN died three years after the fall of Bethther. His successor, Antoninus Pius, was a moderate man who adhered to Roman traditions. He did not leave Italy even once during his entire period of rule. Early in his reign, Palestine was still unruly, although the authorities slowly began to realize that it was not in their power to eradicate the Jews, and thus reconciled themselves to their presence. The emperor allowed the remaining sages to assemble in Usha, and reinstate the presidency of the Sanhedrin. Judaism once again became a "permitted religion," whereby the community was granted legal authorization and could hold property. Even the right to establish rabbinical courts in matters of finance (under the pretext of arbitration) was reinstated, as, with the weakening of Roman rule, was their right of criminal jurisdiction. The city councils of Tiberias and Sepphoris were also returned to Jewish hands. Although Jews were still forbidden to reside in Jerusalem, the authorities tended to "turn a blind eye" when they arrived in the city on pilgrimages, providing they stayed only a short time. The settlements in the south—in the Shephelah and the Jordan Valley—continued to exist, and the percentage of the urban Jewish population in these places increased. The Galilee remained almost entirely Jewish, with settlement based on the "householder" class, small farmers with "a field, a vineyard, and an olive grove." These farmers worked their fields themselves, without slave labor. The large estates of the wealthy and the families of various *nesi'im* (heads of the Sanhedrin), such as R. Tarfon, were outside the Galilee region: in the plain of Esdraelon, the Shephelah, or the Golan. Economically, the lot of the Jewish population improved in the generation following the religious persecutions by Hadrian. However in the beginning, great damage was done, especially to the olive groves, and much of the land that was confiscated was passed on to foreign tax collectors. The economic crisis experienced by the Jewish community after the Hadrianic persecutions compelled the Jewish authorities to enact a number of emergency regulations, such as prohibiting the export of wheat, oil and wine—all essential products—and the raising of small cattle, i.e., goats and sheep, in afforested or cultivated areas. However, with their healthy economy, the Galilean Jews overcame these difficulties, and the prohibitions were slowly lifted. Some Jews who had left the country returned, a few prisoners-of-war managed to return to their settlements, and those already settled never thought of leaving the Holy Land. This state of affairs made it easier for the Jewish leadership to reach a compromise with the Roman authorities by promising to keep the peace of the land.

- Settlement with Jewish population
  :::::: Provincial border of Syria Palaestina
- .... Municipal boundary
- Non-urban area

THE JEWISH DIASPORA IN THE TIME OF ANTONINUS PIUS 138 TO 161 CE

PEACE within the Roman Empire remained undisturbed in the days of the "Antoninian" dynasty. This line of emperors, which came to the throne by way of adoption, ruled from the days of Nerva (96) to the death of Marcus Aurelius (180). Their reign was accompanied by economic growth, despite the troubling omens for the future.

The growth of the urban economy in the west of the empire led to the westward expansion of Diaspora Jewry in the second century. A few of the new communities were the result of external events such as the expulsion of Jews from Rome to Sardinia under Tiberius or the sale of Jews to slave labor after the Bar Kokhba Revolt, but the majority of Jews migrated voluntarily to commercial centers (mainly the provincial capitals) or to large military centers established along the empire's borders. The great majority of the Jews of the Diaspora was still concentrated in the eastern part of the empire. Communities flourished especially in Asia Minor, as evidenced by the remains of splendid synagogues like the one at Sardis. On the other hand, there was somewhat of a decline in Syrian Jewry, perhaps as a result of the negative reactions of non-Jews in the east to the revolts in the days of Trajan and Bar

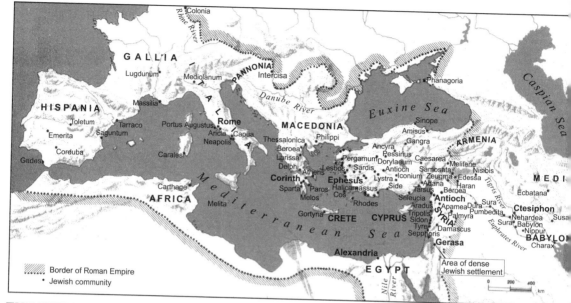

THE JEWISH DIASPORA IN THE TIME OF ANTONINUS PIUS
138–161 CE

Kokhba. The situation of the Jewish communities in Greece is also known to have declined, but this was part of a general phenomenon: Greece at that time began to lose its population. The uprisings during Trajan's reign caused the almost total destruction of the once large Egyptian Diaspora as well as the eradication of Jewish communities in Cyrenaica and Cyprus; only in Alexandria did a small Jewish community remain.

In any event, the Jewish Diaspora was one of the reasons that the Roman government wished to make peace with the Jews of Palestine. The more so because some Jews lived beyond the borders of the empire, in Babylonia and other parts of the Parthian kingdom, in places beyond the reach of Roman rule. In addition, the Jewish communities throughout the empire willingly accepted the leadership of the national authority reestablished in Palestine. With the exception of the *Fiscus Judaicus*, a poll tax of two *drachmae* levied on Jews from the time of Vespasian in place of the half-shekel tax for the Temple, the Jews of the Diaspora willingly continued to pay taxes to the *nesi'im* (pl. of *nasi*) of the Sanhedrin, and they received their emissaries with the highest esteem and followed their directives. The authorization given to these emissaries to teach and judge on behalf of the *nasi* (variously rendered as "prince," "patriarch," or "president") was recognized throughout the Diaspora and, when necessary, they were even authorized to suspend communal leaders. The *nasi* and the Sanhedrin retained the exclusive right of consecrating the New Moon and intercalating the calendar by which Jewish festivals are determined. This proved to be an important tool for the unification of the Jewish people and the status of the *nasi* and the Sanhedrin throughout the Jewish Diaspora.

THE BOUNDARIES OF THE LAND ACCORDING TO
HALAKHAH

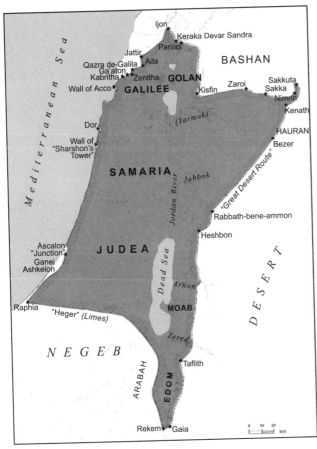

terumot (heave offerings), tithes, and the prohibition of planting and harvesting in the seventh, or Sabbatical year (*shevi'it*)—from other areas that, halakhically speaking, were "land of the Gentiles."

The "boundary of those returning from Babylonia" is listed in three versions: in *Sifrei* (*Ekev*, v. 51), and in *Shevi'it* of both the Tosefta (4:11) and the Jerusalem Talmud (4:36c). These accounts are faulty with regard to many names and to the order in which they are arranged. After making various corrections and changes of order, we arrive at the line depicted on the map. Along the coast, cities considered Gentile were excluded from the Land of Israel: Ascalon (from "the junction," namely, where the Ascalon road intersects the coastal road, a place identified with "Ganei Ashkelon," where the list ends); Caesarea (listed under its old name, Strato's Tower, distorted here to "Sharshon's Tower"); Dora and Acco. From Acco the border continued along the northbound road, to the left (west) of which was the "land of the Gentiles" and to the right (east), the Land of Israel. The boundary passed near several settlements within the townships of Acco and Tyre, and turned northeastward, up to the Ijon Valley, between the Lebanon and Hermon mountain ranges. It then turned southward to "Keraka Devar Sandra," that is, the city of the son of (Li)sandros,

TALMUDIC sources distinguish three borders of Eretz Israel: "the boundary of the Patriarchs," from the river of Egypt (the Nile) to the river Euphrates; "the boundary of those coming out of Egypt," that is, the borders of Joshua's conquests; and "the boundary of those returning from Babylonia." Unlike the first two, which are mainly of historical significance, the third "boundary" had halakhic and practical significance. This boundary generally separated those Jewish settlements that were considered part of Eretz Israel and which were subject to halakhic rules relating to the land—such as

Stone relief of a menorah found at Naveh.

ruler of the Jetherites; this is possibly Antioch, in the Dan region. From there the border passed the vicinity of Panias (mod. Banias), and continued past the Jewish Golan (Gaulanitis) to Kasfon (Kisfin, in the territory of Hippus), and along the borders of Batanea (Bashan) and Trachonitis (Zaroi–Sakka–Kenath–Nimrin to Sakkuta, i.e., Skeia, on the border of Hauran [Auranitis]). From this point the border continued southward along "the Great Desert Route," probably identical to the "new road" of Trajan. It passed close to Bostra (Bezer),

Philadelphia (Rabbath-bene-ammon), Esbus (Heshbon), the Zered Brook, Taflith (et-Tafila), and went south to Gaia, in the vicinity of Petra and Rekem (identified with Petra). The border then continued along the "Heger" (Roman *limes*) to Raphia, and back up to Ascalon.

In this description of borders, despite the difficulty of identifying many of the names (particularly in the north, between the Mediterranean Sea and Panias), or even making an intelligent guess, it is clear that this boundary encompassed all Jewish settlement that existed immediately after the destruction of the Temple and before the easing of the halakhic rules for the land in various areas, by Rabbi Judah ha-Nasi (late second to early third centuries). He permitted this in the case of many cities, such as Sussita (Hippus), Beth-shean (Scythopolis), Panias, Kefar Zemah, and Beth Govrin (Eleutheropolis), and as a result, "the boundary of those returning from Babylonia" became only an abstract concept.

THE URBANIZATION OF THE LAND 63 TO 330 CE

THE Greek culture that predominated in the east, from the Hellenistic period onward, was clearly an urban one, and the cities became the main pillars of that culture from its inception. The Romans, heirs to the Hellenists in the east, continued the path of their predecessors, the kings of the Ptolemaic and Seleucid dynasties. Pompey "restored" the already-existing cities, especially on the northern and southern coasts of the country and in the northern part of Transjordan. Herod and his descendants, interested in creating an urban base for their regime, founded new cities or restored existing ones—Gentile (Sebaste,

Caesarea Philippi [Panias]), mixed (Caesarea, Julias) and Jewish (Tiberias, Antipatris) alike.

The Jewish War of 70 CE was a significant turning point in the urbanization of Palestine: a new city was founded (Neapolis), and several urban centers in Judea became independent cities (Joppa, Azotus, Jamnia, Sepphoris). The establishment of Provincia Arabia turned Charachmoba, Areopolis, Medeba and Esbus into cities. Hadrian's attempt to found Aelia Capitolina on the site of Jerusalem provoked the Bar Kokhba Revolt, but in the end he realized his original plan. After Hadrian, Septimius

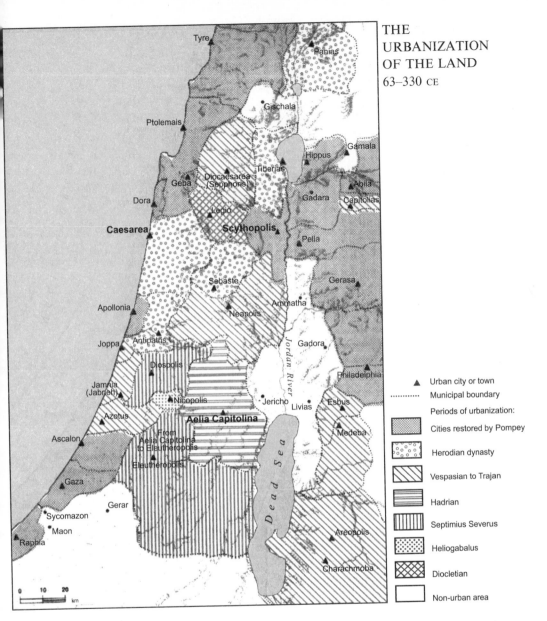

THE
URBANIZATION
OF THE LAND
63–330 CE

Tyre
Panias
Gischala
Ptolemais
Gamala
Hippus
Tiberias
Diocaesarea
(Sepphoris)
Geba
Abila
Dora
Gadara
Capitolias
Legio
Caesarea
Scythopolis
Pella
Sebaste
Gerasa
Ammatha
Apollonia
Neapolis
Joppa
Antipatris
Gadora
Jordan River
Diospolis
Philadelphia
Jamnia
(Jabneh)
Nicopolis
Jericho
Livias
Esbus
Azotus
Aelia Capitolina
Ascalon
From
Aelia Capitolina
to Eleutheropolis
Medeba
Eleutheropolis
Dead Sea
Gaza
Gerar
Sycomazon
Maon
Areopolis
Raphia
Charachmoba

0 10 20
km

▲ Urban city or town
.... Municipal boundary
Periods of urbanization:
Cities restored by Pompey
Herodian dynasty
Vespasian to Trajan
Hadrian
Septimius Severus
Heliogabalus
Diocletian
Non-urban area

Severus in one year (200) founded Diospolis (formerly Lydda or Lod) and Eleutheropolis (Beth Govrin), and in this way caused the urbanization of two more areas. Heliogabalus (Nicopolis) and Diocletian (Maximianopolis, formerly Legio or Kefar-othnay) completed the task of urbanization.

Almost the entire country was urbanized in this manner, apart from two kinds of areas: those with numerous Jews who opposed the Hellenistic culture and which, in the eyes of the Roman authorities, were not suited to an urban regime (these included the Upper Galilee and the Golan), and areas that included royal estates, which, because of their economic importance, the treasury wished to keep under its control. This was the fate of the lower Jordan Valley, on both its banks, and of three estates southeast of Gaza.

MIGRATION ROUTES FROM BABYLONIA TO ERETZ ISRAEL

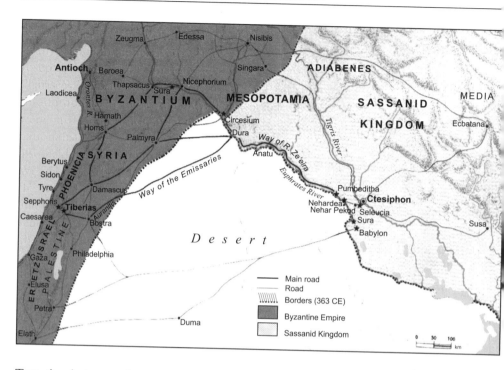

THE ties between the Babylonian Diaspora and the land of the Patriarchs, which had already existed in the days of the Return to Zion, were never broken as long as there remained a strong Jewish presence in the Land. The route generally used was that which ran along the Euphrates River; it was chosen by R. Ze'eira who, despite the ban imposed on him by his teacher, Rav Judah, decided to go and study Torah with R. Johanan himself. Starting out from Dura the travelers went to Circesium, passed Sura (in Syria, not to be confused with Sura in Babylonia), and at Thapsacus (Tiphsah) they turned south to Homs, finally reaching Damascus. Another possible route was the direct one from Dura to Palmyra (Tadmor; or from Circesium to Palmyra), and from there straight to Damascus via Auranitis (the Hauran). The Adiabenes and Medes moved westward on the route taken by the patriarch Abraham—along the Tigris River and then in the land of Haran (Nisibis–Edessa), up to the bridge over the Euphrates at Zeugma, and from there via Beroea (Aleppo) and Antioch.

A particularly short route was "The Way of the Emissaries," which took only seven days (unlike the two weeks required by a more conventional route). Emissaries on behalf of the Sanhedrin traveled directly through the desert to bring the Babylonian Jews news of the intercalation of the calendar and the consecration of the New Moon as determined by the sages of Eretz Israel. Other routes passed through the very heart of the desert—from Petra to Babylon or from Elath via Duma—but these were used chiefly by caravans of Nabateans and their successors, the Saracens.

L. The Talmudic Sages

THE THIRD- AND FOURTH-GENERATION *TANNAIM*
115 TO 175 CE

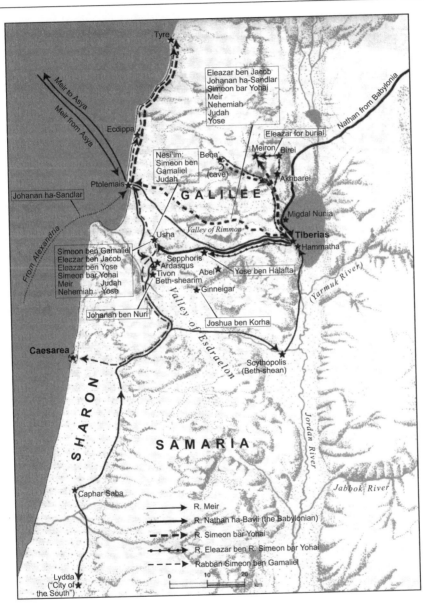

THE mission of these generations of sages was to rehabilitate the nation following the religious persecutions of Hadrian, to establish a renewed national leadership, and to put together the Oral Law, a process which would culminate in the Mishnah, the monumental work of the next generation. Among the nation's outstanding leaders were the *aharonim* (latter elders), disciples of R. Akiva: R. Meir, who returned from Asya when the religious persecutions ended, and R.

Simeon bar Yohai, who hid in a cave near Beqaʻ (Peki'in) with his son, R. Eleazar, and, as legend has it, lived there for thirteen years.

These sages first assembled in the Valley of Rimmon, together with several who had come up from Alexandria (e.g., R. Johanan ha-Sandlar). There was much camaraderie among the assembly: "If anyone did not have a prayer shawl, his friend would cut off half of his and give it to him." When they became aware of the change in the Roman authorities' relationship toward them, the sages gathered once again in Usha, where they reestablished the Sanhedrin. In time, Rabban Simeon ben Gamaliel was appointed *nasi*, R. Meir, *hakham* ("sage") and R. Nathan—who had emigrated from Babylonia—*av bet din* (head of the Sanhedrin). The call went out from Usha to the elders of Galilee: "Let everyone who is learned come and teach, and everyone who is not come and learn." Rabban Simeon slowly took control of the Sanhedrin. As a result, his opponents, led by R. Meir, left for Ardasqus and Tivon, near Usha. Many traditions are connected with R. Meir's later residency in Tiberias. R. Meir was also active in Beth-shean (Scythopolis) and also went south, to Lydda. In the end he was sent to intercalate the Hebrew calendar in Asya, where he died. R. Simeon bar Yohai was also separated from the court of the *nasi*. He purified Tiberias, stayed for some time in Tyre and Sidon, and died and was buried in Meiron. His son R. Eleazar died in Akhbarei, and with the help of the people of Birei was buried next to his father.

Rabban Simeon b. Gamaliel, together with Rabbi Yose and R. Judah, traveled to Ptolemais (Acco), Ecdippa (Achzib), and Caesarea, probably to make contact with the Roman procurator. Some traditions record his public activities in Sidon. Upon Simeon's death his eldest son, R. Judah, served as *nasi*, and during his time the presidency reached its zenith. It has been suggested that "the holy congregation of Jerusalem" mentioned in contemporary sources had lived in Jerusalem in the days of the Severan emperors, when the ban on Jewish settlement in the city was only lightly enforced.

THE FIRST GENERATION OF *AMORAIM* 225 TO 260 CE

ON his deathbed Rabbi Judah ha-Nasi gave these instructions: "My son Simeon [is to be] *hakham* (sage), my son Gamaliel *nasi* (patriarch), Hanina bar Hama shall preside" (*Ketubbot* 103b). The group was largely deprived of its leadership after the Rabbi's death. The deciding power in the nation's affairs passed to the heads of the Sanhedrin and a distinction began to be made between the patriarchy and the Sanhedrin.

After the passing of Rabbi Judah ha-Nasi, R. Aphes ha-Dromi became *av bet din* (head of the Sanhedrin) in Sepphoris, followed by R. Hanina bar Hama, a disciple of Judah ha-Nasi. The *batei hamidrash* (lit., "houses of study") were somewhat dispersed: R. Hoshaya founded an academy at Caesarea, and R. Joshua b. Levi became one of the leading sages at Lydda. In the period of the *amoraim* news surfaced about the sages of Naveh in Transjordan: the "*rabbanan di-Naveh*." Still, the sages from the various places were accustomed to assembling in Sepphoris and in Hammatha (Hammath Gader) during the bathing season there, as well as during public missions, such as those of R. Joshua b. Levi and R. Hanina bar Hama to the Roman governor at Caesarea. When R. Joshua returned from a mission to Rome, R. Hanina went to Ptolemais to welcome him.

During this period, Caracalla ("Antoninus Caesar"), son of Septimius Severus, was murdered, causing a political crisis in the Roman Empire. In the beginning the reigning emperors were of Syrian origin, such as Heliogabalus (218–222) and Alexander Severus (222–235), who were benevolent toward the Jews. They were followed by a period of chaos, power changes, and incessant wars between the various claimants to the throne. Each of these pretenders recruited an army, levied taxes, and commandeered supplies for his soldiers, thereby impoverishing the citizenry. The first indication of distress was the permission to work the land during the Sabbatical year granted by R. Yannai, who resided with his *beth midrash* in Akhbarei. More than others, he and his pupils, who engaged in agricultural work, felt the heavy burden of the property tax. The political crisis brought with it a sapping of Roman power and the easing of old bans, such as that on Jews entering Jerusalem. Thus R. Hanina bar Hama and R. Joshua b. Levi went up to the Holy City. At this time, too, with the weakening of the regime, a feeling of greater security spread among the Jews, who began to lay the groundwork for a change in the ambivalent relationship with Rome.

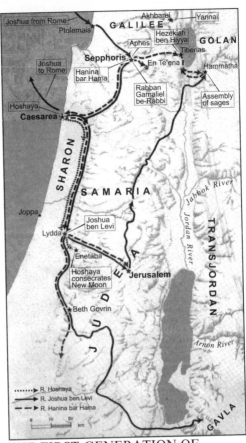

THE FIRST GENERATION OF *AMORAIM* 225–260

This generation also began the compilation and editing of Oral Law literature not included in the Mishnah. The Tosefta—the complement and extension to the Mishnah—was arranged, as were halakhic *midrashim* (homiletic interpretations). First steps were also made in the adaptation to the Mishnah of interpretations and customs—the core of the Palestinian ("Jerusalem") Talmud.

THE SECOND GENERATION OF *AMORAIM* 260 TO 290

STANDING at the head of this generation were the sages R. Johanan, its central figure, and his disciple R. Simeon b. Lakish (known by his Hebrew acronym, "Resh Lakish"). Both resided in Tiberias. R. Johanan would visit his teacher, R. Hoshaya, in Caesarea, and travel to Gennesar and Mamliah, and perhaps also to Naveh. Resh Lakish was active in both Hukkok and Gennesar, he often stayed in Bostra and even went outside the Holy Land. When R. Johanan reached his golden years, R. Eleazar b. Pedat became *av bet din* at Tiberias. Both passed away the same year (279). R. Yose bar Hanina, who had ties with the sages of the south, resided in Caesarea. R. Simeon b. Pazzi, R. Simlai, and R. Samuel b. Nahman were active in Lydda.

The ongoing halakhic deliberations at this time served as the basis for the Jerusalem Talmud. Ties with Babylonia were strengthened, and many disciples came to Tiberias while a few, like R.

Detail of mosaic floor of synagogue found in Tiberias.

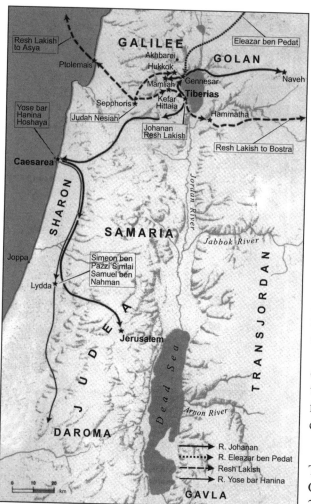

Eleazar b. Pedat, even settled in the land. Furthermore, numerous emissaries were sent to Babylonia to pass on the teachings of the Palestinian sages. In the days of R. Johanan, the crisis in the Roman Empire reached its peak. The emperor Valerian fell prisoner to the Persians (260), and the Palmyrene rulers, Zenobia and Vaballathus her son, seized the eastern half of the empire. Although there were contacts with the court of Palmyra (visited by R. Ammi, one of the younger scholars of this generation), the sages remained wary of the regime. In 271 the emperor Aurelian captured Palmyra and restored Roman rule to the entire east, including Palestine.

In the same period, the economic fallout from the political crisis was severe: taxes multiplied; money lost in value; famine and plagues were prevalent. The economic distress weakened the status of

THE SECOND GENERATION
OF *AMORAIM*
260–290 CE

he *nasi* (Rabbi Judah Nesiah), and caused much friction between the sages and the *nasi*. Resh Lakish would speak harshly in front of the *nasi*, and once was forced to flee Tiberias and hide in Kefar Hittaia. In the end the rights of the *nasi* were restricted and many of his functions, both theoretical and practical, were assumed by the sages. The economic crisis largely undermined the status of Palestinian Jewry in relation to Babylonian Jewry and revived messianic hopes among the people. It also appears that in this generation the percentage of Jews in the Galilee and in all of Palestine fell dramatically. On the other hand, access to Jerusalem was almost unrestricted, so that R. Johanan could say: "Let all those who want to go up [to Jerusalem] go up!" (*Baba Batra* 65b).

THE THIRD GENERATION OF *AMORAIM* 280 TO 320 CE

THE third generation of *amoraim* saw a major turning point in the history of the ancient world: Emperor Diocletian and his heirs solved the political and economic crisis, and from the days of Constantine onward, the Christian "heresy" became the state religion. This radical change disturbed many of the generation, and some, such as the Comes Joseph, abandoned the religion of their forefathers.

The Jewish nation was headed by the *nasi* who, despite his diminished status, was still respected along with the Sanhedrin, headed by R. Ammi and R. Assi, in Tiberias. Meanwhile, though, the academy at Caesarea had become more prestigious and with it the status of R. Abbahu, its head. This sage also had close contacts with the authorities and he often visited Tiberias. R. Judah bar Simon was active in this generation in Lydda. Notably, all the generation's leaders, apart from R. Abbahu, were of Babylonian origin.

The rise of Christianity caused the renewal of disputes with the "heretics" (Judeo-Christians). R. Abbahu was among the defenders of the faith. However, despite internal and external hardships, the creation and compilation of material for the Jerusalem Talmud continued unabated.

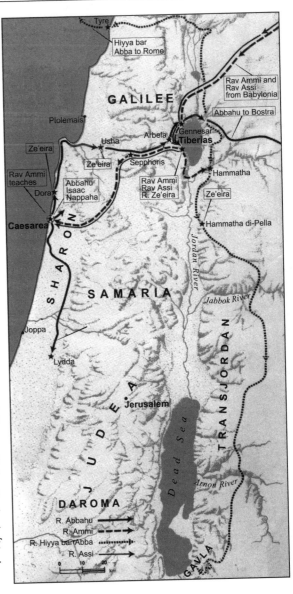

THE FOURTH- AND FIFTH-GENERATION *AMORAIM*
320 TO 400 CE

DURING the fourth generation (320–360) Eretz Israel passed into the hands of a Christian emperor (324), and the authorities put increasing pressure on the Jews—political, religious, and economic. The heads of the Tiberias academy at this time were R. Jeremiah, of Babylonian origin, and after him R. Jonah and R. Yose. R. Jeremiah also saw to it that the burdensome taxes imposed on the city's inhabitants were evenly distributed. He often visited on public business cities such as Ptolemais, Gaulan, Sogane and Lavi, and went to the Dead Sea area (Zoar?). R. Jonah resided for a while in Tyre. R. Yose lived to a ripe old age, and visited Dora and Eshtemoa. R. Haggai, also of Babylonian origin, joined the rabbis in Tiberias. R. Aha was active and taught at Lydda; both R. Jonah and R. Yose came to pay homage, and he in turn would go to Tiberias. R. Aha also served as a teacher in Emmaus and an inspector in Arabiya. In Caesarea, outstanding among his generation was R. Isaac b. Eleazar, who also dealt with the halakhic laws of sea travel.

After the death of Emperor Julian (the Apostate) there came a long and difficult period of legislative restrictions on the Jews, which reached its zenith during the reign of Theodosius II (408–450). At that time the Jews were prohibited from holding public office and forbidden to build new synagogues. Finally, after the death of Rabban Gamaliel VI (c. 425), who left no heirs, the authorities took advantage of the situation and abolished the presidency of the Sanhedrin. The luminaries of the fifth generation of *amoraim* (360–400), among them R. Yose b. Avin and R. Mana, attended to the final editing of the Palestinian Talmud, and brought it to completion. Out of this time of distress there grew great aggadists and homilists, such as R. Phinehas bar Hama, Rabbi Tanhuma bar Abba of Naveh and R. Berechiah, who gave expression to the people's suffering and hopes.

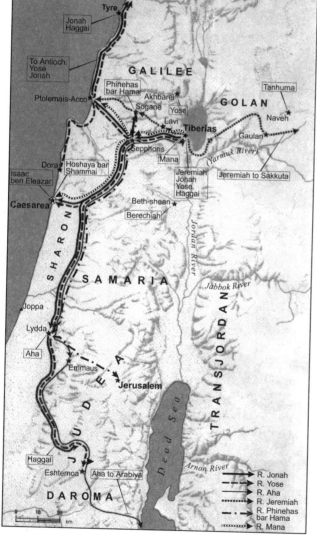

JULIAN'S ATTEMPT TO REBUILD THE TEMPLE
362 TO 363 CE

THE emperor Julian (361–363), successor to Constantius II and brother of Gallus, was from his youth an enthusiastic supporter of the Hellenistic faith and a sworn enemy of Christianity. A friend of the Jews, Julian promised to rebuild the Temple and appointed a special official from among his friends to accomplish this goal. Julian's announcement aroused much excitement throughout Israel and the Diaspora. Large sums of money were raised and building materials amassed. The Jews built a temporary synagogue in Jerusalem, in one of the stoas on the Temple Mount. The Christians in Jerusalem and elsewhere were totally against the rebuilding of the Temple.

The work began in the spring of 363, when Julian crossed the Euphrates in his war against the Persians. An earthquake struck on 27 May 363, during the Temple's construction, and the building materials that were concentrated in the underground vaults of the Temple Mount caught fire. The vaults (known today as "Solomon's Stables") were located at the corner of the southern and eastern porticoes. Gases that had formed within this confined place caused an explosion, killing several laborers.

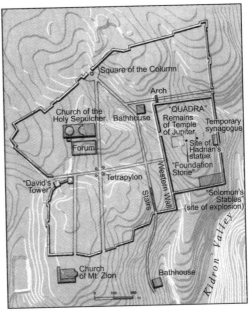

Those responsible for the work stopped construction after this event, because for some time nothing was known of the fate of the emperor and his army. Julian was in fact killed on 16 June 363. His successor, Jovian, was a Christian and reinstated Constantine's policies, thereby aborting any attempt to rebuild the Temple. It is extremely doubtful if this project had the approval of the *nasi* and the Sanhedrin in the first place.

THE FIRST GENERATION OF BABYLONIAN *AMORAIM*
200 TO 254 CE

BABYLONIA was not affected by the troubles that beset the Roman Empire. In the first half of the third century, Ardashir (226–241), of the Sassanid Dynasty, toppled the failing Parthians and regenerated the kingdom. However, the first Sassanid king, influenced by the Zoroastrian priesthood (the "Magis"), began to restrict the rights of the Jews. Toward the end of his reign, however, and particularly in the days of his successor Shapur I, obstacles ceased to be placed in their way. The Jews set up their own law courts and developed the

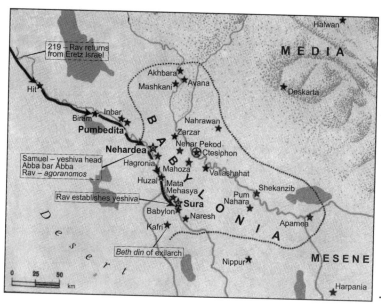

THE FIRST GENERATION OF BABYLONIAN *AMORAIM* 200–254 CE

219 – Rav returns from Eretz Israel

Halwan

MEDIA

Akhbara
Avana
Mashkani
Deskarta
Hit
Inbar
Biram
BABYLONIA
Nahrawan
Pumbedita
Zarzar
Nehar Pekod
Nehardea
Ctesiphon
Samuel – yeshiva head
Abba bar Abba
Rav – *agoranomos*
Hagronia
Mahoza
Vallashphat
Huzal
Mata
Mehasya
Shekanzib
Pum
Nahara
Rav establishes yeshiva
Sura
Babylon
Naresh
Apamea
Kafri
Beth din of exilarch
Nippur
MESENE
Desert

0   25   50
km

Harpania

☆ Teaching center
••••• Babylonian boundary, according to *Kiddushin* 71b

great yeshivas into centers for the teaching and development of talmudic law, as well as for public leadership. The exilarch in this generation, Mar Ukba (210–240), was one of the Torah sages. The head of the Nehardea community, a Jewish center for hundreds of years, was Abba bar Abba, a wealthy silk merchant who had business relations with R. Judah b. Bathyra of Nisibis. His son Samuel (d. 225) headed the yeshiva in Nehardea. He had a good relationship with the royal court, especially with King Shapur I, and supported the Persian campaigns in Asia Minor. Samuel also authored the principle that in civil matters "the law of the state is the law," that is, that Persian law must, according to *halakhah*, be obeyed by the Jews as well. This principle greatly influenced the development of *halakhah* for generations. Nehardea was also the seat of Karna, "*dayyan* (judge) of the *golah* (Diaspora).

However, the decisive impetus toward the development of a Jewish spiritual center in Babylonia came from Rav (Abba Arikha), who had returned to Babylonia from Eretz Israel at the end

of the days of Rabbi Judah ha-Nasi. Rav was first appointed *agoranomos* (inspector of market transactions) on behalf of the exilarch. When the position of *resh sidra* was available in Nehardea and offered to Rav, he respectfully declined the office in favor of Samuel and moved to Huzal (where R. Assi was *resh sidra*). Rav finally settled in Sura—large in population but weak in Torah—founding there a famous academy, which exercised the authority of teaching and appointing the *dayyanim* (pl. of *dayyan*) over the surrounding cities. Rav died in 247.

The Babylonian Jews were proud of their genealogy, and in the opinion of Rav, as told by R. Papa Saba, only Babylonia was in that sense "healthy" within its borders (*Kiddushin* 71b): Akhbara, Avana and Mashkani in the north, near the Tigris River, Nahrawan in the east, and Apamea in the area of the southern Tigris. Furthermore, only the areas adjacent to Babylonia—Nehardea in Media, Halwan, and the Upper Euphrates region "between the rivers"—were considered as "privileged" as Babylonia.

THE SECOND GENERATION OF BABYLONIAN
AMORAIM 254 TO 299 CE

IN 259 Papa ben Nazer, leading the Palmyrene troops (who then owed allegiance to Zenobia and controlled the eastern Roman Empire), destroyed Nehardea, and its sages and disciples were dispersed. In those days R. Hamnuna, and after him R. Huna, continued to preside over the Sura academy, which remained unaffected by the invasion. R. Huna, a luminary of this generation, was born in Drukeret to a distinguished but poor family. Eventually, he acquired wealth from agricultural production. During his time the Sura academy flourished and the number of its permanent students reached eight hundred.

In Sura the traditions of teaching that had drawn Rav from Eretz Israel continued. R. Huna headed the academy for about forty years. He died in 297 and his body was brought to Eretz Israel for burial. After his death R. Hisda (a native of Kafri) became head of the Sura academy until 309. R. Judah bar Ezekiel continued the traditions of Samuel and founded the Pumbedita academy, which was considered to be the continuation of Nehardea. Pumbedita was the "Babylonian" academy par excellence, and its sages, known for their intellectual acumen, shaped the ways of thought of the Babylonian Talmud.

The exilarch had his *beth din* (law court) in the city of Mahoza outside the two main centers. R. Nahman bar Jacob (d. 320) also resided there and had many pupils. R. Sheshet studied under R. Huna in Sura and later taught in Shilhei, on the river Euphrates. R. Mattnah and R. Aha bar Jacob served in Papunia, R. Hiyya bar Joseph in Sikhra (he later immigrated to Eretz Israel), and Rabbah bar Avuha

Shapur I, king of Persia.

in Shekanzib, Shilhei and Mahoza.

Shapur I (241–272), a friend to the sages, still ruled at the start of this generation. In the days of the six kings who succeeded him (273–310), the influence of the Magis greatly increased, and the situation of the Babylonian Jews gradually worsened, although without greatly affecting their spiritual and economic activities.

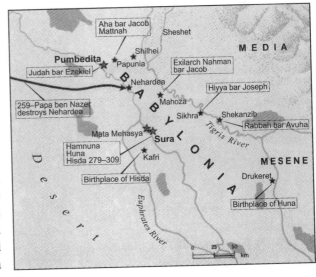

THE THIRD GENERATION OF BABYLONIAN *AMORAIM*
299 TO 330 CE

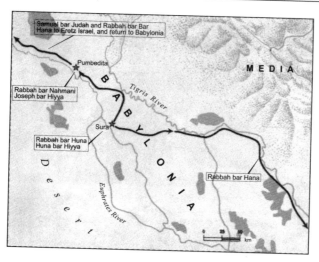

IN the beginning of King Shapur II's reign (309–379) the situation of the Jews worsened, although the queen mother tended to show compassion. The Jews were declared unsuited to hold positions in the service of the state and were frequently sold into slavery for not paying their taxes on time. It reached such a point that the sages received permission to appear as non-Jews in order to survive. Rabbah bar Bar Hana even said that the Jews were better off in the Roman kingdom than under the Persian yoke, but the majority of sages thought otherwise. Many Jews were forced to abandon their lands because of the heavy taxes they had to pay: the *tasqa* and the *karga* (land tax and poll tax, respectively). As a result, in 338, the Persian authorities allotted the Jewish lands around Pumbedita to Arab settlers. Even the spiritual activities of the Jews offended the Persian regime. They complained that because of the periodic general assembly of students (who gathered for Torah study), twelve thousand people failed to pay taxes for two months, and Rabbah bar Nahmani was

hounded for this until he died in his wanderings. Only after his death (320), perhaps because of the lurking dangers to the kingdom on the part of the Romans, did relations between the Persians and the Jews improve.

Despite the pressures, the centers of Torah study in Babylonia in this generation were many. Rabbah bar R. Huna headed the academy in Sura (until his death in 320), but never succeeded in filling his father's place. Characteristic of the attitude of the Jews to the Persian kingdom in the days of Shapur II was the fact that R. Huna bar Hiyya, a natural candidate to inherit R. Judah's position in Pumbedita, was disqualified when it became known that he had served as a government tax collector. He continued to teach in Sura but not as head of the yeshiva.

The outstanding sages of this generation were Rabbah bar Nahmani and R. Joseph bar Hiyya in Pumbedita. Rabbah was head of the academy for twenty-two years (until 320), followed by Rav Joseph, until 323.

In this generation the many ties between Babylonia and Eretz Israel remained intact. Thus R. Samuel bar Judah, who converted together with his father, went up to Eretz Israel and returned, bringing Torah teachings of the Palestinian sages to Babylonia. Rabbah bar Bar Hana often went up to Eretz Israel, and traveled from place to place, as he did in Babylonia. He was renowned for his numerous journeys in different lands and for the tall tales of his sea voyages and travels in the desert.

THE FOURTH GENERATION OF BABYLONIAN
AMORAIM 330 TO 352 CE

THE halakhic activity was now concentrated in Pumbedita. After the death of R. Joseph there were several candidates to head the academy, among them Abbaye and Rava and R. Ze'eira. Abbaye was chosen and he presided over the academy for fourteen years (323–338), the same length of time as his successor, Rava (338–352). Under him, the academy moved to Mahoza, the home of Rava, during whose days R. Nahman bar Isaac headed the general assembly of students. Then, for four years (352–356) he headed the academy, which now returned to Pumbedita, and only one faction moved to Naresh. The sayings of Abbaye and Rava were a high point in the approach to the study of *halakhah* and talmudic law, and became known as "the disputes of Abbaye and Rava." Abbaye, an orphan who was raised by his uncle, Rabbah bar Nahmani, earned his livelihood from a parcel of land that he farmed himself. He subscribed the study and interpretation of *halakhah* to logical reasoning. Rava bar Joseph (also renowned as an aggadist) would add the practical dimension of day-to-day reality, and in the controversies between him and Abbaye, *halakhah* was usually determined according to the latter. Active outside Pumbe-

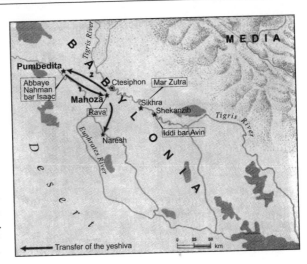

Transfer of the yeshiva

dita were R. Iddi bar Avin, who resided in Shekanzib, and Mar Zutra, son of R. Nahman bar Jacob, who taught in Sikhra.

Toward the end of the fourth generation, the loyalty of Babylonian Jewry was put to the test when the emperor Julian, a known friend of the Jews, invaded Babylonia (363) and stormed the city of Birtha. The Jews of the city left without resistance. Julian's campaign brought about the destruction of Mahoza and Ctesiphon. However, things returned to normal after the death of the emperor and the retreat of the Roman army. Shapur II, who was highly suspicious of the Jews early in his reign, improved later on, as did the economic situation of the Babylonian Diaspora as a whole.

THE FIFTH AND SIXTH GENERATIONS OF
BABYLONIAN *AMORAIM* 352 TO 376 CE

IN the days of Kings Yezdegerd I (399–420) and Bahram V (420–438), the situation of the Jews remained stable. Yezdegerd even showed great respect toward the exilarch, R. Huna bar Nathan, despite the wrath of the Magis. However, under Yezdegerd II (438–457) and Firuz II (457–484), the Jews were

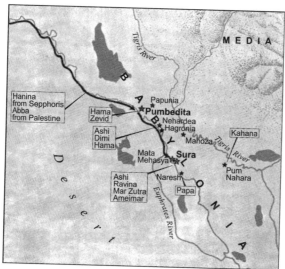

Another center was established in Pum Nahara, in which R. Kahana served, and studies were renewed in Nehardea under R. Zevid, R. Dimi, R. Hama, and others. Smaller assemblies also arose in Hagronia and in Papunia.

After the death of R. Papa, the Sura academy was revitalized and headed by R. Ashi (372–424), although it was now located at Mata Mehasya, adjacent to Sura. The exilarch also moved there, and the heads of the Pumbedita academy would often come to the Sura academy, to which they were subordinate. Here, too, the periodic general assembly of students would be arranged. R. Ashi compiled and edited the Babylonian Talmud but did not live to see its completion. He was assisted by Ravina, R. Abba and R. Hanina of Sepphoris, who transmitted many of the Torah teachings and customs of Palestinian Jewry. The sages Mar Zutra I and Ameimar taught in the *beth midrash* of R. Ashi. The efforts of all these sages brought to a conclusion the tremendous undertaking of completing the Babylonian Talmud, in which the essence of the Oral Law was crystallized and on whose basis the Jewish way of life was determined for the next fifty generations.

persecuted, especially during the struggle against the movement for religious equality led by Mazdak. It reached the point where, in the days of King Kavadh (488–531), the exilarch Mar Zutra II headed an annual rebellion for seven years until he was taken prisoner and beheaded, and his body was suspended from a cross on the bridge at Mahoza (520). His youngest son, Mar Zutra III, escaped to Tiberias, where he was appointed to an academic position in a college (*rosh perek*). This socio-political ferment accelerated the completion of the Babylonian Talmud.

Upon the death of Rava (352), some of his students moved from Mahoza to Naresh, where R. Papa headed the yeshiva until 371, and R. Huna Bereiah de-Rav Joshua served as head of the general assembly of students. The Pumbedita academy was headed by R. Hama (until 377) and after him, R. Zevid (385).

THE POLITICAL DIVISION OF PALESTINE IN THE BYZANTINE PERIOD

THE political rules laid down by Diocletian were the guiding light for all Byzantine rulers who succeeded him, from 324 until the conquests of the Persians (614) and the Arabs (640). The separation of military and state was strictly observed. The division of the old provinces into smaller units finally reached even *Palaestina*, one of the less important areas of the Byzantine Empire. In about 358 the entire southern part of the province (enlarged under Diocletian), along with the *limes* (but not the western estates, namely, Sycomazon, the Constantinian estate and the estate of Gerar)—i.e., the Negeb and the southern Transjordan—became a special province called *Palaestina Salutaris* ("Palestine of Salvation"), with its capital at Petra.

In about 425 the process of decentralization was completed by dividing the rest of the country into two parts: *Palaestina* A (*Prima*), with its capital at Caesarea, formerly the capital of the whole province; and *Palaestina* B (*Secunda*), whose capital was the large "city of weavers," Beth-shean (Scythopolis). *Palaestina* A included the coastal cities and estates therein, the Judean Hills and the Hills of Ephraim, the Jordan Valley, and "Jewish Transjordan" (formerly Perea). *Palaestina* B included the Esdraelon Valley, Lower and Upper Galilee, the cities of Pella, Gadara, Hippus (Sussita), Capitolias and Abila, and also the Golan. This province thus included most of the remaining Jewish settlement in Eretz Israel. With the establishment of *Palaestina* A and B, the authorities changed the name *Palaestina Salutaris* to *Palaestina* C (*Tertia*). These names remained in place until the end of the Byzantine period.

The three provinces were headed by governors of varying ranks (the most senior being the governor of Caesarea). The provinces themselves were divided into urban areas and estates or districts with no urban structure. In the Byzantine period, however, there was already no great significance to an independent urban regime, the cities being administrative units. The decentralization process affected the urban areas as well. The Gaza region was divided in three—Gaza, Constantia (Maiumas Gaza) and Anthedon—as was the Ascalon area: Ascalon, Maiumas Ascalon and Diocletianopolis. Azotus (Ashdod) now became two cities: inland Azotus lost its importance, and Azotus-on-Sea (Azotus Paralios) became

THE POLITICAL DIVISION OF PALESTINE IN THE BYZANTINE PERIOD

a large city, as did Jamnia (Jabneh). A separate unit, Tricomias, may have been formed in the area of Eleutheropolis. Long before this time, Ono had been separated from Lydda Diospolis. The Naim district was separated from Sepphoris after the latter was separated from the Hellenopolis district. These changes completed the urbanization process in the Byzantine period.

THE JEWISH DIASPORA IN THE FIFTH CENTURY

THEODOSIUS I (383–395) was the last Roman emperor to rule over the whole empire. Upon his death the empire was divided between his sons, Arcadeus (Emperor of the East) and Honorius (Emperor of the West). This division remained permanent ever after. The Romans stood their ground in the east, but within three generations the western empire collapsed under the pressure of various invading German tribes. The Ostrogoths ruled in Italy, the Franks and the Burgundians in northern France, the Visigoths in southern France and Spain, and the Vandals in Africa. Thus the Jewish Diaspora in the west came under many rulers, being treated moderately well by some and persecuted by others.

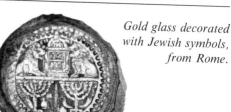

Gold glass decorated with Jewish symbols, from Rome.

By the end of the ancient period the Jewish communities had spread in all directions—northward (to the river Rhine), westward (to France) and southward. The communities multiplied particularly in the south of Spain, despite their harsh treatment by the Visigoth kings, who abandoned Arian beliefs in 589. Communities also multiplied in Italy in the fourth and fifth centuries, some even finding protection in the shadow of the papacy, whose influence was great in the central and southern parts of the country.

In the Byzantine Empire, with the death of Julian and particularly in the time of Theodosius II (408–450), there was a strong anti-Jewish orientation. Christian monks roused the masses to attack synagogues. Although the autho-

rities disapproved of such violent acts, they forbade the establishment of new synagogues. However, they did not as yet interfere with Jewish customs or make it too difficult for the Jews to earn their livelihood. Nevertheless, the situation of the Jews in the Byzantine Empire was rather miserable. The pressure increased even more in the days of Emperor Justinian (525–565) and his successors. It is therefore easy to understand why the Jews turned their backs on the repressive regime and sought allies outside the empire.

The Babylonian Diaspora presented an entirely different picture; in those days it reached its height both materially and spiritually. The kings of the Sassanid Dynasty treated the Jews benevolently. The exilarch, descended from King David, stood at the head of Babylonian Jewry. He oversaw the wide network of administrative and legal institutions spread throughout Babylonia, in the numerous cities inhabited by the Jews. The majority of Babylonian Jews engaged in agriculture and a few in commerce and industry. The generations of Babylonian *amoraim* attest to the spiritual eminence of Babylonian Jewry.

II
THE MIDDLE AGES

Equestrian statue of Charlemagne.

A. FROM THE BARBARIAN INVASIONS OF EUROPE UNTIL THE CRUSADES

THE BARBARIAN INVASIONS OF EUROPE 5TH CENTURY

THE invasions of various tribes, collectively called the barbarians, into the boundaries of the Roman Empire caused great changes in western Europe and only the Eastern Roman Empire—Byzantium—was able to withstand these invasions.

Decoration of a Jewish tombstone found in the catacombs of Rome.

As for the Jews, it was not the barbarian invasions that endangered their survival but rather Byzantium and Christianity. From the time of Constantine the Great (ruled 306–337), who granted imperial favor to Christianity, Christianity sought to populate Palestine with its co-religionists by encouraging both pilgrimages to its holy places and settlement in the country. Bands of Christian monks, "the Christian army," were the standard-bearers of the church militant. Palestine and other Christian centers became arenas for disputations with Jews, and Christianity sought to interpret these disputations as its triumph over Judaism.

Christian tradition tells of whole Jewish communities that converted: for example, the entire Jewish community of Minorca was converted by Bishop Severus in 418. It was during this period that Christianity began laying the first foundation for a comprehensive ideology concerning its ascendancy over Judaism. The Jewish people were punished for crucifying Jesus, and the instruments of this punishment were Vespasian and Titus, who, according to this ideology, supported Christianity. An extensive fabric of legends and folktales was woven around

the allegation that the Jews crucified Jesus, and the Jewish people were branded as "killers of God." The church declared itself the heir of Judaism, *Verus Israel* ("the true Israel"), and sought proof for this in the Bible. The existence of the Jewish people was necessary to enable the conversion of the pagans to Christianity. Augustine (354–430), bishop of Hippo (North Africa), found a justification for the humiliation of the Jewish people in this interpretation of Psalm 59:11—"Slay them not, lest my people forget; scatter them by thy power and bring them down....": "Slay them the Jews not lest my people (the Christians) forget" the prophecies in the Bible foretelling the realization of Christianity. "And bring them [the Jews] down." These were the tenets that guided Christianity in its war against Judaism over the many generations and upon these foundations it built anti-Jewish public opinion, whose effects were apparent during the entire Middle Ages.

Christian propagandists saturated the centers of the ancient world. The most prominent was John Chrysostom (c. 347–407), who determined the character of the

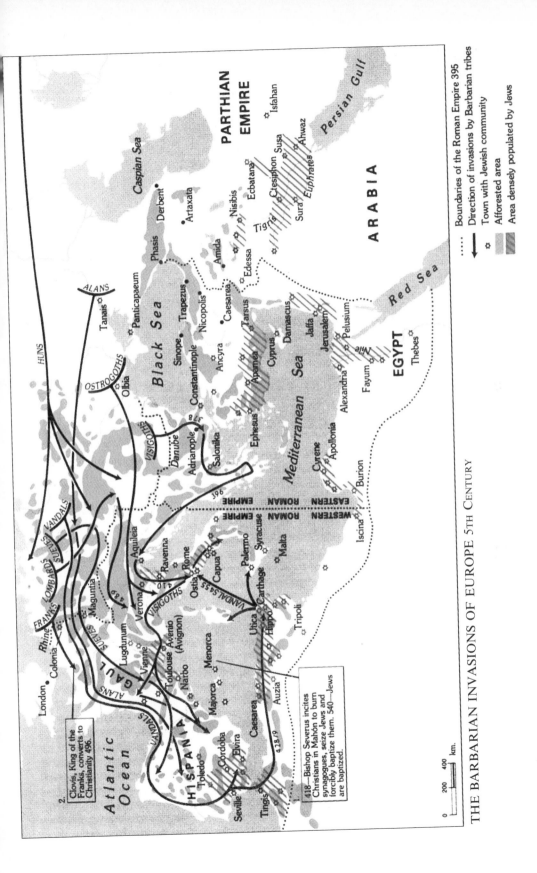

THE BARBARIAN INVASIONS OF EUROPE 5TH CENTURY

Boundaries of the Roman Empire 395
Direction of invasions by Barbarian tribes
Town with Jewish community
Afforested area
Area densely populated by Jews

2. Clovis, King of the Franks, converts to Christianity 496.

418—Bishop Severus incites Christians in Mahón to burn synagogues, seize Jews and forcibly baptize them. 540—Jews are baptized.

PARTHIAN EMPIRE

ARABIA

EGYPT

Caspian Sea

Black Sea

Mediterranean Sea

Red Sea

Persian Gulf

Atlantic Ocean

HISPANIA

GAUL

HUNS

ALANS

OSTROGOTHS

VISIGOTHS

VANDALS

SUEVES

LOMBARDS

FRANKS

Rhine

Danube

EASTERN ROMAN EMPIRE

WESTERN ROMAN EMPIRE

London
Colonia
Maguntia
Lugdunum
Vienne
Toulouse
Narbo
Avernio (Avignon)
Majorca
Menorca
Seville
Córdoba
Elvira
Toledo
Tingis
Caesarea
Auzia
Iscina
Tripoli
Carthage
Utica
Hippo
Malta
Syracuse
Palermo
Capua
Rome
Ostia
Verona
Ravenna
Aquileia
Salonika
Adrianople
Constantinople
Olbia
Tanais
Panticapaeum
Sinope
Trapezus
Nicopolis
Ancyra
Caesarea
Tarsus
Ephesus
Apamea
Cyprus
Damascus
Jaffa
Jerusalem
Pelusium
Alexandria
Fayum
Thebes
Cyrene
Apollonia
Burion
Phasis
Derbent
Artaxata
Nisibis
Amida
Edessa
Caesarea
Tigris
Euphrates
Nile
Ecbatana
Ctesiphon
Sura
Susa
Ahwaz
Isfahan

395
396
410
489
428/9

0 200 400 km.

125

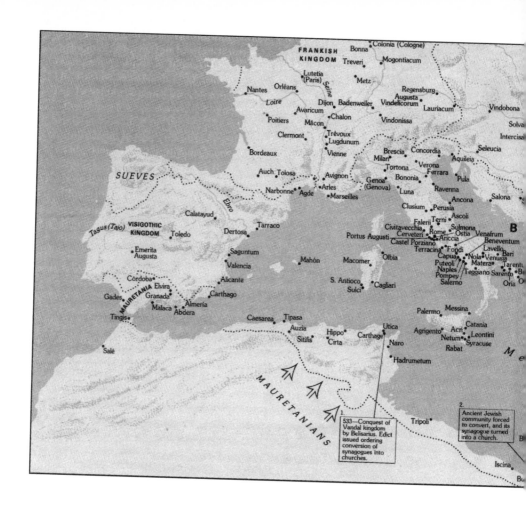

Map labels (reading across the map):

FRANKISH KINGDOM · Bonna · Colonia (Cologne) · Treveri · Mogontiacum · Lutetia (Paris) · Metz · Regensburg · Augusta Vindelicorum · Lauriacum · Vindobona · Nantes · Orléans · Dijon · Badenweiler · Vindonissa · Solva · Loire · Avaricum · Mâcon · Chalon · Intercisa · Poitiers · Trévoux · Lugdunum · Clermont · Vienne · Brescia · Concordia · Seleucia · Milan · Tortona · Verona · Aquileia · SUEVES · Auch · Tolosa · Avignon · Genoa (Genova) · Bononia · Ferrara · Pula · Narbonne · Agde · Arles · Luna · Ravenna · Salona · Marseilles · Ancona · Calatayud · Clusium · Perusia · Ascoli · Tagus (Tajo) · VISIGOTHIC KINGDOM · Toledo · Dertosa · Tarraco · Falerii · Terni · Civitavecchia · Rome · Sulmona · Venafrum · Portus Augusti · Cerveteri · Ostia · Beneventum · Castel Porziano · Ariccia · Emerita Augusta · Saguntum · Terracina · Fondi · Capua · Lavello · Bari · Valencia · Macomer · Olbia · Nola · Venusia · Córdoba · Alicante · Puteoli · Matera · Tarentum · Elvira · S. Antioco · Naples · Teggiano Sarento · Gades · MAURETANIA · Granada · Almería · Carthago · Suici · Cagliari · Pompey · Salerno · Oria · Malaca · Abdera · Tingis · Caesarea · Tipasa · Palermo · Messina · Salé · Auzia · Hippo · Utica · Agrigento · Acri · Catania · Sitifis · Cirta · Carthage · Netum · Leontini · Naro · Rabat · Syracuse · Hadrumetum · MAURETANIANS · Tripoli · Iscina

1. 533—Conquest of Vandal kingdom by Belisarius. Edict issued ordering conversion of synagogues into churches.

2. Ancient Jewish community forced to convert, and its synagogue turned into a church.

struggle against Judaism, a struggle that was necessary for Christianity to emerge victorious in the pagan world. Nonetheless, the church fathers required the assistance of Jewish scholars to interpret and understand the Bible text. One of them, Jerome (Eusebius Sophronius Hieronymus, 342–420, of Bethlehem) required the help of Jewish teachers in Palestine to learn Hebrew for his translation of the Bible into Latin (c. 404).

THE DISPERSION OF THE JEWS MID-6TH CENTURY

INFORMATION regarding the Jewish dispersion is sparse. One may learn about the way of life of the Jewish communities from the canons of the church synods that convened in Europe. For example, one of the rulings of the Council of Elvira in southern Spain at the beginning of the fourth century forbade Jews to bless Christian fields and Christians to eat in the company of Jews. These prohibitions were intended to prevent fraternization between Jews and Christians. From this, one may also infer that Jews engaged in agriculture.

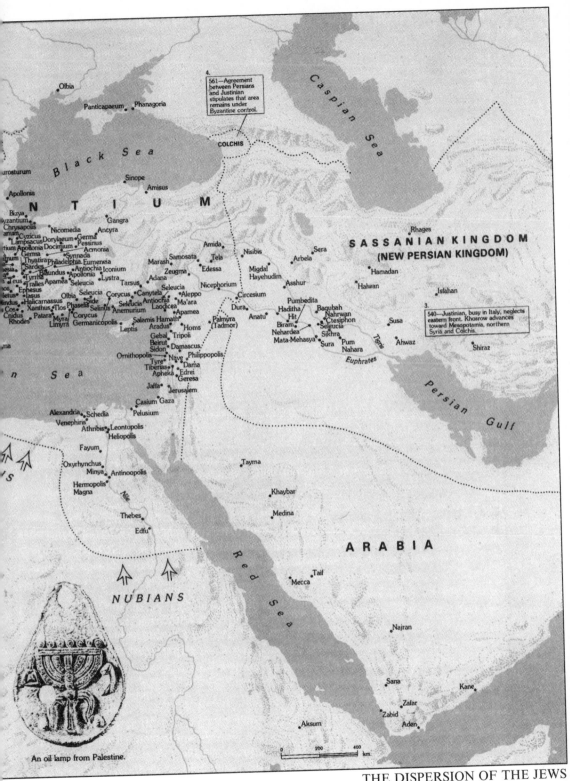

561—Agreement between Persians and Justinian stipulates that area remains under Byzantine control.

Caspian Sea

COLCHIS

Black Sea

Olbia

Panticapaeum   Phanagoria

—rosturum

Sinope

Apollonia   Amisus

Bizya

—yzantium   Nicomedia   Gangra   Ancyra

Chrysapolis

—anium   Cyzicus   Dorylaeum   Germa

—tium   Apollonia   Docimium   Pessinus

—num   Germa   Synnada   Acmonia

—esia   Thyatira   Philadelphia   Eumeneia

—a   Sardes   Antiochia   Iconium

Blaundus   Apollonia   Lystra

—yrrha   Apamea   Seleucia   Tarsus

Ephesus

—iletus   Tralles

—os   Cos   Halicarnassus   Olba   Seleucia   Antiochia

—indus   Cnidus   Xanthus   Tlos   Phaselis   Ide   Selinus

Patara   Myra   Corycus

Rhodes   Limyra   Germanicopolis

Leptis

RHAGES

SASSANIAN KINGDOM
(NEW PERSIAN KINGDOM)

Sera

Arbela

Amida

Nisibis

Tela

Marash   Samosata

Edessa

Zeugma

Adana   Nicephorium

Seleucia

Aleppo

Canytela   Antiochia   Ma'ara

Anemurium   Laodicea   Apamea

Salamis   Hamath

Aradus   Homs

Gebal   Tripoli

Beirut

Sidon   Damascus

Ornithopolis

Tyre   Navs   Philippopolis

Tiberias   Dama

Apheka   Edrei

Jaffa   Geresa

Jerusalem

Circesium

Dura

Anatu

Palmyra
(Tadmor)

Migdal
Hayehudim

Asshur

Hamadan

Halwan

Isfahan

Pumbedita

Haditha   Baqubah

Hit   Nahrwan

Biram   Ctesiphon

Nehardea   Seleucia

Mata-Mehasya   Sihhra

Sura   Pum
Nahara

Susa

Ahwaz

Tigris

3.

540—Justinian, busy in Italy, neglects eastern front. Khosrow advances toward Mesopotamia, northern Syria and Colchis.

Shiraz

Persian Gulf

Euphrates

—n   *Sea*

Casium   Gaza

Pelusium

Alexandria   Schedia

Venephins

Athribis   Leontopolis

Heliopolis

Fayum

Oxyrhynchus

Minya   Antinoopolis

Hermopolis
Magna

Nile

Thebes

Edfu

Tayma

Khaybar

Medina

Red Sea

ARABIA

NUBIANS

Taif

Mecca

Najran

Sana

Kane

Zafar

Zabid

Aden

Aksum

0   200   400
km.

An oil lamp from Palestine.

THE DISPERSION OF THE JEWS
MID-6TH CENTURY

127

In the fifth century church councils increasingly discussed matters involving the Jews. Although Rome was a center of Christianity, the leaders of the church were weak, thus enabling the church councils in various regions to issue canons concerning Jewish affairs.

Anti-Jewish bias was prevalent at the church councils held in France during the Merovingian period and their decisions express the intent to sever social relations between the Jewish and Christian populations. The decisions of these councils determined the relationship of the Merovingian rulers toward the Jews. However, Merovingian France admitted the Jewish refugees who fled from Visigothic persecutions.

Massacre and persecution were the fate of the Jewish communities in the lands conquered by the Byzantine armies. The emperor Justinian I promulgated a series of Novellae (new laws added to the Corpus Iuris Civilis) intended to harm the Jews and restrict the livelihood of the Jewish population in the Roman Empire. One of the Novellae forbade the public reading of the Torah in Hebrew, permitting the reading only in Greek. The Jews got around this law by composing a corpus of Hebrew liturgical poetry that was incorporated in the prayers and contained references to passages in the Pentateuch.

The victory of Belisarius, commander of Justinian's army, over the Vandals in North Africa (533) put an end to their rule in that territory and from then on the status of the Jews declined in the former Vandal kingdom. The Jews, Donatists and Arians were warned against proselytizing. The status of the Jews further declined with the capture of Burion, the fifth city of the Pentapolis, situated at the southwestern edge of Cyrenaica, and the Jews of this ancient community were forced to convert to Christianity and their synagogue was turned into a church. Many Jews fled to the free Berber tribes, who treated them kindly.

The map of Jewish dispersion shows a large Jewish world extending beyond the borders of the Roman Empire, including the Persian Sassanid kingdom. The rulers of this kingdom were generally tolerant toward the Jews, allowing them to establish their own organizations and institutions and thus providing a new political foundation for Jewish self-government through the office of the exilarch, the lay head of the Jewish community.

A distant independent Jewish community in southern Arabia maintained close contact with the Jewish community in the Holy Land and some of its members were priviliged to be buried in Beth She'arim.

SYNAGOGUES IN PALESTINE 2ND TO 6TH CENTURIES

BYZANTINE rule sought to deal a blow to the Jewish communities in Palestine and the Diaspora by abolishing the patriarchate. The death of Rabbam Gamaliel VI in 426 brought an end to the harassment of the patriarchate. (The harassment apparently continued until 429.) In spite of the authorities' attempt to badger the Jewish residents of Palestine by dividing the country into three provinces—Prima in the center, Secunda in the north and Tertia in the south—the Jewish community remained resolute.

A list of synagogues and their mosaics

A section of the floor mosaic of Bet Alfa synagogue showing signs of the Zodiac.

Phoenicia
Kefar Baram   Gush Halav   Dabbura   En Nashut
Mifshata   Sasa   Alma
Zalzula   Dalton   Dabiya
Meiron   Kefar
Nevoraya   Katzrin
Baka   Kh.Shema   Kh. Zemaymira
El-Rama   Chorazin   Khirbet ed Dikka
Sikhni   Kefar   Khirbet Kanaf
Evlayim   Nahum
Kh. Amudim   Arbel   Umm
el-Qanatir
Kafr Cana   Tiberias   Apheka
Bet She'arim   Zippori   Bet Yerah
Husayfa   Simoniya   Japhia
Kh Summaqa   Gader
Caesarea   Bet Alfa   Kokhav Ha-Yarden
Bet She'an   Ma'oz Hayim
Rehob
Tirat Zevi   Secunda
Pahma   Arabia
Palaestina   Gerasa
Palaestina
Prima

☙ Town with synagogue   Neapolis
(Sichem)   0   10   20
Dabiya Modern name   km.

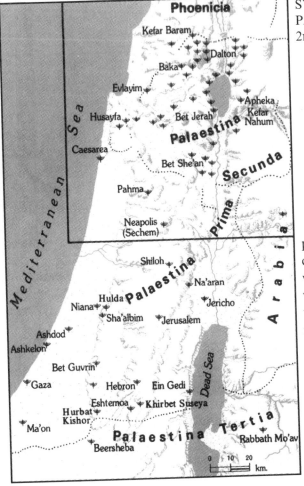

Phoenicia
Kefar Baram
Dalton
Baka
Evlayim
Apheka
Husayfa   Bet Jerah   Kefar
Nahum
Caesarea   Palaestina
Bet She'an   Secunda
Pahma
Neapolis   Prima
(Sechem)
Shiloh
Na'aran
Hulda   Palaestina   Jericho
Niana   Sha'albim   Jerusalem
Ashdod
Ashkelon
Bet Guvrin
Gaza   Hebron   Ein Gedi
Eshtemoa   Khirbet Suseya
Hurbat
Kishor   Tertia
Ma'on   Palaestina   Rabbath Mo'av
Beersheba   0   10   20
km.

SYNAGOGUES IN PALESTINE
2ND TO 6TH CENTURIES

present a picture of a Jewish community attempting to cope with the edicts of the time. Jews were forbidden to reside in Jerusalem, and Tiberias became the most important Jewish center of the period. The Samaritan community was badly decimated as a result of its first revolt against Byzantine rule in 484, when Emperor Zeno built a church on Mount Gerizim, and the revolt in 529 during the reign of Emperor Justinian I.

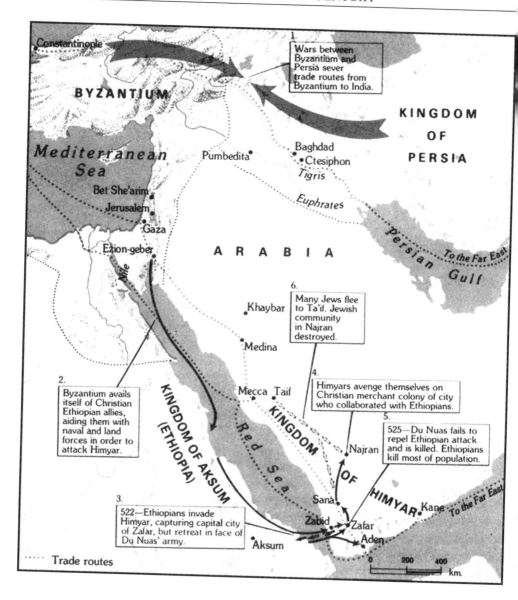

1. Wars between Byzantium and Persia sever trade routes from Byzantium to India.

6. Many Jews flee to Ta'if. Jewish community in Najran destroyed.

2. Byzantium avails itself of Christian Ethiopian allies, aiding them with naval and land forces in order to attack Himyar.

4. Himyars avenge themselves on Christian merchant colony of city who collaborated with Ethiopians.

5. 525—Du Nuas fails to repel Ethiopian attack and is killed. Ethiopians kill most of population.

3. 522—Ethiopians invade Himyar, capturing capital city of Zafar, but retreat in face of Du Nuas' army.

..... Trade routes

THE Jewish kingdom of Himyar in southern Arabia was a thorn in the flesh of Byzantium, particularly during the Byzantine-Persian wars, because it was located on a major trade route. Byzantium's geopolitical motives for moving against Himyar were founded on the strategic necessity of establishing a southern flanking route to the Persian Gulf. This objective required a base on the Red Sea and an alliance with Ethiopia, the only Christian state in the area. The commercial motive was to maintain an open sea route to India in order to

A Himyar inscription.

protect the supply of spices and other goods from India and Arabia to the merchants of Rome. However, the Jewish kingdom prevented the passage of Byzantine traders through its territory in retaliation for the persecution of Jews in Byzantium, and Du Nuas, the last king of Himyar, was particularly zealous in this matter. Persia was too weak an ally to render any significant support to the Jewish kingdom of Himyar because it did not share Himyar's political and strategic needs in its relations with Byzantium. Himyar was threatened by the Christian merchant community in Najran and by the Ethiopians. The latter, having formed an alliance with Byzantium, undertook to fight Byzantium's battle with Himyar to settle a score with that kingdom over Ethiopia's loss of control of the straits that led from the Red Sea to the Indian Ocean. Himyar was also weakened by internal strife. King Du Nuas was defeated and died in a battle on the seashore in 525, an event that signified the end of the Himyar kingdom. The Ethiopians destroyed the Jewish communities and the remnants of the independent Jewish kingdom dispersed to the towns and mountains of the Arabian peninsula; many fled to the city of Taif. The Jewish community in Najran was annihilated.

> The kingdom of Himyar and Himyar ben Saba will become strong in Yemen after the departure from there of the tribes of Saba. And the kings of Himyar were called Tuba in the days when the kings of Egypt were called Pharaoh. Their capital was called Zifar and was near the city known today as Sana. And the most famous ruler, Asad abu-Karb, was the first to become a Jew after his return from his war against Persia. He learned of Judaism from Jewish scholars at Medina when he passed through there on his travels. Many people of his land became Jews with him, and the country of Himyar became Jewish until the days of Yosef Du Nuas, whom the king of Abyssinia fought against because of his war against the Christians of Najran who Yosef pursued when he heard what the Christians had done to the Jews of Najran. Because Christianity had spread in Najran in central Arabia when Himyar was Jewish. And the Abyssinians will become strong in Himyar and Yemen and become a colony of Abyssinia for a long time. And the Abyssinian governor of Sana will build a splendid Christian church in the capital in order to capture the hearts of the inhabitants of Arabia for Christianity.

A. M. Habermann, Sefer Gzerot Ashkenaz ve-Tsarfat, *Jerusalem 1946, p. 29.*

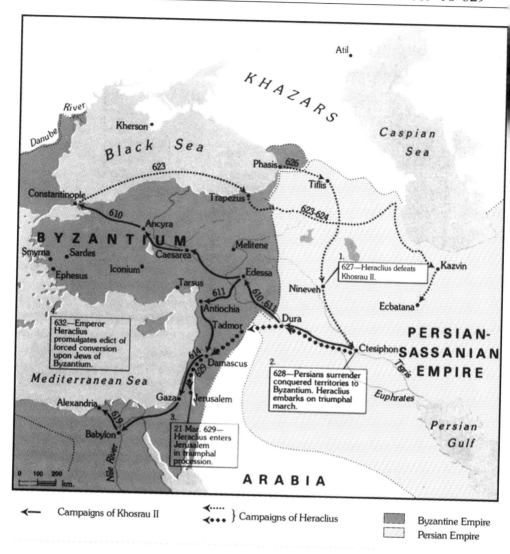

Campaigns of Khosrau II   } Campaigns of Heraclius   Byzantine Empire / Persian Empire

IN 606 the Persian legions invaded Syria, Palestine and Phoenicia and began to dismember the Byzantine Empire. Palestine was a natural center for Persian-Jewish collaboration since it had a large Jewish community that was a potential counterforce to the Christian population and Byzantine rule. Most of the Jewish population was centered in Galilee, in an area that controlled the route leading from Damascus to Palestine. There was also a concentration of Jews in Jerusalem, so large that the governor of the city tried to force them to convert to Christianity. The fall of Antioch to the Persians severed the land route between Constantinople and Palestine and in 613 the Persians entered Damascus. Jerusalem was captured in 614, and in 619 the Persians conquered Egypt. In all these conquests the Jews and Samaritans received the Persians as liberators, turning many cities over to them. The Persian conquest of Palestine was interpreted by the Jews as the advent of the messianic period of redemption. This ferment was reflected in the eschatological literature of the period and in the increasing number of messianic movements among the Jews.

The Jewish community's euphoria over the Persian conquest was short-lived; the Persians did not fulfill their promises to the Jews and were soon favoring the Christian community and persecuting the Jewish one. In a battle near Nineveh (627), the Byzantines defeated the Persians and proceeded to occupy Ctesiphon (628). With the death of Khosrau II (628), the way was open to the conquest of Jerusalem (629), but the days of Byzantine rule too were short-lived. The Islamic conqueror stood at the gate.

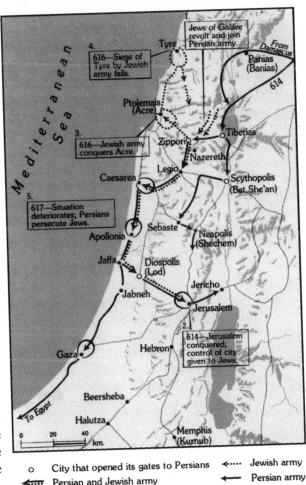

THE PERSIAN INVASION OF PALESTINE
614–618

THE JEWS IN THE ARABIAN PENINSULA
BEGINNING OF THE 7TH CENTURY

WE know very little about the beginnings of Jewish settlement in the Arabian peninsula. It seems that Jews began to live in oases and urban centers in the first centuries CE. The settlers engaged in agriculture and commerce and were organized in clans (or, according to some scholars, tribal groups). Their agriculture consisted mainly of date groves, while in commerce they developed the credit system and in the crafts they were blacksmiths, gold- and silversmiths and expert armor makers. Various families were identified by their occupations. The story is told that Muhammad used to buy goods on credit from the Jews.

Medina had a concentration of Jewish tribes; among the large ones were Banu Nadir, Qurayza, Qaynuqa' and some, who claimed to be of priestly descent,

THE JEWS IN THE
ARABIAN PENINSULA
BEGINNING OF THE 7TH CENTURY

- - - Trade routes
✿ City or town with Jewish community

Rainfall area
Oases
Sands

called Kahinan. Their strongholds were greater in number than those of the Arabs. The Khaybar Jews resided about a hundred kilometers north of the Medina district and it is possible that this Jewish settlement was larger than Medina. In spite of the vicissitudes in their fortune, the Khaybar community played an important role in the history of the Jewish people. The Jewish settlements in Wadi al-Qura and other oases such as Fadak and Tayma served as asylums for the refugees from southern Arabia after the death of Du Nuas. Jewish residents settled in these areas in proximity to nomadic Bedouin tribes and to the Nadirs, who were sedentary farmers. In spite of the influence of these two groups, the Jews persevered in their own special way of life and did not become nomads like the Bedouin, who changed their abode twice a year.

Muhammad had hoped to convert these settlers, but ultimately realizing that he would never succeed, he declared a war of extinction against them.

Relations between Muhammad and the Jews deteriorated, especially after his

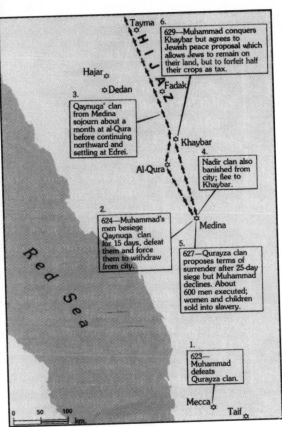

Map labels:
- Tayma 6.
- 629—Muhammad conquers Khaybar but agrees to Jewish peace proposal which allows Jews to remain on their land, but to forfeit half their crops as tax.
- Hajar
- Dedan
- Fadak
- 3. Qaynuqa' clan from Medina sojourn about a month at al-Qura before continuing northward and settling at Edrei.
- Khaybar
- 4. Nadir clan also banished from city; flee to Khaybar.
- Al-Qura
- 2. 624—Muhammad's men besiege Qaynuqa clan for 15 days, defeat them and force them to withdraw from city.
- Medina
- 5. 627—Qurayza clan proposes terms of surrender after 25-day siege but Muhammad declines. About 600 men executed; women and children sold into slavery.
- Red Sea
- 1. 623—Muhammad defeats Qurayza clan.
- Mecca
- Taif
- 0 50 100 km

MUHAMMAD'S WARS AGAINST
THE JEWS 623–629

protection from their allies in Muhammad's camp but Muhammad was determined to destroy them.

The fate of the Jews of Khaybar was different from that of the other Jewish clans. They sought allies amongst the Bedouin tribes of the south but Muhammad succeeded in winning the Bedouin over to his side. In 629, after a siege, the Jews of Khaybar turned to Muhammad and sued for peace. Muhammad, apparently weary of war, agreed to a proposal whereby the Jews were allowed to remain on their land on condition that they paid an annual tax of one half of their date harvest. According to the Hadith, this agreement on the distribution of the spoils served as a model for the conquests of Omar. This may explain and justify Omar's methods in conquest.

victory over Abu Jahl of Mecca (in the second year of the Hegira). He now turned against his enemies in Medina, besieging the stronghold of the Jewish clan of Qaynuqa' and forcing them into exile. The Qaynuqa' went by way of Wadi al-Qura to Transjordan and settled at Edrei. Arab sources number the size of the clan at 750 people, excluding women and children. In 627, after an unsuccessful siege by the Meccans against Medina, Muhammad turned against the Jewish clan of Qurayza and forced them to surrender unconditionally. The Qurayza had hoped for mercy and

THE CITY OF MEDINA

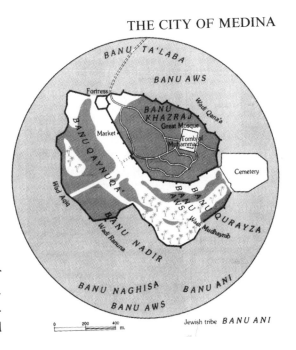

Map labels:
- BANU TA'LABA
- BANU AWS
- Fortress
- Wadi Qana'a
- BANU KHAZRAJ
- Great Mosque
- BANU QAYNUQA'
- Market
- Tomb of Muhammad
- Cemetery
- BANU AWS
- BANU QURAYZA
- Wadi Aqiq
- Wadi Mudhaynib
- BANU NADIR
- Wadi Ranuna
- BANU NAGHISA
- BANU ANI
- BANU AWS
- 0 200 400 m
- Jewish tribe BANU ANI

135

Now came the turn of the Jewish clans in the southern half of the peninsula and in the oases. This stage of the war is reflected in the text of an agreement containing promises given by Muhammad to the Samuel b. Adaya family in return for an undertaking by the family to pay a poll tax and an annual fixed amount of food products. Muhammad now adopted a policy different from the one used against the Jews of Hijaz and Khaybar. He declared that one must not coerce Jews and Christians to accept the new faith and ordered his officers and tax collectors to limit themselves to taking a poll tax (*jizya*) and a land tax (*karga* or *kharaj*). The majority of Jews were at that time concentrated in the Yemen and those in the north, who joined their brethren in the south, were the ones who renewed contacts with the Babylonian *geonim* and subsequently with the secular and religious leaders of the Egyptian Jewish community. Others emigrated to Palestine after it was conquered by the armies of Islam.

After Muhammad's death in 632 his successors continued their conquest and expansion. Knowledge of the map of the world at this period is one of the keys to understanding the fate of Judaism, which was from now on poised between the two world powers—Islam and Christianity.

ARABIAN CONQUEST AND THE RISE OF ISLAM 622–721

ISLAM continued to dominate the Arabian Peninsula, conquering Damascus, Babylonia and Persia. The Arabs invaded Palestine in 634 and by February had already reached the gates of Gaza, defeating the Byzantine army in 636. Jerusalem, still held by the Byzantines, was besieged in 637 and in March to April 638 surrendered to Caliph Omar. In 640 Caesarea, the last Byzantine foothold in Palestine, was taken. The Islamic armies continued their drive through Egypt and North Africa and in 711 crossed the straits separating Europe and Africa, invading and conquering the Iberian Peninsula. They crossed the Pyrenees but were defeated in a battle near Tours (Poitiers) and their advance was halted.

It was clear that the Jews belonged to the *dhimmi* class (the protected people) by virtue of being Jews. Relations with them were therefore determined by the agreements concluded by Muhammad and the practice at that time. However, relations were greatly influenced by the political and social developments in the caliphates.

The Jews tended to live in separate streets, but in this they were not different from members of other faiths. In the Arab city of Fès, Muslims from Kairouan lived in one street and Muslims from Andalusia lived in another street and each community had its own mosque. The Jewish quarter was in the northern part of the city, but there was no fixed Muslim legislation requiring Jews to reside in separate quarters. If such legislation did exist, the Muslims, as a minority, would have segregated themselves in their own quarters. However, in their own quarters Muslims made sure that churches and synagogues were built no higher than mosques and that Muslim houses were no lower than the houses of their neighbors. Segregation existed in the bathhouses, and in many cities

ARABIAN CONQUEST AND THE RISE OF ISLAM
622–721

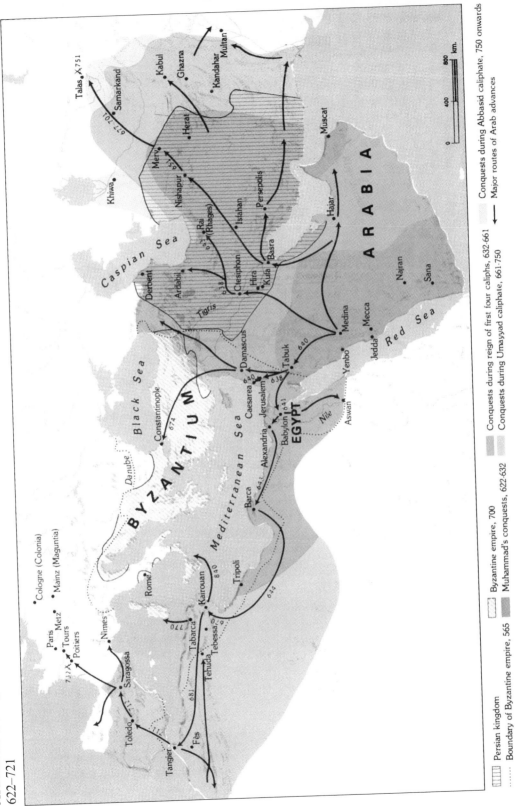

Legend:
- Persian kingdom
- Boundary of Byzantine empire, 565
- Byzantine empire, 700
- Muhammad's conquests, 622-632
- Conquests during reign of first four caliphs, 632-661
- Conquests during Umayyad caliphate, 661-750
- Conquests during Abbasid caliphate, 750 onwards
- → Major routes of Arab advances

separate Jewish baths were built (e.g., Gerona, Granada and elsewhere). Heavy punishment was meted out for sexual intercourse between members of different communities and mixed marriages were strictly forbidden unless the non-Muslim converted to Islam. Muslims were forbidden to bequeath anything to the infidel. In general, *dhimmi* children who converted to Islam lost their right of inheritance and the father of a converted daughter was not entitled to marry her off (and therefore receive her *mohar*).

The superior status of Islam over other religions was further emphasized by distinctions in type and color of clothing. Over the generations, the Muslims added an increasing number of prohibitions and limitations.

VISIGOTHIC SPAIN 7TH CENTURY

1. 589—Third Church Council of Toledo: King Reccared declares Catholicism sole religion of country. Jews forbidden to marry Christian women or own Christian slaves.

2. 589—Regional council of priests compels all residents to rest on Sunday.

FRANKISH KINGDOM

5. 633—Fourth Church Council of Toledo. Restrictions against Jews and persecution of crypto-Jews.

3. 612—King Sisebut orders release of Christian slaves owned by Jews.

4. 613—King Sisebut expels from Spain Jews who refuse to convert to Christianity. Many Jews convert but secretly continue to observe Judaism.

VISIGOTHS

Toulouse • — Agde • — Marseilles • — Béziers — Narbonne — Perpignan — Gerona
Pamplona • — Tudela • — Tarragona — Barcelona
León • — Burgos • — Saragossa • — Tortosa
Zamora • — Calatayud • —
Duero — Escalona •
Lisbon — Badajoz • — Mérida — Toledo • — Guadiana — Valencia •
Seville • — Córdoba • — Lucena • Elvira • — Elche • — Cartagena
Gades • — Granada • — Málaga • — Adra
Tingis • • Ceuta — Algiers •

BASQUES
SUEVES
Ebro

0 100 200
km.

▨ Byzantine provinces taken by Visigoths, 584-585
    Kingdom of Visigoths in 600
○ Place with remains of Jewish residence

THE persecution of the Jews in Visigothic Spain began when the Visigoths converted to Catholicism during the reign of King Reccared (586). From then on the church councils enacted a number of anti-Jewish laws with the intention of eliminating the Jewish community.

King Sisebut, supported by the church councils, inaugurated a series of stringent anti-Jewish laws in 612. The Jewish population was forced to convert and, even then, as converts they were burdened with many restrictions. The church council of 633, during the reign of King Sisenand, was the most severe in its attitude toward the Jewish population and its decisions regarding the Jews were adopted as the law of the land. Nine basic laws (paragraphs 57–65) established a legal network against the Jews and crypto-Jews. Paragraph 65 was the law that forbade Jews and crypto-Jews from holding offices and having any jurisdiction over Christians. This law served in the fifteenth century to forbid Jews and crypto-Jews to hold office and to create anti-Jewish public opinion.

The Visigoths who invaded Spain in 412 ruled for three hundred years as a social upper strata of conquerors that tried to impose the laws of a militant society and church upon the country. They failed to integrate with the indigenous Roman-Spanish community, and also rejected the Jewish minority. Internal intrigues caused their downfall at the beginning of the eighth century.

THE JEWS IN ITALY DURING THE PAPACY OF GREGORY I (THE GREAT)   590 to 604

DESPITE the scant information available on the Jews in Italy in the sixth and seventh centuries, there are sources that indicate Jewish settlement in a number of important Italian cities. Legal autonomy for the Jews of Italy was recognized by an edict of King Theodoric (after 512), in contrast to the policy of the Byzantine emperors, who saw Jewish courts merely as institutions of arbitration. The Jews of Genoa were allowed to repair their synagogue and it was decreed that they were not to be coerced in matters of belief.

The heads of the church in Rome had considerable international influence, but it was only during the papacy of Gregory I (590–604) that the church's attitude to the Jews was given official expression. His papal bull *Sicut Judaeis* determined the church's relationship to the Jews

Pope Gregory I (the Great).

throughout the Middle Ages. The underlying principle of Gregory's bull was the

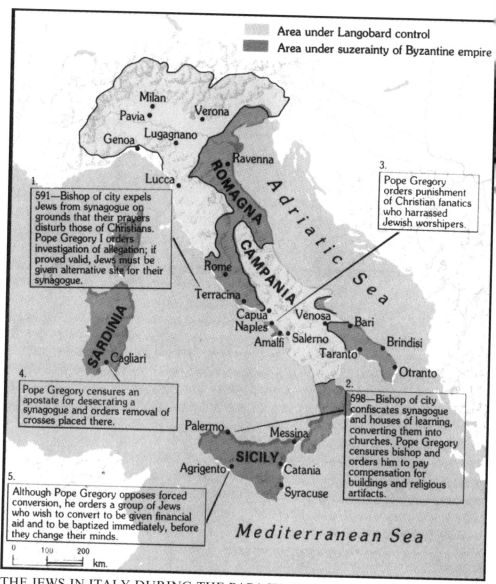

Area under Langobard control

Area under suzerainty of Byzantine empire

1.
591—Bishop of city expels Jews from synagogue on grounds that their prayers disturb those of Christians. Pope Gregory I orders investigation of allegation; if proved valid, Jews must be given alternative site for their synagogue.

3.
Pope Gregory orders punishment of Christian fanatics who harrassed Jewish worshipers.

4.
Pope Gregory censures an apostate for desecrating a synagogue and orders removal of crosses placed there.

2.
598—Bishop of city confiscates synagogue and houses of learning, converting them into churches. Pope Gregory censures bishop and orders him to pay compensation for buildings and religious artifacts.

5.
Although Pope Gregory opposes forced conversion, he orders a group of Jews who wish to convert to be given financial aid and to be baptized immediately, before they change their minds.

0   100   200
km.

THE JEWS IN ITALY DURING THE PAPACY OF
GREGORY I (THE GREAT)
590–604

maintenance of the status quo and so, for example, the extent of synagogue activities was restricted to what had been permissible before the publication of the bull. Successive popes in the Middle Ages continued to be guided by *Sicut Judaeis*. However, Gregory's general policy toward the Jews was to refrain from religious compulsion and serious economic persecution. While he permitted Jews to own pagan slaves, he prohibited them from owning pagan slaves who converted to Christianity and totally forbade trading in these slaves. Pagan slaves who worked on Jewish farms and converted and became colons (594), were obliged to pay a fixed rental fee and forbidden to perform any personal service for their Jewish masters. Gregory also supported the persecution of the Jews by the Visigoths in Spain.

The largest concentration of Jews in Italy seems to have been in Sicily, then under Byzantine rule.

Rome had the most ancient Jewish community and communal organization in Italy. The communal leadership had its early origins in the office of the archisynagogus (head of the synagogue) who was assisted by the elders of the community. The Jews of Rome, like the Greeks, Franks, Saxons, Lombards, and Frisians, were called *schola peregrinorum* (a sect of foreigners), and are mentioned as being present at the coronation of emperors in Rome. Rome became the forum for disputations between Jews and Christians on matters of faith.

CHARLEMAGNE'S EMPIRE

CHARLEMAGNE (768–814), the central Carolingian figure, had his name linked with many Jewish and Christian legends, one of which is the legend concerning the role he played in the Jewish settlements in Narbonne and Mainz and particularly with the tradition that he was instrumental in having Torah study transferred from Baghdad to Narbonne.

Charlemagne was the first western ruler to send a commercial delegation to the caliph Harun al-Rashid, and it was this delegation that renewed and revived trade relations between Christian Europe and eastern Islam. A Jew, called Isaac, was a member of the delegation and was the only one to complete the mission and return safely.

The relationship between Charlemagne and the Jews, and the protection he extended to them, is expressed in his edicts. One can assume that the foundations for the charters of privileges for the Jews were laid during his reign.

There are three extant charters of privileges from the Carolingian period, all dating from the reign of Louis the Pious (814–840): one given to R. Domatus; the second to several Jews from Lyons—David, Joseph and their compatriots; the third to Abraham of Saragossa. The three charters provide a wealth of information about the history of the Jews in Europe and particularly in the Carolingian empire. Probably granted in 825, the charters gave protection to the Jews

> And King Charles sent to the King of Babylonia asking him to send Jews descendants of the House of David. And he agreed and sent him a wise and important person, R. Makhir by name, who was settled in Narbonne...and he was given a big landed property in the time the city was conquered from the Israelites.... And when the city was conquered the King divided it in three parts: one was given to don Eymerich, the city's governor; the second part was given to the local bishop; the third was given to R. Makhir, who became enriched and was granted freedom, and the king gave to the local Jews good laws, signed by the king Charles through privileges, accepted by his descendants. And those who tried to persecute them, they would complain to the King who would order reprisals. And immediately order was restored. Narbonne is under the rule of France. And his R. Makhir's descendants were in their time leaders at the head of various dispersions.

R. Abraham Ibn Daud, The Book of Tradition I, ed. A. Neubaur, Oxford 1888. Addition to manuscript, p.82.

CHARLEMAGNE'S EMPIRE

2.

778—Charlemagne's army defeated when Basques destroy rearguard under command of Roland, prefect of the Breton March, during Charlemagne's campaign against Muslims.

3.

797—Charlemagne sends delegation to Caliph Harun al-Rashid at Baghdad with Jewish merchant Isaac as interpreter. 802— Isaac returns alone and delivers caliph's gift to Charlemagne.

1.

Charlemagne recognizes Jewish autonomy in one third of city and authority of community's nasi.

London
Abbeville
St.-Denis
Paris
Orléans
Tours
Poitiers
Clermont
Bordeaux
Auch
Toulouse
Roncesvalles
Narbonne
Agde
Gerona
Barcelona
Saragossa
Tarragona
Valencia
Granada
Málaga
Tangier

ASTURIAS
EMIRATE OF CÓRDOBA
Duero

Aix-la-Chapelle
Rhine
Elbe
Fulda
Frankfurt
Mainz
Würzburg
Metz
Regensburg
Prague
Lyons
Vienne
Arles
Marseilles
Pavia
Verona
Lucca
Ravenna
Rome
Benevento
Venosa

Volga
Caspian Sea
Atil
Sarkel
KHAZARS
KIEVAN RUSSIA
Kiev
Don
Kaffa
Kherson
Black Sea
Danube
Constantinople
BYZANTIUM

Mediterranean Sea

Kairouan
Alexandria

Tigris
Euphrates
Baghdad
Antiochia
Jaffa
Jerusalem
Gaza
Ramle
CALIPHATE OF BAGHDAD

0   200   400
km.

Frankish kingdom, 768
Charlemagne's conquests
Frontier military districts
Conquered peoples and allies

and defined their rights. Each paragraph dealt with a variety of subjects and problems, for example, exemptions from paying certain taxes and excises that were levied on the general population. We also learn from the charters of the considerable Jewish involvement in the slave trade that extended from Bohemia to Muslim Spain. The importance of defining the legal relations between Jews and Christians can be attested to their prominence in the records of judicial proceedings. It is reasonable to assume that the Carolingians instituted the office of *magister Judaeorum*, an imperial official appointed to supervise matters relating to the Jews. The office and its incumbent were destined to rouse the anger of the church in Carolingian France, but also to be emulated in many places.

A tombstone in Auch (Elimberris).

Relations with the crown were of prime importance since the right of residence for Jews in the Carolingian state, as in every other state, depended upon the crown's approval. A fundamental change

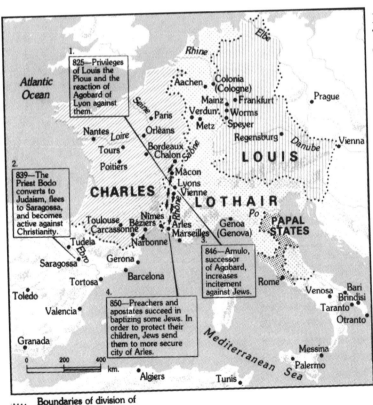

BOUNDARIES OF THE DIVIDED CAROLINGIAN EMPIRE
843

1. 825—Privileges of Louis the Pious and the reaction of Agobard of Lyon against them.

2. 839—The Priest Bodo converts to Judaism, flees to Saragossa, and becomes active against Christianity.

3. 846—Amulo, successor of Agobard, increases incitement against Jews.

4. 850—Preachers and apostates succeed in baptizing some Jews. In order to protect their children, Jews send them to more secure city of Arles.

..... Boundaries of division of the Carolingian empire, according to Treaty of Verdun, 843

143

in relations with the Jews took place in the Carolingian state, which discarded the Theodosian ordinances and replaced them with the ancient Teutonic laws regarding aliens. The new relations were based upon the ruler's patronage and protection in exchange for the payment of a fixed annual tax.

The division of the Carolingian empire after Charlemagne's death did not substantially alter the status of the Jews in the kingdoms. However, the anti-Jewish activities and the writings of Agobard, archbishop of Lyons from 814 to 846, and his pupil, Amulo, archbishop of Lyons from 841, did signify the beginning of a change in attitude. Writings from the second half of the ninth century reveal that there were clergy who preached the forcible conversion of Jews. The Jews strongly objected to these sermons and as a cautionary measure sent their children to take refuge at Arles, where they enjoyed a greater degree of protection.

As a result of the political division in France in the eleventh and twelfth centuries, the Jews found themselves under the jurisdiction either of dioceses that were the owners of cities and towns, or of various feudal barons, to whom the Jewish community paid taxes for right of residence. There were instances where a Jewish community (such as Narbonne) was obliged to pay an annual tax both to the diocese and to the baron who was the lord of the city.

It is from this period that we have increasing knowledge and information about the Jews in France. In Toulouse it was customary to degrade the Jews by publicly slapping the cheek of the head of the community on Good Friday and only in the twelfth century was this practice replaced by an annual payment to the clergy. Sermons on the death of Jesus incited the Christian masses and often resulted in violence against the Jews. In Béziers, the Christian population was allowed to stone the Jewish quarter on Easter and only in 1160 was this license converted to a one-time payment plus a fixed annual tax to the diocese. It is interesting to note that the basic argument for persecuting the Jews was the accusation of collusion between them and the invading Normans in the south of France and their support for the plundering raids of the Muslims.

THE KHAZARS AND PRESSURE FROM THE CHRISTIAN STATES 8TH TO 10TH CENTURIES

THE conversion of the Khazars to Judaism is described in a number of historical sources of the period. Mas'udi, the Arab historian and traveler, in his book *The Meadows of Gold and Mines of Gems* (943–947), tells of the Khazar king who converted during the reign of Harun al-Rashid (786–809); of Muslims, Christians and Jews who settled in the Khazar city of Atil; of Jewish settlers, refugees from Muslim countries and Greeks who settled in the Khazar kingdom as a result of persecution by the Byzantine emperor, Romanus I Lecapenus (919–944). Other Arab sources relate the conversion story, some telling of the king's disappointment with his Christian faith, and of the talented Jewish polemicist who succeeded in convincing the king (after the former had purportedly poisoned his traveling companion, the Muslim emissary). Other sources report that members of the king's

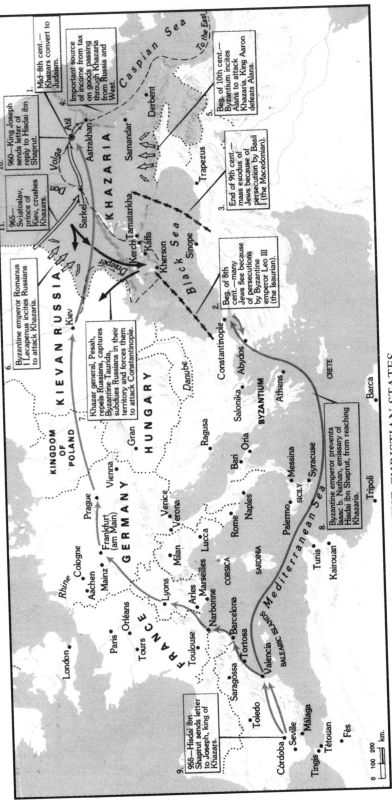

THE KHAZARS AND PRESSURE FROM THE CHRISTIAN STATES
8TH TO 10TH CENTURIES

1. Mid-8th cent.—Khazars convert to Judaism.

4. Important source of income from tax on goods passing through Khazaria from Russia and West.

5. Beg. of 10th cent.—Byzantium incites Alans to attack Khazaria. King Aaron defeats Alans.

10. 960—King Joseph sends letter of reply to Hisdai ibn Shaprut.

3. End of 9th cent.—mass exodus of Jews because of persecution by Basil (the Macedonian).

11. 965—Sviatoslav, prince of Kiev, crushes Khazars.

2. Beg. of 8th cent.—many Jews flee because of persecutions by Byzantine emperor Leo III (the Isaurian).

6. Byzantine emperor Romanus I Lecapenus incites Russians to attack Khazaria.

7. Khazar general, Pesah, repels Russians, captures Byzantine Taurida, subdues Russians in their territory and forces them to attack Constantinople.

8. Byzantine emperor prevents Isaac b. Nathan, emissary of Hisdai ibn Shaprut, from reaching Khazaria.

9. 955—Hisdai ibn Shaprut sends letter to Joseph, king of Khazars.

0 100 200 km.

145

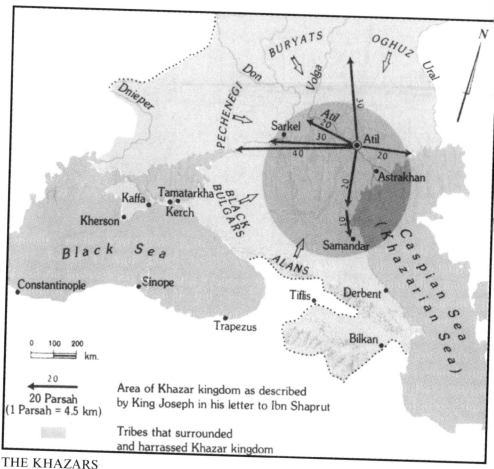

THE KHAZARS

court were Jews; that his judicial court was composed of seven wise men—Jews, Christians, Muslims and pagans; that the basis of the Khazar livelihood was hunting and trading in animal skins, wax and honey. These sources also mention that Jews introduced work methods into the kingdom; that they taught the Khazars to read and write and that only because of their religious separatism were the Jews able to maintain their independence and avoid being crushed between the Byzantine hammer and the caliphite anvil. However, political considerations were certainly not the only factors that prompted the Khazar king to convert.

The Khazars were constantly at war with their neighbors and Byzantium did everything in its power to destroy the kingdom—even inciting the Alan and Russian tribes to attack the Khazars from the north. This constant state of war prevented the Khazars from attending to the internal matter of Jewish consolidation. There is a general consensus that the Khazar kingdom of the ninth and tenth centuries was a Jewish state with Muslim and Christian minorities, in which the presence of Christians acted as a restraint on Byzantium's treatment of its Jewish population. The persecution of the Jews in Byzantium during the reign of Romanus I Lecapenus ould be reciprocated by King Joseph's persecution of the Christians in his kingdom.

Not only international political factors undermined the existence of the Khazar kingdom but also economic ones, such as the lack of a centralized national economy (even by standards of that period). It is true that the capital city of Atil benefited from its strategic location on the crossroads of an important trade route and was, therefore, the major source of national revenue for the kingdom. However, the duties on goods and taxes collected within the state—the extent of which we know practically nothing—still fell short of what the kingdom required.

The apogee of the Khazar kingdom was in the middle of the tenth century, the period of contact between King Joseph and R. Hisdai ibn Shaprut and the emergence of Russian power. According to Russian sources, Sviatoslav, ruler of Kiev (945–972), crushed the Khazars in 965, but they are still mentioned in the Russian Chronicles of 1016 and 1023. Khazars from the city of Tamatarkha (Taman of today) assisted Mstislav the Brave in his campaign against his brother Yaroslav the Wise (ruled 1019–1054). It is known that in 1078 Oleg, grandson of Yaroslav the Wise, resided in Tamatarkha and the Chronicles relate that in 1079 he was siezed by the Khazars and taken captive to Constantinople. However, in 1083 he was able to avenge

"Let not my lord take it ill, I pray, that I enquire about the number of his forces. May the Lord add to them, how many soever they be, an hundredfold. . . . My lord sees that I enquire about this with no other object than that I may rejoice when I hear of the increase of the holy people. I wish too that he would tell me of the number of provinces over which he rules, the amount of tribute paid to him, if they give him tithes, whether he swells continually in the royal city or goes about through the whole extent of his dominions, if there are islands in the neighborhood, and if any of their inhabitants conform to Judaism? If he judges over them? How he goes up to the house of God? With what peoples he wages war? Whether he allows war to set aside the observance of the Sabbath? What kingdoms or nations are on his borders? What are the cities near to his kingdom called Khorasan, Berdaa, and Bab al Abwab? In what way their caravans proceed to his territory? How many kings ruled before him? What were their names, how many years each of them ruled, and what is the current language of the land?"

From letter by Hisdai ibn Shaprut to King of Khazars. Letters of Jews Through the Ages, ed. F. Kobler, Ararat Publishing Society Ltd, London, 1952.

himself on the Khazars on behalf of his brother. The Khazars are still mentioned at the beginning of the twelfth century and so it seems that they were active for a considerable period after their defeat by the Russians in 965 and before they finally dispersed among the many Jewish communities.

THE RADHANITE MERCHANTS

THE beginning of the ninth century saw a change in the function of the Mediterranean ports of the Muslim countries. The Muslim fleets grew stronger and were now able to attack Byzantine garrisons on Cyprus, Crete, Sicily and southern Italy. In fact, the Arabs controlled the Mediterranean and the Byzantine navy ceased to play any practical role in the area. North Africa became the link

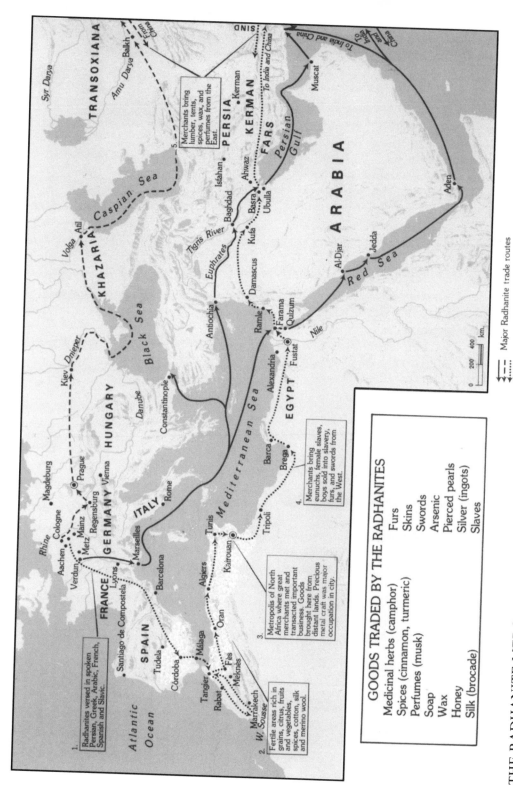

THE RADHANITE MERCHANTS

GOODS TRADED BY THE RADHANITES

Medicinal herbs (camphor)	Furs
Spices (cinnamon, turmeric)	Skins
Perfumes (musk)	Swords
Soap	Arsenic
Wax	Pierced pearls
Honey	Silver (ingots)
Silk (brocade)	Slaves

Major Radhanite trade routes

Trade center

1. Radhanites versed in spoken Persian, Greek, Arabic, French, Spanish and Slavic.

2. Fertile areas rich in grains, citrus, fruits and vegetables, spices, cotton, silk and merino wool.

3. Metropolis of North Africa where great merchants met and transacted important business. Goods brought here from distant lands. Precious metal craft was major occupation in city.

4. Merchants bring eunuchs, female slaves, boys sold into slavery, furs, and swords from the West.

5. Merchants bring lumber, tents, spices, wax, and perfumes from the East.

0 200 400 km.

148

between Muslim ports in the western, southern and eastern Mediterranean. In Egypt, Fustat developed as a trading center, situated between Alexandria and the Red Sea ports on the trade route to India. Due to the political stability of the tenth century, the Muslim countries developed and prospered.

Among the towns that played an important role in developing trade were the new ones—Fès, Marrakech, Meknès, and Rabat—all of them Muslim. Kairouan exceeded them all as the metropolis of North Africa; located on the trade route midway between Alexandria and the ports of western Morocco and Spain and adjacent to the fortified port of Mahdia, it engaged in precious metal crafts, received slaves from Sudan and Byzantium, and goods—oils, dried fruits, turmeric, spices, and leather—from distant places. It was a meeting place for great merchants and their agents and many business transactions were effected there. From the beginning of the ninth until the middle of the eleventh century, considerable wealth was accumulated in Kairouan, and palatial private and public buildings were constructed in the town. Merchants, particularly the Jewish ones known as Radhanites, played a major role in international trade. Their caravans traversed many countries, from Europe through North Africa to the Muslim east and on to India. Another land route took them through Europe to the Far East and China.

The origin of the Radhanites is unknown but some think they came from the east. As Radhanite trade declined in the tenth century, it was taken up by the merchants of Kairouan and Fustat. Documents found in the Cairo Genizah contain a wealth of material relating to the international wholesale trade of North Africa as well as a considerable

A letter from R. Hisdai ibn Shaprut to Joseph, king of the Khazars.

amount of responsa about commercial matters referring to the sages and geonim of Babylon. They reveal the lively trade engaged in by Jewish merchants from different western communities, using Fustat and Kairouan as their centers. Various documents deal with the resolution of credit problems and litigation between various merchants.

Rabbi Naharay b. Nissim, head of the Babylonian Jewish community in Fustat, engaged in a particularly extensive trade that was of international scope. His commercial establishment operated for more than fifty years in the eleventh century, reaching near and distant lands and dealing with a large variety of goods.

The volume and scope of international Jewish trade demanded the use of new methods of credit. It was these Jewish merchants who introduced the use of the *shufatajiyya* (the equivalent of our check), which inter alia was used to protect the merchants from robbery (as well as from merchant association partnerships of a family nature).

ITALY IN THE FRAMEWORK OF BYZANTIUM AND THE HOLY ROMAN EMPIRE 9TH TO 10TH CENTURIES

2. 855—Louis II orders expulsion of Jews from northern Italy. (Decree apparently never implemented.)

3. Bishop Ratherius of Verona complains of excessively tolerant attitude towards Jews.

11. Hananel II gets permission from Byzantine emperor to search empire for family property lost during wars. After peregrinations, settles in Benevento.

1. 850—Church council forbids Jews to serve as tax collectors or arbitrators between Jews and Christians.

4. Shephatiah, head of Jewish community in Oria, cures daughter of Emperor Basil I and consequently obtains cancellation of edict of conversion issued by emperor.

10. 953—Josippon, important Jewish historiographic book, written here.

5. Shephatiah acts as intermediary between Byzantine governor and conquering Arab general.

6. 895—Peace treaty signed, bringing Sicily under Muslim control, but battle for southern Italy continues.

7. 925—Hasadiah and 9 rabbis killed by Arabs because of their loyalty to Byzantium.

9. 950—Paltiel b. Hasadiah backs Imam al-Mu'izz and prophesies that he will conquer southern Italy. The Imam takes him to his court at Kairouan. 969—Al-Mu'izz appoints Paltiel minister at Caliphate in Cairo.

8. Physician and philosopher, Shabbetai Donnolo (born in Oria 913) exiled in his youth (925) to Palermo and Africa (ransomed by relatives in Taranto). Eventually became court physician to Byzantine governor of Calabria.

0   100   200 km.

THE most important political factors for an understanding of this period are the political status of Byzantium in southern Italy, Rome as the papal seat, and the rise of city states in the central and northern parts of the peninsula. This situation did not change very much even after the incorporation of northern Italy into the Holy Roman Empire, nor after the Muslim conquests in southern Italy. In other words, a number of forces, religious or political, combined to rule Italy and within this framework lived the Jewish community, often in very difficult circumstances. In the struggle of power in southern Italy the Muslims tried to oust Byzantium and gain a foothold in Europe.

From 652 until the 820s, Italian cities were at the mercy of Muslim bands based mainly in Tunisia and the adjacent islands, whence they engaged in pillaging raids with no intent to conquer territory. It was only in 827 that actual steps were taken to conquer Sicily and in 831 Palermo became the Muslim capital city on the island. Messina was captured in 843 and Syracuse in 878. In their military campaigns the Muslim invaders took control of the straits of Messina and for a while held Bari and Taranto, presenting a serious threat to Rome. In 846 Rome was invaded and a number of churches were looted. It was only toward the end of the century (895–896) that a peace treaty was signed between Byzantium and the Muslims. Sicily was ceded to the Muslims. At first the island was dependent upon Tunisia, but when Tunisia was conquered by the Fatimids it became part of the Fatimid caliphate. After Cairo became the capital of the Fatimid dynasty their influence on Sicily slackened and the island was ruled by a local family.

The largest Jewish community on the island was at Palermo where the Jewish quarter was located outside the city walls. It was first mentioned in 967 and was probably the residence of the judge Mazliah b. Elijah al-Bazak, believed to be the teacher of the celebrated Talmudist, Nathan b. Jehiel of Rome. In 1030 two Spanish Jews, Hayyim and his son Nissim, assisted the Jews of Sicily by obtaining tax reductions and protection

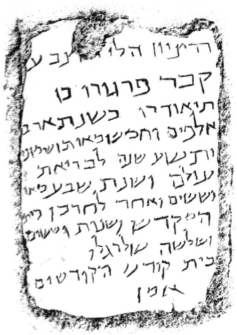

A tombstone in Venosa, southern Italy, from 829.

for Jewish merchants who traded with Sicilians. The Jews of Palermo wrote to the rabbis of Kairouan about the activities of Hayyim and Nissim. A Spanish Jew named Moses served at the court of the ruler of Sicily, Tsamtsam a-Dullah, and accompanied the latter on his journey to Egypt.

The Jews of southern Italy engaged in cloth dyeing and silk weaving; many were also farmers. Otranto and Bari were Torah centers and renowned for their scholarship. Evidence of knowledge of Jewish tradition by the Jews of southern Italy can be found in contemporary tombstones engraved in Hebrew.

Historical evidence from northern Italy indicates the existence of small Jewish communities, located chiefly in small and medium-sized towns (Ferrara, Bologna, Modena, Padua, Mantua, Treviso and Milan). There is further evidence that the famous Kalonymos family settled in

THE NORMAN INVASION OF
SOUTHERN ITALY

Byzantine Empire, 1025
Areas under Muslim rule

Lucca in the state of Tuscany (c. ninth century) and there founded a Talmudic academy. Around the year 1000 some members of the family emigrated to Mainz, where they established themselves and founded a yeshiva. The Jews of Tuscany were known to have owned vineyards and their presence in Modena is mentioned in a document dated 1025. Venice was under the influence of Byzantium and in 945 forbade her ship captains to haul Jewish cargo or carry Jewish passengers to the east.

Louis II, grandson of Charlemagne, in 855 ordered the expulsion of Italian Jews from the territories he ruled, but it is doubtful whether this decree was ever implemented.

In 850 the church council at Ticino forbade the employment of Jews as tax collectors or as arbitrators between Jews and Christians, and in Verona Bishop Ratherius repeated the allegations of Agobard of Lyons against the Jews.

Italy was a repository of Jewish traditions and customs and served as a bridge for Jews who passed from the Holy Land mainly into the Holy Roman Empire through Sicily and from there to Egypt and to Byzantium.

THE AHIMAAZ SCROLL OF GENEALOGIES

THE Jewish community of the small town of Oria, located between Taranto and Brindisi, was a center of Jewry in southern Italy under Byzantine rule. The Amittai family was active in Oria for many generations and their descendants included: Shephatiah b. Shabbetai, the poet (d. 886); the doctor, Shabbetai Donnolo (913–after 983), who composed a number of medical texts in Hebrew; Paltiel (d. 975), astrologer and physician, who was appointed aide to the caliph at

152

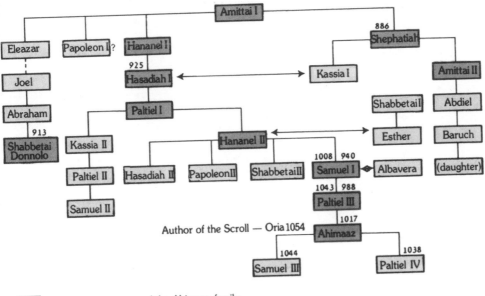

Author of the Scroll — Oria 1054

■ Important personages of the Ahimaaz family

the Fatimid court in Egypt and head of the Egyptian Jewish community; and Ahimaaz, the author of one of the first historical descriptions of the period (1054).

RELIGIOUS FERMENT AND SECTS IN JUDAISM
UNTIL THE 12TH CENTURY

FROM the end of the seventh century the Jewish Middle East was the arena for religious sects that claimed that they had the power to redeem the people of Israel. Between the years 685 and 705 a Jewish sect known as the Isanians was founded in Persia by Abu Isa (Isaac b. Jacob al-Isfahani), also called Obadiah, who claimed to be the Messiah destined to redeem the people of Israel from their dispersion. He led a revolt against the Muslims but was defeated and killed. The basic principles of the sect were asceticism, including the prohibition of eating meat and drinking wine; a ban on divorce; and prayer seven times a day (based on the verse in Psalm 119:164

"seven times daily do I praise Thee"). Some of its tenets anticipate doctrines adopted by Anan, the founder of the Karaite sect. The Isanian sect continued to exist after the death of Abu Isa. Yudghan, Abu Isa's disciple and heir, declared himself to be a prophet and Messiah, founding a sect that was named after him as Yudghanites. Mushka was the founder of another sect, called the Mushkanites. Somewhat more is known about Moses Haparsi, probably Abu Imran; born in Baghdad, he too founded a religious sect, settling in Zafran near Kermanshah before moving to Tiflis (Tbilisi). His sect, which became known as the Tiflisites, rejected the doctrine of

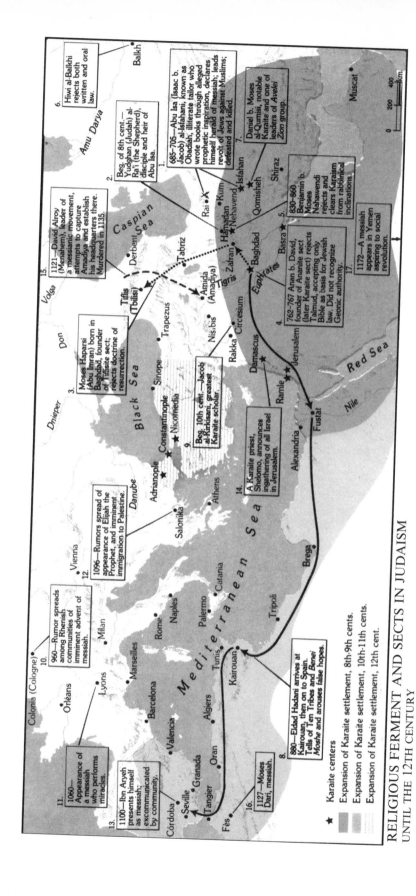

6. Hiwi al-Balkhi rejects both written and oral law.

Beg. of 8th cent.—Yudghan (Judah) al-Ra'i (the Shepherd), disciple and heir of Abu Isa. 2.

1. 685–705—Abu Isa (Isaac b. Jacob) al-Isfahani, known as Obadiah; illiterate tailor who wrote books through alleged prophetic inspiration, declares himself herald of messiah; leads revolt of Jews against Muslims; defeated and killed.

Daniel b. Moses al-Qumisi, notable Karaite and one of leaders of *Aveleí Zion* group. 7.

830–860, Benjamin b. Moses Nahawendi rejects and clears Karaism from rabbinical inclinations. 5.

1172—A messiah appears in Yemen aspiring to social revolution. 17.

15. 1121—David Alroy (Menahem), leader of a messianic movement, attempts to capture Amadiya and establish his headquarters there. Murdered in 1135.

762–767 Anan b. David, founder of Ananite sect (later Karaite sect) rejects Talmud, accepting only Bible as basis for Jewish law. Did not recognize Geonic authority. 4.

Moses Haparsi (Abu Imran) born in Baghdad, founder of Tiflisite sect; rejects doctrine of resurrection. 3.

Beg. 10th cent.—Jacob al-Kirkisani, greatest Karaite scholar. 9.

1096—Rumors spread of appearance of Elijah the Prophet, and imminent immigration to Palestine. 12.

A Karaite priest, Shelomo, announces ingathering of all Israel in Jerusalem. 14.

960—Rumor spreads among Rhenish communities of imminent advent of messiah. 10.

11. 1060—Appearance of a messiah who performs miracles.

13. 1100—Ibn Aryeh presents himself as messiah; excommunicated by community.

16. 1127—Moses Dari, messiah.

8. 880—Eldad Hadani arrives at Kairouan, then on to Spain. Tells of Ten Tribes and *Benei Moshe* and arouses false hopes.

Balkh

Amu Darya

Muscat

Shiraz

Isfahan

Qomisheh

Nehavend

Hamadan

Kum

Rai

Tabriz

Derbent

Caspian Sea

Volga

Don

Dnieper

Tiflis (Tbilisi)

Amida (Amadiya)

Zahran

Baghdad

Basra

Euphrates

Tigris

Circesium

Rakka

Nisibis

Damascus

Jerusalem

Ramle

Fustat

Alexandria

Red Sea

Nile

Nicomedia

Constantinople

Adrianople

Athens

Salonika

Brega

Trapezus

Sinope

Black Sea

Danube

Vienna

Milan

Rome

Naples

Catania

Palermo

Tunis

Kairouan

Tripoli

Marseilles

Lyons

Orléans

Colonia (Cologne)

Barcelona

Valencia

Algiers

Oran

Granada

Seville

Córdoba

Tangier

Fès

Mediterranean Sea

Karaite centers

Expansion of Karaite settlement, 8th-9th cents.

Expansion of Karaite settlement, 10th-11th cents.

Expansion of Karaite settlement, 12th cent.

0   200   400
km

RELIGIOUS FERMENT AND SECTS IN JUDAISM
UNTIL THE 12TH CENTURY

resurrection and other basic tenets of Mosaic law.

The most important sect were the Ananites, named for their founder Anan b. David who, rejecting the Talmudic *halakhah*, and saw Jewish life as based solely on the Bible as interpreted by him and his disciples. The sect was subsequently called Karaite and much of its doctrine was based on Muslim influence. The doctrine was developed by Benjamin b. Moses Nahawendi (between 830 and 860) and other scholars who extended the exegesis and added new tenets. Benjamin's legal works, *Sefer Mitzvot* ("Book of Precepts") and *Sefer Dinim* ("Book of Laws"), represent an attempt at a comprehensive code of Karaite law. Hiwi al-Balkhi, probably born in Balkh in Afghanistan, was a contemporary of Benjamin. A free thinker, he rejected both the written and oral law, being influenced by various Persian religious trends. His doctrines did not survive him by many years.

Three outstanding Karaite personalities were: Salmon b. Jerohim (tenth century), Daniel b. Moses al-Qumisi (ninth to tenth centuries) considered the founder of Karaism in Palestine, and Jacob al-Kirkisani (first half of tenth century), the greatest Karaite philosopher. Most of the Karaites who settled in

A decorated page in a Karaite Bible.

Jerusalem in the first half of the ninth century joined the *Avelei Zion* ("Mourners of Zion"), a group of Jews devoted to mourning the destruction of the Temple and Jerusalem. (The group also included Rabbanite Jews.)

The existence of the Karaite movement was one of the factors that led to the rabbanite examination of biblical texts and the subsequent codification of the spelling and reading of the Hebrew Bible (Masorah).

THE GAONATE IN BABYLONIA

BAGHDAD, founded by Caliph al-Mansur (762), attracted many Jewish settlers.

Although the beginnings of the Jewish Diaspora in Babylon preceded the Muslim conquest, the gaonate period coincided with the period of Muslim rule. The decline of the gaonate began with the death of Rav Hai Gaon in 1038. The gaonate period is of special significance in the history of the Jewish people because the Jewish center in Babylon played a decisive role in the life of the nation and had the vigor to withstand the competition with Eretz Israel for the hegemony over Jewish life, and to prevail.

SURA		PUMBEDITA
Rav Mar bar Huna	589	Mar Hanan of Iskiya
	591	(?) Mar Rav Marib; R. Dimi (formerly of Firuz-Shapur and Nehardea)
Rav Huna		
Rav Sheshna (also called Mesharsheya b. Tahlifa)	650	
	651	Rav Rabbah
		Rav Bosai
Rav Hanina of Nehar-Pekod	689	Rav Huna Mari b. Rav Joseph
		Rav Hiyya of Mershan
		Mar Rav Ravya (or Mar Yanka)
Rav Hilai ha-Levi of Naresh	694	
Rav Jacob ha-Kohen of Nehar-Pekod	712	
	719	Rav Natronai b. R. Nehemiah
		Rav Judah
Mar Samuel	730	
Rav Mari Kohen of Nehar-Pekod	739	Rav Joseph
	748	Rav Samuel b. Rav Mar
	752(?)	Rav Natroi Kahana b. Rav Mar Amunah
		Rav Abraham Kahana
Rav Aha	756	
Rav Yehuidai b. R. Nahman	757	
Rav Ahunai Kahana b. Mar R. Papa	761	Rav Dodai b. Rav Nahman (brother of Rav Yehudai, the Gaon of Sura)
	784	Rav Hananiah b. R of Sharsheya
Rav Haninai Kahana b. Mar R. Huna	769	
	771	Rav Malkha b. R. Aha
	773	Rav Rabbah (Abba) b. R. Dodai
Rav Mari ha-Levi b. R. Mesharsheya	774	
Rav Bebai ha-Levi b. Abba of Nehar-Pekod	777	
	781	Rav Shinoi
	782	Rav Haninai Kahana b. R. Abraham
	785	Rav Huna ha-Levi b. R. Issai
Rav Hilai b. R. Mari	788	Rav Manasseh b. Mar Joseph
	796	Rav Isaiah ha-Levi b. Mar R. Abba
Rav Jacob ha-Koen b. R. Mordecai	797	
	798	Rav Joseph b. R. Shila
	804	Rav Kahana b. R. Haninai
Rav Ivomai	810	Rav Ivomai
Rav Ivomai, uncle of his predecessor	811	
	814	Rav Joseph b. R. Abba
Rav Zadok b. Mar R. Jesse (or Ashi)	816	Rav Abraham b. R. Sherira
Rav Hilai b. R. Hanina	818	
Rav Kimoi b. R. Ashi	822	

THE GAONATE IN BABYLONIA

Jewish means of livelihood in Babylon had changed even before the Arab conquest, when Jews began to assume patterns of life similar to those that would later typify the Jews of Europe during the Middle Ages.

SURA		PUMBEDITA
Rav Moses (Mesharsheya) Kahana b. R. Jacob	825	
	828	Rav Joseph b. R. Hiyya
	833	Rav Isaac b. R. Hananiah
Rav Kohen Zedek b. Ivomai	838	
	839	Rav Joseph b. R. Ravi
	842	Rav Paltoi b. R. Abbaye
Rav Sar Shalom b. R. Boaz	848	
Rav Natronai b. R. Hilai } served jointly	853–58	
Rav Amram b. Sheshna		
	857	Mar Rav Aha Kahana b. Rav
	858	Rav Menahem b. R. Joseph b. Hiyya
	860	Rav Mattathias b. Mar Ravi
	869	Rav Abba (Rabbah) b. R. Ammi
Rav Nahshon b. R. Zadok	871	
	872	Rav Zemah b. R. Paltoi
Rav Zemah b. Mar R. Hayyim	879	
Rav Malkha	885	
Rav Hai b. R. Nahshon		
	890	Rav Hai b. David
Rav Hilai b. R. Natronai	896	
	898	Rav Kimoi b. R. Ahai
Rav Shalom b. R. Mishael	904	
	906	Rav Judah b. R. Samuel (grandfather of R. Sherira)
Rav Jacob b. R. Natronai	911	
	917–26	Rav Mevasser Kahana b. R. Kimoi
Rav Yom Tov Kahana b. R. Jacob	924	
	926–36	Rav Kohen Zedek b. R. Joseph (appointed while predecessor was still living)
Rav Saadiah b. R. Joseph (Rav Saadiah Gaon)	928	
	936	Rav Zemah b. R. Kafnai
	938	Rav Hananiah b. R. Judah
Rav Joseph b. R. Jacob	942–44	
	943	Rav Aaron b. R. Joseph ha-Kohen Sargado
	960	Rav Nehemiah b. R. Kohen Zedek
	968	Rav Sherira b. R. Hananiah
Rav Zemah b. R. Isaac (descendant of Paltoi)	988(?)	
Rav Samuel b. Hophni ha-Kohen	997(?)	
	998	Rav Hai b. R. Sherira
Rav Dosa b. R. Saadiah	1013	
Rav Israel b. R. Samuel b. Hophni	1017	
Rav Azariah ha-Kohen (son of R. Israel?)	1034	
Isaac(?)	1037	
	1038–58	Rav Hezekiah b. David (exilarch and gaon)

Heavy taxation, revolutions, riots and insecurity forced the laborer off his land and obliged him to seek refuge in the cities. This process continued during the entire period of Arab rule. In the first half of the ninth century, Rav Moshe

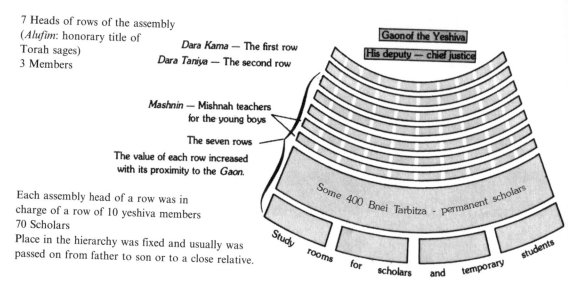

7 Heads of rows of the assembly
(*Alufim*: honorary title of
Torah sages)
3 Members

Dara Kama — The first row
Dara Taniya — The second row

Mashnin — Mishnah teachers
for the young boys

The seven rows
The value of each row increased
with its proximity to the *Gaon*.

Each assembly head of a row was in
charge of a row of 10 yeshiva members
70 Scholars
Place in the hierarchy was fixed and usually was
passed on from father to son or to a close relative.

Gaon of the Yeshiva

His deputy — chief justice

Some 400 Bnei Tarbitza - permanent scholars

Study rooms for scholars and temporary students

THE STRUCTURE OF A YESHIVA

Gaon writes: "In Babylon most people are without land" (*Hemda Genuzah*, 60:65). The small communities and rural settlements diminished, while cities grew and swelled. Jewish population centers disappeared and were replaced by that of Baghdad.

In Baghdad Jewish financial institutions developed to such an extent that their economic influence within the caliphate was considerable. Two Jewish bankers, Joseph b. Phineas and Aaron b. Amram, and their heirs, the sons of Aaron and of Netira, started business operations in the district of Ahwaz (in Persia), later expanding them to trade on an international scale. Documents referring to the two families reveal the extent of their partnership and cooperation in business enterprises. Among their many activities was the lending of money to the vizier of Caliph al Muqtadir, Muhammad ibn Abdullah ibn Yahya (912–913), but there is every indication that they engaged in moneylending prior to this date. They also financed the caliphate, using money deposited with them by Jews and non-Jews and taking as security the tax farming rights in the district of Ahwaz. They engaged in international transfer of funds and were thus able to help in financially supporting the exilarchate and gaonate. Apparently they were the innovators of the *shufatajiyya*, a kind of check-promissory note that could be redeemed by a surrogate.

Even the academies of Sura and Pumbedita could not resist the magnetic pull of Baghdad, and at the end of the ninth century, about 150 years before the waning of the gaonate, they both moved to the city as independent institutions. Each of the academies retained its independence, and preserved its own character, methods of teaching, and public activities. The famous geonim were Rav Saadiah, Rav Samuel b. Hofni and Rav Hai—all residents of Baghdad. However, Babylon could not financially support all its scholars who were taken prisoner in the west, and who, according to legend, brought with them the traditions of the Babylonian Talmud. Poets and grammarians also emigrated to

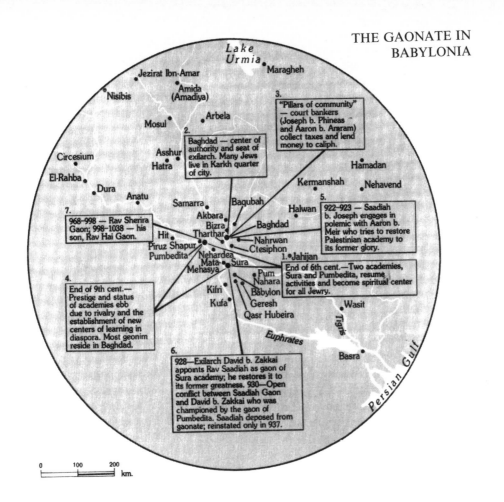

Spain. There was no intrinsic difference between the situation of the Jews in Babylon and their condition in other Islamic countries during the period of Arab rule.

The divisions within the empire of the caliphate and the subsequent founding of emirates in the second half of the eighth century caused basic changes in Jewish life and existence. The following events constituted turning points for the Jews and opened up new opportunities: the separation of Spain from the caliphate in 756 and the subsequent establishing of emirates; Moroccan independence in 788; Tunisian independence in 800; that of Egypt (by Ahmad ibn Tulun) in 868 and

of Persia in 935. There was no basic change in relations within the Jewish community nor was there any change in the affinitive relations between the communities of the Jewish diaspora. They all recognized the authority of the central Jewish organizations, the exilarchate and the gaonate, as powerful elements of unity and instruction for the Jewish people. The Palestinian gaonate was acknowledged as an equal partner with its Babylonian counterpart.

Rav Saadiah (882–942) was among the great geonim. He was born in the Fayum district of Egypt, moved to Palestine and, in 922, to Babylon, where he was appointed gaon of the Sura academy in

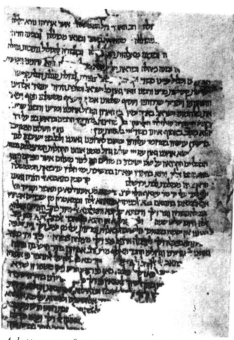

A letter sent from Fustat to R. Hai Gaon.

928. Saadiah waged an unremitting battle against the Karaites and is credited with having stopped their expansion, although his struggle did help them to consolidate as a sect. He was famous for his polemic with the Palestinian gaon, Aaron b. Meir, over the establishing of the Jewish calendar and its festivals, and for his controversy with the exilarch, David b. Zakkai, on matters of authority. His profound spiritual and scholarly activities included works of *halakhah*, exegesis, philosophy, grammar, liturgy, *piyyut* and the translation of the Bible into Arabic.

The Babylonian gaonate came to an end with two great and outstanding figures: Rav Sherira b. Hanina Gaon (c 906–1006), gaon of Pumbedita from 968 to 1006, and his son, Rav Hai Gaon (939–1038). Sherira was among the prolific writers of responsa. One of his famous epistles was written in response to an inquiry from Rabbi Jacob b. Nissim ibn Shahin of the Kairouan community, who asked for information regarding the Mishnah and Talmud. Sherira's reply was a classic work of Jewish historiography in which he listed the generations of Jewish scholars from the men of the Great Sanhedrin until the period of the gaonate. His son and successor, Rav Hai Gaon, gaon of Pumbedita, was one of the great halakhists, a *paytan*, liturgist, judge and writer. With his death, the gaonate in Babylon officially ended.

BONDS BETWEEN BABYLONIA, ERETZ ISRAEL AND THE DIASPORA

THE contacts between the Babylonian geonim and the Diaspora were numerous and widespread. The gaonate became the spirtual and halakhic center for Jewry, issuing instructions and guidance both to the eastern and western Jewish communities. The Diaspora connection was important for establishing a consensus regarding halakhic doctrine. Instrumental in achieving this goal were the emissaries sent by the geonim to the Diaspora—students from the Babylonian academies and Rabbinical judges ordained by the geonim. They were the vanguard of the movement that helped create and maintain the Jewish halakhic consensus during the life span of the Babylonian centers of learning. Ties with

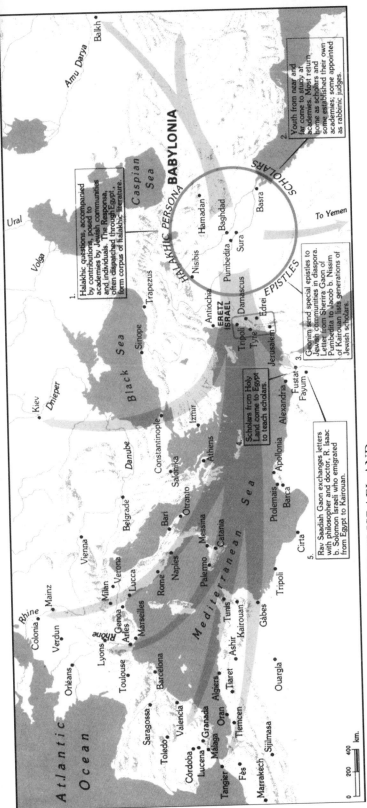

1. Halakhic questions, accompanied by contributions, posed to academies by Jewish communities and individuals. The Responsa, often dispatched through Egypt, form corpus of halakhic literature.

2. Youth from near and far come to study at academies. Most return home as scholars and some established their own academies; some appointed as rabbinic judges.

3. Geonim send special epistles to Jewish communities in diaspora. Letter from Sherira Gaon of Pumbedita to Jacob b. Nissim of Kairouan lists generations of Jewish scholars.

4. Scholars from Holy Land come to Egypt to teach scholars.

5. Rav Saadiah Gaon exchanges letters with philosopher and doctor, R. Isaac b. Solomon Israeli who emigrated from Egypt to Kairouan.

SCHOLARS

EPISTLES

HALAKHIC PERSONA **BABYLONIA**

To Yemen

BONDS BETWEEN BABYLONIA, ERETZ ISRAEL AND
THE DIASPORA

the Diaspora also found expression in the financial support extended by the Jewish communities to the academies, considerable correspondence about which was found in the Cairo Genizah. These relations also helped to foster international commercial ties in which Jews played a very important role.

Other communities, chiefly in Italy and Germany, had very close ties with the academies in Palestine and they adopted the Palestinian (Eretz Israel) tradition primarily in matters of liturgical poetry.

THE GEONIM OF ERETZ ISRAEL; AND ALIYAH TO ERETZ ISRAEL

GENERAL Jawhar conquered Palestine on behalf of the Fatimid caliph al-Mu'izz after subjugating Egypt in 969. The Fatimids were a branch of the Shi'ite sect who ruled over a Muslim population that was predominantly Sunni, and were, therefore, considered foreigners in Palestine, Egypt and Syria. Paltiel (d. 975), a Jew of Oria, served as physician to al-Mu'izz during the conquest of Egypt and was responsible for provisioning the Fatimid army. From his position of influence he was able to assist the Jewish community and when he died he was buried in Eretz Israel. During most of the Fatimid period the rulers employed many Jews, among them the Jewish convert to Islam Yaqub ibn Killis (vizier to Caliph al-Aziz from 978 to 990), who also aided the Jewish community. The Jewish community in Eretz Israel prospered under Fatimid rule, particularly the large communities of Tyre and Sidon. Jerusalem, Tiberias and Ramle were large and important Jewish centers; small Jewish settlements existed in Transjordan. However, prosperity did not last and in 996 the Fatimid throne was occupied by Caliph al-Hakim (996–1021) who persecuted non-Muslims. To make matters worse, there were calamitous earthquakes in 1034 and 1067 in which Ramle was particularly badly hit. Eretz Israel as a whole had its share of al-Hakim's harassment but Jerusalem had a double portion with the caliph's Nubian troops wreaking their violence upon Jews and destroying their synagogues. Many Jews were openly killed and survivors were subjected to hard labor.

It was during this period that the Great Yeshiva of Jerusalem moved to Ramle. From 1024 to 1029 an enormous sum of money was cruelly extorted for the state coffers from the Jews of Jerusalem and from the Karaites who had resided in the city for over a hundred years. Pilgrimage to Jerusalem ceased. Only about fifty Jews resided in the city.

The situation improved somewhat during the reign of al-Hakim's successor, al-Zahir (1021–1034), and the Jewish population slowly recovered. However, the disaster of the Crusades would follow in 1099.

Despite the dangers on land and sea, Jews continued to make pilgrimages to Eretz Israel, especially during the Feast of Tabernacles. Their destinations were chiefly Jerusalem, the Mount of Olives and Hebron. With them came Jews who wished to settle in Jerusalem. Among the settlers were *Avelei Zion* ("Mourners of Zion"), people who "abandoned their families, repudiated their lands of birth, left cities and dwelt in the mountains."

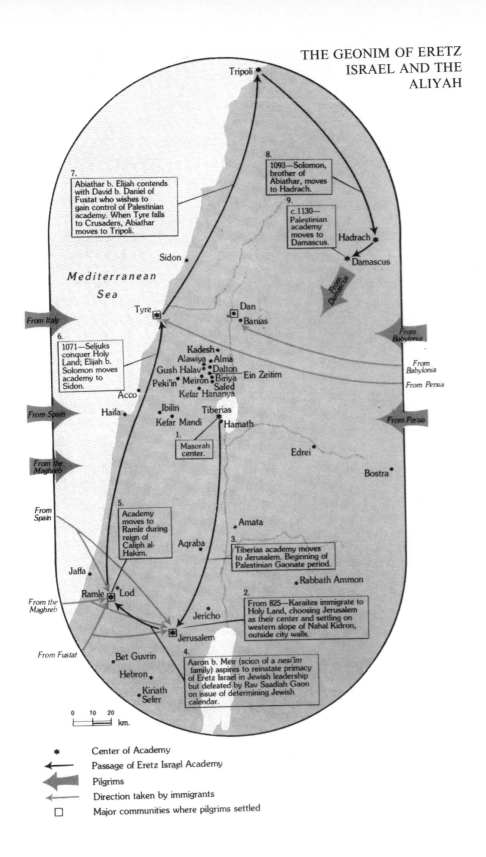

THE GEONIM OF ERETZ
ISRAEL AND THE
ALIYAH

Tripoli

8.
1093—Solomon,
brother of
Abiathar, moves
to Hadrach.

7.
Abiathar b. Elijah contends
with David b. Daniel of
Fustat who wishes to
gain control of Palestinian
academy. When Tyre falls
to Crusaders, Abiathar
moves to Tripoli.

9.
c.1130—
Palestinian
academy
moves to
Damascus.

Hadrach

Damascus

Sidon

Mediterranean
Sea

From Italy

Tyre

Dan
Banias

From
Damascus

From
Babylonia

6.
1071—Seljuks
conquer Holy
Land; Elijah b.
Solomon moves
academy to
Sidon.

Kadesh
Alawiya   Alma
Gush Halav   Dalton
Peki'in Meiron Biriya   Ein Zeitim
Safed
Kefar Hananya

From
Babylonia

From Persia

Acco

From Spain

Haifa

Ibilin
Kefar Mandi

Tiberias
Hamath

From Persia

1.
Masorah
center.

Edrei

Bostra

From
Spain

5.
Academy
moves to
Ramle during
reign of
Caliph al-
Hakim.

Amata

Aqraba

3.
Tiberias academy moves
to Jerusalem. Beginning of
Palestinian Gaonate period.

Jaffa

Rabbath Ammon

From the
Maghreb

Ramle Lod

2.
From 825—Karaites immigrate to
Holy Land, choosing Jerusalem
as their center and settling on
western slope of Nahal Kidron,
outside city walls.

Jericho

From Fustat

Jerusalem

Bet Guvrin

4.
Aaron b. Meir (scion of a nesi'im
family) aspires to reinstate primacy
of Eretz Israel in Jewish leadership
but defeated by Rav Saadiah Gaon
on issue of determining Jewish
calendar.

Hebron

Kiriath
Sefer

0   10   20
              km.

✦   Center of Academy

←   Passage of Eretz Israel Academy

◀   Pilgrims

←   Direction taken by immigrants

☐   Major communities where pilgrims settled

163

c. 844–915	Zemah
c. 915–932	Aaron b. Moses ben Meir
c. 932–934	Isaac (son of Aaron?)
c. 934–948	Ben Meir (brother of Aaron)
c. 948–955	Abraham b. Aaron
c. 955	Aaron
. . .	Joseph ha-Kohen b. Ezron (ruled 2 years)
. . .	. . . (ruled 30 years)
988–?	Samuel b. Joseph ha-Kohen
. . .	Yose b. Samuel
. . .	Shemaiah
1015	Josiah b. Aaron b. Abraham
1020–1027	Solomon b. Joseph ha-Kohen
1027–1051	Solomon b. Judah
1051–1062	Daniel b. Azariah
1062–1083	Elijah b. Solomon b. Joseph ha-Kohen
1084–1109	Abiathar b. Elijah

The gaonate in Palestine.

"People from the east and the west," who "set their sights on settling in Jerusalem, forsook their possessions and renounced the temporal world." The Karaite scholar, Sahl ben Mazliah, relates that "Jerusalem at this time was a haven for all who fled, a comfort for all mourners and a repose for the poor and humble; wherein resided servants of the Lord who were gathered unto her, one from a town, another from a family; wherein resided dirge singers and eulogizers in Hebrew, Persian and Arabic."

Ramle was an important center for Jews from Babylon, known as *Knesset al-Iraquiin*, just as Jews from Eretz Israel who lived in Egypt were known as *Knesset al-Shamiin*. The Karaites had their own synagogue in Ramle. Eretz Israel also served as a transit point for Jews emigrating from east to west.

Bedouin invasions and disturbances in 1029 and 1030 did not hinder Jewish emigration even from Spain, as is attested in a letter sent from Jerusalem to Toledo in 1053 describing the "Sephardim" who resided in Ramle and Jerusalem with their wives and children. Even the Sephardic scholar Joseph ibn Abitur intended to leave Spain and emigrate to Eretz Israel, but one of his friends advised him to go first to Egypt. The story of Rabbi Judah Halevi's *aliyah* typifies a trend among many Jews in those days. Immigrants also came to Eretz Israel from North Africa and Syria. Close ties existed between the Jews of Tripoli and Eretz Israel. Wills from Italy, Egypt and North Africa bear witness to the custom of reinterring the bones of Jewish dead in the Holy Land. There were, however, still many Jews who left Eretz Israel. Those who emigrated to Egypt established communities, such as the one in Alexandria. Many of the émigrés were learned men and graduates of *yeshivot* and it is reasonable to assume that the educational needs of the Diaspora communities were what motivated them to emigrate in order to teach the Torah.

In contrast to the lack of livelihood in Jerusalem, Ramle was a commercial center, and one of the resident Jews held the title of "The Merchants Clerk." He apparently served as a third-party trustee for disputed property or perhaps he was the "Head of the Merchants," as indicated by the Arabic form of this title. In Tyre Jews were engaged in glass blowing and some were shop owners. Here too the Jews had a functionary called "The Merchants Clerk." Tyre was no less an important Jewish center than Ramle, and when the Seljuks conquered Jerusalem in 1071, the Palestinian academy transferred to Tyre. Jews living in the coastal towns seem to have been better off than those residing in the center of the country (excluding Ramle). Jews were engaged in many trades and particularly dyeing, in which they had a monopoly.

Their financial hardships were further aggravated by the burden of taxes; Jerusalem bore the heaviest tax load.

During this period Eretz Israel was renowned for its geonim and its centers of learning. Because of the difficult local conditions, its gaonate was overshadowed by the prosperous Jewish Diaspora of Babylon. A number of geonim in Eretz Israel were members of the ben Meir family, the most important being Aaron b. Meir. The gaon Solomon b. Judah was the head of the community from 1027 to 1051. The gaon Daniel b. Azariah was related to the Babylonian exilarch, David b. Zakkai. The last of the geonim in Eretz Israel were Elijah b. Solomon and his son Abiathar. The latter, who lived during the period of the Crusades, moved to Tripoli where he died in 1109. The Palestinian academy moved to Damascus where it continued to function for about a hundred years under the name "Hatsevi Academy" or "Eretz Hatsevi Academy."

THE JEWS OF NORTH AFRICA 12TH TO 15TH CENTURIES

THE status of the Jews in North Africa as in all other Islamic states was that of a "protected people" (*dhimmi*). The first hundred years of Muslim conquest were rather turbulent; there was no *Pax Islamica*. Naturally this affected Jewish life. During the waning of the Umayyad dynasty and the dawning of the Abbasid rule, a confederation of Berber tribes revolted against the Arab rulers in Kairouan and western Tripolitania. Ibn Rustam, one of the leaders of the revolt, fled and established a new state in central Algeria with its capital at Tiaret. At the same time, another group established a kingdom in the city of Tlemcen. Another Berber tribe established a state in the Tafilalt Oasis, with its capital at Sijilmasa. Despite religious differences, these states became important Jewish centers. Tiaret was the residence of R. Judah ibn Quraysh (Koreish), a well-known ninth-century philologist and renowned author. Jews lived on the island of Jerba, in the region of Jerid to Gabès, and in the area of M'zab, and Ouargla.

When Egypt was conquered and the caliphate established there, Kairouan became "the grand trading center in Africa," as it was designated in a legal document of 978, and a center for Jewish scholars. With the weakening of Fatimid rule in North Africa, government was transferred to the Zirids in Kairouan.

Yusuf ibn Ziri, a Berber and founder of the dynasty, was a loyal servant of the Fatimids in the days when they ruled the

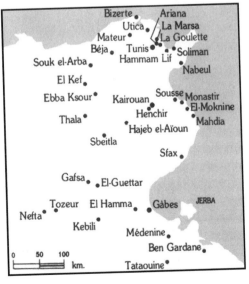

TUNISIA

THE JEWS OF NORTH AFRICA
12TH TO 15TH CENTURIES

Damascus

Jerusalem

Izmir

Athens

M e d i t e r r a n e a n   S e a

Fustat

Nile

N

km.

0   200   400

Alexandria

4. End of 10th cent. — Status of city improves and becomes center for Jewish scholars.

3. Fustat becomes capital of Fatimid Caliphate. 1083–1089—David b. Daniel, head of Fustat academy, strives to impose his authority on Palestinian academy.

Apollonia
Pentapolis
Ptolemais
Barca   Cyrene
Ajdabiyah
Brega
Burion

Taranto

Messina
Catania
Palermo

Labdah
(Lepits Magna)
Misurata
Masallatah
Cirta
Yahudiya

Tunis
JERBA
Tripoli
Jadu

Kairouan
Gàbes

7. 1130–1160 — Almohads establish confederation near Atlas mountains and complete conquest of North Africa. Jews slaughtered and undergo forced conversions; many ostensibly convert to Islam; others, including Maimonides, flee.

2. R. Judah ibn Quraysh (Koreish), author of first comparative study of Semitic languages.

Córdoba
Granada
Málaga
Oran
Ceuta
Tangier   Tlemcen
Algiers
Tiaret
Atlas Mountains
Ashir
Qalat
Bani Hammad

Ouargla

1. Mid. 9th cent. — Berber tribes revolt against Umayyads; establish states whose capitals become centers for Jewish settlement.

5. 1032—City destroyed by Berber sheikh; Jewish activity continues. Some scholars, including *Rif* (Isaac b Jacob Alfasi), establish study centers in Al-Andulas.

Fès
Sijilmasa

Rif
*AL-
MURABITUN*
Marrakech   *Mts.*
Anti-Atlas Mts.

6. 1071—Yusuf ibn Tashfin, leader of Almoravids, imposes large tribute on Jews; many flee to Al-Andulas.

✿   Center of Torah and Jewish life

Berber tribal areas in 9th cent.

Furthest extent of Almohads (al-Muwahhidun)

166

Maghreb. He appointed his sons as governors in various places. Eventually they grew strong and severed their relations with the Fatimids in Cairo, recognizing the sovereignty of the Abbasids in distant Baghdad. Soon they established their city of Ashir and Jews from various places were brought there. Rabbi Sherira Gaon and Rabbi Samuel b. Hofni corresponded with Jews of Ashir. Kairouan was not exclusive in its special status as a center for Torah learning and Jewish life. In southern Tunisia the city of Gabès was famous as a "mother city in Israel" and a Torah center. Fès's status as a Torah center was determined by the residence there in the eleventh century of R. Isaac b. Jacob, known as Alfasi, author of the *Rif* (born c. 1013 in Qal'at Bani Hammad in Algeria, and died 1103 at Lucena in southern Spain). Alfasi was one of the architects of Torah study in Spain and among Jewry in general.

In 1032 Fès was captured by one of the Berber sheikhs who destroyed the town and its Jewish quarter and massacred many of its Jews. However, neither this

EGYPT

MOROCCO

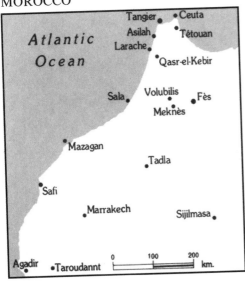

disaster nor those that preceded or succeeded it arrested Jewish activity. The scholars of Fès continued to correspond with the geonim of Babylon on matters of *halakhah* and the Babylonian geonim, Rabbi Sherira, Rabbi Hai and Rabbi Samuel b. Hofni would send their responsa to "Abraham" or "Tanhum." It is possible that these two were heads of the community and its judges. Several important scholars from Fès moved to Spain where they were among the founders of Torah study centers. The Muslims of that period saw Fès as a Jewish town. Even the Jews of Tiaret and Sijilmasa maintained contact with Babylon and the geonim of Palestine. Berber troops, Umayyad armies from Spain, and Fatimid soldiers caused great destruction in these towns. Despite this, however, there was a resurgence of Jews in these towns.

Many engaged in international trade with distant lands. Perhaps the geographical importance of these towns contributed to continuing Jewish settlement. Kairouan played a central role in Jewish relations and contact with Babylon.

In northwestern Africa a number of Berber tribes joined forces to form a religious, social, and military confederation called al-Murabitun, known as the Almoravids, whose doctrines favored a more radical religious orthodoxy. Their leader, Yusuf ibn Tashfin (who founded Marrakech in 1062), set out on campaigns of conquest in Africa and Spain. In 1071 he forced the Jews in his North African domain to pay a huge tribute of 100,000 dinars. Such taxation may explain why so many Jews left North Africa for Spain. However, the rule of the Almoravids cannot be compared to the reign of the Muwahhidun (Almohads), who emerged in the twelfth century and destroyed many Jewish communities.

MUSLIM SPAIN: ECONOMY AND CENTERS OF JEWISH SETTLEMENT 10TH TO 12TH CENTURIES

AL ANDALUS, as the Iberian Peninsula was known, began to prosper during the reign of 'Abd al-Rahman II (822–852).

An ivory vessel from 10th-century Spain. The original is in the museum of the Hispanic Society in New York.

Despite many revolts he built a network of fortifications to defend his kingdom against the Christian incursions and concluded treaties with various Muslim princes. Thus he was able to withstand the Norman invasions of the coastal cities. He also found time to devote to cultural matters and began constructing public building in Córdoba and other places. These buildings are the pride of Spain to this very day. Córdoba also became a center for Jewish spiritual and cultural activity.

At the end of the tenth century, Jacob and Joseph ibn Jau were appointed heads of the Jewish community. Jacob was appointed *nasi* (leader) of all the Jews living in Muslim Spain and in those areas of Morocco and Algeria that were under Muslim Spanish suzerainty. The brothers were wealthy silk merchants and manufacturers. Jacob was appointed tax collector and was allowed to appoint rabbinical judges. Hisdai ibn Shaprut was another major figure in Spanish Jewish life.

Muslim Granada was consolidated in the eleventh century and included the

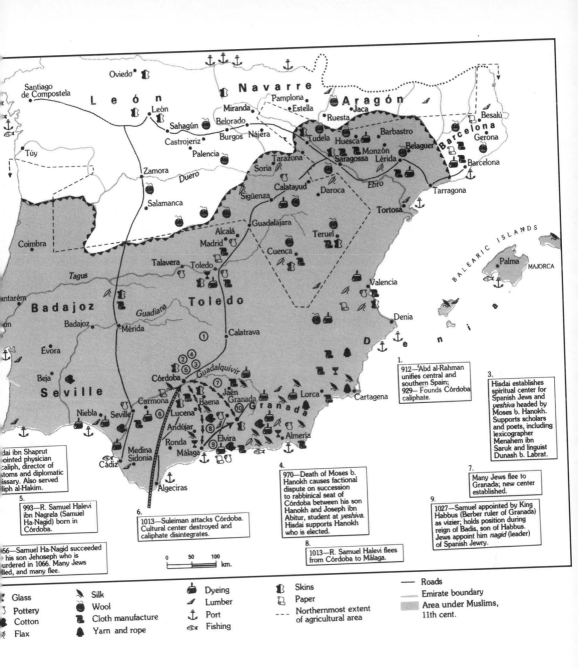

Area under Muslims, 11th cent.

Labels on map (cities, regions):

Santiago de Compostela · Oviedo · León · Navarre · Aragón · Barcelona · Pamplona · Estella · Jaca · Besalú · Gerona · Miranda · Ruesta · Tudela · Huesca · Barbastro · Belaguer · Sahagún · Belorado · Nájera · Monzón · Lérida · Castrojeriz · Burgos · Tarazona · Saragossa · Palencia · Soria · Calatayud · Daroca · Ebro · Tortosa · Tarragona · Zamora · Sigüenza · Duero · Teruel · Túy · Salamanca · Alcalá · Guadalajara · Coimbra · Madrid · Cuenca · Valencia · Talavera · Toledo · Denia · Tagus · Badajoz · Toledo · Guadiana · Calatrava · Mérida · Évora · Córdoba · Guadalquivir · Lorca · Beja · Carmona · Jaén · Granada · Cartagena · Seville · Lucena · Baena · Niebla · Seville · Andújar · Elvira · Almería · Medina Sidonia · Ronda · Málaga · Cádiz · Algeciras · Balearic Islands · Palma · Majorca

1. 912—'Abd al-Rahman unifies central and southern Spain; 929— Founds Córdoba caliphate.

3. Hisdai establishes spiritual center for Spanish Jews and *yeshiva* headed by Moses b. Hanokh. Supports scholars and poets, including lexicographer Menahem ibn Saruk and linguist Dunash b. Labrat.

...dai ibn Shaprut ...pointed physician ...caliph, director of ...stoms and diplomatic ...issary. Also served ...liph al-Hakim.

5. 993—R. Samuel Halevi ibn Nagrela (Samuel Ha-Nagid) born in Córdoba.

...56—Samuel Ha-Nagid succeeded ... his son Jehoseph who is ...urdered in 1066. Many Jews ...lled, and many flee.

6. 1013—Suleiman attacks Córdoba. Cultural center destroyed and caliphate disintegrates.

4. 970—Death of Moses b. Hanokh causes factional dispute on succession to rabbinical seat of Córdoba between his son Hanokh and Joseph ibn Abitur, student at *yeshiva*. Hisdai supports Hanokh who is elected.

8. 1013—R. Samuel Halevi flees from Córdoba to Málaga.

7. Many Jews flee to Granada; new center established.

9. 1027—Samuel appointed by King Habbus (Berber ruler of Granada) as vizier; holds position during reign of Badis, son of Habbus. Jews appoint him *nagid* (leader) of Spanish Jewry.

0 50 100 km.

Glass · Pottery · Cotton · Flax · Silk · Wool · Cloth manufacture · Yarn and rope · Dyeing · Lumber · Port · Fishing · Skins · Paper · Northernmost extent of agricultural area · Roads · Emirate boundary · Area under Muslims, 11th cent.

whole of the southeastern part of the peninsula. Rabbi Samuel b. Joseph Ha-levi ibn Nagrela (Samuel Ha-Nagid) was an outstanding leader of the Jewish community in Granada. Born in Córdoba in 993 he fled to Málaga in 1013 in the wake of the Berber conquest. He had a fine Jewish and general education, including training in Arabic, and soon made a name for himself as a teacher and Arabic stylist to whom people turned for letter-writing skills. Samuel was appointed to the staff of the vizier of Granada. One of his first tasks in Granada was to collect taxes in some of the districts. He soon succeeded in obtaining an important position in King Habbus's administration as minister of finance and later as vizier. His position at court was strengthened during the reign of Badis, son and successor of Habbus. Samuel successfully commanded the king's army from 1038 to 1056. Samuel viewed all his military victories as signs of divine intervention and all of his activities as part of a divine mission in which he was an emissary sent by the Lord to defend his people. Consequently he fulfilled his tasks with a fervor and loyalty uncommon among officials at court. Samuel corresponded with Rabbi Nissim of Kairouan (whose daughter married his eldest son Jehoseph), with R. Hai Gaon, with the heads of the *yeshivot* in Palestine and with the heads of the Jewish community in Egypt. In Spain he maintained a close relationship with, and was patron of, the *paytan* Isaac ibn Khalfun and the poet and philosopher Solomon ibn Gabirol. He exchanged poetry with both of them. In addition to being a poet he was a halakhist and composed a major work in *halakhah*. He was also known as a philologist and writer of theological tracts. During his lifetime there was economic prosperity in Granada, which had many Jewish merchants and craftsmen. The Jewish population of Granada was estimated at five thousand and it was

no wonder that the Muslims called the city *Gharnatat al-Yahud* ("Granada of the Jews"). The yeshiva at Granada had many well-known scholars.

In the Muslim area of northern Spain there was a large concentration of Jews in Saragossa. The rulers were the Banu Tujib dynasty, who maintained proper relations with their Christian neighbors in the city. In the second half of the eleventh century a new family, Banu Hud, came to power, originating from Yemen. The city became one of the richest in all of Spain. Most of the Jewish inhabitants were either furriers or were engaged in the flax, clothing and leather industries. In the environs of Saragossa Jews were engaged in farming and viticulture; they traded with the merchants of Barcelona and southern France. The community had a great number of Torah scholars, doctors and intellectuals. At the ruling court there was an atmosphere of tolerance and Jews found ways of serving these rulers. In the 1030s Abu Ishaq Jekuthiel b. Isaac ibn Hasan served as adviser to King Mundhir II. Jekuthiel had a broad Torah and secular education. He was patron to Torah scholars and poets. In 1039 he was executed by the last of the Banu Tujib kings.

RECONQUISTA: THE RECONQUEST
UNTIL THE MID-12TH CENTURY

INDECISIVE wars and battles were fought over a period of several hundred years between Muslim and Christian princes. Charlemagne helped the Christians create a frontier buffer zone, Marca Hispanica, between Muslim Spain and Carolingian France. Barcelona was one of the first cities in which Christian rule was con-

solidated. It was in this district that Jews developed extensive operations in commerce and in leasing of fields and vineyards. Landholding was either by outright ownership (*allodium*) or by tenancy. Jews often made land transactions with bishops or monastaries, and also with diocesan and parochial

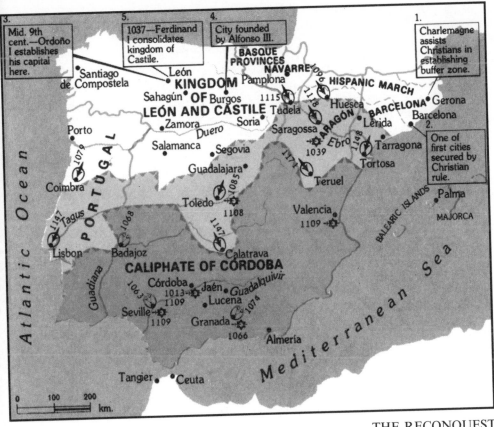

3. Mid. 9th cent.—Ordoño I establishes his capital here.

5. 1037—Ferdinand I consolidates kingdom of Castile.

4. City founded by Alfonso III.

1. Charlemagne assists Christians in establishing buffer zone.

2. One of first cities secured by Christian rule.

⊕ Conquest of city by Christians, with date
⊖ Tribute paid to Christians
✡ Massacres of Jews by Almohads and Almoravids

churches, the deeds of transfer being written in Hebrew or at least bearing a Hebrew signature. Jews developed various spheres of economic activity in the city of Barcelona and in their own neighborhood, which came to an end during riots in 1391. In addition to the official writs of privileges which regulated Jewish life in Barcelona, there was a more ancient writ known as the Book of Usatges (Book of Usage) which defined the legal status of the Jews and was composed between 1053 and 1071. Among its many laws was one which stated that the punishment for doing bodily harm to a Jew or for killing him would be determined by the king. This meant that the Jews were dependent upon the good will of the ruler. The church councils of Gerona (1067–1068 and 1078) forced Jews who purchased land from Christians to pay a regular tithe to the church.

Ordoño I (850–866) invaded the region between Salamanca and Saragossa. He was very active in resettling the north of Spain and chose León as his capital. His son, Alfonso III (866–909), continued his father's policies and conquered territories in northern Portugal only to lose them to the Muslims. Internal dissension and factionalism forced him to halt the

171

Christian advance. Perhaps he was also deterred by the Muslim king 'Abd al-Rahman III, who was then the ruler of Andalusia. During the reign of King Ramiro II (931–950), Count Fernan González of Castile rebelled against the king and from this point the history of Castile actually begins. Ramiro concluded a pact with Tota, queen of Navarre (who negotiated with Hisdai ibn Shaprut). The Jews in Castile were also apparently dependent upon the good will of the ruler. Killing or wounding a Jew was punishable by a heavy fine payable to the ruler, as though the Jews were his property. In fact the regulations in this matter differed in each city and district. The special circumstances of Jewish life are exemplified by the riot of the inhabitants of Castrojeriz in 1035. In order to develop the district, King Sancho III the Great encouraged the Jews to settle on the land, despite the opposition of the Christian population in the district. Upon his death in 1035 the Christian inhabitants of Castrojeriz broke into one of the king's estates in Burgos, killing sixty Jews. Jewish settlement in the rural districts not only required the approval of the ruler but was dependent upon his physical ability to protect these settlers. The settlements themselves were on royal lands and were known as *villa nova de Judaeis*. Such settlements were established in Navarre and Aragón.

Ferdinand I unified Castile, León and Galicia under one crown (1037), thus creating the largest kingdom in Spain. The reign of his second son, Alfonso VI (1065–1109), coincided with the momentous events in Europe during the First Crusade. During this period the behavior toward the Jews in Christian Spain was entirely different from that in the rest of Europe. Alfonso VI, who assumed the title of Emperor of All Spain, carried the battle standard against the Muslims. His preoccupation with the Reconquista, in which he employed French knights, was probably one of the reasons why the Jews were not massacred like their brethren in other parts of Europe.

The services rendered by the Jews to the ruling power stood them in good stead. The Jews of Spain, who were more numerous than their brethren in Ashkenaz (Franco-Germany), remained where they were after the Muslim retreat southward. Those Jews who occupied important posts in the local civil administration of the various Arab emirates were destined later to play a vital role in establishing the rule of the Christian victor.

Alfonso VI defeated the rulers of Seville, Badajoz and Granada and forced them to pay him tribute. He also conquered Coimbra in Portugal and assisted in establishing the Portuguese kingdom.

On 6 May 1085 he captured Toledo and in the terms of capitulation he promised the Muslims that he would honor their rights and their mosques. However, only two generations later the Muslims were forced to leave their dwellings in the city, and the main mosque was converted to a church (1102). Twelfth-century documents from Toledo attest to a sparse Muslim population. The Jews of the city continued to live in the southwest corner of the city which also contained a fortress. (Remains of Jewish edifices have been preserved to this day.)

The Jews were fortunate in having a personality like Joseph ha-Nasi Ferrizuel (called Cidellus). He held office in the royal court and was active on their behalf. He was born in Cabra in the kingdom of Granada, and became the physician of Alfonso VI, and *nasi* of all the Jews residing in Alfonso's kingdom.

He assisted the Jews of Guadalajara when the city was captured by Alfonso and also aided the Jews who migrated from the south to the north. The large estates in and around Toledo that he owned were confiscated by the crown after his death. Extant royal documents bear his signature in Latin characters as a witness verifying the contents of the document. His signature also appears on a purely political document, *Privilegium immunitatis*, dated 1110, one year after the death of Alfonso VI. Joseph adopted a firm stand regarding internal politics and ruthlessly expelled the Karaites from Castile.

JEWISH COMMUNITIES IN ASHKENAZ UP TO 1096

1. End 10th cent.—Emperors Otto I and Otto II issue edicts subordinating Jews to bishops. They are to reside in separate neighborhoods and enjoy certain privileges.

3. Rabbenu Gershom, c.960-1030, head of *yeshiva* and known as *Me'or ha-Golah* (Light of the Exile). Among his important *takkanot* (regulations) are a ban on bigamy and an order forbidding amending Talmudic texts.

4. Henry II expels Jews who refuse to convert. Among forcibly baptized is son of Rabbenu Gershom.

8. Prince Vratislav II (1061-1092) grants autonomy to Jews.

7. 1090 — Henry IV confirms privileges granted by Ruediger and grants additional ones.

6. 1084 — Bishop Ruediger allocates special neighborhood to Jews; encloses it with wall; grants privileges. Group of Jews arrive from Mainz.

5. Rashi (R. Solomon b. Isaac) studies at *yeshivoth* of Worms and Mainz. 1068— Returns to Troyes and establishes *yeshiva*. Composes commentary on Bible and Talmud.

2. 982—Kalonymus, a Jew whose family moved to Mainz in 917, saves life of Otto II.

POLAND

GERMANY

Magdeburg
Merseburg

LORRAINE (LOTHRINGEN)
Xanten
Neuss
Cologne
Aachen Bonn
Mainz Bamberg
Worms
Trier
Speyer
Regensburg
Metz
Prague

London

Paris
FRANCE
Troyes

Lyons
Milan

BURGUNDY

ITALY

PAPAL STATES

Lucca

Marseilles

CORSICA
Rome

SARDINIA

Danube

HUNGARY

CROATIA

SERBIA

Adriatic Sea

Mediterranean Sea

0   200   400   km.

Otto I "the Great" (936–973), the Holy Roman Emperor, and Otto II (973–983) were favorably disposed toward Jews settling in their empire. In fact these were the formative years of the German Jewish communities. Henry II (1002–1024) at first confirmed the rights of the Jews of Merseburg (1004) in their relations with the bishop of the city. However, in 1012 the Jews of Mainz were expelled. Some say this was due to the incident of the priest Wecelinus converting to Judaism; others relate it to the burning of the Church of the Holy Sepulcher in Jerusalem by the Fatimid caliph al-Hakim. The decree was soon revoked, apparently after the intervention of Rabbi Jacob b. Jekuthiel with Pope Benedict VIII (1012–1024).

Mainz was the capital of the state and it was natural that Jews should have dealings with the ruling authorities in many spheres and that these dealings should affect the Jews in other parts of the state. A Jewish community existed in Mainz in the tenth century and perhaps even slightly earlier. The arrival of Kalonymus and his Lucca family inaugurated a period of efflorescence.

Speyer was ideally situated, not only on the Rhine but also on an old Roman road. The official beginnings of its Jewish community date from the time of Bishop Ruediger (1073–1090), who granted the Jews privileges in 1084. Ruediger was a major supporter of Henry IV in the Investiture Controversy. His successor, Johann (1090–1104), continued his predecessor's policies in his relations with the Jews of Speyer.

The significance of Ruediger's privileges granted to the Jews of Speyer transcends their actual value for the community. They were approved in 1090 by the emperor Henry IV and eventually served as a model for many privileges granted to the Jews by other German rulers and in other European countries. The privileges determined the way of life of the Jews and their relations with their Christian neighbors. From what was allowed the Jews in the privileges we can infer what was forbidden. The Jews were obliged to pay a protection tax. In due course, their legal status was defined as belonging to the crown or the state treasury and this implied their subservience to the crown.

Worms was another important community. Construction of its synagogue began in 1014 and was completed in 1034. Shortly afterwards a Jewish neighborhood is mentioned in documents. The local Jews supported Henry IV in the investiture question and were rewarded together with the other citizens of the city, with tax privileges. The commercial contacts of the Jews of Worms extended to Frankfurt, Goslar and other places. From the mid-eleventh century, Worms and Mainz were the Torah study centers of Ashkenaz.

The Jewish neighborhood in Cologne is first mentioned during the term of office of Archibishop Anno (1056–1075). Apparently the synagogue was built in the second decade of the eleventh century, though archaeological remains support a claim that the building is from the end of the tenth century. Relations between Jews and Christians in Cologne were satisfactory during the eleventh century. Archbishop Anno seems to have used the services of Jewish moneylenders. It is known that many Jews brought their goods to the triannual trade fairs in Cologne. Apparently they had a privilege to do so and must have also had protection and exemption from travel tax.

There were smaller Jewish communities in the district like Trier and Metz. Many Jews in this region owned vineyards. Troyes was known for its leather industry and the Jews of that city were known for their manufacture of parchment.

The spring of 1096 saw a bustle of activity related to the march eastward. Peter the Hermit from Amiens was the chief agitator and preacher for launching

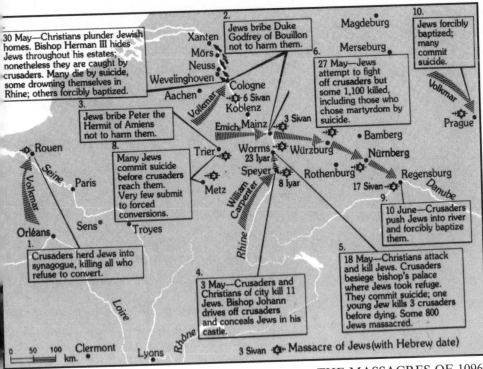

30 May—Christians plunder Jewish homes. Bishop Herman III hides Jews throughout his estates; nonetheless they are caught by crusaders. Many die by suicide, some drowning themselves in Rhine; others forcibly baptized.

2. Jews bribe Duke Godfrey of Bouillon not to harm them.

10. Jews forcibly baptized; many commit suicide.

6. 27 May—Jews attempt to fight off crusaders but some 1,100 killed, including those who chose martyrdom by suicide.

3. Jews bribe Peter the Hermit of Amiens not to harm them.

8. Many Jews commit suicide before crusaders reach them. Very few submit to forced conversions.

1. Crusaders herd Jews into synagogue, killing all who refuse to convert.

9. 10 June—Crusaders push Jews into river and forcibly baptize them.

4. 3 May—Crusaders and Christians of city kill 11 Jews. Bishop Johann drives off crusaders and conceals Jews in his castle.

5. 18 May—Christians attack and kill Jews. Crusaders besiege bishop's palace where Jews took refuge. They commit suicide; one young Jew kills 3 crusaders before dying. Some 800 Jews massacred.

3 Sivan ✡ Massacre of Jews (with Hebrew date)

THE MASSACRES OF 1096: "GEZEROT TATNU" (4856)

the First Crusade. The march of the peasants was the factor that confronted the Jews with a choice between conversion and death. Rabbi Solomon b. Samson, a contemporary Jewish chronicler, describes the massacres of 1096, and cites the cries of the mob: "As they passed through towns where there were Jews they said to one another: 'We are going on a distant journey to seek the [Gentile] house of worship [reference to the Sepulcher of Christ] and to exact vengeance on the Ishmaelites. Yet here are the Jews dwelling in our midst whose forefathers slew him and crucified him without reason. First let us take vengeance on them and destroy them as a people, so that the name of Israel shall no longer be remembered, or so that they should be like us and submit to the son of depravity [Jesus].' "

The Jewish communities, in a state of dreadful apprehensiveness, circulated letters warning of the impending danger and advising on various measures of defense. Peter the Hermit arrived at Trier bearing a letter from the French Jewish communities requesting that their coreligionists in Germany give him and his crusaders money and provisions. The Trier community responded and was thus saved. Perhaps one could infer from this that there was a possibility of avoiding the tragic results by paying a suitable bribe to the leaders of the crusade. However, this could only have succeeded with a leader who had the power to control the mob. Such was not the case with the leader zzof another contingent of crusaders, Godfrey of Bouillon, who was destined to become the first ruler of the crusader kingdom in the Holy Land.

175

Columns of a synagogue in Worms.

A rumor spread that Godfrey had vowed to exact vengeance on the Jews for the blood of Jesus. The Jews of the Rhine communities turned to Kalonymus, the *parnas* of the Mainz Jewish community, asked him to intervene with Henry IV, who was in northern Italy at the time, and requested him to order Godfrey to desist from his plans. However, before Henry's orders reached him, the bloody events took place. Henry ordered his vassals to protect the Jews and guarantee their safety. The Jews of Mainz and Cologne appealed directly to Godfrey and paid him five hundred pieces of silver to dissuade him from his intentions. Godfrey, having succeeded in his extortion, informed the king that he had no intention of harming the Jews.

The first attack on the Jews of France was by Volkmar and his followers, who then went on to Prague, arriving while Vratislav II (1061–1092), king of Bohemia, was fighting in Poland and Cosmas the bishop of Prague was acting as regent. Volkmar gave the Jews of the city a choice between apostasy or death. Many chose to die for *kiddush ha-Shem* (sanctification of God's name); the few that converted later returned to Judaism.

While the Jews of Prague were undergoing their terrible ordeal, the Jewish communities of the Rhine were faced with a similar trial. On 3 May 1096, William, viscount of Melun, surnamed the Carpenter, attacked Speyer at the head of his followers.

The Jewish community was saved by Bishop Johann, who sheltered the Jews in his palace. Those killed were "eleven holy souls who first sanctified their Creator on the holy Sabbath and did not desire to foul the air with their stench. And there was a graceful, prominent woman who slaughtered herself for *kiddush ha-Shem*. And she was the first of the slaughterers and slaughtered amongst all the communities" (*Sefer Gezerot*, p. 25). On 18 May, William and his cohorts arrived at Worms. Here too Bishop Alebrand attempted to protect the Jewish community

"On *Rosh Hodesh* Sivan, the day the Israelites were summoned to Mount Sinai to receive the Torah, those who remained in the bishop's courtyard trembled; the enemies molested them as they had done to the first group, and then put them to the sword. The victims, fortified by the courage of their brethren, died for *kiddush ha-Shem*, extending their necks to the sword. There were some who took their own lives fulfilling the words of the prophet, "when mothers and babes were dashed to death together"; and father fell upon his son. Each his brother did despatch, his kinsman wife and children, also the bridegroom his betrothed, and a merciful woman and her only child. And all with willing hearts accepted the heavenly judgment, making peace with their master they shouted Hear, O Israel! The Lord is our God, the Lord alone."

A. M. Habermann, Sefer Gezerot Ashkenaz ve-Tsarfat, *Jerusalem 1946, p. 29.*

Nov. 1095—At Church [Co]uncil, Pope Urban II calls [a] crusade to forcibly free [Ho]ly Land and redeem Holy [Se]pulcher.

[Chri]stians of Spain, with [th]e's blessing, are [eng]aged in campaigns [agai]nst Muslims; do not [part]icipate in Crusades.

Crusader Kingdom

200   400
km.

1. Following conquest of Palestine (1071) by Seljuk Turks, Alexius I (1048-1118), Byzantine emperor, appeals to pope for aid against them.

THE FIRST CRUSADE 1096 TO 1099

"While sundered children lay twitching in heaps,
They hasten to slaughter the others who wallow in their blood,
Strewn on the floor of Your Sanctuary,
They will seethe before Your eyes forever."

David b. Meshullam of Speyer: God! Be not silent on my blood, *penitential hymn for eve of the Day of Atonement.*

(right) A Crusader seal.

by transferring some of them to his palace. Most of the Jews who were left in the city were massacred. After a week, William informed the Jewish community that he could no longer lay siege to the city and demanded that they submit to baptism. Most of the community was destroyed. A week later William arrived at Mainz, linking up with Count Emich (Emicho) of Leisingen. Emich claimed that divine revelation ordered him either to convert the Jews or to destroy them. The brigands then forced their way into the palace of Archbishop Rothard, who was a relative of Emich. The tragic story of the Jewish community of Mainz is one of the great heroic chapters in the history of the Jewish people. Its members ex-

THE CRUSADER
KINGDOM IN
ERETZ ISRAEL

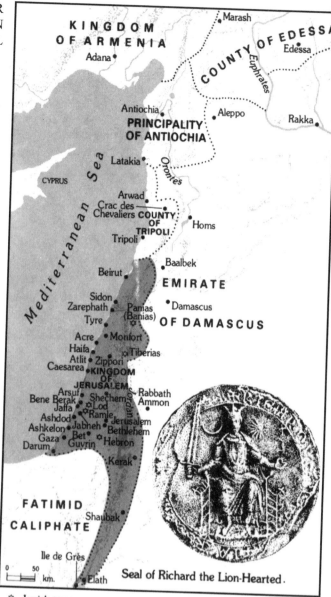

KINGDOM
OF ARMENIA
Adana

Marash

COUNTY OF EDESSA
Edessa

Euphrates

Antiochia • Aleppo
PRINCIPALITY
OF ANTIOCHIA

Rakka

CYPRUS

Latakia

Orontes

Mediterranean Sea

Arwad
Crac des
Chevaliers COUNTY
OF
TRIPOLI
Tripoli

Homs

Baalbek

Beirut

EMIRATE

Sidon
Zarephath
Tyre

Panias
(Banias)

• Damascus

OF DAMASCUS

Acre • Monfort
Haifa
Atlit • Zippori
Caesarea • KINGDOM
OF
JERUSALEM
Arsuf • Shechem
Bene Berak
Jaffa
Lod
Ashdod
Jabneh
Ramle
Ashkelon
Gaza • Bet
Darum
Guvrin
Bethlehem
Hebron

Tiberias

Rabbath
Ammon

Jerusalem

Kerak

FATIMID
CALIPHATE

Shaubak

Ile de Grès

0   50
km.

Elath

Seal of Richard the Lion-Hearted.

✿ Jewish town

emplified the ideology of *kiddush ha-Shem* and whole groups sacrificed themselves as one for their religion and their faith. They saw themselves as a generation chosen to be tested and they were proud to be able to pass the test.

Mainz was not the end of the tragic story. Emich and his followers next moved on to Würzburg and Nürnberg and then to Regensburg, where they arrived on 10 June 1096. Meanwhile, mixed bands of new crusaders composed of English, Flemings and Lotharingians gathered at Cologne, intending to attack the Jews. The archbishop of the city together with some of its citizens at-

178

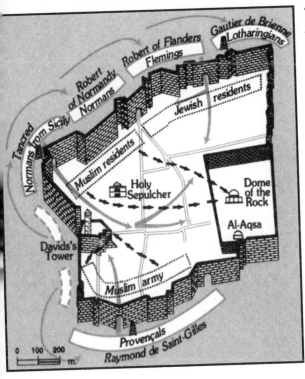

THE CAPTURE OF JERUSALEM
7 JUNE TO 15 JULY 1099

tempted to hide the Jews in the fortress and afterwards to disperse them in the surrounding villages. The brigands contented themselves with plundering Jewish property. For about three weeks the Jewish refugees from Cologne succeeded in finding shelter in their hiding places. However, on 23 June they were discovered in Wevelinghoven, on 24 June in Neuss, and on 30 June in Mörs. Those Jews who did not undergo baptism by force or by consent died for *kiddush ha-Shem*.

During this perod a band of French farmers who had attacked the Jews of Rouen at the end of May reached Cologne. In mid-June the Jewish communities of Trier and Metz were slaughtered.

The destruction of the Ashkenaz communities was almost total. Most of the scholars of Mainz and Worms, the two most important centers, were killed. This was the major reason for the transfer, during this period, of the Jewish cultural center to northern France. The path of the crusaders was a bloody one. Their goal in the Holy Land was Jerusalem and it was there that the Jews, together with the Muslims of the city, fought for their lives. After losing the battle, the entire Jewish community was slaughtered.

FROM CRUSADE TO CRUSADES

ONE whole year elapsed after the fall of Edessa (1144) before a delegation arrived at the court of Pope Eugenius III (1145–1153) in Italy, with a request for aid. In

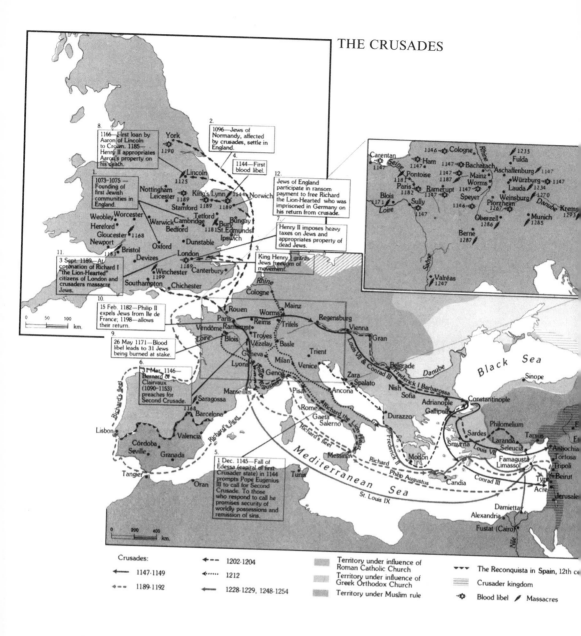

Map labels (clockwise/by region):

8. 1166—First loan by Aaron of Lincoln to Crown. 1185—Henry II appropriates Aaron's property on his death.

2. 1096—Jews of Normandy, affected by crusades, settle in England.

4. 1144—First blood libel.

1. 1073-1075—Founding of first Jewish communities in England.

12. Jews of England participate in ransom payment to free Richard the Lion-Hearted who was imprisoned in Germany on his return from crusade.

Henry II imposes heavy taxes on Jews and appropriates property of dead Jews.

3. King Henry grants Jews freedom of movement.

11. 3 Sept. 1189—At coronation of Richard I "The Lion-Hearted" citizens of London and crusaders massacre Jews.

10. 15 Feb. 1182—Philip II expels Jews from Ile de France; 1198—allows their return.

9. 26 May 1171—Blood libel leads to 31 Jews being burned at stake.

6. 31 Mar. 1146—Bernard of Clairvaux (1090-1153) preaches for Second Crusade.

5. 1 Dec. 1145—Fall of Edessa (capital of first Crusader state) in 1144 prompts Pope Eugenius III to call for Second Crusade. To those who respond to call he promises security of worldly possessions and remission of sins.

Legend:

Crusades:
→ 1147-1149
←·─ 1189-1192
←── 1202-1204
←····· 1212
←── 1228-1229, 1248-1254

Territory under influence of Roman Catholic Church
Territory under influence of Greek Orthodox Church
Territory under Muslim rule

▼▼▼ The Reconquista in Spain, 12th ce[n]
≡ Crusader kingdom
⚙ Blood libel ✦ Massacres

December 1145 the pope issued a bull calling for a Second Crusade and promised those who answered the call an abeyance of their debts and cancellation of the interest. This cancellation particularly affected Jews engaged in money-lending. The pope also declared that participation in the crusade was equivalent to a "sacrament of repentance" and anyone joining a crusade who in his heart repented of his sins would be purified and absolved from the punishment due for those sins. However, there was little response until Bernard of Clairvaux became active. He appeared before a large assembly of French nobles including King Louis VII at Vézelay on 31 March 1146. His rhetoric electrified the assembly, who soon pledged to take up the cross. He continued preaching the crusade for about a year in the Rhenish towns and in 1147 persuaded the German

ing Conrad III (1138–1152) to take up
the cross. During this period a fanatical
Cistercian monk called Rudolf was stirring the masses of the Rhineland to
massacre Jews.

Once again the Jewish communities
faced a repetition of the massacres of
1096. This time, however, the ecclesiastical and political heads of state intervened, fearing that unbridled mob
violence might turn against them. They
appealed to Bernard of Clairvaux as the
person responsible for the crusade propaganda and as a man of stature and
authority in the Christian world in
general and in the Cistercian order—of
which Rudolf was a member—in particular. They urged him to act responsibly
and sagaciously in order to protect the
Jews. Jewish sources express an appreciation for the religious feeling that motivated Bernard to protect the Jews.
Unfortunately he did not succeed in
saving many Jewish communities; the
massacre of French Jewry (in the towns
of Ham, Sully, Carentan and Ramerupt)
had begun before the crusaders reached
Germany. Rabbenu Tam (Jacob b. Meir
Tam, c. 1100–1171) was among the
wounded at Ramerupt. It was fortunate
that Louis VII of France did not heed the
counsel of Peter the Venerable, abbot of
Cluny (c. 1092–1156), who, in a vitriolic
and vituperative letter unprecedented
even for the Middle Ages, called for the
total annihilation of the Jews.

In England King Stephen (1135–1154)
protected the Jews. In Germany the
Jewish communities attacked were those
of Cologne (only a few Jews were saved
by hiding in the Wolkenburg fortress),
Worms, Mainz, Bacharach, Würzburg
and Aschaffenburg. The rioting against
the Jews ended in the summer of 1147.

The Jewish communities of France
continued to be persecuted in the period

Seal of Emperor Frederick Barbarossa.

between the Second and Third crusades.
An example was the blood libel against
the Jewish community of Blois in 1171.
In 1182 the Jews were expelled from the
kingdom of France by King Philip
Augustus (1180–1223). All debts owed
by Christians to Jews were annulled and
the Jews were forced to pay a fifth of the
debt to the state treasury. In 1198 Philip
Augustus authorized their return and
established a special department in his
treasury to deal with the Jews, as had
been done in England.

The crusader defeat at the battle of
Hittin (1178) and Saladin's capture of
Jerusalem aroused enthusiasm for a new
crusade (the Third). Popes Gregory VIII
(1187) and Clement III (1187–1191)
called for Christians to save the Holy
Land. Once again the crusade had its
preacher, Henry of Albano, a monk from
the Clairvaux monastery, who was aided
by the monk Joachim of Fiore, who spent
the winter of 1190–1191 in Palestine. The
Jews of Mainz, Speyer, Worms, Strasbourg and Würzburg, through which the
crusaders were destined to pass, decided
to abandon these towns for places
removed from the crusader route. Fre-

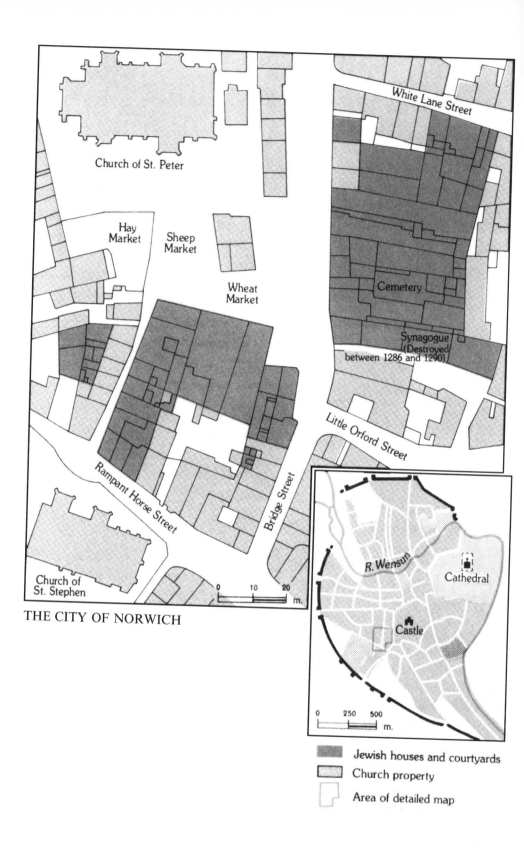

Church of St. Peter

Hay
Market

Sheep
Market

Wheat
Market

Cemetery

Synagogue
(Destroyed
between 1286 and 1290)

White Lane Street

Little Orford Street

Rampant Horse Street

Bridge Street

Church of
St. Stephen

THE CITY OF NORWICH

R. Wensun

Cathedral

Castle

0   250   500
        m.

0   10   20
              m.

Jewish houses and courtyards

Church property

Area of detailed map

Caricature of English Jews from document dated 1233 showing Isaac son of Jurnet of Norwich (with crown) and members of his household.

derick I Barbarossa (emperor 1152–1190) and his son Duke Frederick of Swabia protected the Jews. Even the church intervened on their behalf and undoubtedly both these factors were instrumental in saving the Jews.

In England the crusade was closely linked to the personality of King Richard I "the Lion Hearted" (1189–1199). During an eight-month period (in 1189–1190) the Jews of England suffered from a wave of massacres. Most of the London Jewish community was destroyed. In February–March 1190 most of the rural Jewish communities were destroyed. The massacres were well organized and presaged the eventual expulsion of the Jews from England.

The Fourth Crusade (1202–1204), initiated by Pope Innocent III (1198–1216), ended without achieving its goal. Innocent had hoped that the crusade would bring the Greek Orthodox Church back into the Catholic fold. He saw it as "a return of Samaria to Zion," but his hopes were not fulfilled. This crusade set out for Constantinople but was redirected to Egypt by the Venetians in order to settle some political scores. After this crusade, Germany was endangered by the Children's Crusade (1212), which marched through northern France and the lower Rhineland. The crusade ended dreadfully, as unscrupulous merchants sold the children as slaves in Egypt.

The Fifth Crusade (April 1217 to July 1221), the goal of which was to free the Christians in Muslim captivity, was also unsuccessful. Frederick II (1198–1250) and John of England (1199–1216) were both supposed to participate in the Sixth Crusade but only Frederick arrived in the Holy Land some years later (1228) and stayed in Jerusalem. In 1248 Louis IX (St. Louis, king of France 1226–1270) led the Seventh and last crusade which was also unsuccessful. The Jews of Europe were no sooner free from the nightmare of the crusades than they found other disasters in store for them.

B. UNTIL THE BLACK DEATH

BLOOD LIBELS

ENGLAND had the first recorded case of blood libel, but it was closely followed by other European countries, and the notion even spread to Islamic countries. A libel case occurred in England in 1144 at Norwich where it was alleged that the Jews of the town bought a Christian child named William (who was apparently an epileptic and died after one of his fits) before Easter, allegedly tortured him and then killed him.

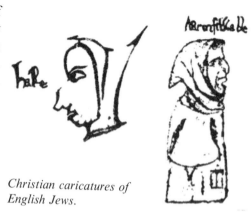

Christian caricatures of English Jews.

The number of libel incidents increased and the emperor of Germany, Frederick II, finally decided to clarify the matter. Consulting with decent and learned Jewish converts to Christianity, he initiated an enquiry as to whether Jews used blood for ritual purposes. The council of the converts concluded that they did not, and Frederick published a statement to this effect. In 1247 Pope Innocent IV issued a bull denouncing blood libels against the Jews. However, the bull did not succeed in eliminating further occurrences.

Pope Gregory X (1271–1276) vigorously combated blood libel, adding a special clause to the Bull of Protection of 1272 (*Sicut Judaeis*).

In 1343 an attempt was made to sell a Christian child born out of wedlock to the head of the Jewish community in Brünn. A similar offer was made in 1699 to Meyer Goldschmidt, the Jewish court jeweler to the king of Denmark.

In 1540 Pope Paul III (1534–1549) issued a bull (*Licet Judaeis*) addressed to the bishops of Poland, Bohemia and Hungary, in which he rejected the allegation that Jews used the blood of Christian children.

There were two major blood libels whose repercussions spread far beyond the place at which they occurred. One concerned Simon of Trent (1475) who was beatified in the eighteenth century and whose beatification was canceled in 1965 by Pope Paul VI. The second libel was that of the "Holy Child of Laguardia" in Spain (1490–1491) whose body was never found. In this libel Jews and conversos were accused of attempting to bring about the annihilation of Christianity, the Inquisition and the inquisitor Tomás de Torquemada by means of the sorcerous use of a child's heart.

Another form of libel was the desecration of the host; Jews were accused of stealing the holy wafer and using it in sorcerous ritual in order to destroy Christianity. Such a libel occurred in 1168 at Saragossa, Spain.

The poisoning of drinking wells was another accusation leveled at the Jews (1320–1321). Europe was rife with these libels, all of which ended tragically for the Jewish people.

THE TRAVELS OF BENJAMIN OF TUDELA 1160 TO 1173

BENJAMIN OF TUDELA was a merchant-traveler who set out on a journey to Palestine either in 1159 or in 1160, returning to Spain in 1172–1173. His book *Sefer ha-Massa'ot* (Book of Travels) contains a vivid description of his travels. In every city that he visited he sought out the Jewish community, enquiring about the life of the Jews in the East, and his account became a major source for the history of that community. Benjamin visited the Holy Land during the period of Crusader rule, meeting a number of Jews, some of them in Jerusalem. After Benjamin had shown the way, and until the time of Judah al-Harizi, a considerable number of Jewish pilgrims from Spain and Ashkenaz visited Palestine, their courage bolstered by a passionate yearning for the Holy Land and the belief that their pilgrimage would hasten the coming of the Redemption. A pupil of the Ramban (Nahmanides,

Memorial plaque to R. Benjamin in the city of Tudela.

(below) Decorated opening pages of the portion Shelah Lekha *(Num. 13–15). Egypt, 11th century.*

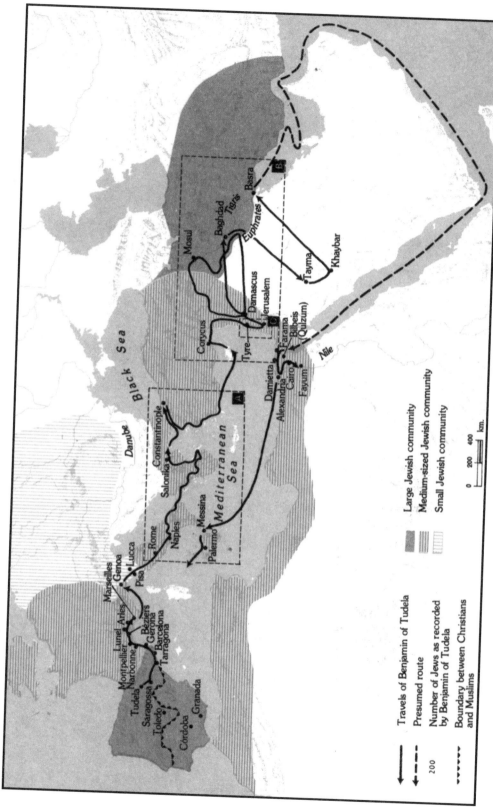

THE TRAVELS OF BENJAMIN OF TUDELA
1160–1173

Travels of Benjamin of Tudela

Presumed route

200 — Number of Jews as recorded by Benjamin of Tudela

Boundary between Christians and Muslims

Large Jewish community

Medium-sized Jewish community

Small Jewish community

0 200 400
km.

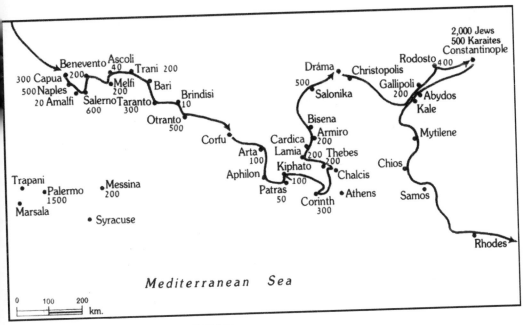

IN ITALY, GREECE AND TURKEY

IN THE
HOLY LAND

IN THE NEAR EAST

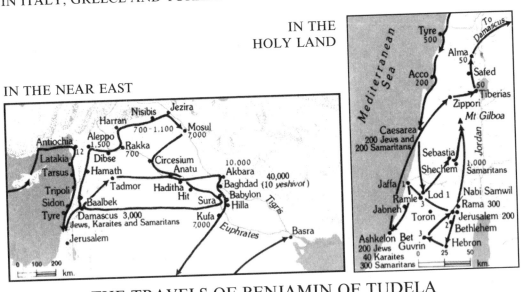

THE TRAVELS OF BENJAMIN OF TUDELA

1194–1270) wrote: "Children of Israel— Torah scholars and pious men of action from all four points of the compass, this one from a city, the other from a family—every man whose heart was prompted to generosity, to a spirit of sanctity and purification and affection for all that is holy—comes to Eretz Israel, and to them the Messiah will reveal himself....And now, many are awakened and volunteer to go to Eretz Israel. And many think that we are approaching the coming of the Redeemer" (A. Yaari: *Massa'ot Eretz Israel*).

JEWISH COMMUNITIES IN THE HOLY LAND
12TH TO 14TH CENTURIES

THE continuous arrival of Christians from Europe did not substantially alter the life style of the country, since they did not establish permanent settlements. The land was desolate and even the crusaders' seignorial system was unable to provide adequate livelihood. During the Crusader period there were a number of rural Jewish settlements which had probably already been established during or before the Arab period. In the second half of the twelfth century Jews were living in Tiberias, the capital of the "Principality of Galilee," and in Safed, the important stronghold of Galilee. Both these cities were surrounded by Jewish villages.

Until Saladin's conquest of Jerusalem, Jews, with the exception of a few families, were forbidden to reside in the city. Nevertheless, when Benjamin of Tudela visited Jerusalem he found Jews engaged in the craft of dyeing, for which they had

Interior of the Ramban synagogue with restored pillars.

The synagogue established by Nahmanides upon his arrival in Jerusalem (apparently a Crusader structure).

purchased a monopoly from the king. These Jews resided either near the king's palace or near the Citadel (David's Tower).

Tyre, Sidon and Ashkelon had the largest Jewish communities in the country. According to Benjamin of Tudela, about five hundred Jews resided in Tyre and two hundred in Ashkelon. Karaites and Samaritans also resided in these cities. Acre, Beirut and Caesarea also had a substantial Jewish population. The crusader conquest opened a period of economic development from which the Jews benefited. Various crafts constituted their major source of income. (In Tyre, for instance, Jews manufactured glass and were tradesmen.) The settlers in the reconstituted *yishuv* (the Jewish population in Eretz Israel) continued to maintain contact with their countries of origin, from where they had come in the

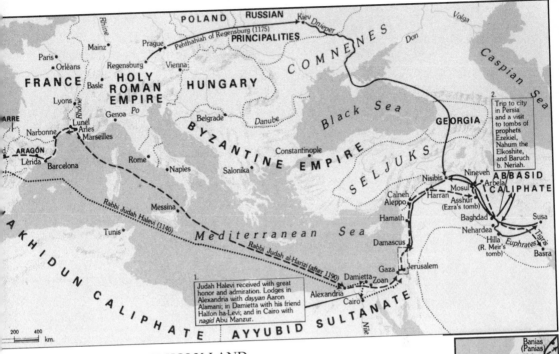

IMMIGRATION TO THE HOLY LAND
12TH CENTURY

wake of the crusaders. The importance of Rabbi Judah Halevi's *aliyah* (immigration) lies not only in its indication of a yearning for Eretz Israel but also in its illustration of the possibility of putting that yearning into practice.

Benjamin of Tudela was the first Jewish traveler to reach the Holy Land in the 1160s. In about 1175 Pethahiah of Regensburg set out on his journey to Eretz Israel. The *aliyah* in 1209 of a group of rabbis and their pupils, headed by Rabbi Samson b. Abraham of Sens, gave a considerable impetus to the revival of the *yishuv*. In 1216 Judah al-Harizi

A section of a sea-poem by Judah Halevi, describing the hardships en route to the Holy Land. Translated by Nina Salaman, Selected Poems of Jehudah Halevi, *Philadelphia 1924. p. 30.*

Call greeting unto daughters and kindred,
Peace to brothers and to sisters,
From the captive of hope who is possessed
By the sea, and hath placed his spirit in the hand of the winds,
Thrust by the hand of the west into the hand of the east:
This one passeth to lead on, and that one to thrust back.
Between him and death is but a step,
Aye, between them but the thickness of a plank;
Buried alive in a coffin of wood,
Upon no floor, with no four cubits of earth, nor even with less.
He sitteth—he cannot stand upon his feet,
He lieth down—he cannot stretch them forth;
Sick and afraid because of the heathen
And because of the marauders and the winds.
The pilot and the mariner, and all their rabble—
They are the rulers and captains there.

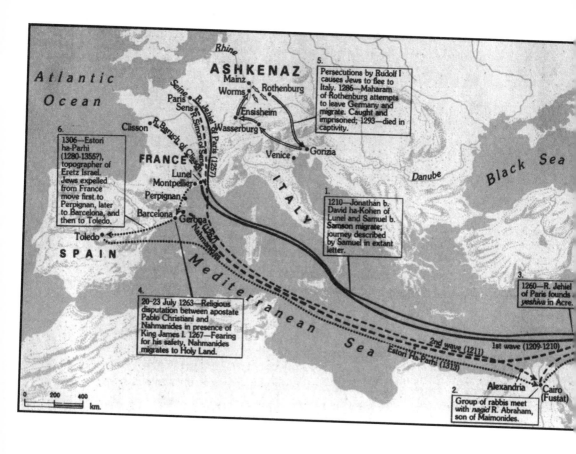

Rhine

ASHKENAZ

Mainz
Worms
Rothenburg
Paris
Sens
Ensisheim
Wasserburg

5. Persecutions by Rudolf I causes Jews to flee to Italy. 1286—Maharam of Rothenburg attempts to leave Germany and migrate. Caught and imprisoned; 1293—died in captivity.

Clisson

6. 1306—Estori ha-Parhi (1280-1355?), topographer of Eretz Israel. Jews expelled from France move first to Perpignan, later to Barcelona, and then to Toledo.

FRANCE

Lunel
Montpellier
Perpignan
Barcelona
Gerona

Venice
Gorizia

ITALY

Danube

Black Sea

Toledo

SPAIN

1. 1210—Jonathan b. David ha-Kohen of Lunel and Samuel b. Samson migrate; journey described by Samuel in extant letter.

Mediterranean Sea

4. 20-23 July 1263—Religious disputation between apostate Pablo Christiani and Nahmanides in presence of King James I. 1267—Fearing for his safety, Nahmanides migrates to Holy Land.

3. 1260—R. Jehiel of Paris founds yeshiva in Acre.

2nd wave (1211)
1st wave (1209-1210)
Estori Ha-Parhi (1315)

Alexandria
Cairo (Fustat)

2. Group of rabbis meet with nagid R. Abraham, son of Maimonides.

0   200   400   km.

was on a visit to the Holy Land and met "the group who came from France," headed by Rabbi Joseph b. Baruch of Clisson and his brother Meir. The Disputation of Paris (1240) and the public burning of the Talmud caused Rabbi Jehiel of Paris and his son to migrate, while the Barcelona Disputation in 1263 caused the Ramban (Nahmanides) to migrate in 1267.

When Rudolf I of Hapsburg, king of Germany, attempted to assert royal authority over the Jews through additional taxation, thousands of Jews, led by the Maharam (Rabbi Meir b. Baruch of Rothenburg), decided to leave Germany. In 1286 Rudolf issued orders to prevent this emigration; the Maharam was arrested while attempting to leave and was delivered to Rudolf who had him im-

prisoned. Rudolf demanded a huge ransom for the Maharam. But the latter refused to be ransomed on the grounds that this would serve as a precedent for the authorities to imprison rabbis and leaders of the community in order to extort large sums of money from them. He died in prison in 1293.

Jews also migrated to the Holy Land from North Africa and Egypt. Ashkelon was the focus for this *aliyah*. In 1209–1210 the Babylonian exilarch visited Eretz Israel (possibly David b. Zakkai II, exilarch in Mosul). From his visit we learn that Safed was a "state," that is, the center of Jewish settlement in the Galilee. Little is known about the Jewish community in Tiberias; Benjamin of Tudela described it as having "about fifty Jewish families." An old tradition relates that

The map contains the following labels:

- Tyre
- 4. 1318–1325 — R. Jacob Sikili and Shem Tov b. Avraham ibn Gaon immigrate to Holy Land.
- Crusaders [...] Acre during [...] rusade. [...] permits [...] ans to visit [...] laces in [...] em.
- Gush Halav
- Safed
- Acco (Acre)
- l of Paris
- Tiberias
- Qarne Hittim
- Nazareth
- 1. 1187—Saladin defeats Crusaders. Jerusalem falls to Muslims and Crusaders succeed in holding only narrow coastal strip.
- Bet Shean
- Caesarea
- Jordan
- Shechem
- E R E T Z
- Jaffa
- I S R A E L
- Estori Ha-Parhi
- Bethlehem
- Jerusalem
- 3.
- shkelon
- 1229—Frederick II takes control of Jerusalem and Bethlehem with corridor to Jaffa, and Nazareth with corridor to Acre.
- 10 20 km.

Depiction of a sea voyage.

the disciples of Maimonides, who died in Fustat in 1204, brought his remains for reburial in Tiberias. Tiberias had favorable conditions for Jews to settle and for the revival of its *yishuv.*

The beginning of the thirteenth century saw a strengthening of the Jewish community in Jerusalem. Rabbi Jehiel b. Isaac ha-Zarefati resided there and maintained contact with the Jewish community of Fustat. Controversies within the community were not resolved until 1240. In 1244 the city was sacked and destroyed by the Khwarizmi Turks.

When the Ramban came to Jerusalem in 1267 he found it in a state of ruin. The *minyan* (quorum) of Jews who gathered for prayers on the Sabbath were "the *she'ar yashuv*" (the remnant that returned—cf. 1 Samuel 7:3). He had a

Torah scroll brought from Shechem and renovated a building for use as a synagogue. In 1268 he moved to Acre, where he died in 1270.

Acre was a large and important Jewish center in the thirteenth century. It had a Jewish quarter and a "Jews' house" in 1206. When the newly crowned king of Jerusalem, John of Brienne, visited Acre, he was received by representatives of the Frankish and Greek communities and by members of the Jewish community holding a Torah scroll. Judah al-Harizi described the community as ignoramuses, "not a man among them who could stand in the breach," and this despite the arrival of three hundred rabbis from France and England in 1211.

The Muslims conquered the city in 1291 and massacred its Christian and

Jewish inhabitants. One of the survivors who reached Spain, Rabbi Isaac of Acre, described the destruction. Among those killed was Rabbi Solomon, the grandson of Rabbi Simon of Sens. The Jewish captives were apparently brought to Egypt where they were ransomed by the community.

The impoverished state and status of the *yishuv* continued until the immigration waves of the fourteenth century inaugurated a process of regeneration.

THE JEWS OF ITALY 13TH CENTURY

EWISH life in Italy in the twelfth and thirteenth centuries was determined by a constantly fluctuating political climate, with the church promulgating anti-Jewish laws. Most of the Jewish population was located from the center of the Italian Peninsula southward. Rome was an important Jewish center, while cities such as Lucca, Pisa and Venice had sparse Jewish populations. Jehiel Anav, a relative of Nathan b. Jehiel, supervised the finances of Pope Alexander III (1159–1181).

The significant political events of this period were the Hohenstaufen rule in Sicily, the Angevin invasion of Italy at the invitation of Pope Boniface VIII (1294–1303), and the wars of the Aragonese dynasty over the rule of south-central Italy. Jews gave financial aid to the war campaigns of the Aragonese.

For its part, the church had already established its attitude toward Jews: at the Third Lateran Council (1179) and the Fourth Lateran Council (1215) a number of anti-Jewish edicts were issued, among them a decree that Jews must dress so as to be easily distinguished from Christians. The distinction soon became institutionalized in the Jewish badge. The council also limited the maximum rate of

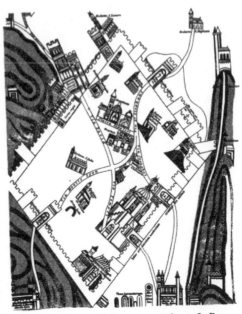

Jerusalem in the 12th century (from J. Prawer, A History of the Crusader Kingdom, Hebrew *ed., Jerusalem 1963, p. 138).*

interest that Jews could charge Christians. This period is also noted for the blood libels in Trani, where in 1290 one such libel resulted in four synagogues being converted into churches. The popularization of the *kabbalah* in Italy began to bear fruit, Bari and Otranto becoming important centers of Torah study.

JEWISH COMMUNITIES IN SPAIN AND THE RECONQUEST 13TH AND 14TH CENTURIES

THE reign of King James I (1213–1276) over the kingdom of Aragón saw the continuation of the Reconquest, which affected Spanish Jewry. King James encouraged Jews from Marseilles and North Africa to settle in his kingdom, and many Jews supported his campaigns of conquest of the Balearic Islands and Valencia. In order to settle and develop the conquered territories, he granted land and property to the Jews and they in turn enjoyed the status of settlers in frontier areas. He exempted communities from payment of taxes and reestablished the Jewish community of Perpignan, which at that time belonged to the kingdom of Aragón. Many of the communities which developed enjoyed preferential status in

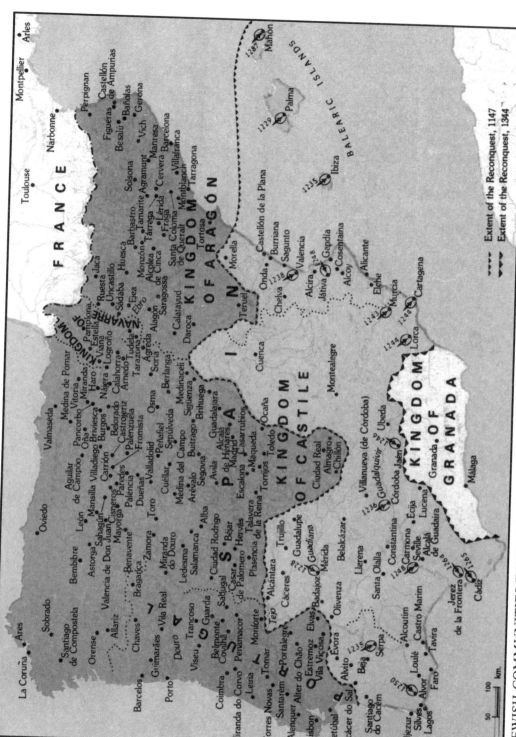

JEWISH COMMUNITIES IN SPAIN AND THE RECONQUEST
13TH AND 14TH CENTURIES

ommerce. Jews held key positions in the court administration, including that of manager of the king's personal property. It would be accurate to say that the major royal administrative posts were held by Jews who were also prominent in the Jewish community. Among the more outstanding of these were Nahmanides of Gerona; the brothers Solomon and Bahya Alconstantini of Saragossa, who assisted the king in his campaigns of conquest and were destined to take part in the controversy regarding the writings of Maimonides; Don Judah (ibn Lavi) de la Cavalleria, who is mentioned from 1257 onward as being the royal treasurer and bailiff of Saragossa. From 1260 Don Judah controlled all the crown revenues, judiciously managing royal expenditure. Nevertheless, from 1260 on, a decline in Jewish power and influence was already apparent.

Despite the prominence of Jews under James, their status in Aragón was not one of total security or welfare. Though no official action was directed against them nor was any specific anti-Jewish policy promulgated, certain changes did occur. During the reign of James I, the laws and edicts of Popes Innocent III and Gregory IX were activated. In 1228, James decreed laws relating to Jews: a fixed 20 percent maximum interest permitted on loan, identical to that of the Christian merchants of Florence; a Jewish oath could not serve as evidence in a court of law; and Jews were excluded from state administrative posts. Although the king was in no way involved, the first instance of a blood libel in Spain, concerning a Christian boy allegedly murdered by Jews, was circulated in Saragossa in 1250.

These events are indicative of the change that took place in the lives of Spanish Jewry. The Barcelona Disputation in 1263, with the participation of

Be advised that we (that is, the *kahal* of Barcelona), the *kahal* of Villafranca del Penedès, the *kahal* of Tarragona, and the *kahal* of Montblanch, maintain a common chest and a common purse for the payment of taxes and imposts levied upon us by the crown. Whenever they wish to pass new regulations governing the assessment of taxes either by the tax-assessors or by the submission of memoranda or by individual declaration, to meet the requirements of the king, we do not impose our will upon them, even though we are in the majority and the city is supreme in all matters. If we should take action without their counsel, they would not heed us. Sometimes we send our men to them, and other times their representatives come to us with their resolutions. Only if they fail to do either of these things at our request do we compel them by the arm of the government to come to us or to adopt in their communities the measures that are in force in ours. In other places however the head community decrees for its dependencies and subjects them to its will.

Solomon b. Abraham Adret, Responsa III No. 411, from Y. Baer, A History of Jews in Christian Spain, vol. 1. Translated from the Hebrew by Louis Schoffman, Philadelphia, 1961, pp. 216–217.

Nahmanides and in the presence of James I, was undoubtedly instigated by the church, particularly by the Dominicans, who were fervent advocates of a militant church policy. In many respects James's policy regarding Jews vacillated between two courses of action: while he used them for his own purposes and had need of many Jews for royal administration, he was nevertheless guided by those church principles and policies that argued for conversion, degradation and limitation. It was church policy that eventually triumphed, although it is difficult to determine the precise date at which this occurred.

The reign of James's son and successor Peter III (1276–1285) is an important chapter in the history of the Jews in the

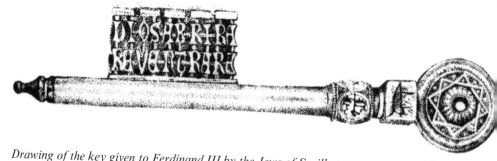

Drawing of the key given to Ferdinand III by the Jews of Seville to commemorate his conquest of the city (23 November 1248). The tongue of the key reads: Dios abrirá, Rey entrará *(God opens and the King enters).*

kingdom of Aragón. The first Spanish ruler to acquiesce to the pressures of Jew-haters, he enacted numerous limitations on them. However, he too was compelled to use the services of Jews in carrying out his foreign and domestic policies. Thus we find Moses Alconstantini and the Abravalia family of Gerona among his courtiers. Their involvement in state administration and finances was reminiscent of the Reconquest period. One of the members of the Abravalia family accompanied Peter on his Sicilian campaign in 1282. During the latter part of his reign Peter himself actively repressed the Jews, removing them from all positions of influence. His son and successor, Alfonso III (1285–1291), heeded the complaints of the urban nobility against the Jews; dark clouds were beginning to gather in Aragón, foreboding days of retrogression and deterioration that would end in the persecutions of 1391.

The reign of James I in Aragón was contemporary with that of two kings of Castile–León—Ferdinand III the Saint (1217–1252) and Alfonso X the Wise (1252–1284). During James I's conquest of the Balearic Islands (1224–1233) and Valencia (1238), Ferdinand III conquered most of the cities of Andalusia (Córdoba in 1236 and Murcia in 1243)

thereby opening an outlet to the Mediterranean that severed the Aragonese advance to the south. Thereafter the military campaigns were Castilian: Jaén in 1246 and Seville in 1248. After Alfonso's completion of his father's campaigns, there followed a truce of about two hundred years in the Reconquest. During its final campaigns in the reign of Ferdinand and Isabella, Jews did not take part in settling the frontier areas; they were only required to pay a special war tax.

Under Alfonso X known as a law-maker, continuing the work of Ferdinand III, a code of laws in the spirit of Roman and canon law was prepared for his country. Called *Las siete partidas* because of its division into seven parts, it went into effect about the middle of the fourteenth century. The prime characteristic of the code was its attempt to organize Spanish society according to the contemporary spirit of Christianity. In the general section of the code (part seven) the regulation requiring modesty of dress applied also to the Jews. The code fixed a maximum rate of interest of 33 1/3 percent for loans extended by Jews to Christians; it established the formula of the Jewish oath, but also forbade breaking into a synagogue. In the fourteenth and fifteenth centuries, the code served as a basis for legal corroboration, but otherwise had little impact on Jewish life. The code was only imperfectly implemented in matters of state appointment and the employment of the services of Jewish physicians. Christians were unhappy with the code because it contained a measure of protection for the Jews. However, the Jewish communities still had the privileges granted to them by Alfonso's predecessors.

Alfonso did not restrict the communal autonomy of Castilian Jewry. The Jewish judiciary remained independent and Jewish judges dispensed justice according to the laws of the Torah. However, the litigants were allowed right of appeal to the king's tribunal. The king also had the right to appoint a Jew as chief justice who would be in charge of Jewish judicial matters in any particular community. He was to act as chief justice of appeals and was known as Rab de la Corte.

THE COLLECTA ORGANIZATION

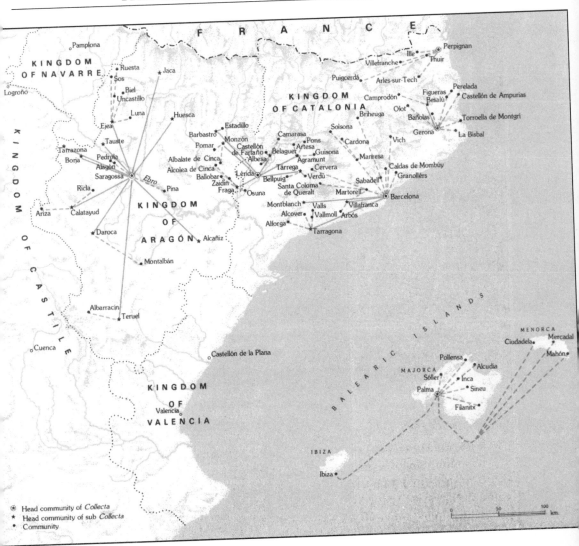

⊗ Head community of *Collecta*
✴ Head community of sub *Collecta*
• Community

Signature of Jews on a bill of sale from 1248. The Magen David forms part of the witness's signature.

THE Collecta was a regional organization of Jewish communities based on tax districts; its purpose was to create a single, central fund for a group of communities, in which a major community extended its authority over a number of smaller satellites. This organizational structure created a mutual alliance based not only on geographical proximity but on a network of relations between large and small communties. Despite the dependence of the smaller communities, the larger were not always able to impose their will upon the smaller dependencies.

SPIRITUAL CREATIVITY

DESPITE the bitter and burdensome trials in the Diaspora, the spiritual creativity of the Jewish people never ceased. Their spheres of creativity were diverse and their contribution to the world of ideas of the Middle Ages and the subsequent generations was great. In Spain Jews participated in the translation from Arabic to Latin of classical works of philosophy. They thus served as a bridge between the culture of the ancient world and that of the Middle Ages.

The specifically Jewish aspects of this creativity had many facets ranging from biblical exegesis to *kabbalah*. Jewish sages and scholars in various countries added their contribution to the spiritual edifice of the people and in a few European countries, between the eleventh and the fourteenth centuries, their achievements were unique. If one country was famous for having the great Bible commentator, Rashi, another was well known for being the cradle of *kabbalah*, and still another for being the home of philosophical and ethical literature. All these achievements became precious assets of the Jewish people.

An examination of the intellectual climate in which the *tosafot* ("additions," i.e., collections of comments on the Talmud) were compiled reveals similar, scholarly activity in the fields of Latin literature of the Middle Ages, Roman and canon law and Christian biblical exegesis. Despite the differences between and the barrier that separated Jews and Christians, they were nevertheless both affected by the same intellectual climate. They not only confronted one another in religious disputations but also met in order to learn from one another. Christian commentators were aided by Jews in deciphering difficult biblical passages and the phrase *Hebraeus meus dicit* ("a Jew told me") is frequently found in the writings of Andreas, the pupil of Abelard, in the twelfth century.

Although the *tosafot* were a collective compilation, like the Mishnah and Talmud, nevertheless one can discern different methodologies and local distinctions among France, Germany, England and other places. Rashi's pupils expanded, elaborated, developed and completed his commentary, ushering in a new period of

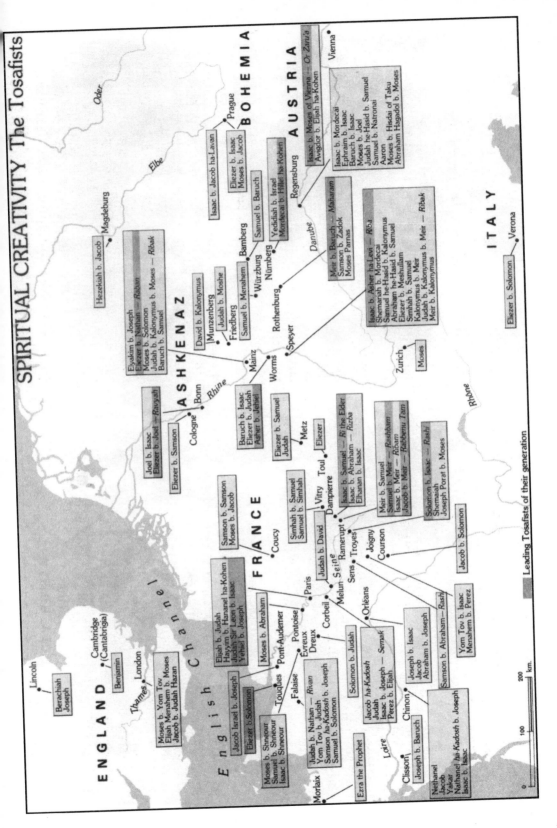

SPIRITUAL CREATIVITY The Tosafists

ENGLAND

Lincoln
Berachiah
Joseph

Cambridge (Cantabrigia)
Benjamin

London
Moses b. Yom Tov
Elijah Menahem b. Moses
Jacob b. Judah Hazan

English Channel

FRANCE

Mortaix
Nathanel
Jacob
Yakar
Nathanel ha-Kadosh b. Joseph
Isaac b. Isaac

Ezra the Prophet

Clisson
Joseph b. Baruch

Chinon
Jacob ha-Kadosh
Judah
Isaac b. Joseph — Semak
Perez b. Elijah

Samson b. Abraham — Rashi

Yom Tov b. Isaac
Menahem b. Perez

Joseph b. Isaac
Jacob
Abraham b. Joseph

Touques
Moses b. Shneour
Samuel b. Shneour
Isaac b. Shneour

Falaise
Judah b. Nathan — Rivan
Yom Tov b. Judah
Samson ha-Kadosh b. Joseph
Samuel b. Solomon

Pont-Audemer
Elijah b. Judah
Hayyim b. Hananel ha-Kohen
Judah Sir Leon b. Isaac
Yehiel b. Joseph

Dreux
Moses b. Abraham

Evreux
Moses b. Abraham

Pontoise
Jacob Israel b. Joseph
Eliezer b. Solomon

Solomon b. Judah

Jacob b. Solomon

Orléans

Corbeil

Paris

Coucy
Samson b. Samson
Samuel b. Samson
Moses b. Jacob

Melun

Seine

Judah b. David

Courson

Joigny

Sens
Solomon b. Isaac — Rashi
Shemaiah
Joseph Porat b. Moses

Troyes

Ramerupt
Meir b. Samuel
Samuel b. Meir — Rashbam
Isaac b. Meir — Ribam
Jacob b. Meir — Rabbenu Tam

Dampierre
Isaac b. Samuel — Ri the Elder
Isaac b. Abraham — Rizba
Elhanan b. Isaac

Vitry

Toul

Eliezer

Metz
Eliezer b. Samuel
Judah

Cologne
Joel b. Isaac
Eliezer b. Joel — Ravyah

Bonn
Elyakim b. Joseph
Eliezer b. Nathan — Raban
Moses b. Solomon
Judah b. Kalonymus b. Moses — Ribak
Baruch b. Samuel

ASHKENAZ

Rhine

Mainz
Baruch b. Isaac
Eliezer b. Judah
Asher b. Jehiel

Worms

Speyer

Zurich
Moses

Friedberg
Samuel b. Menahem

Munzenberg
David b. Kalonymus
Judah b. Moshe

Würzburg

Nürnberg

Rothenburg
Meir b. Baruch — Maharam
Samson b. Zadok
Moses Parnas

Bamberg
Samuel b. Baruch

Regensburg
Yedidiah b. Israel
Mordecai b. Hillel ha-Kohen

Magdeburg
Hezekiah b. Jacob

Oder

Elbe

Prague
Isaac b. Jacob ha-Lavan
Eliezer b. Isaac
Moses b. Jacob

BOHEMIA

AUSTRIA

Vienna
Isaac b. Moses of Vienna — Or Zaru'a
Avigdor b. Elijah ha-Kohen

Isaac b. Mordecai
Ephraim b. Isaac
Baruch b. Isaac
Moses b. Joel
Judah he-Hasid b. Samuel
Samuel b Natronai
Aaron
Moses b. Hisdai of Taku
Abraham Hagadol b. Moses

Isaac b. Asher ha-Levi — Riba
Shemariah b. Mordecai
Samuel he-Hasid b. Kalonymus
Abraham he-Hasid b. Samuel
Eliezer b. Meshullam
Simhah b. Samuel
Kalonymus b. Meir
Judah b. Kalonymus b. Meir — Ribak
Meir b. Kalonymus

Danube

ITALY

Verona

Eliezer b. Solomon

Rhône

Loire

Thames

Leading Tosafists of their generation

0   100   200
km.

199

exegesis. The transitional period is represented by Shemaiah of Troyes (Rashi's responsa) and Simhah b. Samuel of Vitry. However, the most significant work was done by Rashi's two sons-in-law: Judah b. Nathan (Rivan), the father of a family of scholars, who checked Rashi's Talmud commentary, added glosses to it and even composed independent commentaries for most of the Talmud tractates. He frequently used the commentaries of the sages of Mainz and did not refrain from criticizing Rashi. The other son-in-law, Meir b. Samuel of Ramerupt, was sometimes known as "the father of the rabbis." (His sons were Samuel b. Meir—Rashbam, Isaac b. Meir and Jacob b. Meir—Rabbenu Tam, who called his father's commentaries *tosafot*).

These sages witnessed the persecutions and massacres of French Jewry during the crusades and their expulsion from Île de France in 1182. It was they who issued the call to immigrate to the Holy Land. In the towns of France and Ashkenaz they attracted many pupils who then continued their method of learning and it is, therefore, not surprising that Moses b. Jacob of Coucy was able to compile his monumental work *Sefer Mitzvot Gadol* (*Se Ma G*) which became a basic reference book for the study of the *halakhah*.

The works of the tosafists reached Bohemia; pupils from Prague (Eliezer b. Isaac and Isaac b. Jacob ha-Lavan—brother of the famous traveler, Pethahiah of Regensburg) came to Ramerupt to study with Rabbenu Tam. Some of these scholars were active in Ashkenaz and others in Bohemia and Russia. The tosafist Petter b. Joseph of Carinthia in Austria participated in editing *Sefer ha-Yashar* by his teacher, Rabbenu Tam, adding his own glosses. He died a martyr during the Second Crusade. In Hungary

there were two tosafists: Abraham the Proselyte and his son Isaac the Proselyte.

Ramerupt, Regensburg and Dampierre were important tosafist centers, the Regensburg school having such scholars as Joel b. Isaac ha-Levi and his son Eliezer b. Joel ha-Levi (known as Ravyah). The head of the school in Dampierre was Isaac b. Abraham (known as Rizba), who was a grandson of Samson b. Joseph of Falaise and had been privileged to study with Rabbenu Tam. The Rizba was a great halakhist and rabbinical judge (*posek*), whose decisions were accepted by scholars of many generations. Among those who sought his opinion on aspects of Jewish law was Jonathan b. David ha-Kohen of Lunel, an admirer of Maimonides (Rambam). The Rizba was probably familiar with the Rambam's writings, since he was the recipient of one of the letters sent by Meir b. Todros Abulafia of Toledo to the rabbis of southern France regarding the Rambam's doctrine of resurrection. His younger brother was Samson b. Abraham of Sens who was particularly noted for his commentary on several orders of the Mishnah and for his use of the Jerusalem Talmud as a source for halakhic decisions. Little is known of his life but his literary legacy is greater than that of the other tosafists. The bulk of his work has been preserved in his own language and not reworked by his pupils. He emerges from his work as a great scholar whose world was steeped in the *halakhah*.

After Samson of Sens immigrated to the Holy Land at the beginning of the thirteenth century, Paris became the center of Torah study in northern France. Its school was headed by Judah b. Isaac (known as Judah Sir Leon of Paris, 1166–1224), pupil and relative of Isaac b. Samuel of Dampierre (known as

Two pages from a compendium of religious laws from the Rashi school, c. 13th century.

Ha-Zaken). The school was closed in 1182, when the Jews were expelled from the kingdom of France by King Philip II Augustus, but was reopened in 1198, when the Jews were allowed to return. Jehiel of Paris, Moses of Coucy and Isaac of Vienna studied and were active in this school. Asher b. Jehiel (Rosh, 1250–1327) was an outstanding scholar and leader of German Jewry, who, in 1303, left Germany for Spain to take up a position as rabbi in Toledo. He introduced the system of study of Ashkenazic tosafists into Spain.

Jewish creativity in France declined after the Disputation of Paris (1240) and the burning of the Talmud (1242). With the destruction of the French Jewish villages and their expulsion in 1306, this great spiritual achievement came to an end.

The Ashkenazic Hasidic movement developed in Germany during the twelfth and thirteenth centuries. Samuel b. Kalonymos he-Hasid of Speyer and his son Judah he-Hasid of Regensburg (c. 1150–1217) were the founders of the movement and their most important work was *Sefer Hasidim*, a book of pragmatic true-to-life ethical teachings which reflect the contemporary life of German Jewry in their Christian environment. The book

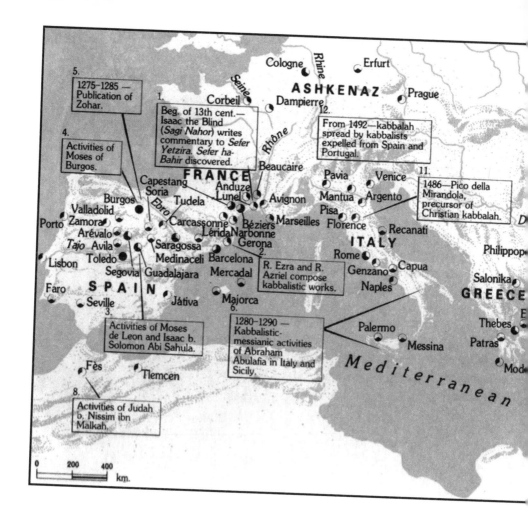

5.
1275–1285 — Publication of Zohar.

1.
Beg. of 13th cent.— Isaac the Blind (*Sagi Nahor*) writes commentary to *Sefer Yetzira. Sefer ha-Bahir* discovered.

4.
Activities of Moses of Burgos.

12.
From 1492—kabbalah spread by kabbalists expelled from Spain and Portugal.

11.
1486—Pico della Mirandola, precursor of Christian kabbalah.

2.
R. Ezra and R. Azriel compose kabbalistic works.

3.
Activities of Moses de Leon and Isaac b. Solomon Abi Sahula.

6.
1280–1290 — Kabbalistic-messianic activities of Abraham Abulafia in Italy and Sicily.

8.
Activities of Judah b. Nissim ibn Malkah.

Cologne · Rhine · Erfurt
Corbeil · Dampierre · Prague
ASHKENAZ
Seine · Rhône
FRANCE
Capestang · Anduze · Pavia · Venice
Soria · Lunel · Avignon · Mantua · Argento
Burgos · Tudela · Pisa
Valladolid · Ebro · Marseilles · Florence
Porto · Zamora · Carcassonne · Béziers
Arévalo · Lérida · Narbonne · Recanati
Tajo · Avila · Saragossa · Gerona · ITALY · Philippop
Lisbon · Toledo · Medinaceli · Barcelona · Rome
Segovia · Guadalajara · Mercadal · Genzano · Capua
Faro · SPAIN · Naples · GREECE
Seville · Játiva · Majorca · Salonika
Palermo · Thebes
Fès · Tlemcen · Messina · Patras
Mediterranean · Mod

0   200   400 km

preaches spiritual revival and instructs the pious on avoiding sin and on leading a righteous life that will ensure his salvation in the life to come. Various weltanschauungen are expressed in the book and scholars believe that some of these were influenced by ideas prevalent in the area; even the languages of the text, German and French, indicate such influences. The Hasid, the protagonist, is portrayed as the ideal—in his conduct, his full Jewish life, and in his relations with his Christian neighbors. While he is fully aware of the grim realities which surround his people, he is called upon to bear the burden of the community and lead it along the true path.

THE SPREAD OF THE KABBALAH

JEWISH mysticism in its various guises was another manifestation of spiritual creativity. It was rooted in theosophy as expressed by the creation, the revealed Shekhinah and the promised redemption in time to come. The *kabbalah*, with all its

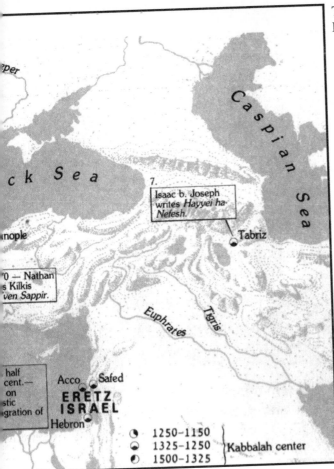

Isaac b. Joseph
writes *Hayyei ha-
Nefesh.*

Caspian Sea

7.

Tabriz

ck Sea

'per

nople

'0 — Nathan
s Kilkis
ven Sappir.

Euphrates

Tigris

half
cent.—
on
stic
gration of

Acco   Safed
**ERETZ
ISRAEL**
Hebron

- 1250–1150
- 1325–1250
- 1500–1325

Kabbalah center

social and historical implications for the people of Israel, held a special place among all the mystical philosophies. A prolific literature created a world of values which found expression in *Sefer ha-Zohar*, the greatest book on *kabbalah*, and in the literature which developed around it, for example, *Tikkunei Zohar* and *Ra'aya Meheimna* ("The Faithful Shepherd"). At the beginning of the thirteenth century, kabbalistic works flourished in southern France and north-eastern Spain, eventually spreading even beyond the Spanish border. According to Isaac b. Samuel of Acre, who arrived in Spain in 1305, *Sefer ha-Zohar* was written by Moses de León between 1275 and 1285.

Kabbalistic literature gives further expression to a protest against the moral decline in a Jewish society which must mend its ways, as *Sefer ha-Zohar*, *Tikkunei ha-Zohar* and *Ra'aya Meheimna* do. In this literature, with its wealth of symbols, Jewish sages sought solutions to the problems of *galut* (being dispersed in the Diaspora), apprehension of the Shekhinah and even practical instruction on hastening the redemption (see map on p. 269 for details of the Lurianic *kabbalah* in Safed of the seventeenth century).

THE writings and activities of Moses b. Maimon (Rambam, 1135–1204) encompassed all aspects of contemporary Jewish life, extending even beyond his lifetime and domicile.

The range of his writings was wide and varied, covering commentaries, *halakhah* (*Mishneh Torah*), medicine, responsa, epistles, philosophy and science. In the *Guide of the Perplexed* he attempted to formulate a complete philosophical system for the interpretation of Jewish scripture. The book set out to grapple with the weltanschauungen of both Christianity and Islam and the threat they posed to the spiritual and physical survival of the Jewish people.

Drawing of a personal seal belonging to Nahmanides, found in 1972 near Acre. The text reads: Moshe b'Rabbi Nahman. Nuah Nefesh, Gerondi Hazak—*"Moses the son of Rabbi Nahman of restful soul, the Gerundian Be Strong!"*

Autographed responsum of Maimonides.

The Rambam's halakhic approach and his views on resurrection caused a furious controversy which almost divided the Jewish people, lasting about a hundred years and which engulfed Jews in the east and west, in Islamic countries and in Christian Europe.

The four controversies associated with the Rambam's methods, philosophy and writings, were in fact merely stages in an ongoing polemic which emerged during the Rambam's lifetime, at the end of the twelfth century. The first controversy arose from reservations regarding the *Mishneh Torah*, the Rambam's system of defining *halakhot*, and his views on resurrection. The second (1232) was associated with the *Guide of the Perplexed* and *Sefer ha-Madda*; in the third (end of the thirteenth century), an attempt was made to ban the *Guide*; while the fourth dealt with the study of philosophy, with the Rambam's writings assuming a secondary role. The second

THE MAIMONIDEAN CONTROVERSY

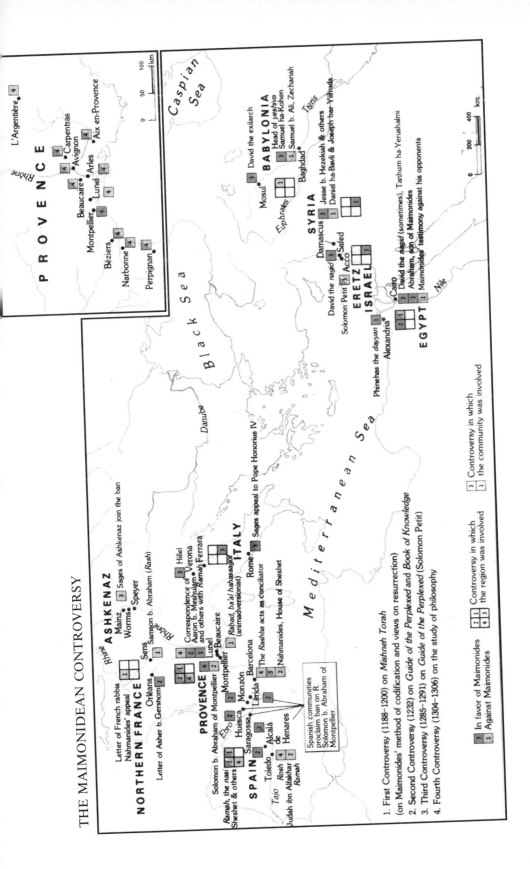

1. First Controversy (1188–1200) on *Mishneh Torah*
   (on Maimonides' method of codification and views on resurrection)
2. Second Controversy (1232) on *Guide of the Perplexed* and *Book of Knowledge*
3. Third Controversy (1285–1291) on *Guide of the Perplexed* (Solomon Petit)
4. Fourth Controversy (1304–1306) on the study of philosophy

Statue of Maimonides in the Tiberias Plaza in Córdoba.

Abraham Gerondi, with the support of the rabbis of northern France, issued a ban on the study of the Rambam's philosophical works. A counterban against Solomon of Montpellier and his pupils was issued in the summer of 1232 by the Aragonese *aljamas* (communities) and David Kimhi, a pro-Maimonist, tried to enlist support from the elders of Toledo for this counterban. Nahmanides attempted to reach a compromise by proposing an educational program for the study of the philosophical writings geared to different age groups and communities. His prime concern was to avoid a schism in Jewry. One of the consequences of this polemic was the drawing of the papal Inquisition's attention to Jewish religious matters and writings.

The third controversy involved a number of Jewish sages from the Islamic countries. Solomon b. Samuel (Petit), one of the important kabbalists in Acre, tried to revive the ban on the *Guide of the Perplexed* by enlisting the support of rabbis in Ashkenaz, France and Italy. He failed, arousing the opposition of the heads of the community of Damascus and Mosul, and that of the *nagid* David b. Abraham, the grandson of the Rambam. In Italy, Hillel b. Samuel of Verona (c. 1220–c. 1295), and in Spain, Solomon b. Abraham Adret (Rashba) tried to mediate between the antagonists.

The last controversy occurred at the beginning of the fourteenth century in Provence and Spain. Abba Mari of Montpellier (b. Moses b. Joseph of Lunel) induced the Rashba to issue a ban on the study of science and metaphysics by anyone under twenty-five years of age. The Rambam's writings were not specifically mentioned in the ban and gradually the polemic abated.

controversy was the bitterest polemic, occurring at a time when there were spiritual and religious conflicts in Christianity and Islam as well. (In those days a savage crusade was taking place in southern France against the Albigensian heretics.) This second controversy, in which the greatest Jewish scholars of the age were involved, had far-reaching ramifications regarding the nature of Jewish education. In 1232, Solomon b. Abraham of Montpellier and his two pupils David b. Saul and Jonah b.

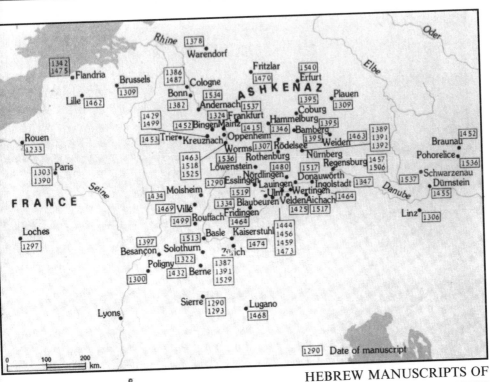

HEBREW MANUSCRIPTS OF
ASHKENAZ AND FRANCE

IN various Jewish communities scribes were engaged in copying books required for study and reference. The profession developed as patrons employed scribes to copy books especially for them.

(left) Illuminated page of prayer for Yom Kippur in second volume of Worms Mahzor, Germany, c. 1270.

207

Opening of the Book of Numbers, The Duke of Sussex Pentateuch, *showing the four leading tribes of Israel camping around the Tabernacle, c. early 14th century, Ashkenaz.*

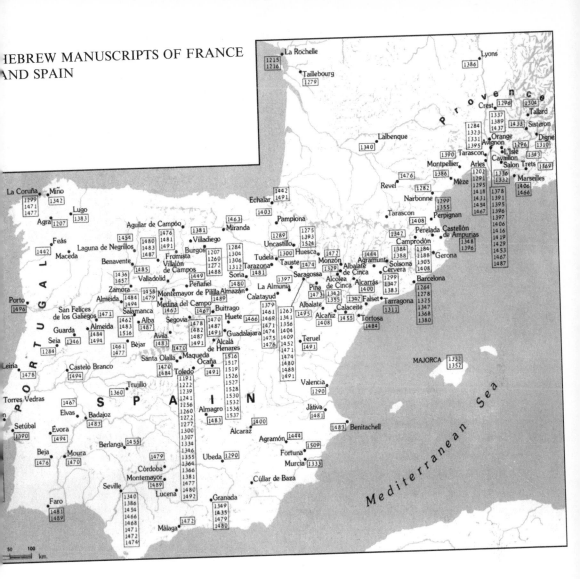

THE JEWS OF ENGLAND UP TO THE EXPULSION

THE history of the Jews in England in the thirteenth century can be described as one of persecutions and oppression by the state and the population at large. The state and the English church had, from the beginning, intended to convert the Jewish community to Christianity and for this purpose a home for converted Jews (*domus conversorum*) was established in London in 1232.

The tax policy toward the Jews was one of merciless exploitation. King Edward I (1272–1307) approved the church's attempts at converting Jews. Many towns expelled the Jews, while others received priviliges permitting them "not to tolerate Jews." (Leicester was the first to receive such a privilege in 1231.) The Jews moved to towns owned by Edward I after being expelled in 1275 by Eleanor,

North Sea

• Newcastle
↗1233

1.
1219—William of Blois, bishop of
Worcester, forbids Jews to employ
Christians as servants or wet nurses,
to accept sacred vessels as security
for loans, and to earn interest on
moneys received from Christians.

York •

E N G L A N D

Beaumaris
↗• Conwy Rhuddlan
↗ • ↗•Flint
6.

Lincoln ✿–1263/4
↗1255

8.
1287—All Jewish heads of fam
arrested and held hostage unti
payment of £20,000 ransom.

Bala ↗•
Harlech↗

1275—Jews forbidden to
engage in usury; allowed to
reside only in towns owned
by king; obliged to wear
identifying badge from age
8, and to pay taxes from age
12.

Nottingham •
• Derby ✿–1264

A t l a n t i c
O c e a n

3.
1241—"Parliament of
Jews" (representatives
of recognized Jewish
communities) summoned
to levy a tax of £14,000.

Bridgnorth •

1231 ↗• Leicester • Stamford

• King's Lynn
Norwich•–✿
1239

• Coventry

Huntingdon •

Tetford •

Bungay

Warwick •
1263 ✿–/ •Worcester ✿
Weobley • 1275 ↗•
Hereford • 1240 ▲   Avon

Northampton •
1263 ✿– •

Bury St. Edmunds •↗

Cambridge •↗
1275

Ipswich •

Gloucester •◉↗ 1275

4.
1244—Students attack
Jews of town.

• Bedford
✿–1263
• Dunstable

Sudbury •

Colchester • ✿–

7.
17 Nov. 1278—
Mass arrests an
executions of
Jews.

↗•Caerleon

1244 ✿–• 1242 ↗•
1220 ▲ Oxford •Berkhamsted

Newport •
1263 ✿–•

5.
Jews obliged to wear an
identifying badge and forbidden
to build synagogues.

Bristol •

Wycombe •
Wallingford ↗• London ✿– 1215,1239,1263/4
Marlborough• ↗ 1283
Windsor ↗ 1244
Devizes ↗•1275 •Newbury Merton ↗ 1261
1258 ▲?

• Ospringe

2.
1232—Synagogue
confiscated by king
and converted to
church.

• Canterbury
✿– 1261,1263
Hythe • Dover
New Romney

Wilton •
Salisbury •
1256▲ Winchester ✿–1263
Romsey↗• ↗ 1192
Southampton↗•
• Chichester

Winchelsea •↗

S t r a i t   o f   D o v e

↗ Blood libel
↗ Expulsion
✿– Pogroms
▲ Church council
◉ Towns in ownership of Queen Eleanor

1281▲ ↗• Exeter

▲1240
• Newport

9.
18 July 1290—Edict of Banishment
compels Jews to leave England by
1 Nov. under punishment of death;
Jews permitted to take or sell their
possessions. Jewish houses and
synagogues destroyed.

FRAN

English Channel

0   50   100
km.

the queen mother, from the towns in her
possession. However, local expulsions
did not cease.

In 1275 Edward I issued a decree,
Statutum de Judaismo, in which he
endeavored to change the occupations
of his Jewish subjects from moneylending
and usury to crafts and agriculture. The

attempt failed because by that time the
Jewish community was completely impoverished. Pressured by the townspeople he ordered the *archae* (chirograph
chests) containing records of their debts
to the Jews to be closed. It soon became
clear that there was nothing left to extort
from the Jews.

A Hebrew quitclaim of Jose son of Elias, Jose son of Moses, and Judah the Frenchman. H. Loewe, Starrs and Jewish Charters Preserved in the British Museum, London 1932, Plate IX.

On 18 July 1290 Edward issued an edict for the banishment of the Jews from England by the beginning of November. The Jews were allowed to take only their personal possessions; the rest of their property was confiscated. To replace the loss of income the crown was authorized by parliament to levy a tithe on ecclesiastical property and a 15 percent tax on the property of the nobles and citizens. These taxes were but a pittance in comparison to those paid by Jews a hundred years earlier. The number of Jews expelled has been estimated at four thousand, most of them going to France and Ashkenaz.

THE JEWISH COMMUNITIES OF FRANCE 13TH CENTURY

THIRTEENTH-CENTURY France underwent a process of centralization and the increased power of the king caused a worsening in the condition of the Jews. The years 1236 to 1239 were characterized by a revival of anti-Jewish feeling together with preachings for a new crusade. Jewish quarters in Anjou, Poitou and Brittany were attacked, prompting an order from Pope Gregory IX in 1236 to the bishops of France to denounce the assaults, despite his usually unfavorable attitude toward the Jews.

The expulsion of the Jews from England made a profound impression in France. Philip IV the Fair ordered the expulsion of the Jews in 1291 and again on 6 June 1299, but his orders were not implemented. The crown forbade the expelled Jews from Gascony (an English possession) and England to enter France and, judging by Philip's policies and extortionary methods, Jewish expulsion from France was inevitable. Thus in 1306 Philip ordered their expulsion from all districts under his control. This order and

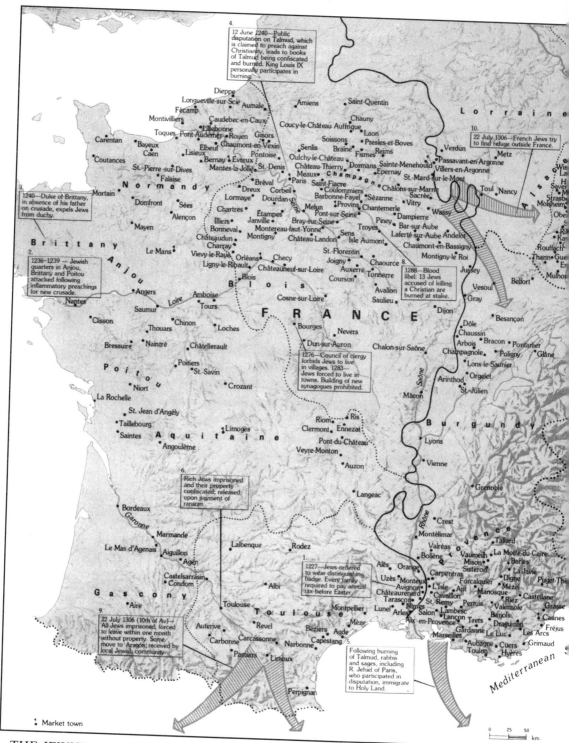

4.
12 June 1240—Public disputation on Talmud, which is claimed to preach against Christianity, leads to books of Talmud being confiscated and burned. King Louis IX personally participates in burning.

10.
22 July 1306—French Jews try to find refuge outside France.

Dieppe
Longueville-sur-Scie Aumale
Fécamp
Montivilliers
Caudebec-en-Caux
Toques Pont-Audemer Rouen Gisors
Carentan Bayeux Elbeuf Chaumont-en-Vexin
Coutances Caen Lisieux Pontoise
St-Pierre-sur-Dives Bernay Evreux Mantes-la-Jolie St-Denis
Falaise
Mortain
Domfront Sées Bréval Dreux Corbeil
Lormaye Dourdan
Mayen Chartres Étampes Janville
Illiers Bonneval Montereau-faut-Yonne
Châteaudun Montigny Château-Landon
Charray
Le Mans Vievy-le-Rayé Orléans Checy
Ligny-le-Ribault Châteauneuf-sur-Loire
Blois Cosne-sur-Loire
Angers Amboise Courson
Nantes Saumur Tours
Clisson Chinon Loches Bourges
Thouars Nevers
Bressuire Naintré Châtellerault
Poitiers St-Savin Dun-sur-Auron
Niort Crozant
La Rochelle Chalon-sur-Saône
St. Jean d'Angély Riom Ris
Taillebourg Clermont Ennezat
Saintes Limoges Pont-du-Château
Angoulême Veyre-Monton
Auzon
Langeac

Amiens Saint-Quentin
Chauny
Coucy-le-Château Auffrique Laon
Soissons Braine Presles-et-Boves
Senlis Fismes Reims
Oulchy-le-Château
Château-Thierry Dormans Sainte-Menehould
Meaux Épernay
Paris Saint-Fiacre Châlons-sur-Marne
Coulommiers St-Mard-sur-le-Mont
Barbonne-Fayel Sézanne
Melun Provins Vitry Wassy
Pont-sur-Seine Chantemerle
Bray-sur-Seine Dampierre
Sens Troyes Piney Bar-sur-Aube
Isle Aumont Laferté-sur-Aube Andelot
St-Florentin Chaumont-en-Bassigny
Joigny Auxerre Chaource Montigny-le-Roi
Tonnerre
Avallon Dijon
Saulieu

Verdun
Metz
Passavant-en-Argonne
Villers-en-Argonne
Toul Nancy
Sacrée
Molsheim

8.
1288—Blood libel: 13 Jews accused of killing a Christian are burned at stake.

Jussey
Vesoul
Gray Belfort
Besançon
Dôle
Chaussin
Arbois Bracon Pontarlier
Champagnole Poligny Glane
Lons-le-Saunier
Arinthod Orgelet
St-Julien
Mâcon

B u r g u n d y

Lyons
Vienne

Grenoble

7.
1276—Council of clergy forbids Jews to live in villages. 1283—Jews forced to live in towns. Building of new synagogues prohibited.

6.
Rich Jews imprisoned and their property confiscated; released upon payment of ransom.

Bordeaux
Garonne Marmande
Le Mas d'Agenais Aiguillon
Agen
Castelsarrasin Condom
Gascony
Aire

1.
1227—Jews ordered to wear distinguishing badge. Every family required to pay annual tax before Easter.

Lalbenque Rodez
Albi
Toulouse T o u l o u s e
Auterive Revel
Carbonne Carcassonne Béziers Agde Mèze
Pamiers Limoux Capestang
Perpignan

Crest
Montélimar
Valréas Tallard
Bollène Vaumeil La Motte-du-Caire
Mison Barles
Orange Sisteron La Javie
Alès Carpentras Forcalquier Digne Puget-The
Uzès Monteux L'Isle Apt Mézel
Avignon Cavaillon Manosque Castellane
Châteaurenard St. Remy Riez Grasse
Tarascon Pertuis Valensole
Nîmes Salon Lambesc Barjols Cannes
Lunel Arles Lançon Trets Draguignan
Montpellier Aix-en-Provence Gardanne Le Luc Les Arcs Fréjus
Marseilles Aubagne Cuers Grimaud
Toulon Hyères

9.
22 July 1306 (10th of Av)— All Jews imprisoned; forced to leave within one month without property. Some move to Aragon; received by local Jewish community.

5.
Following burning of Talmud, rabbis and sages, including R. Jehiel of Paris, who participated in disputation, immigrate to Holy Land.

Mediterranean

• Market town

0   25   50
km.

THE JEWISH COMMUNITIES OF FRANCE
13TH CENTURY

212

its purpose were similar to the expulsion of 1182, except that in 1182 it was ordered by a boy king (Philip Augustus) who depended upon irresponsible advisers, while in 1306 it was a well-calculated decision. The 1182 expulsion encompassed a relatively small area of France while that of 1306 covered all the areas of the king's domain, which was most of France. Philip the Fair hoped to achieve great financial gain from the expulsion of the Jews and the seizure of their property.

A small number of those expelled moved to Gascony while the majority were welcomed by the kingdoms of Aragón (including Provence) and Navarre (Barcelona took in sixty families). In 1315 they were allowed to return, only to be finally expelled in 1394.

King David, from an illuminated manuscript, eastern France, 1280.

PERSECUTIONS IN ASHKENAZ 13TH AND 14TH CENTURIES

DURING the second half of the thirteenth century anti-Jewish propaganda seriously affected the Jewish communities in Germany. On 20 April 1298 a massacre instigated by a host-desecration libel spread from the Franconian town of Röttingen to many other areas. The inflamed mob, led by a German knight called Rindfleisch, went from town to town inciting the population of Franconia, Swabia, Hesse and Thuringia to slaughter the Jews. This they did with extreme cruelty, destroying entire Jewish communities. Among those killed in Nürnberg were Rabbi Mordecai b. Hillel and his family.

Depictions of Jewish figures of the 13th century.

213

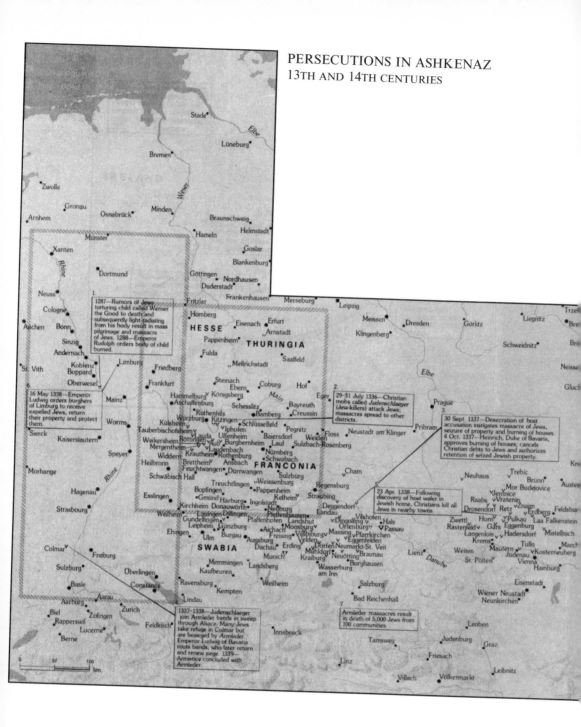

PERSECUTIONS IN ASHKENAZ
13TH AND 14TH CENTURIES

1.
1287—Rumors of Jews torturing child called Werner the Good to death and subsequently light radiating from his body result in mass pilgrimage and massacre of Jews. 1288—Emperor Rudolph orders body of child burned.

16 May 1338—Emperor Ludwig orders burghers of Limburg to receive expelled Jews, return their property and protect them.

2.
29-31 July 1336—Christian mobs called *Judenschlaeger* (Jew-killers) attack Jews; massacres spread to other districts.

3.
30 Sept. 1337—Desecration of host accusation instigates massacre of Jews, seizure of property and burning of houses. 4 Oct. 1337—Heinrich, Duke of Bavaria, approves burning of houses; cancels Christian debts to Jews and authorizes retention of seized Jewish property.

5.
23 Apr. 1338—Following discovery of host wafer in Jewish home, Christians kill all Jews in nearby towns.

1337-1338—Judenschlaeger join Armleder bands in sweep through Alsace. Many Jews take refuge in Colmar but are besieged by *Armleder*. Emperor Ludwig of Bavaria routs bands, who later return and renew siege. 1339. Armistice concluded with Armleder.

7.
Armleder massacres result in death of 5,000 Jews from 100 communities.

Between 1336 and 1339 a group of lawless German bands known as Armleder (so called after the leather armpiece they wore) attacked Jewish communities in Franconia and Alsace leaving slaughter and destruction behind them. Of particular note was the massacre of Jews in the communities of Rouffach, Ensisheim, Ribeauvillé and Mülhausen (Mulhouse). In Colmar the local population massacred the Jews. When the Armleder began to menace the general

214

MASSACRES IN THE RHINE DISTRICTS

Emmerich
Kleve
Rees
Goch
Xanten Wesel
Rheinberg Dinslaken
Geldern Mülheim Essen Dortmund
a.d. Ruhr
Kempen Duisburg Iserlohn *Ruhr*
Dülken Uerdingen Wolfhagen
Gladbach Neuss Kaiserswerth
Wassenberg Wevelinghoven
Erkelenz Dormagen
Grevenbroich Monheim
Rödingen Kaster Stommeln
Jülich Lövenich Bergheim Mülheim
Aldenhoven Cologne (Köln)
Düren Kerpen Biedenkopf
Lechenich Brühl Siegburg Siegen
Nideggen Bonn Beuel *Sieg* Siegen
Zülpich Heimerzheim Marburg
Euskirchen Königswinter Hachenburg
Münstereifel Remagen Linz am Rhein
Ahrweiler Westerburg Giessen Grünberg
Altenahr Sinzig Heinbach Wetzlar
Andernach Siershahn Münzenberg
Koblenz Montabaur Nidda
Mayen Kobern Diez Limburg
Gerolstein Münstermaifeld Lahnstein Weilnau Friedberg
Ehrenburg Brauback Assenheim Büdingen
Cochem Kamp
Karden Boppard Königstein Kronberg Gelnhausen
Beilstein Oberwesel Kaub Frankfurt Mülheim
Bacharach Lorch Eltville Offenbach Hanau
Wittlich Krov Trarbach Mainz Seligenstadt Steinheim
Bernkastel Rheinbollen Bingen Babenhausen Aschaffenburg
Neumagen Kirchberg Langenlonsheim Grossostheim
Bretzenheim Oppenheim Dieburg
Trier Kirn Kreuznach Klingenberg
Sobernheim Lichtenberg am Main
Obermoschel Alzey Bensheim Freudenberg
Saarburg Rockenhausen Worms Miltenberg
Heppenheim Amorbach
Weinheim Waldürn
St. Wendel Kusel Altleiningen Schriesheim Buchen
Kaiserslautern Dürkheim Ladenburg Eberbach
Wachenheim Deidesheim Heidelberg Mosbach
Neustadt an der Speyer Wiesloch Möckmühl
Weinstrasse Neudenau
Landau Germersheim
Hornbach in der Pfalz Bruchsal Eppingen Weinsberg
Saargemund Zabern Kleingartach Heilbronn
Wissembourg Bretten Güglingen
Woerth Lauterbourg
Pforzheim
Neuwiller Haguenau Seltz
Bischwiller Sinzheim Leonberg Stuttgart
Saverne Weil der Stadt Esslingen
Herrlisheim
Wolfsheim Strasbourg Herrenberg
Molsheim Oberkirch
Rosheim Enheim
Erstein Offenburg
Benfeld
Rhinau Lahr *Neckar*
Châtenois Sélestat Ettenheim Haslach
St. Hippolyte Bergheim
Ribeauville Riquewihr Kenzingen Hornberg
(Rappoltsweiler) Marckolsheim Rottweil
Kaysersberg Turckheim Endingen
Munster Colmar Waldkirch
Sulzbach Breisach Villengen
Herrlisheim Freidburg
Guebwiller Rouffach
Thann Soultz Ensisheim
Masevaux Wattwiller Oberlingen
Rougemont Sentheim Radolfzell
Mulhouse
Belfort Altkirch Constance Ailingen
Delle Waldshut Diessenhofen Friedrichshafen
Basle Säckingen
Ferrette Rheinfelden Baden Winterthur

0 10 20 km.

Jewish community
Major community (before 1239)
Massacres before 1298 (excluding that of Werner the Good)
Werner the Good blood libel, 1287
Rindfleisch massacres, 1298
Armleder massacres, 1336-1339

peace and security, a number of towns concluded a ten-year armistice with John Zimberlin, one of the Armleder leaders in Alsace.

The local authorities tried to restore calm by concluding additional agreements in the Rhine and other areas but the armistice was short-lived. The Armleder massacres were portents of and preludes to the destruction of European Jewry during the Black Death.

THE PASTOUREAUX AND "LEPERS" MASSACRES
1320 TO 1321

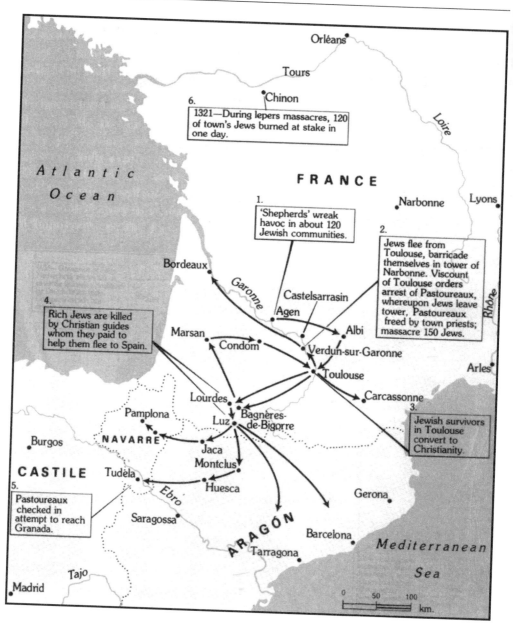

6.
1321—During lepers massacres, 120 of town's Jews burned at stake in one day.

FRANCE

1.
'Shepherds' wreak havoc in about 120 Jewish communities.

2.
Jews flee from Toulouse, barricade themselves in tower of Narbonne. Viscount of Toulouse orders arrest of Pastoureaux, whereupon Jews leave tower, Pastoureaux freed by town priests; massacre 150 Jews.

4.
Rich Jews are killed by Christian guides whom they paid to help them flee to Spain.

3.
Jewish survivors in Toulouse convert to Christianity.

5.
Pastoureaux checked in attempt to reach Granada.

Atlantic Ocean

Orléans
Tours
Chinon
Narbonne
Lyons
Bordeaux
Castelsarrasin
Agen
Albi
Arles
Marsan
Condom
Verdun-sur-Garonne
Toulouse
Carcassonne
Lourdes
Pamplona
Luz
Bagnères-de-Bigorre
NAVARRE
Jaca
Montclus
Gerona
Burgos
CASTILE
Tudela
Huesca
Barcelona
Saragossa
Tarragona
ARAGÓN
Madrid
Mediterranean Sea

Garonne *Rhône* *Ebro* *Tajo* *Loire*

0   50   100 km.

A POPULAR religious movement of Pastoureaux ("shepherds") in the town of Agen in southern France soon turned into a crusade bent on storming Granada and freeing the last portion of Christian European soil from Muslim rule. Along their route they turned first on Jewish communities in southern France and then on communities across the Pyrenees in the kingdoms of Aragón and Navarre.

216

ope John XXII opposed the crusaders and so did James II of Aragón, who, in order to protect the communities of northern Iberia, dispatched his son, crown prince Alfonso, to suppress them. This is one of the rare instances of a movement for liberating Christian soil from Muslim domination being destroyed by the party it wished to serve. As if this were not enough, the Jews of Chinon (in central France) were, in 1321, accused of poisoning wells in conspiracy with the lepers (who lived as outcasts from society).

THE BLACK DEATH 1348

MANY countries—from Spain in the southwest to Poland in the east—were hard hit by the great bubonic plague that reached Europe in 1348. The non-Jewish population accused the Jews of causing the plague by poisoning the wells. While Jewish casualties of the plague were relatively low in proportion to those of the Christians, the number of Jewish dead was swelled by the massacres. Jews were cruelly tortured in order to extract confessions that they were responsible for disseminating the plague. In many places they were burned at the stake. Pope Clement VI (1342–1352), recognizing the absurdity of the allegations against the Jews, issued a bull from the papal court at Avignon in 1348 denouncing the allegations.

Charles IV, emperor of Germany, and King Peter IV of Aragón tried to protect their Jewish communities, but, nonetheless, Jewish casualties were great. The Black Death and its aftermath proved a critical turning point for the Jewish communities. In Spain it represents the beginning of a decline for the communities in Castile and Aragón, not only in numbers but also politically, culturally and economically.

Woodcut depicting the burning of Jewish martyrs in Ashkenaz. From Schedel's Weltchronik, *1493.*

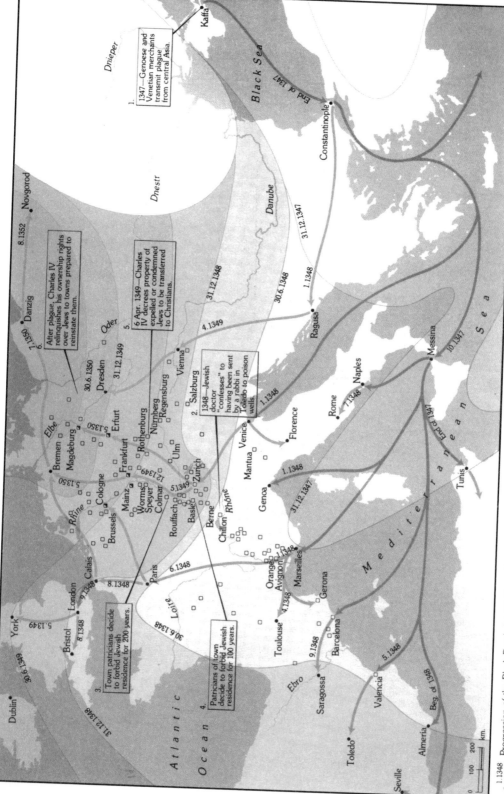

THE BLACK DEATH
1348

1. 1347—Genoese and Venetian merchants transmit plague from central Asia.

2. 1348—Jewish doctor "confesses" to having been sent by a rabbi in Toledo to poison wells.

3. Town patricians decide to forbid Jewish residence for 200 years.

4. Patricians of town decide to forbid Jewish residence for 100 years.

5. 6 Apr. 1349—Charles IV decrees property of expelled or condemned Jews to be transferred to Christians.

6. After plague, Charles IV relinquishes his ownership rights over Jews to towns prepared to reinstate them.

□ Jewish community stricken by massacre
▪ Jewish community which defended itself

1.1348   Progression of the Black Death (month & year)
→   Spread of the Black Death at six-month intervals
)   End of the Black Death

Black Sea
Dnieper
Dniestr
Danube
Mediterranean Sea
Atlantic Ocean
Rhine
Loire
Rhône
Elbe
Oder
Ebro

Kaffa
End of 1347
Constantinople
31.12.1347
1.1348
Ragusa
30.6.1348
31.12.1348
4.1349
Vienna
Salzburg
Regensburg
Nürnberg
Rothenburg
Ulm
Zurich
Basle
Berne
Chillon
Colmar
Rouffach
Speyer
Worms
Mainz
Frankfurt
12.1349
5.1349
Cologne
5.1350
Brussels
Erfurt
5.1350
Magdeburg
Bremen
Dresden
30.6.1350
31.12.1349
Danzig
7.1350
8.1352
Novgorod
Paris
6.1348
8.1348
Calais
9.1348
London
8.1348
Bristol
York
30.6.1349
5.1349
Dublin
31.12.1348
Mantua
Venice
1.1348
Florence
Rome
7.1348
Naples
7.1348
Messina
10.1347
Tunis
End of 1347
Genoa
1.1348
31.12.1348
Orange
Avignon
1.1348
Marseilles
4.1348
Toulouse
30.6.1348
Gerona
Barcelona
Saragossa
9.1348
Valencia
5.1348
Almeria
Beg. of 1348
Toledo
Seville

km.
0 100 200

C. UNTIL THE EXPULSION FROM SPAIN

DESTRUCTION OF THE JEWISH COMMUNITY IN FRANCE 14TH CENTURY

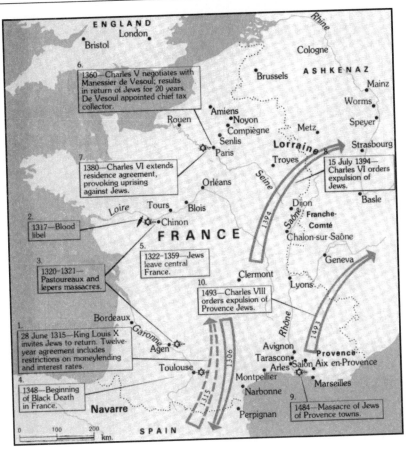

THE Hundred Years War (between England and France, 1337–1453) further impoverished France. An attempt was made between the years 1359 and 1361 to renew Jewish settlement in the country. Privileges of protection were extended to the Jews and, for a period of twenty years, they were even allowed to charge a high rate of interest on loans. In 1365 and 1366 certain factions tried to influence the crown to expel the Jews. Charles V (1364–1380) did in fact sign a decree to this effect on 6 January 1367, but it was never implemented. The king also ordered an inventory of Jewish property. Similar decrees were issued in 1368 and 1370. When Charles V died in 1380, the population attacked the Jews, killing many. They died as martyrs and their children were kidnapped. In Paris, the provost Hugues Aubriot tried to thwart the rioters, even returning kidnapped children to their parents, but was dismissed and imprisoned. Aubriot and the Jews were both casualties of the anti-crown riots of 1382. Charles VI succumbed to popular pressure and on 15 July 1394 decreed the expulsion of the

Jews from France by 3 November—seven years short of the twenty-year period granted in the charter of resettlement issued by his father Charles V.

The Jews were also expelled from Toulouse on 7 December 1394. (There were twelve families and an additional seven from the environs of Toulouse.) Jewish communities remained in Franche-Comté, Lorraine in the north, Provence and Navarre. In 1481, when Provence was annexed to France, the edict of expulsion was applied there as well; however, the king acquiesced to the plea of the Jews of Marseilles, Arles, Aix-en-Provence, Tarascon and Salon-de-Provence and renewed their privileges. In 1484 there was an outbreak of riots in the towns of Provence (except Salon) and on 19 August 1484 Charles VIII (1483–1498) forbade Jewish settlement in Arles. In 1486 the town council turned to its representatives in the Assembly of Estates demanding the expulsion of the Jews, a similar demand being made in Marseilles. Anti-Jewish feelings were particularly strong after the Spanish expulsion (1492) and Charles finally yielded to the pressure. At the end of July 1493 he ordered all Jews to either convert or leave Arles within three months.

The Jews of Arles and Marseilles succeeded in obtaining a number of postponements of the decree but in 1500–1501 the remnant was forced to leave. Only a few Jews remained in the French papal territories. The renewal of Jewish settlement in southwest France became the task of the conversos who fled the Iberian Peninsula, but many years were to pass before they were allowed to live openly as Jews.

THE BEGINNING OF JEWISH SETTLEMENT IN POLAND

IT was only in the thirteenth century that the Jews of Poland began to enjoy privileges, although there is evidence of Jews in Poland at an earlier period. In 1264 King Boleslav V the Pious of Kalisz granted the Jews privileges, being influenced by those granted them by the emperors of Germany. The first privilege was to ensure protection against blood libels. It also recognized the status of the Jews as the *servi camerae regis* ("servants of the royal chamber").

In 1334 Casimir III the Great conferred privileges upon the Jews of Poland, ratifying these privileges in 1336 for other parts of his kingdom—Lesser Poland (western Galicia with Cracow, its capital) and Red Russia (Ruthenia, eastern Galicia with Lvov, its capital). After the unification of Poland and Lithuania in 1386, Grand Duke Vitold granted the same privileges to Lithuania (1388).

In the fourteenth and fifteenth centuries many Jewish refugees from Germany arrived in Poland. The Polish nobles and townspeople wanted to expel the Jews and consequently, during the reign of Ladislaus (Wladyslaw) II Jagiellon (1386–1434), the Jews were persecuted.

A blood libel in 1399 in Poznan resulted in the massacre of the Jews and the looting of their neighborhood. In 1407 there was an anti-Jewish outbreak in Cracow by the students of the university (founded in 1400).

There is little information about early Jewish communities in Lithuania. The important centers were Brest Litovsk,

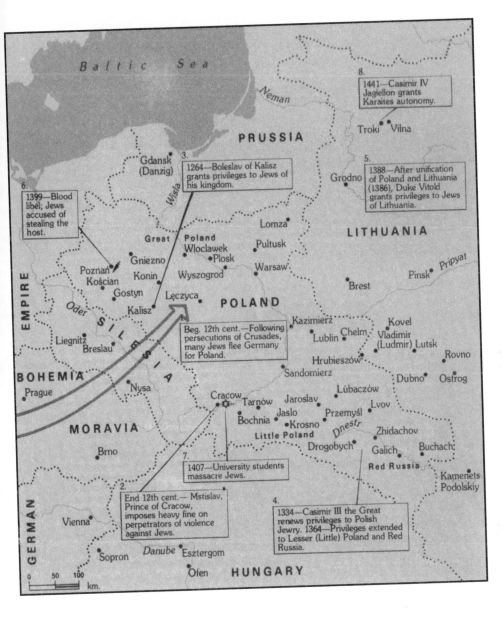

Map labels:

Baltic Sea

Neman

PRUSSIA

Troki • Vilna

8.
1441—Casimir IV
Jagiellon grants
Karaites autonomy.

Gdansk
(Danzig)

3.
1264—Boleslav of Kalisz
grants privileges to Jews of
his kingdom.

Grodno

5.
1388—After unification
of Poland and Lithuania
(1386), Duke Vitold
grants privileges to Jews
of Lithuania.

6.
1399—Blood
libel; Jews
accused of
stealing the
host.

Wisła

LITHUANIA

Lomza

Great Poland
Wloclawek
• Plosk
Pultusk

Gniezno

Warsaw

Pinsk • *Pripyat*

Poznan
Kościan

Konin

Wyszogrod

Brest

Gostyn

Łęczyca

Kalisz

POLAND

Kazimierz

Kovel
Vladimir
(Ludmir) Lutsk

Beg. 12th cent.—Following
persecutions of Crusades,
many Jews flee Germany
for Poland.

Lublin Chelm

Rovno

Liegnitz
Breslau

Oder S I L E S I A

Hrubieszów

Sandomierz

Dubno • Ostrog

BOHEMIA

Prague

Nysa

Cracow

Tarnów

Jaroslav

Lúbaczów

Bochnia • Krosno

Jaslo

Przemyśl

Lvov

MORAVIA

Dnestr

Zhidachov

Little Poland

Drogobych

Galich

Buchach

Brno

7.
1407—University students
massacre Jews.

Red Russia

Kamenets
Podolskiy

2.
End 12th cent.— Mstislav,
Prince of Cracow,
imposes heavy fine on
perpetrators of violence
against Jews.

4.
1334—Casimir III the Great
renews privileges to Polish
Jewry. 1364—Privileges extended
to Lesser (Little) Poland and Red
Russia.

G E R M A N   E M P I R E

Vienna

Sopron

Danube Esztergom

Ofen   HUNGARY

0 50 100
km.

Troki, Grodno and perhaps Lutsk. In Volhynia the Jewish community of Ludmir (Vladimir in Volhynia) was already known in the thirteenth century. (Volhynia was annexed to Lithuania in 1336.) Many Lithuanian Jews were farmers, but the nobles from time to time attempted to drive them off the land. Slowly, Jewish urban settlement developed, with Jews engaged in operating lease concessions, an activity that in due course extended over all of Poland, Lithuania and the Ukraine.

In 1441 Casimir IV Jagiellon recognized the Karaite community, granting them equal rights with Christians.

The expulsion of the Jews from Spain in 1492 also had repercussions in Poland and Lithuania, and in 1495 the Jews were expelled from Lithuania and Cracow. (However, they were allowed to reside in Kazimierz, a suburb of Cracow.)

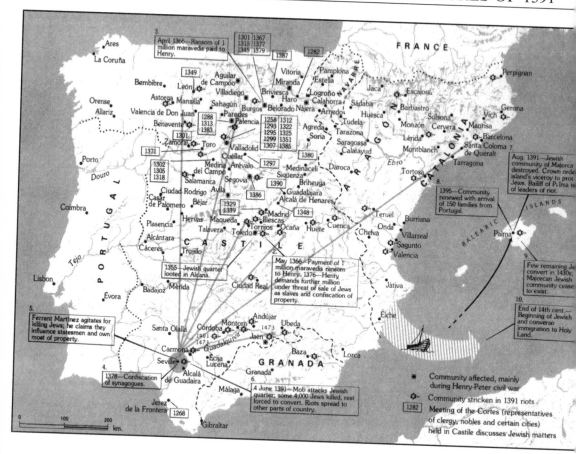

Map labels and boxes:

April 1366—Ransom of 1 million maravedis paid to Henry.

FRANCE

Ares
La Coruña
Bembibre
León
Orense
Allariz
Astorga
Mansilla
Sahagún
Valencia de Don Juan
Benavente
Paredes
Palencia
Zamora
Toro
Valladolid
Cuéllar
Medina del Campo
Arévalo
Segovia
Ciudad Rodrigo
Avila
Casar de Palomero
Béjar
Plasencia
Hervás
Maqueda
Talavera
Toledo
Alcántara
Cáceres
Trujillo
Porto
Douro
Coimbra
PORTUGAL
Tejo
Lisbon
Évora
Badajoz
Mérida
Ciudad Real

1349
1301
1315
1345
1367
1377
1379
1387
1282
Vitoria
Pamplona
Estella
Miranda
Aguilar de Campóo
Villadiego
Briviesca
Haro
Logroño
Calahorra
Jaca
Escalona
Sádaba
Barbastro
Huesca
Monzón
Cervera
Solsona
Vich
Gerona
Manresa
Belorado Nájera
Arnedo
Tudela
Agreda
Tarazona
Soria
Saragossa
Calatayud
Lérida
Montblanch
Santa Coloma de Queralt
Barcelona
Tarragona
Ebro
Tortosa
1288
1313
1383
1301
1371
1302
1305
1318
1258 1312
1293 1322
1295 1325
1299 1351
1307 1385
1297
1380
Medinaceli
Sigüenza
Briheuga
Daroca
1390
1386
Guadalajara
Alcalá de Henares
1329
1339
Madrid
1348
Illescas
Torrijos
Ocaña
Huete
Cuenca
Teruel
Burriana
Onda
Villarreal
Chelva
Sagunto
Valencia
Játiva

Aug. 1391—Jewish community of Majorca destroyed. Crown orde island's viceroy to prot Jews. Bailiff of P. lma is of leaders of riot.

1395—Community renewed with arrival of 150 families from Portugal.

ISLANDS
BALEARIC
Palma

Few remaining Je convert in 1430's Majorcan Jewish community cease to exist.

End of 14th cent.— Beginning of Jewish and converso immigration to Holy Land.

1355—Jewish quarter looted in Alcana.

May 1366—Payment of 1 million maravedis ransom to Henry. 1376—Henry demands further million under threat of sale of Jews as slaves and confiscation of property.

Ferrant Martínez agitates for killing Jews; he claims they influence statesmen and own most of property.

1378—Confiscation of synagogues.

Santa Olalla
Carmona
Sevilla
Écija
Lucena
Alcalá de Guadaira
Jerez de la Frontera
Málaga
Granada
Córdoba
Montoro
Guadalquivir
Jaén
Andújar
Ubeda
Baza
Lorca
Elche
Játiva
GRANADA
1473
1461
1471
1268
Gibraltar

4 June 1391—Mob attacks Jewish quarter; some 4,000 Jews killed, rest forced to convert. Riots spread to other parts of country.

0   100   200   km.

● Community affected, mainly during Henry-Peter civil war
✦ Community stricken in 1391 riots
1282 Meeting of the Cortes (representatives of clergy, nobles and certain cities) held in Castile discusses Jewish matters

---

THE Black Death, which reached Aragón in 1348, brought with it a wave of murderous attacks on Jews, who were accused of causing the plague. The kingdom of Castile underwent a radical decline in population during the second half of the fourteenth century, not so much as a result of the plague as of a general increase in mortality and of population migration. The Jews were not held responsible for these factors. Thus, the 1354 attack on the Jews of Seville, which seemed a distant echo of the Black Death, proved to have had a local cause—an accusation of a host desecration.

The rule of Peter the Cruel (1350–

1369), king of Castile, was contested by his half-brother Henry of Trastámara and during their bitter struggle many Jewish communities suffered. Henry was the first ruler to use an anti-Jewish line as the basis of his political policy, declaring that he was waging war against his brother in order to free Castile from the harmful influence of Peter's Jewish advisers. Toledo was one of the first communities to be affected when in the spring of 1355 some of Henry's forces entered the town attacking and looting the small Jewish quarter of Alcana. According to the contemporary Spanish historian Pedro López de Ayala, more than one thousand Jews were killed in

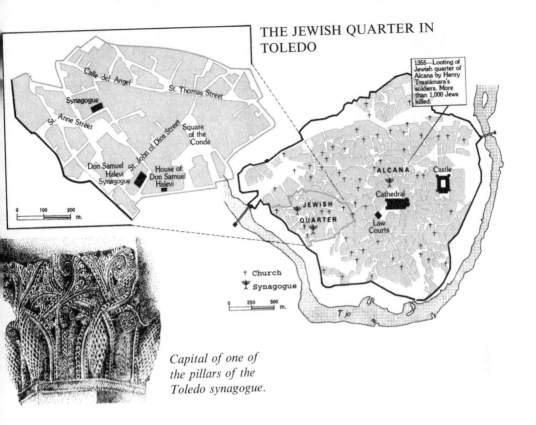

THE JEWISH QUARTER IN
TOLEDO

1355—Looting of
Jewish quarter of
Alcana by Henry
Trastámara's
soldiers. More
than 1,000 Jews
killed.

Calle del Angel
Synagogue
St. Thomas Street
St. Anne Street
St. John of Dios Street
Square
of the
Conde
Don Samuel
Halevi
Synagogue
House of
Don Samuel
Halevi

0 100 200 m.

ALCANA   Castle
Cathedral
JEWISH
QUARTER
Law
Courts

† Church
Synagogue

0 250 500 m.

Tajo

Capital of one of
the pillars of the
Toledo synagogue.

Alcana. The attackers were not able to penetrate the larger Jewish quarter of Toledo, which was protected by mercenaries hired by the Jewish community.

Other Jewish communities in Castile were also attacked. In 1360 Henry advanced from northern Castile, attacking Jewish communities and populations along the way. In April 1366 Henry took the town of Burgos, demanding one million maravedis from the Jewish community in ransom money; in May when he entered Toledo, he made the same demand of its Jewish community, which had to sell the Torah crowns in order to pay the ransom. A year later Henry again entered Burgos, forcing the Jews to pay a further ransom of one million maravedis. The first rioters were French and English mercenary troops enlisted by Peter and Henry in their civil war. They were responsible for the destruction of most

of the Jewish communities of Castile. Even the southern communities were not spared; Peter, the avowed protector of the Jews, allowed the Muslims of Granada, who aided him, to sell the Jews of Jaén into slavery.

The persecutions of 1391 were preceded, in 1378, by the confiscation of synagogues in Seville, instigated by the anti-Jewish agitation of the archdeacon of Écija, Ferrant Martínez. On 4 June 1391 anti-Jewish disorders broke out in Seville, spreading through the other Jewish communities of Andalusia and subsequently through most of the communities in Spain. Clergy, nobles, townspeople and peasants all participated in the riots. At the beginning of July news of the attacks reached Aragón, causing general agitation. In Catalonia, where most of the Jewish communities were destroyed, the riots were accompanied by

223

Interior of a synagogue in the Jewish neighborhood of Toledo, founded in the 13th century. After the riots of 1391, it was converted into Santa Maria La Blanca church.

John I (1387–1395) ordered an invento of the property of Jews killed in the rio who had no heirs, since it was the custo in those days for the crown to inher such property.

Two communities in the kingdom (Aragón were unharmed—those of Sara gossa, the capital and royal residenc and Perpignan. In Saragossa Rabb Hasdai Crescas was active and instru mental in organizing the defense of th town's Jews, collecting money to hire on of the nobles, Francisco d'Aranda, an his troops for this purpose. At the end o 1391 the king left Saragossa to tour th kingdom and pacify the population Every place he visited he began negotia tions on the size of fines to be paid an the procedures for procuring a roya pardon. The population of a number of towns succeeded in placing the blame for the riots on the Jews.

Very few Castilian Jewish communities were spared; even the large ones disap peared as if they had never existed. Only Navarre escaped almost unscathed from the riots. But the Jews were attacked during the riots of 1328.

Many Spanish Jews saved their lives by apostasy, so that entire communities together with their leaders were obliterated. Even great Jewish personalities converted prior to the riots of 1391, some of them under the influence of Friar Vincent Ferrer. This gave rise to a new phenomenon: the creation of a community of conversos who wished to return to Judaism and who secretly practiced Jewish observance alongside openly professing Jewish communities that began to recuperate and rebuild their lives during the fifteenth century.

a revolt of the indentured artisans and peasants against their lords. However, this revolt was only a secondary factor in the crusade against the Jews, although the authorities were wary of its side effects. The crown took advantage of the disturbances: the king of Aragón,

JEWISH SETTLEMENT IN PORTUGAL

13TH AND 14TH CENTURIES

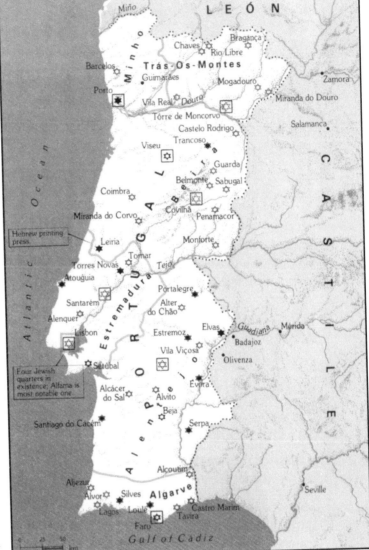

Jewish community in 13th century (1279–1325)
New Jewish settlement in reighn of Afonso IV, 1325–1357
New Jewish settlement in reign of Pedro. 1357–1467
New Jewish settlement in reign of Ferdinand, 1367–1383
Boundary of regional organization under *arrabi môr*
Regional capital

EVER since Portuguese independence, during the reign of Afonso III (1248–1279), the Jewish communities of Portugal developed their own unique organizational structure. The crown appointed a single head of all the Jews in Portugal called the *arrabi môr*, who in turn appointed seven regional heads, or *arrabi menors*, each heading one of the seven regional divisions of Portugal. The *arrabi môr* had a wide range of authority in supervising Jewish communal life. He was the intermediary between the crown and the community; he represented the latter before the crown and conveyed the crown's wishes to the community. He also advised the crown on matters of taxation and obligations imposed on the Jewish community. However, he was not a "chief rabbi" in the conventional sense, but rather a crown administrator.

The fourteenth century was relatively tranquil for the Jews of Portugal notwithstanding anti-Jewish agitation and church pressure, for example, with regard to the wearing of identifying badges and restriction of residence. Although the anti-Jewish atmosphere fomented by the church resulted in the massacres of 1449, Jewish communal life continued to function unperturbed.

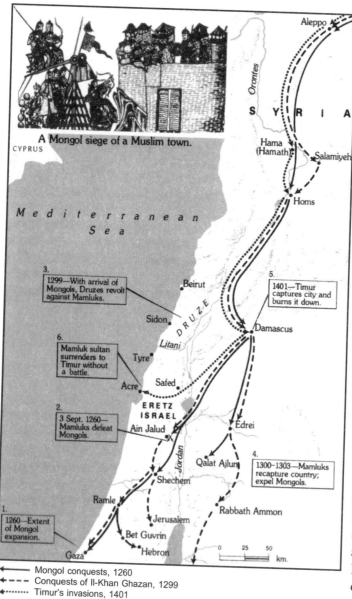

A Mongol siege of a Muslim town.

CYPRUS

Aleppo

Orontes

S Y R I A

Hama
(Hamath)
Salamiyeh

Homs

M e d i t e r r a n e a n
S e a

3.
1299—With arrival of
Mongols, Druzes revolt
against Mamluks.

Beirut

5.
1401—Timur
captures city and
burns it down.

Sidon

D R U Z E

Damascus

6.
Mamluk sultan
surrenders to
Timur without
a battle.

Litani

Tyre

Acre

Safed

ERETZ
ISRAEL

2.
3 Sept. 1260—
Mamluks defeat
Mongols.

Ain Jalud

Edrei

Jordan

Qalat Ajlun

4.
1300–1303—Mamluks
recapture country;
expel Mongols.

Shechem

Ramle

Rabbath Ammon

1.
1260—Extent
of Mongol
expansion.

Jerusalem

Bet Guvrin

Gaza

Hebron

0   25   50
km.

⟶ Mongol conquests, 1260
⟵- - - Conquests of Il-Khan Ghazan, 1299
⟵······· Timur's invasions, 1401

THE Mongol invasion of Europe and the Middle East from the end of the twelfth century brought radical changes to those areas. Nations were destroyed and whole populations annihilated. The world was engulfed by a powerful wave of conquest the like of which it had never known before.

Before the death of Genghis Khan (1227) the Mongols had reached the Dnieper in Europe and in 1421 they crossed the Oder, annihilating a German and Polish army in a battle near Liegnitz. In 1258 the Mongols, led by Il-Khan Hülegü, conquered Mesopotamia, from which they proceeded to Palestine, reaching Gaza in 1260. In September 1260, at the battle of Ain Jalud (Ein Harod) in the Valley of Jezreel, they were decisively defeated by Baybars and the Mamluk army, thus ensuring Mamluk rule over Palestine. In 1299, under the leadership of Il-Khan Ghazan, they launched an invasion with the aid of an Armenian army and Druse from the Lebanon. At the end of the fourteenth century the Tartar prince Timur (Tamerlane) revived the Mongol Empire and in 1401 conquered and set fire to Damascus. Palestine surrendered without battle, accepting the Tartar yoke until the death of Timur in 1405.

The Mongol campaigns directed against Muslims in the east as well as

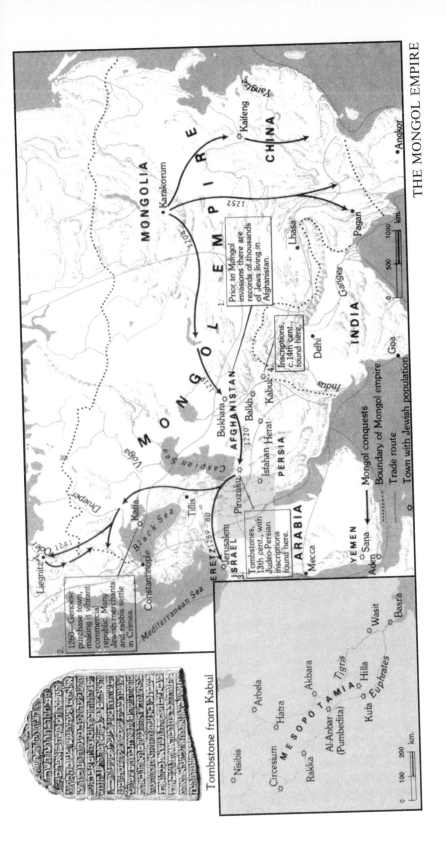

THE MONGOL EMPIRE

Prior to Mongol invasions there are records of thousands of Jews living in Afghanistan.

Inscriptions, c.14th cent., found here.

Tombstones, 13th cent., with Judeo-Persian inscriptions found here.

1260—Genoese purchase town, making it vibrant commercial republic. Many Jewish merchants and rabbis settle in Crimea.

Mongol conquests

Boundary of Mongol empire

Trade route

Town with Jewish population

MONGOLIA

CHINA

Karakorum

Kaifeng

Yangtze

Pagan

Lhasa

Angkor

INDIA

Ganges

Delhi

Goa

Indus

MONGOL EMPIRE

1254

1252

1219

Bukhara

Balkh

AFGHANISTAN

Kabul

1220

Herat

Isfahan

PERSIA

Firuzkuh

Caspian Sea

Volga

Kaffa

Tiflis

Black Sea

Constantinople

Dnieper

Liegnitz

Oder

1241

1259–60

ERETZ

Jerusalem

ISRAEL

Mediterranean Sea

ARABIA

YEMEN

Sana

Mecca

Aden

0   500   1000 km.

Tombstone from Kabul

Nisibis

Arbela

Circesium

Hatra

Akbara

MESOPOTAMIA

Tigris

Rakka

Al-Anbar (Pumbedita)

Hilla

Kufa

Euphrates

Wasit

Basra

0   100   200 km.

227

their expansion in Europe caused great dread both in the east and in the west. The Muslims in the east were the chief victims of these campaigns although in the course of events the Mongols became closer to Islam, some even converting. The Jewish communities were saved in a number of places, including Baghdad (1258), Aleppo (in 1260 Jews found asylum in the central synagogue, which was left untouched) and Damascus. The Mongol invasions aroused messiani hopes for an imminent redemptio among the Jews of Italy and Spain. Som believed the Mongols to be descendant of the ten tribes. In Christian Europ some Jewish communities were suspecter of contact with the Mongols, and accusec of being associated with their invasion and devastations. The Jewish commu nities in Silesia and Germany sufferec from the Mongol advance westward.

IMMIGRATION TO THE HOLY LAND
14TH AND 15TH CENTURIES

Wood engraving of a map of Jerusalem by Erhard Reuwich, 1486.

THE massacres in 1391 in Spain increased the number of immigrants to Eretz Israel. Among the newcomers, of whose travels we do not have details, were many conversos, such as Isaac Nifoci of Majorca. They went to Palestine despite the difficult living conditions and the persecutions of the Mamluk regime. Jews came not only from Spain but also from Ashkenaz. Two important personalities from Italy came in the 1480s: Meshullam of Volterra (1481) and Obadiah of Bertinoro (1485). The involvement of the latter in the life of the Jerusalem community was both considerable and significant. Every traveler had to choose his own way from among the existing routes to Palestine, a particularly difficult

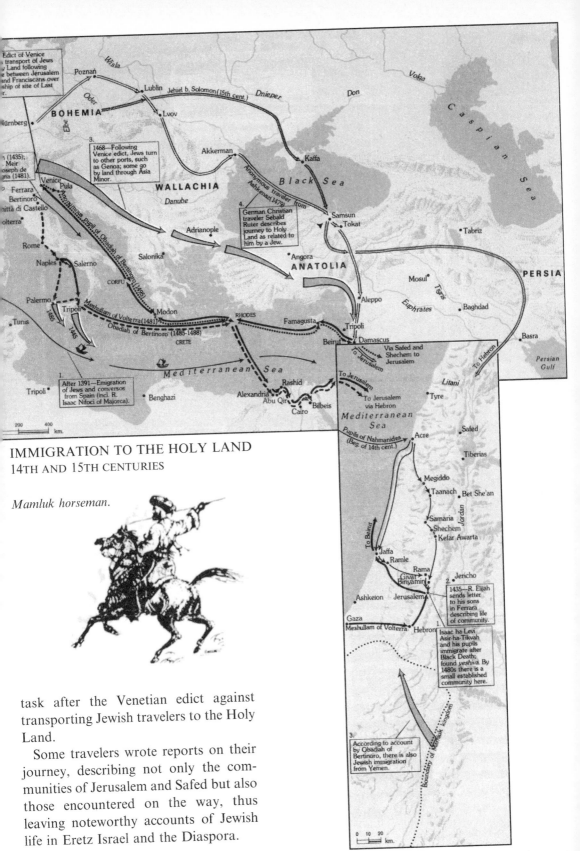

Nürnberg

Poznań

Wisła

Oder

Lublin Jehiel b. Solomon (15th cent.)

Dniepr

Volga

Don

BOHEMIA

Lvov

Elbe

Caspian Sea

(1435); Meir Joseph de [...]ma (1481).

Ferrara Bertinoro [...]nitta di Castello [...]olterra

Venice Pula

Akkerman

Kaffa

3.
1468—Following Venice edict, Jews turn to other ports, such as Genoa; some go by land through Asia Minor.

WALLACHIA

Danube

Black Sea

Samsun
Tokat

Tabriz

Anonymous traveler from Ashkenaz (1479)

4.
German Christian traveler Sebald Ruter describes journey to Holy Land as related to him by a Jew.

PERSIA

Rome

Adrianople

Salonika

ANATOLIA
Angora

Mosul

Tigris

Baghdad

Naples Salerno

CORFU

Anonymous pupil of Obadiah of Bertinoro (1491)

Aleppo

Euphrates

Palermo

1435   1445

Tripoli Modon

Meshullam of Volterra (1481)

RHODES

Famagusta

Tripoli

Beirut Damascus

Basra

Tunis

Obadiah of Bertinoro (1485–1488)

CRETE

Via Safed and Shechem to Jerusalem

To Hebron

Persian Gulf

Mediterranean Sea

To Jerusalem

Litani

1.
After 1391—Emigration of Jews and conversos from Spain (incl. R. Isaac Nifoci of Majorca).

Rashid

To Jerusalem via Hebron

Tyre

Tripoli

Benghazi

Alexandria
Abu Qir

Cairo Bilbeis

Mediterranean Sea

Safed

200   400
km.

Pupils of Nahmanides (Beg. of 14th cent.)

Acre

IMMIGRATION TO THE HOLY LAND
14TH AND 15TH CENTURIES

Tiberias

Megiddo

Taanach Bet She'an

Mamluk horseman.

Samaria
Shechem
Kefar Awarta

Jordan

To Beirut

Jaffa
Ramle

Rama
Givat Binyamin

Jericho

2.
1435—R. Elijah sends letter to his sons in Ferrara describing life of community.

Ashkelon

Jerusalem

Gaza
Meshullam of Volterra

Hebron

1.
Isaac ha-Levi Asir-ha-Tikvah and his pupils immigrate after Black Death; found *yeshiva*. By 1480s there is a small established community here.

task after the Venetian edict against transporting Jewish travelers to the Holy Land.

Some travelers wrote reports on their journey, describing not only the communities of Jerusalem and Safed but also those encountered on the way, thus leaving noteworthy accounts of Jewish life in Eretz Israel and the Diaspora.

Boundary of Mamluk kingdom

3.
According to account by Obadiah of Bertinoro, there is also Jewish immigration from Yemen.

0 10 20
km.

THE BEGINNINGS OF THE OTTOMAN EMPIRE

Jewish tombstone found in cemetery near Istanbul.

OTTOMAN incursions into the Byzantine Empire occurred over an extended period, gradually undermining Byzantine rule in Asia Minor and the Balkan peninsula. Region upon region was wrenched from Byzantium, even by Venice and Genoa, which took control over various islands in the eastern Mediterranean. It was in these regions that Jewish life was revived. The Turks captured Gallipoli in 1354 and Adrianople in 1361. From this point the way was open to additional conquests in Europe and the course of the wars between 1361 and 1430 determined the fate of Macedonia. Salonika held out after being under Venetian rule from 1423 until it was occupied by the Turks in 1430. From that date the Ottoman Empire became a serious threat to the Christian states of Europe.

In the fourteenth century there were few Jewish settlements in Asia Minor or in the areas ruled by Byzantium. Constantinople had a small Jewish community as well as a Karaite one. The Romaniot (Byzantine Jews) failed to develop a rich cultural or spiritual life under the Byzantines and after the Ottoman conquest they integrated with the newly established communities. The fall of Constantinople to Muhammad II in 1453 was seen by Jewry as a second fall of Rome. Constantinople epitomized hatred of Jews in all its dreadful manifestations. Its conquest became associated with messianic hopes for the beginning of the redemption, arousing Jews and conversos to leave Spain for the east, the Holy Land and other places under Ottoman rule; in the words of the emigres, "to be taken under the wings of the Shekhinah (divine presence)."

After the conquest of Constantinople the Ottomans established their capital there (also called Kosta by the Jews) and repopulated the almost deserted city by the forcible transfer of Jews and other populations from Salonika, Adrianople and other towns.

In 1470 the first group of Jewish emigrants from Ashkenaz settled in Salonika, followed by a large number of Sephardic refugees from Spain, after the Expulsion (1492), Portugal, Sicily, Calabria and Naples. The city soon became a thriving Jewish center along with Constantinople, Adrianople, Bursa and other places.

The conquest of Damascus and Aleppo in 1516 and the Ottoman subjugation of Palestine (1516) and Egypt (1517) opened new horizons for the Jews of the Diaspora.

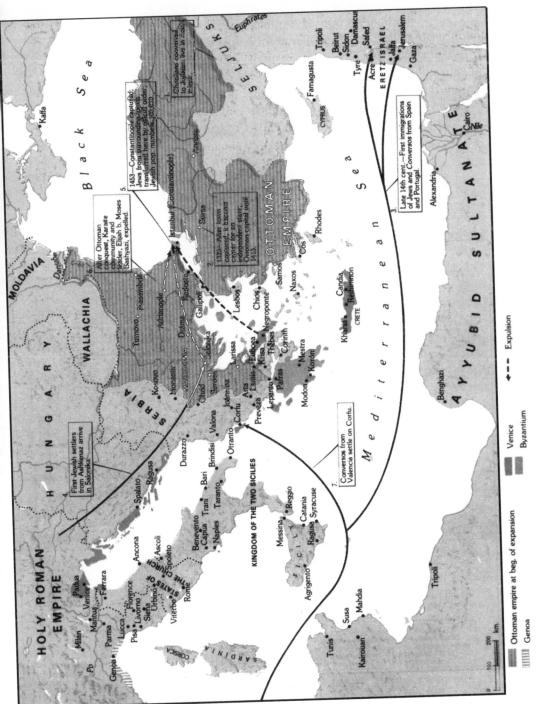

THE
BEGINNINGS
OF THE
OTTOMAN
EMPIRE

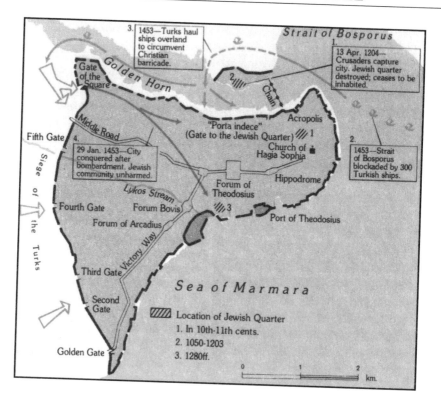

THE volunteers and the Venetian and Catalonian residents of the city's trading cantons were unable to withstand the Ottoman siege. The Jewish Romaniot community was dispersed and its quarter destroyed.

Detail from a woodcut of Constantinople (1520). Jewish cemetery in center indicated by an arrow.

COMMERCE IN THE MEDITERRANEAN BASIN
14TH TO 15TH CENTURIES

JEWISH economic activity in the Mediterranean basin in the fourteenth and fifteenth centuries covered a variety of commercial fields including maritime trade to many countries. Jews were partners to trade agreements with ship captains. The captain carried out the commercial transaction and the Jew financed the merchandise. Sometimes special joint ventures would be organized

COMMERCE IN THE MEDITERRANEAN BASIN
14TH–15TH CENTURIES

Atlantic Ocean

POLAND

HOLY ROMAN EMPIRE

HUNGARY

MOLDAVIA

WALLACHIA

FRANCE

NAVARRE

ARAGON

CASTILE

PORTUGAL

MUSLIM KINGDOMS

MAMLUKS

Black Sea

Mediterranean Sea

CORSICA

SARDINIA

BALEARIC ISLANDS

SICILY

JERBA

Boxed notes:

1. Embarkation port for Jews; only four Jews allowed per voyage.

2. Jews are partner to maritime trade agreements.

3. 1322–1330—Under Venetian rule.

4. Jews supply inhabitants with grain, wine, perfume and spices.

5. Until 1480—Jewish merchants from Europe stayed at local inns.

6. Venice and Genoa control immigration routes to Holy Land. 1428—Captains prohibited from transporting Jews to Holy Land.

7. Jews are partners in ships carrying copper.

8. Jewish merchants lend money to Christian Venetian merchants.

9. Jews control manufacture of sugar.

Place names:

Kaffa, Istanbul (Constantinople), Angora, Antiochia, Tripoli, Damascus, Acre, Jerusalem, Beirut, Tyre, Jaffa, Gaza, Damietta, Alexandria, Cairo (Fustat), Toron, Famagusta, Candia, Smyrna, Negroponte, Gallipoli, Adrianople, Nicopolis, Kosovo, Alessio, Salonika, Modon, Corfu, Otranto, Ragusa, Syracuse, Ragusa, Messina, Naples, Venice, Genoa, Marseilles, Narbonne, Barcelona, Valencia, Málaga, Gold, Sijilmasa, Tangier, Tunis, Tripoli, Santiago de Compostela, Lisbon

Silk, pearls

Spices, flax, olive oil, wool

Sugar, pepper, cotton

metal

Copper, slaves, wood

km.
0 200 400

Legend:

Major trading areas of Venice and Genoa in Mediterranean
- Venice
- Genoa

Trade routes of Venice and Genoa

Inn for Jewish merchants

Ottoman empire

Byzantium

233

Italian merchant.

Christian merchants money for payment of customs duty on the goods they were delivering. A number of ports (e.g., on Crete) had special inns for Jewish travelers. Many Jews served as agents in the trade between Europe and Muslim countries.

Jewish commercial activity was considerable despite many restrictions: Jewish passengers were limited to four per ship per voyage; some captains refused to carry Jewish passengers to Egypt; Venice forbade sea captains to carry Jewish passengers bound for the Holy Land; and Mamluk rulers in Syria and Egypt generally oppressed their Jewish citizens.

European trade in the fourteenth and fifteenth centuries developed considerably in comparison with that of the Radhanites in the ninth to the eleventh centuries. Credit facilities and methods of finance improved, and trade routes were shorter and safer. Jews in their various places of residence played an important role in this trade.

between Jewish and Christian merchants, including Jewish residents of Muslim countries who would lend the Venetian

THE JEWS OF GERMANY IN THE SHADOW OF EXPULSIONS AND MASSACRES 14TH AND 15TH CENTURIES

ALTHOUGH the Jewish communities were persecuted even before the period of the Black Death, neither the massacres nor the plague itself and its consequences were able to eliminate the Jews of Ashkenaz. However, conditions within the communities deteriorated; in some places Jewish residence was limited to ten years. Only a few communities were able to recuperate, but by the middle of the fifteenth century the network of Jewish communities had grown despite the continued harrassment of the population. The Jews of Prague who were saved during the Black Death were massacred

in 1389. In the 1380s a long list of expulsions from various places were added to the list of massacres.

During the second half of the fifteenth century John of Capistrano preached in German cities, inciting people against the Jews. Many of the expulsions in the fifteenth century were initiated by the townspeople. The Jewish privilege of temporary residence in Cologne was not renewed. King Sigismund requested that the expulsion be postponed and Duke Adolf was appointed as a judge-arbitrator. In his judgment of 24 July 1425 he asserted that the city was entitled to carry

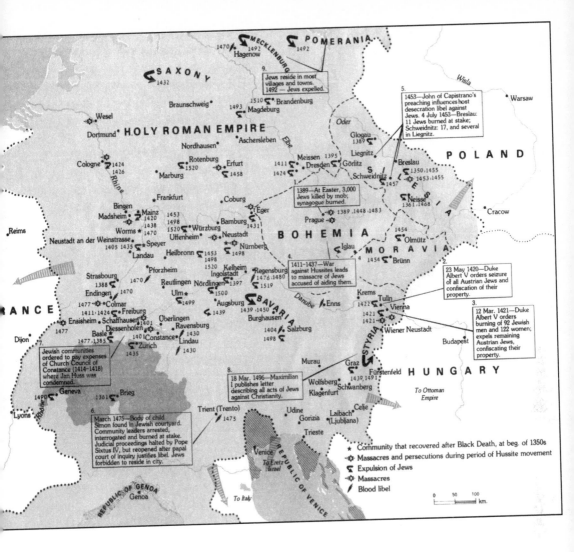

Map labels (reading across):

470● Hagenow   MECKLENBURG 1492   POMERANIA

9.
Jews reside in most
villages and towns.
1492 — Jews expelled.

SAXONY
1432

Braunschweig ●   1510 ⌇ Brandenburg
1493 ⌇ Magdeburg

Wesel ●
Dortmund ●-⌖- HOLY ROMAN EMPIRE
Nordhausen ●
Aschersleben ●

Oder

Glogau
1389 ⌇

5.
1453—John of Capistrano's
preaching influences host
desecration libel against
Jews. 4 July 1453—Breslau:
11 Jews burned at stake;
Schweidnitz: 17, and several
in Liegnitz.

Wisla

● Warsaw

POLAND

Cologne ⌇ 1424
1426
Marburg ●
Frankfurt ●
Rotenburg ⌇1520 -⌖- Erfurt
⌇ 1458

Meissen 1395
1411 ⌇● ● Dresden ⌇● Görlitz
1424 ⌇

Liegnitz
⌇ 1350,1455
Schweidnitz ● 1453,1455
1457

S Neisse
1361,1468

Cracow ●

MORAVIA

Bingen ●
Madsheim ● ⌇ Mainz 1453
1420 1498
Worms ● 1438 1520 ⌇● Würzburg
● 1470 Uffenheim ● -⌖- Neustadt
Neustadt an der Weinstrasse
1405 1435 ⌇● Speyer
Landau ● Heilbronn ⌇ 1453 ⌇ 1498

Coburg ●
-⌖- Eger

Bamberg ● 1431
Nürnberg ⌇

1389 ,1448 ,1483 ●
Prague -⌖-

BOHEMIA

1389—At Easter, 3,000
Jews killed by mob;
synagogue burned.

⌇ Iglau
⌇● Olmütz
4 1454 ⌇● Brünn

Reims ●

Strasbourg
1388 ⌇ 1470
Endingen ⌇ 1470
1477 -⌖-● Colmar
1411·1424 ⌇● Freiburg
-⌖-● Ensisheim ● Schaffhausen ● 1401
Diessenhofen
1477·1385 ⌇ Basle ●
Dijon ● 1477
⌇ Zürich
1435

Pforzheim ●
1520 Kelheim
Reutlingen Nördlingen 1397
Ulm ● ⌇ 1500
⌇ 1499
-⌖- Augsburg ⌇ 1439 ,1450
Burghausen
Überlingen
Ravensburg
140 ⌇ Constance ● 1430
● Lindau
/ 1430

Ingolstadt
⌇● Regensburg 1476 ,1480
⌇ 1519

4.
1411-1437—War
against Hussites leads
to massacre of Jews
accused of aiding them.

Danube / ● Enns

BAVARIA

1404 ● Salzburg
1498 ⌇

Krems
⌇ Tulln
1422 ⌇● Vienna
1421 ⌇
1421 -⌖-
Wiener Neustadt

23 May 1420—Duke
Albert V orders seizure
of all Austrian Jews and
confiscation of their
property.

12 Mar. 1421—Duke
Albert V orders
burning of 92 Jewish
men and 122 women;
expels remaining
Austrian Jews,
confiscating their
property.

Budapest ●

Jewish communities
ordered to pay expenses
of Church Council of
Constance (1414-1418)
where Jan Huss was
condemned.

1490 ⌇ ● Geneva
Lyons ● 1361 ⌇ ● Brieg

6.
March 1475—Body of child
Simon found in Jewish courtyard.
Community leaders arrested,
interrogated and burned at stake.
Judicial proceedings halted by Pope
Sixtus IV, but reopened after papal
court of inquiry justifies libel. Jews
forbidden to reside in city.

Murau ●

STYRIA

Graz
⌇
⌇ Fürstenfeld HUNGARY
Wolfsberg ● 1439,1491
Schwanberg
Klagenfurt ●

To Ottoman
Empire

8.
18 Mar. 1496—Maximilian
I publishes letter
describing all acts of Jews
against Christianity.

Trient (Trento)
/ 1475

Udine ●
Gorizia ●
● Laibach
(Ljubljana)
Trieste ●

Celje ●

Venice ●
To Eretz
Israel

REPUBLIC OF VENICE

To Italy

REPUBLIC OF GENOA
Genoa ●

★ Community that recovered after Black Death, at beg. of 1350s
-⌖- Massacres and persecutions during period of Hussite movement
⌇ Expulsion of Jews
-⌖- Massacres
/ Blood libel

0   50   100
km.

out its decision, but the Jews had already
been expelled in October 1424. The
refugees settled in a region adjacent to
the archbishop's diocese, but a dispute
between the archbishop and the townspeople of Mainz led to the expulsion of
the Jews from the diocese. Albert III,
elector of Brandenburg (1470–1486),
wrote in 1462: "Every ruler is entitled
to appropriate Jewish property, even to
kill them, except for those few who must
be allowed to live as a testimony. The
Jews can avert this fate by giving one-
third of their property to every ruler
upon his investiture." Albert slightly

altered this text in 1463 but basically it
remained the same.

The emperor Maximilian I (1493–1519)
adopted the same tactic of expelling the
Jews, publishing an edict of expulsion of
the Jews of Styria on 18 March 1496, in
which he enumerates *all* the Jewish
offences against Christianity such as
kidnapping and killing of Christian
children, thus giving official sanction to
the legendary lies and superstitions current among Christians. Maximilian did
leave an opening for Jews to return to
Styria, but the local authorities obtained
extensions of the expulsion order. He

235

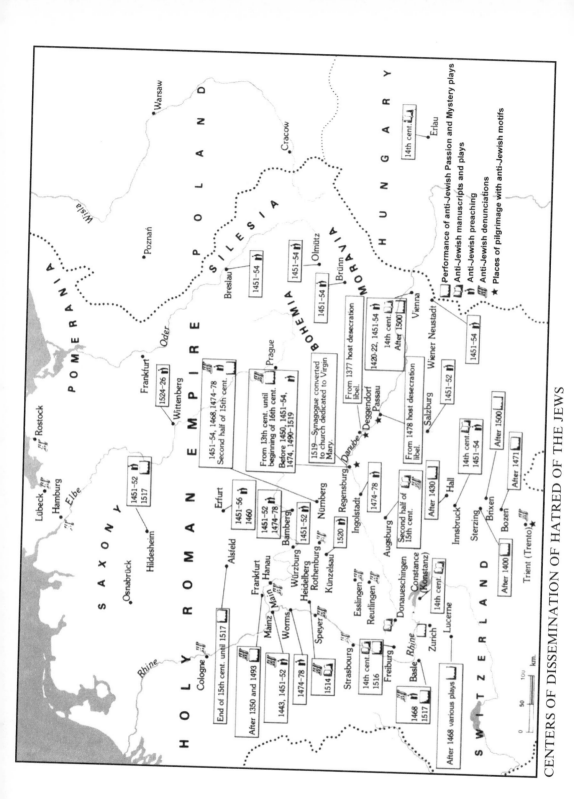

CENTERS OF DISSEMINATION OF HATRED OF THE JEWS

Legend:
- Performance of anti-Jewish Passion and Mystery plays
- Anti-Jewish manuscripts and plays
- Anti-Jewish preaching
- Anti-Jewish denunciations
- ★ Places of pilgrimage with anti-Jewish motifs

POMERANIA
POLAND
Warsaw
Poznań
Cracow
SILESIA
Breslau — 1451–54
Olmütz — 1451–54
Brünn — 1451–54
MORAVIA
HUNGARY
Erlau — 14th cent.

HOLY ROMAN EMPIRE
BOHEMIA
Oder
Rhine
Elbe
Wisła

Rostock
Lübeck
Hamburg
Hildesheim — 1451–52 / 1517
Osnabrück
SAXONY
Frankfurt
Wittenberg — 1524–26
Prague — From 13th cent. until beginning of 16th cent. Before 1450, 1451–54, 1474, 1490–1519
Erfurt — 1451–56 / 1460
Bamberg — 1451–52 / 1474–78
Nürnberg — 1451–54, 1468, 1474–78 Second half of 15th cent.
Würzburg
Rothenburg
Künzelsau — 1520
Regensburg — 1519—Synagogue converted to church dedicated to Virgin Mary.
Deggendorf — ★ From 1377 host desecration libel.
Passau — 1420–22, 1451–54
Danube
Ingolstadt — 1474–78
Augsburg — Second half of 15th cent.
★ From 1478 host desecration libel.
Vienna — 14th cent. / After 1500
Wiener Neustadt
Salzburg — 1451–52
Hall — After 1430
Innsbruck — 14th cent. / 1451–54
Sterzing
Brixen — After 1500
Bozen — After 1471 / After 1400
Trient (Trento)

Cologne — End of 15th cent. until 1517
Alsfeld
Frankfurt — After 1350 and 1493
Hanau
Mainz — 1443, 1451–52
Worms — 1474–78
Speyer — 1514
Heidelberg
Strasbourg — 14th cent. / 1516
Freiburg
Esslingen
Reutlingen
Donaueschingen
Constance (Konstanz) — 14th cent.
Lucerne
Zurich
Basle — 1468 / 1517
SWITZERLAND
After 1468 various plays

0 50 100 km.

236

efrained from molesting the Jews of Moravia and Bohemia and opposed their expulsion from Regensburg.

One would have thought that upon the election of Charles I of Spain as Emperor of the Holy Roman Empire (Charles V 1519–1556]) he would have treated the Jews of Ashkenaz in as harsh a way as did his grandparents Ferdinand and Isabella. However, he made a distinction between his Jewish policy in the two realms, particularly since he was preoccupied with the problems of Lutheranism in Germany. At Charles' court the Jew Joseph (Joselmann) b. Gershon of Rosheim (c. 1478–1554) was successfully active as the *shtadlan* (intercessor) for the Jews of Germany. There was very little change in conditions for the Jews of Germany in the sixteenth century, the Ashkenazic center of gravity moving to Poland-Lithuania, Bohemia and Moravia. Already in the fourteenth and particularly in the fifteenth and sixteenth centuries there were the beginnings of Jewish immigration to northern Italy and in the direction of the Ottoman Empire, including Palestine. The persecutions, massacres and expulsions took their toll on the Jews of Germany and sapped their creative strength.

THE JEWS OF SWITZERLAND 13TH TO 15TH CENTURIES

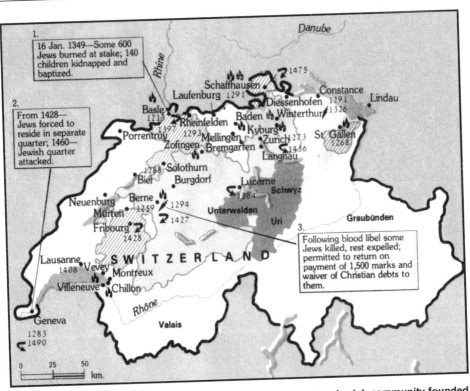

1. 16 Jan. 1349—Some 600 Jews burned at stake; 140 children kidnapped and baptized.

2. From 1428—Jews forced to reside in separate quarter; 1460—Jewish quarter attacked.

3. Following blood libel some Jews killed, rest expelled; permitted to return on payment of 1,500 marks and waiver of Christian debts to them.

Three Forest cantons, 1291
Cantons that joined Confederation, till 1353
Cantons that joined Confederation, till 1513
Jews burned during well-poisoning libel, 1348-1349

1384 Jewish community founded
Burning of Jews in 1401
Blood libel
Expulsion

A 15th century woodcut depicting Jews bleeding the child Simon—subject of a blood libel in 1475.

thirteenth century were in Constance, Lucerne, Berne, Zurich, Geneva and Lausanne. Although most of their members were engaged in moneylending there were also merchants, tailors, metal craftsmen and owners of vineyards and orchards. The Jews of these towns, who came mainly from Alsace and Germany, were soon destined to be persecuted and expelled from Switzerland. Among other things they were accused of causing the Black Death and the Jews of Chillon were accused of poisoning wells. The fate of the Jews of Geneva, Lucerne and Berne was similar; many were expelled or burned at the stake.

Jewish life in Switzerland was reconstituted on a small scale toward the end of the fourteenth century, a few Jewish doctors being given permits of residence. It was only in the German-speaking areas that a number of communities took root. The scholar Moses of Zurich was known for his notes and additions on the *Semak* (*Sefer Mitzvot Katan*).

THE oldest Jewish community in Switzerland seems to have been in Basle, where Jews are first mentioned in 1213. Additional communities in the area in the

THE JEWS OF SPAIN ON THE EVE OF THE EXPULSION
15TH CENTURY

THE expulsion of Spanish Jews in 1492 had its roots in the persecutions of 1391, when a large Jewish population of about two hundred thousand was forcibly converted and continued to live alongside both the surviving Jewish community, to which they no longer belonged, and the Christian community, which had not accepted them. The apostates Pablo de Santa María in Castile (formerly Solomon ha-Levi, rabbi of Burgos) and Jerónimo de Santa Fé (formerly the doctor Joshua ha-Lorki of Alcañiz) became prominent figures within the Christian community, both working ac-

tively against their former coreligionists, each in his own way inducing the authorities to convert the remaining Jewish population. Upon the advice of Jerónimo, the antipope Benedict XIII in 1413 convened a religious disputation in Tortosa, inviting twelve rabbis from the kingdom of Aragón to participate. The disputation, which continued for about two years (1413 and 1414) caused considerable stress among the Aragonese communities, bereft of their rabbis and leaders, who were struggling with the apostates in Tortosa. These years were characterized by much apostasy. The

SPANISH
JEWISH
COMMUNITIES

Legend:
- ● Town with Jewish residents
- ○ Town with converso residents
- ✡ Massacres of Jews, with date
- +1473
- 1480 Meeting of Castilian Cortes at which Jewish matters were discussed and decisions taken

Boxed notes:

1. Jewish community not renewed after persecutions of 1391.

3. Jerónimo de Santa Fé, formerly Joshua ha Lorki, doctor of Alcañiz, influenced by Pablo de Santa María.

4. 1413–1414—Antipope Benedict XIII, on advice of Jerónimo de Santa Fé, convenes religious disputation with 12 Aragonese rabbis.

5. 1432—Abraham Benveniste, Rab de la Corte in Castile, convenes Jewish representatives and scholars to revive Jewish schools and courts.

2. 1390—Solomon ha-Levi, rabbi of Burgos, converts; adopts name of Pablo de Santa María.

8. 1474—Riots in town and environs force conversos to flee, some refuse to flee, to Palma (de Mallorca), inflicting casualties on attackers in self-defense.

7. 1449—Riots against conversos. Mid 15th cent.—Controversy over acceptance of conversos into Christian society.

9. 1474–1475—Conversos appeal to Ferdinand and Isabella requesting permission to settle here with promises to defend town and pay taxes. Crown rejects request fearing invasion by Muslims of North Africa.

6. 1449—Pogrom against city's Jews.

Place names (selected):
FRANCE, Rhône, Avignon, Toulouse, Burgos, Perpignan, Besalú, Gerona, Avch, Solsona, Santa Colomo de Queralt, Cervera, Balaguer, Tàrrega, Barcelona, Jaca, Huesca, Monzón, Lérida, Fraga, Alcañiz, Tarragona, Tortosa, Peñíscola, Castellón de la Plana, CATALONIA, Biarritz, Pamplona, Estella, NAVARRE, Tudela, Tarazona, Ágreda, Saragossa, Calatayud, Daroca, Belchite, Montalbán, Albarracín, Teruel, Segorbe, Valencia, Denia, Alicante, VALENCIA, ARAGON, Durango, Medina de Pomar, Vitoria, Haro, Nájera, San Pedro, Calahorra, Soria, Almazán, Medinaceli, Cifuentes, Cuenca, Laredo, Valmaseda, Oviedo, Aguilar de Campóo, Fromista, Castrojeriz, Palencia, León, Villadiego, Benavente (de Duero), Dueñas, Atienza, Sigüenza, Huete, Requena, Astorga, Zamora, Medina del Campo, Olmedo, Arévalo, Ávila, Segovia, Madrid, Guadalajara, Illescas, Ocaña, Maqueda, Tembleque, Salamanca, Alba, Ciudad Rodrigo, Plasencia, Talavera de la Reina, Toledo, Escalona, La Guardia, Ainagro, Almadén, Ciudad Real, CASTILE, Coria, Trujillo, Mérida, Medellín, Chillón, Almodóvar del Campo, Montealegre, Arévalo, Murcia, Cartagena, Lorca, Santiago de Compostela, La Coruña, Tuy, Miranda do Douro, Gouveia, Coimbra, Santarém, Lisbon, Évora, Porto, Douro, Badajoz, Belalcázar, Llerena, Córdoba, Bujalance, Baena, Écija, Jaén, Úbeda, Andújar, Guadalquivir, Granada, GRANADA, Vélez Málaga, Málaga, Gibraltar, Almería, Cádiz, Jerez de la Frontera, Sevilla (Seville), SEVILLE, Carmona, Osuna, Palma del Río, Faro, Atlantic Ocean, Mediterranean Sea, BALEARIC ISLANDS, MENORCA, MAJORCA (MALLORCA), Palma (de Mallorca), IBIZA

Dated entries near towns:
1490, 1405, 1438/1478, 1467, 1461/1464/1467/1471, 1480, 1449/1467/1477, 1473 & 1477, 1473, 1477

0 50 100 km

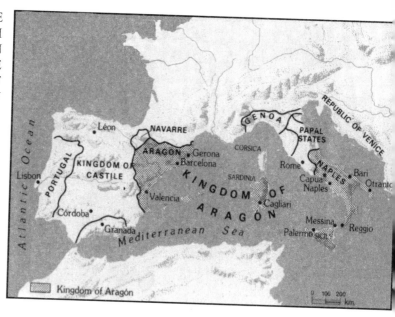

THE KINGDOM OF ARAGÓN AT THE TIME OF ALFONSO V

Kingdom of Aragón

Dominican friar Vincent Ferrer traveled from place to place preaching conversion and exerting pressure on the Jewish population.

Only at the beginning of the 1430s could signs of recuperation be discerned among the communities of Castile, particularly in their attempt to establish a nationwide Jewish organization with a code of regulations. In 1432 Abraham Benveniste of Soria, "Rab de la Corte," convened representatives of the Castilian Jewish communities in order to reestablish the Jewish judicial and educational systems, determine methods of tax collection, combat informers and establish norms for a more modest life style in Jewish society.

Unlike those of Castile, the large Jewish communities in Aragón were not revived after the persecutions of 1391, and in the 1430s the Jewish communities of the Balearic Islands ceased to exist.

The riots against the conversos in 1449 in Toledo and Ciudad Real must be viewed against the background of an antagonistic Christian society unwilling to accept the "new Christians" and their descendants. The instigator of the riots in Toledo was Pedro Sarmiento, appointed by King John II of Castile as commander of the fortress. A heavy war tax imposed on the city, to be collected by the converso tax farmers, served as the pretext for the riots which were directed against the conversos and did not affect the Jews. Riots recurred against the conversos in Toledo in 1467 and in the towns of Andalusia in 1473–1474.

The status of the conversos in the intensely religious environment of a militant Christian state striving for religious unification became the subject of considerable polemical literature. The disputes between those favoring integration and those opposing it, gave rise to anti-Jewish as well as anticonverso literature. Alfonso de Espina, a Franciscan friar, published a major work around 1460 in which he argued that the continued observance of Mosaic law by the conversos resulted from their contact

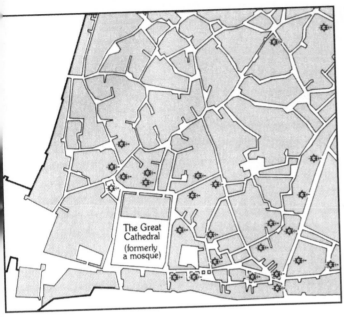

VIOLENT ATTACKS
AGAINST THE
CONVERSOS OF
CÓRDOBA

The Great
Cathedral
(formerly
a mosque)

with Jews and could be remedied only by the expulsion of the Jews. Alfonso was also the principal originator of the idea of the national Spanish Inquisition.

The ascent of Ferdinand and Isabella to the throne of Castile in 1474 and of the united kingdoms of Castile and Aragón in 1479 raised hopes for a respite among the Jews. In 1474 the converso request to settle in Gibraltar, on a promise of fidelity to Christianity, was rejected out of hand by Ferdinand and Isabella. The Catholic Monarchs conceived a plan for the organization of the united kingdom to be implemented in stages: stabilizing their rule by creating a calm atmosphere and preventing revolts of the nobles and townspeople; establishing a national Spanish Inquisition to deal with the problem of converso fidelity to Christianity; the conquest of Granada, the last Muslim foothold in western Europe and the expulsion of the Jews. By these methods they intended to create a united Christian kingdom of Castile and Aragón of "one flock and one sword." The

crown's first step in 1475–1476 was to quell the revolt of the marquis of Villena that supported the union of Portugal and Castile through the marriage of crown princess Joana, daughter of Henry IV of Castile, to Afonso V, king of Portugal. Ferdinand and Isabella then turned to deal with the "Jewish heresies" of the conversos.

In 1477 they appealed to Pope Sixtus IV for permission to establish a national Inquisition in Spain, which was granted in 1478, and in 1480 two Dominican monks, Miguel de Murillo and Juan de San Martín, were appointed as the first inquisitors. They began their activities on 1 January 1481 in Seville for the whole of Andalusia and Spain. In 1483 an expulsion order was issued against all Jews of Andalusia giving them one month to leave. During that time the Dominican Tomás de Torquemada was appointed inquisitor-general of the Spanish kingdom, and it was he who was responsible for the Andalusian and other expulsions—Saragossa and Albarracín in

241

THE CONQUEST OF GRANADA
1 JANUARY 1492

3. 1482–1491—Heavy war tax on Jewish communities; collected annually according to a tax map.

4. 1483—Expulsion of Andalusian Jews.

2. Pope Sixtus IV approves establishment of Inquisition tribunal when Catholic Monarchs undertake to conquer Granada (1478).

6. Granada, last Muslim stronghold in Europe, falls to Christians; some of Muslims leave for North Africa. 2 Jan. 1492—Catholic Monarchs enter city.

5. 1487—After capture of Málaga, Jews of city held prisoners of war; ransom of 20 million maravedis demanded for their release.

1. 1477—Ferdinand and Isabella request permission from pope to establish Inquisition tribunal; 1478—permission granted; 1480—Miguel de Morillo and Juan de San Martín first inquisitors; Jan. 1481—begins functioning.

0   50   100   km.

↙ 1492 Conquest and date
↙   Expulsion

→ Christian attacks
→ Muslim attacks

242

ANNUAL TAXES PAID IN 1474 BY JEWS OF CASTILE AND WAR TAX PAID IN 1491 FOR THE CONQUEST OF GRANADA

Town	1474	1494	Town	1474	1494
Alaejos	—	3,770	Jerez de la Frontera	1,500	—
Alcalá	5,000	45,000	León	2,600	44,870
Alfara	1,000	15,120	Lorca	—	11,785
Almagro	800	—	Madrid	1,200	11,825
Almansa	1,100	5,200	Madrigal	4,000	42,120
Almazán	4,500	76,234	Medina del Campo	8,500	64,000
Arnedo	3,000	—	Merida	2,500	38,000
Avila	1,200	83,750	Miranda	2,000	13,350
Ayllón	2,000	33,120	Olmeda	500	5,800
Badajoz	7,500	65,750	Palencia	2,000	14,500
Belvis	—	13,539	Plasencia	5,000	53,400
Benavente	3,500	16,000	Salamanca	4,800	51,020
Briviesca	2,500	38,550	Saldaña	2,000	23,970
Burgos	700	28,350	Segovia	11,000	140,000
Cáceres	8,200	42,000	Seville	2,500	—
Cartagena	—	3,742	Talavera de la Reina	2,500	52,000
Castrojeriz	1,100	6,120	Toledo	3,500	107,560
Córdoba	1,200	—	Toro	2,000	16,070
Coria	3,300	25,030	Trujillo	7,500	111,400
Escalona	1,000	4,000	Vallodolid	5,500	60,120
Estadillo	1,800	12,600	Vitoria	3,000	30,870
Guadalajara	6,500	90,620	Zamora	6,500	100,650
Huete	4,000	44,750			

(In 1474 the tax was paid in maravedis. The war tax in gold coins [castellanos]; 1 castellano = 485 marevedis.)

1486. The latter, postponed at the request of Ferdinand, did not take place until the general expulsion of 1492. Inquisition tribunals were systematically established throughout Spain.

During the war against Granada the Jewish communities of Castile were heavily taxed, the amounts increasing each year. On 25 November 1491 Granada, the last Muslim foothold in the Iberian Peninsula, capitulated. On 6 January the Catholic Monarchs entered the city in a triumphal procession and on 31 March 1492 they signed the Edict of Expulsion of the Jews from the whole of Spain. The edict specifically stated that the reason for the act was religious, namely that so long as Jews continued to reside in Spain there would be no hope for the integration of the conversos with Christianity. There is no doubt that the ideas embodied in the edict were those of Torquemada, who based his anti-Jewish ideology on the writings of Alfonso de Espina.

THE JEWISH COMMUNITIES IN ITALY
14TH TO 16TH CENTURIES

THE distribution of Jews in Italy underwent a change after the Black Death, beginning with emigration from the south and the arrival in northern Italy of Jews, some of whom had been expelled from Germany. Communities were founded where previously there had been none. The changing political climate in the Italian Peninsula also created favorable conditions for Jewish settlement. Jewish loan-bankers gave great impetus to Jewish settlement in northern Italy and greatly assisted in the development of town and rural centers. Settlement was facilitated by the founders of banks receiving a *condotta* (privilege) for a period of time adequate for the establishment of a community.

Among the popes who reigned at the end of the fourteenth century it was Urban V (1362–1370) who

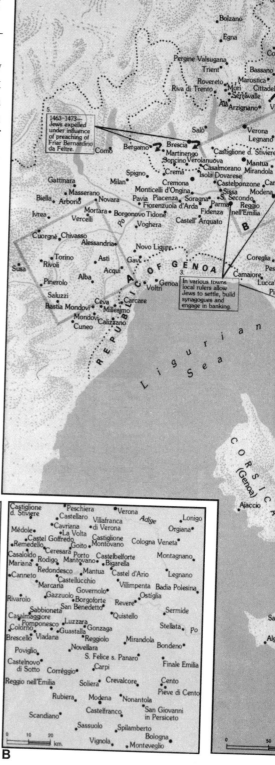

A

B

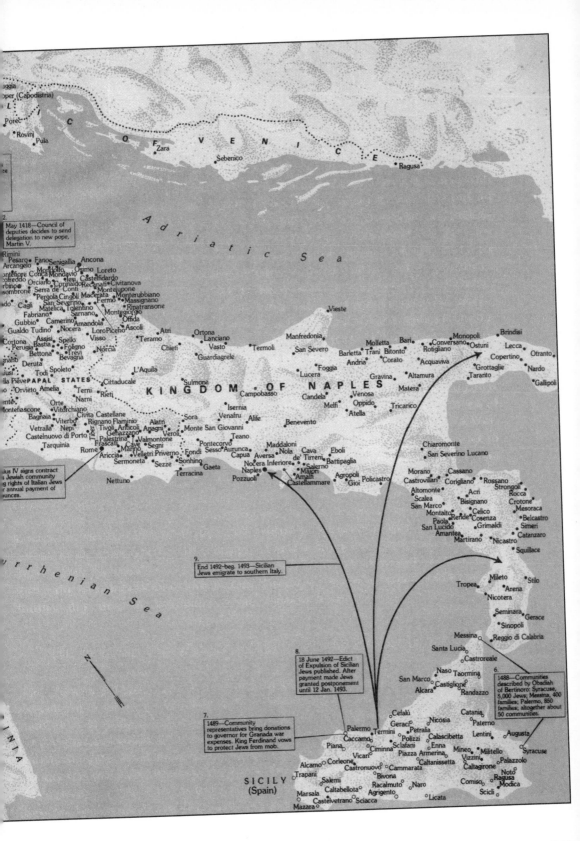

GULF OF VENICE

Poret
Rovini
Pula
Zara
Sebenico
Ragusa

Adriatic Sea

2.
May 1418—Council of
deputies decides to send
delegation to new pope,
Martin V.

Rimini
Pesaro Fano Senigallia Ancona
Arcangelo Montolfo Osimo Loreto
Montefiore Corinaldo Mondavio Iesi Castelfidardo
Urbino Orciano Cornaldo Recanati Civitanova
sombron Serra de' Conti Montelupone
Pergola Cingoli Macerata Monterubbiano
Fabriano San Severino Fermo Massignano
Matelica Tolentino Sarnano Ripatransone
Cagli Montegiorgio
Gubbio Camerino Amandola Offida
Gualdo Tadino Nocera Loro Piceno Ascoli
Cortona Assisi Spello Visso Teramo Atri Ortona Lanciano
Perugia Bastia Foligno Norcia Chieti Vasto
Deruta Bettona Bevagna Guardiagrele
Todi Spoleto Sulmona L'Aquila
Orvieto Amelia Terni Rieti Campobasso
Montefiascone Orte Vitorchiano Narni
Bagnaia Viterbo Civita Castellane Isernia Venafru
Vetralla Nepi Rignano Flaminio Sora Alife
Castelnuovo di Porto Tivoli Articoli Apagni Monte San Giovanni Benevento
Tarquinia Palestrina Gehazzano Veroli Teano
Frascati Valmontone
Rome Marino Segni Pontecorvo Maddaloni
Ariccia Velletri Priverno Fondi Sesso Aurunca Capua Aversa Nola
Sermoneta Sonhing Sezze Gaeta Nocera Inferiore Salerno
Nettuno Terracina Naples Magon Cava de' Tirreni Eboli
Pozzuoli Amalfi Battipaglia
Castellammare Agropoli
Gioi Policastro

PAPAL STATES
Cittaducale

KINGDOM OF NAPLES

Vieste
Manfredonia
San Severo
Termoli
Foggia
Lucera
Candela
Melfi
Atella
Oppido
Venosa
Tricarico
Gravina
Altamura
Taranto
Matera
Molfetta Bari
Trani Bitonto
Barletta Rotigliano
Andria Corato
Acquaviva
Conversano Monopoli
Ostuni
Lecce
Copertino
Grottaglie
Nardo
Gallipoli
Brindisi
Otranto

Chiaromonte
San Severino Lucano
Morano Cassano
Castrovillari Rossano
Altomonte Coriglano Strongoli
Scalea Acri Rocca
San Marco Celico Crotone
Montalto Bisignano Mesoraca
Paola Rende Cosenza Belcastro
San Lucido Grimaldi Simeri
Amantea Martirano Catanzaro
Nicastro
Squillace

9.
End 1492-beg. 1493—Sicilian
Jews emigrate to southern Italy.

Tyrrhenian Sea

Julius IV signs contract
a Jewish community
g rights of Italian Jews
r annual payment of
unces.

N

Mileto
Tropea
Nicotera
Arena Stilo
Seminara Gerace
Sinopoli
Messina Reggio di Calabria
Santa Lucia
Castroreale
San Marco Naso Taormina
Castiglione
Alcara Randazzo

8.
18 June 1492—Edict
of Expulsion of Sicilian
Jews published. After
payment made Jews
granted postponement
until 12 Jan. 1493.

6.
1488—Communities
described by Obadiah
of Bertinoro: Syracuse,
5,000 Jews; Messina, 400
families; Palermo, 850
families; altogether about
50 communities.

7.
1489—Community
representatives bring donations
to governor for Granada war
expenses. King Ferdinand vows
to protect Jews from mob.

Cefalù Nicosia Catania
Geraci Petralia Paterno
Palermo Termini Polizzi Calascibetta Lentini Augusta
Caccamo Sclafani Enna Mineo Militello
Piana Ciminna Piazza Armerina Vizzini Syracuse
Vicari Caltanissetta Caltagirone Palazzolo
Alcamo Corleone Castronuovo Cammarata Noto
Trapani Bivona Comiso Ragusa Modica
Salemi Caltabellota Racalmuto Naro Scicli
Marsala Agrigento Licata
Mazara Castelvetrano Sciacca

SICILY
(Spain)

245

Illustration from a Hebrew illuminated manuscript, Arba'a Turim, *by Jacob b. Asher, Mantua, Italy, 1435.*

Ark of the Law in a synagogue.
Detail from a drawing in an Italian Haggadah, 1453.

issued a bull of protection for the Jews, as did Boniface IX (1389–1404) after him. The antipope Benedict XIII (1394–1417) was extremely hostile toward the Jews, his animosity reaching its peak during the Disputation of Tortosa (1413–1414). He was deposed in 1417; his successor Martin V (1417–1431) issued two bulls favorable to the Jews and also attempted to restrain the anti-Jewish agitation of the Franciscan friars. Other popes were either indifferent to the Jews or assisted in their persecution. Calixtus III (b. Alfonso Borgia, 1455–1458), the Spanish pope, showed his disdain for Judaism when he intentionally dropped a Torah scroll given him by the Jews of Rome at his election. Another pope, Sixtus IV (1471–1484), was instrumental in establishing the national Spanish Inquisition and in 1475 a papal court of inquiry justified the Trent libel, which the pope endorsed in a bull of 1478. Rodrigo Borgia, later elected as Pope Alexander VI (1492–1503), had a considerable influence upon late fifteenth-century popes while he held the post of vice chancellor of the papal curia.

The expulsion from Spain also caused changes in Italy, particularly in the

Area of Jewish residence

territories under Aragonese rule—Sicily, Sardinia and southern Italy—since Jews were also expelled from those territories. Until the end of April 1492 no expulsion order similar to that of Spain had been published. Furthermore, on 23 May the municipality of Palermo declared that it was forbidden to harm the Jews. However, on 9 June Ferdinand and Isabella forbade emigration from Sicily and the transfer of money to the Ottoman Empire. Jews were obliged to prepare an inventory of their possessions and deposit their bills of exchange with notaries. On 18 June the expulsion order was published, causing a wave of protest. On 20 June the citizens of Messina warned the king of the harm that would be done to the city if the Jews left. Palermo argued that the exodus of Jewish craftsmen would affect arms and agricultural supplies. At the request of the Jews the governor issued an order for their protection, continuing to protect them even though he was compelled to rescind the order. The Jews succeeded in postponing the expulsion until 12 January 1493. In the interim period there were continuous attempts to persuade the crown to rescind the order. Ferdinand, however, insisted that all Jews leave, including those of Malta and Sardinia.

About forty thousand Jews left Sicily alone. The numbers expelled from Sardinia were comparatively small. Pope Alexander VI did not prevent the refugees from residing in districts of the Papal States. Others went to the Ottoman-dominated Balkans and still others to the kingdom of Naples, where refugees from Spain had arrived.

In 1503 the kingdom of Naples was won by the Spanish and on 25 November 1510 an order was issued for the expulsion of the Jews, the date of implementation being fixed for the end of March 1511. By this order the Jews were forbidden ever to return. The expulsion order enabled the conversos of Apulia and Calabria and those who were tried

247

and condemned in absentia by the Inquisition to put their affairs in order and leave the kingdom within a few months. They were allowed to take all their movable possessions other than gold and silver. Despite the edict, two hundred families were allowed to remain on condition that they annually paid three thousand ducats to the crown. Most of the Jews left the kingdom and in 1541 a total expulsion was ordered which included the conversos.

JEWISH DEMOGRAPHIC CHANGES
FROM THE 13TH CENTURY UNTIL THE EXPULSION FROM SPAIN

IT is difficult to estimate the size of the Jewish population in the Middle Ages. Even were we able to surmise the number of Jews in a particular place, we would still be ignorant of their composition by age and sex or the birth and death rate. We lack not only the absolute numbers but also other factors. It is certain that there were great population fluctuations resulting from expulsions, or from persecutions and massacres, which often destroyed entire communities. Therefore any estimate can be based only upon actual available statistics such as tax records or martyrology lists. These figures are more or less accurate but relate only to a particular time and place. It is clear that we are dealing primarily with an urban Jewish population having diverse occupations which differed from place to place.

Jewish figures from the 15th century.

MAJOR EXPULSIONS

1290	Edward I expels Jews of England
1306	Philip IV expels Jews of France (Louis X readmits Jews for a twelve-year period)
1322	Charles IV again expels Jews from France
1367	Expulsion from Hungary
1381	Expulsion from Strasbourg
1394	Charles VI expels Jews of France
1421	Expulsion from Austria
1426	Expulsion from Cologne
1439	Expulsion from Augsburg
1450	Expulsion from Bavaria
1453	Expulsion from Breslau
1467	Expulsion from Tlemcen
1483	Expulsion from Andalusia
1492	Expulsion from Spain
1493	Expulsion from Sardinia
1495	Expulsion from Lithuania
1496	Expulsion from Portugal (replaced in 1497 by forced conversion)

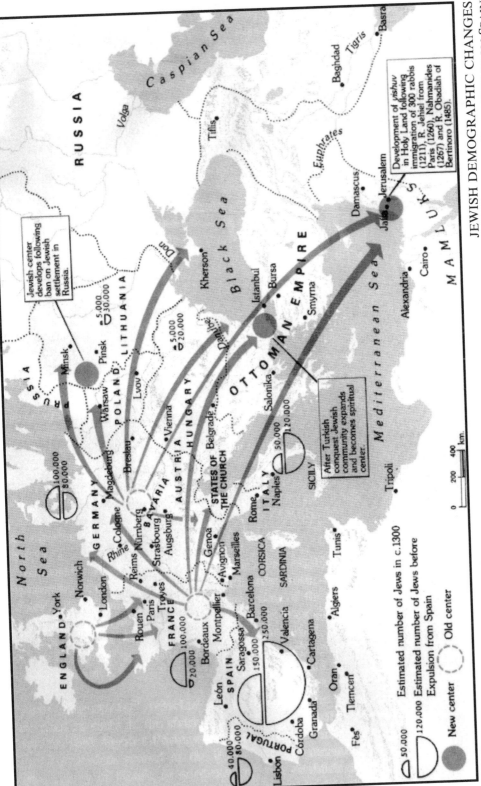

JEWISH DEMOGRAPHIC CHANGES
FROM THE 13TH CENTURY UNTIL THE EXPULSION FROM SPAIN

Jewish center develops following ban on Jewish settlement in Russia.

Development of *yishuv* in Holy Land following immigration of 300 rabbis (1211), R. Jehiel from Paris (1260), Nahmanides (1267) and R. Obadiah of Bertinoro (1485).

After Turkish conquest Jewish community expands and becomes spiritual center.

Estimated number of Jews in c.1300

120,000 Estimated number of Jews before Expulsion from Spain

Old center

New center

249

ENGLAND

THE statistical information on England relates only to the period of the expulsion. Basing himself on tax records, the historian Georg Carol (1867–1912) estimated the size of the Jewish population in 1280 to 1283—that is, before the expulsion—at between 2,500 and 3,000. This is a considerably smaller figure than is arrived at by various other calculations, which place the number at between 15,000 and 17,500. The historian S. W. Baron (1895–1989) assumed that the correct figure lies between the two estimates. In London there were apparently no more than 2,000 to 2,500 Jews and the bulk of the Jewish population resided in the rest of England. Therefore it would seem that the total number of Jews in England at the time of expulsion (1290) was about 10,000—a very small number in relation to the general population, which is estimated at 3,500,000.

FRANCE

THE statistics for French Jewry are also meager. In the south of what is today France, there was a dense Jewish population. According to Benjamin of Tudela, the town of Arles had two hundred Jewish families when he stopped there in 1160, while in 1194 the Jews were more than 25 percent of the town's population. A similar situation existed in the town of Tarascon. On the other hand, in September 1341, King Robert found that there were 1,205 Jews living in 203 houses in Aix-en-Provence, that is, no more than 10 percent of the general population. Narbonne experienced a decline in Jewish population and in 1305 there were no more than 1,000 Jews in comparison to 15,000 residents (about 7 percent). Toulouse had 15 Jewish families in 1391 and the situation was similar in Béziers, Albi and other towns in southern France. Only in the port town of Marseilles was there a large Jewish community. In 1358 at Avignon, 210 heads of Jewish families swore allegiance to the pope. Its Jewish population grew toward the end of the century and in 1414 the community requested permission to enlarge the area of the cemetery. In the 1490s refugees from Spain arrived at Avignon, but it is still difficult to calculate the size of the Jewish community in a town which was one of the largest in Europe, having 30,000 inhabitants in 1355. Carpentras had 64 Jewish family heads in 1276 and despite the expulsion in 1322, the community grew to 90 family heads in 1343. In 1486 the townspeople exerted pressure to reduce the area of the Jewish quarter, whose members in 1476 numbered 12 percent of the town's population.

In northern France, in the town of Troyes, there were no more than 100 Jews during Rashi's time (1040–1105). While the expulsion of 1182 put a halt to Jewish population growth it did not affect the Jews of Champagne, Burgundy, Poitou and Normandy. In 1182 there were equal numbers of Jews and Christians residing in Paris. There was a large concentration of Jews residing in Villejuif near Paris; however, in the thirteenth and fourteenth centuries their numbers in Paris were on the decline. Jews resided in hundreds of small towns and the historian Heinrich Graetz (1817–1891) estimated that in 1306 there were 100,000 Jews who were expelled by Philip IV the Fair.

GERMANY

GERMANY'S Jewish population increased between the eleventh and thirteenth centuries. During the subsequent two hundred years the population grew only gradually. The Hohenstaufen rulers founded many towns that attracted Jewish settlers. The number of Jews massacred in Mainz during the First Crusade is indicative of the size of this major Jewish community. Jewish sources give a figure of 1,100 to 1,300 killed, while Christian sources cite 1,014. The Nürnberg Jewish community is recorded in a tax list from 1338 as having 212 persons, decreasing to 150 by 1449. Another reliable demographic source is the Nürnberg *memorbuch* in which the names of the 628 martyrs of the Rindfleisch massacres in 1298 were recorded. Apparently the community recuperated since the massacres of 1349 claimed 570 victims. To these numbers one must add those Jews who escaped. The community numbered some 1,000 in the thirteenth and fourteenth centuries. Nürnberg recovered after the Black Death and became one of the largest communities in Germany. In 1498, when the Jews were expelled from the town, it had a population of about 20,000.

According to S. W. Baron the total Jewish population of Germany and Austria at the beginning of the fourteenth century was about 10,000. In 1500 there were in all of Germany (the Holy Roman Empire) about 12 million people. Therefore the percentage of Jews was very small. Because the Jewish population was primarily an urban one, it is difficult to calculate the population of every town and village.

ITALY

THE demography of Jews in Italy differed considerably in the north and the south. In the 1260s Benjamin of Tudela found 500 families (or taxpayers) in Naples, 600 in Salerno, 500 in Otranto, 300 in Capua, 300 in Taranto, 200 in Benevento, 200 in Melfi and 200 in Trani. He found 20 families in the port of Amalfi—at this time the town was in a depression. In this period Sicily was heavily populated with Jews: 200 in Messina, 1,500 families in Palermo—the largest single concentration of Jews in southern Italy. Until the expulsion of 1493 Sicily was the center of Italian Jewish life. Palermo and Syracuse had about 5,000 Jews each at the time of the expulsion. Therefore, Nicolo Ferorelli estimated the number of Jews in Sicily at about 50,000 (1492). This figure seems accurate, since Attilio Milano (1907– 1969) arrived at a figure of 37,046 Jews for Sicily—with its 45 communities, and Malta, Gozo and Pantelleria. There was also a community in Sardinia during the period of Aragonese rule. In the sixteenth and seventeenth centuries the community of Rome developed considerably (in 1527 there were 1,738 Jews). Venice in the sixteenth and seventeenth centuries was the largest and most important of the northern communities, numbering several hundred Jews.

During the fifteenth to seventeenth centuries the Jews of Italy migrated from place to place, achieving a degree of communal organization similar to that achieved by the Jews of Ashkenaz and Spain in the thirteenth century.

Frequently the number of Jewish immigrants exceeded those who were native

JEWISH POPULATIONS IN EUROPE
(BY PERCENTAGES)

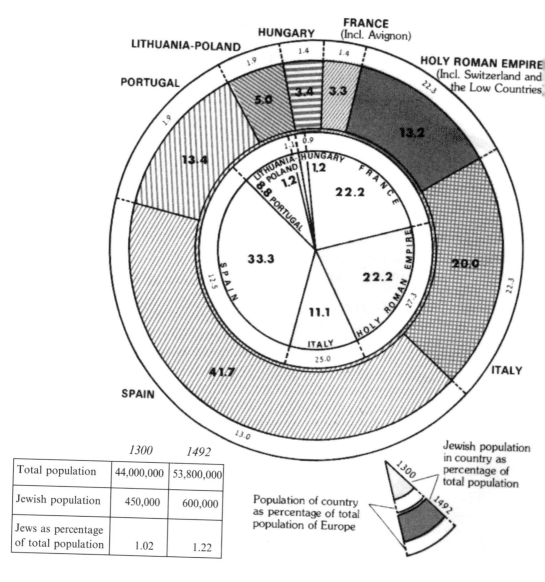

	1300	1492
Total population	44,000,000	53,800,000
Jewish population	450,000	600,000
Jews as percentage of total population	1.02	1.22

born. Expulsion of the Jews from the southern towns in 1492 to 1511 shifted the Jewish center of gravity to Rome and northward, where the Jewish population was about 25,000 to 30,000, a figure that remained unchanged for centuries.

SPAIN

THE Jewish population of Castile grew from 60,000 in 1300 to 160,000 by 1492. By contrast the Jewish population in Aragón decreased to 75,000. Navarre had 15,000 Jews. A knowledge of the number of Jews in Spain in 1492 is an essential factor in estimating the size of the Jewish population of Europe, Asia and Africa from the sixteenth century onward. The number of Jews expelled from Spain has been estimated by both Jewish and Christian sources. The priest-historian Andrés Bernáldez, a contemporary of the expulsion period, estimated that in 1492 there were 35,000 heads of family in Castile and 6,000 in Aragón. One Jewish document calculates 50,000 heads of family, while another estimates that 53,000 were expelled. Isaac Abrabanel (1437–1508) estimated the number that left and crossed the Portuguese border on foot at 300,000 "young and old, children and women," which would mean that in Castile there were between 150,000 and 200,000 Jews at the time of the Expulsion. Another method of calculation is by the size of the communities. For example the Jewish community of Cáceres in Estremadura numbered 130 persons and in the neighboring Talavera de la Reina between the years 1477 and 1487 there were 168 families, these numbers being typical of many other communities. A conservative estimate of the Castilian communities will show that between 1486 and 1491 there were 14,400 to 15,300 families. Estimating six people per family we would reach a figure of under 100,000. If we add to the number of Jews who left Spain some of the conversos, we will arrive at the total Jewish population toward the end of the fifteenth century. A further source of information is the tax paid by the refugees crossing the Portuguese border, each of whom had to pay eight cruzados for permission to cross over and to reside for eight months in the kingdom of Portugal. Here a figure of 120,000 can be reached. We also know that those who went to North Africa in hired ships numbered approximately 50,000. Several thousand refugees crossed the border of the kingdom of Navarre in 1493, having been given certificates of passage and protection so that they might get to Spanish ports whence they could embark. About 50,000 Jews went to Italy and several thousand to Avignon. All these figures bring us close to the estimate of 200,000.

These figures refer only to the Jews of Europe to whom we must add the Jews of Poland-Lithuania estimated at about 50 to 60 communities (30,000 persons) in the fifteenth century. Hungary and the Balkans had very few Jewish communities until the arrival of the Spanish refugees.

By comparison with our knowledge of European Jewish demography we are in the dark concerning the number of Jews in North Africa (including Egypt) and Asia. North Africa had sizable Jewish communities in the tenth and eleventh centuries but there was a decline in the twelfth and thirteenth centuries. After the persecution of 1391 and the expulsion of 1492, Jews from Spain reached North Africa. In Asia concentrations of Jews could be found in Iran and Iraq and it is reasonable to assume that they numbered several thousands. We have no information about the size of sixteenth-century Jewish communities in Yemen, the Ottoman Empire, Byzantine Asia Minor and Palestine. However, we know that the revival of the Jewish *yishuv* in Palestine in the sixteenth century brought with it a substantial increase in the number of Jews in the Holy Land.

THE EXPULSION ORDER

Don Fernando and Doña Isabela...by the Grace of God...etc....To the Prince heir don Juan, our very dear and beloved son, to the Infantes, Prelates, Dukes, Marquises, Counts, Masters of Orders, Priors, Ricos omes, Commanders, Alcaldes of Castles and Fortified houses of our Kingdoms and Domains, to all Councils, Alcaldes, Alguasils, Merinos, Calealleros, Escuderos, officials and notables of the very noble and loyal town of Avila, and all the other towns, villages and places of its Bishopry, and to all other Archbishopries and Bishopries and Dioceses of our Kingdoms and Domains, and to the Aljamas of the Jews in the named town of Avila and to all other towns, villages and places of its Bishopry, and to all other towns and villages and Places of our Kingdoms and Domains, and to all other Jews and persons, males and females of any age, and to all other persons of any standing, dignity, preeminence and state they may be, to whom the contents of this Order may concern in any way, grace and greetings.

Know indeed or you must know, that we have been informed that in our kingdoms there were some bad Christians who judaized and apostatized against our holy Catholic Faith, mainly because of the connection between the Jews and the Christians. In the *Cortes* of the past year which we held in Toledo in 1480, we ordered the separation of the above-mentioned Jews in all cities, villages and places in our kingdoms and domains, and to give them Jewish quarters and separate quarters where they should live, hoping that through this separation the matter would be remedied. We further ordered that an inquisition be held in our kingdoms and domains. As you know, this was done and has been the practice for more than twelve years and through it, as is well known, many sinners have been found by the inquisitors, churchmen and many other secular authorities.

Thus the great damage caused to Christians by their participation, connection and conversation they had and are having with the Jews which is proven which they do to subverse and remove from our holy Catholic Faith the devoted Christians and apart them from it and attract and pervert them to their damned faith and opinion instructing them in their ceremonies and observances of their law, organizing meetings in which they read to them and teach them in what they have belief and keep according to their Law, circumcising them and their children, providing them with books in whic they recite their prayers, informing them when the have to fast in their fasting days, coming togethe for readings and teaching them histories of thei Law, notifying them the days of their holy days t come, informing them how they are to be observed giving and bringing from their homes Matzoth an meats slaughtered according to their rituals, advis ing them from what to abstain in food and in othe matters in observance of their Law, convincing them as much as they are able to observe and keep the Law of Moses, making them to understand tha there is no other Law nor truth, but theirs, which has been proven through many confessions by the Jews themselves as well by those whom they perverted and deceived, which all caused great damage in detriment of our holy Catholic Faith.

Although we were informed about this before-hand and we know that the real remedy to all the damages and inconveniences is to separate the said Jews and the Christians in all our kingdoms and to expel them from our realm. We had thought it sufficient to order them out of the cities and villages and settlements in Andalusia, where they had already caused great damage, thinking that this would be enough for those living in other cities, villages and places in our kingdoms and domains who would stop acting and sinning as described above.

And because we are aware that this matter, and punishments inflicted on some of these Jews who were found guilty of these great sins and transgressions against our holy Catholic Faith, proved to be insufficient as a complete remedy, in preventing and remedying the great sin and transgression against the holy Catholic Faith and religion; it is not enough for a full remedy in order to cease this great offence to the faith, since we have discovered and seen that Jews pursue their evil and damaging intentions wherever they are found and are in touch; in order that there should be no further damage to our holy Faith, both through those whom God preserved so far and those who failed, but reformed their conduct and were brought back to the fold of the holy Catholic Church—our Holy Mother—and what is bound to happen bearing in mind our human weakness and the deceit and intrigues of the Devil who is continuously fighting us, something that can easily occur, we have decided to remove the main cause for this through the expulsion of the Jews from our kingdoms.

Whenever a grave and detestable crime is committed by any member of any society or group, it is proper that that society or group be dissolved or that the low disappear or suffer for the sake of the lofty, the few for the sake of the many. Those who corrupt the good and decent life in towns and villages and contagiously injure others, they should be expelled from these places. If for matters far less consequential which may cause damage to the state we act this way, all the more so for a very serious crime, one of the most dangerous and contagious crimes as this is.

Therefore, in consultation and agreement with the clergy, the higher and lower nobility in our realm, other men of science and conscience from our Council and having deliberated much on the matter, we have agreed to order the expulsion of all Jews and Jewesses in our kingdoms. Never should any one of them return nor come back. We have therefore issued this order. Thus we order all Jews and Jewesses of any age, who live, dwell and are found in our kingdoms and domains, whether born here or elsewhere, and are present here for any reason, must leave our kingdoms and domains until the end of the next month of July this year, together with their sons and daughters, their male and maidservants and their Jewish relatives, old and young, whatever their age. They should not dare to return and live where they previously lived, not for passage or in any other form, under a penalty, that if they fail to do so and to obey the order, and if they are found living in our kingdoms and domains, or come here in any way, they should be put to death, their property being confiscated by our Court and Royal Treasury. These punishments will be inflicted on the basis of the act and law, without trial, verdict and proclamation.

We order and prohibit that no man in our kingdoms, whatever his status, position and level should receive under his protection, should accommodate or defend, openly or secretly, any Jew or Jewess, from the above-mentioned date, the end of next July and onwards, for ever, neither in their lands nor in their houses, or anywhere in our kingdoms and domains, under the penalty of having their property, their vassals, their fortresses and any other thing that passes in inheritance confiscated. They will also lose any acts of mercy they have from us to the advantage of the Court and Royal fisc.

In order that these Jews and Jewesses can sell in a proper way their goods and property during this time until the end of the month of July, we take them and their property, throughout this period, under our protection, auspices and royal defense, so that during this period until the last day of July, could securely move around, sell, exchange or transfer their movables and land, and decide freely and willingly anything connected with them. During this period no harm, evil or injustice should be inflicted on the people and their property against the law, under a penalty against anyone who contravenes the royal safety of the kingdom.

We hereby as well authorize and permit these Jews and Jewesses to take out from our kingdoms and domains their property and goods, by sea or land, as long as they do not take away gold, silver and coins and any other article forbidden by the law of the kingdom, apart from goods which are not prohibited and exchange bills. We also instruct all the Councils and Courts of Justice, the *regidores*, the *caballeros* and *escuderos*, the officials and notables in the city of Avila, and cities, villages and other places in our kingdoms and domains, all vassals who are under our dominion and natives, that they should keep and fulfil our order and everything written in it, do and give any help and support to anyone who needs it, under the penalty of losing our mercy and having all their property and positions confiscated by the Court and Royal Treasury.

In order that this may reach everyone, and that no one should pretend ignorance, we command that our order be proclaimed in the usual places and squares in this city and major cities, in villages and places in the bishop's domain by the herald and in the presence of the notary public.

No one should act against this under penalty of our mercy and deprivation of all offices and confiscation of his property. And we order any person who would be summoned to appear before us in our Court, wherever we may be, from the day of summons till fifteen days coming, and under the same penalty to appear. And we order any notary public who will be summoned for it, to present the order stamped by his seal so that we shall be informed how our order is carried out.

Given to our city of Granada, the 31st of the month of March in the year 1492. I, the King and I, the Queen. I, Juan de Coloma, the secretary of the King and Queen our Lords, have written as ordered.

(Original text: R. León Tello, Judíos de Avila, *Avila 1964. pp. 91–95.)*

THE expulsion order came as a surprise to the Jews of Spain. During the month of April unsuccessful efforts were made to rescind the edict, in which Micer Alfonso de la Caballeria among others was involved. On 1 May the edict was promulgated in Castile, and two days earlier in Saragossa. The Jews were allowed three months to wind up their affairs and leave Spain. Spanish Jewry immediately began to prepare to leave. Among those who left for Italy was the family of Don Isaac Abrabanel from the port of Valencia. Compelled to forego loans he had advanced to the crown, he was permitted to take gold, silver and jewelry out of the country although this was forbidden in the edict. Others attempted to smuggle their valuables out. The authorities were interested in a calm and orderly expulsion. Various personalities, among them descendants of conversos Luis de Santangel and Francisco Pinelo, negotiated with and gave guarantees to ship captains for chartering vessels to carry the evacuees to North Africa and other places. This was a trying period for the communities whose leaders had the additional task of disposing of community property—synagogues, schools, public ritual baths (mikvaot), and cemeteries, etc. The value of property declined drastically; houses, fields and vineyards were sold for the price of a donkey or a mule. By contrast, the price of cloth and silk rose because the refugees were allowed to take such goods with them. The Christians at first hoped for a loss of faith on the part of Spanish Jews and a subsequent readiness to convert and remain in the land where they had resided for close to fifteen hundred years. They were astounded by the Jews' spiritual fortitude as they left for the ports of embarkation with hymns on their lips.

Jews were forbidden ever to return to Spain on pain of death unless they were prepared to convert to Christianity. As a result, Spain was without Jews for hundreds of years. The Spanish expulsion served as a model for expulsions in Lithuania (1495) and Portugal (1496), though the latter was changed by King Emanuel (Manuel I, 1495–1521), for a forced conversion of the Jewish population.

Contemporary descriptions of the hardship and suffering of the banished Jews produced epics unequalled in the annals of human history.

"I heard it told by elders, exiles from Spain, that a certain ship was smitten by pestilence and the owner cast the passengers ashore on a desolate site. Whereupon most of them died of starvation, a few attempting to walk until they could find a place of habitation. One Jew among them with his wife and two sons struggled to walk and the woman being barefooted swooned and expired, while the man, carrying his sons, both he and they collapsed from hunger and upon recovering from his swoon, he found the two boys dead. Arising in great distress he cried 'God of the Universe! You do much to cause me to abandon my faith. Know you that despite those who dwell in Heaven, I am a Jew and will remain a Jew, despite all you have brought upon me or will bring upon me.' And so saying he gathered dust and grass, covered the youths, and went to seek an inhabited place."

From Solomon Ibn Verga (late 15th to early 16th centuries), Shevet Yehudah, Hebrew edition by A. Schochat, Jerusalem 1947, p. 122.

JEWISH EXODUS FROM SPAIN AND PORTUGAL
1492 TO 1497

Capital of a column from a synagogue that was to be inaugurated in 1496–1497 in Gouveia, Portugal.

THE Expulsion from Spain altered the map of Jews in Europe, creating a Diaspora within a Diaspora—Spanish Jewish communities formed within existing Jewish communities. This situation poses two questions. How many Jews left Spain and what were their destinations? It is difficult to calculate the number expelled, but an estimate may be hazarded, on the basis of the number of Jewish residents in various places. The majority of Spanish Jews in the fifteenth century resided in Castile. A conservative estimate of this population is 30,000 families, that is, between 120,000 to 150,000 people. In Aragón the estimate is about 50,000 people. This gives us a total of 200,000 expelled—an approximate estimate given in both Jewish and non-Jewish sources.

Most of those banished went to Portugal, where they were offered a temporary eight-month haven for the per capita price of eight cruzados. Twenty-five ships led by Pedro Cabron left Cádiz for Oran but the Jewish passengers fearing to disembark—despite the reassurance of a Genoese pirate named Fragosso—returned to Arsila in North Africa. Storms forced the ships to anchor at Cartagena and Málaga where many of the Jews converted while others died of an epidemic. Those who disembarked at Arsila remained there until 1493. They were joined by a group of Jews who had settled in Portugal and were now on their way to the east (except for 700 heads of family who went to Morocco), paying a considerable sum of money for this privilege.

Other refugees went to North Africa, Italy and farther eastward. Some went to the papal state in France. Their journeys were beset with hardship, suffering and affliction, robbery, extortion, and even murder. Many lost their lives on the way.

A cruel fate awaited those Jews who fled to Portugal. John II (1481–1495)

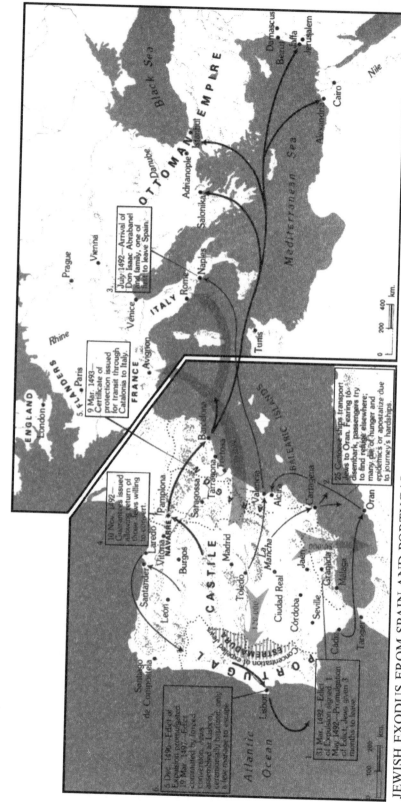

Black Sea

OTTOMAN EMPIRE

Danube

Nile

Damascus
Beirut
Jaffa
Jerusalem

Cairo

Alexandria

Adrianople
Istanbul

Salonika

Mediterranean Sea

3. July 1492—Arrival of Don Isaac Abrabanel and family, one of the last to leave Spain.

Vienna

Prague

Naples

Rome

ITALY

Venice

5. 9 Mar. 1493—Certificate of protection issued for transit through Catalonia to Italy.

Avignon

FRANCE

Rhine

FLANDERS

Paris

ENGLAND

London

Tunis

BALEARIC ISLANDS

Barcelona

Tortosa

Tarragona

Saragossa

Pamplona

NAVARRE

Valencia

Alcira

Cartagena

2.

Oran

4. 10 Nov. 1492—Guarantees issued allowing return of those Jews willing to convert.

Santander

Laredo
Vitoria
Burgos

León

CASTILE

Madrid

La Mancha

Toledo

Ciudad Real

Córdoba

Jaén

Granada

Málaga

Seville

PORTUGAL

EXTREMADURA

Santiago de Compostela

Atlantic Ocean

Lisbon

Cádiz

Tangier

2. 25 Genoese ships transport Jews to Oran. Fearing to disembark, passengers try to find refuge elsewhere; many die of hunger and epidemics or apostatize due to journey's hardships.

1. 31 Mar. 1492—Edict of Expulsion signed. 1 May 1492—Promulgation of Edict. Jews given 3 months to leave.

6. 5 Dec. 1496—Edict of Expulsion promulgated. 19 Mar. 1497—Edict commuted by forced conversion; Jews assembled at Lisbon, ceremonially baptized; only a few manage to escape.

km.
100   200

km.
0   200   400

JEWISH EXODUS FROM SPAIN AND PORTUGAL
1492–1497

258

ccepted 600 wealthy families and skilled craftsmen, granting them permanent residence; others, who were given only temporary residence, were enslaved if they failed to leave on time.

The reign of John II's successor, Manuel I (1495–1521) was a tragic one for the Jews of Portugal. Isabella, daughter of Ferdinand and Isabella, agreed to marry him on condition that he rid Portugal of the Jews. Thus, on 5 December 1496 the edict of expulsion was promulgated, the text being an abridged copy of the Spanish edict. In February 1497 Jewish children up to the age of fourteen whose parents intended emigrating, were seized and forcibly baptized. Soon the age limit was extended to twenty, and Jews began to flee the country in every possible way. Many children were detained and transferred to the Portuguese colony on the island of São Tomé in the Gulf of Guinea off the African coast, where they were cruelly ill-treated and most of them died in the jungle.

On 19 March 1497 the expulsion edict was replaced by forced conversion, a change in policy which possibly stemmed from the desire to retain the Jewish population within a sparsely populated nation of about one million people that had recently undertaken large settlement commitments in western Africa. The act of conversion was accomplished through deception, by assembling at Lisbon, the only officially sanctioned port of embarkation, all those wishing to leave. Those assembled were then ceremonially baptized and declared citizens of the realm. Only a few, among them Abraham b. Samuel Zacuto, were able to resist and later escaped. On 30 May 1497 the king issued orders that those who converted should be safe from persecution and from

"And I Judah, son of my lord the wise and pious R. Jacob may he rest in Peace, while residing in Spain savored a smidgen of honey, mine eyes saw the light and my mind was given to seek wisdom and inquire thereof. I went from strength to strength gathering all that was found in the aforementioned book, gleaning a morsel here and a morsel there until I possessed most of what it contained. In true faith I believe it was this knowledge that enabled me to withstand the terrible hardships that befell me upon my expulsion from Spain; and that whosoever heareth of it, both his ears shall tingle; to relate all the hardships, from I know not the numbers thereof but of some I will tell and I shall speak the praises of the Lord.

We traveled, I and my family, with 250 other souls in one vessel, in mid-winter 1493, from Lisbon the great city of the Kingdom of Portugal at the command of the king. The Lord struck us with pestilence to fulfill his word 'I will smite them with pestilence and destroy them...' and this was the reason why no place would receive us—'Depart ye! unclean! men cried unto them' and we left wandering ceaselessly, four months on the sea with 'meager bread and scant water.' "

R. Judah Hayyat, Ma'arekhet ha-Elohut, Mantua, 1558, introduction.

the Inquisition for a twenty-year period. From this it would appear that Manuel I was already contemplating the institution of a national inquisition modeled on that of Spain.

Many new communities were established by the Spanish exiles in the Mediterranean Basin; the Ottoman Empire proved particularly congenial to Jews and conversos, who developed a comprehensive spiritual network in their communities. The Holy Land also attracted the Spanish exiles and its conquest by the Turks (1517) served as a fulcrum for the expansion and development of the Jewish communities in the country.

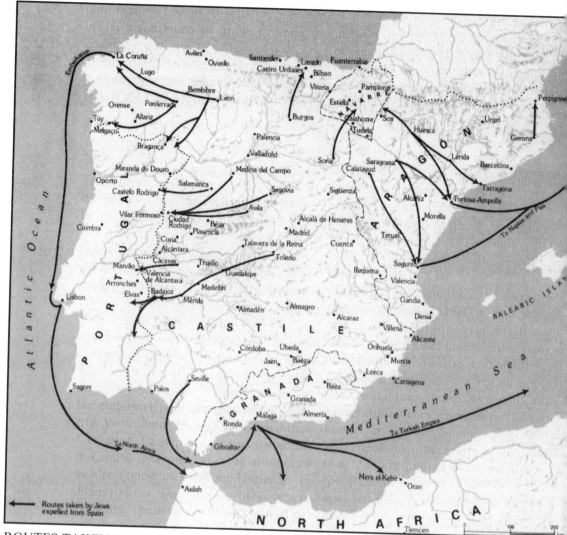

ROUTES TAKEN BY JEWS EXPELLED FROM SPAIN

THE WANDERINGS OF R. JUDAH HAYYAT

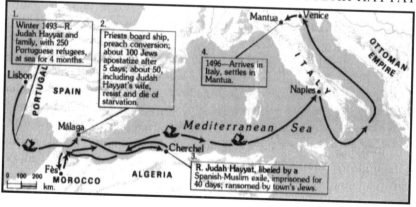

1. Winter 1493—R. Judah Hayyat and family, with 250 Portuguese refugees, at sea for 4 months.

2. Priests board ship, preach conversion; about 100 Jews apostatize after 5 days; about 50, including Judah Hayyat's wife, resist and die of starvation.

3. R. Judah Hayyat, libeled by a Spanish-Muslim exile, imprisoned for 40 days; ransomed by town's Jews.

4. 1496—Arrives in Italy, settles in Mantua.

D. UNTIL THE CHMIELNICKI MASSACRES AND SHABBATEAN MOVEMENT

THE OTTOMAN EMPIRE AT THE HEIGHT OF ITS EXPANSION UNTIL 1683

The Turkish fleet besieging a city. Late 15th century.

THE expansion of the Ottoman Empire in Europe aroused deep fear in the Christian world, since it seemed that with the fall of Constantinople in 1453 there was no power that could halt this expansion. With great momentum the empire annexed the whole of the southern Mediterranean Basin, excluding a few areas under Spanish rule in Morocco. Attempts by various popes to arouse the Christian world to forestall the danger were unsuccessful, particularly since the Christian world was disunited and engaged in wars over the Lutheran Reformation.

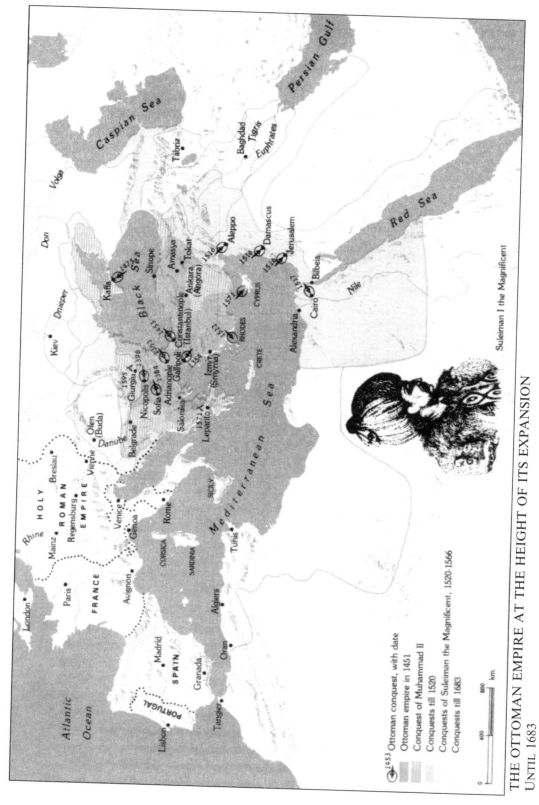

Suleiman I the Magnificent

1453 Ottoman conquest, with date
Ottoman empire in 1451
Conquest of Muhammad II
Conquests till 1520
Conquests of Suleiman the Magnificent, 1520-1566
Conquests till 1683

THE OTTOMAN EMPIRE AT THE HEIGHT OF ITS EXPANSION
UNTIL 1683

262

The victory of the allied Christian forces in the naval battle of Lepanto (1571) led by Don John of Austria, half-brother of King Philip II of Spain (1556–1598), dealt a blow to the Ottoman navy but did not affect the foundation of its empire. Philip had made his plans for war against England and was therefore interested in preserving calm on his Mediterranean flank. Thus in 1578 he succeeded in negotiating an armistice with the Turks. In 1580 Philip ascended the throne of Portugal, intensifying his plans for war with England, which he attacked in 1588, only to be defeated.

For their part, the Turks turned to central Europe, where they already controlled large areas of Hungary, threatening the Holy Roman Empire. On 28

A 15th-century woodcut depicting characters from different nations. On the right is a Jew.

October 1595 the Turks were defeated in the battle of Giurgiu and their expansion was halted.

The existing political climate enabled the Jews to promote immigration to the Holy Land and revitalize the Jewish

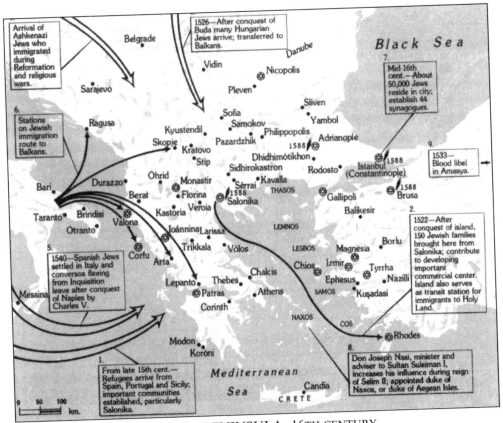

Arrival of Ashkenazi Jews who immigrated during Reformation and religious wars.

1526—After conquest of Buda many Hungarian Jews arrive; transferred to Balkans.

7. Mid-16th cent.—About 50,000 Jews reside in city; establish 44 synagogues.

6. Stations on Jewish immigration route to Balkans.

1533—Blood libel in Amasya.

2. 1522—After conquest of island, 150 Jewish families brought here from Salonika; contribute to developing important commercial center. Island also serves as transit station for immigrants to Holy Land.

5. 1540—Spanish Jews settled in Italy and conversos fleeing from Inquisition leave after conquest of Naples by Charles V.

1. From late 15th cent.—Refugees arrive from Spain, Portugal and Sicily; important communities established, particularly Salonika.

8. Don Joseph Nasi, minister and adviser to Sultan Suleiman I, increases his influence during reign of Selim II; appointed duke of Naxos, or duke of Aegean Isles.

Black Sea

Mediterranean Sea

Belgrade, Danube, Vidin, Nicopolis, Pleven, Sliven, Sofia, Samokov, Yambol, Philippopolis, Adrianople, Pazardzhik, 1588, Dhidhimótikhon, Sidhirokastron, Rodosto, Istanbul (Constantinople), 1588, Brusa 1588, Sérrai, Kavalla, THASOS, Gallipoli, Balikesir, Borlu, Magnesia, LEMNOS, LESBOS, Chios, Izmir, Tyrrha, Nazilli, Ephesus, SAMOS, Kuşadası, COS, Rhodes, NAXOS, Sarajevo, Ragusa, Kyustendil, Skopje, Kratovo, Stip, Ohrid, Monastir, Florina, Salonika 1588, Veroia, Kastoria, Bari, Durazzo, Berat, Taranto, Brindisi, Valona, Otranto, Corfu, Arta, Joánnina, Larissa, Trikkala, Vólos, Chalcis, Lepanto, Thebes, Athens, Patras, Corinth, Messina, Modon, Koróni, Candia, CRETE

0 50 100 km.

THE JEWS OF THE BALKAN PENINSULA 16TH CENTURY

Tombstone of Samuel son of Joel ibn Shuaib from the Aragonese congregation in Salonika.

centers. Thus, for example, Jews were ordered to settle in Constantinople after its conquest by the Turks in 1453. In Salonika the Spanish, Portuguese and Italian refugees joined the indigenous Romaniots and the more recently arrived Ashkenazic Jews (1470). The communal organization in Salonika was of a special character, each immigrant group forming its own congregation (*kahal kadosh*) named after its native country or town. At the height of its development the city had thirty such congregation.

population there. Within the Ottoman Empire Jews engaged in international trade, particularly with Europe. Philip II of Spain even suspected them of both covertly and overtly supporting Turkish expansion, suspecting the Jewish exiles from Spain who had settled in large numbers in Ottoman-dominated European territories of collusion. Refugee communities were established in many towns in the Balkan Peninsula, the Turks encouraging their residence in important

"CONGREGATIONS" (SYNAGOGUES) IN SALONIKA, 16TH CENTURY

* Aragón	Italy
Ashkenazi	* Lisbon (Old and New)
Astruc	Majorca (*Baalei*
Baalei Teshuva—	*Teshuva*)
"Community of the	Midrash (Castile)
Penitent"	*Neot Hen*
Calabria (Old)	Otranto
Castile	Portugal (New)
* Castile (Expulsion)	Provence
Catalonia	* Pugliese
* Catalonia (Expulsion)	*Shalom* (or *Neve*
Corfu	*Shalom*)
Etz Hayyim (or *Etz*	Sicily (Old)
Hada'at)	Sicily (New)
Évora	Spain (Expulsion)
Ishmael	

* Large congregation

IMMIGRATION TO THE HOLY LAND
16TH TO 17TH CENTURIES

THE instability stemming from frequent changes of rule in Palestine, the harassment encountered there by Jews, and the heavy taxation imposed upon them all failed to deter Jews immigrating to the country. The immigration wave of the sixteenth century brought new life to the local Jewish population that is described in the accounts left by pilgrims. The Jews resided in a few towns, chiefly Jerusalem, Safed, Tiberias and in some agricultural villages in Galilee. For hundreds of years the Jews of Italy played a special role in strengthening Palestine's Jews by direct support to the communities and by serving as a transit station en route for the immigrants.

Some of the refugees from Spain as well

PALESTINE UNDER OTTOMON RULE
16TH CENTURY

3.
Safed becomes major Jewish center in country with a population of 15,000 engaged in farming, cloth manufacturing and export of finished goods to Damascus.

5.
Late 16th cent.—Beginning of decline; 1576-77—About 1,000 Jews expelled to Cyprus to counterbalance Christian community.

4.
Jews in Safed live in their own quarters, in Shechem and Jerusalem in mixed quarters. Four ethnic groups exist: Musta'rabs (native born), Maghrebis (from North Africa), Ashkenazim and Sephardim (refugees from expulsions).

1.
1516—Turkish Sultan Selim I conquers Palestine.

2.
1522—Traveler relates of 1,570 Jews (300 families) living in city.

···· Boundary of Sanjak (province)

as kabbalists came in the hope of imminent redemption.

Safed of the sixteenth century had an established and growing Jewish community and was the home of many great scholars, among them Jacob (I) Berav, Joseph Caro and Moses Trani. In 1548, nineteen hundred taxpaying families, of whom 716 were Jewish, lived in the town.

In 1560 Doña Gracia Mendes-Nasi obtained concessions in Tiberias from the sultan (confirmed and extended for Joseph Nasi, her nephew, in 1561), intending to rebuild the town and reestablish the Jewish community. Joseph Nasi ordered the reconstruction of the town's walls (completed in 1565) and the planting of mulberry trees for the silk industry. A call was issued to Jewish communities in the Mediterranean Basin inviting them to settle in Tiberias and the entire community of Cori (south of Rome) made preparations to emigrate. After Joseph Nasi's death in 1579 the Tiberias venture was continued by Solomon Abenaes (Ibn Yaish), a Portuguese converso statesman, wealthy merchant and successor of Joseph Nasi at the Turkish court in Constantinople.

The decline in the seventeenth century of the Jewish population in the Holy Land in general and in Galilee in particular reflected the erosion of the Ottoman Empire during this period. The Jewish community of Safed was severely affected by the continuing wars between the Ottoman rulers and the Druse of Lebanon, as well as by epidemics and a plague of locusts. Despite attempts at reconstituting the Safed community in the 1720s, it never regained its sixteenth-century status and glory. The center of gravity shifted to Jerusalem. Rabbi Isaac ha-Kohen Sholal (Solal), the last *nagid* in Mamluk Egypt from 1502, settled in Jerusalem in 1517. The beginning of the seventeenth century saw a stream of immigrants to Jerusalem, particularly from Italy. The distinguished rabbi, Isaiah b. Abraham ha-Levi Horowitz

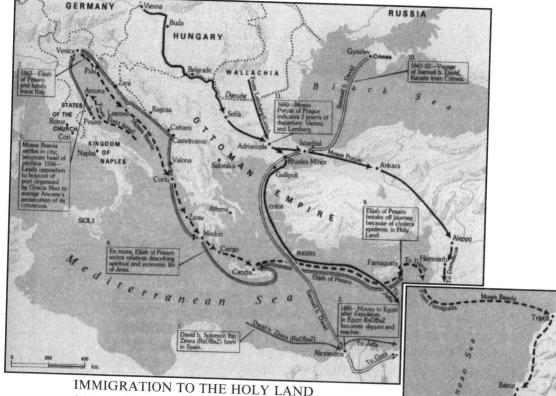

IMMIGRATION TO THE HOLY LAND
16TH TO 17TH CENTURIES

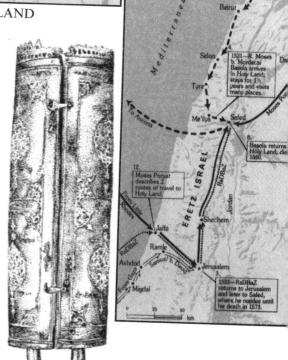

(called ha-Shelah ha-Kadosh), settled in Jerusalem in 1622.

There was a unique upsurge of support for the Jews of Palestine among Protestants, especially in England and Holland, concurrent with a wave of renewed assistance by the Jewish Diaspora, especially for Jerusalem. The Jews of Italy and the Low Countries were particularly generous.

For many generations the Jews in the Holy Land were dependent upon the financial support of the Diaspora, brought by travelers or immigrants via treacherous routes, often at great risk to their lives.

Cover of Torah scroll from Damascus, 1565. Incised copper with silver decoration.

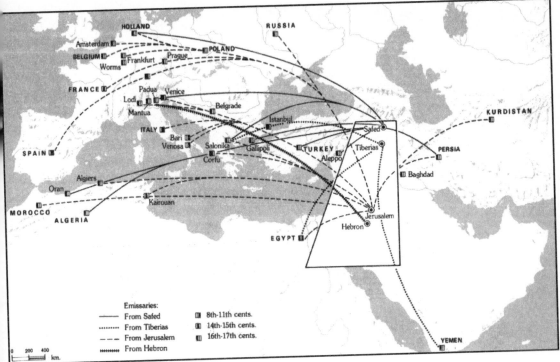

EMISSARIES FROM THE HOLY LAND TO THE DIASPORA
15TH TO 16TH CENTURIES

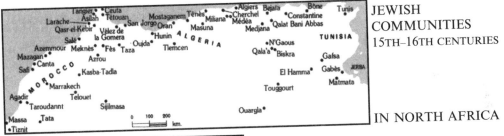

**JEWISH
COMMUNITIES
15TH–16TH CENTURIES**

IN NORTH AFRICA

**IN THE EGYPTIAN
DELTA**

However, such support was inadequate, and the local community was forced to send emissaries known as *shadarim* (from *sheluhei de-rabbanan*) out to the entire Diaspora, east and west, to procure contributions. The despatch of these emissaries attested to the close ties between the Jews of the Diaspora and those of the Holy Land.

KABBALISTS AND KABBALISTIC CENTERS
16TH AND 17TH CENTURIES

THE persecutions of 1391 in Spain and the subsequent events, culminating in the Expulsion of 1492, made a deep impression upon the kabbalists of the period and resulted in far-reaching changes in kabbalistic thought. The problem of redemption was heightened, particularly because hopes that the Messiah would come in 1492 (based on the passage in Job 38:7, "When the morning stars sang together"—the numerical value of the Hebrew word, *bron*, for "sung," is 1492) proved baseless. The messianic frustration and the catastrophe of expulsion precipitated a soul searching by the kabbalists.

Two books by anonymous authors, published about 1500, were particularly significant: *Sefer ha-Meshiv*, a commentary on the Pentateuch, and *Kaf ha-Ketoret*, a commentary on the book of Psalms. The authors attempted to highlight the apocalyptic meaning of every word in the Bible. There were "seventy modes of expounding the Torah" (Num. R. 13:15) and each generation had its own mode; thus it was expulsion and redemption that occupied their generation, proving to be a particularly dominant theme in *Kaf ha-Ketoret*, which expressed the new weltanschauung of Safed kabbalists and was founded on messianic eschatology.

In the kabbalistic center of Safed, outstanding personalities were: Moses b. Jacob Cordovero, author of *Tomer Devorah*; Elijah b. Moses de Vidas, author of *Reshit Hokhmah*; Eleazar b. Moses Azikri, author of *Sefer Haredim*; Hayyim b. Joseph Vital, author of *Sha'arei Kedushah*; Joseph b. Ephraim Caro, author of the *Shulhan Arukh*, one of the great halakhists of all time, who apparently met Solomon Molcho, kabbalist and pseudo-messiah, in Salonika and was so deeply impressed by him that when Molcho was martyred at the stake in Mantua in 1532, Caro also expressed a desire to meet a martyr's death. Caro wrote a mystical diary called *Maggid Mesharim* in which he recorded messages revealed to him by a "heavenly mentor" (*maggid*). Another kabbalist living in Safed was Solomon b. Moses ha-Levi Alkabez. Born in 1505 in Salonika, he studied with the greatest of its rabbis, Joseph Taitazak. Around 1535 he settled in Safed, where he died in 1584. Alkabez is the author of the *piyyut Lekhah Dodi*, a hymn welcoming the Sabbath that is woven out of strands of kabbalistic imagery expressing messianic yearning for redemption. Another personality active in the Holy Land was the Hebrew poet, Israel b. Moses Najara (1555?–1625?). Born in Damascus he settled in Gaza around 1587, serving as a rabbi until his death.

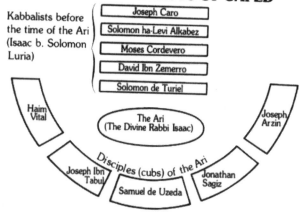

NOTED KABBALISTS OF SAFED

Kabbalists before the time of the Ari (Isaac b. Solomon Luria)

- Joseph Caro
- Solomon ha-Levi Alkabez
- Moses Cordevero
- David Ibn Zemerro
- Solomon de Turiel

The Ari (The Divine Rabbi Isaac)

Disciples (cubs) of the Ari

Haim Vital
Joseph Ibn Tabul
Samuel de Uzeda
Jonathan Sagiz
Joseph Arzin

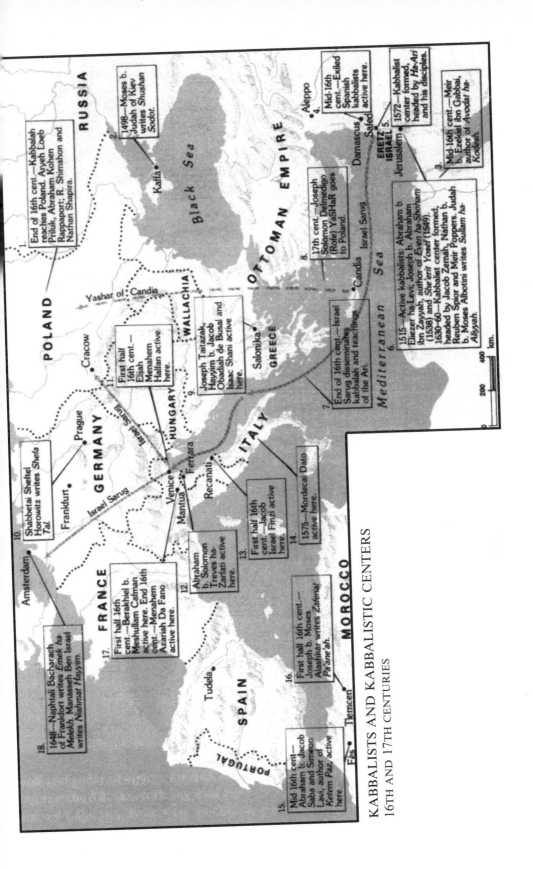

KABBALISTS AND KABBALISTIC CENTERS
16TH AND 17TH CENTURIES

The outstanding kabbalist of the sixteenth century was Isaac b. Solomon Luria, known as ha-Ari. He was born in 1534 and was active in Safed from about 1569 until his death in 1572. Luria's originality is in his pioneering conception of the theoretical aspect of *kabbalah* and its permeation with messianic eschatology. In Safed he gathered around him a group of disciples who subsequently expounded, expanded and propogated his teachings. Mid-sixteenth-century Safed was like thirteenth-century Gerona as a center of theoretical *kabbalah*.

JEWISH PRINTERS AND ADMISSION OF JEWS TO UNIVERSITIES 15TH TO 16TH CENTURIES

ABOUT twenty years after Johann Gutenberg developed a new method of printing and printed his forty-two-line Bible in 1455, there are verified accounts of Jewish printers printing books in Hebrew. Books printed before 1501 are known as incunabula and at present there are 175 extant editions of books printed with Hebrew letters. These deal with the whole Bible or various parts of it, biblical commentaries, tractates of the Babylonian Talmud, prayer books, Passover *haggadot*, and books on the *halakhah*. Italy was the cradle of Jewish printing in the fifteenth century with presses operating in at least eleven towns including Piove di Sacco and Reggio di Calabria, 1475; Mantua, 1476; Soncino, 1483; and Brescia, 1491. Jewish printing continued in the sixteenth and seventeenth centuries with presses operating in Venice, Cremona and Sabbioneta. Both Jewish and non-Jewish craftsmen contributed to the development of Hebrew printing.

Spain was the next largest center for Jewish printers and their presses. In 1476 Solomon b. Moses Alkabez (grandfather of the kabbalist Solomon Alkabez) established a press in Guadalajara and Eliezer Alantansi in Híjar in Aragón in 1485; one was set up in Zamora in 1487. For Portugal there are extant incunabula

Printers in the 16th century.

attesting to printing presses in Lisbon in 1473; in Faro in 1487 operated by Eliezer Toledano the printer; and in Leiria in 1492 operated by the printers Samuel D'Ortas and sons.

Constantinople had one incunabulum, *Arba'a Turim* by Jacob b. Asher, completed in December 1493 by the printers David and Samuel ibn Nahmias.

In the sixteenth century presses were established in other Jewish centers such as Prague (1512), Salonika (1513), Fès (1516) and Augsburg (1533). Amsterdam became an important center for Hebrew printing in the seventeenth century, after Manasseh ben Israel established the first press in 1626.

Christian printers were also active in printing Hebrew texts both for Jewish and non-Jewish clients; such presses operated in Basle (1516) and Lyons (1520).

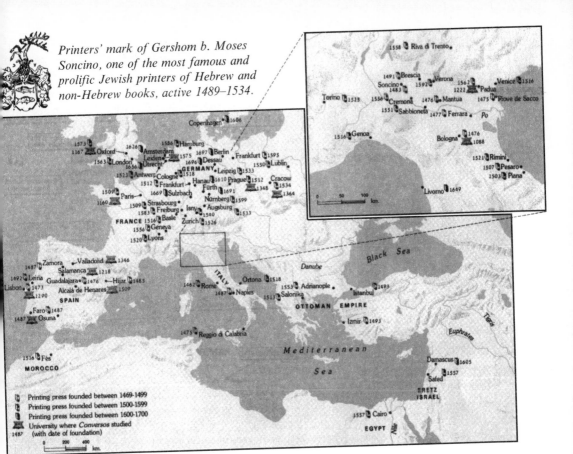

Printers' mark of Gershom b. Moses
Soncino, one of the most famous and
prolific Jewish printers of Hebrew and
non-Hebrew books, active 1489–1534.

UNIVERSITIES

THE medieval universities founded in the twelfth and thirteenth centuries were naturally closed to Jews, since their curriculum was largely theologically oriented. The few "Jews" who were able to attend these universities were apostates. The universities of Oxford, Paris and Salamanca established faculties for the study of Hebrew and Judaica, particularly for men studying to be priests. Medicine was one of the few subjects that interested Jews, but few places were open to them. Eventually a number of Jews were able to study medicine at the University of Padua. At the beginning of the seventeenth century a larger number succeeded in gaining admission to Dutch universities, particularly Leiden.

In Spain the conversos were able to study at many of the universities until the end of the fifteenth century, when a number of universities limited the intake of conversos, thus compelling some of them to obtain forged documents attesting to their Christian ancestry. The University of Salamanca established a faculty of Hebrew in 1314 and when the University of Alcalá de Henares was founded in 1509 some conversos were admitted. However, the major converso admittance into universities was in the sixteenth and seventeenth centuries, some of them even attained high status. The Inquisition kept a close watch on university students, fearing the spread of heretical ideas.

THE history of the Jews in Italy in the sixteenth and seventeenth centuries is as complex as that of the two preceding centuries. The Italian Peninsula was fragmented into many states, between which constant rivalry played an important part in both the establishment of new Jewish communities and in the expulsion of Jews and and their constant emigration. Jewish emigrants from Germany, most of whom settled in northern Italy, as well as refugees from Spain and Portugal, among them conversos who reverted to Judaism, were assimilated by the Italian Jewish communities. Each group of immigrants brought with it customs and traditions of communal organization which they reestablished and continued to practice for many generations in their new communities, quite distinct from one another.

Bronze Italian Hanukkah lamp from the 16th century showing the lily of Florence.

The Jewish fate in sixteenth-century Italy was one of expulsions from various towns and areas. Persecutions, as in Spain, were uniformly applied in the Spanish-ruled territories of southern Italy. After Spain took control of Milan and northern Italy, it was extended to these areas as well. In the 1570s Spain exerted its influence upon Savoy and its environs. With regard to the Jews, Spain was concerned about the rise of Islam and the expansion of the Ottoman Turks and saw the Jews as collaborators with the Turks. Philip II of Spain, who succeeded in uniting the kingdoms of Spain and Portugal in 1580, was particularly troubled by this matter, seeing himself as the protector of Christianity against its external enemies and guardian of the faith against internal heresy.

Internal power struggles in sixteenth-century Italy and external pressures also affected the popes, some of whom (particularly popes Julius II, 1503–1513, and Leo X, 1513–1521) were patrons of the arts. They encouraged and supported artists, philosophers and architects, and transformed their domains into centers of culture. Others, assisted by the Inquisition, supported the persecution and expulsion of Jews.

During the papacy of Leo X (Giovanni de' Medici) Rome blossomed, its population increased from forty to ninety thousand, the Jewish community also grew. Elijah (Bahur) Levita, Hebrew philologist, grammarian and lexicographer, lived and worked in Rome from 1514 to 1527.

The papacies of Julius III (1550–1555) and Paul IV (1555–1559) were years of grief and suffering for the Jews of Italy. Paul IV revived the Inquisition and was the author of the bull *Cum nimis absurdum* ("because it is absurd") of 14 July

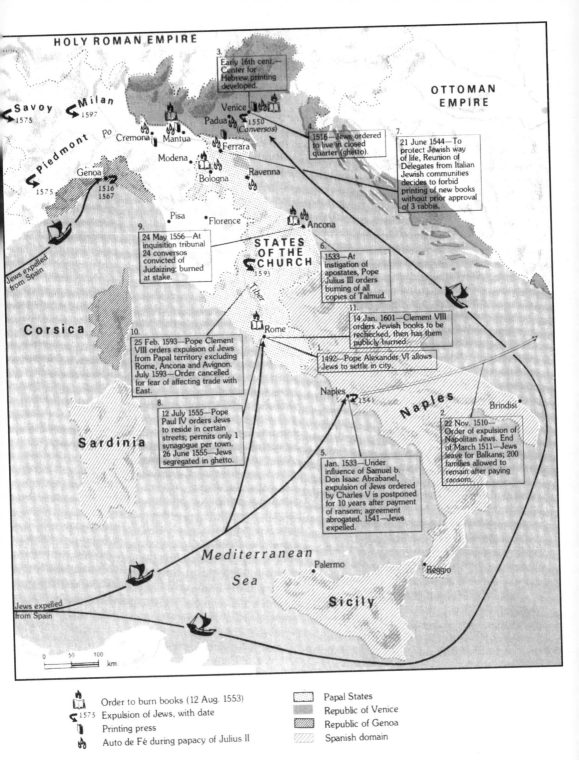

HOLY ROMAN EMPIRE

OTTOMAN EMPIRE

Savoy 1575

Milan 1597

Piedmont

Genoa 1575 1516 1567

Po Cremona Mantua

Venice 1550 (Conversos)

Padua

Ferrara

Modena

Bologna

Ravenna

Pisa

Florence

Ancona

3. Early 16th cent.— Center for Hebrew printing developed.

4. 1516—Jews ordered to live in closed quarter (ghetto).

7. 21 June 1544—To protect Jewish way of life, Reunion of Delegates from Italian Jewish communities decides to forbid printing of new books without prior approval of 3 rabbis.

STATES OF THE CHURCH 1593

9. 24 May 1556—At inquisition tribunal 24 conversos convicted of Judaizing; burned at stake.

6. 1533—At instigation of apostates, Pope Julius III orders burning of all copies of Talmud.

Jews expelled from Spain

Corsica

Tiber

Rome

11. 14 Jan. 1601—Clement VIII orders Jewish books to be rechecked, then has them publicly burned.

1. 1492—Pope Alexander VI allows Jews to settle in city.

10. 25 Feb. 1593—Pope Clement VIII orders expulsion of Jews from Papal territory excluding Rome, Ancona and Avignon. July 1593—Order cancelled for fear of affecting trade with East.

8. 12 July 1555—Pope Paul IV orders Jews to reside in certain streets; permits only 1 synagogue per town. 26 June 1555—Jews segregated in ghetto.

Sardinia

Naples 1541

Naples

Brindisi

2. 22 Nov. 1510—Order of expulsion of Napolitan Jews. End of March 1511—Jews leave for Balkans; 200 families allowed to remain after paying ransom.

5. Jan. 1533—Under influence of Samuel b. Don Isaac Abrabanel, expulsion of Jews ordered by Charles V is postponed for 10 years after payment of ransom; agreement abrogated. 1541—Jews expelled.

Mediterranean Sea

Palermo

Reggio

Jews expelled from Spain

Sicily

0   50   100 km.

📖 Order to burn books (12 Aug. 1553)

🔔1575 Expulsion of Jews, with date

🕯 Printing press

🔥 Auto de Fé during papacy of Julius II

▦ Papal States

▦ Republic of Venice

▨ Republic of Genoa

▨ Spanish domain

1555, which determined the official attitude of the church toward the Jews. The bull decreed the segregation of Jews into separate streets or quarters (ghettos) and the wearing of a yellow badge and hat. On 30 April 1556 he ordered the arrest of the conversos who had come from Portugal and settled in Ancona. An inquisition tribunal sentenced fifty of them; twenty-four were burned at the stake. Doña Gracia Nasi and her nephew Joseph Nasi, former conversos, attempted to intervene on behalf of those condemned to the stake by organizing a boycott of the port of Ancona and transferring commerce to nearby Pesaro. The boycott was unsuccessful but the attempt was significant as an instance of exertion of Jewish power through the use of economic sanctions against Christian authorities. The policies of Pope Gregory XIII (1572–1585) toward the Jews were less severe.

Despite their hardships, the Jews of Italy continued to maintain an active community life and even increased their support of the Jews of the Holy Land.

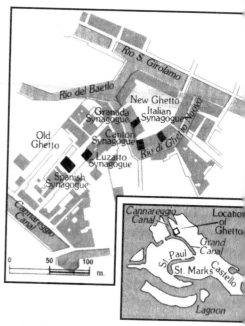

THE JEWISH GHETTO IN VENICE

THE TRAVELS OF DAVID REUVENI 16TH CENTURY

IN 1524–1525, shortly after Palestine was conquered by Sultan Selim, David Reuveni appeared from the east and proposed the grandiose scheme of organizing a Jewish-Christian military campaign against the Ottoman Empire, which was threatening Christianity. His plan called for Pope Clement VII to make peace between the emperor Charles V and King Francis I of France, and then to give him a letter of recommendation to the emperor of Ethiopia. The combined forces would execute a flanking military campaign against the Ottoman Empire while the Jews of Habor, led by Reuveni's brother, would join the forces and conquer Palestine. The plan was based upon the belief that the soldiers of Habor were brave warriors who lacked only weapons for their assured victory.

It is important to note that this plan was proposed by a Jew to the Christian world for a war against the Ottomans who, after conquering Palestine, opened their gates to Jewish and converso refugees from Spain. Reuveni relates in his diary that the pope found the plan plausible but said he was unable to make peace between Charles V and Francis I, who was at that time negotiating for a treaty with the Turks. The pope referred Reuveni to John III, king of Portugal, giving him a letter of recommendation. In referring Reuveni to Portugal, the pope no doubt wished to rely on Portuguese experience of voyages and discovery. In particular, he may have borne in mind their reputation for voyages to the east, perhaps thinking that they might operate from their overseas colonies or

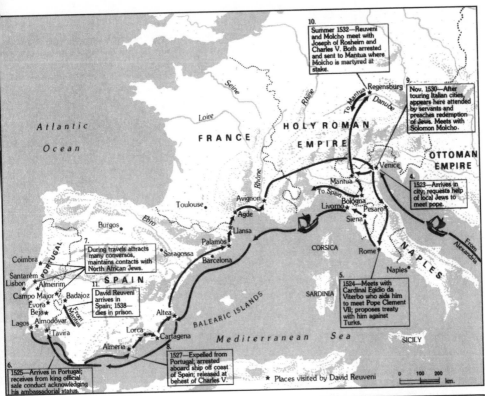

10. Summer 1532—Reuveni and Molcho meet with Joseph of Rosheim and Charles V. Both arrested and sent to Mantua where Molcho is martyred at stake.

9. Nov. 1530—After touring Italian cities, appears here attended by servants and preaches redemption of Jews. Meets with Solomon Molcho.

4. 1523—Arrives in city; requests help of local Jews to meet pope.

7. During travels attracts many converos, maintains contacts with North African Jews.

11. David Reuveni arrives in Spain; 1538—dies in prison.

5. 1524—Meets with Cardinal Egidio da Viterbo who aids him to meet Pope Clement VII; proposes treaty with him against Turks.

6. 1525—Arrives in Portugal; receives from king official safe conduct acknowledging his ambassadorial status.

8. 1527—Expelled from Portugal; arrested aboard ship off coast of Spain; released at behest of Charles V.

★ Places visited by David Reuveni

0   100   200
km.

from places discovered in their voyages around Africa. However, doubt has been cast on this supposition by a non-Jewish source. A letter by Marco Foscari, the Venetian representative in Rome, written on 13 March 1524 (while Reuveni was still in Rome) states that it was Reuveni who suggested the visit to Portugal.

Reuveni requested and also received a second letter to the emperor of Ethiopia, from which we learn that he promised the pope his loyalty to the Holy See and the Christian world if his plan succeeded. His appearance before the king of Portugal had a resounding effect upon the conversos, one of whom, Diogo Pires, inspired by Reuveni, returned to Judaism, circumcised himself and took the Hebrew name of Solomon Molcho.

Solomon probably spent some time

1. 1480s—Presumed birth date.

3. Meets Abraham Castro.

2. Journey along Nile.

0   100   200
km.

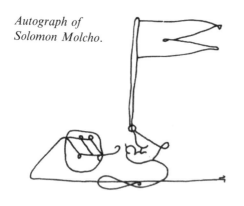
Autograph of Solomon Molcho.

studying *kabbalah* in Salonika, where he possibly met Joseph Caro, who was greatly impressed by Molcho. Returning to Italy in 1529 he was by then convinced he was the Messiah. In 1530 he appeared before Pope Clement VII, who recognized him as a visionary, after he correctly predicted the Tiber's flooding of Rome in 1530. The strange appearance of David Reuveni and Solomon Molcho jointly and severally before pope and kings, the protection proferred by the pope—particularly to Molcho (considering that he was a converso who returned to Judaism)—and their combined mission to Emperor Charles V is food for thought. It is difficult to determine

whether this was a messianic phenomenon linked to a political plan, for this was the period of eschatological fervor. Even a personality like Don Isaac Abrabanel had calculated the year of redemption first 1503 and then 1531, as the year for the coming of the Messiah.

David Reuveni and Solomon Molcho were arrested by order of Charles V. Reuveni imprisoned, died in an inquisition prison in Spain (in the town of Llerena) while Molcho died as a martyr at the stake. Despite their tragic end, the fact that Jews were able to negotiate openly with heads of state is most significant. If we examine this fact in conjunction with the activities of former conversos during the sixteenth century, we may perhaps gain some insight into the origin of the new ideas and weltanschauung in Jewish thinking. There is no doubt that they were fully acquainted with the political climate and balance of power within Christianity and the rest of the world and were therefore able to present a plausible case to the heads of state. The appearance of David Reuveni caused a great stir amongst Jews and conversos.

THE EMIGRATION OF CONVERSOS FROM PORTUGAL AND THEIR DISPERSION; THE READMISSION OF JEWS TO ENGLAND 16TH AND 17TH CENTURIES

ONE of the outcomes of the Expulsion of Jews from Spain was a Sephardic diaspora within the existing Diaspora—a new reality in the history of the Jews. Those expelled settled and established communities in many places in the countries of the Mediterranean Basin, particularly in the domains of the Ottoman Empire. In due course, these communities absorbed the indigenous Jewish communities, transplanting their communal organization from Spain. However, the refugees from Spain were not alone in establishing the new Sephardic communities. At the beginning of the sixteenth century the first refugees from the forced conversions in Portugal in 1497 joined the newly established Sephardic communities, after first forming communities of their own.

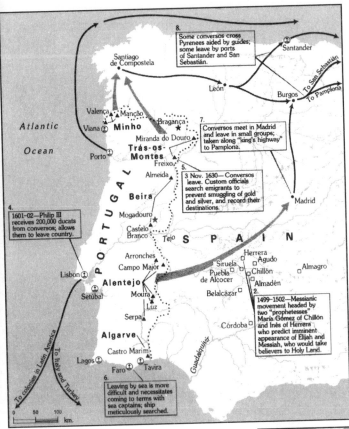

8. Some conversos cross Pyrenees aided by guides; some leave by ports of Santander and San Sebastián.

7. Conversos meet in Madrid and leave in small groups; taken along "king's highway" to Pamplona.

5. 3 Nov. 1630— Conversos leave. Custom officials search emigrants to prevent smuggling of gold and silver, and record their destinations.

4. 1601-02—Philip III receives 200,000 ducats from conversos; allows them to leave country.

2. 1499–1502—Messianic movement headed by two "prophetesses" María Gómez of Chillón and Inés de Herrera who predict imminent appearance of Elijah and Messiah, who would take believers to Holy Land.

6. Leaving by sea is more difficult and necessitates coming to terms with sea captains; ship meticulously searched.

Atlantic Ocean

Santiago de Compostela · Santander · León · Burgos · To San Sebastián · To Pamplona

Valença · Mançâo · Bragança · Minho · Viana · Miranda do Douro · Trás-os-Montes · Porto · Freixo · Almeida · Beira · Madrid · Mogadouro · Castelo Branco · Tejo · S P A I N · Arronches · Campo Major · Siruela · Herrera · Agudo · Chillón · Almagro · Puebla de Alcocer · Almadén · Lisbon · Alentejo · Setúbal · Moura · Belalcázar · Luz · Serpa · Córdoba · Algarve · Castro Marim · Guadalquivir · Lagos · Faro · Tavira

To Italy and Turkey · To colonies in Latin America

P O R T U G A L

☐ Center of Messianic movement
★ Major converso community
▲ Customs post
⊕ Port of embarkation

0   50   100   km.

From the sixteenth century these new Jewish communties were joined by conversos who had succeeded by various means and routes in escaping from the Iberian Peninsula. By the mid-sixteenth century many conversos settled in Jewish centers in France and in the Low Countries. They were the first Jews to settle in Amsterdam toward the end of the sixteenth century, as well as in Hamburg and Glückstadt at the beginning of the seventeenth century.

Manasseh ben Israel (1604–1657) was a man of considerable achievements who undertook to work for the readmission of Jews to England, believing in its messianic significance (to scatter the Jews to "the end of the earth" ([Deut 28:64], the medieval Hebrew for *Angle-Terre*). He was also interested in the reported

Dublin · Danzig · Glückstadt · POLAND · Bristol · Amsterdam · Hamburg · Rotterdam · London · Antwerp

3. 1520—Conversos settle in city establishing banks and businesses after Belgium's annexation to Germany. 1529— Conversos forbidden to enter city; those already in residence expelled.

9. Conversos arrive at Zamość after invitation to settle here by local prince.

From Canary Is. · Paris · GERMANY · Nantes · Orléans · La Rochelle · FRANCE · Santander · San Sebastián · Bordeaux · Avignon · STATES OF THE CHURCH · Bayonne · Toulouse · Burgos · Pamplona · CORSICA · Rome · NAPLES · Barcelona · SARDINIA · Naples · SPAIN · Valencia

1. Route taken by early converso emigrants.

Mediterranean Sea · To Turkey

0   100   200   km.

⊙ Town where conversos settled

discovery in South America of the Ten Lost Tribes. In 1655 Manasseh nego-

277

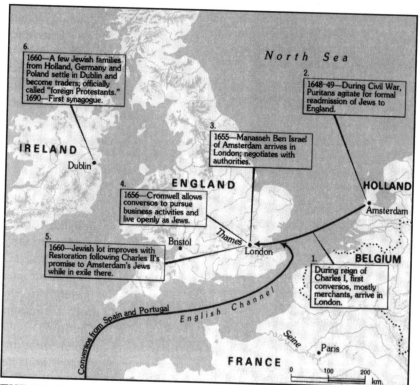

THE READMISSION OF JEWS TO
ENGLAND 17TH CENTURY

Map labels:

6.
1660—A few Jewish families from Holland, Germany and Poland settle in Dublin and become traders; officially called "foreign Protestants." 1690—First synagogue.

2.
1648–49—During Civil War, Puritans agitate for formal readmission of Jews to England.

3.
1655—Manasseh Ben Israel of Amsterdam arrives in London; negotiates with authorities.

4.
1656—Cromwell allows conversos to pursue business activities and live openly as Jews.

5.
1660—Jewish lot improves with Restoration following Charles II's promise to Amsterdam's Jews while in exile there.

1.
During reign of Charles I, first conversos, mostly merchants, arrive in London.

North Sea

IRELAND
Dublin

ENGLAND
Bristol
London
Thames

HOLLAND
Amsterdam

BELGIUM

Conversos from Spain and Portugal

English Channel

Seine
Paris

FRANCE

0   100   200
km.

tiated unsuccessfully with Oliver Cromwell for the formal readmission of Jews to England. However, in 1656 the small converso community was allowed to live openly as Jews, thus de facto renewing the community that had been expelled in 1290.

The conversos of Spain and Portugal who continued in secret to observe the precepts of the Torah had powerful spiritual resources. During the years 1499 to 1502 a turbulent messianic movement developed, based on the anticipation of—and expressing the yearning for—the coming of Elijah and the Messiah, both of whom would lead the Jews to the Promised Land. Among the leaders of the movement were two "prophetesses": María Gómez of Chillón and Inés, the twelve-year-old daughter of the shoemaker Juan Estéban from the

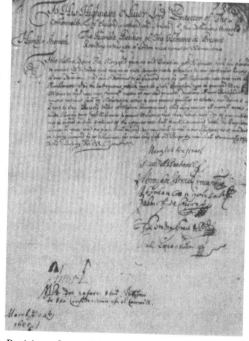

Petition from Manasseh ben Israel (first signator) and six Jews living in London to Oliver Cromwell, requesting permission to conduct services in their homes, 24 March 1655.

278

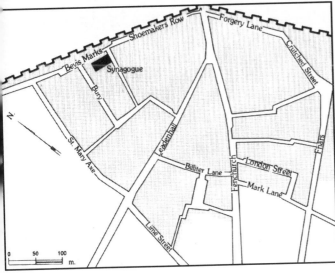

AREA OF JEWISH SETTLEMENT IN THE CITY OF LONDON

Printers' mark of Manasseh ben Israel.

town of Herrera. The remembrance of their Judaism sustained the conversos for hundreds of years until they were able to cast off their disguise and openly join Jewish communities and profess and practice their religion.

In the 1630s, Jacob Cansino (d. 1666), the Jewish interpreter of the governor of Algeria, negotiated with the count-duke of Olivares (1587–1645), prime minister of Philip IV of Spain, for the return of Jews to Spain and the founding of a community in Madrid. Although the plan was foiled by the Inquisition, it is significant that the prime minister was prepared to give serious consideration to Cansino's private proposal.

During the sixteenth and seventeenth centuries Sephardic Jews developed a wide range of economic activities which included distant voyages of trade to the Far East and the New World. The Jews and conversos expelled from Spain developed a particular spiritual tradition that reached its peak in Holland with the works of Juan de Prado, Baruch Spinoza, Isaac Orobio de Castro and Daniel Levi De Barrios.

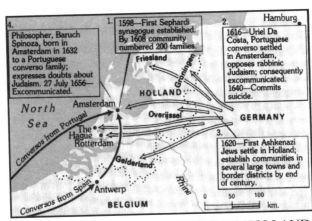

Document of excommunication pronounced upon Baruch Spinoza.

4. Philosopher, Baruch Spinoza, born in Amsterdam in 1632 to a Portuguese converso family; expresses doubts about Judaism. 27 July 1656—Excommunicated.

1. 1598—First Sephardi synagogue established. By 1608 community numbered 200 families.

2. Hamburg
1616—Uriel Da Costa, Portuguese converso settled in Amsterdam, opposes rabbinic Judaism; consequently excommunicated. 1640—Commits suicide.

3. 1620—First Ashkenazi Jews settle in Holland; establish communities in several large towns and border districts by end of century.

JEWISH COMMUNITIES IN HOLLAND
17TH CENTURY

279

JEWISH SETTLEMENT IN AMERICA AND THE FAR EAST
16TH AND 17TH CENTURIES

ALTHOUGH Jewish and converso settlement in South American colonies was forbidden, in the sixteenth century conversos succeeded in gradually settling in the Spanish colonies of Mexico and Peru. Occasionally the crown would permit entry for commercial reasons and the conversos fully exploited these opportunities to infiltrate and settle in Spanish and Portuguese colonies. During the seventeenth century there was an increase of immigrants to the New World; but

The Dutch fleet anchored in Paraíba (1640).

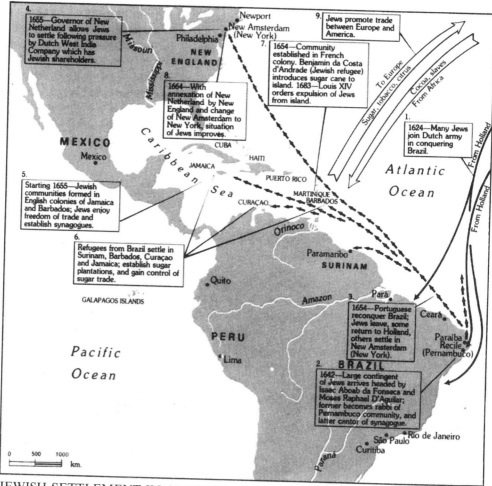

4.
1655—Governor of New Netherland allows Jews to settle following pressure by Dutch West India Company which has Jewish shareholders.

9.
Jews promote trade between Europe and America.

7.
1654—Community established in French colony. Benjamin da Costa d'Andrade (Jewish refugee) introduces sugar cane to island. 1683—Louis XIV orders expulsion of Jews from island.

8.
1664—With annexation of New Netherland by New England and change of New Amsterdam to New York, situation of Jews improves.

1.
1624—Many Jews join Dutch army in conquering Brazil.

5.
Starting 1655—Jewish communities formed in English colonies of Jamaica and Barbados; Jews enjoy freedom of trade and establish synagogues.

6.
Refugees from Brazil settle in Surinam, Barbados, Curaçao and Jamaica; establish sugar plantations, and gain control of sugar trade.

3.
1654—Portuguese reconquer Brazil; Jews leave, some return to Holland, others settle in New Amsterdam (New York).

2.
1642—Large contingent of Jews arrives headed by Isaac Aboab da Fonseca and Moses Raphael D'Aguilar; former becomes rabbi of Pernambuco community, and latter cantor of synagogue.

JEWISH SETTLEMENT IN AMERICA 17TH CENTURY

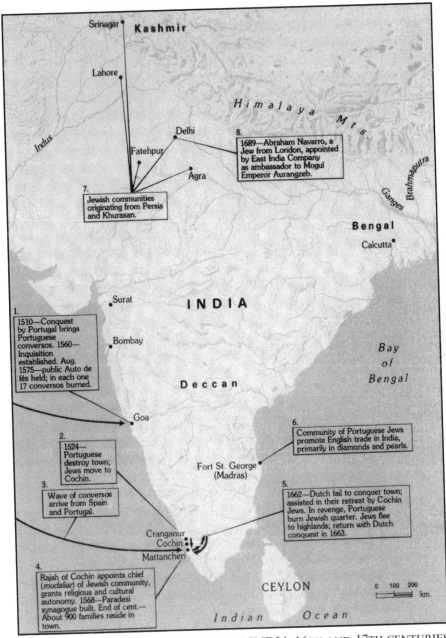

Map labels:

Srinagar • **Kashmir**

Lahore •

Himalaya Mts.

Indus

Delhi •

Fatehpur •

8.
1689—Abraham Navarro, a Jew from London, appointed by East India Company as ambassador to Mogul Emperor Aurangzeb.

Agra •

Ganges

Brahmaputra

7.
Jewish communities originating from Persia and Khurasan.

Bengal
Calcutta •

Surat •

I N D I A

1.
1510—Conquest by Portugal brings Portuguese conversos. 1560—Inquisition established. Aug. 1575—public Auto de fés held; in each one 17 conversos burned.

Bombay •

Bay of Bengal

D e c c a n

Goa •

6.
Community of Portuguese Jews promote English trade in India, primarily in diamonds and pearls.

2.
1524—Portuguese destroy town; Jews move to Cochin.

Fort St. George (Madras) •

5.
1662—Dutch fail to conquer town; assisted in their retreat by Cochin Jews. In revenge, Portuguese burn Jewish quarter. Jews flee to highlands; return with Dutch conquest in 1663.

3.
Wave of conversos arrive from Spain and Portugal.

Cranganur
Cochin
Mattancheri

4.
Rajah of Cochin appoints chief (*mudaliar*) of Jewish community, grants religious and cultural autonomy. 1568—Paradesi synagogue built. End of cent.—About 900 families reside in town.

CEYLON

0   100   200 km.

Indian Ocean

JEWISH SETTLEMENT IN INDIA 16TH AND 17TH CENTURIES

significant Jewish settlement began in 1624 with the conquest of the northern region of Brazil by the Dutch—a campaign in which Jews participated—later settling in Pernambuco and leading full Jewish lives. Following Dutch colonial expansion, Jews also settled in the Caribbean islands. The Jewish community in Brazil was short-lived, dispersing after the reconquest of the northern territories by the Portuguese in 1654. Some of the refugees arrived in the same year at New Amsterdam, settling there despite the governor's opposition. They were the first Jewish settlers in North America.

Conversos also reached India, settling chiefly in the Portuguese colony of Goa, which also had an active inquisition tribunal. The converso commercial ties in the Far East brought spices and precious gems to Europe.

Cochin in India had a Jewish community whose origin and foundation date are uncertain. There are accounts of Jews from Egypt and Aden trading with India and of Jewish merchants who stayed on in the country for several years on business. We also know that the Rambam's brother drowned in the Indian Ocean (1169) while on a business trip.

The first news of a Jewish community in Kaifeng, China, reached Europe in 1605 in a report from the Italian Jesuit missionary, Matteo Ricci, who resided in Peking. Jewish merchants probably arrived in Kaifeng via Persia and Afghanistan in the first quarter of the twelfth century.

The Inquisition standard at Goa.

INQUISITION TRIBUNALS 15TH TO 17TH CENTURIES

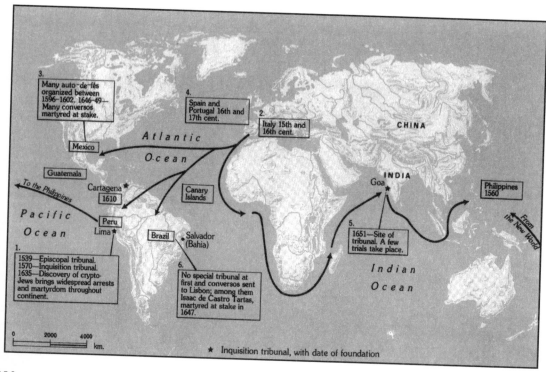

3. Many auto-de-fés organized between 1596-1602, 1646-49—Many conversos martyred at stake.

4. Spain and Portugal 16th and 17th cent.

2. Italy 15th and 16th cent.

CHINA

Atlantic Ocean

Mexico

Guatemala

Cartagena ★ 1610

Canary Islands

INDIA
Goa ★

Philippines 1560

To the Philippines

Pacific Ocean

Peru
Lima ★

Brazil

Salvador (Bahia)

5. 1651—Site of tribunal. A few trials take place.

From the New World

1. 1539—Episcopal tribunal. 1570—Inquisition tribunal. 1635—Discovery of crypto-Jews brings widespread arrests and martyrdom throughout continent.

6. No special tribunal at first and conversos sent to Lisbon; among them Isaac de Castro Tartas, martyred at stake in 1647.

Indian Ocean

0 2000 4000 km.

★ Inquisition tribunal, with date of foundation

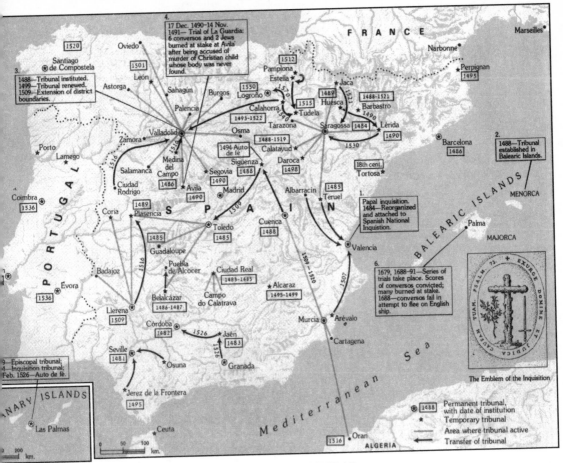

4. 17 Dec. 1490–14 Nov. 1491— Trial of La Guardia: 6 conversos and 2 Jews burned at stake at Avila after being accused of murder of Christian child whose body was never found.

3. 1488—Tribunal instituted. 1499—Tribunal renewed. 1509—Extension of district boundaries.

2. 1488—Tribunal established in Balearic Islands.

1. Papal inquisition. 1484—Reorganized and attached to Spanish National Inquisition.

6. 1679, 1688–91—Series of trials take place. Scores of conversos convicted; many burned at stake. 1688—conversos fail in attempt to flee on English ship.

1494-Auto de fé

5. Episcopal tribunal; Inquisition tribunal; Feb. 1526—Auto de fé.

F R A N C E — Marseilles — Narbonne — Perpignan 1495 — Pamplona — Estella 1512 — Jaca — Huesca 1489 — Barbastro 1488-1521 — Lérida 1490 — Saragossa 1484 — Barcelona 1486 — BALEARIC ISLANDS — MENORCA — Palma — MAJORCA

Santiago de Compostela 1520 — Oviedo 1501 — León — Astorga — Sahagún — Burgos — Palencia — Logroño 1550 — Calahorra 1495-1522 — Tarazona — Tudela 1515 — Osma — Valladolid — Zamora — Medina del Campo 1486 — Sigüenza 1488 — Calatayud 1488-1519 — Daroca 1498 — Albarracin — Teruel 1485 — Tortosa 18th cent.

Porto — Lamego — Coimbra 1536 — Salamanca — Ciudad Rodrigo — Coria 1489 — Plasencia — Segovia 1490 — Avila 1490 — Madrid — S P A I N — Cuenca 1488 — Valencia 1485

P O R T U G A L — Badajoz — Évora 1536 — Guadaloupe — Puebla de Alcocer — Ciudad Real 1483-1485 — Campo do Calatrava 1495-1499 — Alcaraz — Toledo 1485 — Belalcázar 1486-1487 — Llerena 1509 — Córdoba 1482 — Jaén 1483 — Arévalo — Murcia — Cartagena — Osuna — Granada — Seville 1481 — Jerez de la Frontera 1495 — Ceuta

CANARY ISLANDS — Las Palmas

Oran 1516 — ALGERIA

The Emblem of the Inquisition

EXURGE DOMINE ET IUDICA CAUSAM TUAM PSALM 73

⊛ 1488 Permanent tribunal, with date of institution
★ Temporary tribunal
— Area where tribunal active
← Transfer of tribunal

INQUISITION TRIBUNALS IN SPAIN AND PORTUGAL

THE Inquisition organized its activities most methodically, slowly spreading its network in Spain. A tribunal was founded in Seville in 1481 and in Córdoba in 1482; the tribunal whose jurisdiction was over all Castile was at first located at Ciudad Real (1483); later it moved to Toledo in 1485. Thus the Inquisition organized tribunals throughout the country, eventually extending its authority to the New World, first in Mexico (1532), later founding tribunals in Cartagena (Colombia) and in Lima (Peru). In Portugal the Inquisition had three centers—Lisbon, Évora and Coimbra—and when it began its activities against the conversos in Brazil, the Inquisition sent visiting commissaries.

HOLY ROMAN EMPIRE — After 1540 — Milan — 1557-1711 — VENICE — Venice — Genoa (Genova) — Mantua — 1532 — GENOA — Pisa — Livorno — Anconna — OTTOMAN EMPIRE — End of 16th cent. — STATES OF THE CHURCH — 1556—Inquisition trial. 25 conversos burned at stake. — CORSICA — Rome — KINGDOM OF NAPLES — Naples — SARDINIA — **1.** From 1492—Isolated trials. — Adriatic Sea — 1511 Palermo — SICILY — 1482 — MALTA — **2.** 1530—Inquisition commissioner for Sicily stationed on island. — Mediterranean Sea

▨ Under Spanish rule
★ Inquisition tribunal

IN ITALY

283

HEADS OF THE INQUISITION

Tomás de Torquemada	1481–1489	Prior of Santa Cruz in Segovia
Diego Deza	1498–1506	Bishop of Palencia
Francisco Jiménez de Cisneros	1505–1517	Archibishop of Toledo
Adrian of Utrecht	1517–1522	Cardinal; later Pope Adrian VI
Alfonso Manrique	1523–1538	Archbishop of Seville
Juan Pardo de Távira	1538	Archbishop of Toledo
García de Loaysa	1538–1546	Cardinal; Father-Confessor to Charles V
Fernando Valdés	1546–1566	
Diego Espinosa	1566–1571	Cardinal and Bishop of Sigüenza
Pedro Ponce de León	1571–1573	Bishop of Plasencia
Gaspar de Quiroga	1573–1594	Archbishop of Toledo
Jerónimo Manrique de Lara	1594–1595	
Pedro de Portocarrero	1595–1599	Bishop of Córdoba
Fernando Nuño de Guevara	1599–1602	Cardinal; Archbishop of Seville
Juan de Zúñiga	1602–1603	Bishop of Cartagena
Juan Bautista de Azevedo	1603–1607	Head of the Church in South America
Bernado Sandoval y Rojas	1607–1618	Cardinal; Archbishop of Toledo; Adviser to the Crown
Luis de Aliaga	1618–1625	Dominican; Father-Confessor to Philip III
Andrés Pacheco	1621–1625	
Antonio de Zapata	1626–1643	Cardinal; Archbishop of Burgos; Head of the Church in South America
Antonio de Sotomayor	1632–1643	Dominican; Father-Confessor to the King
Diego de Arce y Reinoso	1643–1665	
Pascual de Aragón	1665–1666	Cardinal; Archbishop of Toledo
Juan Eduardo Nithard	1666–1669	German; Father-Confessor to the Queen
Diego Sarmiento de Valderas	1669–1694	Archbishop; Head of the Council of Castile
Juan Tomás de Rocaberti	1694–1699	Archbishop of Valencia
Alfonso Fernández de Córdoba y Aguilar	1699	
Balthasar de Mendoza y Sandoval	1699–1705	Bishop of Segovia
Vidal Marin	1705–1709	Bishop of Ceuta
Antonio Ibáñez de la Riva Herrara	1709–1710	Archbishop of Saragossa
Francisco Giudici	1710–1716	Italian priest
José de Molinas	1717–1720	
Juan de Arcemendi	1720	Counselor of the Suprema
Diego de Astorga y Cespedes	1720	Bishop of Barcelona
Juan de Camargo	1720–1733	Bishop of Pamplona
Andrés de Urban y Lariategui	1733–1740	Archbishop of Valencia; Chairman of Council of Castile
Manuel Isidoro Manrique de Lara	1742–1758	Archbishop of Santiago
Francisco Pérez de Pardo y Cuesta	1745–1758	Bishop of Teruel
Manuel Quintana Bonifas	1758–1761	
Felipe Beltrán	1761–1783	Bishop of Salamanca
Agustin Rubib de Celoallos	1783–1792	Bishop of Jaén
Manuel Abad y la Sierra	1792–1794	
Francisco Antonio de Lorenzano	1794–1797	Cardinal; Archbishop of Toledo
Ramón José de Arce	1797–1808	Head of the Church in South America
Francisco de Mier y Campillo	1814–1820	

The Amraphel Scroll. Sermon held by R. Abraham b. Eliezer ha-Levi exhorting Jews and conversos not to lose heart because of the persecutions. He advises those tried to declare openly that they are Jews and not to be frightened when put on trial. He alludes to the auto-de-fés of the Inquisition. The sermon is based on the Midrash Shir ha-Shirim Raba. The power of the person's love of the Almighty is stronger than earthly fire. By permission of the keeper of the Michael Collection, Bodleian Library, Oxford.

Seal of the Catholic Monarchs Ferdinand (1474–1506) and Isabella (1474–1504) after unification of the Kingdom of Castile and Aragón.

In 1621 the first tribunal was founded in Brazil in the Bahia district, but most of the suspects were sent to Portugal for trial.

Both the Spanish and Portuguese inquisition tribunals persisted in persecuting the conversos who returned to Judaism, even though they managed to leave the Peninsula and settle in regions where the Inquisition did not function.

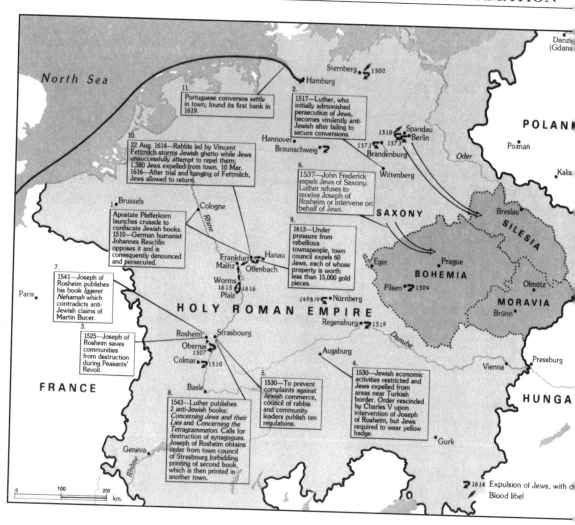

North Sea

Sternberg • ⚡ 1500

↳ Hamburg

11.
Portuguese conversos settle in town; found its first bank in 1619.

2.
1517—Luther, who initially admonished persecution of Jews, becomes virulently anti-Jewish after failing to secure conversions.

POLAN

Poznań

10.
22 Aug. 1614—Rabble led by Vincent Fettmilch storms Jewish ghetto while Jews unsuccessfully attempt to repel them; 1,380 Jews expelled from town. 10 Mar. 1616—After trial and hanging of Fettmilch, Jews allowed to return.

Hannover •
Braunschweig • ⚡

1510 ⚡ Spandau
⚡ Berlin
1573 ⚡ 1573
Brandenburg
Oder

Wittenberg

Kalis

Brussels •

1.
Apostate Pfefferkorn launches crusade to confiscate Jewish books. 1510—German humanist Johannes Reuchlin opposes it and is consequently denounced and persecuted.

Cologne •

6.
1537—John Frederick expels Jews of Saxony. Luther refuses to receive Joseph of Rosheim or intervene on behalf of Jews.

SAXONY

Breslau •

SILESIA

Paris •

7.
1541—Joseph of Rosheim publishes his book *Iggeret Nehamah* which contradicts anti-Jewish claims of Martin Bucer.

Rhine

9.
1613—Under pressure from rebellious townspeople, town council expels 60 Jews, each of whose property is worth less than 15,000 gold pieces.

Frankfurt • Hanau
Mainz • Offenbach
Worms
1615 ⚡ 1616
Pfalz

Eger •

• Prague

BOHEMIA

Pilsen ⚡ 1504

Olmütz •

1498/9 ⚡ • Nürnberg

HOLY ROMAN EMPIRE

Regensburg • ⚡ 1519

MORAVIA

Brünn •

3.
1525—Joseph of Rosheim saves communities from destruction during Peasants' Revolt.

Rosheim •
Obernai
1507
Colmar • ⚡ 1510

Strasbourg

Danube

FRANCE

Basle •

8.
1543—Luther publishes 2 anti-Jewish books: *Concerning Jews and their Lies* and *Concerning the Tetragrammaton.* Calls for destruction of synagogues. Joseph of Rosheim obtains order from town council of Strasbourg forbidding printing of second book, which is then printed in another town.

Geneva •

Rhône

5.
1530—To prevent complaints against Jewish commerce, council of rabbis and community leaders publish ten regulations.

Augsburg •

4.
1530—Jewish economic activities restricted and Jews expelled from areas near Turkish border. Order rescinded by Charles V upon intervention of Joseph of Rosheim, but Jews required to wear yellow badge.

• Gurk

Vienna •

• Pressburg

HUNGA

⚡ 1614 Expulsion of Jews, with d
Blood libel

0 100 200
km.

Danzi
(Gdans

THE sixteenth century was not auspicious for the Jews of Germany-Austria. Though they resided in many villages and towns, pressures exerted by the German emperors and the many expulsions greatly depleted the Jewish communities. The rise of Protestantism did not encourage the renewal of Jewish settlement. Charles V, the Holy Roman Emperor, fought the spread of Protestantism but was not antagonistic toward the Jews, who were represented at court by the *shtadlan* (intercessor) Joseph b. Gershon of Rosheim. Martin Luther was at first tolerant toward the Jews, hoping to attract and convert them to Protestantism, but later, disappointed at their rejection, he became violently hostile to them. The Jews of Germany were subjected to the anti-Jewish polemic of the apostate Antonius Margarita (1530), who followed in the footsteps of another apostate and anti-Jewish agitator, Johannes Pfefferkorn. The activities of these agitators were opposed by a number of humanists led by Johannes Reuch-

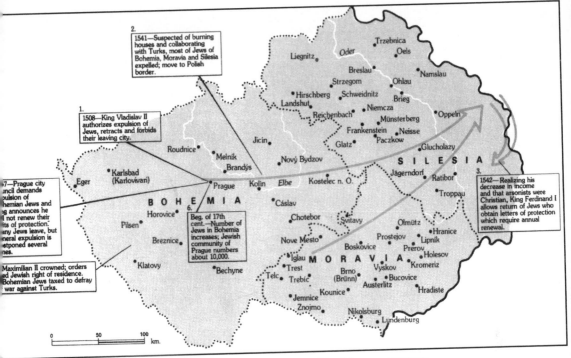

2. 1541—Suspected of burning houses and collaborating with Turks, most of Jews of Bohemia, Moravia and Silesia expelled; move to Polish border.

1. 1508—King Vladislav II authorizes expulsion of Jews, retracts and forbids their leaving city.

...7—Prague city ...uncil demands ...pulsion of ...hemian Jews and ...ing announces he ...l not renew their ...ts of protection. ...any Jews leave, but ...neral expulsion is ...stponed several ...nes.

3. 1542—Realizing his decrease in income and that arsonists were Christian, King Ferdinand I allows return of Jews who obtain letters of protection which require annual renewal.

6. Beg. of 17th cent.—Number of Jews in Bohemia increases; Jewish community of Prague numbers about 10,000.

...Maximilian II crowned; orders ...d Jewish right of residence. ...Bohemian Jews taxed to defray ...war against Turks.

Liegnitz · Oder · Trzebnica · Oels

Breslau · Namslau

Strzegom · Schweidnitz · Ohlau

Hirschberg · Brieg

Landshut · Reichenbach · Niemcza · Oppeln

Münsterberg

Frankenstein · Neisse

Glatz · Paczkow

Glucholazy

S I L E S I A

Jägerndorf · Ratibor

Troppau

Roudnice · Jicin · Nový Bydzov

Melník · Brandýs

Eger · Karlsbad (Karlovivari) · Prague · Kolin · Elbe · Kostelec n. O.

B O H E M I A · Cáslav

Horovice · Chotebor · Svitavy · Olmütz · Hranice

Pilsen · Lipnik

Breznice · Nove Mesto · Prostejov · Prerov · Holesov

Boskovice · Kromeriz

Klatovy · Iglau · M O R A V I A

Bechyne · Trest · Vyskov · Bucovice

Telc · Trebic · Brno (Brünn) · Austerlitz · Hradiste

Jemnice · Kounice

Znojmo · Nikolsburg · Lundenburg

0 · 50 · 100 km.

THE JEWS OF SILESIA, MORAVIA AND BOHEMIA 16TH CENTURY

The expulsion of Jews from Frankfurt-on-the-Main in 1614. Engraving by Georg Keller.

(left) Entrance to the Pinkus synagogue in Prague.

Within the map image:
ENGLAND
London
Amsterdam
HOLLAND
Antwerp
Paris
FRANCE
Berne
SWITZERLAND
Avignon
Genoa
Mediterranean Sea
Rome
North Sea
Hamburg
Berlin
HOLY ROMAN EMPIRE
Frankfurt "The White Mountain" Prague
Regensburg
Rhine
Danube
Venice
Adriatic Sea
Elbe
Baltic Sea
Danzig
Poznań
Breslau
Vienna
Buda
Pest
HUNGARY
Belgrade
Bucharest
Wisła
Vilnius (Vilna)
Warsaw POLAND

3. 1648—Jews participate in defense of city during siege by Swedes; even messenger sent to bring re-enforcements is a Jew.

1. Jews protected by Emperor Ferdinand II after his victory at Battle of White Mountain—8 Nov. 1620.

2. 1624—Ferdinand II allocates separate quarter for Jews; grants them autonomy under Rabbi Yom Tov Lipman Heller; heavily taxed to cover war expenditure.

0 100 200 km.

Boundary of Holy Roman Empire at end of Thirty Years' War — Peace of Westphalia (1648)

lin, who engaged Pfefferkorn in written and verbal attacks and counterattacks from 1511 to 1521. Anti-Jewish propaganda also found its expression in a number of plays depicting the Jews as the killers of Christ.

The Jewish center of gravity moved eastward. Despite the adverse effect on the Jewish community of the expulsions from the crown cities in Bohemia and Moravia to the countryside and villages, Jews somehow managed to withstand the trials and tribulations of this period.

The Thirty Years' War destroyed these communities and increased the numbers who fled to eastern Europe, Poland and Lithuania, joining the already established and growing Jewish communities of these countries within the superbly organized structure known as the Council of Four Lands.

THE JEWS OF HUNGARY UNDER TURKISH AND AUSTRIAN RULE

THOUGH there is very little information about early Jewish presence in Hungary, it seems there was a well integrated settlement in the eleventh century, Esztergom (Gran) being the most important community. The church council of Szabolcs in 1092 prohibited Jews from marrying Christian women, working on Christian festivals and purchasing slaves. During the First Crusade King Kálmán (1095–1116) protected the Jews of his domain against attacks by remnants of the crusader army passing through Hungary. From the twelfth century Jews played a role in the economic life of the country, but in 1222 an order was issued forbidding them to hold any office that would give them authority to judge Christians or to receive titles of nobility.

We do not know what befell the Jews

luring the Mongol invasion of Hungary n 1241 when King Bela IV (1235–1270) vas severely defeated and the country overrun and devastated. But in 1251 the king granted a privilege to the Jews that was similar to those granted in Germany. It would appear that Bela wished to encourage Jewish settlement. Despite this privilege, the church council of Buda in 1279 ordered Jews to wear a distinguishing badge.

The Black Death led to the first expulsion of Jews in 1349 and to a further general expulsion decree in 1360. In 1364 Jews were allowed to return, subject to restrictions. In 1365 the king instituted the office of "judge of the Jews," appointing one of the nobles to represent the Jews before the crown in matters relating to collection of taxes and protection of their rights. Only in the second half of the fifteenth century, during the reign of Matthias Corvinus (1458–1490), did the status of the Jews improve, despite the animosity of the townspeople, who were mostly of German origin. The Jewish population increased and Buda emerged as the largest community in the kingdom.

A blood libel case in Tyrnau (Trnava;

6. 1599—Emperor Rudolf II offended by inclusion of Jews in delegation from Sultan Mehmed III; sentences them to imprisonment with hard labor.

4. 21 May 1529—Blood libel results in 30 Jews being burned at stake. Children forcibly baptized and many Jews expelled.

3. Hungarians accuse Jews of treason and expel them from towns.

2. Sultan Suleiman's army captures capital. Several wealthy Jewish families leave town with queen; most Jews remain; give keys of fortress to Turks.

1. 1526—Turks defeat Hungarian army; King Louis II killed.

5. Sultan Suleiman transfers more than 2,000 Jews from Hungary; resettles them in various districts of Ottoman Empire.

——— Boundary of Holy Roman Empire, 1550

  Territory under Austrian control

  Territory under Turkish control

1494) led to both the arrest of sixteen Jews who were then burned at the stake and to anti-Jewish riots in the town. At the beginning of the sixteenth century there were anti-Jewish riots in Pressburg and Buda, but none during the reign of Louis II (1516–1526).

The Turks first invaded Hungary in 1526, the year in which the Jews were expelled from Esztergom (Gran) in northern Hungary—an expulsion that is thought to have been the result of a accusation of Jewish collusion with th invading Turks. From this point ther was a distinct difference between th status of the Jews living in Turkish-hel territories and those living in the domain of the Holy Roman Empire. In th former, they enjoyed satisfactory treat ment while in the latter they wer persecuted. Jews even emigrated to othe parts of the Ottoman Empire.

THE JEWS OF EASTERN EUROPE Until the 1650s

In 1495 Alexander Jagiellon, grand prince of Lithuania and later (1501) king of Poland and Lithuania, expelled the Jews of Lithuania. Though some of the leading wealthy Jews apostatized, the majority immigrated to Kaffa (Feodosiya in Crimea), to Constantinople or to Poland (where they were allowed to remain an additional year). The folly of the expulsion was soon recognized and in 1503 the Jews were allowed to return, their communal property being restored. Conditions for those who returned were difficult, since they had to redeem their property from the German inhabitants, pay a special tax, and pay for the annual upkeep of one thousand cavalry.

The major Jewish communities in Poland were Cracow, Poznań and Lvov, the latter being a commercial center for the trade routes to Kiev and Istanbul.

Two outstanding rabbinic personalities in Poland were Rabbi Jacob b. Joseph Pollack, who opened the first yeshiva in Poland, and his pupil Rabbi Shalom Shakhna b. Joseph (died in Lublin in 1559), founder of Talmudic scholarship in Poland. R. Pollack (1460/1470–after 1522) was born and studied in Bavaria and was later rabbi in Prague, from which he moved to Cracow.

Ivan the Terrible.

There was a considerable growth of Jewish communities during the reign of Sigismund II Augustus (1548–1572), partly due to immigration from Moravia and Bohemia; in some places the Jewish population doubled toward the end of the sixteenth century. A conspicuous example was the community of Lublin, a town that, in the mid-sixteenth century, was famous for its trade fair.

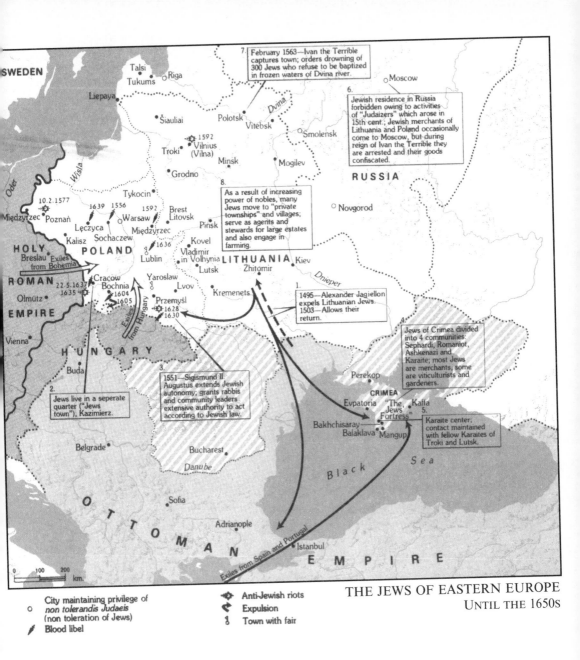

7. February 1563—Ivan the Terrible captures town; orders drowning of 300 Jews who refuse to be baptized in frozen waters of Dvina river.

6. Jewish residence in Russia forbidden owing to activities of "Judaizers" which arose in 15th cent.; Jewish merchants of Lithuania and Poland occasionally come to Moscow, but during reign of Ivan the Terrible they are arrested and their goods confiscated.

8. As a result of increasing power of nobles, many Jews move to "private townships" and villages; serve as agents and stewards for large estates and also engage in farming.

1495—Alexander Jagiellon expels Lithuanian Jews. 1503—Allows their return.

Jews of Crimea divided into 4 communities: Sephardi, Romaniot, Ashkenazi and Karaite; most Jews are merchants, some are viticulturists and gardeners.

1551—Sigismund II Augustus extends Jewish autonomy; grants rabbis and community leaders extensive authority to act according to Jewish law.

2. Jews live in a seperate quarter ("Jews town"), Kazimierz.

Karaite center; contact maintained with fellow Karaites of Troki and Lutsk.

SWEDEN

Talsi
Tukums
Riga
Liepaya
Šiauliai
Polotsk
Vitebsk
Dvina
Moscow

Troki
Vilnius (Vilna) 1592
Minsk
Smolensk
Mogilev
Grodno
RUSSIA

Tykocin
10.2.1577
Międzyrzec
Poznań
1639 1556
Warsaw
1592
Brest Litovsk
Pinsk
Novgorod

Łęczyca
Sochaczew
Międzyrzec
Kalisz
POLAND
1636
Lublin
Kovel
Vladimir in Volhynia
Lutsk
LITHUANIA
Kiev
Zhitomir
Dnieper

Breslau
Exiles from Bohemia
HOLY
ROMAN
22.5.1637
1635
Olmütz
EMPIRE
Cracow
Bochnia
1604
1605
Przemyśl
1628
1630
Yaroslaw
Lvov
Kremenets

Vienna

HUNGARY
Buda

Perekop

CRIMEA
Evpatoria
"The Jews Fortress"
Kaffa
Bakhchisaray
Balaklava Mangup

Belgrade
Bucharest
Danube
Black Sea

OTTOMAN
Sofia
Adrianople
Istanbul
EMPIRE
Exiles from Spain and Portugal

0 100 200 km.

City maintaining privilege of *non tolerandis Judaeis* (non toleration of Jews)

Blood libel

Anti-Jewish riots

Expulsion

Town with fair

THE JEWS OF EASTERN EUROPE
UNTIL THE 1650s

In the middle of the sixteenth century the major Jewish communities in Lithuania were Brest Litovsk (which had 160 Jewish homes in 1566; though they were all burned in 1568, the community succeeded in rehabilitating itself); and Grodno, out of which developed the community of Tykocin and Pinsk. The Vilna community developed slowly; being a town with the privilege of *non tolerandis Judaeis* (1527) very few Jews could reside there, but by 1568 there are records of an organized community. Toward the end of the sixteenth century communities also developed in Lutsk, Kovel and Kremenets.

The death of Sigismund II (1572), the last of the Jagiellon dynasty, and the election of Henry III of Valois in 1574 resulted in a deterioration of Jewish status in Poland-Lithuania that was ameliorated beyond recognition with the election in 1576 of Stephen Báthory, who reigned until 1586. Jews were active in his court, successfully representing the interests of the Jewish community at large. During the reign of Sigismund III Vasa (1587–1632) the situation deteriorated for Poland in general and for the Jews in particular.

Polish-Lithuanian Jewry was fortunate in having great rabbinic leaders and a central institution of self-government called the Council of the Lands (also known as the Council of Four Lands). The council led the communities from the middle of the sixteenth century until 1764 and among its many achievements was support of the development of a study of Torah that was a synthesis of Ashkenazic erudition, *Kabbalah* and Talmudic sophistry (*pilpul*).

THE JEWS OF POLAND WITHIN THE COUNCIL OF FOUR LANDS 17TH CENTURY

THE Jews of Poland created a national institution for self-government known as the Council of Four Lands, consisting of representatives of the four lands or provinces: Great Poland, Little Poland, Red Russia and Volhynia. Lithuania was a separate entity; its council probably functioned as early as the 1560s.

Basically there was cooperation and coordination between the two councils in matters relating to Jewry at large, though relations were sometimes strained over divergent approaches to local problems.

The two councils, initially established to deal with matters of taxation and protection of the Jewish community, soon became institutions dealing with internal community affairs. In the first half of the sixteenth century we have evidence of a central rabbinical court for the Jews of Poland; a similar court already existed in Lithuania.

Representatives of the four provinces (*roshei ha-glilot*) formed a council of elders who governed Polish Jewry. They would usually assemble at the annual fairs of Lublin in February and Jaroslaw in September and deal with such subjects as the election of rabbis, taxation and personal matters. In 1549 the Polish government, realizing its administrative inability to collect Jewish poll taxes,

The Jewish quarter in Kazimierz.

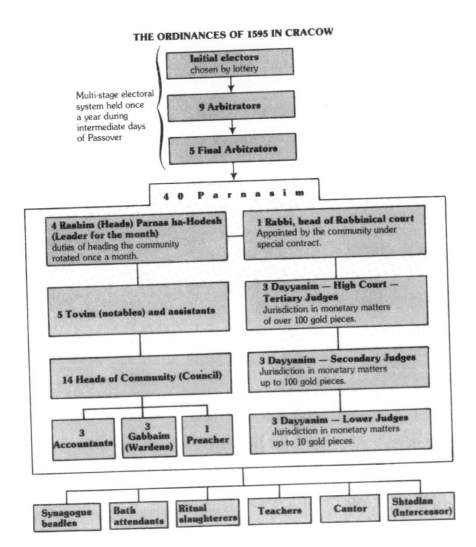

THE ORDINANCES OF 1595 IN CRACOW

Multi-stage electoral system held once a year during intermediate days of Passover

Initial electors
chosen by lottery

9 Arbitrators

5 Final Arbitrators

40 Parnasim

4 Rashim (Heads) Parnas ha-Hodesh (Leader for the month)
duties of heading the community rotated once a month.

1 Rabbi, head of Rabbinical court
Appointed by the community under special contract.

5 Tovim (notables) and assistants

3 Dayyanim — High Court — Tertiary Judges
Jurisdiction in monetary matters of over 100 gold pieces.

14 Heads of Community (Council)

3 Dayyanim — Secondary Judges
Jurisdiction in monetary matters up to 100 gold pieces.

3 Accountants

3 Gabbaim (Wardens)

1 Preacher

3 Dayyanim — Lower Judges
Jurisdiction in monetary matters up to 10 gold pieces.

Synagogue beadles

Bath attendants

Ritual slaughterers

Teachers

Cantor

Shtadlan (Intercessor)

imposed this task upon the council. The Council of Four Lands probably started functioning from the middle of the sixteenth century (the earliest extant record from its official minute book [*pinkas*] is dated 1580) and was dissolved by the Polish Sejm in 1764.

The nonrabbinical delegates (*roshei ha-medinot*) of the provinces elected one of their number as the *parnas* (community leader) of the House of Israel of the Four Lands; he headed the council, presided at the assemblies, and negotiated on its behalf with the king. They also elected a *ne'eman* (trustee) of the House of Israel of the Four Lands to serve as a treasurer and secretary. This appointment was for one year, with salary and expenses, and was also open to rabbinical candidates (rabbis qualified to be elected to the assembly of judges). In later years a number of trustees were elected, dividing the tasks among them.

In Lithuania the council's executive consisted of an elected *parnas* and a number of *shelihim* (emissaries) whose duties were to visit the Jewish communities, check the population rolls and

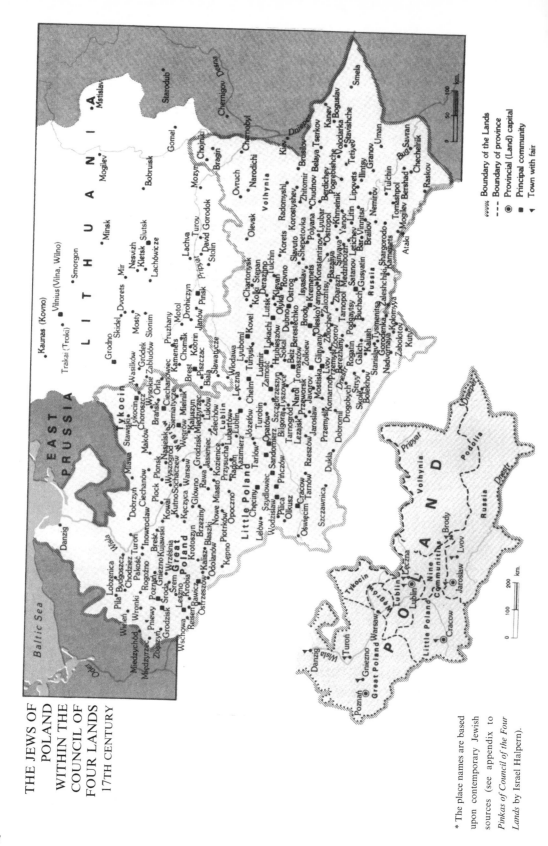

THE JEWS OF
POLAND
WITHIN THE
COUNCIL OF
FOUR LANDS
17TH CENTURY

* The place names are based
upon contemporary Jewish
sources (see appendix to
*Pinkas of Council of the Four
Lands* by Israel Halpern).

〰〰 Boundary of the Lands
--- Boundary of province
◉ Provincial (Land) capital
■ Principal community
▼ Town with fair

assess their ability to pay taxes. These emissaries were eventually replaced by appointed clerks who dealt with tax collection in the province. The trustees were responsible for tax collection and the secretaries of the council recorded the regulations.

Representatives of the two councils would meet to discuss and settle matters relating to the obligations of Polish-Lithuanian Jewry as well as determining their relations with one another.

The institution declined following the destruction of the Polish-Lithuanian community in the Chmielnicki massacres of 1648–1649 and in the Russian and Swedish wars against Poland.

THE CHMIELNICKI MASSACRES 1648–1649

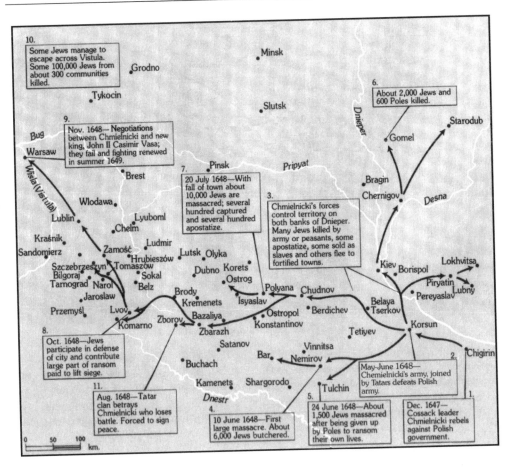

10. Some Jews manage to escape across Vistula. Some 100,000 Jews from about 300 communities killed.

6. About 2,000 Jews and 600 Poles killed.

9. Nov. 1648— Negotiations between Chmielnicki and new king, John II Casimir Vasa; they fail and fighting renewed in summer 1649.

7. 20 July 1648—With fall of town about 10,000 Jews are massacred; several hundred captured and several hundred apostatize.

3. Chmielnicki's forces control territory on both banks of Dnieper. Many Jews killed by army or peasants, some apostatize, some sold as slaves and others flee to fortified towns.

8. Oct. 1648—Jews participate in defense of city and contribute large part of ransom paid to lift siege.

11. Aug. 1648—Tatar clan betrays Chmielnicki who loses battle. Forced to sign peace.

4. 10 June 1648—First large massacre. About 6,000 Jews butchered.

5. 24 June 1648—About 1,500 Jews massacred after being given up by Poles to ransom their own lives.

2. May-June 1648— Chmielnicki's army, joined by Tatars defeats Polish army.

1. Dec. 1647— Cossack leader Chmielnicki rebels against Polish government.

TOWARD the latter half of the seventeenth century two calamitous events shattered Polish Jewry: externally, the Cossack rebellion led by Bogdan Chmielnicki (Bohdan Khmelnytsky; 1599–1657) and the major wars on Polish territory which followed; and internally, the Shabbetai Zevi crisis, which shook the very foundations of the community. Repercussions were still felt in the second half of the eighteenth century.

The massacres of 1648–1649 decimated

> Of some they removed their skins and the flesh they threw to the dogs; some they cut off their arms and legs and cast them on the wayside to be driven over by carriages and horses; on some they inflicted many wounds but not enough for them to die, and threw them out so that they would not die soon and would convulse in their blood until their spirit would depart from them; and many they buried alive, and slaughtered children in the presence of their mothers; they cut up many children like fish; and they cut the stomachs of pregnant women and wrenched the foetus from them and beat their faces; some, they cut their stomachs and put a live cat in them and sewed up the stomach, and cut off their hands so that they could not tear out the live cat; and they hung children on the breasts of their mothers; and they speared children on sticks and burned them on the fire and brought them to their mothers to be eaten by them: and sometimes they took the children of Jews and made bridges of them to pass over. There was no form of gory death which they spared them—the four forms of death, by trial, stoning, burning and strangulation.

From Yeven Metzula *by Nathan Nata Hanover, Venice 1653 (ed. Ein Harod 1945, p. 32).*

Polish Jewry, scattering the survivors throughout many countries. The anti-Jewish propoganda presented the Jewish lessee as an exploiter of the peasants and agent of the nobility. Many Jews died in the rebellion of Pavoloch and other uprisings. In 1637 three hundred Jews were killed east of the Dnieper and many communities were destroyed. The anti-Jewish agitation in the 1640s found a leader in Chmielnicki, whose rebellion dealt a crushing blow to the Polish army near Korsun (1648). In the course of his campaigns against the Poles, Chmielnicki, at the head of a Cossack army and the peasant-serf paramilitary bands of Haidamacks, destroyed Polish Jewry and their communities. The Jews were betrayed by the Poles despite their mutual defense pacts, the latter suggest-ing apostasy as a mode of rescue. Entire communities resisted this temptation, preferring martyrdom. Following the never-to-be-forgotten slaughter of the Tulchin and Nemirov communities, the shocked Polish nobility went to battle against the Cossacks and Haidamacks but were defeated. Chmielnicki's forces lashed out on all fronts, wreaking havoc and death while those taken captive were sold by the Tatars as slaves. The Jewish communities of Istanbul, Salonika, Venice, Rome, Hamburg and Amsterdam did everything in their power to ransom the captives. The Russian and Swedish invasions of Poland completed the destruction of the Jewish communities.

Jews did not reside in the principality of Moscow. In the area that was the Soviet Union and was then Polish, Jews resided in Vitebsk, Smolensk and Polotsk and the adjacent villages. By 1667, following the wars involving Russia, Poland and Sweden, the grand duchy of Lithuania was destroyed and the Jews who were taken captive were ransomed under the terms of the Truce of Andrusovo (1667). Jewish refugees fleeing westward were also caught by the invading Swedes and Brandenburgers and very few succeeded in reaching Amsterdam or Hamburg. In other towns, such as Lublin, the Jews were handed over to the Russians, many being sold into slavery. In Lvov they were spared after paying a huge ransom. The deteriorating situation brought complete ruin upon the Jews of Lithuania, Reisen, Podolia and Volhynia.

The Truce of Andrusovo stabilized Poland's eastern border, the entire area east of the Dnieper remaining in Russian hands. Attempting to rationalize their defeats, the Poles laid the blame on those who had forsaken Catholicism—the Eastern Orthodox, Protestants and Jews.

In Lvov and Cracow there were anti-Jewish pogroms. John III Sobieski (1674–1696)—exemplary for the privileges he granted the Jews of Zolkiew, his town of residence—did much to revive the Jewish communities during his reign and with his death in 1696 the Jews lost a patron. In 1699 a blood libel in Sandomir (Sandomierz) had grave consequences for the community.

Renewed invasions by the Russians, Swedes and Saxons dealt crushing blows to the Jewish communities. On the eve of the eighteenth century the Jews of Poland faced a crisis of actual existence.

Jews had been predominant in the Polish economy for several centuries—in national and international trade and commerce, in leasing large estates and salt mines, banking and crafts and participation at the trade fairs of Lublin and Jaroslaw; but this predominance was gravely affected by anti-Jewish propaganda and the consequent molestation was one of the major factors that contributed to the destruction of the Polish economy.

SHABBETAI ZEVI—ACTIVITIES AND TRAVELS

MORDECAI Zevi orginated from Greece (probably Patras), and settled in Smyrna (Izmir) where his son Shabbetai was born on the Sabbath, Ninth of Av (August) 1626. As a youth Shabbetai Zevi studied with Rabbi Joseph Escapa and seems to have been ordained a *hakham* (scholar) when he was eighteen. Shabbetai Zevi early began showing signs of mental instability—extreme manic-depressive psychosis—which plagued him for his entire life. During his manic spasms he committed acts that ran counter to religious law, including pronouncing the Ineffable Name of God and proclaiming himself the Messiah. These repeated violations led the rabbis to banish him from Smyrna at some time between 1651 and 1654. Wandering through Greece and Thrace, visiting Athens, Patras and Salonika, he arrived at Constantinople in 1658, staying there for eight months, before being expelled because of his blasphemous pronouncements and behavior. Returning to Smyrna, he remained there until 1662, when he decided to settle in Jerusalem.

Shabbetai Zevi.

Traveling via Rhodes and Cairo, where he established contacts with leaders of the Jewish community, he arrived in Jerusalem at the end of 1662. In the autumn of 1663 he was sent by the community as an emissary to Egypt to raise money. On 31 March 1664 in Cairo he married Sarah, his third wife, who was rumored to be a woman of easy virtue. Returning from Egypt, he stopped at Gaza in April 1665, where he met

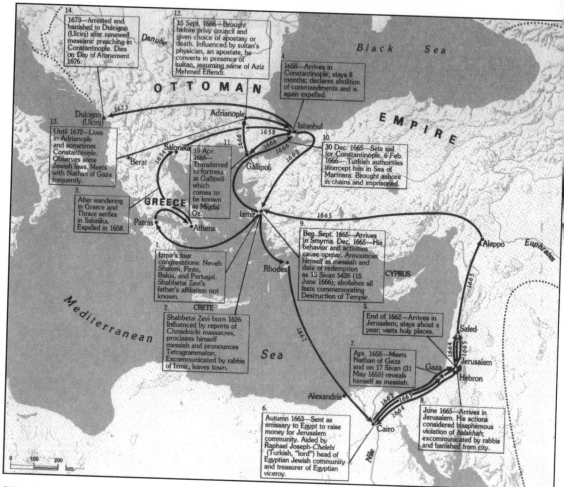

14. 1673—Arrested and banished to Dulcigno (Ulcinj) after renewed messianic preaching in Constantinople. Dies on Day of Atonement 1676.

12. 15 Sept. 1666—Brought before privy council and given choice of apostasy or death. Influenced by sultan's physician, an apostate, he converts in presence of sultan, assuming name of Aziz Mehmed Effendi.

4. 1658—Arrives in Constantinople; stays 8 months; declares abolition of commandments and is again expelled.

13. Until 1672—Lives in Adrianople and sometimes Constantinople. Observes some Jewish laws. Meets with Nathan of Gaza frequently.

11. 19 Apr. 1666—Transferred to fortress at Gallipoli which comes to be known as Migdal Oz.

10. 30 Dec. 1665—Sets sail for Constantinople. 6 Feb. 1666—Turkish authorities intercept him in Sea of Marmara. Brought ashore in chains and imprisoned.

3. After wandering in Greece and Thrace settles in Salonika. Expelled in 1658.

1. Izmir's four congregations: Neveh Shalom, Pinto, Bakis, and Portugal. Shabbetai Zevi's father's affiliation not known.

9. Beg. Sept. 1665—Arrives in Smyrna. Dec. 1665—His behavior and activities cause uproar. Announces himself as messiah and date of redemption as 15 Sivan 5426 (15 June 1666); abolishes all fasts commemorating Destruction of Temple.

2. Shabbetai Zevi born 1626. Influenced by reports of Chmielnicki massacres, proclaims himself messiah and pronounces Tetragrammaton. Excommunicated by rabbis of Izmir, leaves town.

5. End of 1662—Arrives in Jerusalem; stays about a year; visits holy places.

7. Apr. 1655—Meets Nathan of Gaza and on 17 Sivan (31 May 1655) reveals himself as messiah.

6. Autumn 1663—Sent as emissary to Egypt to raise money for Jerusalem community. Aided by Raphael Joseph-*Chelebi* (Turkish, "lord") head of Egyptian Jewish community and treasurer of Egyptian viceroy.

8. June 1665—Arrives in Jerusalem. His actions considered blasphemous violation of *halakhah*; excommunicated by rabbis and banished from city.

Black Sea
Danube
OTTOMAN EMPIRE
Istanbul
Adrianople
Salonika
Berat
Gallipoli
GREECE
Patras
Athens
Izmir
Rhodes
CRETE
Mediterranean Sea
Dulcigno (Ulcinj)
Aleppo
Euphrates
CYPRUS
Safed
Jerusalem
Gaza
Hebron
Alexandria
Cairo
Nile

0 100 200 km

SHABBETAI ZEVI—ACTIVITIES AND TRAVELS

Abraham Nathan b. Elisha Hayyim Ashkenazi. Nathan convinced Shabbetai Zevi of his messianic destiny and on 17 Sivan (31 May 1665) Shabbetai Zevi proclaimed himself the Messiah.

Letters despatched from Palestine, Egypt and Smyrna to the many communities of the Jewish Diaspora proclaiming the need for repentance to facilitate the coming redemption, created a fervent revivalist atmosphere which developed into a mass movement of people who believed in Shabbetai Zevi as the revealed Messiah of the Jewish people. In eastern Europe the Chmielnicki massacres and the Russian-Swedish war provided fertile soil for the growth of such a movement.

The messianic revelation had special significance in Poland-Lithuania, and in several places it resulted in massacres (Pinsk—20 March 1666; Vilna—28 March; Lublin—27 April). A number of delegations were despatched from Poland to Shabbetai Zevi, both while in Smyrna and when he was imprisoned in Migdal Oz in Gallipoli. His meeting with one of the emissaries, Nehemiah ha-Kohen, was destined to play a crucial role in Shabbetai's life. Other prominent Jewish communities, such as Salonika, Amsterdam and Livorno (Leghorn) were caught up in the fervor, and many became his followers.

The movement's vital energy sprang from the Holy Land and the belief in redemption which would originate from it, as well as from the renewal of prophecy that was confirmed by the rabbi of Gaza, Jacob Najara, and some other scholars. The overwhelming enthusiasm that swept over and united Jews all over the world brought people from all walks of life to the movement: from the punctiliously observant kabbalists to the simple folk, all were united in repentance and in anticipation of the coming redemption. Ashkenazim, Sephardim, conversos returning to Judaism, Jews from Yemen and Persia, and in fact the entire Diaspora, were engulfed by these expectations.

The Shabbatean movement included many rabbis and scholars among its adherents: David Yitshaki of Salonika, Samuel Primo of Bursa, Judah Sharaf, and Mattathias Bloch Ashkenazi. It also had many opponents, the greatest of whom was Jacob Sasportas, rabbi and erudite scholar, who narrated the story of his polemic with the Shabbateans in a book called *Zizat Novel Zevi*. Shabbetai Zevi also had many opponents in Egypt, Jerusalem and Safed.

The tumult and messianic fever caused by Shabbetai Zevi and his followers prompted the authorities to arrest and imprison him in Constantinople (30 December 1665). He was later transferred to the fortress at Gallipoli (19 April). On 3 or 4 September he was visited by the Polish kabbalist Nehemiah ha-Kohen. After an angry debate with Shabbetai, he declared his willingness to convert to Islam and was taken to Adrianople where

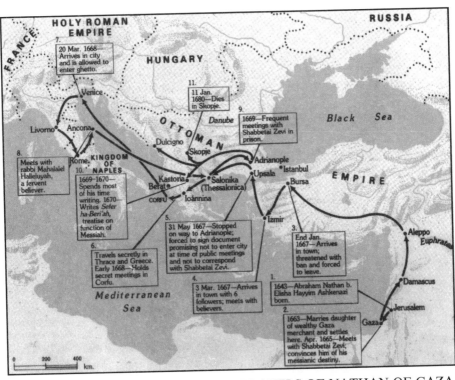

THE TRAVELS OF NATHAN OF GAZA

LEADERS
OF THE
SHABBATEAN
MOVEMENT
AFTER THE
DEATH OF
SHABBETAI
ZEVI

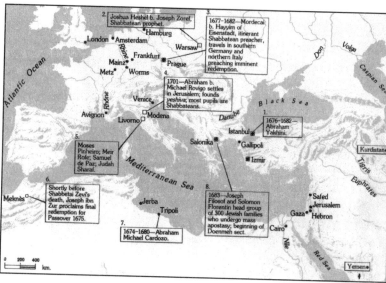

2. Joshua Heshel b. Joseph Zoref, Shabbatean prophet.

3. 1677–1682—Mordecai b. Hayyim of Eisenstadt, itinerant Shabbatean preacher, travels in southern Germany and northern Italy preaching imminent redemption.

4. 1701—Abraham b. Michael Rovigo settles in Jerusalem; founds yeshiva; most pupils are Shabbateans.

1. 1676–1682—Abraham Yakhini.

5. Moses Pinheiro; Meir Rofe; Samuel de Paz; Judah Sharaf.

6. Shortly before Shabbetai Zevi's death, Joseph ibn Zur proclaims final redemption for Passover 1675.

7. 1674–1680—Abraham Michael Cardozo.

8. 1683—Joseph Filosof and Solomon Florentin head group of 300 Jewish families who undergo mass apostasy; beginning of Doenmeh sect.

• Shabbatean center during lifetime of Shabbetai Zevi
□ Shabbatean center after death of Shabbetai Zevi

he denounced Shabbetai Zevi. On 15 September Shabbetai was brought to Adrianople and given the choice of death or apostasy. He converted, assuming the name of Aziz Mehmed Effendi. His apostasy was emulated by many of his adherents.

News of Shabbetai Zevi's apostasy spread quickly, causing shock and consternation amongst the Jews. For some, it was proof of their errors while others tried to rationalize the apostasy, continuing to believe in Shabbetai Zevi and his

Nathan of Gaza.

mission. Shabbetai Zevi continued his activities even after his apostasy trying to persuade adherents to follow him into Islam. Denounced and arrested in Constantinople on 16 August 1672, he was exiled to Dulcigno in January 1673, dying there on the Day of Atonement (17 September) 1676.

Following the apostasy, secret sects of believers sprang up in various places. In Turkey a sect of believers arose called the Doenmeh, who followed in Shabbetai Zevi's footsteps by converting to Islam without renouncing their Judaism.

Nathan of Gaza persisted in his activities even after the apostasy and on his travels secretly visited Shabbetai Zevi in Adrianople (mid-1667). Nathan continued writing, preaching and explaining Shabbetai Zevi's actions, defending his apostasy and his messianic mission. For the next ten years (from 1670) he remained in Macedonia and Bulgaria, staying mainly in Sofia, Adrianople and Kastoria. He died in Skopje on 11 January 1680. The crisis caused by the Shabbatean messianic movement was felt in the Jewish world for many years.

III
MODERN TIMES

Detail of Emigrants' Ship *by Lasar Segall (1891–1957).*

A. JEWISH DEMOGRAPHY
MODERN TIMES IN JEWISH HISTORY

THE concept "modern times" embraces two distinct periods in Jewish history. One, from the seventeenth or eighteenth century until 1939, will here be called the "modern period." The other, from 1948 on, will be called the "contemporary period." Separating the two are those fateful years from 1939 to 1948 that changed the course of Jewish history.

The modern period did not begin at the same time for the various Jewish communities. The Spanish-Portuguese Jews

living in Amsterdam and London were already "modern" in the early seventeenth century. For the majority of European Jews, different events in the late seventeenth and the eighteenth centuries marked the dawn of the modern period: the new direction of Jewish migration, from Eastern Europe westward; the effects of the partitions of Poland; the European Enlightenment; and the civic emancipation granted to Jews in the wake of the French Revolu-

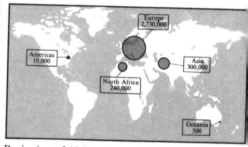

End of 17th century: fewer than 1,000,000 Jews

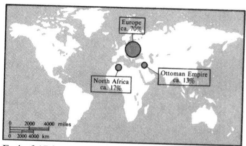

Beginning of 19th century: 3,280,500 Jews

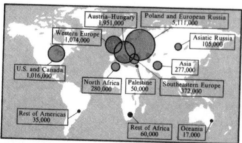

End of 19th century: 10,348,000 Jews

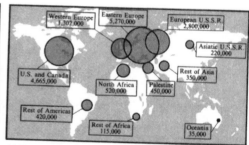

1939: 16,147,000 Jews

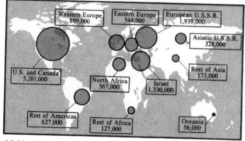

1951: 11,791,000 Jews

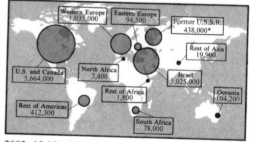

2002: 12,880,000   * Including Asian regions

302

on. For the Jews in many Muslim countries and certain regions in Eastern Europe, modernity came only in the twentieth century.

For all Jews, wherever they lived, "modernization" meant basically the same thing: to cope with the new ideas and forms of social, cultural, and political life developing in the general society, and to adjust Judaism and Jewish society to them. This pattern—adapting to the general environment while maintaining Jewish identity—repeated a process that had occurred again and again in Jewish history. What made the modern situation more acute were the depth of the changes and the fateful implications, both positive and negative, that some of them had for the continuing existence of the Jewish people.

It was in Europe that most of the characteristics of Jewish "modern times" originated. And it was in Europe that most of the Jewish people were concentrated: more than 80 percent at the end of the nineteenth century. The largest Jewish communities were in Eastern Europe, most of them originating from historic Poland, the Poland before the partitions of the late eighteenth century. These communities retained many elements of the social and cultural distinctiveness of the old community (some to a lesser, some to a greater degree). The encounter between the traditional values and the new ideas circulating in the general European society produced a rich array of ideas and movements: the Jewish enlightenment (*haskalah*); different religious trends ranging from extreme Reform to ultra-Orthodoxy; the "Science of Judaism"; a flowering of Yiddish and Hebrew creativity; and the rise of Jewish nationalism, Jewish socialism, autonomism, and Zionism.

Almost all these new ideas and move-ments took hold also in Jewish communities in other parts of the world, such as the Americas and the Muslim countries, in each place being adapted to local conditions and needs. But it was in Europe that the drama of Jewish modernization was to be played out to a tragic dénouement. Although the relationship between the general and the Jewish society in modern times offered many new opportunities, it spelled some awesome dangers. The growth of modern antisemitism and its terrible outcome, the Holocaust, revealed how perilous Jewish life in modern conditions could become.

The developments of the 1940s—the destruction of European Jewry and the re-creation of the Jewish state—closed one chapter in Jewish history and opened another. These two events were of opposite historical significance, although together they caused an upheaval in Jewish life of far-reaching consequences. In the tempest that swept the Jewish people during World War II, large, well-established communities were obliterated; many of those that survived could not recover from the internal demographic and spiritual havoc wrought by the Holocaust. And the events surrounding the establishment of the Jewish state shortly afterward shook the foundations of even older Jewish communities in Muslim countries and caused their ultimate dissolution.

The establishment of Israel led to the concentration there of Jews from all over the world. Two new centers—in Israel and in the United States—became the pillars of Jewish life. Substantive changes took place in the character of the Jewish people and in its relations with non-Jewish societies and countries. This process continued as the Jewish people moved toward the threshold of the twenty-first century.

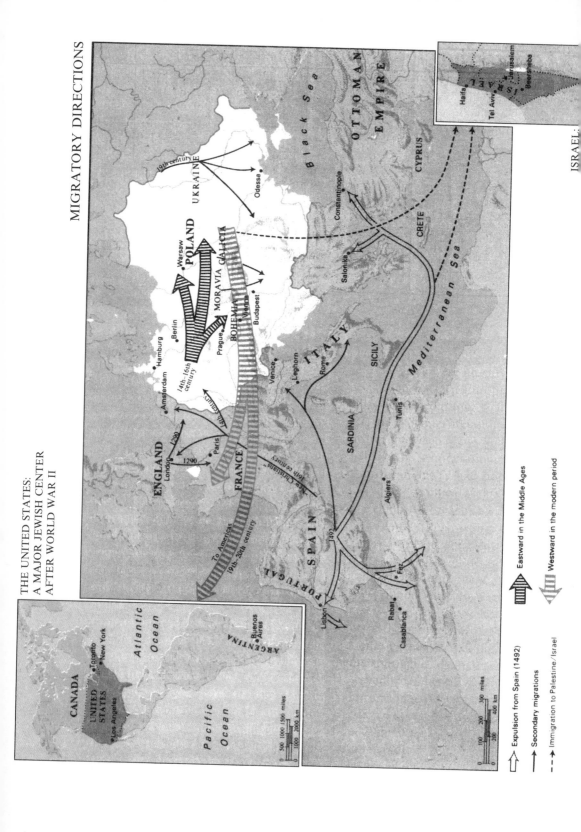

MIGRATORY DIRECTIONS

THE UNITED STATES:
A MAJOR JEWISH CENTER
AFTER WORLD WAR II

ISRAEL:

Eastward in the Middle Ages

Westward in the modern period

Expulsion from Spain (1492)

Secondary migrations

Immigration to Palestine/Israel

MIGRATORY DIRECTIONS:
THE MIDDLE AGES TO THE MODERN PERIOD

FROM the end of the thirteenth century, Western Europe was gradually depleted of most of its Jews, as a result of their expulsion from England (1290), France (fourteenth century), Spain (1492), Portugal (1496–1497), most of the Italian peninsula (sixteenth century), and most of the German cities and principalities (sixteenth century). The bulk of these banished Jews migrated eastward, many settling in Poland. Others went from Spain and Portugal to North Africa and the eastern part of the Mediterranean basin, toward the Ottoman Empire.

Beginning in the late seventeenth century, Jewish migration changed direction. From Eastern Europe, Jews started moving westward, back to Central and Western Europe. The trend began in the wake of the pogroms in the Ukraine in 1648 and 1649 and the upheavals caused by the Russian-Swedish wars of 1648 to 1656. The westward migration resumed, eventually, during the great migration that started in the second half of the nineteenth century, bringing masses of Jews to the Americas. After World War II, other migratory patterns developed, reflecting the new Jewish situation.

JEWISH MIGRATIONS 19TH AND 20TH CENTURIES

THE migratory movement of the Jews in modern times showed two main patterns, which overlapped starting at some point in the nineteenth century: one extended from the mid-seventeenth century to the late nineteenth century; the other, from then until the present. In the first period, Jews migrated inside Europe, both between and within the different countries. The migration brought about the reconstitution of Jewish communities that had disappeared in earlier centuries, as well as the establishment of new ones. A trickle of Jewish immigrants crossed the Atlantic Ocean and founded the first Jewish communities in the Americas.

Three main factors may explain this new development of European Jewry. First, changes in European political and social philosophy beginning in the late seventeenth century improved the attitude of the general society toward the Jews and made possible their resettlement in countries from which they had been expelled in earlier centuries. Second, natural increase among Jews grew enormously; in the nineteenth century, it was much higher than among non-Jews, especially in Eastern Europe. Toward the end of the nineteenth century, there were about 7.5 million Jews in Eastern Europe, or 70 to 75 percent of the entire Jewish people. Third—connected with these two factors—Jews began emigrating in large numbers and settling all over the world. Before World War II, when the Jewish people reached its greatest size, established Jewish communities existed in Europe, the Americas, Africa, Palestine, and Oceania.

The mass emigration of Jews from Europe, which started in the 1870s, is one of the most important developments in modern Jewish history, since it completely changed the demographic structure of the Jewish people. Jewish

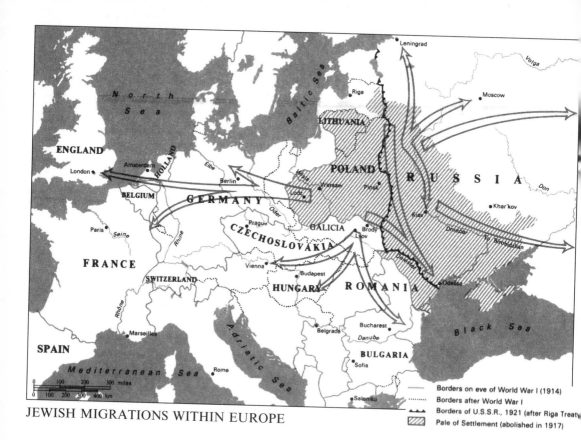

JEWISH MIGRATIONS WITHIN EUROPE

Borders on eve of World War I (1914)
Borders after World War I
Borders of U.S.S.R., 1921 (after Riga Treaty)
Pale of Settlement (abolished in 1917)

emigration was part of the enormous migration of tens of millions of people from the Old World. But proportionately more Jews emigrated, relative both to the total number of Jews in Europe and to the percentage of non-Jews emigrating. Jewish emigration was also of a more conclusive character: it was family-oriented, with a high percentage of women and children and a very low percentage of people who later returned to the Old World. More than other emigrating groups, Jews burned the bridges connecting them to Europe. Furthermore, the growth of new Jewish centers as a result of the mass migration was to prove decisive after the Holocaust for the continuing existence of the Jewish people.

Jewish migration continued strongly in the late twentieth century. Between 1881 and 1939, an average of about 64,000 Jews immigrated yearly to different countries. From 1948 to 1982, the average was even higher, about 75,000 a year. But the countries of destination changed. Before World War II, almost all Jewish emigrants came from Europe, more than 90 percent of them from Eastern Europe. Their main destination was the Americas (83 percent), especially the United States (68 percent). After 1948, Israel became the main destination of Jewish emigrants (68 percent), and Europe again became the objective for many Jews (13 percent), most coming from African and Asian Muslim countries. In the 1960s, a new factor appeared on the map of Jewish migration: Jews leaving Israel. In the early 1980s, their number reached about 400,000, including children born after leaving Israel. Finally, during the 1960s and 1970s, almost 240,000 Jews were permitted to leave the Soviet Union, the majority (67 percent) settling in Israel.

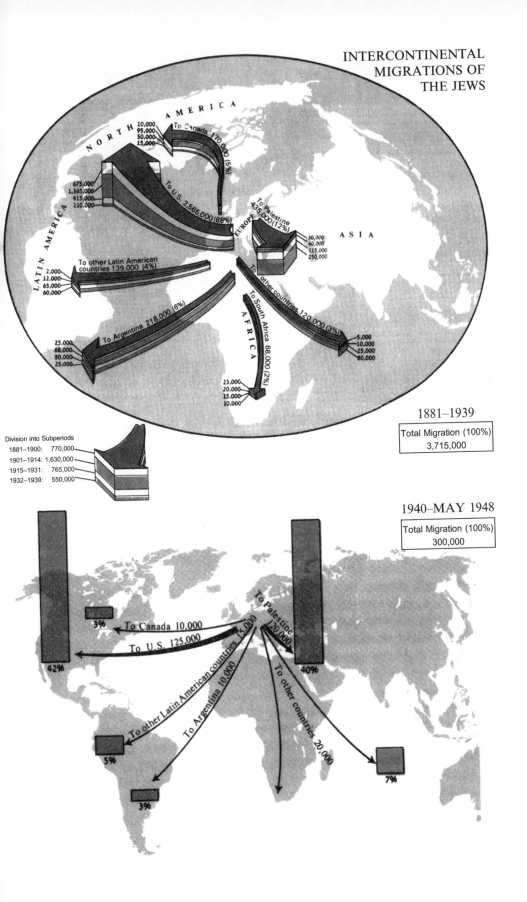

INTERCONTINENTAL MIGRATIONS OF THE JEWS

NORTH AMERICA

To Canada 170,000 (5%)
10,000
95,000
50,000
15,000

To U.S. 2,565,000 (68%)
675,000
1,365,000
415,000
110,000

LATIN AMERICA

To Palestine 435,000 (12%)
30,000
40,000
115,000
250,000

ASIA

To other Latin American countries 139,000 (4%)
2,000
12,000
65,000
60,000

To other countries 120,000 (3%)
5,000
10,000
25,000
80,000

To Argentina 218,000 (6%)
25,000
88,000
80,000
25,000

EUROPE

AFRICA

To South Africa 68,000 (2%)
23,000
20,000
15,000
10,000

1881–1939

Total Migration (100%)
3,715,000

Division into Subperiods
1881–1900:   770,000
1901–1914: 1,630,000
1915–1931:   765,000
1932–1939:   550,000

1940–MAY 1948

Total Migration (100%)
300,000

3%

To Canada 10,000

To U.S. 125,000

42%

To Palestine 120,000

To other Latin American countries 15,000

To Argentina 10,000

To other countries 20,000

40%

5%

3%

7%

307

THERE is not much demographic information about the Jews at the beginning of the nineteenth century is sparse, and assessments have yet to be made on a continental basis. Only toward the end of the nineteenth century did better demographic data become available, and even then we must still depend on estimates regarding many places in Asia, Africa, the Americas, and even in major European

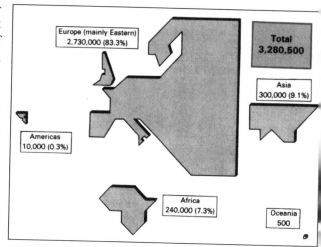

Europe (mainly Eastern)
2,730,000 (83.3%)

Total
3,280,500

Asia
300,000 (9.1%)

Americas
10,000 (0.3%)

Africa
240,000 (7.3%)

Oceania
500

EARLY 19TH CENTURY

THE JEWISH PEOPLE:
LATE 19TH CENTURY

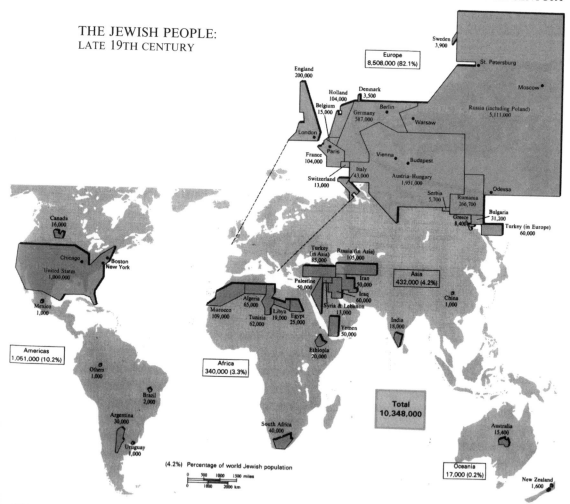

Europe
8,508,000 (82.1%)

Sweden
3,900

St. Petersburg

Moscow

England
200,000

Holland
104,000

Denmark
3,500

Belgium
15,000

Berlin

Germany
587,000

Warsaw

Russia (including Poland)
5,111,000

London

France
104,000

Paris

Vienna

Budapest

Italy
43,000

Switzerland
13,000

Austria-Hungary
1,951,000

Odessa

Serbia
5,700

Rumania
266,700

Bulgaria
31,200

Greece
8,400

Turkey (in Europe)
60,000

Canada
16,000

Chicago

Boston
New York

United States
1,000,000

Mexico
1,000

Turkey
(in Asia)
85,000

Russia (in Asia)
105,000

Asia
432,000 (4.2%)

Palestine
50,000

Iran
50,000

Iraq
60,000

China
1,000

Algeria
65,000

Libya
19,000

Egypt
25,000

Syria & Lebanon
13,000

India
18,000

Morocco
109,000

Tunisia
62,000

Yemen
50,000

Ethiopia
20,000

Americas
1,051,000 (10.2%)

Others
1,000

Africa
340,000 (3.3%)

Brazil
2,000

Argentina
30,000

Uruguay
1,000

South Africa
40,000

Total
10,348,000

Australia
15,400

Oceania
17,000 (0.2%)

New Zealand
1,600

(4.2%) Percentage of world Jewish population

0   500   1000   1500 miles
0   1000   2000 km

countries like France and England. Nevertheless, some demographic trends shown by Jews during the nineteenth century seem clear enough.

The most significant trend was the huge increase in the number of Jews, primarily in Eastern Europe. The general population of Europe grew considerably in the nineteenth century, but the increase among the Jews was even more rapid. The Jews were an estimated 1.4 percent of the European population during the first decades of the nineteenth century, but 2 percent at the end of the century. About 82 to 83 percent of all Jews lived in Europe in the nineteenth century. Fifty percent of the Jewish people was concentrated in the Russian Empire (Russia and Poland), and another 20 percent in the Hapsburg Empire (Austria–Hungary, from 1867). An important demographic development of those years was the rise of American Jewry. At the beginning of the nineteenth century, there were a few thousand Jews in the United States. By the end of the century, American Jewry numbered about 1 million, the result of the growing emigration of Jews from Europe, especially Eastern Europe, beginning in the second half of the century. Those emigrants settled in other parts of the world as well: in Central and Western Europe and, from the beginning of the twentieth century, in Argentina and South Africa. East European Jewry played a central role in the Jewish demographic changes in modern times.

Toward the end of the nineteenth century, there were indications that the large natural increase among the Jews had begun to slow down. The rate of natural increase of Jews fell in line with that of the general society, and in Western Europe was even lower. Another typical demographic tendency was the growing concentration of Jews in larger cities, in both Europe and the Americas. These two characteristics—a declining birth rate and urban concentration—were to continue in the twentieth century.

The percentage of Jews living in Muslim countries in Asia and Africa decreased in the nineteenth century. It was only toward the end of the century that the social and economic factors that had caused the demographic changes in Western Jewry began to have an impact in Muslim countries, where the Jews were among the first to be influenced by the modernizing trends. From the beginning of the twentieth century, the demographic characteristics of European Jewry during the nineteenth century—increasing birth rates and gradual urbanization—began to appear in Asian and African Jewries.

THE JEWISH PEOPLE ON THE EVE OF WORLD WAR II

THE Jewish people reached a demographic high point in the late 1930s: more than 16 million Jews in the world, 90 percent of whom lived in Europe and North America. The largest Jewish community was that in the United States, but 60 percent of all Jews still lived in Europe. The Jewish community in Palestine, which in 1939 consisted of only 3.6 percent of all Jews, was nevertheless the fifth biggest.

Never in Jewish history had such large and well-organized Jewish communities existed simultaneously in so many countries. This was one of the results of the migration of Jews in the preceding decades, which had created new Jewish communities in lands outside Europe and enlarged those in Central and Western Europe. But the signs of the impending catastrophe of the Jewish people were already discernible on the eve of World War II: three important Jewish communities in Europe—in Germany, Austria, and Czechoslovakia—were, under German domination, disintegrating.

The gradual urbanization of the Jewish people added another characteristic to its demographic situation. In 1939, more than 30 percent of all Jews lived in communities of more than 100,000 Jewish inhabitants. Nevertheless, even the largest Jewish communities (New York, Warsaw) were minorities in their cities, 25 to 30 percent of the population. Most Jews lived in smaller communities, although also in major urban centers.

As a result of the demographic, cultural, and religious developments of the modern era, the Jews in the 1930s were highly diversified in differing, often opposing, religious and ideological positions. Furthermore, the integration of the Jews into different nations, and their acculturation to the ways of life of the societies in which they lived, produced significantly different types of Jews in various countries. For instance, Jews living in South America, Western Europe, North America, or Israel were inevitably influenced by different cultural attitudes and political conceptions. That process continued in later years.

The outbreak of World War II changed the Jewish situation and its characteristic trends. The year 1939 closed an era in Jewish history. The next decade was one of the most unsettling periods in Jewish annals.

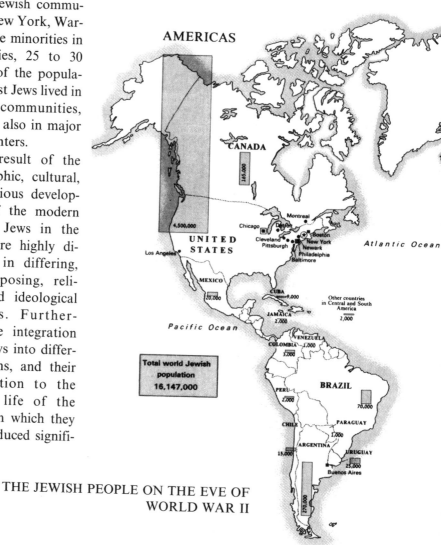

AMERICAS

THE JEWISH PEOPLE ON THE EVE OF WORLD WAR II

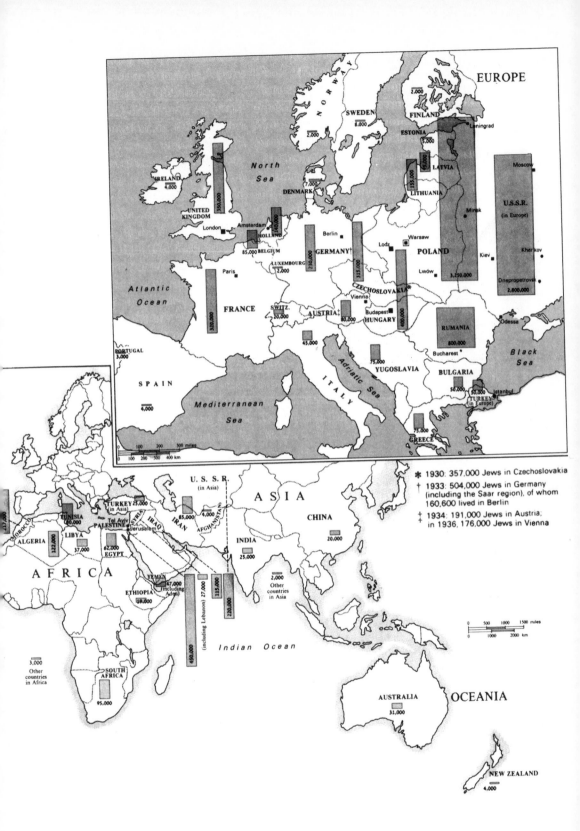

EUROPE

NORWAY
2,000

SWEDEN
8,000

FINLAND
2,000

ESTONIA
5,000

Leningrad

North
Sea

DENMARK
7,000

LATVIA
95,000

LITHUANIA
155,000

U.S.S.R.
(in Europe)

Moscow

IRELAND
4,000

UNITED
KINGDOM
350,000

London

Amsterdam
HOLLAND
140,000

BELGIUM
85,000

Berlin

Warsaw
Lodz

POLAND
3,250,000

Kiev

Lwów

Minsk

Kharkov

Dnepropetrovsk
2,800,000

Atlantic
Ocean

Paris

LUXEMBOURG
2,000

GERMANY†
240,000

CZECHOSLOVAKIA*
335,000

Vienna

FRANCE
320,000

SWITZ.
20,000

AUSTRIA‡
50,000

Budapest

HUNGARY
400,000

RUMANIA
800,000

Bucharest

Odessa

Black
Sea

PORTUGAL
3,000

SPAIN

4,000

Mediterranean
Sea

45,000

Adriatic
Sea

ITALY

75,000
YUGOSLAVIA

BULGARIA
50,000

50,000
TURKEY
(in Europe)

Istanbul

100   200   300 miles
100 200 300 400 km

75,000
GREECE

AFRICA

MOROCCO
177,000

ALGERIA
122,000

TUNISIA
60,000

LIBYA
37,000

U.S.S.R.
(in Asia)

TURKEY 25,000
(in Asia)

PALESTINE
Tel Aviv
Jerusalem

SYRIA
(including Lebanon) 27,000

IRAQ

EGYPT
67,000

YEMEN
67,000
(including
Aden)

ETHIOPIA
50,000

IRAN
85,000

AFGHANISTAN
4,000

ASIA

INDIA
25,000

CHINA
20,000

2,000
Other
countries
in Asia

115,000

220,000

450,000

Indian   Ocean

* 1930: 357,000 Jews in Czechoslovakia

† 1933: 504,000 Jews in Germany
(including the Saar region), of whom
160,600 lived in Berlin

‡ 1934: 191,000 Jews in Austria;
in 1936, 176,000 Jews in Vienna

0   500   1000   1500 miles
0   1000   2000 km

3,000
Other
countries
in Africa

SOUTH
AFRICA
95,000

AUSTRALIA
31,000

OCEANIA

NEW ZEALAND
4,000

311

B. EUROPEAN JEWRY UNTIL WORLD WAR I

THE SPANISH-PORTUGUESE JEWS IN EUROPE AND IN THE AMERICAS 17TH AND 18TH CENTURIES

THE Spanish-Portuguese Jews (Sephardim) were among the harbingers of the modern era in Jewish history. Some were descendants of the Jews expelled from Spain (1492) and Portugal (1496–1497). Most, however, were "New Christians"—Jews who had been forced to convert in those countries, continued to observe Judaism secretly, and returned to open Jewish life when circumstances allowed. They then created new Jewish communities, some of which became very important.

The New Christians who left Spain and Portugal during the sixteenth century (frequently because of the Inquisition) settled mainly in northern Italy, the

Netherlands, and southern France. During the next century, many moved northward, still to the Netherlands, and from there to northern Germany (Hamburg, Altona), England, and even North and South America. Some settled (without establishing communities) in Central and Eastern Europe.

The great center of Sephardic Jewry was Amsterdam. In the seventeenth century, Amsterdam was a city of intense economic and cultural life, with a relatively tolerant religious atmosphere. The Jewish community in Amsterdam, which began to organize itself at the end of the sixteenth century, was very small (in modern terms)—between 2,500 and

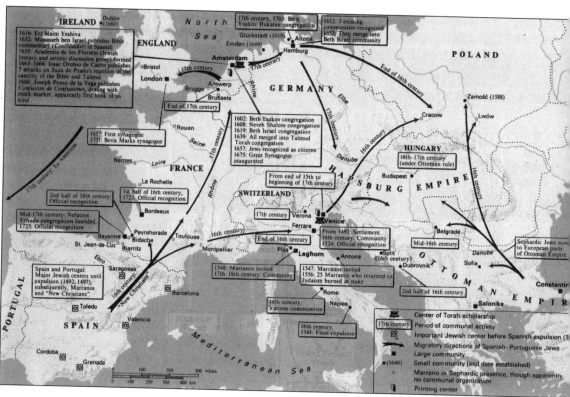

5,000 Jews, or 1 to 2 percent of the city's population. Other Spanish-Portuguese communities of the seventeenth century were not larger: 500 Jews lived in London; 3,000 lived in Leghorn, one of the oldest communities. Important communities existed in Venice, Bordeaux (recognized by the authorities only in the 1720s), and Hamburg. The Amsterdam community was the economic and cultural center for the whole Sephardic dispersion, and its spiritual influence was felt far beyond Jewish circles. Its cultural creativity, influenced by the fecund amalgamation of Jewish and non-Jewish spiritual elements, was highly original and expressed itself in important religious and philosophical works. One important center of Amsterdam Jewry's religious activity was the Etz Haim Yeshiva. The influence of the European Spanish-Portuguese Jews declined in the late eighteenth century, their gradual assimilation into the general society.

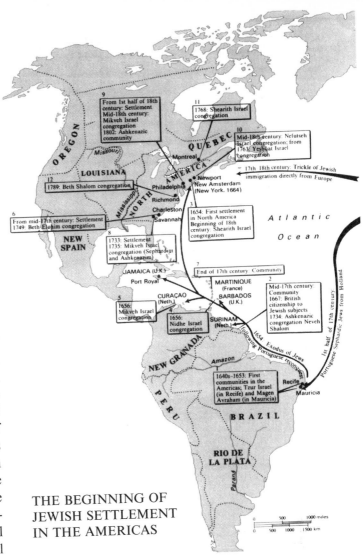

THE BEGINNING OF
JEWISH SETTLEMENT
IN THE AMERICAS

Ashkenazic Jews began to settle in Amsterdam at the end of the seventeenth century, their number rising to about 10,000 in the eighteenth century. The relations between them and the older, patrician strata of Sephardim were mostly strained.

"NEW CHRISTIANS" traveled to the Americas as early as the sixteenth century. In 1630, Spanish-Portuguese Jews from Amsterdam arrived in the Portuguese colony of Recife, in northeastern Brazil, then under Dutch domination.

They established two communities, the first in the New World. With the expulsion of the Dutch from Recife in 1654, the Jews also left. Some of them went northward, to Dutch or English settlements: Surinam, Curacao, Jamaica, Barbados, and New Amsterdam, which in 1664 came under English domination and changed its name to New York. Other Jews, mostly Spanish-Portuguese, migrated from England and Holland in the seventeenth and eighteenth centuries and established about a dozen communities in North America. Ashkenazic

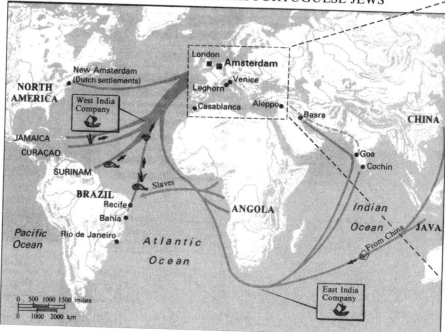

Jews started arriving in the eighteenth century.

The legal situation of the Jews in the English and Dutch colonies was much better than in Europe. European rulers wished to attract settlers to the New World, and various laws in the seventeenth and eighteenth centuries (the law regarding Surinam in 1665, and the Plantation Act of 1740) guaranteed the Jews broad social and civil rights. With American independence in 1776, the Jews there became full and equal citizens of the republic. Their social and economic situation was satisfactory, too. The number of Jews in the Americas remained small: no more than about 3,000 at the end of the eighteenth century, two-thirds of them in North America, which also became the main destination of Jewish immigration: in about 1820, some 15,000 Jews lived in North America.

ECONOMIC ACTIVITIES 17TH AND 18TH CENTURIES

SPANISH-PORTUGUESE Jews were influential in international commerce in the seventeenth and eighteenth centuries. Their experience, financial means, and international family connections enabled them to build a network of economic relations that spanned the entire known world. Operating out of Amsterdam, London, Hamburg, Leghorn, and other commercial centers, these Jewish entre-preneurs carried commodities from and to the Mediterranean countries, Africa, the Americas, India, and even China. In many of these places, they were represented by family members or Sephardic acquaintances. Sugar, tobacco, silk, and precious stones were among the main products that the Spanish-Portuguese Jewish merchants imported into Europe. They were also involved in the printing

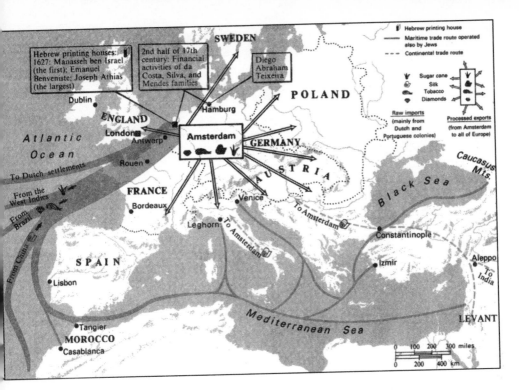

Hebrew printing houses:
1627: Manasseh ben Israel
(the first); Emanuel
Benveniste; Joseph Athias
(the largest)

2nd half of 17th
century: Financial
activities of da
Costa, Silva, and
Mendes families

Diego
Abraham
Teixeira

SWEDEN

POLAND

Hebrew printing house
Maritime trade route operated
also by Jews
Continental trade route

Sugar cane
Silk
Tobacco
Diamonds

Raw imports
(mainly from
Dutch and
Portuguese colonies)

Processed exports
(from Amsterdam
to all of Europe)

Dublin

ENGLAND

London

Antwerp

Hamburg

Amsterdam

GERMANY

Atlantic Ocean

Rouen

A U S T R I A

Caucasus Mts.

To Dutch settlements

FRANCE

Venice

Black Sea

From the
West Indies

Bordeaux

To Amsterdam

From Brazil

Leghorn

To Amsterdam

Constantinople

From China

SPAIN

Izmir

Aleppo

To India

Lisbon

Mediterranean Sea

LEVANT

Tangier

MOROCCO

Casablanca

0   100   200   300 miles

0   200   400 km

industry in Europe, producing books with both Latin and Hebrew characters. They participated in two large commercial concerns: the East India Company, active in India and Asia in general; and the West India Company, active in the Western Hemisphere. They also played a role in the development of the modern banking system.

The Sephardic Jews did not act independently, but as part of the economic life of the centers where they lived. They were far from being among the most important merchants in places like Lon-don or Amsterdam. In general, they belonged to the more prosperous segment of the population, but many Christian merchants were much richer. Jews were usually forced to take greater business risks, and the competition from the Christian guilds of merchants and craftsmen gradually drove them from dealing in many profitable goods, such as sugar and silk. Only in one field, precious stones, have Jews, mainly of Ashkenazic stock, maintained a leading presence throughout the modern era.

THE COURT JEWS IN CENTRAL EUROPE
17TH AND 18TH CENTURIES

FEW Jews lived in Central Europe at the beginning of the seventeenth century. Most had been expelled in the fifteenth and sixteenth centuries and had moved eastward, to the large Polish kingdom. From the mid-seventeenth century, new social and political conditions in Europe made possible the gradual return of the Jews. In Western Europe after the Reformation, religion began to lose its influence on political and intellectual life, and the first indications of what was later

Samuel Oppenheimer, Court Jew in Vienna.

known as the "secular" society began to appear, generating, among other things, greater tolerance toward Jews. The Jews' position was also enhanced by such developments as the rise in Western Europe of the absolute state and the economic system related to it, mercantilism. The ambitions of the new absolute ruler, his growing financial needs, and the tensions between him and the social classes in his land whose rights he was trying to curtail combined to make possible and necessary the appearance of some new element in the ruler's court who would be loyal to him and could satisfy his various needs. That task was fulfilled by a specific Jewish type, the Court Jew (*Hofjude*). From the ruler's point of view, the Court Jew offered the great advantage of being dependent on him and neutral in the struggle between the ruler and the three social groups disputing his growing power in the state: the nobles, the cities, and the clergy.

The Court Jew helped the ruler obtain money, organized supplies for his army (now under the ruler's command, and no longer mobilized through the feudal-type services of the nobles), executed diplomatic services, and supplied the court with the luxury articles that were such an important sign of status in that era. Indeed, so important were the missions of Court Jews that from the mid-seventeenth to the late eighteenth century, there was virtually no king or ruling noble in Central Europe who did not employ at least one Court Jew. Court Jews were especially prominent in such important states as Prussia, Bavaria, Saxony, and Württemberg.

The Court Jews did not act alone, but were helped by family members and other Jews, collaborated with one another and with Sephardic merchants in Hamburg and Amsterdam, and maintained close relations with wealthy Jews in Eastern Europe.

The activities of the Court Jew were a fascinating mixture of great opportunities and equally great dangers. He could rise to enormous riches and great political influence, or lose everything, including his freedom and even his life. The most rewarding and dangerous of his tasks was supplying the ruler's army. This was a time of ceaseless wars, and the Court Jew depended on their outcome, on the outcome of court intrigues, and on the whims of his royal protector. The difficult life of the Court Jew was well exemplified by the well-known Samuel Oppenheimer, Court Jew of Emperor Leopold I of Austria. For thirty years (1673–1703), Oppenheimer organized and financed the supply system of the emperor's armies; he knew periods of enormous wealth and utter despondency, and he died penniless. His fate taught other Court Jews to avoid dealing in military supplies.

One important result of the existence of

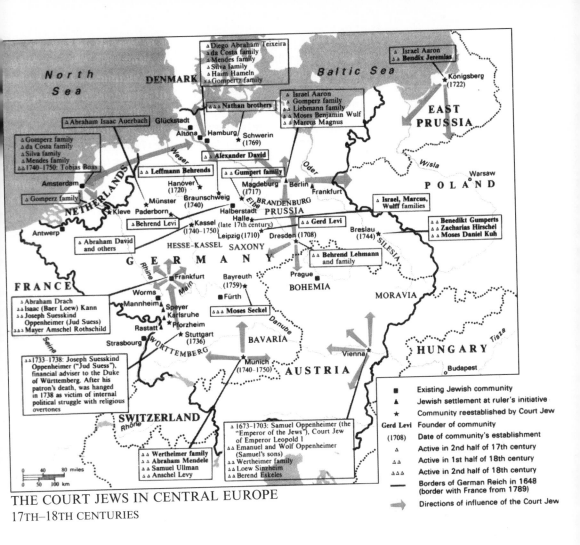

Map labels:

North Sea

Baltic Sea

DENMARK

▲ Diego Abraham Teixeira
▲ da Costa family
▲ Mendes family
▲ Silva family
▲ Haim Hameln
▲▲ Gompertz family

■ Israel Aaron
■ Bendix Jeremias
Königsberg (1722)

EAST PRUSSIA

▲▲▲ Nathan brothers

▲ Israel Aaron
▲ Gompertz family
▲ Liebmann family
▲▲ Moses Benjamin Wulf
▲▲ Marcus Magnus

▲ Abraham Isaac Auerbach Glückstadt
Altona ■ Hamburg ■ Schwerin (1769) ★

Wisla

Warsaw

▲ Gompertz family
▲ da Costa family
▲ Silva family
▲ Mendes family
▲▲ 1740–1750: Tobias Boas

Amsterdam

▲ Gompertz family

NETHERLANDS

Antwerp

Kleve ▲ Paderborn
Münster ★

▲▲ Leffmann Behrends
Hanover (1720) ★

▲▲ Alexander David

▲▲ Gumpert family
Magdeburg (1717) ★ Berlin
Braunschweig (1740) ★

Weser

Oder

Elbe

BRANDENBURG
PRUSSIA

Frankfurt

POLAND

▲ Israel, Marcus, Wulff families

Halberstadt
Halle (late 17th century) ★
Kassel (1740–1750) ★
Leipzig (1710) Dresden (1708)

▲▲ Gerd Levi
Breslau (1744) ★

SILESIA

▲▲ Benedikt Gumperts
▲▲ Zacharias Hirschel
▲▲ Moses Daniel Kuh

▲ Behrend Levi

▲ Abraham David
and others

HESSE-KASSEL

SAXONY

GERMANY

▲▲ Behrend Lehmann
and family

Rhine

▲ Frankfurt
Worms

Bayreuth (1759) ★
Fürth ■

Prague

BOHEMIA

MORAVIA

FRANCE

▲ Abraham Drach
▲▲ Isaac (Baer Loew) Kann
▲▲ Joseph Suesskind
Oppenheimer (Jud Suess)
▲▲▲ Mayer Amschel Rothschild

Mannheim
Speyer ▲
Karlsruhe ★
Rastatt Pforzheim ★
Strasbourg
Stuttgart (1736) ★

Main

▲▲▲ Moses Seckel

Danube

BAVARIA

Munich (1740–1750)

AUSTRIA

Vienna ★

HUNGARY

Tisza

Budapest

▲▲ 1733–1738: Joseph Suesskind
Oppenheimer ("Jud Suess"),
financial adviser to the Duke
of Württemberg. After his
patron's death, was hanged
in 1738 as victim of internal
political struggle with religious
overtones

WÜRTTEMBERG

Seine

SWITZERLAND

Rhône

▲▲ Wertheimer family
▲▲ Abraham Mendele
▲▲ Samuel Ullman
▲▲ Anschel Levy

▲ 1673–1703: Samuel Oppenheimer (the
"Emperor of the Jews"), Court Jew
of Emperor Leopold I
▲▲ Emanuel and Wolf Oppenheimer
(Samuel's sons)
▲▲ Wertheimer family
▲▲ Loew Sinzheim
▲▲ Berend Eskeles

Legend:

■ Existing Jewish community
▲ Jewish settlement at ruler's initiative
★ Community reestablished by Court Jew
Gerd Levi Founder of community
(1708) Date of community's establishment
▲ Active in 2nd half of 17th century
▲▲ Active in 1st half of 18th century
▲▲▲ Active in 2nd half of 18th century
— Borders of German Reich in 1648
(border with France from 1789)
➡ Directions of influence of the Court Jew

scale: 0 40 80 miles 0 50 100 km

THE COURT JEWS IN CENTRAL EUROPE
17TH–18TH CENTURIES

so many Court Jews and of the Jews who served them was the return of Jews to places from which they had been expelled in earlier centuries. Many new communities were established by Court Jews or by rulers interested in the presence of Jews for economic reasons.

The institution of Court Jew was transitory, and toward the end of the eighteenth century, his services were no longer needed or were performed by others. The gradual development of state bureaucracies and the better organization of the European armies rendered many of the Court Jew's tasks superfluous. However, the new atmosphere of greater religious tolerance during the Age of Enlightenment in Europe, together with the expanding economic opportunities brought about by the Industrial Revolution, not only made it possible for Jews who had returned to Central and Western Europe to remain and prosper, but also attracted a growing number of Jewish immigrants from Eastern Europe. The Court Jews entered new economic fields; for instance, some of them established private banks, several of which were to play major financial roles in the nineteenth century.

THE JEWS IN POLAND AND LITHUANIA BEFORE THE EIGHTEENTH-CENTURY PARTITIONS

IN the mid-eighteenth century, shortly before the partitions of the Polish state, more than two-thirds of all Jews in the world lived in that large kingdom, which extended from the Baltic Sea and Silesia in the west to the Dnieper River and the Ukrainian steppe in the east. The origins of Polish Jewry go back to the Middle Ages. Its beginnings were at times difficult, but by the eighteenth century, it had built a firm position for itself in the kingdom and was well organized in hundreds of small and large communities. Polish Jews engaged in a variety of economic activities, had a rich cultural and religious life, and were well served by a large degree of internal autonomy.

Considering the conditions in Poland in the seventeenth and eighteenth centuries, Polish Jewry of that time had a mainly "urban" character. More than 70 percent of the Jews lived in cities or small towns, in many of which they were the majority of the population. Even the Jews who lived in villages were not serfs or peasants, but renters of mills, producers of alcoholic beverages, owners of inns, or administrators of the estates of the largely absent Polish nobles.

In 1580, a general Jewish authority, the Council of the Lands (*Vaad Haaratzot*), was established. Its purpose was to represent the Jews before the Polish rulers, especially regarding the payment of the poll taxes to the king. These taxes were collected internally, according to a system agreed on by the members of the council. The council (or the regional councils) also dealt with internal Jewish matters, such as regulations for the nomination of rabbis and religious-court judges (*dayanim*), communal elections, resolution of quarrels between communities or between individuals and communities, and communal authorizations for book printings. The original council had representatives from Great Poland (main community, Poznań), Little Poland (main community, Cracow), Reissen (or Ruthenia; main community, Lwów) and Lithuania—thus the common name Council of the Four Lands. In 1623, the Lithuanian communities established their own council. There were additional changes in the number of lands, circuits (*glilot*), and communities represented in the councils, and in the extent of the influence of each of these bodies.

In Poland in the mid-seventeenth century, after the rebellions and wars that took their toll in the Jewish communities as well, Polish Jewry reorganized itself, and the period that followed was one of relative prosperity and population increase. But the inability of the Polish state to solve its own social and political problems and the gradual decline of the central authority also weakened the authority of the Jewish central institutions. Tensions developed between the Jewish communities and the Christian population of the cities. Sources of income disappeared; the centralized collection of taxes became impossible; and many communities sank deeply into debt. In the end, the authorities decreed the dissolution of the councils—of Poland in 1764, and of Lithuania in 1765.

The Partitions of Poland
The internal weakness of the Polish-Lithuanian kingdom and its growing internal anarchy awakened the ambitions of the neighboring countries, whose more

leveloped centralist and absolute regimes were served by armies organized according to modern principles. Poland's neighbors (Prussia, Austria, and Russia) decided to conquer and partition Poland and Lithuania. In 1772, 1793, and 1795 (Austria did not participate in the second partition), they divided the Polish kingdom among them. Independent Poland disappeared until 1919.

The partitions opened a new period for Polish Jewry, whose life had followed the autonomous communal pattern characteristic of the Middle Ages. Polish Jewry now found itself living in states whose political systems were, or strove to be, of the absolute type and, as such, very different from that of the semifeudal Polish state. The subsequent development of each part of Polish Jewry was influenced by the very different economic, social, and political conditions of each of the states to which the Jews now belonged. Meanwhile, Polish Jewry continued to grow in number; at the beginning of the nineteenth century, there were about 1.25 million Jews living in the territories of former Poland, about 70 percent of all the Jews in the world.

The Russian Empire and the Jews
There were very few Jews in Russia before the partitions of Poland. Since the late Middle Ages, Jews (the "enemies of Christ") had not been admitted into the principality of Moscow, the nucleus of the future empire—an example of Jew-hatred without Jews. The annexation of the Polish and Lithuanian territories, with their large and well-rooted Jewish populations, forced the Russian authorities to deal with what gradually came to be regarded as the "Jewish problem." In the 1780s and 1790s, during the reign of Catherine II, the Jews of the annexed territories received the status of city

PARTITIONS OF POLAND

— Polish border, 1772

FIRST PARTITION, 1772

SECOND PARTITION, 1793

* After 1815, the borders of Poland, now part of the Russian Empire, were those on page 325.

THIRD PARTITION, 1795*

319

POLAND AND LITHUANIA
18TH CENTURY

Baltic Sea

Ż

M

Königsberg

Belonged to prince-elector of
Brandenburg (Prussia) but
vassalage of king of Poland

Gdańsk

PRUSSIA

ROYAL PRUSSIA

WARMIA

DUCHY OF PRUSSIA

Belonged to
Polish Crown

Brda

Wisla

● Chelmno

Mlawa

Narew

Lomza

Wysokie

Pila ●

Bydgoszcz
Canal

Noteć

Bydgoszcz

Toruń

Ciechanów ●

Maków

M A Z O V I A

Wieleń ●

Chodziez ● Kcynia

Dobrzyń ● Drobin

Wronki ●

Rogożno ●

Pakość ●

☐ ● Inowroclaw

1527 to end of 18th
century: Ban on
Jewish residence.
Communities beyond
city limits

Miedzychód ●

Gniezno ●

Brześć
Kujawski ●

● ☐ Plock
(Plotsk)

Plońsk ●

Miedzyrzecz ●
(Mezhirech)

Poznań ☐

Września ●

Kleczew ●

Kowal ●

Wyszogród ●

Warsaw ●

L U B

Grodzisk ●

Kórnik ● Środa

Kutno ●

Sochaczew ●

☐ ● Praga

Leszno
(Lissa)
◉(5,000)

Srem ●

Osieczna ●

G R E A T

Sobota ●

Leczyca ●

Lowicz ●

Mszczonów ●
(Amshinov)

Wschowa ●

Krobia ●

G R E A T   P O L A N D

Dobra ●

Brzeziny ●

Rawa ●

Grójec ●

Zelechów ●

Rawicz ●

Krotoszyn ◉

☐◉ Kalisz

Warta ●

Lutomiersk ●

☐ Rawa

Goszczyn ●

Pilica

Kozienice ●

Sieradz ●

Nowe Miasto ●

Wisla

Kepno ●

Wieluń ●

Kamieńsk ●

Piotrków ●

Opoczno ●

Przysucha ●

Radom ●

Kazimierz ●

Prosna

S I L E S I A

Ostrowiec ●

Checiny ●

T S U Z M I R

Opatów ●
(Apta)

Koniecpol ●

Lelów ●

Raków ●

Chmielnik ●

Sandomie
(Tsuzmir)

San

Pilica ●

C R A C O W

Pilica ●

Wodzislaw ●

◉ Pińczów

Szydlów ◉

Stopnica ●

L I T T L E

Olkusz ◉

Nida

Cracow - Kazimierz ◉
(3,500)(Kuzhmir)

Oświecim ●

Bochnia ●

Wiśnicz ●

Dunajec

Pilzno ●

Rzeszów ●
(Raishe)

Strzy

1495–1868: Jews forbidden
to live in Cracow. Community
in nearby town of Kazimierz

Biecz ●

Jaslo ●

Zmigród ●

Dukla ●

Nowy Sacz ●
(Zanz)

H A P S B U R G

dwellers and merchants, and the first steps were taken to establish a territorial sphere where they could live—the beginning of what later developed into the Pale of Settlement. From 1794, the Jews in Belorussia and the Ukraine had to pay a double poll tax, and their settlement in the eastern part of the empire was limited. However, Catherine II also decided that the Jews should continue to maintain their autonomous internal administration in the form of their communities (the *kahal*), and for the next generation, the Russian authorities virtually did not interfere with the internal life of the Jews.

PINSK	Region with Jewish administration
POLESIE	Polish or foreign region
●	Jewish community
◉	Head community
(3,500)	Number of Jews in community of at least
⊲	Venue of Council meetings
☐	Province (*województwo*) capital
(Mezhirech)	Jewish name of locality
⌄⌄⌄⌄⌄	Traffic canal

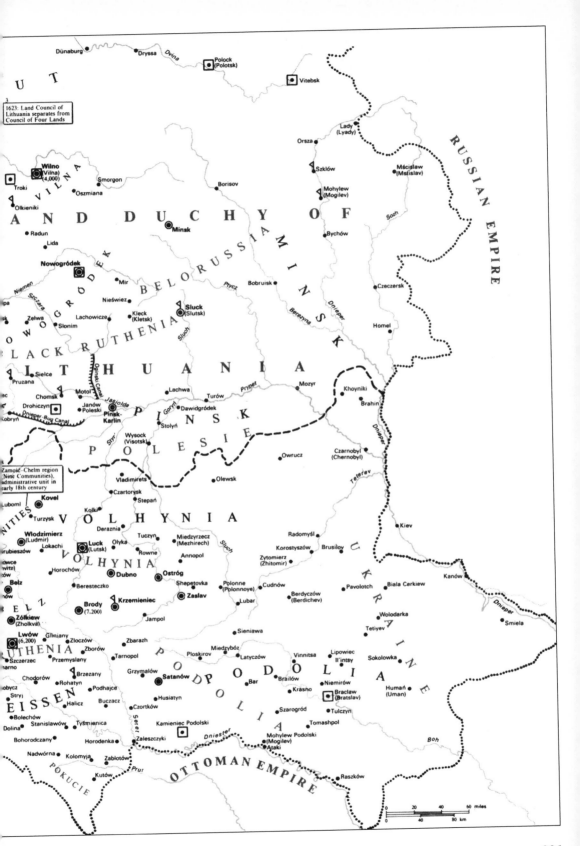

Dünaburg • • Dryssa • *Dvina* ⊡ Polock (Polotsk)

□ Vitebsk

1623: Land Council of
Lithuania separates from
Council of Four Lands

Lady (Lyady)

Orsza • • Mścisław (Mścisław)

U T

◉ Wilno (Vilna) (4,000)   • Smorgon   Szkłów ▷

Borisov •

□ ◉ Troki   • Oszmiana   Mohylew (Mogilev) ▷

◁ Olkieniki

A N D   D U C H Y   O F   M I N S K

• Radun   • Lida   ◉ Minsk   • Bychów

• Zelwa   NOWOGRÓDEK   Niemen   • Nieśwież   • Mir   B E L O R U S S I A   • Bobruisk   Sozh   • Czeczersk

◉ Nowogródek   SZCZARA   • Lachowicze   • Kleck (Kletsk)   Ptycz   Berezyna   Dnieper   • Homel

O W O G R Ó D E K   • Słonim   Słuck (Slutsk) ◉▷   Słuch

B L A C K   R U T H E N I A   ◁ Sielce   L I T H U A N I A

• Pruzana   Oginski Canal   Goryn   • Lachwa   • Turów   Prypet   • Mozyr   Khoyniki •   Dnieper

• Chomsk   • Motol   Jasiołda   • Drohiczyn   Janów Poleski   Pinsk- Karlin   P I N S K   • Dawidgródek   • Stolyń   Brahin •

• Kobryń   Dnieper-Bug Canal   ⊡   P O L E S I E   Styr   • Wysock (Visotsk)   Czarnobyl (Chernobyl) •

Zamość-Chelm region
(Nine Communities),
administrative unit in
early 18th century

• Vladimirets   • Olewsk   • Owrucz   Teterev

• Czartorysk   • Stepań

• Luboml   ◉ Kovel   V O L H Y N I A   • Kolki   • Deraznia   • Tuczyn   Miedzyrzecz (Mezhirech)   Sluch   Radomyśl •   • Kiev

• Włodzimierz (Ludmir)   • Lokachi   ⊡ Luck (Lutsk)   • Olyka   • Rowne   Annopol   Korostyszów •   Brusiłov •   U K R A I N E

• Hrubieszów   V O L H Y N I A   • Horochów   ◉ Dubno   ◉ Ostróg   Zytomierz (Zhitomir)   Dnieper

B e ł z   ◉ Bełz   • Beresteczko   Shepetovka   • Polonne (Polonnoye)   Cudnów   Berdyczów (Berdichev)   Pavolotch •   Biala Cerkiew •   • Kanów

• Żółkiew (Zholkva)   ◉ Brody (7,200)   ◉ Krzemieniec   ◉ Zaslav   • Lubar   Wolodarka •   Dnieper

◉ Lwów (6,200)   • Jampol   Tetiyev •   • Smiela

R U T H E N I A   • Glniany   • Złoczów   • Zbarazh   • Sieniawa

• Szczerzec   • Zborów   Tarnopol   Ploskirov •   Miedzybóz •   Latyczów •   Vinnitsa •   Lipowiec   Sokolowka

• Przemyślany   • Zbarazh   • Grzymałów   Il'intsy   P O D O L I A

W E I S S E N   Brzezany   ◉ Satanów   P O D   Bar •   Brailów •   Niemirów •   Humań (Uman)

• Chodorów   • Rohatyn   • Podhajce   • Buczacz   • Husiatyn   • Krasno   Braclav (Bratslav)   • Tulczyn

• Stryj   • Halicz   • Czortków   Szarogród •   Tomashpol •

E I S S E N   • Bolechów   Seret   Kamieniec Podolski ⊡   • Tulczyn

• Dolina   • Stanisławów   • Tyśmienica   Dniester   Mohylew (Mogilev) •   Boh   • Raszków

• Bohorodczany   • Horodenka   • Zaleszczyki   • Ataki

• Nadwórna   • Kolomyja   • Zabłotów   Prut   O T T O M A N   E M P I R E

P O K U C I E   • Kutów

R U S S I A N   E M P I R E

0   20   40   60 miles

0   40   80 km

321

In 1815, after the end of the Napoleonic wars and as a result of the new political arrangements approved by the Treaty of Vienna, Russia acquired most of the Grand Duchy of Warsaw, thus significantly enlarging its Polish holdings. An autonomous kingdom of Poland (known as Congress Poland) was now established as part of the Russian Empire and ruled by the czar. The special status of Poland was reflected in its large Jewish population, whose situation was somewhat better than that in the western provinces of Russia (which had also belonged to Poland before the partitions).

In spite of the regional differences, the large and growing Polish-Russian Jewry was, to a large extent, characterized by internal Jewish cohesiveness. In the later nineteenth century, it would become a source of the emigration movement that would spread throughout the world and establish new Jewish communities, and the cradle of most ideological and spiritual movements in modern Jewry.

THE JEWS IN THE RUSSIAN EMPIRE LATE 19TH CENTURY

MORE than 5 million Jews—about 50 percent of the Jewish people—lived in the Russian Empire (Poland included) at the end of the nineteenth century. More than 90 percent lived in the Pale of Settlement, which in its final form (1835) included fifteen provinces in western Russia and the ten provinces that formed the kingdom of Poland, incorporated into the empire in 1815. The kingdom had its own administrative status, and only in 1868 were the Jews permitted to pass freely from the Polish to the Russian region. Several other limitations existed in the Pale: Jews were forbidden to live in certain cities or, in part of the nineteenth century, along the empire's western frontier. At the end of the nineteenth century, the Jews made up about 11 percent of the Pale's population, but 36 percent of its Durban population (about 50 percent, if Poland is excluded).

Complex relations developed between the Russian government and the large Jewish population, so different in religion and culture from the empire's other populations, and possessing a well-rooted tradition of autonomy. The government's policy was expressed in a long series of edicts, the most significant being the 1804 Jewish Statute of Alexander I and the May Laws (or Temporary Laws) of 1882. The basic intention of the 1804 edict was to integrate the Jews gradually into Russian society in the social, cultural, and economic spheres—that is, to bring about their "Russianization." The Russian czars tried to attain that goal by various means: by exerting pressure (Nicholas I, 1825–1855); by granting rights (Alexander II, 1855–1881); or by combining the two (Alexander I, 1801–1825). The regime of Nicholas I was particularly harsh; among many other steps, special military duties were forced on the Jews (1827, the cantonist system), and the Jewish communal structure (the *kahal*) was abolished in 1844.

The May Laws, or Temporary Laws, of 1882 marked a radical change in the government's policy toward Russian Jewry. They reflected new ideological trends in Russian governmental circles, such as the growing influence of pan-Slavic and anti-Western attitudes, combined with disillusionment over the results of the efforts to Russianize the Jews. The official position was now to discourage the integration of the Jews into Russian society, to keep them apart, and

SWEDEN

Baltic Sea

ST. PETERSBURG
★ St. Petersburg

BELORUSSIA
724,000 (13.6%)

KURLAND
Riga

LIVONIA

PSKOV

LITHUANIA
697,900 (14.7%)

KOVNO
212,700

Dvinsk

VITEBSK
175,600

Polotsk

Moscow ★

LITHUANIA

Kovno

SUWALKI
59,200

Vilna

VILNA
204,700

Vitebsk

SMOLENSK

Dnieper

★ Smolensk

Kaluga ★

Tula ★

POLAND
1,321,100 (14.1%)

GERMANY

51,500 PLOCK

Lomza

Grodno

★ Mogilev

Minsk

LOMZA
91,400

Bialystok

BELORUSSIA
203,900

MOGILEV

Plock

KALISZ POLAND
71,700

Kalisz

Lodz

WARSAW

Siedlce

GRODNO
280,000

Slonim

Slutsk

Bobruysk

Gomel

OREL

Orel ★

351,900 Warsaw

SIEDLCE
121,100

Brest Litovsk

MINSK
345,000

PIOTRKOW RADOM
222,600 112,300

Czestochowa

Radom

Pinsk

CHERNIGOV
114,500

★ Chernigov

Kursk ★

Kielce

Lublin

UKRAINE
1,425,500 (9.7%)

KURSK

Bedzin

KIELCE
83,200

LUBLIN
156,200

VOLHYNIA
395,800

UKRAINE

Kiev

AUSTRIA-HUNGARY

Dniester

Prut

PODOLIA

Zhitomir

Berdichev

KIEV
433,700

POLTAVA
110,900

Poltava

Khar'kov ★

KHAR'KOV

Kamenets Podolskiy

370,600

Cherkassy

Kremenchug

Mogilev Podolskiy

Uman

NEW RUSSIA

RUMANIA

Balta

Beltsy

Yelizavetgrad

Yekaterinoslav

YEKATERINOSLAV
101,100

Rostov ★

KHERSON
339,900

Kishinev

Odessa

Nikolayev

Dnieper

Bendery

Kherson

T A U R I D A

In European Russia
outside Pale of Settlement
211,200 (0.4%)

In Pale of Settlement
4,899,300 (11.6%)

Total Jewish
population in Russia
5,215,800 (4.15%)

In Asia
48,500 (0.4%)

BESSARABIA
228,500 (11.8%)

60,800

CRIMEA

NEW RUSSIA
501,800 (8%)

In Caucasia
56,800 (0.6%)

Black Sea

Sevastopol

Yalta

◉ Large city with at least 40,000 Jews
◉ Community of 30,000–40,000 Jews
● Community of 20,000–30,000 Jews
○ Community of 10,000–20,000 Jews
★ City barred to Jewish residence
  (by order of Nicholas I)
── Pale of Settlement
── Regional boundary
⋯⋯ Provincial boundary
724,000 Jewish population of region
(13.6%) Jewish percentage of total population
345,000 Jewish population of province

to encourage their emigration from the country (reigns of Alexander III, 1881–1894, and Nicholas II, 1894–1917). A difficult period began for Russian Jewry, a time of discrimination and several waves of pogroms, which continued until the revolution of 1917.

During the nineteenth century, Russian–Polish Jewry underwent gradual cultural modernization, which became pronounced beginning in the reign of Alexander II. New concepts about Jewish life, together with the pressures faced by the Jews in Russia, spurred Jewish intellectuals to seek new ways for Russian Jewry. The emigration movement—

to other parts of Europe or overseas—gradually grew to enormous proportions. New ideological movements arose, such as socialism and Zionism. All these trends expressed the deep dissatisfaction of Jews with the conditions in which they lived.

The data show that at least in Poland

(and perhaps also in Russia), the number of Jews continued to grow, in spite of emigration and the first signs of a decline in the natural increase. Approximately 1.3 million Jews lived in Poland at the end of the nineteenth century (14 percent of the whole population), and close to 2 million in 1913 (15 percent of the population). World War I and its consequences were to alter radically the political and demographic conditions of the Jews in both Russia and Poland.

THE JEWS IN THE HAPSBURG EMPIRE LATE 18TH CENTURY

THE Hapsburg Empire, with Austria at its center, was a major European power in the eighteenth and nineteenth centuries. The empire was a conglomeration of countries and peoples, each with its own culture and language, and each maintaining many of its own customs and laws. Consequently, the position of the Jews varied from land to land, and in some cases was rooted in relations established in the Middle Ages. Restrictions were in force regarding the settlement of Jews in the "German lands" of the empire (Upper Austria, Lower Austria, Vorarlberg, Tyrol, Styria, Carinthia, Carniola). Their presence was forbidden in Croatia, Slavonia, and the militarized border region in southern Hungary. In Transylvania and Banat, in southern Hungary, the Jews could (in theory) live in only one town in each region, and their presence was forbidden in certain parts of Hungary. A small Jewish community lived in the capital, Vienna, subject to many restrictions. Furthermore, Jews were not permitted in the "free cities" of the empire, cities with their own charters of rights. In Moravia, the Jews were not permitted to live in the villages.

The Jews could live (in some instances, under certain restrictions) in Bohemia, in some cities in Moravia, and in most parts of the Hungarian lands reconquered from the Turks in the seventeenth century. The largest number of Jews lived in Galicia, which had been annexed to the Hapsburg Empire only in 1772 (as a result of the first partition of Poland) and was not subject to the limitations imposed on other parts of the empire. In the 1780s, about one-half of the Jews of the empire lived in Galicia, one-quarter in the lands belonging to the Bohemian Crown (Bohemia, Moravia, and Silesia), and one-quarter in the Hungarian lands, most of them immigrants from Galicia and Moravia. In the eighteenth and nineteenth centuries, the Jewish population in Galicia increased significantly. Emigration from there was a major factor in the development of Jewish settlements in other parts of the Hapsburg Empire and in some provinces of the Russian Empire: 70,000 to 150,000 Jews left Galicia between 1765 and 1830; over 50 percent settled in Hungary, the others going to Bukovina, Moldavia, Bessarabia, southern Russia, and parts of central (Congress) Poland, formed in 1815 as part of the Russian Empire. Most of the Jewish population in Galicia and Moravia lived in small towns, although there were also some major communities in cities. In Hungary and Bohemia, there was a larger percentage of Jews living in villages.

The Jewish Policies of Joseph II

Joseph II (1781–1790), a ruler of the enlightened absolute type, promulgated several decrees (*Toleranzpatenten*) between 1781 and 1789. These were a

THE JEWS IN THE HAPSBURG EMPIRE
LATE 18TH CENTURY

POLAND

1798: 52 official communities
1849: 27 communities receive
autonomous municipal status

1789–1848: 131 Jewish communities
with recognized legal status

1772–1809: Included in
Galicia, in period of
Joseph II. 10 Jewish
communities in region with
recognized legal status

1846: Annexed to Galicia.
Formerly free city

1789–1848: 2 communities
with recognized legal status

MORAVIA

Aussee
Gewitsch
Boskowitz
Meseritsch
Neu-Raussnitz
Triesch
bitsch
Eibenschitz
Misslitz
Schaffa
Nikolsburg
Pohrlitz
Strassnitz
Steinitz
Bisenz
Kanitz
Ungarisch-Brod
Prossnitz
Kremsier
Holleschau
Weisskirchen
Leipnik

20 30 miles
40 km

Teplitz
Eidlitz
Raudnitz
Prague
Bunzlau
Nachod
Kolin
Elbe

BOHEMIA

1781

1781

Zamość

Cracow

Boskowitz
New Raussnitz
Prossnitz
Holleschau
Trebitsch
Nikolsburg
Holics
Ungarisch-Brod
Trentschin
Szobotist
Szenicz
Nove Mesto
Verbo

1782

MORAVIA

Sokal
Zolkiew
(Zholkva)
Brody
Tarnopol

Tarnów
Rzeszów
Jaroslau
Przemyśl

1785
1789

GALICIA

Stryj

Stanislau

Kolomea

Czernowitz

1782

LOWER

UPPER
AUSTRIA

BAVARIA

Danube

AUSTRIA

Stomfa
Neutra
Pressburg
Vienna
Eisenstadt
Deutschkreutz
Mattersdorf
Lackenbach
Rechnitz

Duna
Szerdahely
BURGENLAND

OBERLAND

Szécsény
Balassagyarmat

Aszod

Nagykároly

Unsdorf

BUKOVINA
Suczawa
(Suceava)

Prut

SALZBURG

STYRIA

Pápa
Tata

Danube

Ó-Buda

1783

Tisza

TRANSYLVANIA

VORARLBERG

TYROL

CARINTHIA

Drava

Nagykanisza
Bonyhád

Paks

H U N G A R Y

Gyulafehérvár
(Karlsburg)

CROATIA

Sava

CARNIOLA

Trieste

SLAVONIA

Makó
Temesvar

Mureşul

B A N A T

W A L A C H I A

Military border area

Military border area

1-2%
2-3%
3-5%
5-7%
7-9%

Percentage
of Jews
in total
population
late 1780s

A d r i a t i c   S e a

0 20   40   60 miles
0 40   80 km

Danube

Border of Hapsburg Empire in 1918 ——
(excluding areas of Italy, mainly Lombardy and Tuscany, and Belgium and part of Galicia, which were part of the empire at various times during the 18th and 19th centuries)
Border between Hungary and other parts of the empire – – –
Border of Bohemia, Moravia, Galicia, and Hungary ·····
Border between the other lands ········
500–1,000 Jews, or smaller but important communities ○
1,000–2,000 Jews ●
2,000–5,000 Jews ◉
5,000–10,000 Jews ⊡
Toleranzpatent (edict of rights) 1781
of Joseph II and date

Zamość

Cracow

Ulanów
Sokal
Tartaków
Mielec
Kolbuszowa
Lezajsk
Uhnów
Krystynopol
Dabrowa
Glogów
Sokolów
Cieszanów
Rawa Ruska
Tarnów
Debica
Rzeszów
Oleszyce
Lubaczów
Kamionka
Strumiłowa
Brody
Przeworsk
Podkamien
Tyczyn
Lańcut
Jaroslau
Jaworów
Busk
Zolkiew
(Zholkva)
Yarychev
Złoczów
Wiśnicz
Strzyzów
Przemyśl
Lemberg
Gliniany
Zbarazh
Neusandez
(Zanz)
Dynów
Mościska
Gródek
Przemyślany
Gologory
Zborów
Tarnopol
Zmigród
Rymanów
Komarno
Bobrka
Pomórzany
Skalat
Lisko
Dobromil
Rozdól
Khodorov
Brzezany
Grzymałów
Drohobycz
Rohatyn
Podhajce
Trembowla
Stryj
Dniester
Buczacz
Husiatyn
Turka
Monasterzyska
Czortków
Skole
Bolechów
Kalusz
Jazłowiec
Jezierzany
Dolina
Stanislau
Tyśmienica
Bohorodczany
Horodenka
Nadwórna
Kolomea
Sniatyn
Zabłotów
Kuty

Wisła
San

G   A   L   I   C   I   A

W E S T

E A S T

Emperor Joseph II.
Medallion minted on occasion of
first Toleranzpatent, *1781.*

0 10   20   30 miles
0 20   40 km

combination of concessions and restrictions aimed at "improving" (according to the emperor's concepts) the ways of life, the cultural level, and the economic activities of the Jews. General schools for the Jewish population were established in many communities. In 1785, most of the rights of the communities as autonomous bodies were abolished, especially regarding their juridical powers. Some communities were recognized as religious bodies: 141 communities in Galicia (including 10 in Zamość province), 52 in Moravia, 1 in Bohemia (Prague), and 2 in Bukovina. In 1788, it was decided to enlist the Jews into the army. Furthermore, restrictions were imposed on Jewish estate-renting in Galicia, to remove the Jews from the rural population and concentrate them in the towns. It was decided in 1783 to open the "free cities" in Hungary to the Jews, but they still were not permitted to live in the German lands of the empire. The various edicts put heavy pressure on the Jews in Galicia, about 50,000 of whom lived in villages. The economic regulations and the enlistment into the army were among the factors that impelled many Jews to migrate to Hungary and other countries. After the death of Joseph II in 1790, many of his decrees were disregarded, except in Bohemia and Moravia, where the central government had more influence.

THE JEWS IN AUSTRIA-HUNGARY EARLY 20TH CENTURY

IN 1867, the Hapsburg Empire was reorganized politically: the Austro-Hungarian monarchy was established, ruled by the Hapsburg dynasty. All subjects were granted full civil and political rights, and all the restrictions regarding the Jews were abolished. The number of Jews continued to grow in the nineteenth century, especially in Hungary and Galicia. Many Jews settled in cities, which until the mid-nineteenth century had been closed to them (until 1840 in Hungary, and until 1848 in the rest of the empire). In the early twentieth century, Vienna and Budapest were among the largest Jewish centers in Europe.

In Galicia, there were demographic and cultural differences between the Jews of the larger, eastern part (east of the San River), where 75 percent of them lived, and those of the western part. In 1910, the Jews made up 31.2 percent of the population in the eleven largest cities in western Galicia (but only 8 percent of the total population), and 38.5 percent of the inhabitants of the nineteen largest cities in eastern Galicia (12.3 percent of the total population). The occupational structure of the Jews throughout the monarchy reflected their urban character: a small percentage in farming (although higher in Galicia than in other European countries), and more in commerce.

Until the 1890s, natural increase among the Jews remained higher than among other religious groups in the empire. This changed between 1890 and 1900, and in a relatively short period, natural increase of the Jews fell below that of other groups. In addition, from the end of the nineteenth century, Jews began to emigrate in growing numbers from Austria–Hungary (especially Galicia) to Western Europe or overseas. Both trends brought the increase of the Jewish population in Austria–Hungary to a halt. Although the number of Jews in Galicia grew from 686,600 in 1880 to 871,900 in 1910, their proportion in the total popu-

Map legend:

City with Jewish majority ✡
International border ——
Border between Austria and Hungary ——
Border between states within Austria-Hungary ————
Border between East and West Galicia ————

Community at end of 18th century ● Community at beginning of 20th century ●

Community of 500–1,000 Jews
Community of 1,000–2,000 Jews
Community of 2,000–5,000 Jews
Community of 5,000–10,000 Jews
Community of 10,000–20,000 Jews
Community of 20,000–200,000 Jews
Community of 200,000 or more Jews

lation fell from 11.5 to 10.9 percent. In contrast, neighboring Polish Jewry (under Russian rule) continued to increase until World War I, both absolutely and relative to the general population.

THE JEWS IN AUSTRIA-HUNGARY

THE JEWS IN FRANCE 18TH AND 19TH CENTURIES

IN the second half of the eighteenth century, 30,000 to 40,000 Jews lived in France; the expulsion decrees of the fourteenth century were still in effect; and only Jews who had arrived later in special circumstances or who lived in territories later added to France were permitted to stay. This was the case with the "New Christians," who had settled mainly in Bordeaux and Bayonne in the sixteenth century, or in the Comtat Venaissin region and in Avignon in Provence, which had belonged to the pope—altogether, about 3,000 Jews, most of them merchants, who were well integrated into the general society and well off economically. The main Jewish settlement was in eastern France, in Alsace-Lorraine, which had become French under the Treaty of Westphalia (1648) and other treaties. These Jews were of Ashkenazic stock, supporting themselves by lending money and peddling, and living in a tenuous relationship

327

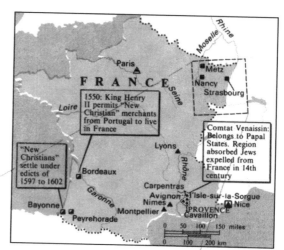

1550: King Henry II permits "New Christian" merchants from Portugal to live in France

Comtat Venaissin: Belongs to Papal States. Region absorbed Jews expelled from France in 14th century

"New Christians" settle under edicts of 1597 to 1602

▲ Jews of Comtat Venaissin and Avignon
■ Ashkenazim
□ North African and Italian Jews
◪ Portuguese Sephardim
▲ Mixed communities
● Locality with 250–500 Jews in 1789
···· 1789 border
······ Border of Alsace

Until the French Revolution, city was virtually shut to the Jews. After 1791, their number grew rapidly and the city became the main Jewish center in Alsace

THE JEWS IN ALSACE-LORRAINE
LATE 18TH CENTURY

Joseph David Sinzheim, the first chief rabbi of the Central Consistory of Jews in France.

with the general population. A few hundred Jews lived in Paris illegally.

Long debates about the civil status of the Jews took place in the wake of the French Revolution. Among the revolutionaries, there were doubts about whether the Declaration of the Rights of Man and of the Citizen, approved in August 1789, applied to the Jews. The first debate on the question took place in December 1789. The Sephardic Jews of Provence were recognized as full citizens in January 1790. But the debate continued regarding the Jews of Alsace-Lorraine, who were not granted full citizenship until September 1791.

Napoleon Bonaparte, emperor from 1804 to 1815, sought to ensure the civil integration of the Jews in France and to formalize their position, like that of all other religious groups, in the framework of the state and under its supervision. With that aim in mind, Napoleon acted in two directions. First, in July 1806, the Assembly of Jewish Notables convened. More than 100 elected delegates from France and northern Italy (then under French domination) participated. The

ENGLAND

London

GERMANY

Krefeld

1829: Local yeshiva
recognized as official
rabbinical seminary.
1859: Transferred to Paris

Koblenz
Mainz

Trier

Paris

Metz

Nancy

Strasbourg

Wintzenheim

Colmar

FRANCE

1871: 3 consistories
annexed to Germany

1823: Consistory
moves from Wintzenheim
to Colmar

Lyons

1846: New
consistory formed

Turin

Casale

Bordeaux

1857: New
consistory formed

Bayonne

Marseilles

CORSICA

SPAIN

— French border in 1789
  French regional borders
◉ Seats of the 13 consistories
  formed in 1808

0 40 80 miles
0 50 100 km

1845: 3 new consistories formed
in Algeria: Algiers, Oran, and
Constantine

Total Jewish population in France
in 1808: 47,200
① Paris and suburbs: 3,000 Jews
② North: 200 Jews
③ East: 37,100 Jews
④ Paris basin: 500 Jews
⑤ West: 100 Jews
⑥ Southwest: 3,500 Jews
⑦ Southeast: 200 Jews
⑧ Mediterranean littoral: 2,600 Jews

Jewish delegates were asked to answer twelve questions dealing with various aspects of Jewish life and religion, economic activities, and the position of the Jews vis-à-vis other citizens and the state. The answers, formulated by the delegates with great care, achieved a balance between loyalty to the state and adherence to the obligations of Jewish religious law (*halakhah*). The answers were approved by Napoleon, who then convened a second body, a Sanhedrin, made up of seventy-one rabbis and lay leaders. At its meeting in Paris in February 1807, the Sanhedrin endorsed the recommendations of the Assembly of Jewish Notables and declared them to be binding on all French Jews.

Second, in March 1808, Napoleon issued a decree deferring for ten years all debts owed to Jews by people in Alsace-Lorraine and laying down certain restrictions on the economic activity of Jews. An additional step was the establishment in 1808 of the consistory system, organizing all Jewish communities within an official frame attached to the French Ministry of Religions. Every French district (*département*) or group of districts organized a consistory, and all consistories were under the authority of the Central Consistory in Paris. The whole system was under official control. Its tasks were mainly religious, although it also dealt with educational and social-welfare matters. Originally, thirteen regional consistories were established, but over the years the system underwent several modifications, reflecting also the territorial changes of France. The law of separation of church and state, approved in 1905, abolished the system's official status, although part of its authority continued, as a matter of tradition.

C. Major Themes in Modern Jewish History

Jewish Entrepreneurs 19th and 20th Centuries

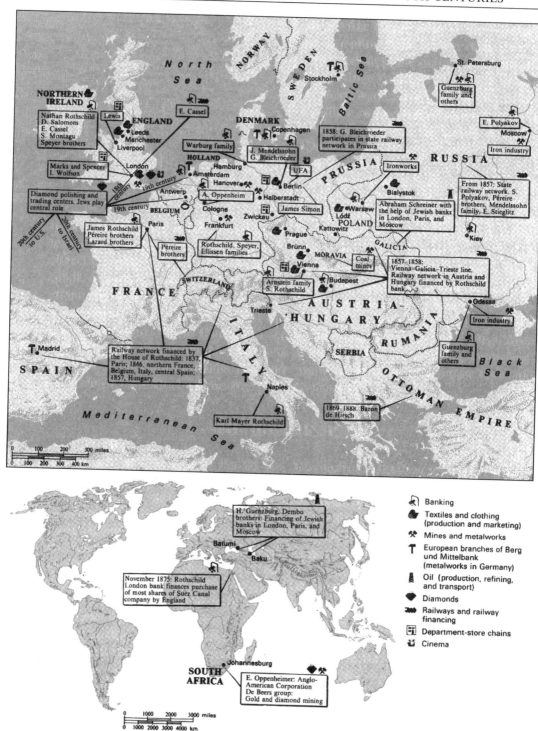

Map labels (top European map):

NORWAY
SWEDEN
North Sea
Baltic Sea
St. Petersburg

Stockholm
Guenzburg family and others

NORTHERN IRELAND
Lewis
ENGLAND
E. Cassel
DENMARK
Copenhagen

Nathan Rothschild
D. Salomons
E. Cassel
S. Montagu
Speyer brothers

Leeds
Manchester
Liverpool

Warburg family

1858: G. Bleichroeder participates in state railway network in Prussia

E. Polyakov
Moscow
Iron industry

RUSSIA

Marks and Spencer
I. Wolfson

London
Amsterdam
Hanover
Hamburg
HOLLAND
J. Mendelssohn
G. Bleichroeder
UFA
Berlin
Ironworks
Halberstadt

18th century
19th century

PRUSSIA

From 1857: State railway network. S. Polyakov, Péreire brothers, Mendelssohn family, E. Stieglitz

Diamond polishing and trading centers. Jews play central role

19th century
BELGIUM
Antwerp
A. Oppenheim
Cologne
James Simon
Bialystok
Warsaw
Lódź
POLAND
Kattowitz

Abraham Schreiner with the help of Jewish banks in London, Paris, and Moscow

20th century to U.S.
20th century to Israel

James Rothschild
Péreire brothers
Lazard brothers
Paris
Péreire brothers

Frankfurt
Zwickau

Rothschild, Speyer, Ellissen families

Prague
Brünn
MORAVIA
GALICIA
Kiev

Coal mines

1857-1858: Vienna-Galicia-Trieste line. Railway network in Austria and Hungary financed by Rothschild bank

FRANCE
SWITZERLAND
Vienna
Budapest
Arnstein family
S. Rothschild

AUSTRIA-HUNGARY

Odessa
Iron industry

Trieste

ITALY

RUMANIA
SERBIA

Guenzburg family and others

Madrid
Railway network financed by the House of Rothschild: 1837, Paris; 1846, northern France, Belgium, Italy, central Spain; 1857, Hungary

SPAIN

Naples

OTTOMAN EMPIRE

Black Sea

Mediterranean Sea

Karl Mayer Rothschild

1869-1888: Baron de Hirsch

0 100 200 300 miles
0 100 200 300 400 km

Map labels (bottom world map):

H. Guenzburg, Dembo brothers: Financing of Jewish banks in London, Paris, and Moscow

Batumi
Baku

November 1875: Rothschild London bank finances purchase of most shares of Suez Canal company by England

SOUTH AFRICA
Johannesburg

E. Oppenheimer: Anglo-American Corporation De Beers group: Gold and diamond mining

0 1000 2000 3000 miles
0 1000 2000 3000 4000 km

Legend:

- Banking
- Textiles and clothing (production and marketing)
- Mines and metalworks
- European branches of Berg und Mittelbank (metalworks in Germany)
- Oil (production, refining, and transport)
- Diamonds
- Railways and railway financing
- Department-store chains
- Cinema

THE intensive development of modern Europe (and later of the United States) created economic opportunities for the Jews. Jews were among the entrepreneurs active in the expanding commerce. The earliest modern Jewish entrepreneurs were the Spanish-Portuguese Jews of Amsterdam and London in the seventeenth century, whose economic activities embraced the entire known world. A later type was the Court Jews of Central Europe in the eighteenth century, who established a broad network of business connections, often with Jews in other countries. In the nineteenth century, Court Jews, their descendants, and other Jews also went into banking. Prominent among them were the Rothschilds, who started in Frankfurt and eventually established bank branches and other banking connections in Germany, France, Italy, England, the Hapsburg Empire, and even Russia. Characteristically, Jewish entrepreneurs and bankers entered new economic fields, to avoid the competition of the guilds of craftsmen or merchants, which often forbade Jewish participation in established occupations. Jews were active (and sometimes impor-

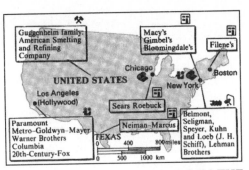

JEWISH ENTREPRENEURS IN THE
UNITED STATES

tant) in the sugar industry and trade, the development of the railroad system in Europe (and later in the United States), and the nascent petroleum industry. Jews were also prominent in the diamond industry and trade from the seventeenth century on.

Another field in which Jews pioneered was the garment industry, especially in the United States. In the twentieth century, Jews played a major role in the establishment of large department stores, including some famous chains in Europe and the United States. They were also prominent in communications and entertainment: journalism, the theater, the film industry, radio, and, later, television.

Notwithstanding this wide range of activities, the Jews were only one factor, and with few exceptions not the most important one, in the economic development of the Western world in modern times.

Rothschild home in Frankfurt-on-the-Main, 16th century.

(right) Schocken department store in Chemnitz. Designed by architect Eric Mendelsohn.

THE LEGAL SITUATION OF THE JEWS UNTIL WORLD WAR I

NEW social and political concepts that developed in Europe in modern times changed the legal position of the Jews, in each country according to a pattern of its own. Until the rise of the absolute states in the seventeenth and eighteenth centuries, the Jews were regarded as a foreign people in the European countries or cities, and their presence was based on and regulated by a legal contract ("privilege") between them and the local ruler. The ruler's interest in the Jews was economic; the attitude of the general society was strongly influenced by the historical tensions between non-Jews and Jews. Under the absolute rulers, the legal situation of the Jews changed: from foreigners, they became subjects. Their new status involved some rights and many duties, since it was thought that the Jews had to be "improved." The absolute ruler considered it his right and duty to intervene in the life of the Jewish community (as he did in the lives of his other subjects), in order to move it in the "desirable" direction.

In Western and Central Europe (but not in Eastern Europe), absolutism gradually gave way to regimes and systems inspired by the French Revolution, which also had a far-reaching influence on the situation of the Jews. The French National Assembly decided in 1791 that Jews should be granted citizenship with full civil and political rights. But in many countries, this so-called Jewish emancipation involved an implicit or explicit accord between non-Jews and Jews: in exchange for their new rights, Jews were supposed to relinquish much (or most) of their distinctiveness, such as their separate group existence. These conditions

were not specifically mentioned in the emancipation laws, but were clearly expressed in the discussions related to them. During the debate on the Jews in the French National Assembly, in December 1789, Count Clermont-Tonnerre formulated it thus: "Everything must be refused to the Jews as a nation but everything must be granted to them as individuals; they must be citizens." These and similar statements expressed the uneasiness and doubt about the new status of the Jews and set conditions for their full integration into the general society. The conditions were not and could not be clearly defined and were interpreted differently by each ideological sector of the general society. Together, however, these conditions and interpretations placed a question mark on the Jews' position and cast a shadow on the whole process that was to prove fateful, with the development of modern antisemitism. That ambivalence in the new situation of the Jews, that combination of many new possibilities with as many problems attached to them, became one of the main characteristics of the modernization of European Jewry.

Nevertheless, the granting of citizenship rights to the Jews by the French National Assembly was a landmark in modern Jewish history: it put the Jews on an equal footing with all other French citizens and provided a model that sooner or later was followed by most other West European countries. For the Jews, it set a goal and a challenge that deeply influenced the subsequent internal development of Jewish society, in each country according to local conditions. But in many of the countries where Jews gained

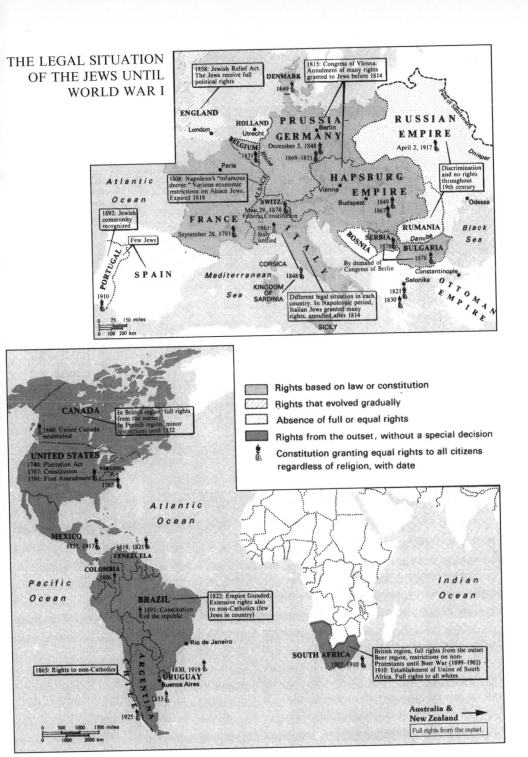

THE LEGAL SITUATION OF THE JEWS UNTIL WORLD WAR I

1858: Jewish Relief Act. The Jews receive full political rights

1815: Congress of Vienna. Annulment of many rights granted to Jews before 1814

DENMARK
1849

ENGLAND

HOLLAND
London
Utrecht
BELGIUM
1831

PRUSSIA-GERMANY
Berlin
December 5, 1848
1869–1871

RUSSIAN EMPIRE
April 2, 1917
Pale of Settlement
Dnieper

1808: Napoleon's "infamous decree." Various economic restrictions on Alsace Jews. Expired 1818

Atlantic Ocean

1892: Jewish community recognized

Few Jews

PORTUGAL

SPAIN

1910

FRANCE
Paris
September 28, 1791

ALSACE
Rhine
SWITZ.
May 29, 1874: Federal Constitution
1861: Italy unified

HAPSBURG EMPIRE
Vienna
Budapest   1849
1867

Discrimination and no rights throughout 19th century
Odessa

ITALY

BOSNIA
SERBIA
1878
RUMANIA
Danube
BULGARIA
1878

Black Sea

By demand of Congress of Berlin

CORSICA

KINGDOM OF SARDINIA

Mediterranean Sea
1848

Different legal situation in each country. In Napoleonic period, Italian Jews granted many rights, annulled after 1814

Constantinople
Salonika
1821
1830

OTTOMAN EMPIRE

SICILY

CANADA
In British region, full rights from the outset. In French region, minor restrictions until 1832
1840: United Canada established

UNITED STATES
1740: Plantation Act
1787: Constitution
1791: First Amendment
VIRGINIA
1785

Atlantic Ocean

- Rights based on law or constitution
- Rights that evolved gradually
- Absence of full or equal rights
- Rights from the outset, without a special decision
- Constitution granting equal rights to all citizens regardless of religion, with date

MEXICO
1857, 1917
VENEZUELA
1819, 1821
COLOMBIA
1886

Pacific Ocean

BRAZIL
1891: Constitution of the republic

1822: Empire founded. Extensive rights also to non-Catholics (few Jews in country)

Rio de Janeiro

Indian Ocean

1865: Rights to non-Catholics
ARGENTINA
CHILE
1830, 1919
URUGUAY
Buenos Aires
1853
1925

SOUTH AFRICA
1902–1910

British region, full rights from the outset. Boer region, restrictions on non-Protestants until Boer War (1899–1902). 1910: Establishment of Union of South Africa. Full rights to all whites

Australia & New Zealand
Full rights from the outset

civil and political rights, an undeniable gap remained between theory and practice, and the new laws were unable to persuade non-Jews to overcome their deep-rooted prejudices. And in several countries, there was a semiofficial (or tacit) preference for the religion of the majority group.

In Eastern Europe after World War I, a positive approach was adopted (or imposed) regarding the cultural and national rights of minority groups (including the Jews), opening new possibilities for Jewish life and self-definition in the countries of that region.

Although the development of American Jewry showed European influences, the legal situation of American Jews was quite different from that of European Jews. No separate discussion took place in the United States about the legal rights of the Jews. The Plantation Act of 1740 granted full civil rights to Jews and members of other religious groups who had been living in the British colonies in America for at least seven years. The law, characteristic of the mercantilist age, aimed to attract settlers to the undeveloped and uncolonized Crown lands in the New World, and it established a basis for the legal equality of the Jews in America long before the colonies declared and won their independence. Consequently, in the United States there was never a "Jewish emancipation" as it evolved in Europe, with all the attendant problems and conditions. Some laws

discriminating against Jews existed in several American states, but they were rescinded during the nineteenth century.

The situation in the Latin American countries (most became independent in the nineteenth century) was not much different from that in the United States, although Roman Catholicism was recognized in most South American states as the predominant or official religion. Jews also enjoyed full equality in other nations established in the nineteenth and twentieth centuries—for example, Australia, Canada, and South Africa.

THE LEGAL SITUATION OF THE JEWS IN MUSLIM COUNTRIES

THE legal situation of the Jews in Muslim countries has a long history. It is based on the prophet Mohammed's prescript that non-Muslims who believe in one God be considered protected subjects (*dhimmis*) and pay a special annual tax (*jizya*). There eventually evolved an additional set of laws of a discriminatory character, associated with the Caliph Omar II. In practice, much depended on local conditions or on the whims of local rulers. European penetration into Mus-

lim countries beginning in the nineteenth century, and the attainment of independence by these countries in the twentieth century, improved the legal situation of the Jews and, in many places, led to civil and political equality—at least in theory. Growing Arab nationalism and the worsening Arab-Zionist conflict undermined the position of the Jews in most Muslim countries around the mid-twentieth century and was one of the reasons for their emigration.

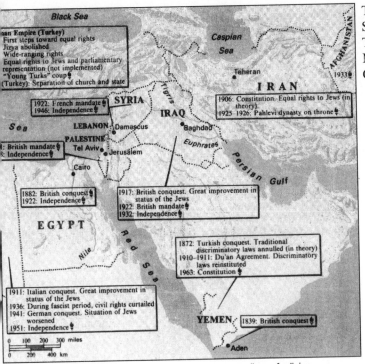

Black Sea

an Empire (Turkey)
First steps toward equal rights
Jizya abolished
Wide-ranging rights
Equal rights to Jews and parliamentary
representation (not implemented)
"Young Turks" coup
(Turkey): Separation of church and state

Caspian
Sea

Teheran
1933

IRAN

1906: Constitution. Equal rights to Jews (in
theory).
1925–1926: Pahlevi dynasty on throne

1922: French mandate
1946: Independence

SYRIA

IRAQ

Tigris

LEBANON   Damascus

Baghdad

Euphrates

PALESTINE

: British mandate
: Independence

Tel Aviv

Jerusalem

Persian Gulf

Cairo

1882: British conquest
1922: Independence

1917: British conquest. Great improvement in
status of the Jews
1922: British mandate
1932: Independence

EGYPT

Nile

Red Sea

1872: Turkish conquest. Traditional
discriminatory laws annulled (in theory)
1910–1911: Du'an Agreement. Discriminatory
laws reinstituted
1963: Constitution

1911: Italian conquest. Great improvement in
status of the Jews
1936: During fascist period, civil rights curtailed
1941: German conquest. Situation of Jews
worsened
1951: Independence

YEMEN   1839: British conquest

Aden

0   100   200   300 miles
0   200   400 km

♀ Constitution or law granting all citizens equal rights, regardless of religion

JEWISH ENLIGHTENMENT (*HASKALAH*) IN EUROPE
18TH AND 19TH CENTURIES

JEWISH enlightenment, in the sense of the cultural interaction of Jews with the general society and their absorption of spiritual values from it, was always part of Jewish history. It was the characteristic of Jewish life in the Diaspora: to maintain cultural bridges with the non-Jewish environment, while preserving Jewish specificity. It varied in kind and in degree from generation to generation. The modern Jewish enlightenment in Europe differed from former enlightenment patterns in three respects: the significance of the values adopted from the general culture; the influence of these values not only on Jewish culture, but also on Jewish social life and self-definition; and the struggle that developed in European Jewry between the advocates and the opponents of the *haskalah* movement.

Western Europe
Jewish enlightenment in Western Europe began in the 1780s with Moses Mendelssohn and his *Ha-Meassef* circle in Germany. Its main centers were in Berlin, Breslau, Königsberg, and Vienna. The program of the Western *maskilim* for the modernization of Jewish society envisaged deep changes in education and culture as well as in the socioeconomic structure of Jewish society ("productivization"). At the beginning of the nineteenth century, the *maskilim* began to focus their efforts on reforming tradi-

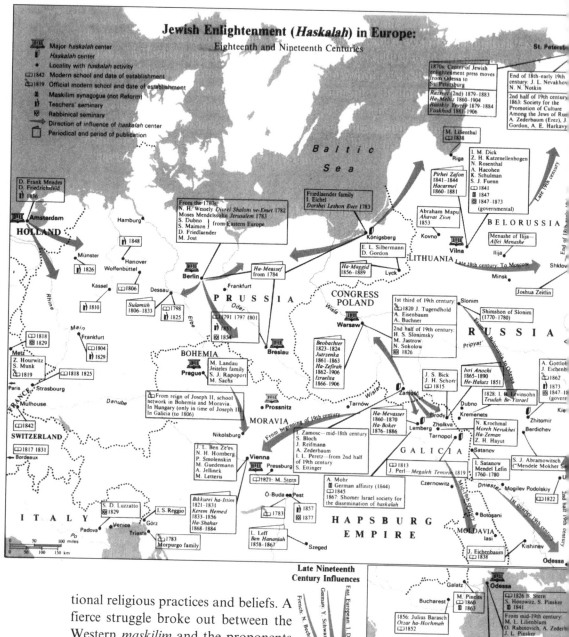

Jewish Enlightenment (*Haskalah*) in Europe:
Eighteenth and Nineteenth Centuries

tional religious practices and beliefs. A fierce struggle broke out between the Western *maskilim* and the proponents of classical Judaism, especially (but not only) over religious changes, which led to a deep and lasting breach.

West European *haskalah* was inspired by its own vision of the place of Jews and Judaism in modern society, and by its hopes for Jewish social and cultural "emancipation." But since the number of Jews in

Western Europe was small and their communal structures were relatively weak, many of them lost their identification with Judaism as a result of the influence of modernizing trends.

The founding of the Association for the Culture and Science of Judaism (the Kulturverein), which was active in Berlin from 1819 to 1824, may be regarded as the final activity of Western *haskalah* as a separate tendency. From then on, *haskalah* was active as a basis for or part of other trends and movements in Western and Central Europe, such as the "Science of Judaism" and the Reform movement.

Eastern Europe

Small circles of *maskilim* began to appear in Belorussia in the mid-eighteenth century. New groups were formed toward the end of the century in Galicia, Lithuania, Bohemia and Moravia, St. Petersburg, and Warsaw. By the early nineteenth century, several distinct types of East European *haskalah* were apparent: the Galician, the Lithuanian, and the Polish. Important centers of Jewish enlightenment gradually emerged: Zamość, Warsaw (Poland), Brody, Tarnopol, Lemberg (Lwów [Galicia]), Odessa, St. Petersburg, and Vilna (Russian Empire). Circles of *maskilim*, each with its own characteristics, appeared in Vienna and Prague (Hapsburg Empire), influenced by both Western and Eastern Jewish enlightenment.

At first, East European *maskilim* met with little opposition from the other segments of Jewish society, since their main interests were cultural and scientific. But by the end of the eighteenth century, they began to turn their attention to the social improvement of Jewish society, a matter raised by the authorities as well, first in the Hapsburg Empire, and then in czarist Russia. By the 1820s, the *maskilim* were working to modernize Jewish society and severely criticizing its ways of life. These efforts led to a confrontation with the more traditional sector of East European Jewry, composed of both Hasidim and Mitnagdim, who together still made up a huge majority. The struggle intensified from the middle of the century, partly as a result of pressure from the authorities, who tried by various means to force modernization on the Jewish masses and to undermine the traditional structure of Jewish society. However, the mounting tendencies toward assimilation among the Jewries of Western Europe undergoing modernization only strengthened the traditionalists' opposition to Jewish enlightenment.

The *maskilim*, who often collaborated with the authorities, began to create their own institutions, such as schools and synagogues. Their numbers and influence increased greatly during the relatively liberal reign of Czar Alexander II (1855–1881). Many were attracted by the schools that the authorities established for Jewish children beginning in the 1840s, both because of their growing interest in modernization and because of the exemption from military service offered to Jews who acquired a general education. The publication of Jewish newspapers (another expression of *haskalah*) in German, Hebrew, Yiddish, and Russian contributed greatly to the movement's expansion. From the 1860s, new organizations were formed for the propagation of *haskalah*. Additional centers of *haskalah* were the rabbinical seminaries established with governmental support in Warsaw (1826), Vilna, and Zhitomir (1847–1873). The official rabbinate (*mitaam*) was also a tool of the enlightenment. All these enterprises combined to give the East European *haskalah* movement a framework within which to function.

Since East European Jewry was sizable, concentrated in strong Jewish centers, spiritually very active, and relatively secluded from the general population, most *maskilim* sought to implement their new ideas *inside* Jewish society, not *outside* it, as those in Western Europe had done. East European *haskalah* grew in different directions, and its proponents adopted a wide range of attitudes to the problems of Jewish life. But even the later *maskilim*, who supported religious reforms, had reservations about the West European brand of Jewish reform, which defined Jews and Judaism on a very narrow religious basis. Most major cultural or social initiatives inspired by ideas rooted in East European *haskalah* aimed to preserve Jewish group life and to develop it, even if according to the new ideological approaches gradually being formulated.

Three main ideological trends emerged under the influence of East European *haskalah* in the last quarter of the nineteenth century. One, similar to the West European pattern, favored a high level of social and cultural integration into the general society. This position was expressed by the associations for the propagation of *haskalah*, and even more so by the circles that issued Jewish publications written in Russian, such as *Dien* (Odessa, 1869–1871) and the important *Voskhod* (St. Petersburg, 1881–1906). The second trend, partly influenced by the first, turned to Jewish nationalism in its different forms. This approach involved important authors who wrote in Hebrew and Hebrew-language publications, such as *Ha-Shahar*, *Ha-Maggid*, *Ha-Melitz*, and *Ha-Zefirah*, as well as Russian-language newspapers. Two significant cultural enterprises of these circles were the transformation of Hebrew into a living language and the fostering of Yiddish. The third current turned to socialism. Its beginnings were already apparent in the 1870s, and it reached its fullest expression with the creation of the Jewish socialist party, the Bund, in 1897.

A different kind of *haskalah* developed in Palestine beginning in the late nineteenth century. It was a combination of East European, German, and French elements, brought to the country by immigrant Jews. In the new Jewish centers in North and South America the *haskalah* was part of Jewish life, since conditions of modernity already prevailed there. Consequently, the kind of confrontation between Jewish modernism and traditionalism that had been so important in shaping Jewish life in the Old World did not occur in the New.

SHABBATEANISM, FRANKISM, AND EARLY HASIDISM

Two streams of mysticism were evident among the Jews in southeastern Poland in the early eighteenth century: Shabbateanism and Hasidism. Shabbateanism, a religious movement whose members believed that Shabbetai Zevi was the Messiah, had been strong in the second half of the seventeenth century but later declined. Hasidism arose toward the mid-eighteenth century and became one of the most influential movements in modern Jewish history. At first glance, the geographical proximity of the centers of the two might suggest mutual influence. Jacob Frank led a sect that continued the Shabbatean tradition, and in the winter

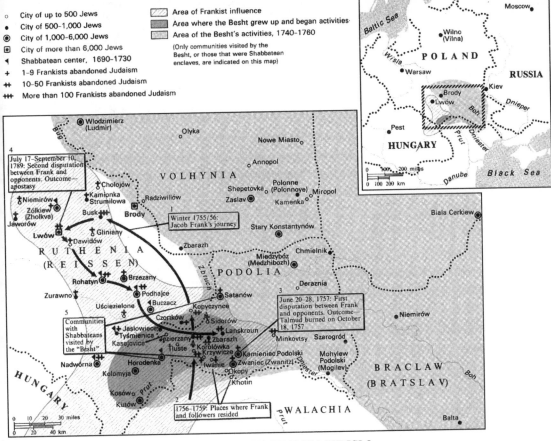

SHABBATEANISM, FRANKISM, AND EARLY HASIDISM

of 1755 visited Jewish communities in Poland that apparently were Shabbatean centers. His appearances generated local religious tensions and heated discussions between his critics and his supporters. About 500 of the latter converted to Christianity in 1759 and 1760.

A closer examination of the geographical data, however, raises doubts about a relationship between the two streams. It is true that Rabbi Israel Baal Shem Tov (the "Besht"), the creator of Hasidism, was born and grew up in a region where there apparently were Shabbatean influences (west of the River Zbruch, near the River Prut). Around 1740, however, he

ישראל בב׳ר אליעזר

Autograph of Israel Baal Shem Tov (the "Besht"), son of Eliezer.

began to propagate his new ideas in Medzhibozh (Miedzybóz) and other areas that were free of those influences. This analysis is based mainly on the writings of Rabbi Jacob Emden, the list of the Shabbateans who converted in Lwów in 1759 (which includes their places of residence), and the book *Shivhei Habesht*.

HASIDISM: BEGINNINGS AND EXPANSION

HASIDISM, a movement of religious renewal, appeared in Poland in the mid-eighteenth century. Scholars, kabbalists, and common folk banded together in groups led by a *zaddik* or *admor*. The *zaddik*, a new type in Jewish religious leadership, was an essential figure in the development of Hasidism. Typically, he was a mystic (*mekubbal*, or kabbalist) dedicated to a personal life of holiness, who now agreed to lead a sect of followers. The *zaddik* was believed to connect the higher spheres of holiness with the lower spheres of daily life, as explained in Jewish mysticism (kabbalah).

The founder of the Hasidic movement was Rabbi Israel Baal Shem Tov (the "Besht," 1700–1760), who became known in Podolia from about 1735. His most important successor was Rabbi Dov Baer (the "Great Maggid"), who led the Hasidic movement from 1760 to 1772 from Mezhirech (Miedzyrzecz), a small town in Volhynia. After his death, his many followers dispersed over the country, and the movement gradually split into many Hasidic courts, led by a descendant or disciple of the Besht or the Great Maggid.

The expansion of Hasidism brought it into conflict with sectors of the Jewish population opposing its views—the Mitnagdim (opponents), who tried to stop its expansion and even to excommunicate the Hasidim. The best-known leader of the Mitnagdim was Rabbi Elijah (the "Gaon of Vilna"). Nevertheless, Hasidism continued to grow, and since its adherents upheld religious law (*halakhah* and *mitzvot*) and did not attempt to change the traditional structure of the Jewish community, a total schism between the factions was avoided. The growth of Hasidism was aided by the fact that the Polish state was disintegrating at the time; the weakness of the Polish central government also weakened the established Jewish institutions and their possible reaction against the new current. Later, the rise of the Jewish enlightenment drew the Mitnagdim and Hasidim together to combat what they considered a common threat.

By the end of the eighteenth century, Hasidism had become a substantial movement, large sectors of the Jewish population in central Poland, Galicia, parts of the Ukraine, and even some parts of Lithuania having accepted it.

RELIGIOUS TENDENCIES IN MODERN JUDAISM

THE process of religious transformation in modern Jewry generated one of the great internal spiritual struggles in Jewish history, with important social and even political overtones and consequences.

Until the end of the eighteenth century, Jews were mostly "traditional" in outlook and way of life and accepted the strict religious practices and beliefs of Jewish religious law (*halakhah*) as God's command handed to Moses at Mount Sinai. This was true even of those small segments of the Jewish people that were already "modern" and relatively well adapted to the societies in which they lived, such as the Spanish-Portuguese Jews of Amsterdam and London. Furthermore, on the eve of the modern period, East European Jewry underwent a profound religious revival of a "tradi-

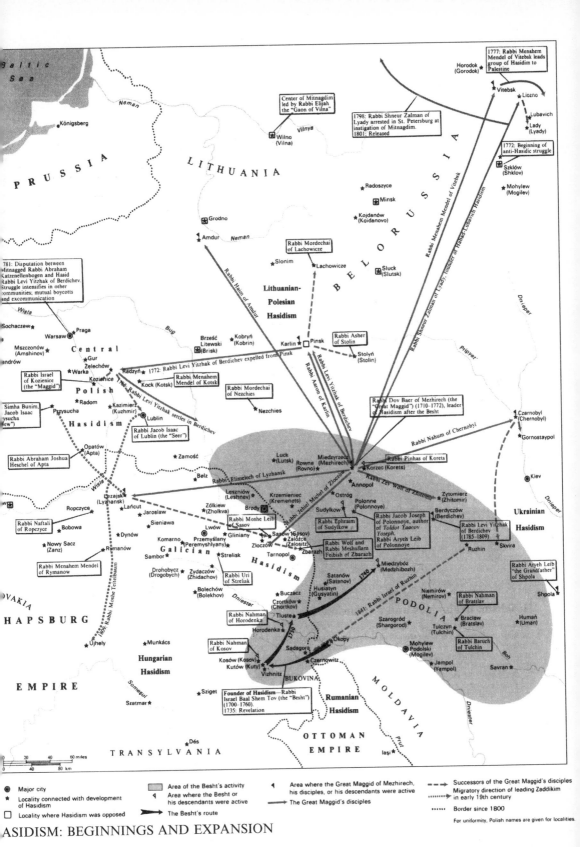

Baltic Sea

PRUSSIA

LITHUANIA

BELORUSSIA

* Königsberg

Neman

* Horodok (Gorodok)

1777: Rabbi Menahem Mendel of Vitebsk leads group of Hasidim to Palestine

✠ Vitebsk

Liozno

Lubavich

Lady (Lyady)

Center of Mitnagdim led by Rabbi Elijah the "Gaon of Vilna"

Vilnya

1798: Rabbi Shneur Zalman of Lyady arrested in St. Petersburg at instigation of Mitnagdim.
1801: Released

✠ Wilno (Vilna)

* Radoszyce

* Minsk

✠ Grodno

Neman

* Amdur

Rabbi Haim of Amdur

Rabbi Menahem Mendel of Vitebsk; founder of Habad-Lubavich Hasidism

Rabbi Shneur Zalman of Lyady; founder of Habad-Lubavich Hasidism

Mohylew (Mogilev)

1772: Beginning of anti-Hasidic struggle

✠ Szklów (Shklov)

Dnieper

Rabbi Mordechai of Lachowicze

* Slonim

Lachowicze

Lithuanian-Polesian Hasidism

✠ Sluck (Slutsk)

Kojdanów (Koidanovo)

781: Disputation between Mitnagged Rabbi Abraham Katzenellenbogen and Hasid Rabbi Levi Yitzhak of Berdichev. Struggle intensifies in other communities; mutual boycotts and excommunication

Wisla

Sochaczew *

Brześć Litewski (Brisk)

Kobryń (Kobrin)

Karlin

Pinsk

Rabbi Asher of Stolin

Pripyat

Warsaw * * Praga

Mszczonów * (Amshinov)

andrów

* Gur

Zelechów

Radzyń

Bug

Central

1772: Rabbi Levi Yitzhak of Berdichev expelled from Pinsk

Rabbi Aaron of Karlin

Stolyń (Stolin)

Rabbi Israel of Kozienice (the "Maggid")

Polish

* Radom

Warka

Kozienice

Rabbi Menahem Mendel of Kotsk

Rabbi Levi Yitzhak of Berdichev

Rabbi Dov Baer of Mezhirech (the "Great Maggid") (1710–1772), leader of Hasidism after the Besht

Czarnobyl (Chernobyl)

Kock (Kotsk)

Rabbi Mordechai of Nezchies

Rabbi Nahum of Chernobyl

Gornostaypol

Simha Bunim, Jacob Isaac ysucha ew")

Przysucha

Kazimierz (Kuzhmir)

Lublin

Hasidism

Nezchies

Rabbi Pinhas of Korets

Kiev

Rabbi Jacob Isaac of Lublin (the "Seer")

* Zamość

Luck (Lutsk)

Rowne (Rovno)

Miedzyrzecz (Mezhirech)

Korzec (Korets)

Rabbi Zev Wolf of Zhitomir

Rabbi Abraham Joshua Heschel of Apta

Opatów (Apta)

Belz

Rabbi Elimelech of Lyzhansk

Annopol

Zytomierz (Zhitomir)

Ukrainian Hasidism

Wisla

Leszniów (Leshnev)

Krzemieniec (Kremenets)

Ostróg

Polonne (Polonnoye)

Berdyczów (Berdichev)

Rzajsk (Lyzhansk)

Rabbi Naftali of Ropczyce

Ropczyce

Lańcut

Jaroslaw

Sieniawa

Żółkiew (Zholkva)

Brody

Sudyłkow

Rabbi Ephraim of Sudylkow

Rabbi Jacob Joseph of Polonnoye, author of Toldot Yaacov Yoseph. Rabbi Aryeh Leib of Polonnoye

Rabbi Levi Yitzhak of Berdichev (1785–1809)

Skvira

Bobowa

Lwów

Gliniany

Sasów (Sasov)

Zaloźce (Zalositz)

Zloczów

* Nowy Sacz (Zanz)

Komarno

Przemyslany (Peremyshlyany)

Galician

Rabbi Wolf and Rabbi Meshullam Feibish of Zbarazh

Ruzhin

Rabbi Aryeh Leib "the Grandfather" of Shpola

Rymanów

Rabbi Moshe Leib of Sasov

Tarnopol

Zbaraz

Rabbi Menahem Mendel of Rymanow

Sambor

Strelisk

Hasidism

Miedzybóż (Medzhibozh)

Shpola

VAKIA

Drohobycz (Drogobych)

Zydaczów (Zhidachov)

Rabbi Uri of Strelisk

Satanów (Satanov)

Husiatyn (Gusyatin)

1740

Rabbi Israel of Ruzhin

Niemirów (Nemirov)

Rabbi Nahman of Bratslav

Humań (Uman)

HAPSBURG

Bolechów (Bolekhov)

Dniester

Czortków (Chortkov)

PODOLIA

Braclaw (Bratslav)

SVAKIA

Rabbi Nahman of Horodenka

Tluste

1841: Rabbi Israel of Ruzhin

Szarogród (Shargorod)

Tulczyn (Tulchin)

Rabbi Baruch of Tulchin

Rabbi Moshe Teitelbaum

Horodenka

1790

Buczacz

1740

Mohylew Podolski (Mogilev)

Jampol (Yampol)

Ujhely

Munkács

Rabbi Nahman of Kosov

Kosów (Kosov)

Kutów (Kuty)

Viznitza

Sadagora

Okopy

Czernowitz

Savran

EMPIRE

Hungarian Hasidism

Someşul

BUKOVINA

MOLDAVIA

Dniester

Szatmar

Sziget

Founder of Hasidism—Rabbi Israel Baal Shem Tov (the "Besht") (1700–1760).
1735: Revelation

Rumanian Hasidism

Prut

Dés

OTTOMAN EMPIRE

Iaşi

TRANSYLVANIA

20   40   60 miles
40   80 km

• Major city

★ Locality connected with development of Hasidism

☐ Locality where Hasidism was opposed

▨ Area of the Besht's activity

◀ Area where the Besht or his descendants were active

▶ The Besht's route

◀ Area where the Great Maggid of Mezhirech, his disciples, or his descendants were active

→ The Great Maggid's disciples

⇢ Successors of the Great Maggid's disciples

⋯⋯ Migratory direction of leading Zaddikim in early 19th century

⋯⋯ Border since 1800

For uniformity, Polish names are given for localities.

ASIDISM: BEGINNINGS AND EXPANSION

tional" character in the form of Hasidism combined with the opposition (*hitnagdut*) it evoked. The two together invigorated traditional Jewish religious life and strengthened it against the challenges of the modern era, which were posed by the Jewish enlightenment and one of its major consequences, the "acculturation" of Jewish society.

From the early nineteenth century, different segments of Jewish society in Western Europe became estranged from Jewish religious matters. Other groups criticized the beliefs and life ways of classical Judaism. They developed new concepts about the practice and principles of Judaism, which led to the Reform movement. Both the trend toward religious indifference and the efforts to introduce religious changes drew a fierce reaction from the defenders of classical Judaism.

Acculturation, meaning the gradual integration into the social and cultural life of the general society, was a central theme in the religious quest of nineteenth-century Jewry. It began among West European Jews in the late eighteenth century (in some instances, even earlier), advanced gradually through Central Europe during the nineteenth century, and later touched a growing part of East European Jewry.

Acculturation presented Jewish society with a wide gamut of new and intellectual questions that evoked the most diverse responses. Since modern European culture had strong secular overtones, one consequence of acculturation was the slackening adherence to the precepts of classical Judaism or a critical attitude toward them. In Western Europe, some—although relatively few—Jews were able to combine their cultural integration into the general society with strict religious practice. But the majority

accepted the idea that the Jewish religion should be reformed. Large sectors of East European Jewry, however, reacted differently. Set in their traditional ways, deeply attached to classical Judaism, and relatively isolated from the surrounding non-Jewish society, they were wary of the new influences and tended to reject them, fearing that they would lead to changes in the *halakhah* and *mitzvot* (religious duties). The tradition-minded response to the challenges of acculturation expressed itself in a new religious attitude, Orthodoxy. This produced several currents, which varied with time and place: in Western Europe, it produced Orthodoxy and neo-Orthodoxy; in Eastern Europe, Haredut; and in Hungary, ultra-Orthodoxy. What they had in common was the uncompromising observance of Jewish religious law and the total rejection of any reforms in Judaism.

Viewed historically, the retreat from the extreme religious way of life was but one feature of Jewish society undergoing modernization. At the beginning of the twentieth century, most East European Jews still lived according to the *halakhah*; in Western Europe, the Reform position already had the upper hand, while many other Jews had become indifferent to religious matters. Later, the growing influence of secularization further weakened the religious life of Jewish society. This tendency was even sharper among Jews who emigrated from Europe: their traditional Jewish institutions, religious and other, lost influence in their adopted countries. In the former Soviet Union, the regime's antireligious ideology made the practice of all religion difficult. Finally, the Holocaust destroyed the main centers of classical Judaism in Europe.

In Palestine, and later in Israel, religious life developed a logic of its own.

The emergence of an autonomous Jewish society, which later won political independence, made the question of the character of that society a matter of principle. The different currents in classical Judaism were impelled to participate in the public and political life of the country—not only to safeguard their interests, but also to promote their own conception of Jewish life. After a period of uncertainty and defensiveness, Orthodox Jewry gained self-assurance and became very active in Israeli public life, while other religious positions continued to struggle to gain recognition.

The Reform Movement

The Reform movement aimed to adapt the forms of classical Jewish ritual and to explain the concepts of Judaism, according to the forms and ideas absorbed from the general society. It introduced changes in Jewish ritual from the early nineteenth century, first in German-speaking countries, then in other places in Europe, and later in the United States. From the 1830s, new concepts about the character of Judaism were presented, and gradually the Reform position in modern Jewry was formulated. The movement's thinkers and leading figures (Abraham Geiger, Samuel Holdheim, Isaac Mayer Wise, and others) did not consider religious law (*halakhah* and *mitzvot*) to be binding and immutable. They distinguished between what they considered to be the essence and the forms of Judaism. Their intention was, as stated by Abraham Geiger in his younger years, to free the spirit, the eternal ideas, of Judaism from the "petrified" forms in which it had been imprisoned. They hoped that their proposed changes would remold the Jewish religion and bring it into harmony with the concepts of a modern and progressive general society. Judaism, according to most of the reformers, should be limited to the realm of religion, while in the civil and cultural domains, the Jews should live as loyal and integrated citizens of their respective countries.

In its more developed form, the Reform trend in Europe was known as the Liberal movement; only its more extreme sector, which was limited in size, called itself "Reform." In the United States, the movement became large and significant during the last two decades of the nineteenth century and adopted the name "Reform." The American movement was usually more extreme than its European counterpart.

In order to unify their positions regarding the envisaged changes in Jewish ritual and belief, the Reform rabbis in Germany convened assemblies of rabbis (1844, 1845, 1846) and later meetings of rabbis and lay leaders (the Synods, 1869, 1871). No agreement was reached in those discussions, as the gap between the moderate and the radical attitudes on many precepts of Judaism was apparently too wide to bridge. In Hungary, the supporters of the Reform movement adopted the name "Neology." The reforms it introduced were on the whole moderate. In Eastern Europe, the Reform movement did not become popular, and the proposed changes dealt more with ritual than with religious conception. In the Jewries of the Muslim countries, there never was a Reform movement. In the United States, the radical Pittsburgh Platform of 1885 provided a basis for most of the developing Reform congregations.

Toward the end of the nineteenth century, Liberal and Reform Jews started taking positions also on Jewish issues that were not of a purely religious nature, such as the expanding Zionist movement, which they fiercely opposed.

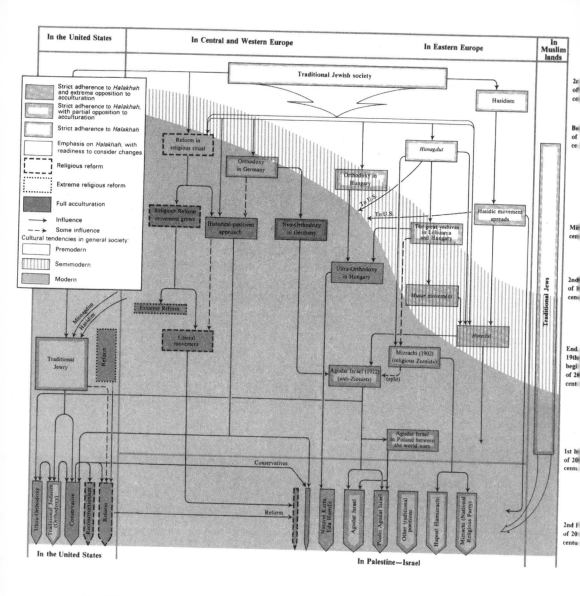

The Historical-Positivist Approach

The proponents of the historical-positivist approach, who lived mostly in Central and Western Europe, stood between the Orthodox and Reform movements, although somewhat closer to the former. They considered the *halakhah* to be an imposing religious historical creation. Most believed that it was rooted in divine revelation, but had undergone transformations in the course of Jewish history. Indeed, many regarded revelation as a continuing process, and not as a unique, one-time event. The outstanding representative of the historical-positivist approach was Zacharias Frankel, who from 1854 headed the Juedisch-Theologisches Seminar in Breslau. The advocates of historical positivism proposed moderate reforms, but they had difficulty establishing clear criteria for them. They insisted on belief in the *halakhah*, but the pressures of modernization frequently pushed them to a middle position between Orthodoxy and Reform. Many maintain that the historical-positivist position, as developed in Germany, later influenced the Conservative movement in the U.S.

West European Orthodoxy

West European Orthodox Jews (like Liberal Jews) accepted the definition of Judaism as being a religion only, but their attitude toward Jewish religion was comprehensive. Most were close to the position of Moses Mendelssohn, one of the main figures of the Jewish enlightenment, who in his treatise *Jerusalem* (1783) asserted that Judaism was divine legislation revealed to the Jewish people by God at Mount Sinai and therefore binding, eternal, and irrevocable, both in its principles and in its laws. However, almost all West European Orthodox Jews accepted the principle of the separation of church (religion in general) and state, and regarded their duties as citizens as no less binding than their duties as Jews. It should be noted that among many Orthodox Jews in Western Europe (and later in America), religious practice often diverged from religious principle, objective conditions making full observance of all the details of classical Judaism exceedingly difficult.

A serious confrontation between the Orthodox and the Liberal (Reform) currents took place in Germany. In the nineteenth century, most Jewish communities in Germany, which originally had held the classical position, became Liberal. Synagogues that introduced organ playing during the religious service, for example, often lost the Orthodox members of their congregations.

Neo-Orthodoxy in Germany

The leading figure of what came to be known in the second half of the nineteenth century as neo-Orthodoxy was Samson Raphael Hirsch, rabbi of the Orthodox segment of the Jewish community in Frankfurt-on-the-Main. Hirsch formulated the principle of *Torah im derech eretz*, meaning the Jewish classical observant position combined with full participation in general German cultural life. Hirsch and his followers were extreme on both counts: they were equally scrupulous in the total observance of *halakhah* and *mitzvot*, in the performance of their civic duties as German citizens, and in their participation in German culture. They organized their own communities (Secession Laws of 1876 and 1878), in which they isolated themselves in order to follow their own Jewish way of life. But not all those associated with neo-Orthodoxy agreed with the separatist tendencies of the Frankfurt group. For instance, Rabbi Azriel Hildesheimer, who served the neo-Orthodox community of Berlin (Adath Israel) and in 1873 founded an Orthodox rabbinical seminary there, was more open-minded about working with other Jewish institutions, and later became interested in the Hibbat Zion movement.

Ultra-Orthodoxy in Hungary

The confrontation between reformers and defenders of classical Judaism in Hungary was particularly bitter. The latter developed a position that, because of its extremism, has been called ultra-Orthodoxy. Rabbi Moses Sofer ("Hatam Sofer"), yeshiva head in Pressburg, Hungary, from 1806 to 1839, laid the foundations of ultra-Orthodoxy by interpreting a passage in the Talmud, *Hehadash assur min ha-Torah* (New is forbidden by the Torah), as meaning that any innovation, merely by virtue of being an innovation, is forbidden—not only in religious practice, but in all aspects of life. Some of his disciples were even more extreme (decisions of the

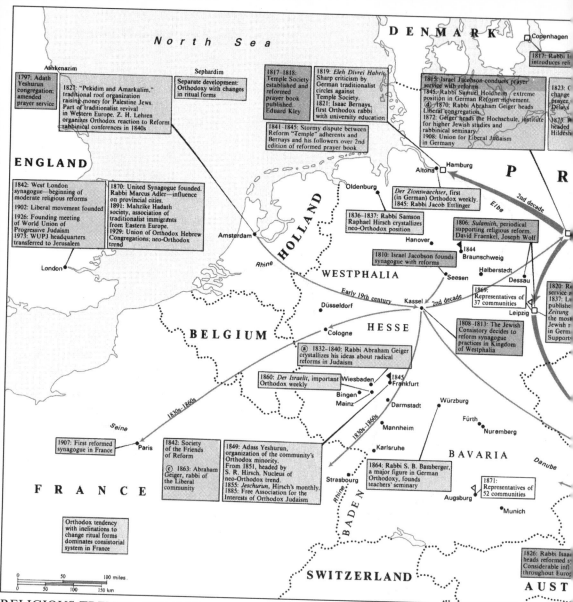

North Sea

DENMARK

Copenhagen

1817: Rabbi I
introduces reli

Ashkenazim

Sephardim

1797: Adath
Yeshurun
congregation;
amended
prayer service

1827: "Pekidim and Amarkalim,"
traditional roof organization
raising money for Palestine Jews.
Part of traditionalist revival
in Western Europe. Z. H. Lehren
organizes Orthodox reaction to Reform
rabbinical conferences in 1840s

Separate development:
Orthodoxy with changes
in ritual forms

1817-1818:
Temple Society
established and
reformed
prayer book
published.
Eduard Kley

1819: Eleh Divrei Habrit.
Sharp criticism by
German traditionalist
circles against
Temple Society.
1821: Isaac Bernays,
first Orthodox rabbi
with university education

1843: Israel Jacobson conducts prayer
service with reforms
1845: Rabbi Samuel Holdheim – extreme
position in German Reform movement.
(d.) 1870: Rabbi Abraham Geiger heads
Liberal congregation.
1872: Geiger heads the Hochschule, institute
for higher Jewish studies and
rabbinical seminary.
1908: Union for Liberal Judaism
in Germany

1823: C
change
prayer.
Delays

1873: I
headed
Hildesh

1841-1845: Stormy dispute between
Reform "Temple" adherents and
Bernays and his followers over 2nd
edition of reformed prayer book

ENGLAND

1842: West London
synagogue—beginning of
moderate religious reforms
1902: Liberal movement founded
1926: Founding meeting
of World Union of
Progressive Judaism
1973: WUPJ headquarters
transferred to Jerusalem

1870: United Synagogue founded.
Rabbi Marcus Adler—influence
on provincial cities.
1891: Mahzike Hadath
society, association of
traditionalist immigrants
from Eastern Europe.
1929: Union of Orthodox Hebrew
Congregations; neo-Orthodox
trend

HOLLAND

Amsterdam

Rhine

London

Oldenburg

Altona ☐ Hamburg

P R

R

Der Zionswaechter, first
(in German) Orthodox weekly.
1845: Rabbi Jacob Ettlinger

Elbe

2nd decade

1836-1837: Rabbi Samson
Raphael Hirsch crystallizes
neo-Orthodox position

1806: Sulamith, periodical
supporting religious reform.
David Fraenkel, Joseph Wolf

Hanover

1844
Braunschweig

1810: Israel Jacobson founds
synagogue with reforms

Halberstadt

Dessau

WESTPHALIA

Seesen

Early 19th century

Kassel

2nd decade

1869:
Representatives of
37 communities

Leipzig

1820: R
service w
1837: L
publishe
Zeitung
the most
Jewish r
in Germa
Supports

Düsseldorf

BELGIUM

Cologne

HESSE

1808-1813: The Jewish
Consistory decides to
reform synagogue
practices in Kingdom
of Westphalia

Ⓐ 1832-1840: Rabbi Abraham Geiger
crystallizes his ideas about radical
reforms in Judaism

1860: Der Israelit, important
Orthodox weekly

Wiesbaden

1845
Frankfurt

Bingen

Darmstadt

Würzburg

Mainz

1830s-1860s

1907: First reformed
synagogue in France

Seine

Paris

1842: Society
of the Friends
of Reform

Ⓒ 1863: Abraham
Geiger, rabbi of
the Liberal
community

1849: Adass Yeshurun,
organization of the community's
Orthodox minority.
From 1851, headed by
S. R. Hirsch. Nucleus of
neo-Orthodox trend.
1855: Jeschurun, Hirsch's monthly.
1885: Free Association for the
Interests of Orthodox Judaism

Fürth

Nuremberg

Mannheim

Karlsruhe

BAVARIA

Danube

Strasbourg

1864: Rabbi S. B. Bamberger,
a major figure in German
Orthodoxy, founds
teachers' seminary

Augsburg

1871:
Representatives of
52 communities

Munich

FRANCE

1830s-1860s

Rhine

BADEN

Orthodox tendency
with inclinations to
change ritual forms
dominates consistorial
system in France

1826: Rabbi Isaac
heads reformed s
Considerable infl
throughout Europ

0   50   100 miles
0 50 100 150 km

SWITZERLAND

AUST

RELIGIOUS TRENDS AND INSTITUTIONS AMONG EUROPEAN JEWS

Michalovce Orthodox convention, Jewish groups that did not adopt their position. But their principles were not accepted by the majority of Hungarian Orthodox rabbis, and their influence was limited mainly to the northeastern part of the country.

The religious split inside Hungarian Jewry was officially recognized after the General Jewish Congress, held in Buda-

pest from the end of 1868, whose aim had been to create an overall Jewish organization. Under pressure of the ultra-Orthodox, the Orthodox also rejected collaboration with the reformers, the Neologists. In the following years, Hungarian Jewry remained divided into three main camps: the Neologists, the Orthodox (including the ultra-Orthodox), and the Status Quo Ante communities, which

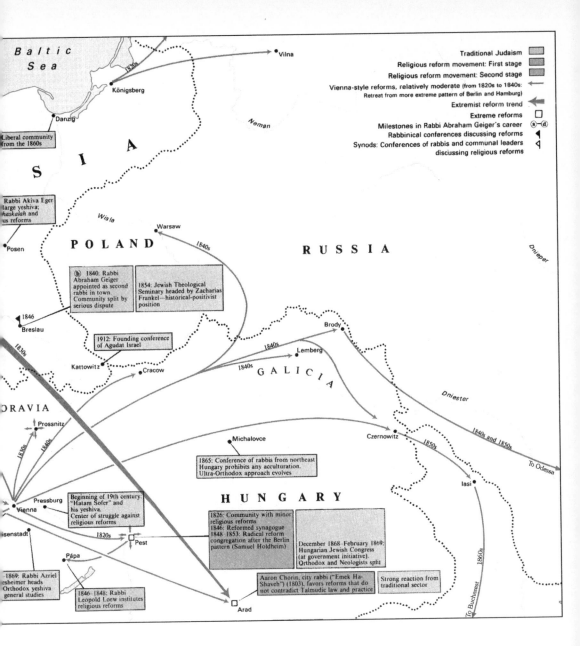

Traditional Judaism ▭
Religious reform movement: First stage ▭
Religious reform movement: Second stage ▭
Vienna-style reforms, relatively moderate (from 1820s to 1840s: ←
Retreat from more extreme pattern of Berlin and Hamburg) ◄
Extremist reform trend ◄
Extreme reforms ▢
Milestones in Rabbi Abraham Geiger's career ⓐ–ⓓ
Rabbinical conferences discussing reforms ◄
Synods: Conferences of rabbis and communal leaders discussing religious reforms ◁

Baltic Sea

Vilna

Königsberg

Danzig

Liberal community from the 1860s

S I A

Neman

Rabbi Akiva Eger large yeshiva; *haskalah* and us reforms

Posen

Wisla

Warsaw

1840s

POLAND

RUSSIA

Dnieper

ⓑ 1840: Rabbi Abraham Geiger appointed as second rabbi in town. Community split by serious dispute

1854: Jewish Theological Seminary headed by Zacharias Frankel—historical-positivist position

1846
Breslau

1912: Founding conference of Agudat Israel

Brody

1840s
Lemberg

Kattowitz

Cracow

1840s

G A L I C I A

Dniester

ORAVIA

Prossnitz

Czernowitz

1850s

1840s and 1850s

To Odessa

Michalovce

1865: Conference of rabbis from northeast Hungary prohibits any acculturation. Ultra-Orthodox approach evolves

Iasi

H U N G A R Y

Pressburg

Vienna

Beginning of 19th century: "Hatam Sofer" and his yeshiva. Center of struggle against religious reforms

1826: Community with minor religious reforms
1846: Reformed synagogue
1848–1853: Radical reform congregation after the Berlin pattern (Samuel Holdheim)

December 1868–February 1869: Hungarian Jewish Congress (at government initiative). Orthodox and Neologists split

1820s

isenstadt

Pest

Pápa

1869: Rabbi Azriel esheimer heads Orthodox yeshiva general studies

1846–1848: Rabbi Leopold Loew institutes religious reforms

Aaron Chorin, city rabbi ("Emek Ha-Shaveh") (1803), favors reforms that do not contradict Talmudic law and practice

Strong reaction from traditional sector

1860s

To Bucharest

Arad

remained loyal to classical Judaism but were ostracized by the Orthodox. Some of the ultra-Orthodox settled in Jerusalem, where they formed a small and extremist faction in the Orthodox community, the Natorei Karta. Another faction emigrated to the United States in the wake of World War II and, led by Rabbi Joel Teitelbaum (the "Satmar Rebbe"), attained a certain influence, notwithstanding its small size.

Religious Zionism

The issue of Zionism also split religious Jewry. The neo-Orthodox, the ultra-Orthodox, Agudat Israel, and, on the opposite religious side, the Reform and Liberal movements vehemently opposed Zionism, each on its own grounds. But broad segments of traditional Jewry very enthusiastically adopted the Zionist idea. Important rabbis were among the leaders and activists of the Hibbat Zion movement. Later, the World Zionist Organization was one of the few modern Jewish institutions in which religious and non-religious Jews coexisted and worked together in spite of the deep differences between them regarding the character of the Jewish society that Zionism aimed to create in Palestine. In 1902, the Mizrachi organization was established, representing the classical religious position in the Zionist movement. Mizrachi quickly became a worldwide organization with hundreds of branches.

ORTHODOXY (*HAREDUT*) IN EASTERN EUROPE

FROM the early nineteenth century on, the leadership of classical East European Judaism was well aware that new spiritual trends developing among Jews, such as the *haskalah* (Jewish enlightenment), ran counter to the traditional Jewish ways of life. But only toward the end of the century did it become clear that those new trends, which had meanwhile grown and assumed many different forms and expressions, posed a danger to classical Judaism. The response to this was resistance, which expressed itself in the formation of the Russian–Polish brand of Orthodoxy, or *Haredut*, in which Mitnagdim and Hasidim collaborated.

The main forum of public activity of the Haredim was Agudat Israel, founded in 1912, with the participation of German neo-Orthodoxy. Its initial aim was to combat the growing Zionist movement. After World War I, Agudat Israel's main center of activity was in Poland, where it also participated in the public life of Polish Jewry, to protect the interests of its adherents.

THE GREAT YESHIVAS IN EASTERN EUROPE AND THE *MUSAR* MOVEMENT

UNTIL the second half of the seventeenth century, the most important yeshivas were in Eastern Europe. Then they declined, and from the late seventeenth to the beginning of the nineteenth century, important centers of religious learning were established in Bohemia, Moravia, and several German-speaking countries. These yeshivas were dependent on the local communities, and were usually headed by the local rabbi. Outstanding among these heads of yeshivas

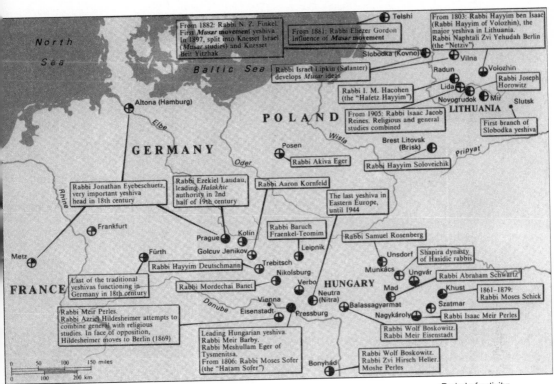

THE GREAT YESHIVAS IN EASTERN EUROPE AND THE *MUSAR* MOVEMENT

Period of activity:
- 18th century
- First half of 19th century
- Second half of 19th century
- First half of 20th century

was Rabbi Jonathan Eybeschuetz, who taught in Prague, Metz, and Altona. The students came from all over Europe, and they were exposed to the different spiritual trends of the time, such as Shabbateanism, on the one hand, and *haskalah*, on the other. In the nineteenth century, the "great yeshivas" were created in Eastern Europe.

Rabbi Jonathan Eyebeschuetz.

The Lithuanian Yeshivas

In 1803, Rabbi Hayyim ben Isaac (Volozhiner) established a yeshiva in Volozhin that soon became the outstanding academy of its kind in Lithuania. The yeshiva (later named Etz Hayyim) differed from others in at least two respects. It was independent of the local community, being supported by contributions from all over Lithuania and beyond. And it accepted only long-term students, most

of whom came from outside Volozhin. Other yeshivas were established in Lithuania on similar principles, but none became as famous as Etz Hayyim.

The *Musar* movement developed out of the great yeshivas in the second half of the nineteenth century, under the inspiration of Rabbi Israel Lipkin of Salant, commonly known as Rabbi Israel Salanter. The movement stressed pietism and ethical-moral conduct, combined with formal religious studies. It reflected the spiritual restlessness characteristic of East European Jewry at the time, but it was an inner-directed trend that paid little attention to the non-Jewish environment and concentrated on traditional Jewish issues.

Toward the end of the nineteenth century, Rabbi Israel's influence gave rise to yeshivas of a new type, the *Musar* yeshivas. Existing yeshivas, too, adopted many of his ideas. The *Musar* yeshivas had a considerable influence on the religious life of East European Jewry.

The Hungarian Yeshivas
Of far-reaching importance was the institution founded in Pressburg in 1807 by Rabbi Moses Sofer (the "Hatam Sofer"). In 1857, the authorities recognized it as a rabbinical seminary, thus qualifying its students for exemption from military service. In 1866, that exemption was extended to students at other Hungarian yeshivas.

The Pressburg yeshiva inculcated in its students total and unquestioning adherence to classical Judaism, and, together with related yeshivas, it played an important role in the struggle against the Reform movement in Hungary. After World War I, parts of Hungary were incorporated into other countries. Pressburg, in the Slovakian "Oberland," became part of Czechoslovakia (and was renamed Bratislava). The eastern part of the country was turned over to Romania. The original yeshiva continued to function, and several new ones were established in a now smaller Hungary.

THE HASIDIC MOVEMENT 19TH CENTURY

THE political changes in Eastern Europe influenced the development of Hasidism during the nineteenth century. The partitions of Poland (where the movement originated) in the second half of the eighteenth century divided its Jewish population (and Hasidism) between Russia, Prussia, and Austria. In the nineteenth century, the movement spread to Hungary, Romania, Palestine, and, later (to a smaller extent), the new centers of Jewish immigration in Western Europe and North America.

The structure of the Hasidic movement underwent changes in two main directions: first, the Hasidic leaders dispersed as the sons and grandsons of the founders themselves became heads of Hasidic groups; second, there arose large, new, and powerful Hasidic dynasties, whose influence extended far beyond the areas of their leaders' residence.

The major Hasidic centers in Europe were destroyed in the Holocaust. Hasidic leaders and followers who survived created new centers in America and Israel.

THE RELIGIOUS ORGANIZATION OF AMERICAN JEWRY MID-19TH AND EARLY 20TH CENTURIES

THE few Jewish communities in North America in the eighteenth century were tradition-minded, although their members were not fully observant. From the mid-nineteenth century on, Jewish immigrants brought with them the ideas about ritual and religion being debated in Europe. In the American environment,

⊚ Main city
★ Locality linked to Hasidism

– – Borders in mid-19th century
– – Borders of Poland and Galicia

these ideas developed along new lines, resulting in the different American Jewish religious currents.

The Reform movement developed during the period of the German Jewish immigration (the late nineteenth century) and was the first to establish its own institutions (rabbinical seminary, union of congregations, and organization of rabbis). In 1885 at the Pittsburgh Con-

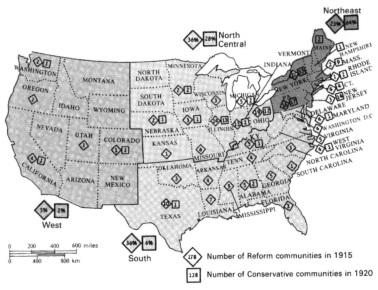

THE RELIGIOUS
ORGANIZATION
OF AMERICAN
JEWRY
EARLY 20TH
CENTURY

178 Number of Reform communities in 1915

128 Number of Conservative communities in 1920

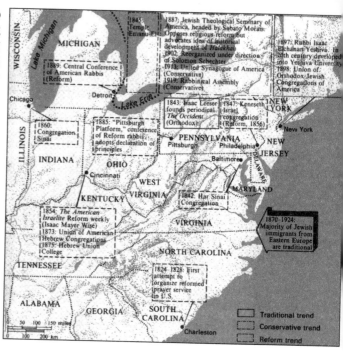

REFORM AND
CONSERVATIVE
CONGREGATIONS IN
THE UNITED STATES
EARLY 20TH CENTURY

vention, the Reform leaders (Isaac Mayer Wise and his colleagues) elaborated the principles of the American Reform movement, which was extreme in its position, adopting far-reaching religious innovations and, later, becoming anti-Zionist.

The large mass immigration from Eastern Europe brought mostly Orthodox Jews to the United States. But under the impact of American conditions, Orthodoxy lost most of the public overtones that characterized it in Eastern Europe. At the beginning of the twentieth century, a new religious movement was established, the Conservative trend. As formulated by Solomon Schechter, Conservative Judaism was traditional and strictly observant, but geared to the English language and the American way of life. It had a certain affinity with the European historical-positivist position.

Over the years, as American Jewry underwent deep changes, so did the different religious positions in its midst. There was a general trend away from Orthodoxy and toward more flexible religious positions, and second- and third-generation Jews became Reform, Conservative, or religiously indifferent. The religious trends themselves also changed. The Reform movement gradually became less radical, developing a new interest in tradition and, over the years, a more positive attitude toward Zionism. The Orthodox trend split in several directions, and many of its members were impelled to compromise regarding many mitzvoth, such as traveling on the Sabbath. The Conservative movement was caught in the middle, although it aspired to create an original position. One offshoot of it was the Reconstructionist movement, created in the 1930s and 1940s by Mordecai M. Kaplan.

Hasidic leaders who arrived in the United States before and after World War II established Hasidic courts and yeshivas there, and strengthened the classical Orthodox camp.

MODERN ANTISEMITISM: IDEOLOGICAL SOURCES

ONE of the great hopes of nineteenth-century Jewry was that the strengthening of liberal trends in the general society would banish the age-old hatred of the Jews. Indeed, certain developments during the 1860s and early 1870s in France, England, Germany, Austria-Hungary, and even Russia seemed to bear out this hope. But from the end of the 1870s, changes occurred in the attitude of large sectors of European society to the Jews, and the old tensions between non-Jews and Jews reappeared. A review of the century from 1850 to 1945 reveals a fateful symmetry between the progress that the Jews in Europe made toward civil equality and the growing animosity of the general society toward them: the better the civil status of the Jews, the more threatening the antisemitic manifestations erupting in the very society that was recognizing them as full citizens.

New expressions of animosity against Jews now appeared—"modern" antisemitism—although the older forms continued to exist among certain segments of the population. Modern antisemitism had many carriers: social groups pushed aside by modern development, especially in the larger cities; urban dwellers who in the late nineteenth century acquired full political rights but remained economically deprived; the lower middle class, which feared absorption into the proletariat; and intellectuals trying to understand and explain the transformations that modern society was undergoing. These and other groups resented the new Jewish presence in modern society: Jews were now full citizens, quite successful culturally and economically, yet somehow they seemed to be different, keeping to themselves and enjoying all the advantages of modern society without fulfilling all the conditions implicit in their new rights. The resentment of the antisemites was fed by populist ideas tinged with romantic and nationalistic overtones. New racial and social theories influenced public opinion. Most of these had little to do with the Jews: Social Darwinism, race anthropology, or the social conditions in the new large cities had no intrinsic antisemitic significance. Under the influence of the old anti-Jewish hatred, however, they became the components of modern antisemitism. The traditional negative stereotype of the Jew remained unchanged, although it now assumed new expressions. The classical image of the base, cringing Jew was replaced by one of the mighty, aggressive, domineering Jew. It was now said that a historical struggle existed between the Jews and the Germans (Marr, 1879) or between Judaism and Christianity (Dostoyevsky, 1877), in which the Jews had the upper hand. It was said that the Jews dominated the German stock exchanges and its press (Treitschke, 1880) and French finances (Drumont, 1886). Racial theory, which became popular in the late nineteenth century, was used to maintain that there were basic differences between the Jewish race and the Aryan race, the latter being represented in its purest form by the Germanic peoples (Chamberlain, 1899). Close to this line of thought was the belief in the existence of an international Jewish conspiracy to take over the world. This canard was spread throughout Europe before and especially after World War I, receiving its most elaborate exposition in the book *The Protocols of the Learned Elders of Zion.*

Whereas in the older kind of antisemitism religious beliefs had played a central role, modern antisemitism was secular in

The Ideology of Modern Antisemitism

The negative image (stereotype) of the Jew as developed in Christian consciousness over the centuries appears from the end of the 18th century with new expressions, mostly along nonreligious lines.

Voltaire French philosopher, *Dictionnaire philosophique* (1764): Jews as fanatics and barbarians

J. G. Fichte German philosopher (end of 18th century): Jews as a powerful group spread throughout Europe and in strife with everybody

J. F. Fries German writer (beginning of 19th century): Jews are acceptable as citizens, but Judaism has to be rejected

P. J. Proudhon French socialist (mid-19th century): Jews as a domineering people, enemies of mankind

B. Bauer (1843), **K. Marx** (1844) Leftist intellectuals: critical of the social position and economic role of the Jews

A. Toussenel French writer, *Les Juifs rois de l'époque* (1845)

K. Freigedank [R. Wagner] German composer (1850): Jews have a destructive influence on European arts

M. A. Bakunin Russian revolutionary (second half of 19th century): Jews as exploiters dominating Europe; extreme hatred of Jews, which influenced other revolutionaries

F. M. Dostoyevsky Russian writer, *Diary* (1877): Jews as a separate nation, very talented, dominating the Christian world

P. A. de Lagarde German Orientalist, *Deutsche Schriften* (1878): against liberalism, against the Jews; influenced populist (*voelkisch*) circles

W. Marr German writer (1879): Judaism conquered Germanism and dominates it

H. von Treitschke German historian (1880): Jews should give up their excessive influence on German life and assimilate into the German nation

T. Mommsen German historian (1880): not an antisemite, but against a specific Jewish presence in the German nation

K. E. Duehring German philosopher (1881): extreme racial hatred of Jews, proposes their extermination

E. A. Drumont French writer, *La France juive* (1886): Jews dominate the economic, social, and cultural life of France

G. von Schoenerer Austrian politician (end of 19th century): racial antisemite, forerunner of the National Socialist position; influenced Hitler

H. Class [D. Frymann] German politician (1912): pan-Germanism and racial antisemitism; forbid Jewish immigration into Germany and limit civil rights of Jews living in the country

The Development of Race Theory

Racialism	Anthropology
Qualitative approach to certain races	From end of 18th century, development of modern anthropology, one branch of which is the race theory: distinction among races according to such traits as skin color, body structure, head form, and hair texture

Count J. de Gobineau French intellectual (mid-19th century): stresses the social importance of racial traits; not an antisemite, but later influenced extreme antisemites

19th century philology: the common roots of Indo-European (or Indo-German languages seem to indicate kinship between these peoples

F. Nietzsche German philosopher (second half of 18th century): despises antisemites, but elements of his ideas were incorporated into extremist racial antisemitism

E. Renan French intellectual (second half of 19th century): moderate racist; superiority of Aryans over Semites; Jews as race

The racist approach uses the conclusions of scientific research on races for its own purposes

G. Vacher de Lapouge French writer (end of 19th century): racist; the moral superiority of the Aryan peoples

Growing influence of populist (*voelkisch*) ideas in the 19th century: emphasis on the "soul" of the German people and its historical roots. Approach found among many antisemites; close to the racist position

H.S. Chamberlain Anglo-German writer, *Foundations of the Nineteenth Century* (1899): importance of race; superiority of German race, and negative influence of Jews

The Development of Social Darwinism

H. Spencer English philosopher, *Social Statics* (1851), *The Principles of Biology* (1864–1867): idea of the survival of the fittest, meaning the socially fittest

C. Darwin Engl anthropologist, *the Origin of Spec* (1859): idea of n ural selection in evolution of speci with no social mea ing

Darwinism (second half of 19th century) The struggle for survival among groups (als human groups) as a central characteristic life

Social Darwinism (beginning of 20th century): the struggle for survival among human groups or racial groups as typical and even necessary characteristic of life

Tendencies close to antisemitism

Antisemitic tendencies

Scientific or philosophical theories used by antisemitic ideologists

Protocols of the Elders of Zion (anonymous, first quarter of 20th century): international Jewish conspiracy to dominate the world; disseminated mainly after World War I in many languages

A. Hitler, *Mein Kampf* (1925–1927): Hitler's political program, in which the struggle against Jews and Judaism has a central role

ts views and its solutions to the Jewish threat. Some of these solutions were "moderate": the total integration of the Jews into the general society, meaning also renunciation of their specific group characteristics (Treitschke, 1880). The more extreme attitude advocated curtailing the civil rights of the Jews and halting Jewish immigration from Eastern Europe (Class, 1912). The most extreme approach declared that there was no possibility of integrating the Jews and that, in any event, such a step was highly dangerous for German society, and therefore the best solution was the "elimination" of the Jews (Duehring, 1881; Hitler, 1919).

Antisemitic agitation reached a peak in the last two decades of the nineteenth century, and subsided early in the twentieth. But it did not disappear, and the new antisemitic ideas gradually insinuated themselves into the general anti-Jewish feeling of many segments of the general population, capable of flaring up again under the right conditions.

The emergence of modern antisemitism was a bitter disappointment to those sectors of Jewish society that had integrated culturally and socially into the general society. They had trouble coping with the new phenomenon, because its irrational and intolerant character was so out of tune with the liberal and enlightened principles that were part of the ideological basis for Jewish acculturation. Only gradually did they create organizations aimed (among other things) at combating antisemitism by means of the law and of publicity, such as the Centralverein in Germany (1893) or the Anti-Defamation League of B'nai B'rith in the United States (1913). But these measures could not halt the growth of modern antisemitism or change its character. The more extreme trends prevailed and brought about the near extermination of European Jewry by the Germans (with the active or passive participation of other European peoples) during World War II.

Antisemitism did not disappear in the second half of the twentieth century, although it changed many of its slogans. The emergence of the Jewish state, the continuing Arab-Israeli conflict, and the perpetuation of historical anti-Jewish attitudes created new expressions of contemporary antisemitism. Although the Zionist movement and the state of Israel served as central themes in this new version, the antisemites of the late twentieth century made little distinction between Jews in Israel and Jews elsewhere. The tension between Jews and non-Jews seemed to be a persistent phenomenon, its forms changing according to circumstances.

ANTISEMITIC PARTIES AND ORGANIZATIONS IN EUROPE LATE 19TH AND EARLY 20TH CENTURIES

THE new ideology of antisemitism found diverse public, political, and organizational expressions in different European countries. Antisemitic congresses were held in Germany in the 1880s, antisemitic parties were formed in Germany and Austria–Hungary, and antisemitic planks were included in the political platforms of existing parties even if antisemitism was not their main political aim (the Conservative Party in Germany, 1892).

The May Laws against the Jews promulgated in Russia in 1882 indicated a new and much more negative attitude by

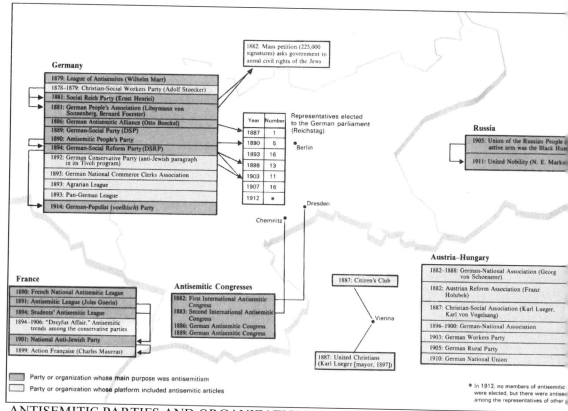

Germany

1879: League of Antisemites (Wilhelm Marr)	
1878–1879: Christian-Social Workers Party (Adolf Stoecker)	
1881: Social Reich Party (Ernst Henrici)	
1881: German People's Association (Libermann von Sonnenberg, Bernard Foerster)	
1886: German Antisemitic Alliance (Otto Boeckel)	
1889: German-Social Party (DSP)	
1890: Antisemitic People's Party	
1894: German-Social Reform Party (DSRP)	
1892: German Conservative Party (anti-Jewish paragraph in its Tivoli program)	
1893: German National Commerce Clerks Association	
1893: Agrarian League	
1893: Pan-German League	
1914: German-Populist (*voelkisch*) Party	

1882: Mass petition (225,000 signatures) asks government to annul civil rights of the Jews

Year	Number
1887	1
1890	5
1893	16
1898	13
1903	11
1907	16
1912	*

Representatives elected to the German parliament (Reichstag)

Berlin

Dresden

Chemnitz

Russia

1905: Union of the Russian People (active arm was the Black Hun
1911: United Nobility (N. E. Marko

France

1890: French National Antisemitic League
1891: Antisemitic League (Jules Guerin)
1894: Students' Antisemitic League
1894–1906: "Dreyfus Affair." Antisemitic trends among the conservative parties
1901: National Anti-Jewish Party
1899: Action Française (Charles Maurras)

Antisemitic Congresses

1882: First International Antisemitic Congress
1883: Second International Antisemitic Congress
1886: German Antisemitic Congress
1889: German Antisemitic Congress

1887: Citizen's Club

Vienna

1887: United Christians (Karl Lueger [mayor, 1897])

Austria–Hungary

1882–1888: German-National Association (Georg von Schoenerer)
1882: Austrian Reform Association (Franz Holubek)
1887: Christian-Social Association (Karl Lueger, Karl von Vogelsang)
1896–1900: German-National Association
1903: German Workers Party
1905: German Rural Party
1910: German National Union

Party or organization whose main purpose was antisemitism

Party or organization whose platform included antisemitic articles

* In 1912, no members of antisemiti were elected, but there were antise among the representatives of other

ANTISEMITIC PARTIES AND ORGANIZATIONS IN EUROPE

the government toward its large Jewish population and helped to create the conditions that led to the anti-Jewish riots in later years. The Dreyfus Affair in France (from 1894) injected antisemitism into the discussion of the political problems of the Third Republic, causing a sharp increase in antisemitism among all strata of the French population. French antisemites did not organize into separate parties, but were active in the existing right-wing parties.

THE "HEP-HEP" DISTURBANCES 1819

THE violent expression of anti-Jewish feeling gradually intensified from the nineteenth to the twentieth century.

In 1819, a wave of riots, called the "Hep-Hep" disturbances, erupted against Jews in Germany and Denmark. The first incidents occurred in southern Germany, and from there they spread to the north and west. Jews were attacked in several large cities—Frankfurt, Hamburg, Copenhagen—and in small towns and villages in Baden, Württemberg, and Bavaria, where they had been living for many generations. The main reasons for the incidents were traditional anti-Jewish hatred and economic tensions. Much damage was done to Jewish property, but few Jews were physically attacked. Almost without exception, the authorities took steps against the assailants and order was quickly restored. Nevertheless, the "Hep-Hep" incidents deeply affected

THE "HEP-HEP" DISTURBANCES

the Jews and caused many of those who had been hopeful about Jewish acculturation in German society to reevaluate their situation. An indirect outcome of the incidents was the formation of the Gesellschaft zur Foerderung der Wissenschaft des Judentums (Society for the Advancement of Jewish Scholarship) in 1819, which over the years generated a new cultural trend in Jewry on the road to modernization.

Sketch of "Hep-Hep" disturbances of 1819, printed in Frankfurt at that time.

ANTI-JEWISH RIOTS DURING THE 1848 REVOLUTIONS

SERIOUS anti-Jewish riots erupted in many of the countries swept by the 1848 revolutions, from Alsace in France to Hungary. The riots were not related to the revolutions and their aims or to Jewish participation in them in several important cities, such as Berlin and Vienna. They were a product of the general situation of upheaval, and the rioters were mainly farmers, apprentices, and members of the lower middle class. The authorities and the social groups

Map labels:
North Sea
Baltic Sea
HOLLAND
PRUSSIA
RUSSIAN EMPIRE
Weser
Elbe
Berlin
Poles rampage against the Jews during the revolution in Prussia
Posen
Trzemeszno
Buk
Wreschen
Wisla
Warsaw
BELGIUM
Rhine
Rimbach
Rotenburg
THURINGIA
SAXONY
POLAND
Oder
February-March
Reichelsheim
Würzburg
Prague
Zabern
Bruchsal
Bamberg
Kolín
FRANCE
Brumath
BAVARIA
April-May
Prossnitz
April-May
Thann
Marmoutier
Ungarisch-Brod
Eperjes
Altkirch
BADEN
Waag-Neustadtl
Seppois
Müllheim
March-April
Danube
Vienna
Sered
HAPSBURG
Pfirt
Durmenach
Pressburg
EMPIRE
SWITZERLAND
Eisenstadt
Budapest
0 50 100 150 miles
0 100 200 km
Stuhlweissenburg
Klausenburg

★ Anti-Jewish attacks
⊛ Areas where attacks caused great damage
April-May │ Period of disturbances

ANTI-JEWISH RIOTS DURING THE REVOLUTIONS OF 1848

active in the revolutions—the middle class and the intellectuals—acted forcefully to stop the riots.

The riots of 1848 were a source of bitter disillusionment for the Jews, especially those who had supported the revolutions.

Many concluded that it was more realistic to seek a better future elsewhere and migrated to the United States, where they were part of the immigrant group that came to be known as "the '48ers."

ANTI-JEWISH RIOTS IN RUSSIA 1881 TO 1906

AN additional chapter in the increasingly bloody story of anti-Jewish violence unfolded in Russia in the last half of the nineteenth century. Serious anti-Jewish riots broke out in Odessa in 1871 (on a smaller scale, also earlier). In 1881, after the assassination of Czar Alexander II, a wave of anti-Jewish riots swept southern Russia. A result of the old antagonism between non-Jews and Jews, this violence reflected the general unrest following the czar's death. There is no evidence that the authorities had a hand in the riots, but the railway network being built in southern Russia facilitated the movement of the rioters from place to

place. The attacks spread to Poland and the Baltic states, continuing until 1884.

A much more murderous wave of riots swept the Pale of Settlement between 1903 and 1906. Although the government may not have encouraged the incidents, persons or groups connected with the authorities organized or planned the attacks, and soldiers or policemen participated. From Kishinev in 1903 to Siedlce in 1906, thousands of Jews were killed or wounded and Jewish life in Russia was seriously disrupted. The mass emigration of Jews from Russia and Poland to Western Europe and across the ocean to America during these years

Anti-Jewish Riots in Russia, 1881–1906

Nizhniy Novgorod★
June 1884

Baltic Sea

Dvina

LITHUANIA

○ Vilna

Shklov ○

Neman

Dnieper

Oka

RUSSIAN EMPIRE

2
1881: Railroads facilitate the spread of the riots. Many rioters are laborers streaming to the south in search of work and railroad workers living in camps along the lines

GERMANY

○ Mogilev

Bialystok ○
June 1906

BELORUSSIA

Gomel ★
September 1903

Warsaw ★
Siedlce ○
August 1906

Pripyat'

Chernigov ⊛
Konotop ⊛

Kiev ⊛
May 1905

POLAND

Rovno ○

Zhitomir ○
U K R A I N E

Romny ⊛
October 1905

Don

Wisła

Autumn 1904

Volochisk ★

Fastov ★
Smela
Autumn 1904 ⊛

Kremenchug
□

Lozovaya ★

Dnieper

Kamenets Podolskiy □

Zhmerinka
Yelizavetgrad

Yekaterinoslav ⊛

Rostov ★

AUSTRIA–HUNGARY

Balta ⊛

Aleksandriya □

Spring 1883

Kishinev ⊛
April 1903

Odessa □
Nikolayev ⊛

Melitopol' ○

N E W

★ Aleksandrovsk

1
1821, 1859, 1871, 1881:
Religious tension and business competition turn the city into a center of repeated riots

Odessa ⊛

R U S S I A

April 1905

1882–1884: Riots spread throughout New Russia and the Ukraine

Feodosiya ○
February 1905

0   50   100   150 miles
0   100   200 km

October 1905 (300 dead)

Simferopol' □

Black Sea

— Pale of Settlement
★ Major community hit by the riots of 1881–1884
(relatively few casualties)
○ Major community hit by the riots of 1903–1906

□ Riots of October–November 1905 (most serious wave)
★ Jewish self-defense groups
⊪⊪⊪⊪ Rail line

The City of Slaughter by H. N. Bialik

Arise and go now to the city of slaughter;
Into its courtyard wind thy way;
There with thy own hand touch, and with the eyes
  of thine head,
Behold on tree, on stone, on fence, on mural clay,
The spattered blood and dried brains of the dead.
Proceed thence to the ruins, the split walls reach,
Where wider grows the hollow, and greater
  grows the breach;
Pass over the shattered hearth, attain the broken
  wall
Whose burnt and barren brick, whose charred
  stones reveal
The open mouths of such wounds, that no
  mending

Shall ever mend, nor healing ever heal.
There will thy feet in feathers sink, and stumble
On wreckage doubly wrecked, scroll heaped on
  manuscript,
Fragments against fragmented —
Pause not upon this havoc; go thy way....

Descend then, to the cellars of the town,
There where the virginal daughters of thy folk
  were fouled,
Where seven heathen flung a woman down,
The daughter in the presence of her mother,
The mother in the presence of her daughter,
Before slaughter, during slaughter, and after
  slaughter!

(Written after 1903 Kishinev pogrom)

attested to the panic that had seized the Jewish communities.

In the late nineteenth and early twentieth centuries, anti-Jewish riots occurred also in some Muslim countries. They were generally connected with the tensions arising from the domination of these countries by European powers and the internal upheaval caused by the gradual process of modernization. In Algeria, where the Jews acquired French citizenship in 1870 (Crémieux Decree), they were sporadically attacked until the beginning of the twentieth century. The French occupation of Morocco in 1912 generated severe riots against the Jews of Fez.

BLOOD LIBELS 19TH AND 20TH CENTURIES

THE blood libel—the accusation that Jews use Christian blood, especially that of children, for various ritual purposes, such as the preparation of *matzot* (unleavened bread for Passover)—was one of the most terrible superstitions to develop in the Middle Ages. The fact that the blood libel continued into the modern period showed how deeply hatred of Jews was ingrained in popular culture. Although in modern times, blood libels happened mostly in the more backward parts of Europe, their influence was widely felt, since they were the subject of trials that received extensive newspaper coverage. Antisemitic groups everywhere exploited the blood libels for their own purposes, even when they did not believe in them. Several blood libels were of particular significance in modern times.

The Damascus Affair
In February 1840, a French monk and his Muslim servant disappeared in Damascus, and the local Jews were accused of murdering them to use their blood. Through collaboration between the French consul in Damascus and the Turkish governor, several Jewish notables were imprisoned and tortured. Two died and the others "confessed," but since they were unable to produce the corpses, the tortures continued. Leading Jewish figures, including Adolphe Crémieux in France and Moses Montefiore in England, asked their governments to intercede on behalf of the Damascus Jews, who were finally freed.

The Beilis Affair
Menahem Mendel Beilis was accused in March 1913 of killing a Christian boy near Kiev, Russia. Various antisemitic leaders and organizations demanded a blood-libel trial. The trial, held in Kiev in 1913, attracted international attention. A jury acquitted Beilis.

The Leo Frank Affair
Blood-libel accusations were heard even in the United States, although rarely. In April 1913, Leo Frank of Atlanta, Georgia, was accused of killing a fourteen-year-old girl. In an atmosphere charged with prejudice, in which Frank's Jewishness featured prominently, he was tried, convicted, and sentenced to death. When the governor of Georgia commuted his sentence to a life term, an incensed mob took Frank from jail and lynched him.

In 1928, a little Christian girl vanished in Massena, New York, a few days before Yom Kippur. The police were question-

ing the local rabbi about the alleged Jewish custom of using the blood of Christian children for ritual purposes, and a mob was preparing a lynching, when the girl was found in the nearby woods, unharmed.

Jewish organizations and individuals reacted vigorously against the resurgent blood libel, taking steps to persuade the authorities and the public that such accusations were utterly false.

BLOOD LIBELS
19TH–20TH CENTURIES

JUDAIC STUDIES 19TH AND 20TH CENTURIES

THE "Science of Judaism" (*Wissenschaft des Judenthums*) was an outgrowth of the Jewish enlightenment. The scholars engaged in it aimed to examine the cultural and spiritual creations of Judaism, using the scientific methods and tools developed in Europe since the eighteenth century. A major definer of its aims was Leopold Zunz, who in 1818 drew up a plan dividing the scientific study of Judaism according to different themes. He and other scholars of his time (Zacharias Frankel, Samuel David Luzzatto, Solomon Rapoport, Abraham Geiger) established the gradual division of the Science of Judaism into various fields, including history, literature, philology, and philosophy.

The attitude to the Science of Judaism varied over the years. The first generation of scholars, especially those from Western and Central Europe, were inclined to regard their work as no different from the study of any past culture—such as ancient Greek or Roman culture—whose spiritual creativity had ended. They tried to show that Judaism, like other great classical cultures, was part of and had helped to shape Western civilization. This provided an additional argument in support of Jewish integration into modern European society: the spiritual contribution of the Jewish people. Different aims for the Science of Judaism were formulated from the second half of the nineteenth century by a new generation of Jewish scholars, who regarded the study and research of Judaism as an expression of a living, developing culture.

The progress of Jewish studies led to the creation of institutions of higher learning, scientific journals, and societies

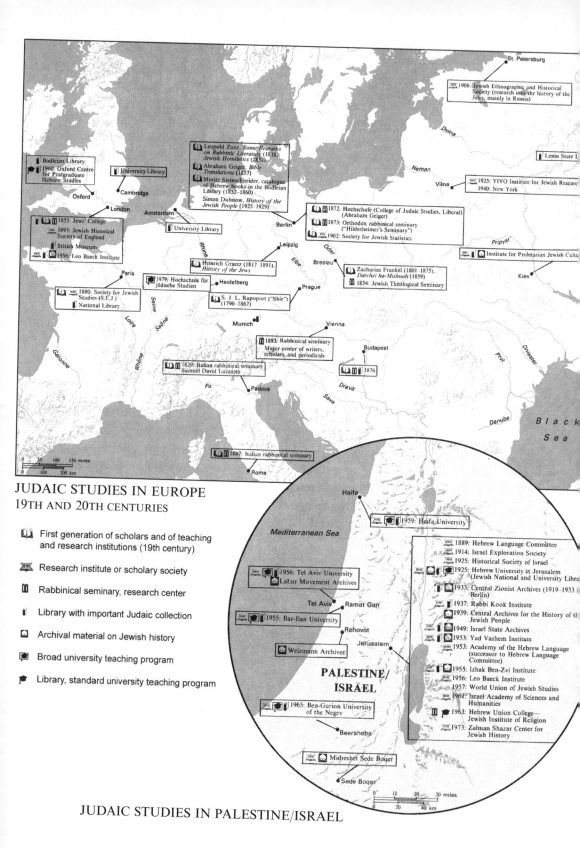

JUDAIC STUDIES IN EUROPE
19TH AND 20TH CENTURIES

📖 First generation of scholars and of teaching and research institutions (19th century)

📜 Research institute or scholary society

📖 Rabbinical seminary, research center

🎗 Library with important Judaic collection

🗔 Archival material on Jewish history

📖 Broad university teaching program

📌 Library, standard university teaching program

Europe map labels:

Bodleian Library
1960: Oxford Centre for Postgraduate Hebrew Studies
Oxford

University Library
Cambridge
London

1855: Jews' College
1891: Jewish Historical Society of England
British Museum
1956: Leo Baeck Institute

Paris
1880: Society for Jewish Studies (S.E.J.)
National Library

Amsterdam
University Library

Leopold Zunz, *Some Remarks on Rabbinic Literature* (1818); *Jewish Homiletics* (1832)
Abraham Geiger, *Bible Translations* (1857)
Moritz Steinschneider, catalogue of Hebrew books in the Bodleian Library (1852–1860)
Simon Dubnow, *History of the Jewish People* (1925–1929)
Berlin

1872: Hochschule (College of Judaic Studies, Liberal) (Abraham Geiger)
1873: Orthodox rabbinical seminary ("Hildesheimer's Seminary")
1902: Society for Jewish Statistics

1979: Hochschule für jüdische Studien
Heidelberg

Heinrich Graetz (1817–1891), *History of the Jews*
Leipzig

Breslau
Zacharias Frankel (1801–1875), *Darchei ha-Mishnah* (1859)
1854: Jewish Theological Seminary

S. J. L. Rapoport ("Shir") (1790–1867)
Prague

Munich
Vienna
1893: Rabbinical seminary Major center of writers, scholars, and periodicals

1829: Italian rabbinical seminary Samuel David Luzzatto
Padova

Budapest
1876

1887: Italian rabbinical seminary
Rome

St. Petersburg
1908: Jewish Ethnographic and Historical Society (research into the history of the Jews, mainly in Russia)

Lenin State L

Vilna
1925: YIVO Institute for Jewish Research
1940: New York

Institute for Proletarian Jewish Cultu

Kiev

Rivers labeled: Dvina, Neman, Pripyat, Oder, Elbe, Rhine, Seine, Loire, Saône, Rhône, Po, Garonne, Drava, Sava, Prut, Dniester

Black Sea

Mediterranean Sea

JUDAIC STUDIES IN PALESTINE/ISRAEL

Palestine/Israel map labels:

Haifa
1959: Haifa University

1956: Tel Aviv University Labor Movement Archives
Tel Aviv
Ramat Gan

1955: Bar-Ilan University
Rehovot

Weizmann Archives
Jerusalem

PALESTINE/ ISRAEL

1965: Ben-Gurion University of the Negev
Beersheba

Midreshet Sede Boqer
Sede Boqer

1889: Hebrew Language Committee
1914: Israel Exploration Society
1925: Historical Society of Israel
1925: Hebrew University in Jerusalem (Jewish National and University Libra
1933: Central Zionist Archives (1919–1933 Berlin)
1937: Rabbi Kook Institute
1939: Central Archives for the History of th Jewish People
1949: Israel State Archives
1953: Yad Vashem Institute
1953: Academy of the Hebrew Language (successor to Hebrew Language Committee)
1955: Izhak Ben-Zvi Institute
1956: Leo Baeck Institute
1957: World Union of Jewish Studies
1961: Israel Academy of Sciences and Humanities
1963: Hebrew Union College— Jewish Institute of Religion
1973: Zalman Shazar Center for Jewish History

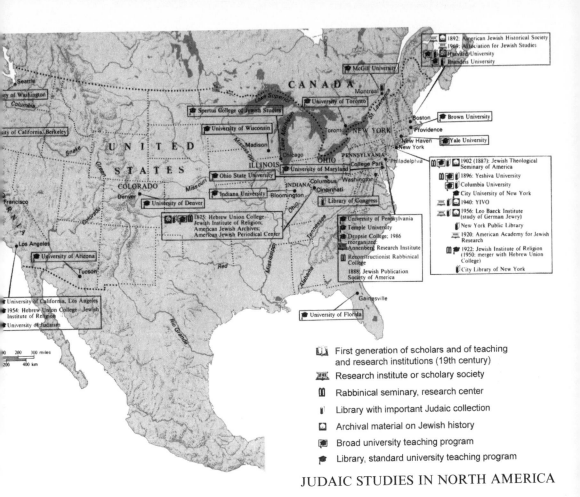

Seattle
ity of Washington
Columbia

ity of California, Berkeley

CANADA

McGill University

University of Toronto

Montreal

St. Lawrence

1892: American Jewish Historical Society
1969: Association for Jewish Studies
Harvard University
Brandeis University

Spertus College of Jewish Studies

University of Wisconsin

UNITED

STATES

Lake Michigan

Lake Superior

Toronto

NEW YORK

Boston

Brown University

Providence

New Haven
New York

Yale University

Chicago

Madison

ILLINOIS

OHIO

PENNSYLVANIA

University of Maryland

College Park

Philadelphia

1902 (1887): Jewish Theological
Seminary of America
1896: Yeshiva University
Columbia University
City University of New York
1940: YIVO
1956: Leo Baeck Institute
(study of German Jewry)
New York Public Library
1920: American Academy for Jewish
Research
1922: Jewish Institute of Religion
(1950: merger with Hebrew Union
College)
City Library of New York

Ohio State University

COLORADO

Denver

Missouri

INDIANA

Columbus

Cincinnati

Indiana University

Bloomington

Ohio

Library of Congress

Washington

University of Denver

1875: Hebrew Union College–
Jewish Institute of Religion;
American Jewish Archives;
American Jewish Periodical Center

University of Pennsylvania
Temple University
Dropsie College; 1986
reorganized:
Annenberg Research Institute
Reconstructionist Rabbinical
College
1888: Jewish Publication
Society of America

Francisco

Los Angeles

University of Arizona

Tucson

Red

Alabama

Mississippi

Rio Grande

Gainesville

University of California, Los Angeles
1954: Hebrew Union College–Jewish
Institute of Religion
University of Judaism

University of Florida

Tennessee

200   300 miles
200   400 km

First generation of scholars and of teaching
and research institutions (19th century)

Research institute or scholary society

Rabbinical seminary, research center

Library with important Judaic collection

Archival material on Jewish history

Broad university teaching program

Library, standard university teaching program

JUDAIC STUDIES IN NORTH AMERICA

of scholars. In the late twentieth century, the different branches of Jewish studies were included in the curricula of universities around the world, especially in the United States and Israel. The results of the scientific labors of hundreds of scholars were published in many languages. Archives and a large and ever-growing body of literature were the source material for the continuing work in the Science of Judaism.

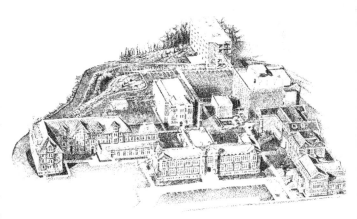

Hebrew Union College campus, Cincinnati, Ohio.

A specific language is a main characteristic of a human group with its own historical consciousness and continuity. The Jewish people carried to its Diasporas two closely related languages: Hebrew and Aramaic. Over the centuries, the Jews also adopted (and adapted) the local languages of different countries, infusing into them Hebrew or Aramaic words or sentence structures, writing them in Hebrew characters, and taking them along to new Diasporas. The resultant variety of "Jewish languages" makes their definition difficult, but in general they can be defined as the languages used by Jews in particular places, but differing up to a point from the vernaculars from which they evolved. Clear examples are Yiddish and Ladino. Each was adopted in one country (Germany and Spain, respectively, in the Middle Ages) and taken by wandering Jews to other places, where they differed from the local tongues, although they were slightly influenced by them. They were the main languages of the Jews, both for daily use and for literary expression, and were written in Hebrew characters. The Judeo-Arabic language had many of the same characteristics.

Another type of language spoken by smaller Jewish groups were local dialects, generally residues of older tongues. These had certain unique elements, but they can hardly be considered "Jewish languages." Among them were remnants of Judeo-Greek, spoken by Jews on some Aegean islands, and the Haketia dialect (a mixture of old Castilian, Hebrew, and Arabic), used in parts of northern Morocco.

With the gradual modernization of the Jewish people and their acculturation to the general society, most Jewish languages fell into disuse, becoming the second tongue of fewer and fewer Jews. Yiddish underwent a different process: at the beginning of the modernization of Jewish society, there was a most interesting flowering of Yiddish, first in Eastern Europe, and then, from there, among the Jewish immigrants in the United States and in other major centers of Jewish life—London, Paris, Montreal, and Buenos Aires, for example. Besides being the spoken language, Yiddish was the language of newspapers, belles-lettres, theater, and Jewish political groups. In the years between the two world wars, it was either the first or the second language of about two-thirds of the Jewish people. Later, the Holocaust and the sociological changes in the new Jewish settlements sent Yiddish into a sharp decline.

Another impressive development was the renaissance of the Hebrew language. Although the use of Hebrew had shrunk drastically, it had never ceased, even for everyday purposes. The Enlightenment produced a renewed interest in Hebrew among both Jews and non-Jews. The Zionist movement set as one of its major objectives the use of Hebrew as the spoken language of the Jewish people. The two main centers of the evolution of modern Hebrew were Eastern Europe and Palestine. In Eastern Europe, the development was primarily literary, while Yiddish remained the main spoken language. In Palestine, Hebrew provided the necessary link among Jews of different origins even before the Zionist enterprise got under way, and it later became the spoken language of the Jewish population and the second language of the non-Jewish population. From the mid-twentieth century, efforts have been made to establish Hebrew as the Jewish language of Diaspora Jewry.

LANGUAGES
OF THE JEWS

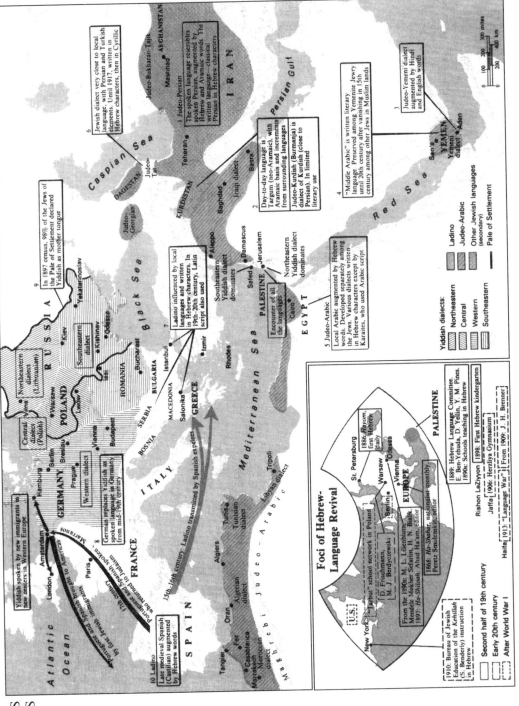

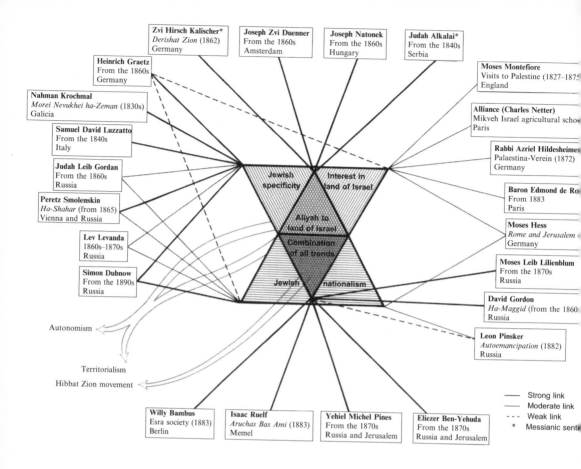

Zvi Hirsch Kalischer*
Derishat Zion (1862)
Germany

Joseph Zvi Duenner
From the 1860s
Amsterdam

Joseph Natonek
From the 1860s
Hungary

Judah Alkalai*
From the 1840s
Serbia

Heinrich Graetz
From the 1860s
Germany

Moses Montefiore
Visits to Palestine (1827–187?)
England

Nahman Krochmal
Morei Nevukhei ha-Zeman (1830s)
Galicia

Alliance (Charles Netter)
Mikveh Israel agricultural school
Paris

Samuel David Luzzatto
From the 1840s
Italy

Rabbi Azriel Hildesheimer
Palaestina-Verein (1872)
Germany

Judah Leib Gordan
From the 1860s
Russia

Baron Edmond de Ro?
From 1883
Paris

Peretz Smolenskin
Ha-Shahar (from 1865)
Vienna and Russia

Moses Hess
Rome and Jerusalem ?
Germany

Lev Levanda
1860s–1870s
Russia

Moses Leib Lilienblum
From the 1870s
Russia

Simon Dubnow
From the 1890s
Russia

David Gordon
Ha-Maggid (from the 1860?)
Russia

Jewish
specificity

Interest in
land of Israel

Aliyah to
land of Israel

Combination
of all trends

Jewish nationalism

Leon Pinsker
Autoemancipation (1882)
Russia

Autonomism

Territorialism

Hibbat Zion movement

Willy Bambus
Esra society (1883)
Berlin

Isaac Ruelf
Aruchas Bas Ami (1883)
Memel

Yehiel Michel Pines
From the 1870s
Russia and Jerusalem

Eliezer Ben-Yehuda
From the 1870s
Russia and Jerusalem

——— Strong link
——— Moderate link
- - - Weak link
* Messianic senti?

THE ROOTS OF JEWISH NATIONALISM LATE 19TH CENTURY

THE gradual integration of certain sectors of the Jewish people into the general society had contradictory results. One group reduced the Jewish component of its self-definition to a minimum, or even lost it and assimilated. Another sector began considering its Jewishness in light of new ideas absorbed from the general culture, but emphasized the Jewish component. From the latter trend emerged, after some elaboration, Jewish nationalism—a very complex interplay of Jewish

Rabbi Zvi Hirsch Kalischer   *Rabbi Azriel Hildesheimer*   *Leon Pinsker*

nd general ideological influences, with various ramifications.

Among the general influences were the unification of Italy and of Germany, and the national awakening of peoples in the Balkans and Austria-Hungary, all of which caused the Jews to think about themselves in national terms. East European Jewish intellectuals were led in that direction by reflections about the vagueness of Jewish self-definition in the conditions of modern European society: neither the traditional position nor the new Jewish attitudes in Western Europe seemed to offer satisfactory answers. Another factor was the historical attachment of the Jews to the land of Israel, now sharpened by the growing attention of the European powers to the Holy Land. Some Jewish notables, such as Moses Montefiore, began to take an interest in Palestine and in the situation of the Jews there, without considering Jewish immigration to Palestine or nationalistic conceptions about modern Jewry.

The various ideological components—questions about the specific character of the Jewish people, reflections about the relation between modern Jewry and nationalism, interest in Palestine and in the Jewish community there—often appeared independently, totally unrelated to one another. The first proto-Zionists (David Alkalai, Zvi Hirsch Kalischer, David Luria) and the men interested in the Jews of Palestine (Charles Netter of the Alliance Israélite Universelle, Moses Montefiore), for example, could not have been further apart ideologically. Others asked why a national definition of the Jewish people should apply only to the past and not also to the present and future. But the very perception of the Jewish people in national terms was a complex proposition. Some sought a spiritual definition of Jewish nationality (Heinrich Graetz, Samuel David Luzzatto); others proposed a political definition (David Gordon, Eliezer Ben-Yehuda). Jewish national, or quasi-national, ideas began appearing also in mystical, social or spiritual formations.

That difficult and widespread process of ideological elaboration continued unabated in the last quarter of the nineteenth century. It received further impetus from the continuing acculturation of large segments of East European ideologies, and the emergence of new and threatening patterns of antisemitism. The outcome of these ideological labors were four social and political trends: the Hibbat Zion movement, which began in the 1880s and led in the late 1890s to the Zionist movement; Jewish socialism; Jewish autonomism; and Jewish territorialism.

JEWISH NATIONALISM: IDEOLOGICAL AND ORGANIZATIONAL TENDENCIES

FROM the end of the nineteenth century, four main nationalist trends developed in European Jewish society: Zionism, socialism, autonomism, and territorialism. These tendencies existed separately or in different combinations, such as Zionism and socialist territorialism.

The trends spawned a bewildering array of movements and parties, usually centered in Eastern Europe, although they appeared also in Western Europe and in the countries of Jewish immigration, especially the United States. They were further distinguished by their posi-

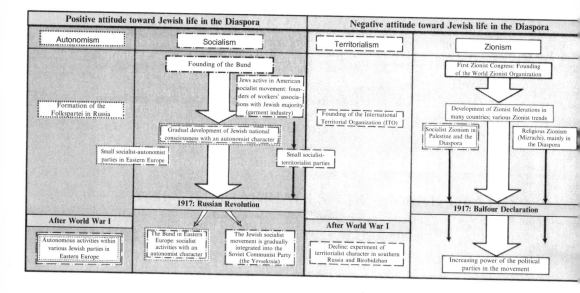

Positive attitude toward Jewish life in the Diaspora			Negative attitude toward Jewish life in the Diaspora	

Autonomism | Socialism | Territorialism | Zionism

Founding of the Bund

Jews active in American socialist movement: founders of workers' associations with Jewish majority (garment industry)

Formation of the Folkspartei in Russia

First Zionist Congress: Founding of the World Zionist Organization

Development of Zionist federations in many countries; various Zionist trends

Founding of the International Territorial Organization (ITO)

Gradual development of Jewish national consciousness with an autonomist character

Socialist Zionism in Palestine and the Diaspora

Religious Zionism (Mizrachi), mainly in the Diaspora

Small socialist-autonomist parties in Eastern Europe

Small socialist-territorialist parties

1917: Russian Revolution

1917: Balfour Declaration

After World War I

Autonomous activities within various Jewish parties in Eastern Europe

The Bund in Eastern Europe: socialist activities with an autonomist character

The Jewish socialist movement is gradually integrated into the Soviet Communist Party (the Yevsektsia)

After World War I

Decline: experiment of territorialist character in southern Russia and Birobidzhan

Increasing power of the political parties in the movement

tive or negative position regarding the continued existence of the Jews amid other peoples. The Jewish socialists and autonomists belonged to the "positivists"; Zionists and territorialists (with their socialist offshoots) to the "negativists." In spite of the differences among the many parties, trends, and movements, they shared a deep dissatisfaction with the prevailing relationship between the Jewish and the general society and a desire to change that relationship, according to their respective conceptions.

Jewish socialists believed that the transformation of the capitalist economic and social structure of general society would solve the Jewish problem. The Zionists thought that the problems of modern Jewry would be solved through the creation of an independent Jewish home in Palestine. The territorialists sought to direct part of the Jewish people—especially those emigrating from Europe—to some underdeveloped region where Jews would be a majority, perhaps even with a state of their own. The autonomists strove for broad rights, including national rights, in the countries where the Jews were already established, especially in Eastern Europe.

All these programs marked a new phase in the interpretation of the relationship between Jews and non-Jews. Whereas the "integrationist" segments of European Jewry had hoped to attain full civil and political rights for the Jews in the countries in which they lived, the new organizations wanted more: the recognition of the specificity of the Jews as a group with well-defined characteristics, even national ones.

The boundaries between the different trends were not always clear. Obviously, some of the envisaged solutions were not mutually exclusive. The different movements split, split again, and recombined. However, real hostility, bitter and uncompromising, expressing itself in long and fierce struggles, existed between the Bund—the main Jewish socialist organization—and the Zionist movement.

IN Central and Western Europe, Jews with socialist leanings did not form separate political organizations, but became active in the general socialist parties. In Eastern Europe (and in some major centers of Jewish immigration), Jewish socialism developed as an independent movement. Its foremost example was the Bund.

At the beginning of the twentieth century, the Bund (League of the Jewish Workers in Lithuania, Poland, and Russia, 1897) was the best-organized Jewish association in the Pale of Settlement. Its members were also among the founders and outstanding activists of the general Russian Socialist Party. Other Jewish socialist groups in the Pale were the Poalei Zion (Labor Zionists) and some smaller groups of territorialist or autonomist orientation.

The center of the Jewish socialist movement was in Lithuania, in Vilna and its vicinity. From there, it spread to Poland and then to the Ukraine (southern Russia). The ideological orientation of the Bund was Marxist, directed toward the revolution of the international working class, and only hesitantly did it formulate a Jewish national-cultural program. The fourth convention of the Bund, held in 1904, decided that the

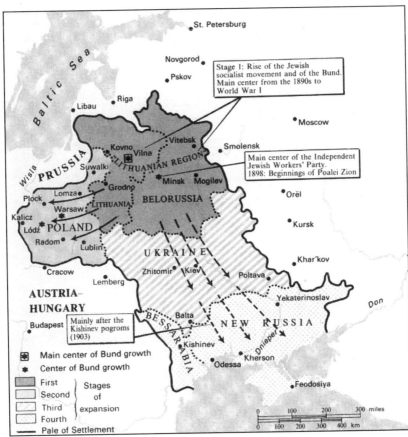

THE RISE OF THE BUND AND ITS SPREAD
IN THE PALE OF SETTLEMENT

concept of "nationality" applied also to the Jewish masses. This development was influenced by both the strengthening of the national idea in other sectors of East European Jewry and the nationalistic tendencies that appeared in the general socialist movement, especially in Poland and Austria-Hungary. The Bund maintained that the Russian social-democratic movement should be reorganized on a federative basis, joining together the major national groups of the Russian working class. This approach was rejected by the party's centralist-minded leadership, headed by Lenin, who also opposed the definition of the Jews as a national group. As a result of these differences, the Bund withdrew from the Russian Social Democratic Party in 1903, returning in 1906, after a compromise had been worked out guaranteeing it virtual autonomy inside the Russian movement.

Relations between the Bund and other Jewish groups were usually strained. The Bund stressed the class differences in Jewish society, totally opposed all religious tendencies, and was usually very wary about participating in activities of a Jewish communal character. Neverthe-less, it campaigned vigorously for the rights of Jewish workers, and during the anti-Jewish riots in Russia in the early twentieth century, it was very active organizing its members in self-defense groups.

After the Bolshevik Revolution in Russia in 1917, the Bund split. Its pro-communist faction merged with the Soviet Communist Party, with many Bund members becoming active in the Yevsektsia—the Jewish section of the Communist Party. The Bund's social-democratic faction gradually disappeared. The Bund continued to be active in other East European countries, especially Poland, where it became a recognized Jewish political party. During World War II, Bund members played an important role in the underground. The extermination of Polish Jewry brought about the end of the Bund in Europe.

In the United States, to which many Bundists migrated in the early twentieth century, the Bund did not organize as a separate political party; rather, its members became active in existing professional, social, and political organizations with a leftist orientation.

ZIONISM: IDEOLOGICAL COMPONENTS AND THE BEGINNING OF THE ZIONIST MOVEMENT

FEW movements in modern Jewish (or even modern general) history were as ideologically complex as the Zionist movement. The Zionist idea had three indispensable components: yearning for Zion (that is, the historical attachment of the Jewish people to the land of Israel), nationalism (that is, the influence of European national and civil concepts), and antisemitism. Combined in a certain way, these components produced an additional idea that became characteristic of Zionism: negation of Galut (*Sh'lilat Hagalut*), the rejection, on both pragmatic and ideological grounds, of the idea of continued Jewish group existence in non-Jewish societies.

A broad array of positions developed inside the Zionist movement, based on these elements and their various constellations. In addition, local conditions inevitably influenced the conceptions of the regional Zionist organizations. The later Zionist parties—such as socialist

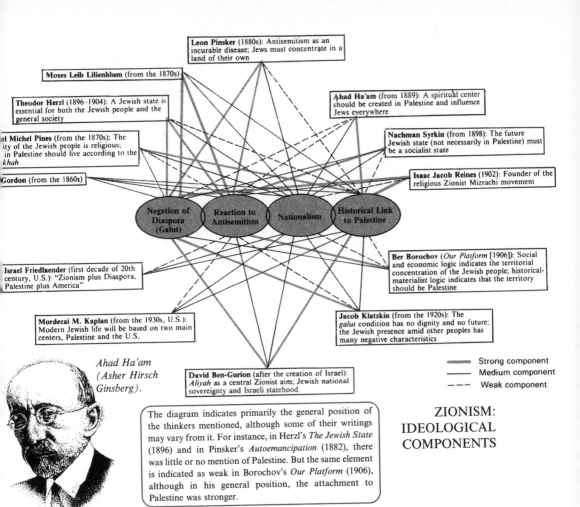

Leon Pinsker (1880s): Antisemitism as an incurable disease; Jews must concentrate in a land of their own

Moses Leib Lilienblum (from the 1870s)

Theodor Herzl (1896–1904): A Jewish state is essential for both the Jewish people and the general society

el Michel Pines (from the 1870s): The ity of the Jewish people is religious; in Palestine should live according to the khah

Gordon (from the 1860s)

Ahad Ha'am (from 1889): A spiritual center should be created in Palestine and influence Jews everywhere

Nachman Syrkin (from 1898): The future Jewish state (not necessarily in Palestine) must be a socialist state

Isaac Jacob Reines (1902): Founder of the religious Zionist Mizrachi movement

Negation of Diaspora (Galut)

Reaction to Antisemitism

Nationalism

Historical Link to Palestine

Israel Friedlaender (first decade of 20th century, U.S.): "Zionism plus Diaspora, Palestine plus America"

Ber Borochov (*Our Platform* [1906]): Social and economic logic indicates the territorial concentration of the Jewish people; historical-materialist logic indicates that the territory should be Palestine

Mordecai M. Kaplan (from the 1930s, U.S.): Modern Jewish life will be based on two main centers, Palestine and the U.S.

Jacob Klatzkin (from the 1920s): The *galut* condition has no dignity and no future; the Jewish presence amid other peoples has many negative characteristics

Ahad Ha'am (*Asher Hirsch Ginsberg*).

David Ben-Gurion (after the creation of Israel): *Aliyah* as a central Zionist aim; Jewish national sovereignty and Israeli statehood

━━━ Strong component
──── Medium component
– – – Weak component

The diagram indicates primarily the general position of the thinkers mentioned, although some of their writings may vary from it. For instance, in Herzl's *The Jewish State* (1896) and in Pinsker's *Autoemancipation* (1882), there was little or no mention of Palestine. But the same element is indicated as weak in Borochov's *Our Platform* (1906), although in his general position, the attachment to Palestine was stronger.

ZIONISM:
IDEOLOGICAL
COMPONENTS

Zionism or religious Zionism—added their own ideological perspectives to the basic components of the Zionist idea, enriching it, but also making it more complex. A trenchant debate started at the beginning of the twentieth century between religious and nonreligious Zionists as to the cultural content of the Zionist program. Religious Zionists (and religious Jews in general, many of whom were anti-Zionists) believed that the Jewish society in Palestine should live according to the *halakhah* (Jewish religious law). This discussion continues to this day in other forms.

Containing so many ideological elements, the Zionist movement was an arena for conflicting trends. But the existence of common goals established a basis for joint action. The "Uganda Scheme" (1903) ended by emphasizing Palestine, the historical land of Israel, as the sole objective of Zionist endeavors. The Helsingfors Conference of the Russian Zionist movement (December 1906) adopted the principle of work in and for the Diaspora communities (*Gegenwartsarbeit*) as one of the means to attain the Zionist ends. In the first decade of the twentieth century, three political and cultural trends became active in the movement, each stressing a different aspect of Zionist activity. "Synthetic Zionism," formulated toward the end of the decade, brought these trends together.

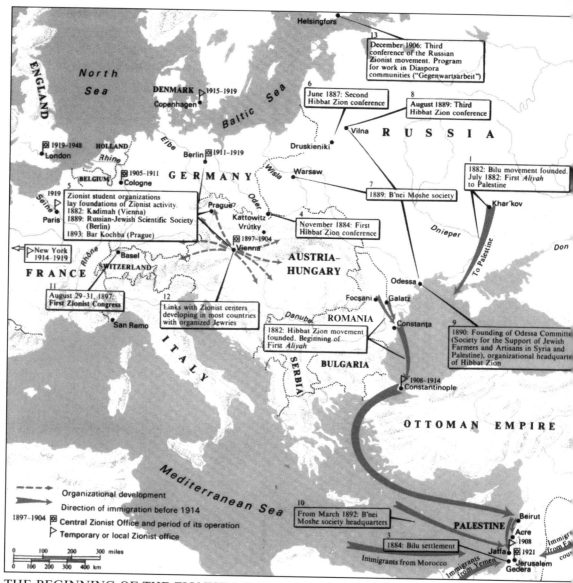

The following labels and annotations appear on the map:

Helsingfors

13 December 1906: Third conference of the Russian Zionist movement. Program for work in Diaspora communities ("Gegenwartsarbeit")

North Sea

ENGLAND

DENMARK ▷ 1915-1919
Copenhagen

Baltic Sea

6 June 1887: Second Hibbat Zion conference

8 August 1889: Third Hibbat Zion conference

Elbe

⊠ 1919-1948 HOLLAND
London
Rhine

Vilna

R U S S I A

Berlin ⊠ 1911-1919

Druskienieki

BELGIUM ⊠ 1905-1911
Cologne
Warsaw

GERMANY

Wisła

1 1882: Bilu movement founded. July 1882: First *Aliyah* to Palestine

5 1919 ▷ Zionist student organizations lay foundations of Zionist activity. 1882: Kadimah (Vienna) 1889: Russian-Jewish Scientific Society (Berlin) 1893: Bar Kochba (Prague)

Prague

Oder

7 1889: B'nei Moshe society

Khar'kov

Dnieper

Kattowitz
Vrútky

4 November 1884: First Hibbat Zion conference

Don

⊠ 1897-1904
Vienna

Seine

Paris

▷ New York 1914-1919

Rhône

Basel
SWITZERLAND

AUSTRIA-HUNGARY

Odessa

To Palestine

FRANCE

11 August 29-31, 1897: First Zionist Congress

12 Links with Zionist centers developing in most countries with organized Jewries

Focşani
Galatz

Danube

ROMANIA

Constanța

9 1890: Founding of Odessa Committee (Society for the Support of Jewish Farmers and Artisans in Syria and Palestine), organizational headquarters of Hibbat Zion

San Remo

ITALY

2 1882: Hibbat Zion movement founded. Beginning of First *Aliyah*

SERBIA

BULGARIA

▷ 1908-1914 Constantinople

OTTOMAN EMPIRE

Mediterranean Sea

- - - Organizational development
→ Direction of immigration before 1914
1897-1904 ⊠ Central Zionist Office and period of its operation
▷ Temporary or local Zionist office

10 From March 1892: B'nei Moshe society headquarters

PALESTINE
Beirut
Acre
⊠ 1908

3 1884: Bilu settlement

Immigrants from Morocco

Immigrants from Yemen

Immigrants from Eastern countries

Jaffa
Jerusalem ⊠ 1921
Gedera

0   100   200   300 miles
0 100 200 300 400 km

THE BEGINNING OF THE ZIONIST MOVEMENT

The Zionist program generated more dissension inside modern Jewry than existed between Jews and non-Jews, and it was the subject of heated debates. It was fiercely opposed by the Jewish socialists, the Orthodox, and those segments of Jewish society committed to integration into the general society. Yet the struggle for Jewish statehood in 1947 and 1948 united almost all ideological sectors of the Jewish people.

ORGANIZED Zionism began in the 1880s with the Hibbat Zion movement, whose practical achievements were modest. The First Zionist Congress, convened by Theodor Herzl at Basel in 1897, ushered in a new era. The congress approved the Zionist (Basel) Program, and founded the World Zionist Organization. From 1901, the congress met every two years. Branches of the World Zionist Organization were organized around the world.

Until World War I, the settlement of Jews in Palestine faced many difficulties, yet it continued to grow at a small but steady pace. The invasion of Palestine led to the Balfour Declaration (November 2, 1917). The declaration, which reflected a complex mixture of British interests and sentiments, created a great political opportunity for the Zionists. The Zionist Commission, led by Chaim Weizmann, which went to Palestine in 1918; the San Remo Conference, held in April 1920; and the British Mandate on Palestine (approved by the League of Nations in July 1922) were some of the first political steps taken toward the creation of a Jewish national home in Palestine. Parallel to this, Jewish immigration into Palestine resumed, and the Zionist Executive began development work in the country. In 1914, there had been about 85,000 Jews in Palestine. During the war, about 30,000 left the country or died. By 1922, the Jewish population again numbered about 85,000, still only 11.1 percent of the population.

Zionism and Palestine

1897: First Zionist Congress
World Zionist Organization founded

1897–1904: "The political period"
Effort to obtain Charter

1901: Fifth Zionist Congress
Debate over religious and secular culture and its place in the Zionist undertaking

1903: Sixth Zionist Congress
Uganda Scheme. In reaction, strengthening of Palestine-directed tendency

1903–1909: Debate between practical and political Zionists about course of Zionist activity

December 1906: Helsingfors Conference
Diaspora work accepted as part of Zionist program

1907–1911: Crystallization of synthetic trend in Zionist activity, combining political, practical and Zionist activities

1908: Zionist Office in Jaffa

1917: Balfour Declaration

1917–1918: British conquer Palestine

1920: Civil administration headed by High Commissioner Herbert Samuel

1922: British Mandate over Palestine confirmed

1922: Transjordan separated from Palestine

THE STRUCTURE OF THE WORLD ZIONIST ORGANIZATION 1929

THE Zionist movement functioned through a number of parallel or interrelated bodies that together composed the World Zionist Organization. Its supreme organ was the Zionist Congress, which generally met every two years. Its delegates, elected from all over the world, formed a large Jewish parliament whose interest was inevitably drawn also to issues beyond Zionism. The Zionist Congress adopted resolutions of an organizational and political character and elected the president of the Zionist movement (Chaim Weizmann, for most of the years between 1920 and 1946). It also chose the bodies that led the movement between the convening of congresses; the Greater Actions Committee (today called the Zionist General Council), which met between one and three times a year and had thirty to forty members and led the movement in its day-to-day activities. The Executive was served by the Central Zionist Office, which was divided into departments. Until 1920, both bodies were variously based in Vienna, Cologne, or Berlin. Thereafter, the Executive and the Central Office each had sections in both London and Jerusalem. Although during the

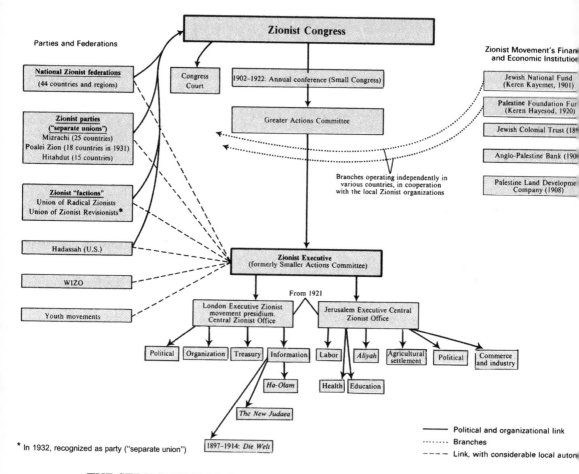

Zionist Congress

National Zionist federations
(44 countries and regions)

Zionist parties
("separate unions")
Mizrachi (25 countries)
Poalei Zion (18 countries in 1931)
Hitahdut (15 countries)

Zionist "factions"
Union of Radical Zionists
Union of Zionist Revisionists*

Hadassah (U.S.)

WIZO

Youth movements

Congress
Court

1902–1922: Annual conference (Small Congress)

Greater Actions Committee

Branches operating independently in
various countries, in cooperation
with the local Zionist organizations

Zionist Movement's Financial
and Economic Institutions

Jewish National Fund
(Keren Kayemet, 1901)

Palestine Foundation Fund
(Keren Hayesod, 1920)

Jewish Colonial Trust (1899)

Anglo-Palestine Bank (1902)

Palestine Land Development
Company (1908)

Zionist Executive
(formerly Smaller Actions Committee)

From 1921

London Executive Zionist
movement presidium.
Central Zionist Office

Jerusalem Executive Central
Zionist Office

Political | Organization | Treasury | Information | Labor | Aliyah | Agricultural settlement | Political | Commerce and industry

Ha-Olam

Health | Education

The New Judaea

* In 1932, recognized as party ("separate union")

1897–1914: Die Welt

——— Political and organizational link
········· Branches
– – – – Link, with considerable local autonomy

THE STRUCTURE OF THE WORLD ZIONIST ORGANIZATION, 1929

1920s and 1930s the seat of the movement's political leadership was in London, the tasks and powers of the Jerusalem-based Zionist Executive gradually increased.

The Zionist Executive acted in different countries or regions through Zionist federations. In 1929, there were forty-four such federations, each with its own organizational structure, central administration, local branches, annual or biennial conventions, and bodies for financial affairs, propaganda, education, youth, and the like. Besides the federations, which were organized on a geographical basis, there were the ideological Zionist parties ("separate unions")—such as Mizrachi, Poalei Zion, and the Revisionists—each of which also had world headquarters. In the 1920s and 1930s, the party structure in the Zionist movement gradually grew stronger (especially in Europe), while many of the federations lost support. Other important Zionist associations were the women's organizations; in the 1930s, the Women's International Zionist Organization (WIZO) functioned in dozens of countries, and the well-organized Hadassah was active in the United States. There were also the Zionist youth movements, organized on a worldwide basis. In the early 1930s, there were seven such groups, most of them connected with the Hehalutz movement, which prepared many of their members for pioneering *aliyah* to Palestine, where they became members of kibbutzim.

An important organizational development was the formation in 1929 of the (enlarged) Jewish Agency, which brought together Zionists and non-Zionists interested in the creation of a national Jewish home in Palestine. As it turned out, the success of the Jewish Agency was more one of principle than of practice; it expressed the idea that the development of Palestine was the concern of the whole Jewish people, and not only of the Zionist movement. In practice, the work for and in Palestine remained mainly in the hands of the World Zionist Organization and its affiliated bodies.

The Zionist enterprise in Palestine was financed by several agencies, the most important of which were the Jewish National Fund (Keren Kayemet le-Israel), dedicated to land redemption in Palestine, and the Palestine Foundation Fund (Keren Hayesod), dedicated to Zionist development projects. Both functioned in close cooperation with local Zionist bodies, but non-Zionists were prominent in the Keren Hayesod.

In many countries, especially in Eastern Europe, the Zionists were among the most active element in Jewish public life. Their activities were supported by a large Zionist press. About 200 periodicals were published in 1931 by the various Zionist bodies, and another 50 Jewish magazines or newspapers supported Zionism.

After the creation of the state of Israel, the World Zionist Organization underwent important internal changes. New statutes, adopted in 1960, opened the door to participation in the Zionist movement of Jewish organizations that accepted the Zionist program, such as the Jewish Reform movement in the United States.

THE POLITICAL COMPOSITION OF ZIONIST CONGRESSES 1921 TO 1939

Two main tendencies characterized the development of the Zionist movement: the gradual growth of the party system, and the increasing power of the leftist parties. At the Twelfth Zionist Congress, held in 1921, the General Zionists (politically unaligned) had 73 percent of the delegates, and Labor, 8 percent. At the Twenty-first Congress, convened in 1939, Labor had 42.5 percent of the delegates, and the General Zionists, only 32.4 percent. The General Zionists had meanwhile become affiliated; the politicization of the movement in the 1920s and 1930s had compelled them to define themselves politically. By 1935, they were repre-

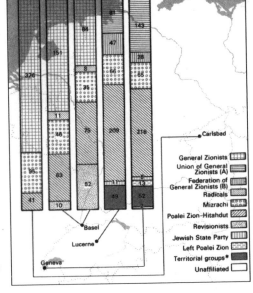

* Delegates from countries (mainly Germany) where it was not possible to hold elections for the Zionist Congress

sented by two parties (A and B), speaking for the Jewish middle class, with its characteristic social and economic positions. The B group, also called Progressives, supported Chaim Weizmann. The Labor representation consisted of a broad array of ideological positions, all of which were leftist-oriented (Poalei Zion–Hitahdut, Hashomer Hatzair, and, from 1938, Left Poalei Zion), that outside the Zionist Congress acted independently. The most important representation of religious Zionism was Mizrachi although many religious Zionists voted for other Zionist parties. Another important Zionist party was the Revisionists, organized in 1925, which was mostly middle class and extremely nationalistic. In 1935, the Revisionists left the World Zionist Organization and founded the New Zionist Organization, which existed independently until 1946.

JEWISH STUDENT ORGANIZATIONS AND YOUTH MOVEMENTS

SEVERAL very interesting functions in modern Jewish life (especially in Europe) were fulfilled by the younger strata of Jewish society, organized in youth movements and student organizations. A significant number of the future Jewish leaders belonged to these groups. The Zionist and pioneer youth movements played important roles in the building of the Jewish national home in Palestine.

There were basic conceptual differences between the Jewish student organizations, which appeared in Europe from the last decade of the nineteenth century, and the youth movements, which appeared from the beginning of the twentieth century. Both represented a part of society that was critical of the Establishment and dissatisfied with the situation of modern Jewry in general society. Each

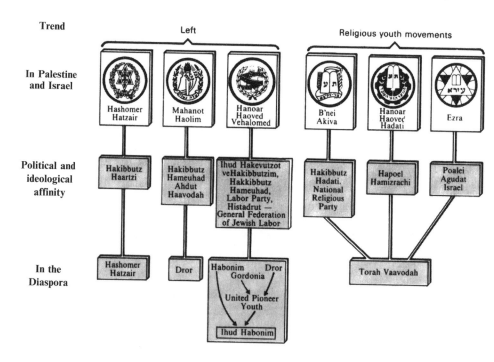

group, however, developed its own ideological expression and form of organized action.

The Jewish youth movements were divided into two quite diverse branches. The first developed in Western Europe, especially in Germany. The main movements there were Blau-Weiss (before World War I), Jung-juedischer Wanderbund (JJWB), Kameraden, and what later became Habonim-Noar Halutzi (after World War I). The Jewish youth associations were influenced by the classic German youth movement (the Wandervogel), which aimed to create a new type of person through spiritual development in a unique social framework. The Jewish organizations added their own objectives: to foster Jewish consciousness and attachment to Jewish values. That internal development gradually brought most of their members to Zionism.

The other branches of the Jewish youth movement, whose center was in Eastern Europe (although it also appeared in Western Europe and in some Muslim countries), produced a new type between the two world wars, the Zionist youth movement. Its aims were better defined than those of the classic youth movement, and to some extent it managed to avoid the inevitable fate of youth movements: to disappear as its members reached adulthood, or to become a section of a political party. An outstanding example of a Zionist youth movement was Hashomer Hatzair. It began in Vienna as a group of young scouts, according to the classic pattern, and developed strongly in Eastern Europe; later, it adopted Zionism, socialism, and pioneering ideals; established kibbutzim in Palestine from the mid-1920s that combined to form an independent kibbutz federation (Hakibbutz Haartzi); and eventually founded a political party—all while maintaining the youth movement as a structure for the younger generation.

The Zionist youth movements reflected the political divisions within the Zionist movement: rightist (Betar), leftist, or religious with a leftist orientation. The leftist-oriented movements, which based themselves on a pioneering lifestyle (*halutziut*), became large and influential. They emphasized personal implementation (*hagshamah*) of their ideals, in which settlement in Palestine occupied a prime place. The attainment of this goal, together with other basic ideals of the classic youth movement, had not only a

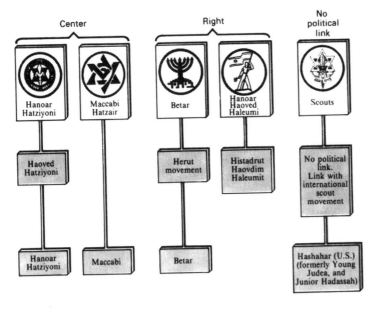

YOUTH MOVEMENTS: IDEOLOGICAL CONNECTIONS

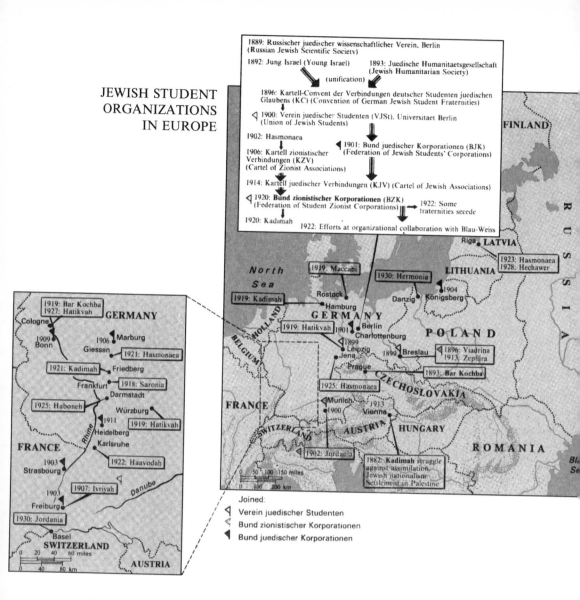

JEWISH STUDENT
ORGANIZATIONS
IN EUROPE

1889: Russischer juedischer wissenschaftlicher Verein, Berlin
(Russian Jewish Scientific Society)

1892: Jung Israel (Young Israel)   1893: Juedische Humanitaetsgesellschaft
(Jewish Humanitarian Society)

(unification)

1896: Kartell-Convent der Verbindungen deutscher Studenten juedischen
Glaubens (KC) (Convention of German Jewish Student Fraternities)

1900: Verein juedischer Studenten (VJSt). Universitaet Berlin
(Union of Jewish Students)

1902: Hasmonaea

1906: Kartell zionistischer   1901: Bund juedischer Korporationen (BJK)
Verbindungen (KZV)   (Federation of Jewish Students' Corporations)
(Cartel of Zionist Associations)

1914: Kartell juedischer Verbindungen (KJV) (Cartel of Jewish Associations)

1920: Bund zionistischer Korporationen (BZK)
(Federation of Student Zionist Corporations)   1922: Some
fraternities secede

1920: Kadimah

1922: Efforts at organizational collaboration with Blau-Weiss

FINLAND

R U S S I A

Riga LATVIA

1923: Hasmonaea
1928: Hechawer

LITHUANIA

1919: Maccabi   1930: Hermonia

North
Sea

Rostock   Danzig   1904
Königsberg

1919: Kadimah   Hamburg

GERMANY   Berlin   POLAND
1919: Hatikvah 1901 Charlottenburg
1899   1896: Viadrina
Leipzig   1899 Breslau   1913: Zephira
Jena   Prague
1893: Bar Kochba
1925: Hasmonaea
CZECHOSLOVAKIA

FRANCE   Munich   1913
1900   Vienne

SWITZERLAND   AUSTRIA   HUNGARY
ROMANIA

1902: Jordania   1882: Kadimah struggle   Bla
against assimilation,   Se
Jewish nationalism
Settlement in Palestine

0 50 100 150 miles
0   100   200 km

1919: Bar Kochba
1927: Hatikvah   GERMANY
Cologne
1909   1906 Marburg
Bonn   Giessen   1921: Hasmonaea
1921: Kadimah   Friedberg
Frankfurt   1918: Saronia
Darmstadt
1925: Haboneh   Würzburg
1911   1919: Hatikvah
Heidelberg
Karlsruhe
FRANCE
1903   1922: Haavodah
Strasbourg
1903   1907: Ivriyah   Danube
Freiburg
1930: Jordania
Basel
SWITZERLAND
0 20 40 60 miles
0   40   80 km
AUSTRIA

Joined:
◁ Verein juedischer Studenten
◁ Bund zionistischer Korporationen
◀ Bund juedischer Korporationen

spiritual and personal significance, but also a profound impact on the shape of the Jewish society and body politic developing in the land of Israel.

The Hehalutz (Pioneer) movement provided an umbrella organization for Zionist youth on their way to Palestine, where they became the spearheads of the Zionist enterprise. The pioneer youth movements were instrumental in the development of the different kibbutz federations in Palestine.

Branches of the Zionist youth move-

ments were established in most Jewish communities around the world. Young Judea, the youth movement of the Zionist Organization of America, founded in the first decade of the twentieth century, was typical of the American youth movements: it was active in Zionist education, but lacked the dimension of social rebellion characteristic of the European youth movements. Although it supported *aliyah*, it did not oblige its members to settle in Palestine.

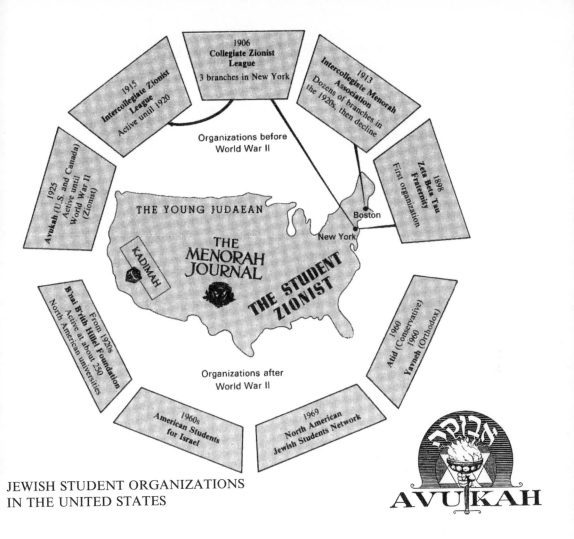

**JEWISH STUDENT ORGANIZATIONS
IN THE UNITED STATES**

The Bund, the Jewish Socialist Party in Eastern Europe, created its own youth movement, which belonged in the category of associations that were youth sections of political parties.

The creation of separate organizations of Jewish students in Europe was a clear expression of the tensions between non-Jewish and Jewish students at European universities, especially in Germany; German student associations were hotbeds of antisemitism. But the desire of Jews to associate with one another to achieve goals advantageous to Jews was also a factor in the formation of the Jewish associations. Jewish student organizations also sprang up in the United States, for reasons somewhat different from those in Europe, although in the first decades of the twentieth century discrimination against Jews was not uncommon at American universities.

Another development was the associations of Jewish students from Eastern Europe at many West European universities from the last years of the nineteenth century. Because of discriminatory laws in Russia, many young Jews were forced to seek university education in the West. There they founded associations that had a very dynamic intellectual life.

D. The Jews in Muslim Countries

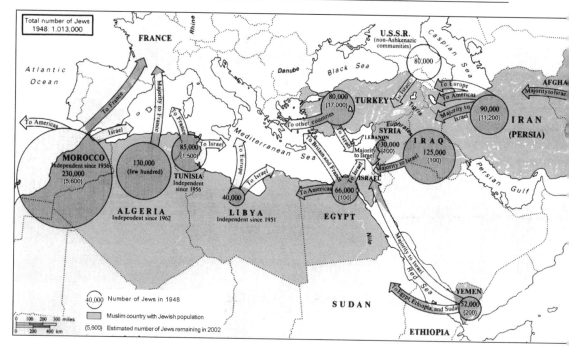

Total number of Jews
1948: 1,013,000

FRANCE

U.S.S.R.
(non-Ashkenazic
communities)

80,000

*Atlantic
Ocean*

Danube

Black Sea

AFGHA

Majority to Israel

To Americas

To France

Majority to France

Israel

80,000
{17,000}

TURKEY

To Europe

To Americas

Majority to
Israel

90,000
{11,200}

IRAN
(PERSIA)

*Mediterranean
Sea*

85,000
{1,500}

To Israel

To other countries

SYRIA
30,000
{400}

LEBANON

IRAQ
125,000
{100}

MOROCCO
Independent since 1956
230,000
{5,600}

130,000
(few hundred)

TUNISIA
Independent
since 1956

To Israel

To Europe

Majority
to Israel

Majority to Israel

ISRAEL

*Persian
Gulf*

40,000

66,000
{100}

To Americas

ALGERIA
Independent since 1962

LIBYA
Independent since 1951

EGYPT

Nile

Majority to Israel

Red Sea

YEMEN
52,000
{200}

To Egypt, Ethiopia, and Sudan

SUDAN

ETHIOPIA

40,000 Number of Jews in 1948

Muslim country with Jewish population

{5,600} Estimated number of Jews remaining in 2002

0 100 200 300 miles
0 200 400 km

In the nineteenth and twentieth centuries, an important segment of the Jewish people lived in Muslim countries, in a broad belt extending from Morocco in the west to Afghanistan in the east, and including about a dozen countries in North Africa and the Middle East.

These Jewries evolved very differently from one another. Tradition has it that the Jews lived in Yemen in southern Arabia and in Morocco in North Africa since the Second Temple period, and perhaps even earlier. Other communities, such as those in Turkey and Greece, underwent radical transformations in the fifteenth and sixteenth centuries, with the arrival of the Jewish refugees from Spain and Portugal, who imposed their culture, language, and customs on the older Jewish society, the Romaniots. Another group was Egyptian Jewry: Jews had been in Egypt since times immemorial; but relatively few lived there in the eighteenth and nineteenth centuries, and new communities arose in the nineteenth century.

In spite of these differences, several important characteristics linked almost all Jewish communities in Muslim lands. Their life in these countries and their situation within Islamic society were based on two common legal foundations: (1) the principle established by the prophet Mohammed that non-Muslims believing in one God (such as Jews and Christians) were protected subjects (*dhimmi*), although they had to pay a special annual tax (*jizya*); and (2) a set of discriminatory laws adopted in the time of the caliph Omar II (717–719). These laws reflected a harsher attitude of Muslim society to the Jews. Their implementation, however, varied greatly, depending on which religious trend was dominant in a given time and place.

Most of these Jewish communities were

also affected by the rise of the Ottoman Empire in the fifteenth century. The Turks came to dominate all the countries from northwestern Africa to the Middle East, conquering a large segment of southeastern Europe as well, and imposing a certain degree of unity in their empire. The decline of the Ottoman Empire, which began in the second half of the sixteenth century, was reflected in the conditions of its subjects, including the Jews. The "modernization" that began in Europe in the sixteenth and seventeenth centuries reached the Ottoman Empire only in the second half of the nineteenth century.

The third important factor in the development of the Jewries in Muslim lands was the growing European presence in the nineteenth and twentieth centuries. Many Muslim countries became European colonies—from the French conquest of Algeria in 1830 to the British occupation of Iraq in World War I. The situation of the Jews improved immensely under the colonial or semicolonial European regimes. They adapted quickly to the cultural and political changes that swept the Muslim countries from the mid-nineteenth century, and participated in the economic development associated with the European presence. The process was facilitated by another characteristic of most of the Jewries in Muslim countries: their urban or semiurban character. Even in countries where a large number of Jews lived in villages or small towns—such as Morocco, Yemen, and Kurdistan—the Jews' occupational structure was more urban than was that of the general population. The trend toward urbanization among these Jews, once modernization started in the Muslim countries, had interesting similarities to the behavior of the Jewish communities in Eastern Europe.

Finally, all the Jewries in Muslim countries faced a common crisis caused by the establishment of Israel. A combination of external pressures (strong hostility by the general population) and internal aspirations (the yearning for Zion component in their Jewish consciousness) brought about the dissolution of most of these Jewish communities. Most of the Jews migrated to Israel; many settled in Europe or North America. In the second half of the twentieth century, the Jewries of the Muslim countries and of the Christian West, who had been separated for centuries, met and were reuniting in Israel and several other countries.

THE JEWS IN MOROCCO

THE largest Jewish community in the Muslim lands in the twentieth century was in Morocco. It is estimated that early in the century, about 100,000 Jews lived there, increasing in the 1940s to between 200,000 and 250,000 (including those in the Tangier international zone).

Jews had lived in Morocco for many centuries. They apparently arrived in Roman times, and, with occasional setbacks, their organized existence continued until the mid-twentieth century. In the modern period, Moroccan Jewry comprised three distinct groups: city dwellers along the Atlantic coast; villagers in the south or interior; and mountain dwellers, alongside the Berber population. The city dwellers were divided into the autochthonous Jews and the "newer" Sephardic Jews, descendants

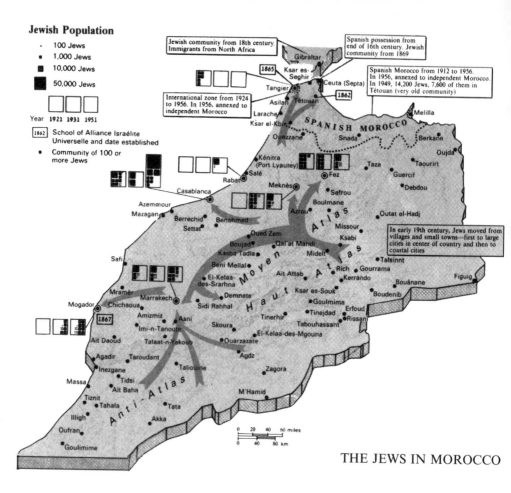

Jewish Population

- · 100 Jews
- ■ 1,000 Jews
- ■ 10,000 Jews
- ■ 50,000 Jews

Year 1921 1931 1951

[1862] School of Alliance Israélite Universelle and date established

• Community of 100 or more Jews

Jewish community from 18th century. Immigrants from North Africa

Spanish possession from end of 16th century. Jewish community from 1869

Spanish Morocco from 1912 to 1956. In 1956, annexed to independent Morocco. In 1949, 14,200 Jews, 7,600 of them in Tétouan (very old community)

International zone from 1924 to 1956. In 1956, annexed to independent Morocco

In early 19th century, Jews moved from villages and small towns—first to large cities in center of country and then to coastal cities

0   20   40   60 miles
0   40   80 km

THE JEWS IN MOROCCO

of refugees who had come from Spain and Portugal in the late Middle Ages.

Until the French conquest in 1912, Jewish life in Morocco was regulated by the traditional Muslim pattern: the Jews were protected subjects of the local ruler, and they paid special taxes. In the nineteenth century, their situation varied: those living in cities, where the power of the Moroccan sultan was effective, were well protected. Those living farther away were frequent victims of persecution, which occupied European Jewish public opinion. In 1864, Moses Montefiore visited Morocco and persuaded the sultan to revoke anti-Jewish laws. But later, under pressure from Muslim clergymen and local rulers, the sultan changed his mind.

The situation of the Jews improved considerably with the establishment of the French protectorate over Morocco in 1912. The following decades were a period of peace and prosperity for the Jewish community (although only in 1956 did the Jews become full citizens), and Moroccan Jewry underwent radical internal changes. Many villagers settled in the coastal cities. Toward the middle of the century, about half of the country's Jews lived in several larger cities, especially Casablanca. The Jews in Morocco, like those in Algeria and Tunisia, were deeply influenced by French culture, a process spurred by the Alliance Israélite Universelle school system. In 1948, there were more than fifty Alliance schools in Morocco.

After 1948, Moroccan Jewry began to emigrate—the majority to Israel, some to France, some to other European countries or North America.

The Jewish Quarter (Mellah) of Fez
The *mellah* of Fez was in the New City, close to the sultan's palace. It was a small, very crowded neighborhood, which in 1912 contained about 12,000 Jews. It consisted of two parts divided by a main street. The more affluent Jews lived in the northwestern part, higher and close to the palace; the poorer Jews lived in the southern, lower part. A large section of the *mellah* was burned down in 1912, when the Muslim population rioted against the French occupiers.

THE JEWS IN ALGERIA

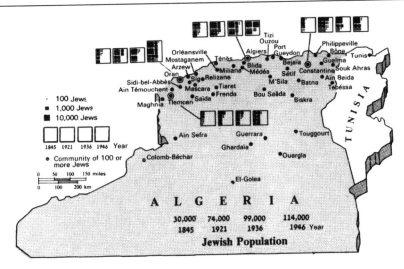

JEWS lived in Algeria from time immemorial. In the nineteenth century, most were concentrated in several large and well-organized communities on the Mediterranean coast: Algiers, Constantine, Tlemcen, and others. The communities were led by a *mukadam* (the Jewish elder, or *sheikh al-Yahud*), who had broad powers. The Spanish-Portuguese Jews had their own communal organization. Relations with the Muslim population were relatively good.

The French conquest of Algeria in 1830 brought many benefits for the Jews. Their civil situation improved, becoming the best of any Jewry in the Muslim world. In 1870, the Crémieux Decree granted French citizenship to the Jews in the major coastal cities. This aroused resentment among the Muslim and French (Christian) inhabitants, leading to riots and antisemitic incidents, which later subsided.

The authorities established for the organization of the Jewish communities the consistorial system that existed in France. Three consistories were formed —in Algiers, Constantine, and Oran— connected with the Central Consistory in Paris and the French administration in Algiers. The Jews underwent a rapid and rather extreme process of French acculturation. The richer families sent their sons to study at universities in France. On their return to Algeria, they eventually occupied leading positions in the Algerian administration and in the professions.

Algerian Jewry underwent difficult times during World War II, when the French Vichy regime revoked the Crémieux Decree. After the struggle for Algerian independence (1956–1962), the Jews concluded that their future in the new state was doubtful. Most (in 1955, they numbered 130,000 to 140,000) emigrated to France; some went to Israel and other countries.

THE JEWS IN TUNISIA

IN the nineteenth and twentieth centuries, Tunisian Jewry consisted of two separately organized groups: authocthonous Jews (Touansa) and Spanish-Portuguese Jews (Grana), some of whom had come from Italy. The two communities were at odds with each other, which caused problems within Tunisian Jewry and in its relations with the Muslim authorities. An ancient and highly interesting community, the subject of many legends, lived on the island of Djerba.

More than half the country's Jews lived in the capital, Tunis. They worked chiefly in commerce and the crafts. Some larger Jewish merchants were active in the country's international commerce, especially with France and Italy.

In 1881, Tunisia became a French protectorate. The Jewish community was reorganized in one unified frame, the Tunisian Jewish Welfare Fund, in which the various bodies participated. It dealt with both religious and social matters. Tunisian Jewry came under the influence of the French language and culture. Many young Jews went to France to study, and later occupied important positions in the professions.

During World War II, Tunisia was under German military occupation from 1942 to 1943, very difficult years for the Jews. Tunisia became independent in 1956, and the Jews were granted the civil rights enjoyed by the rest of the popula-

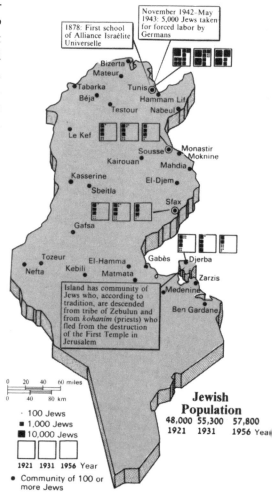

November 1942–May 1943: 5,000 Jews taken for forced labor by Germans

1878: First school of Alliance Israélite Universelle

Bizerta
Mateur
Tabarka
Béja
Tunis
Hammam Lif
Testour
Nabeul
Le Kef
Sousse
Monastir
Moknine
Kairouan
Mahdia
Kasserine
El-Djem
Sbeitla
Sfax
Gafsa
Tozeur
El-Hamma
Gabès
Djerba
Nefta
Kebili
Matmata
Zarzis
Medenine
Ben Gardane

Island has community of Jews who, according to tradition, are descended from tribe of Zebulun and from *kohanim* (priests) who fled from the destruction of the First Temple in Jerusalem

0   20   40   60 miles
0   40   80 km

· 100 Jews
■ 1,000 Jews
■ 10,000 Jews

Jewish Population
48,000 55,300 57,800
1921   1931   1956 Year

☐ ☐ ☐
1921 1931 1956 Year
● Community of 100 or more Jews

tion. Until 1967, the Tunisian government took a relatively moderate position regarding the Arab-Israeli conflict. Nevertheless, most Jews left the country in the 1950s and 1960s, mainly for France and Israel.

THE JEWS IN LIBYA

EWS are believed to have lived in Libya since the Second Temple period. In modern times, Libyan Jewry was relatively small—about 25,000 in 1931. Two-thirds lived in Tripoli, where they made up 20 percent of the population. Benghazi was the second largest community. Amruz (near Tripoli) also had an important community, and there were several smaller communities in towns along or near the Mediterranean coast. Libyan Jews were cohesively organized according to traditional patterns, and their relations with their Muslim neighbors were relatively good. In 1911, the Italians conquered Libya, their domination continuing until 1943, when the British took it. The situation of Libyan Jews had been good under the Italians, but deteriorated on the eve of and during World War II, when Italy allied itself with Germany and the country was a major arena of the military operations in North Africa.

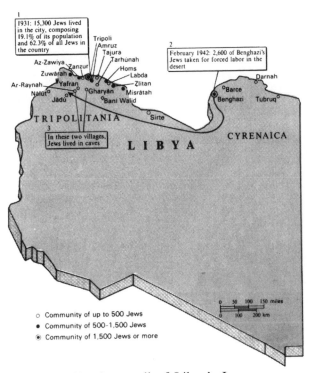

1
1931: 15,300 Jews lived in the city, composing 19.1% of its population and 62.3% of all Jews in the country

2
February 1942: 2,600 of Benghazi's Jews taken for forced labor in the desert

3
In these two villages, Jews lived in caves

Tripoli, Amruz, Tajura, Tarhūnah, Homs, Labda, Zlitan, Az-Zawiya, Zanzur, Zuwārah, Ar-Raynah, Yafran, Nalūt, Gharyān, Misrātah, Jādū, Bani Walid, Sirte, Darnah, Barce, Benghazi, Tubruq

TRIPOLITANIA   LIBYA   CYRENAICA

○ Community of up to 500 Jews
● Community of 500–1,500 Jews
◉ Community of 1,500 Jews or more

0   50   100   150 miles
0   100   200 km

After 1948, almost all of Libya's Jews migrated to Israel, most in 1948 and 1951, and the rest later.

THE JEWS IN EGYPT

JEWS lived in Egypt almost as long as in Palestine, although there were different and noncontinuous Jewish settlements. In the seventeenth and eighteenth centuries, most Egyptian Jews were concentrated in two large and well-organized communities, Alexandria and Cairo, in such smaller ones as Rosetta, Mansura, and Damietta; and in several villages. In the early nineteenth century, there was a total of only 5,000 to 7,000 Jews, including about 1,200 Karaites.

A small segment of the Jewish population consisted of veteran, well-established settlers, usually Ottoman citizens. In the eighteenth century, European Jewish merchants settled in Alexandria, mostly under the protection of the Capitulations (as subjects of foreign powers). In the 1820s, Jews from Greece and the Greek islands arrived, followed later in the century by more Jews from Greece and some from Italy, Iraq, and even Morocco. There was also a significant immigration of Ashkenazic Jews from Eastern and Central Europe. Many of these newcomers settled in Alexandria, Egypt's gateway to Europe and a city of cosmopolitan character and very active economic life.

Under Mohammed Ali (1805–1848), Egypt opened to European modernizing

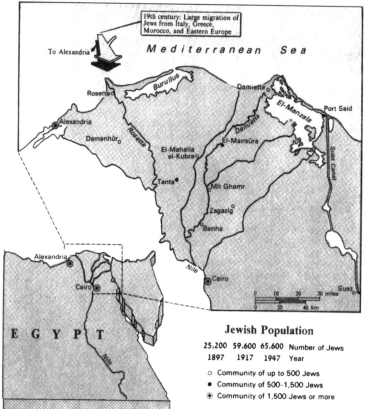

Inside map:
19th century: Large migration of Jews from Italy, Greece, Morocco, and Eastern Europe

To Alexandria

Mediterranean Sea

Rosetta
Burullus
Damietta
El-Manzala
Port Said
Alexandria
Damanhûr
Rosetta
Damietta
El-Mahalla el-Kubra
El-Mansûra
Tanta
Mît Ghamr
Zagazig
Benha
Suez Canal
Nile
Cairo
Suez

Alexandria
Cairo
E G Y P T
Nile

Jewish Population

25,200	59,600	65,600	Number of Jews
1897	1917	1947	Year

○ Community of up to 500 Jews
● Community of 500–1,500 Jews
◉ Community of 1,500 Jews or more

influences. The more affluent part of the population began to adopt European customs and languages. The Jews, too, accepted the Europeanizing trend. When Great Britain took over Egypt in 1882, the Jews' legal status was made equal to that of the rest of the population. Many Jews prospered.

The Jewish population was concentrated in the cities. In the late nineteenth century, most breadwinners were in commercial occupations—from clerks to middle-size or large merchants. The European origin or cultural tendencies of the Jews eased their way toward professions connected with Egypt's growing commercial contact with Europe. Many also acquired higher education, in Egypt or abroad, and Jews gradually became prominent in the professions.

In the nineteenth century, the Cairo and Alexandria communities dominated the country's Jewish social and religious life, with the support of the authorities. Newcomers had to struggle to establish their own synagogues. In 1854, Italian Jews in Alexandria created their own communal organization. In 1865, an Ashkenazic community was established in Cairo, over the opposition of the incumbent Jewish leadership. Over the years, the diversity of Egyptian Jewry expressed itself also in the separate Jewish institutions that each group created.

The relatively good situation of Egyptian Jewry continued until the mid-twentieth century. After the establishment of Israel, most Jews gradually left Egypt, emigrating to Israel and France, as well as to Latin America, the United States, and other countries.

THE JEWS IN THE OTTOMAN EMPIRE AND TURKEY

THE Ottoman Empire underwent many political changes in the nineteenth and twentieth centuries that gradually reduced its size. Greece became independent in 1830 (although its northern part, with the great Jewish center in Salonika, became part of Greece only in 1913). Between 1859 and 1878, the empire lost Walachia and Moldavia (which formed Romania), Bosnia (to Austria–Hungary), Serbia, and Bulgaria. Great Britain conquered Egypt in 1882, and Italy took over Libya and Rhodes in 1911 and 1912. As a result of World War I, the Turks had to yield large parts of the Middle East (the Arabian Peninsula, Iraq, Syria, Lebanon, and Palestine). The Ottoman Empire was dissolved, and the core that remained became modern Turkey.

Large and varied Jewish communities lived in the lands that had been under Ottoman domination. The Jewish population usually consisted of groups that had settled in a particular place over the centuries. There was usually a small older stratum, the Romaniots (or Gregos), which was augmented by a large influx of Jewish refugees from Spain and Portugal in the sixteenth century. The Sephardim strongly influenced Jewish life and culture during the succeeding centuries. In Palestine and in several other places in the empire, there were also Ashkenazic Jews. Constantinople was an important center of the Karaite sect. An interesting community, with specific characteristics, lived in Rhodes. In general, the particular conditions in the different parts of the empire were a factor in the shaping of the local Jewish communities.

On the whole, the legal situation of the Jews in the empire was good. However, local traditions regarding relations be-

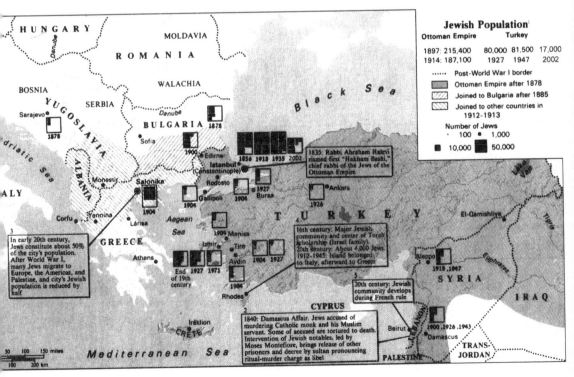

tween Jews and non-Jews, and the whims of the local ruler, affected the status of each community. As "non-believers" (Islamically speaking), Jews paid a special tax (*jizya*, or *haradj*), were protected subjects (*dhimmi*), had internal autonomy, were unhindered in their economic activities, and could, in principle, travel freely. Social reforms in the empire in the nineteenth century (the *tansimat*) bestowed new civil rights on Muslim subjects and, as a result of pressure by the European powers, also on non-Muslims. The *hakham-bashi* (head *hakham*, or chief rabbi) of Constantinople was recognized by the authorities as the official religious leader of the Jews of the empire, with a considerable voice in the nomination of rabbis (*hakhamim*) in the larger provincial communities. Two commissions were established in each community, one for religious and one for social matters, and together with the *hakhamim* they administered the life of the Jewish general community (*millet*, or nation).

The growing European cultural influence left its mark. A specific type of *haskalah* (Jewish enlightenment) developed among the Jews of the major Ottoman centers, especially Constantino-ple and Salonika. One of its results was the flowering of Ladino, which began to be used in newspapers and books.

The Jews acquired full civil rights in the new Turkish state created by Mustafa Kemal (Atatürk) in the early 1920s. Most Jews now lived in the larger cities. In 1927, half of Turkey's 81,500 Jews lived in Istanbul (Constantinople). In the 1920s and 1930s, many Jews emigrated, mainly to the Americas.

After 1948, 30,000 to 40,000 Jews emigrated to Israel. Emigration to other countries continued as well.

Syria and Lebanon
Syria and Lebanon became separate French mandates after World War I, and independent countries after World War II. Only 15,000 Jews lived in Syria in the 1940s, but the two main communities, Aleppo and Damascus, were old and well established. Most Jews left Syria after 1948, for Israel or other countries. About 4,000 Jews lived in Lebanon in the 1940s, mainly in Beirut. In the 1950s, the Jews in Lebanon were better off than in other Arab countries, but in the 1960s most Jews emigrated.

THE JEWS IN CONSTANTINOPLE (ISTANBUL)

JEWS lived in Constantinople continuously since antiquity. Their status and conditions were affected by the changing character of the city over the centuries, from Christian-Byzantine to Muslim-Turkish times. There was no permanent Jewish quarter, and in different periods the Jews moved from one part of the city to another, although they settled for longer periods on the southern shore of the Golden Horn.

The long presence of the Jews in Constantinople was reflected in their

Gate of Etz Hayyim synagogue in Ortaköy, Istanbul. Synagogue burned down in 1934 and was rebuilt.

internal organization. There was an older group of Romaniots, the remnants of the first Jewish settlers. A large number of Jews exiled from Spain and Portugal arrived in the sixteenth century. They prospered in Constantinople, attaining important positions in public life, and created a new Jewish type and culture in the Ottoman Empire. Additional Jewish settlers came in later centuries, including, in the eighteenth century, Ashkenazic Jews. The various Jewish groups did not organize in a common framework, but maintained separate communities, according to their origins. Severe fires in the seventeenth and eighteenth centuries destroyed large sections of the Jewish neighborhoods, which led the diverse groups to seek greater cooperation with one another.

The sixteenth and seventeenth centuries marked a high point in the development and influence of Constantinople Jewry. In the nineteenth century, the Jews were strongly influenced by the gradual penetration of European culture. In 1864, the authorities reorganized the minority groups (*millets*, or nations), including the Jews. The post of *hakham-bashi* (chief rabbi) was created in 1835, with broad powers over the religious and internal life of the Jewish communities in the empire.

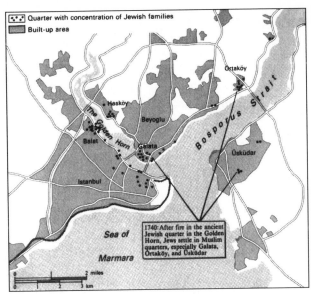

THE JEWS IN CONSTANTINOPLE

This strengthened the position of Constantinople Jewry. In the late nineteenth century, 40,000 to 50,000 Jews lived in the city, and perhaps even more in the early twentieth century, but their number decreased after World War I. With the establishment of the Turkish republic, Jews became full citizens, and their economic and professional situation improved. Nevertheless, many emigrated, mostly to Europe, America, and, after 1948, Israel.

THE JEWS IN SALONIKA

UNTIL the nineteenth century, the Jewish communities of Salonika and Constantinople were the two largest in the world. In Salonika, the Jews were able to create a much more unified community than in Constantinople. In the early twentieth century, there were more than 50,000 Jews in the city, about half of Salonika's total population. There was also a large community of "Doenmeh," descendants of seventeenth-century followers of the false messiah Shabbetai Zevi who had become Muslims without renouncing Judaism, which they interpreted according to new principles. Most of the Jews were Sephardim, descendants of Spanish-Portuguese Jews who had arrived in the sixteenth century. Salonika became a major religious and spiritual center of Sephardic Jewry, known for its rabbis

THE JEWS IN SALONIKA

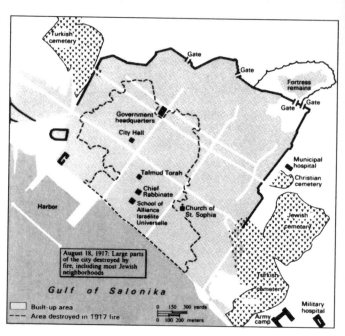

and sages. In the nineteenth century, Salonika also became a center of Jewish enlightenment (*haskalah*). A small but very influential element were the Francos—European Jewish merchants from Central and Western Europe, who were important transmitters of modern ideas.

Particularly interesting was the occupational structure of Salonika Jewry. Jews were in all the occupations: manual laborers, stevedores (the large Salonika port was said to have closed down on the Sabbath and other Jewish holy days), artisans, as well as large merchants, professionals, and bankers. A group of Jewish intellectuals and Doenmeh belonged to the Young Turk revolutionaries in the first decade of the twentieth century. In 1913, the city was handed over to Greece.

Large fires in the city in 1890 and 1917 destroyed the Jewish neighborhoods and ruined their inhabitants. After World War I, many Jews left Salonika, while Christian Greeks settled in the city. The portion of Jews in the total population decreased in the interwar years to 25 percent, but Salonika remained an important Jewish center.

The end of the Jewish community came in the summer of 1943. The German conquerors sent most of the 40,000 to 50,000 Jews living in Salonika (including many previously deported there from other places) to death camps in Poland.

THE KARAITES

THE Karaite sect dates to the eighth century. Karaism opposed the mainstream talmudic-rabbinic tradition, rejecting the "Oral Law" and adhering to a fundamentalist, literal reading of the written text of the Bible.

In modern times, most Karaites lived in Russia (Lithuania and the Crimea), Poland, Egypt, and Palestine. In the eighteenth century, when the Russian Empire absorbed Lithuania, the Karaites were recognized as a separate religious sect; the same happened in 1840 regarding the Crimean Karaites. At the end of the nineteenth century, there were about 13,000 Karaites in Russia, mostly in the Crimea. The Karaites spoke a variety of languages: an Arabic dialect in Iraq and Egypt, a Turkish dialect in Constantinople, and Crimean-Tataric in the Crimea.

In the twentieth century, their number decreased to about 12,000 (1930). Most

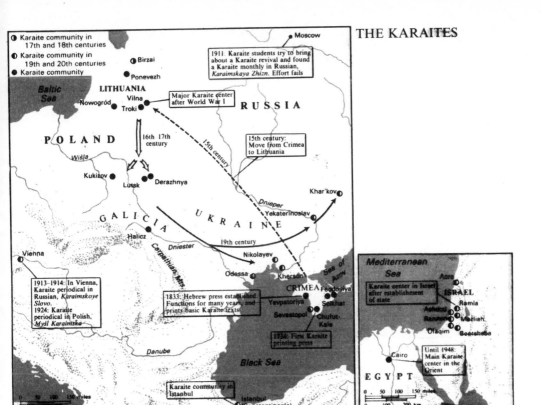

Map legend:
- ◐ Karaite community in 17th and 18th centuries
- ◑ Karaite community in 19th and 20th centuries
- ● Karaite community

1911: Karaite students try to bring about a Karaite revival and found a Karaite monthly in Russian, *Karaimskaya Zhizn*. Effort fails

Major Karaite center after World War I

15th century: Move from Crimea to Lithuania

16th 17th century

15th century

19th century

1913–1914: In Vienna, Karaite periodical in Russian, *Karaimskoye Slovo*. 1924: Karaite periodical in Polish, *Myśl Karaimska*

1833: Hebrew press established. Functions for many years, and prints basic Karaite texts

1734: First Karaite printing press

Karaite community in Istanbul

Karaite center in Israel after establishment of state

Until 1948: Main Karaite center in the Orient

Labels: Moscow, Birzai, Ponevezh, LITHUANIA, Vilna, Nowogród, Troki, RUSSIA, POLAND, Wisła, Kukizov, Lutsk, Derazhnya, Khar'kov, Dnieper, Yekaterinoslav, GALICIA, UKRAINE, Halicz, Carpathian Mts., Dniester, Vienna, Nikolayev, Odessa, Kherson, Sea of Azov, CRIMEA, Feodosiya, Yevpatoriya, Solkhat, Sevastopol, Chufut-Kale, Danube, Black Sea, Baltic Sea, Mediterranean Sea, Acre, ISRAEL, Ramla, Ashdod, Rehovot, Rishon, Ofaqim, Beersheba, Cairo, EGYPT, Istanbul (Constantinople)

lived in the former Soviet Union, and the rest in Poland (Vilna became a Karaite center), Turkey, Iraq, Egypt, and Palestine. During World War II, the Germans granted a Karaite request for recognition as an independent religious group. Nevertheless, their centers in Europe were destroyed.

Most Karaites from Muslim countries emigrated to Israel after the establishment of the state. The largest concentration of them settled in Ramla, which became the seat of their leading institutions: a synagogue, a yeshiva, and a religious court; unlike the Muslim or Druse religious courts, however, the Karaite one did not have state sanction. Smaller Karaite communities were established in other Israeli localities.

In Israel, they are defined as "Karaite Jews." Since the Karaites strictly obey the biblical prohibition against "counting the people," there are no exact data about their number. Estimates range from 10,000 to 18,000, most in Israel, and the rest in the United States, Canada, France, and Turkey.

THE ETHIOPIAN JEWS

THE Jews of Ethiopia (generally called Falashas; they call themselves Beta Esrael, or "House of Israel") consider themselves descendants of King Solomon and the Queen of Sheba. Researchers think that they are black tribes that adopted the Jewish religion in the Middle Ages. Their holy books are the Bible and part of the Apocrypha. They did not know the Mishnah or the Talmud.

THE ETHIOPIAN JEWS

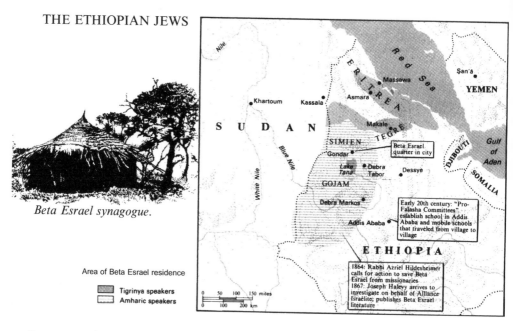

Beta Esrael synagogue.

Area of Beta Esrael residence

Tigrinya speakers

Amharic speakers

Early 20th century: "Pro-Falasha Committees" establish school in Addis Ababa and mobile schools that traveled from village to village

1864: Rabbi Azriel Hildesheimer calls for action to save Beta Esrael from missionaries. 1867: Joseph Halevy arrives to investigate on behalf of Alliance Israélite; publishes Beta Esrael literature

It seems that until the seventeenth century, they were a largely autonomous community, even independent at times. They retained their identity even when subjected to persecutions instigated by Christian missionaries. "Pro-Falasha Committees" were organized among European Jews in the twentieth century, to help the Ethiopian Jews.

Their number in the early twentieth century is estimated to have been 50,000. They lived in northern Ethiopia, near the Sudanese border, in or around the city of Gondar. They worked in agriculture and crafts. Their language was Amharic, the official language of Ethiopia, but they read the Bible in Ge'ez, the classical holy language of the Ethiopian church. They were organized in communities led by religious leaders.

The Jewish Agency established contact with the Ethiopian Jews before the creation of the state of Israel. In 1969, they numbered 25,000 to 30,000. Their situation deteriorated considerably in the 1960s and 1970s, due to the political situation in Ethiopia, and efforts were made to rescue them. In the course of 1991, the overwhelming majority of Ethiopian Jewry was brought to Israel.

THE JEWS IN IRAQ

IRAQ became part of the Ottoman Empire in 1638. Jews (referred to in Hebrew as Babylonian Jews) had lived in the country since the dawn of Jewish history. In the modern period, they were divided in two groups: the inhabitants of the lowlands (living mainly in the capital, Baghdad), and the mountain Jews of Kurdistan. They were defined as a minority (*millet*), and although their situation depended considerably on the whims of the local ruler (the pasha), it was usually better than that of the Jews in most other Muslim countries and that of the Christian *millet*. Conditions improved further starting in 1839, with the implementation of the social reforms (*tanzimat*) in the Ottoman Empire. The special poll tax (*jizya*) was abolished in 1855, and new rights were gradually granted. With the British conquest of Iraq in 1917, the Jews acquired civil rights equal to those of the Muslims. After Iraq achieved independence in 1932, Jews became full citizens of the new state. Parts of the community integrated into the cultural and political life of the general society and underwent "Iraqization." But their situation was ambivalent: first signs of discrimination began to appear, reflecting nationalistic and anti-European tendencies in Iraqi society. In mid-1941, there were severe riots against the Jews in Baghdad and other parts of the country. Hundreds of Jews were killed.

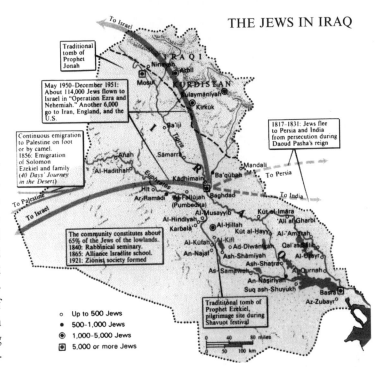

Map labels:

To Israel

Traditional tomb of Prophet Jonah

I R A Q

Ninivah · Mosul · Arbil

K U R D I S T A N

Sulaymaniyah

Kirkuk

May 1950–December 1951: About 114,000 Jews flown to Israel in "Operation Ezra and Nehemiah." Another 6,000 go to Iran, England, and the U.S.

Ba'iji

1817–1831: Jews flee to Persia and India from persecution during Daoud Pasha's reign

Continuous emigration to Palestine on foot or by camel. 1856: Emigration of Solomon Ezekiel and family (40 Days' Journey in the Desert).

Anah · Sāmarrā

Al-Hadithah

Mandali

Kādhimain · Ba'qubah · To Persia

Tigris · Euphrates

Hit · Ar-Ramadi · Fallujah · Baghdad · To India

To Palestine · (Pumbedita)

To Israel

Al-Hindiyah · Al-Musayyib · Kūt al-Imāra · 'Ali al-Gharbi

Karbalā · Al-Hillah · Kūt al-Hayy · Al-Amarah

The community constitutes about 65% of the Jews of the lowlands. 1840: Rabbinical seminary. 1865: Alliance Israélite school. 1921: Zionist society formed

Al-Kūfah · Al-Kifl · Ad-Diwaniyah · Qal'at Sālih

An-Najaf · Ash-Shāmiyah · Ash-Shatra · Al-Ujayr

As-Samawah · Al-Qurnah

An-Nāsiriyah

Suq ash-Shuyukh · Basra · Az-Zubayr

Traditional tomb of Prophet Ezekiel, pilgrimage site during Shavuot festival

o Up to 500 Jews
• 500–1,000 Jews
◉ 1,000–5,000 Jews
▣ 5,000 or more Jews

0   40   80 miles
0   50   100 km

In the twentieth century, more than two-thirds of Iraqi Jewry lived in Baghdad, which was the spiritual center for all Jews who lived east of Damascus. Its leading position had been established in the nineteenth century, in the days of Rabbi Joseph Haim (1833/5–1909), the community's leading religious figure from 1859. While the religious authority was in the hands of the rabbi, the community was headed by the sheikh (or *nasi*), usually a rich Jew who was well connected with the authorities and had the power to veto communal appointments. Baghdad Jewry was a community primarily of merchants, some very important, whose activities extended over the whole country and beyond.

Iraqi Jewry had always maintained contact with Palestine. In the twentieth century, immigration to Palestine increased, and by 1948, about 11,000 Iraqi Jews already lived in the country. The creation of Israel caused severe tension between the Jews and the general Iraqi population. An agreement was reached in 1950 that enabled all the Jews to emigrate from Iraq to Israel. Almost the entire community of about 120,000, including the Kurdish Jews, left in a short time in what is known as "Operation Ezra and Nehemiah." Most went to Israel; others, to Europe and the United States.

THE JEWS IN KURDISTAN

THE majority of Kurdish Jewry lived in the mountain region of northern Iraq. They constituted a well-defined group among Middle Eastern Jewry, with their own Jewish culture and traditions, very different from those of the Jews in the

The map contains the following labels:

Kurdistan
District capital in Iraqi Kurdistan

SOVIET UNION

THE JEWS IN KURDISTAN

TURKEY

IRAN

Lake Van

Traditional tomb of Prophet Nahum

Diyarbakir
Mardin
Nusaybin
Urfa
El-Qamishliye

Atrush
Amadiyah
Nerva
Zakho
Zhuxt
Zibar
Dihok
Aqrah Rawandiz
Mosul Nineveh
Arbil Qala Dize
Shaqlawa Koi Sanjaq Ranya Banen
Sulaymaniyah
Kirkuk Halabja
Tuz Khurmatu
Khanaqin

Urmia Maragheh
Miandowab
Naqadeh Shahin Dezh
Takab
Saqqez
Bijar
Sanandaj

1900, 1906: Alliance Israélite schools

SYRIA

Mislawi Jews of Mosul understand Kurdish but speak Arabic

1912: Alliance Israélite school

IRAQ

1880, 1888, 1889: Drought years. Many Jews fled to Baghdad. Committee formed to look after refugees. 1894–1895, 1910: Riots. Jews flee to Baghdad

0   40   80 miles
0   50   100 km

Tigris

Iraqi lowlands, and much older. In the twentieth century, there were 15,000 to 20,000 Kurdish Jews living in about 150 small mountain villages in Iraq and about 50 villages in northeastern Iran, southeastern Turkey, and Syria—the other areas into which Kurdistan extends. They lived in greater hardship than the Jews of the Iraqi lowlands. The rule of the local Kurdish chieftain (the *aga*),

to which they were subject, was often oppressive. The portion of Kurdish Jews in agriculture was higher than that of other Jewries, but many were virtually serfs. Other Kurdish Jews were artisans or small tradesmen. They spoke Judeo-Kurdish, an Aramaic dialect used also by other minorities of the region, as well as Kurdish, an Indo-European language akin to Persian.

The political changes in Iraq in the 1930s and 1940s made the situation of Kurdish Jews increasingly difficult. Riots against the Jews in the lowlands spread to the mountains. Many Kurdish Jews began to emigrate to Palestine, to which the community had a longstanding attachment, and when Israel was established it already had a sizable Kurdish community. Most Kurdish Jews—from Iraq and the neighboring countries—went to Israel in "Operation Ezra and Nehemiah."

THE JEWS IN IRAN

THE Jewish communities in Persia (renamed Iran in 1935) were among the oldest in Jewish history. In the early nineteenth century, when Persia dominated Afghanistan in the east and regions in Central Asia in the north, it had about 50,000 Jews. When those lands were later lost, the number of Jews in Persia fell to about 25,000. It rose again to 50,000 in the twentieth century, reaching a peak on the eve of the creation of Israel—about 90,000, including 13,000 Jews in Iranian Kurdistan. On the eve of Israel's establishment, 20,000 to 30,000 Iranian Jews were living in Palestine. More came later, but in 1975 there were still about 80,000

Jews in Iran. The Jews were a tiny part of the total population: 0.5 percent at the beginning of the century, and 0.2 percent in the 1970s.

The legal situation of the Jews conformed to the traditional Muslim pattern: protected subjects, who had to pay the poll tax (*jizya*), and from time to time were subjected to discriminatory regulations. There were occasional persecutions, such as under the Safawid dynasty (1502–1736), which tried to convert the Jews. Legislation in 1906 broadened the civil rights of the non-Muslim minorities, including the Jews. The *jizya*, however, was abolished only in

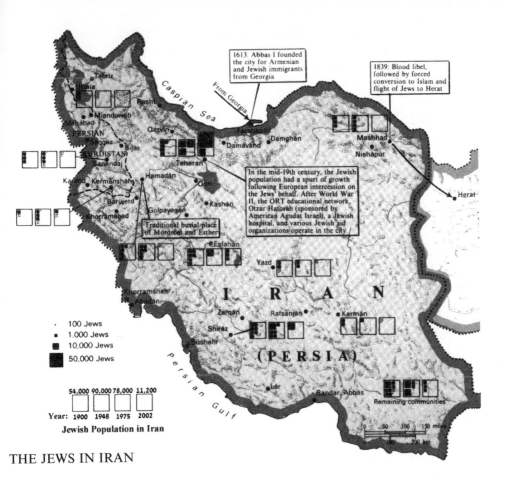

THE JEWS IN IRAN

1926—much later than in other Muslim countries—after Reza Shah Pahlavi rose to power, and equal rights were granted to all the country's inhabitants.

The Jews were scattered throughout Iran, living mainly in cities. In the early twentieth century, the largest Jewish center was Shiraz and its vicinity—although only 10 to 15 percent of all Persian Jews lived there. In the coming years, the Jewish population gradually became concentrated in several larger centers, especially the capital, Teheran: about 30 percent of the country's Jews in 1948, and about 75 percent in 1975, when more than 90 percent were living in three major centers. Parallel to the concentration in cities, Iranian Jewry was influenced by modern European manners and

concepts, and integrated into the country's social and cultural life.

The occupations of the Jews reflected their urban character. Until the early twentieth century, they were mainly small tradesmen and craftsmen. Later they branched out into new fields: as professionals, merchants (some of them very large), real-estate agents, and the like.

Like other Middle Eastern Jewish communities, Iranian Jewry had a twin leadership, religious (the *mullah*, or rabbi) and secular (the *kadkhuda*). The *kadkhuda* was responsible for the collection of the *jizya* and the community's relations with the authorities. The *mullah* acted also as religious judge, teacher, and *shohet* (ritual slaughterer). Sometimes the same prestigious figure occupied both offices, bearing the title *nasi*. Sometimes the *nasi* served with a council of elders, the "eyes of the community." In the second half of the twentieth century, most matters regarding Iranian Jewry were dealt with by the Organization of Teheran Jews, which aimed to represent all the country's Jews.

After 1948, part of Iranian Jewry migrated to Israel. The Islamic revolution in 1979 completely changed the internal life of the Jewish community. The new regime regarded all Jews as Zionists, and most Jewish institutions were forced to cease operations. Several leading Jewish figures, including the former head of the Teheran community, were executed. Most Jews managed to leave the country, settling mainly in Europe, America, and Israel.

THE JEWS IN AFGHANISTAN

ALTHOUGH there are documents from the early Middle Ages mentioning Jews in Afghanistan, most Afghan Jews in the modern period were of Persian origin. They lived mainly in the western part of the country, in Harat (about 2,000 Jews in the mid-nineteenth century) and Balkh (about 100 Jews in the early twentieth century). In 1948, there were about 4,000 Jews in the country. Laws enacted in 1933 granted the Jews equal rights.

Afghan Jews were mostly traders, many of them in the international commerce between Persia, Bukhara (until the Russian Revolution), and India. They had close social and economic relations with the Jewish community of Meshed, in northeastern Persia.

Most Jews left Afghanistan in 1951 and 1952, the majority emigrating to Israel, and others to Europe and America.

THE JEWS IN YEMEN

As in many other countries, Jews had been living in Yemen for centuries; legends place them there even before the Second Temple period. In the nineteenth and twentieth centuries, they were in hundreds of communities throughout Yemen, some of them very small. The largest was in San'a, the capital, where 5,000 to 10,000 Jews lived in the early twentieth century, making up 5 to 10 percent of its population.

Most Yemenite Jews were concentrated in three regions: the central plateau, in and around San'a; the south, the Shar'ab region; and the north, the Heidan-ash-Sham region, where the main community lived in Sa'dah. Two additional, smaller Jewish settlements were in Habban and its environs and in Aden, Arabia's important southwestern port, under British domination from 1839. In each region, the Jews had their distinct dialect

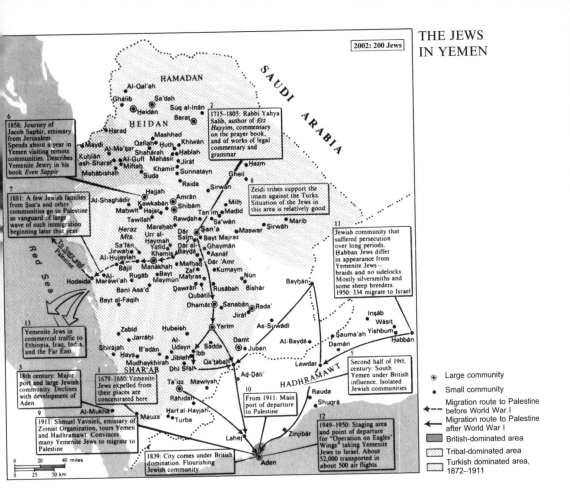

THE JEWS
IN YEMEN

2002: 200 Jews

HAMADAN

Al-Qal'ah
Ghālib   Sa'dah
    Heidān   Sūq al-Inān
HEIDAN   Barat

6
1858: Journey of
Jacob Saphir, emissary
from Jerusalem.
Spends about a year in
Yemen visiting remote
communities. Describes
Yemenite Jewry in his
book Even Sappir

SAUDI ARABIA

1715–1805: Rabbi Yahya
Salih, author of Etz
Hayyim, commentary
on the prayer book,
and of works of legal
commentary and
grammar

Harad   Mashhad
    Qaflah Huth Khiwan
Maydi Al-Ma'sar Shaharah Hablah
Kublan Al-Guft Mahasir Jirat
esh-Sharat Miftah Khamir Sunnatayn
Mahabishah   Suda Hazm
              Raida Sirwah

7
1881: A few Jewish families
from San'a and other
communities go to Palestine
as vanguard of large
wave of such immigration
beginning later that year

Hajjah   Amran
Al-Shaghadir Kawkaban Shibam Milh
    Mahwit Hajar Tan'im Madid
        Tawilah Rawdah Sa'wan
Heraz Marahab Dar Maswar Sirwah Marib
Mts. Urr al- Salm Bayt Majraz
Sa'fan Haymah Yafid Ghaymān
Jirwah Khamis Baydā Asnaf
Al-Hujaylah   Mafhad Dar 'Amr
    Baji Rugab Bayt Kumaym Nun
Marawi'ah Maymun Mahras Bayhan
Hodeida   Dawran Rusabah Bishar
    Bani Asa'd Qubati
Bayt al-Faqih   Dhamar Sanaban Rada'
            Jirat

8
Zeidi tribes support the
imam against the Turks.
Situation of the Jews in
this area is relatively good

11
Jewish community that
suffered persecution
over long periods.
Habban Jews differ
in appearance from
Yemenite Jews—
braids and no sidelocks.
Mostly silversmiths and
some sheep breeders.
1950: 334 migrate to Israel

Red Sea

To Suez and Palestine

13
Yemenite Jews in
commercial traffic to
Ethiopia, Iraq, India,
and the Far East

Zabid Hubeish   Yarim
    Jarrahi   Damt As-Suwadi
Shirajah B'adan Al- Sadda Al-Bayda Daman
Hays   Udayn Juban
Mudhaykhirah Jibleh Ibb Qa'tabah
Dhi Sfal   Lawdar   HADHRAMAWT

Insāb
    Wāsit
        Yishbum
Sauma'ah   Habbān

5
Second half of 19th
century: South
Yemen under British
influence. Isolated
Jewish communities

3
18th century: Major
port and large Jewish
community. Declines
with development of
Aden

1
1679–1680: Yemenite
Jews expelled from
their places are
concentrated here
SHAR'AB

Ta'izz Mawiyah
        Rahidah

10
From 1911: Main
port of departure
to Palestine

Rauda
Shuqra

9
Al-Mukha Mauza
        Turba
Harf al-Hayjah

1911: Shmuel Yavnieli, emissary of
Zionist Organization, tours Yemen
and Hadhramawt. Convinces
many Yemenite Jews to migrate to
Palestine

Lahej   Zinjibar

12
1949–1950: Staging area
and point of departure
for "Operation on Eagles'
Wings" taking Yemenite
Jews to Israel. About
52,000 transported in
about 500 air flights

1839: City comes under British
domination. Flourishing
Jewish community
Aden

0   20   40 miles
0 25   50 km

● Large community
• Small community
←-- Migration route to Palestine
    before World War I
← Migration route to Palestine
    after World War I
▨ British-dominated area
▨ Tribal-dominated area
▨ Turkish dominated area,
    1872–1911

(in both Hebrew and Arabic), dress, customs, occupations, and pattern of relations with the local populations.

As was usual in the Muslim lands, the Jews were, in principle, protected subjects, paying the *jizya* and practicing their own religion and customs. In fact, however, they were subjected to many discriminatory regulations: the prohibitions on building houses higher than those of their Muslim neighbors and on riding horses. But there were no restrictions on their occupations, and they were permitted to own real estate and businesses. The Jews were frequent victims of Yemen's internal troubles, such as the protracted struggles between the central ruler (the imam) and the local chieftains,

or between both of these and the Ottoman overlords. The seventeenth century was a particularly troubled one. The Shabbatean movement (1667) swept Yemenite Jewry, which incensed the Yemeni rulers. In 1679, many Jews were exiled briefly to the remote southern city of Mauza. New restrictive laws were imposed on the Jews in the eighteenth and nineteenth centuries: San'a's synagogues were closed for thirty years (1762–1792); Jews were forced to do menial cleaning jobs; and the community had to deliver Jewish orphans for conversion. These regulations were enforced mainly in the central and southern regions, where the imam's authority was more effective. In the north and east, where the tribal heads

Final page of 15th-century San'a Bible.

ing it for some months. He reinstituted the traditional laws regarding the Jews. They were reaffirmed in 1911, when the imam and the Turks reached an agreement, giving the imam control over the country's internal affairs.

Yemen's Jews were not centrally organized. Each community had full local responsibility. The local leadership was divided between the *mori* (rabbi) and the *haakil* (or sheikh, head, *nasi*). The *mori* was responsible for the community's internal affairs; the *haakil* dealt with matters between the community and the local rulers. Since his position was recognized by the authorities, his standing was higher than the *mori*'s.

Most Yemenite Jews were craftsmen (few Yemeni Muslims worked in crafts) or small businessmen. A few Jews became large merchants, some even on an international scale, and had connections with India, Iraq, and Ethiopia. Many Jews owned land, although the farming was done by Muslims.

Yemenite Jews began to emigrate from the country in the early nineteenth century, establishing communities in India, Egypt, Ethiopia, and Sudan. In 1881, they began to emigrate to Palestine in growing numbers. It is estimated that in early 1948, about 52,000 Jews lived in Yemen, and tens of thousands of Yemenite Jews were already in Palestine. Most of the others migrated to Israel after its establishment.

were powerful, the situation of the Jews was sometimes easier. The best place for Jews was Aden, under the British.

After the Ottoman reconquest of Yemen in the second half of the nineteenth century, most restrictions against the Jews were abolished. But Ottoman power did not extend equally over the whole country; it was effective only in the central plateau and along the Red Sea coast. In other parts of Yemen, especially in the north and east, the local tribes remained semi-independent; toward the end of the nineteenth century, they rebelled against the Turks. In 1905, Imam Yahya occupied the capital, San'a, hold-

THE JEWS IN INDIA

THE Jews in India historically consisted of three groups. Two of them, Bene Israel and Cochin Jews, had lived in the country since ancient times; there is no documentary information about their origins. The third group was composed of Jews who had emigrated from various countries since the sixteenth century.

The Cochin Jews lived on the Malabar Coast, in southwestern India. The Bene Israel lived in villages in the Konkan region, south of Bombay. In the second

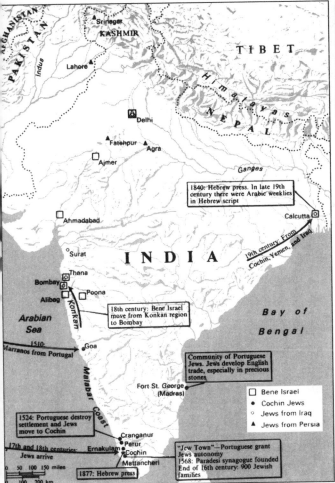

Tamil inscription on copper plate in which Hindu ruler of Malabar grants privileges to Cochin Jews.

Map labels:

AFGHANISTAN
PAKISTAN
KASHMIR
Srinegar
Lahore
Indus
TIBET
Himalayas
NEPAL
Delhi
Fatehpur
Agra
Ajmer
Ganges
Ahmadabad
Calcutta
1840: Hebrew press. In late 19th century there were Arabic weeklies in Hebrew script
Surat
INDIA
19th century: From Cochin, Yemen, and Iraq
Thana
Bombay
Poona
Alibag
Konkan
Arabian Sea
18th century: Bene Israel move from Konkan region to Bombay
Bay of Bengal
1510: Marranos from Portugal
Goa
Malabar Coast
Community of Portuguese Jews. Jews develop English trade, especially in precious stones
Fort St. George (Madras)
1524: Portuguese destroy settlement and Jews move to Cochin
Bene Israel
Cochin Jews
Jews from Iraq
Jews from Persia
17th and 18th centuries: Jews arrive
Cranganur
Parur
Ernakulam
Cochin
Mattancheri
"Jew Town"—Portuguese grant Jews autonomy 1568: Paradesi synagogue founded End of 16th century: 900 Jewish families
1877: Hebrew press
0 50 100 150 miles
0 100 200 km

THE JEWS IN INDIA

half of the eighteenth century, they began to move to Bombay, and only then was contact established between the two groups. The Cochin Jews guided the Bene Israel in Jewish matters. The European Jews who arrived in the sixteenth century were mostly Spanish-Portuguese, but they also included Ashkenazim. They settled in the towns along the Malabar Coast. Some mixed with the Cochin Jews, creating yet another Jewish group. Additional Jewish settlers migrated from Yemen, Persia, and Iraq. At the end of the eighteenth century and especially during the nineteenth century, hundreds of Iraqi Jews, mostly from Basra and Baghdad (and therefore designated "Baghdadis"), came to India. They settled mostly in Bombay and Calcutta, where they formed their own communities. The Baghdadis were large-scale merchants, with international connections (the Sassoon, Kedoorie, Gabai, and Yehuda families), who traded throughout Asia.

The situation of the Jews in India was good. Under Dutch domination in Cochin (1663–1795), the Jews enjoyed the same rights as Jews in Holland. After the British conquest of India in the 1770s, their situation remained unchanged. Nevertheless, the rigid caste system in

399

Hindu society kept the Jews isolated in their own social stratum. In the twentieth century, in Israel, questions arose regarding the religious status of the two older groups of Indian Jews (especially the Bene Israel), since they observed only part of the *halakhah*. Most of the problems were solved.

There were about 7,000 Bene Israel in 1880. In the early twentieth century, there were 3,500 Jews in Cochin. In 1948, there were 28,000 Jews in India, more than half of whom were Bene Israel, and the others mainly Baghdadis and Cochin Jews. From the 1950s, many Jews left the country, emigrating to Israel, Australia, the United States, and Canada.

THE JEWS IN THE FAR EAST

JEWISH traders visited the Far East in the Middle Ages and established commercial relations in different countries, but did not settle there. Jews settled in China in the nineteenth century, in the wake of the European penetration, mainly in Hong Kong, Shanghai, and Tientsin. Most of these Jews were British citizens, from India or Iraq. In 1937, there were about 10,000 Jews in China, many of them refugees from Europe. From 1938 to 1941, 18,000 to 20,000 Jews fled from Europe to Shanghai, then under Japanese domination. In the 1940s, their number rose to between 25,000 and 30,000. In 1948, after the Communist victory in China, most Jews left the country. They emigrated to Israel, the United States, or the former Soviet Union. Several hundred Jews remained in Hong Kong.

In 2001, there were about 1,000 Jews in Japan (mainly in Tokyo and Yokohama), about 1,000 Jews in China (mainly Hong Kong), and a few hundred in Singapore, Thailand, and the Philippines. Most of them had arrived in these countries in the second half of the twentieth century from Europe, Israel, and elsewhere.

China 2002: 1,000 Jews

1937: City has about 5,000 Jews, mostly refugees from the Russian Revolution

Community grows after World War II

Community grows after Russo–Japanese War and 1923 earthquake in Yokohama

1937: About 2,500 Jews in city

1894: First Jewish community in Japan

1937: About 2,000 Jews in city
1938–1941: About 20,000 Jewish refugees arrive from Europe

17th–18th century: Marranos arrive
1898: Jewish settlement in wake of American conquest
1937: About 1,200 Jews in city
1976: About 200 Jews

1842: Jews come from Baghdad with British conquest (Sassoon and Kadoorie families). Develop town's commerce
1900: Ohel Leah synagogue founded
1976: About 200 Jews in city

Mid-19th century: Jews come from Baghdad with British army. Merchants among them
1942: About 2,500 Jews in Burma. Most immigrate to Israel

Several dozen Jews in city from beginning of 20th century

1890: About 200 Jews in city
1939: About 2,500, mostly Sephardim
1975: About 500 Jews

E. European Jewry in the Interwar Years

THE JEWS IN EAST CENTRAL EUROPE

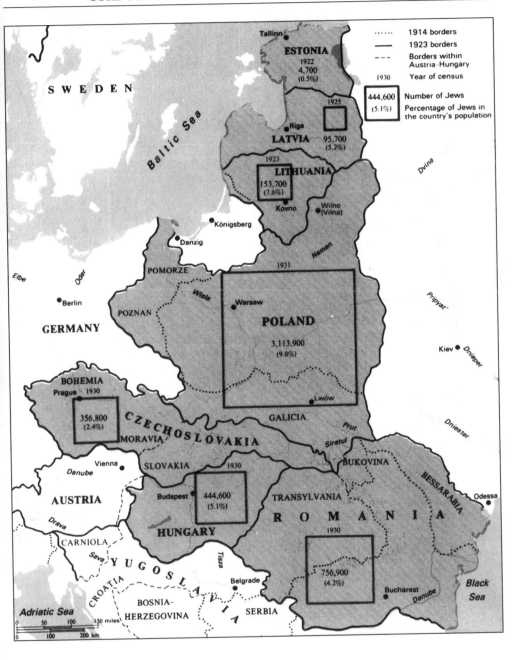

Legend:
- `......` 1914 borders
- `———` 1923 borders
- `- - -` Borders within Austria-Hungary
- 1930 Year of census
- 444,600 (5.1%) Number of Jews / Percentage of Jews in the country's population

SWEDEN

ESTONIA 1922 / 4,700 (0.5%)

Tallinn

Baltic Sea

Riga

LATVIA 1925 — 95,700 (5.2%)

Dvina

1923

LITHUANIA 153,700 (7.6%)

Kovno · Wilno (Vilna)

Königsberg

Danzig

Neman

Elbe · Oder

POMORZE

Wisła

1931

Berlin

POZNAN

Warsaw

POLAND 3,113,900 (9.8%)

Pripyat'

GERMANY

Kiev · Dnieper

BOHEMIA Prague 1930

356,800 (2.4%)

CZECHOSLOVAKIA

MORAVIA

Lwów

GALICIA

Prut

Dniester

Siretul

BUKOVINA

Vienna

Danube

SLOVAKIA 1930

BESSARABIA

Odessa

AUSTRIA

Budapest · 444,600 (5.1%)

TRANSYLVANIA

R O M A N I A

Drava

CARNIOLA

HUNGARY

1930

Save **Y U G O S L A V I A**

Tisza

756,900 (4.2%)

Belgrade

Bucharest · Danube

Black Sea

Adriatic Sea

CROATIA

BOSNIA-HERZEGOVINA

SERBIA

0 50 100 150 miles
0 100 200 km

EASTERN Europe underwent far-reaching political changes in the wake of World War I. The Austro-Hungarian Empire was dissolved, and the considerably reduced Austrian state (whose Jewish population was concentrated in the capital, Vienna) belonged culturally to Western Europe. Large parts of the former

Russian Empire became independent countries.

About 8 million Jews, half of the Jewish people, lived in Eastern Europe in the interwar period. Politically, they were divided into two groups: one in the Soviet Union, and the other in East Central Europe. The large Jewish group in the Soviet Union found itself in conditions very different from those of other European Jewries, as a result of the Russian Revolution. In the southern part of East Central Europe (the Balkans), several Jewish communities bore the mark of their particular history, influenced by the former Turkish presence in part of the region and by their unique ethnic composition, including Sephardim.

About 5 million Jews lived in seven countries of East Central Europe, from Estonia in the north to Romania in the south. Most of those countries became politically independent after World War I, or gained territory (Romania) or lost it (Hungary). The Jewries of Central Europe were one of the most vital segments of the Jewish people, with well-established religious and cultural traditions, social characteristics that distinguished them from the general populations, and a very high level of Jewish consciousness. In most countries (the main exception being Czechoslovakia), relations between Jews and non-Jews were not good, and they deteriorated in the 1930s. This was partly a continuation of former tensions. In addition, political conditions in most of the new states were unstable, and the economic situation was difficult. Many new states contained large national minorities, including Jews, who did not live peacefully either with one another or with the majority group. The influence of the Nazi regime in Germany beginning in 1933 exacerbated the already deteriorating situation of the Jews in almost all the East Central European countries. The development of East Central European Jewry had a tragic dimension, presaging the impending disaster of World War II.

THE JEWS IN EASTERN EUROPE AFTER WORLD WAR I

MOST of the states carved out of Eastern Europe and the Balkans after the dissolution of the Russian and Austro-Hungarian empires were multinational. The Paris Peace Conference (1919) established the principle that the rights of minorities should be protected. The issue was much debated between the representatives of the victorious Entente powers and of the new states. The latter stressed that civil rights also guaranteed national rights, while the representatives of the national groups (including the Jews) demanded explicit recognition of their national status in addition to civil rights.

The Jews were one of the largest minority groups in several of the new states. Jewish delegates from these countries, as well as from Jewish organizations in Western Europe and America, went to Paris to lobby for Jewish rights in the new states. They disagreed among themselves about whether the Jews should content themselves with full civil rights or insist on recognition as a national group. On March 28, 1919, the Committee of Jewish Delegations to the Peace Conference was formed, comprising those seeking national recognition for East European Jews: the delegates of the East European Jewish national councils and the American Jewish Congress. Those who did not support the quest for national rights acted separately: the Joint Foreign Committee (representing part of British Jewry), the Alliance

Israélite Universelle, and members of the American Jewish Committee. The Zionists, who were the driving force behind the Committee of Jewish Delegations, also appeared separately before the peace conference's Council of Ten, on February 27, 1919. Led by Chaim Weizmann, they presented the case for a Jewish national home in Palestine.

The treaty with Poland, approved on June 28, 1919, was the most important document to come out of the conference on the minorities question. Several articles guaranteed the rights of the minorities living in Poland, but no mention was made of *national* rights. The treaty also included two "Jewish" clauses (numbers 10 and 11), which guaranteed the Jews control over their schools and recognized Saturday as the Jewish day of rest. Similar treaties were signed with the other new or restructured states. In practice, few of the new states fully upheld the Jewish minority clauses. During the 1930s, growing internal problems

POGROMS IN RUSSIA AND POLAND
1917–1921

in most East European states and the influence of the German Nazi regime worsened the general situation of the East European Jewries.

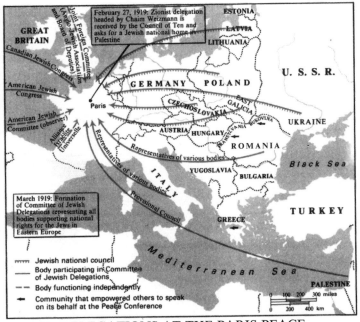

JEWISH DELEGATIONS AT THE PARIS PEACE
CONFERENCE, 1919

While negotiations were going on in Paris, the situation of the Jews in the lands bordering Poland and the Soviet Union deteriorated. The political uncertainty during the establishment of the Soviet and Polish states, and the internal struggle between the Red Russians and their opponents (White Russians and other groups), led to civil war in a region densely inhabited by Jews, in Galicia and in the former Pale of

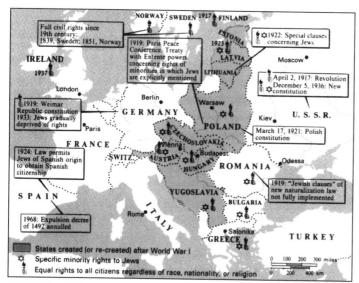

Full civil rights since
19th century:
1839, Sweden; 1851, Norway

IRELAND
1937

1919: Paris Peace
Conference. Treaty
with Entente powers
concerning rights of
minorities in which Jews
are explicitly mentioned

1922: Special clauses
concerning Jews

Moscow

London

Berlin

1919: Weimar
Republic constitution
1933: Jews gradually
deprived of rights

GERMANY

Warsaw

Paris

FRANCE

POLAND

Kiev

U. S. S. R.

March 17, 1921: Polish
constitution

April 2, 1917: Revolution
December 5, 1936: New
constitution

1924: Law permits
Jews of Spanish origin
to obtain Spanish
citizenship

SWITZ.

CZECHOSLOVAKIA

Vienna

AUSTRIA

Budapest

HUNGARY

ROMANIA

Odessa

YUGOSLAVIA

BULGARIA

1919: "Jewish clauses" of
new naturalization law
not fully implemented

SPAIN

1968: Expulsion decree
of 1492 annulled

Rome

ITALY

Salonika

GREECE

TURKEY

States created (or re-created) after World War I
Specific minority rights to Jews
Equal rights to all citizens regardless of race, nationality, or religion

0   100   200   300 miles
0   200   400 km

EQUAL RIGHTS AND MINORITY RIGHTS AFTER
WORLD WAR I

Settlement. The Jewish population suffered terribly from the soldiers' violence. The forceful intervention of the new Soviet regime improved the situation in the territories under its control. This did not apply to other armies, such as the Poles in the north and the bands led by Simon Petlyura and other chieftains in the Ukraine, who killed tens of thousands and destroyed hundreds of communities. The pogroms that erupted between 1917 and 1921 were the worst anti-Jewish outbreaks since the Cossacks' rebellion in 1648 and 1649.

THE JEWS IN POLAND 1921 TO 1931

ABOUT 3 million Jews lived in Poland in the interwar years, making it the largest Jewish community outside the United States. The Jews made up about 10 percent of the Polish population, but about 30 percent of all city dwellers.

The treaty signed by Poland on June 28, 1919, gave the Jews full Polish citizenship and guaranteed specific Jewish interests (religion, language, education). In practice, however, the attitude of the authorities was at least suspicious, and became increasingly negative. Antisemitic traditions and efforts to "Polonize" the state found expression in a variety of limitations imposed on the Jews. The difficult economic situation and the growing power of right-wing

political groups increased the pressure on the Jewish population.

Although the conditions in Poland spurred many Jews to emigrate, the interwar years were a period of cultural and educational blossoming and intense public and political activity. Communal institutions were established, including an impressive Jewish school system in which instruction was mostly in Yiddish or Hebrew.

Jewish life in Poland came to an end in World War II. More than 90 percent of Polish Jews were exterminated in the Holocaust. One of the most important communities in the history of the Jewish people disappeared.

HISTORICAL SUBGROUPS IN POLISH JEWRY

THE Polish state, reborn in 1919, was multinational. One-third of its population consisted of minorities: Ukrainians, Jews, White Russians, and Germans. The

Jews, the second largest national group in Poland, belonged to five different historical subgroups.

Congress (Central) Poland Jewry. In

Free city-state.
7,300 Jews in 1923
Danzig

350 Jews in the town.
2,900 Jews living in 32
localities in the province

WILNO

Dzisna

Glebokie

Dokszyce

Wilno
(Vilna)
56,200 (36.1)

Lida
Iwje

NOWOGRÓDEK

Nowogródek
Mir
Zdzieciol
Nieśwież
Kleck
Baranowicze

Suwalki
Augustów
Grajewo
Szczytno
Sokółka
Kolno
Krynki
Wolkowysk
Slonim
Grodno
18,700 (53.9)
Skidel

POMORZE
Bydgoszcz
Canal
Toruń

Wloclawek
Rypin
Mlawa
Przasnysz
Ostroleka
Lomza
Zambrów
BIALYSTOK
Bialystok
39,600 (51.6)

Bielsk
Brańsk
Ostrów Mazowiecki

Różana
Pruzana
Bereza Kartuska
Motol
Luninets
Pripyat'

Pinsk
17,500 (74.7)

Dawidgródek
Stolyn

POZNAŃ
Lipno
Sierpc
Gabin
Plock
Plońsk
Nasielsk
Wyszogród
Nowy
Dwor
Serock
Pultusk
Wyszków
Radzymin
Wolomin

Ciechanów
Maków

WARSAW

Warsaw
310,300 (33.1)

Narew
Siemiatycze
Sokolów
Wegrów

Kobryń
Brześć nad Bugiem
(Brest Litovsk)
15,600 (53.1)

POLESIE
Dubrovitsa
Sarny

penań
arra
Konin
Kolo
Turek
Kalisz
Warta
Blaszki
Sieradz
Wielun

Kutno
Leczyca
Ozorków
Aleksandrów
Zduńska
Wola
Pabjanice
Lask
Sochaczew
Zychlin
Grodzisk
Lowicz
gierz
Skierniewice
Brzeziny
Mszczonów
(Amshinov)
Grójec
Rawa
Mazowiecka
Mogielnica
Piaseczno
Zyrardów
Warka
Góra
Kalwaria

Lódź
156,200 (34.5)

Pilica

Minsk
Mazowiecki
Kaluszyn
Otwock
Siedlce
Biala Podlaska
Losice
Lukow
Miedzyrzec
Radzyń
Parczew
Wlodawa

VOLHYNIA
Berezno

Piotrków
Belchatów
Sulejów

Radomsko

Częstochowa
22,700
(28.2)

L Ó D Ź

Tomaszów Mazowiecka
Opoczno
Przysucha
Konskie
Szydlowiec
Wierzbnik

Radom
24,600 (39.7)
Zwoleń

Kozienice
Ryki
Kock
Pulawy
Kurów
Lublin
37,300 (39.6)
Opole
Piaski

Lubartów
Leczna
Chelm

Luboml
Kovel
Rozhishche
Luck
Olyka
Rowne
21,700
(71.2)
Dubno

Styr'
Tuczyn
Korzec
Ostrog

Zarki
Jedrzejów
Przedbórz
KIELCE
Ostrowiec
Wloszczowa
Chmielnik
Szczekociny
Kielce
Checiny
 Opatów
Ozarów
Sandomierz
Janów Lubelski
Krasnik
Izbica
Hrubieszów
Zamość

Szczebrzeszyn
Tarnobrzeg
Bilgoraj

Horochów
Wloclawek
(Ludmir)
Wlodzimierz

Wiszniowice
Krzemieniec

Zawiercie
Wodzisław
Staszów
Stopnica

Pinczów
Miechów
Dzialoszyce
Nowy Korczyn
Mielec
Dabrowa

e of Jewish
nmunities in 1921
2,000-5,000
5,000-10,000
10,000-20,000
20,000-100,000
100,000 or more

) Number of Jews in city
) Percentage of Jews
in total population
Border of province

Bedzin
17,900 (62.1)
Chorzów
Katowice
SILESIA
Dabrowa
Sosnowiec
13,600
(15.8)
Chrzanów
Kraków
45,200
(24.6)
Oświęcim
Bielsko Biala

Wolbrom
Olkusz

Bochnia
Tarnów
15,600 (44.1)

Jaslo
Gorlice
Nowy
Sacz
Sanok
Lesko

Rzeszów
Jaroslaw
Przemyśl
Dobromil
Sambor

Tarnogród
Tomaszów Lubelski
Rawa Ruska
Krystynopol'
Belz
Sokal

LWÓW
Jaworów
Gródek
Mościska
Zamarstynów
Zólkiew
Kamionka
Lwów
76,900
(35.0)
Zloczów
Przemyślany

TARNOPOL
Zbaraż
Podvolochisk
Tarnopol
Skalat

Brody
Krzemieniec

Komarno
Brzeżany
Drohobycz
Borysław
Tustanowice
Stryj
Turka
Skole
Bolechów
Dolina
Kalusz
Knihinin

STANISLAWÓW
Stanislawów
23,200 (45.2)
Tlumacz
Nadwórna
Horodenka

Dniester
Rohatyn
Podhajce
Buczacz
Czortków
Kopyczynce
Zaleszczyki

Prut
Kosów
Kutów
Sniatyn
Kolomyja

0   20   40   60 miles
0   40   80 km

the nineteenth century, Central Poland, although under Russian domination, was the heart of ethnic Poland. Some Jews in the larger cities were influenced by the dominant Polish culture, although the Hasidic movement was very strong in Central Poland.

Galician Jewry. Until the end of World War I, Galicia belonged to the Austro–Hungarian Empire, where Jews had enjoyed full civil rights since 1867. In the interwar years, the Polish cultural influence became stronger than the former German one. Jewish enlightenment had deep roots in Galicia, but the opposing Hasidic movement was also very influential.

405

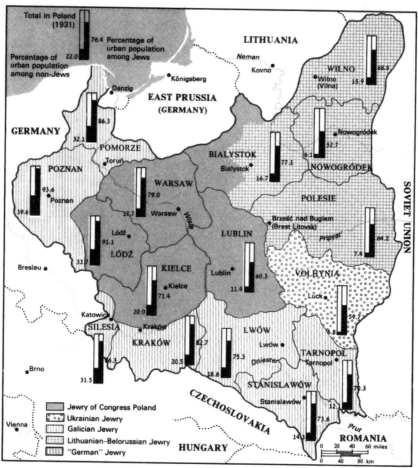

Total in Poland (1931)
76.4 Percentage of urban population among Jews
22.0 Percentage of urban population among non-Jews

Map labels: LITHUANIA, Neman, Kovno, Königsberg, Danzig, EAST PRUSSIA (GERMANY), WILNO, Wilno (Vilna) 15.9, 68.8, GERMANY, 86.3, 32.1, POMORZE, Toruń, BIALYSTOK, Bialystok 16.7, 77.1, 6.1, Nowogródek, NOWOGRÓDEK 52.7, POZNAN, WARSAW, 79.0, 93.6, Poznan, 39.6, Warsaw 17.7, Wisła, POLESIE, LUBLIN, Brześć nad Bugiem (Brest Litovsk), Pripyat, 64.2, 7.4, Łódź 91.1, LÓDŹ 33.7, Breslau, LUBLIN, Lublin 11.4, 60.3, VOLHYNIA, Łuck, KIELCE, Kielce 71.4, 20.0, 59.7, 6.8, Katowice, Kraków, SILESIA, KRAKÓW 82.7, LWÓW, Lwów, TARNOPOL, Tarnopol 70.3, 16.3, 20.5, 75.3, Dniester, 12.1, 31.5, 18.6, STANISLAWÓW, Stanisławów 73.6, 14.3, Prut, ROMANIA, Brno, Vienna, CZECHOSLOVAKIA, HUNGARY, SOVIET UNION

Legend:
- Jewry of Congress Poland
- Ukrainian Jewry
- Galician Jewry
- Lithuanian-Belorussian Jewry
- "German" Jewry

Scale: 0 20 40 60 miles / 0 40 80 km

HISTORICAL SUBGROUPS IN POLISH JEWRY

Belorussian and Lithuanian Jewry. Both Belorussia and Lithuania, which had been parts of the Russian Empire, were divided after World War I among four countries: the Soviet Union, Poland, Lithuania, and Latvia. In Poland, the area involved was called *kresy*, the borderlands, whose Jews were less open to external influences than were those of Congress Poland and Galicia. Besides Yiddish, they spoke Russian rather than Polish. The Lithuanian region, with its well-known major city, Wilno (Vilna), was a strong center of *haskalah* and of opposition to the Hasidic movement. From the late nineteenth century, Jewish national movements developed here, both the socialist Bund and Zionism.

Ukrainian Jewry. Until World War I, the province of Volhynia was part of the Russian Ukraine. In the view of the Poles, it, too, belonged to the *kresy*. As in the Lithuanian region, the Jewish intelligentsia was oriented to Russian rather than to Polish culture. Yet the Ukrainian Jews there were a distinct group.

"German" Jewry. Upper Silesia, Poznań (Posen) and Pomorze (Pomerania) belonged to Germany until the end of World War I, and the Jews there leaned toward German culture. Few Jews remained in these provinces in the interwar period.

THE JEWS IN WARSAW

UNTIL the late eighteenth century, Jews were not permitted to settle in Warsaw, although a few thousand had special permits to live there. After the partitions of Poland, the city came under Prussian domination (1796–1807), and in spite of continuing restrictions, the number of Jews grew to about 7,700. Most concentrated in the Marywil neighborhood (later called Theater Square) and the nearby streets. During the time of the Warsaw Duchy (1807–1815), most Jews were forced to move to the southern and southwestern parts of the city. They settled around Marszalkowska, Krolewska, and Twarda streets, up to the southern border of Jerozolimska Boulevard. In the mid-nineteenth century, the Jews were again forced to move to the northern part of the city. In 1862, the Jews in Congress Poland were granted the same rights as the rest of the population, and could now live freely in Warsaw. The city's Jewish population grew rapidly, reaching 337,000 in 1914, and expanded around the old nucleus, especially southward. Warsaw's Jewish community became the largest in Europe and, unlike in other cities with large Jewish populations, remained concentrated in the central part of the city, relatively few Jews settling beyond it. There they made up about 37 percent of the total popula-

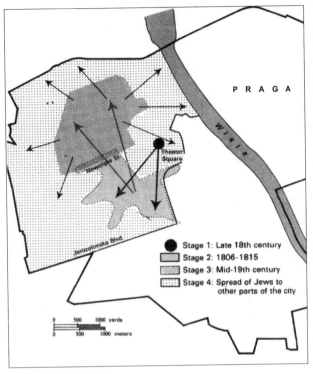

Stage 1: Late 18th century
Stage 2: 1806–1815
Stage 3: Mid-19th century
Stage 4: Spread of Jews to other parts of the city

tion, a percentage that remained stable in the interwar period. In some neighborhoods, as many as 90 percent of the inhabitants were Jews.

Warsaw was a major center of Jewish culture and public life. All parties and movements active in modern Jewry organized, met, and struggled in Warsaw: Zionists and assimilationists, socialists and capitalists, Hasidim and Mitnagdim, religious and secular Jews.

THE JEWS IN THE BALTIC STATES IN THE INTERWAR YEARS

A large and well-established Jewish community lived in historical Lithuania. After World War I, the country was divided between Poland and the Soviet Union, and only the northwestern part became independent. Vilna, the foremost Jewish center of old Lithuania, became part of Poland.

The Jews acquired extensive national and cultural rights in the new state, and the government included a minister for Jewish affairs. The *kehillot* (community councils) had official recognition; Jews controlled their own education and culture; Jewish parties organized on the Polish pattern and participated in the general political life.

In 1926, there was a right-wing revolution in Lithuania, and all democratic institutions were abolished. The policy toward the Jews changed completely, and strong antisemitic trends developed. Economic pressure was exerted against the Jews, aimed at reducing their numbers in various occupations.

Lithuania was occupied by the Germans in 1941. During the war, 90 percent of the Lithuanian Jews were exterminated.

About 100,000 Jews lived in Latvia in the interwar period, enjoying relatively good conditions until 1934. Their rights as citizens and as a minority were recognized, and they organized their own communal institutions and schools, formed parties, and elected representatives to parliament. Latvian Jews came under various cultural influences, which found expression in the languages used in the Jewish schools: Russian, German, Yiddish, or Hebrew. Economically, they were better off than the Jews in neighboring countries. They concentrated in the cities; in 1935, about half of all Latvian Jews lived in the capital, Riga.

After a fascist revolution in Latvia in 1934, all autonomous institutions were abolished. Jews were now defined as a religious group only. Antisemitism

THE JEWS IN THE BALTIC STATES
IN THE INTERWAR YEARS

surged in the late 1930s. Latvia was conquered by the Russians in 1939, and by the Germans in 1941. The Germans, with the help of part of the non-Jewish population, killed about 90 percent of the Latvian Jews.

Fewer than 5,000 Jews lived in Estonia in the interwar years, half of them in the capital, Tallinn. Their legal situation was among the best in East European Jewry. They had full civil rights and were recognized as a national minority. Although Estonia, too, was conquered by the Germans in World War II, 60 percent of its Jews escaped to the Soviet Union. Most of those who remained were exterminated by the Germans.

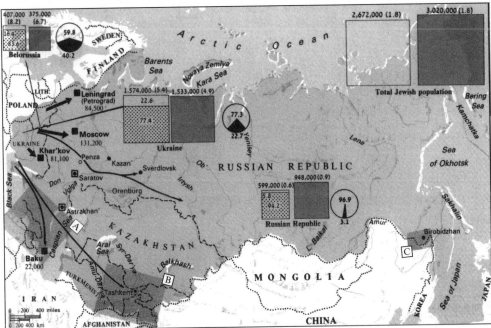

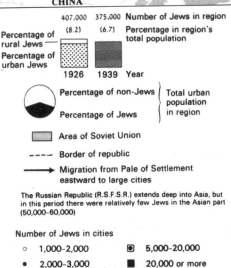

407,000 375,000 **Number of Jews in region**
(8.2) (6.7) **Percentage in region's total population**

Percentage of rural Jews
Percentage of urban Jews

1926 1939 Year

Percentage of non-Jews | Total urban population in region
Percentage of Jews |

Area of Soviet Union

---- Border of republic

⟶ Migration from Pale of Settlement eastward to large cities

The Russian Republic (R.S.F.S.R.) extends deep into Asia, but in this period there were relatively few Jews in the Asian part (50,000-60,000)

Number of Jews in cities

○ 1,000-2,000 ◉ 5,000-20,000
• 2,000-3,000 ■ 20,000 or more

WORLD War I and the 1917 revolutions caused drastic changes in the situation of Russian Jewry. Large areas in western Russia, with large Jewish populations, became independent countries (Poland, the Baltic States) or were incorporated into other states (Bessarabia, in Romania). About half of the Jews of 1897 Russia now lived outside the Soviet Union. In 1926, the Soviet Union was politically and administratively reorganized into eleven republics, and 95 percent of its Jews were concentrated in three of them: the Russian Republic (Russian Socialist Federal Soviet Republic), the Ukraine, and Belorussia.

After 1917, all Russians became citizens with full political and civil rights, and the right to national self-definition. The Jews, too, were recognized as a national group, although many of their national rights could be exercised only in districts or towns where they were the majority of the population. In the 1930s,

there were about 200 Jewish councils in locales with Jewish majorities.

The abolition of the Pale of Settlement and the economic and political changes in the Soviet Union radically transformed the demography of Jewish society. Jews moved from the Pale outward to the interior of the country, or into cities that had been barred to them. In

1897, 6 percent of all Jews had lived outside the Pale, 26 percent in 1926, and 37 percent in 1939. Jews entered new occupations: many became public servants, and others learned a trade or profession or acquired a higher education. The number of Jews in agriculture increased (especially in southern Russia and the Crimea), although this was only a temporary trend. All together, these changes in Jewish life created a new class of acculturated Jews who came to occupy positions of influence in Soviet political, cultural, and economic life.

Many Soviet Jews were among the victims of the purges in Russia in the late 1930s. Later, after the German invasion, hundreds of thousands were exterminated by the German *Einsatzgruppen*.

THE CAUCASIAN "MOUNTAIN JEWS" AND THE JEWS IN GEORGIA

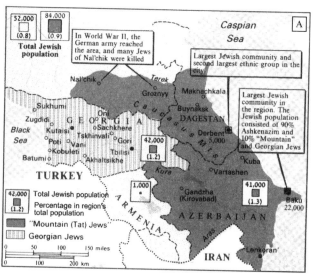

In the Caucasus Mountains, mainly in the Dagestan region and in northern Azerbaijan, there lived for many generations the "Mountain Jews," who spoke their own Tatic language and had no contact with other Jews until the Russians conquered the region in the early nineteenth century. In the twentieth century, due to tensions with the Muslims, many Mountain Jews moved to the cities, especially to Derbent. During World War II, many Jewish refugees from the German-occupied parts of western Russia settled in the Caucasus.

Another Caucasian group were the Jews of Georgia. In the early nineteenth century, when the Russians occupied the region, these Jews lived in villages and towns and were so integrated into their society that the Russian authorities did not distinguish between them and the general population and did not apply to them the special laws promulgated for Jews in other parts of Russia. In the nineteenth century, "European" Russian Jews settled in Georgia, as did Karaites.

THE JEWS IN BUKHARA

THE Jews in the large Bukharan region (which included parts of Uzbekistan, Turkmenistan and Kazakhstan) were influenced by Persian Jewry, but developed their own Jewish life and spoke a specific dialect, Tajik. After the anti-Jewish riots in the nineteenth century in Meshed (Persia), many Jews emigrated from there to Bukhara. With the Russian conquest, from the mid-nineteenth century, many moved from the Muslim to the Russian parts, mainly to the cities of Samarkand and Kokand.

Bukharan Jews began to emigrate to

Palestine toward the end the nineteenth century, without any connection with European Zionism. In 1892, the Bukharan Quarter was established in Jerusalem.

THE JEWISH AUTONOMOUS REGION IN BIROBIDZHAN

BIROBIDZHAN was part of Khabarovsk territory in the Soviet Far East. The Russian authorities decided to establish an autonomous Jewish region there, to fortify the frontier with China, win over Jewish public opinion in the West, and create a Jewish national territory. Jewish settlement began in 1928, and six years later the Jewish autonomous region was officially founded. The Jewish population grew from 3,500 to about 20,000 in the 1930s, and to 30,000 in 1948. In the late 1940s, many Jews left the region. In 1959, there were 14,300 Jews in Birobidzhan (only 8.8 percent of the total population), 84 percent of whom lived in cities. In 1970, there were 11,500 Jews, 6.6 percent of the total population.

THE JEWS IN BUKHARA

THE JEWISH AUTONOMOUS
REGION IN BIROBIDZHAN

THE JEWS IN CZECHOSLOVAKIA IN THE INTERWAR YEARS

As formed after World War I, Czechoslovakia was a mosaic of various national groups living in five regions. There were old Jewish communities in all parts of the new state. Because of the diversity of general cultural influences, there were profound differences between the Jews in the western regions (Bohemia, Moravia, Silesia), which had belonged to the Austro-German part of the Hapsburg Empire, and the Jews in the eastern regions (Slovakia and Sub-Carpathian Ruthenia), which had belonged to the Hungarian part of the empire. The western Jews were urban; those in the eastern regions lived in villages or small towns. Additional differences were related to patterns of acculturation, religious tendencies, socioeconomic structure, and demographic trends. For example, while the Jewish population in the eastern part of the country was still growing, the Jews in the western part were experiencing the demographic prob-lems characteristic of Western Jewry in general—no numerical growth and gradual aging.

The Czechoslovakian state scrupulously respected the national rights of

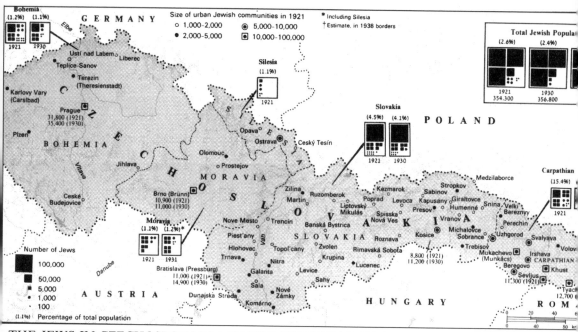

Map labels (clockwise / by region):

Bohemia (1.2%) (1.1%) 1921 1930

G E R M A N Y

Size of urban Jewish communities in 1921
○ 1,000-2,000   ◉ 5,000-10,000
● 2,000-5,000   ⊡ 10,000-100,000

*Including Silesia
†Estimate, in 1938 borders

Total Jewish Popula[tion]
(2.6%) (2.4%)
1921   1930
354,300 356,800

Ústí nad Labem   Liberec
Teplice-Sanov
Terezin
(Theresienstadt)

Silesia
(1.1%)
1921

Karlovy Vary
(Carslbad)

Prague
31,800 (1921)
35,400 (1930)

Plzeň

B O H E M I A

Opava   Ostrava   Český Těšín

P O L A N D

Slovakia
(4.5%) (4.1%)
1921   1930

Olomouc
Prostějov

Jihlava

Brno (Brünn)
10,900 (1921)
11,000 (1930)

M O R A V I A

Žilina   Ružomberok   Kežmarok   Medzilaborce
Martin   Poprad   Levoča   Stropkov
Liptovský   Spisská   Giraltovce   Snina
Mikuláš   Nová Ves   Presov   Humenné   Velki
                                          Berežnyy

Carpathian
(15.4%)
1921

České
Budějovice

Moravia
(1.1%) (1.2%)*
1921   1931

Bratislava (Pressburg)
11,000 (1921)
14,900 (1930)

Danube

Nove Mesto   Trenčín
Piešťany
Hlohovec
Trnava
Galanta   Nitra
Šaľa   Levice
Nové   Sahy
Zámky

Banská Bystrica
Topoľčany   Zvolen
Krupina
Lučenec

S L O V A K I A

Rimavská Sobota

Vranov
Michalovce
Sobrance
Trebišov
Mukachevo
(Munkács)

Roznava   Košice

8,800 (1921)
11,200 (1930)

Perechin
Uzhgorod
Svalyava
Volov
Irshava
Beregovo
11,300 (1921)
Sevljus
Khust
Tyach
12,700 (1930)

CARPATHIA

Number of Jews
100,000
50,000
5,000
1,000
100
(1.1%) Percentage of total population

A U S T R I A

Dunajska Streda
Komárno

H U N G A R Y

R O M [ANIA]

THE JEWS IN CZECHOSLOVAKIA IN THE INTERWAR YEARS

its different groups, including the Jews. But there were severe tensions among the nationalities themselves. Since the Jews were not territorially concentrated but lived among other nationalities, they were accused by the Czechs of being representatives of German culture, or by the Slovaks of propagating Hungarian influences. In fact, between 1921 and 1930, there was an increase in the number of Jews who defined themselves as Czech nationals. Furthermore, fewer Jews regarded themselves as Germans or Hungarians, and relatively more defined themselves as Jewish nationals.

Czechoslovakia was conquered by the Germans in the spring of 1938. Many Jews left the country before the start of World War II. Of those who remained, about 85 percent (according to the 1938 borders) were exterminated during the Holocaust.

THE JEWS IN HUNGARY IN THE INTERWAR YEARS

HUNGARY as reconstituted after the Trianon Treaty of 1920 was a much smaller country than it had been in 1914. All the national minorities that had lived in Hungary were incorporated into other states, together with several million Hungarians—including hundreds of thousands of Jews (mainly in Czechoslovakia and Romania). In theory, the Jews were full citizens, and since Hungary was a country of only one nationality, they were recognized as a religious group. In practice, antisemitism was rampant; Hungary was the only European country besides Germany to adopt explicit antisemitic laws before World War II (1938–1939).

Hungarian Jewry decreased in the interwar period, from 473,400 in 1920 to about 400,000 in 1939—mainly because of a low fertility rate and emigration. About 45 percent of Hungarian

412

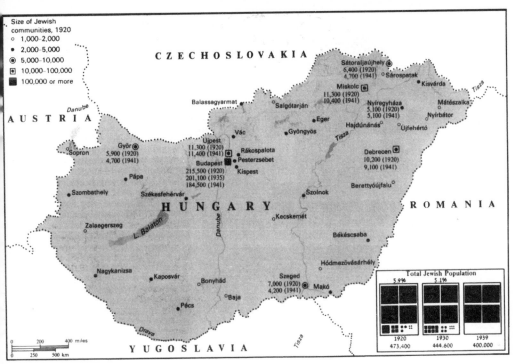

CZECHOSLOVAKIA

Sátoraljaújhely ◉
6,400 (1920)
4,700 (1941) ○ Sárospatak
Kisvárda •

Miskolc ▣
11,300 (1920)
10,400 (1941)

Balassagyarmat •   • Salgótarján   Nyíregyháza
5,100 (1920)
5,100 (1941) Nyírbátor ○   Mátészalka ○

AUSTRIA   Danube

• Eger   Hajdúnánás ○   • Újfehértó
○ Gyöngyös
Vác ○

Sopron ○   Győr ◉   Újpest
5,900 (1920)   11,300 (1920)
4,700 (1941)   11,400 (1941) ▣   Rákospalota   Debrecen ▣
Budapest ■   • Pesterzsébet   10,200 (1920)
215,500 (1920)   Kispest   9,100 (1941)
• Pápa   201,100 (1935)
184,500 (1941)

Berettyóújfalu ○

• Szombathely   Székesfehérvár ○   Szolnok ○   ROMANIA

HUNGARY

Zalaegerszeg ○   L. Balaton   ○ Kecskemét   Danube

Békéscsaba •

• Nagykanizsa   Hódmezővásárhely ○
• Kaposvár   ○ Bonyhád   Szeged
7,000 (1920) ◉ Makó ○   Tisza
○ Baja
• Pécs

Drava

0   200   400 miles
0   250   500 km

YUGOSLAVIA   Tisza

THE JEWS IN HUNGARY IN THE INTERWAR YEARS

Jews lived in the capital, Budapest, which was one of the major Jewish centers in Europe at the time. Although their percentage in the city's population was decreasing (23.2 percent in 1920, to 18.9 percent in 1935), the Jews remained an important element in Budapest's cultural and economic life. In 1930, 55.1 percent of the lawyers in Budapest were Jews, as were 40.2 percent of the doctors and 36.1 percent of the journalists. Similar percentages obtained in the country as a whole: in 1920, 50.6 percent of the Hungarian lawyers, 59.9 percent of the doctors, and 34.3 percent of the journalists and editors were Jews. Budapest was Hungary's only large Jewish center. A significant part of the Jewish population lived in dozens of relatively small communities in the northeastern part of the country.

Hungarian Jewry suffered heavy losses in the Holocaust. About 75 percent of the Jews who lived within the borders of Trianon Hungary perished, most of them in 1943 and 1944.

THE JEWS IN ROMANIA IN THE INTERWAR YEARS

As a result of World War I, Romania became a multinational state: Transylvania in the west (formerly Hungarian), Dobrogea (Dobruja) in the south (from Bulgaria), Russian Bessarabia in the east, and Austrian Bukovina in the north became part of the new Romania. Many of these territories contained large Jewish communities. Records show that Romania's Jewish population had risen by 1930 to 757,000. But there are many indications that its actual, undeclared number was about 20 percent higher. Culturally, these Jewries continued to belong to their

413

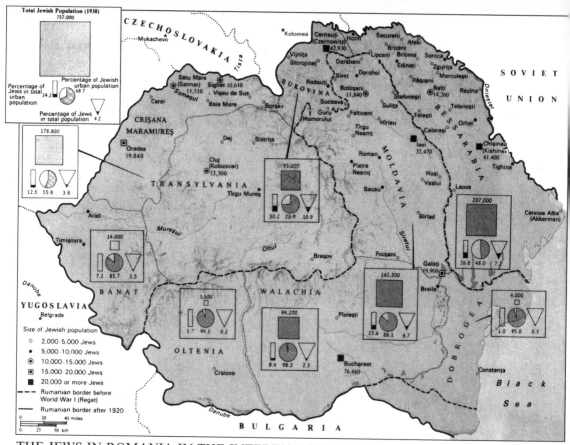

THE JEWS IN ROMANIA IN THE INTERWAR YEARS

historical groups, only the Jews of the Regat (the Old Kingdom) coming under Romanian cultural influence.

Seventy percent of Romanian Jews lived in cities, as compared with 20 percent of the general population. Their urban character found expression in their occupational structure: in 1930, 73.2 percent of the general population lived from agriculture, while only 6.5 percent of Jews did so; the rest were concentrated in commerce, crafts, and industry.

The legal situation of Romanian Jews remained problematic in the enlarged state. At the Paris Peace Conference, Romania had pledged to grant full citizenship to all the inhabitants of its new lands. Where the Jews were concerned, however, only those of the Regat became citizens, while difficulties were created regarding all the others. Antisemitism, a serious problem even before 1919, became worse in the interwar period: antisemitic parties were organized, and the Jews were subjected to pogroms and economic pressure. This resulted in a sizable Jewish emigration.

Romania, which fought in World War II on the German side, underwent several territorial changes during the war that affected its large Jewish population. The Jews in Bukovina, Bessarabia, and Transylvania suffered considerably, under either a German or a Romanian military presence, with many sent to extermination camps. In the Old Kingdom, despite Romanian antisemitism, the Jews fared better. About half of the Jews living within the country's 1939 borders perished during the war.

THE JEWS IN SOUTHEASTERN EUROPE

EARLY 20TH CENTURY

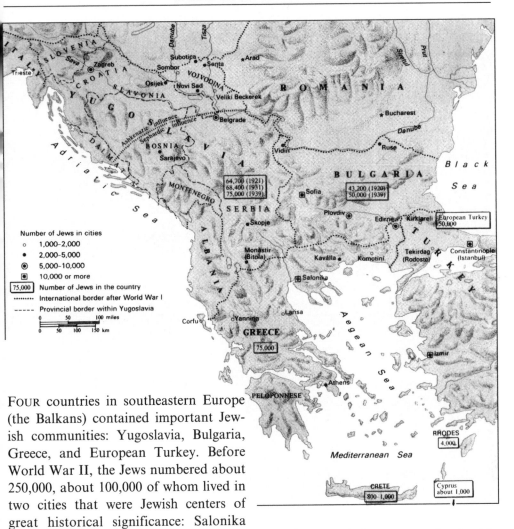

Number of Jews in cities
- ○ 1,000–2,000
- • 2,000–5,000
- ◉ 5,000–10,000
- ◼ 10,000 or more
- 75,000 Number of Jews in the country
- ········· International border after World War I
- ----- Provincial border within Yugoslavia

0   50   100 miles
0   50   100   150 km

FOUR countries in southeastern Europe (the Balkans) contained important Jewish communities: Yugoslavia, Bulgaria, Greece, and European Turkey. Before World War II, the Jews numbered about 250,000, about 100,000 of whom lived in two cities that were Jewish centers of great historical significance: Salonika (which after 1913 belonged to Greece) and Constantinople.

Sixty percent of the Jews in these countries were Sephardim, descendants of Jews expelled from Spain and Portugal at the end of the fifteenth century. They had gradually settled in the Ottoman Empire, where they had been well received, prospered, and created influential Jewish centers. Parts of southeastern Europe were under Turkish domination until the nineteenth century, and Jews had settled there, too.

In the twentieth century, the Jewish communities in southeastern Europe were very different from one another. The Jews of Sofia, the capital of Bulgaria, and of Salonika were organized in a more unified structure than were those of Constantinople (Istanbul), who were divided into many independent communities. In Yugoslavia, Jewish groups of various historical roots found themselves living in the same state as a result of World War I. An imaginary line divided the Ashkenazic and Sephardic spheres of

415

Jewish influence in Yugoslavia, evident also in the country's three major Jewish centers: Zagreb, Sarajevo, and Belgrade. In Sarajevo, in Bosnia, the Sephardic community was more influential, while in Zagreb, the capital of Croatia, the Ashkenazic element was dominant. Belgrade, in Serbia, was on the line dividing the two spheres: the community had originally been Sephardic, but in the nineteenth century there was a large Ashkenazic influx. In the interwar period, the two groups were equally represented.

The Jews in all four countries were well integrated into and acculturated to the general society. But unlike those in Western Europe, the Jewish communities in the Balkans maintained distinct social patterns. Assimilation and out-marriage were relatively low.

In World War II, Bulgaria allied itself with the Germans. Yet in spite of many antisemitic measures, the Bulgarian government refused (after some vacillation) to hand over its Jewish citizens to the Germans. Yugoslavia and Greece were occupied by the Italians and the Germans, and most of the Jews there were sent to extermination camps. About 86 percent of Greek Jews and about 80 percent of Yugoslavian Jews perished in the Holocaust.

THE JEWS IN WESTERN EUROPE IN THE 1930s

ALMOST 1.7 million Jews lived in Western Europe in the 1930s, 70 percent of them in Germany, the United Kingdom, and France. Most lived in cities, especially in the capitals. Half were concentrated in six large centers: Berlin, London, Paris, Amsterdam, Antwerp, and Vienna. In a few countries, about 50 percent or more of the Jews lived in the capital: Austria (91 percent), the Netherlands (56 percent), France (46 percent), and the United Kingdom (67 percent). The same applied to several countries with smaller Jewish populations.

West European Jewry in the interwar period was very much the product of the large Jewish immigration from Eastern Europe that began in the second half of the nineteenth century. Between 1897 and 1939, the Jewish population of France trebled, and that of Great Britain grew four- or fivefold. The West European Jewries may be said to have been "East European" in some of their basic characteristics, even if the second and third generations underwent rapid and far-reaching acculturation to the societies into which they were born. An additional Jewish group in almost all the countries were the refugees from Germany, who arrived after 1933.

British Jewry underwent two basic transformations in the modern era. At its beginnings, in the seventeenth century, its composition was mainly Spanish-Portuguese. Toward the end of the eighteenth century, Ashkenazic Jews, mostly from Central Europe, settled in England. And from the mid-nineteenth century, British Jewry gradually became predominantly East European. From the start, most Jews who settled in the United Kingdom were attracted to London. Although from the late eighteenth century, Jewish communities were established in other English cities, they remained much smaller than the London center. The second largest community in England was in Manchester, which in the 1930s had fewer than 40,000 Jews.

The Jewish community in the Netherlands was the fourth largest in Western

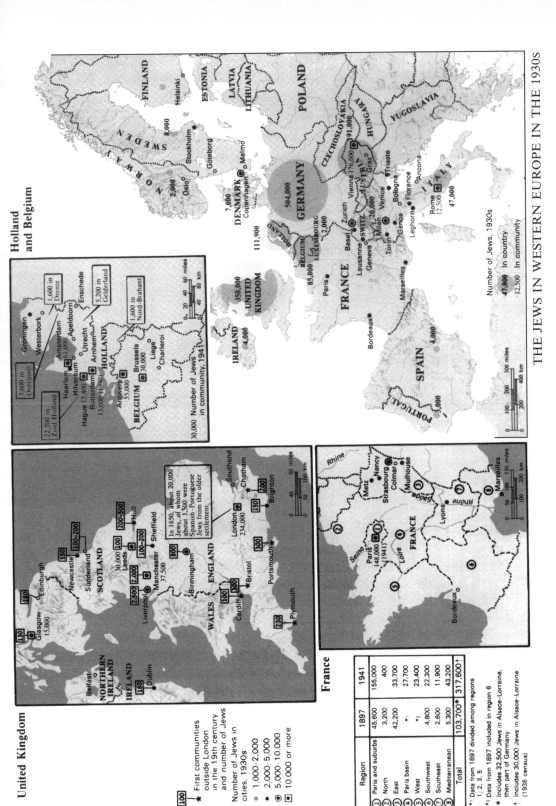

Holland and Belgium

United Kingdom

★ First communities outside London in the 19th century and number of Jews

Number of Jews in cities, 1930s

○ 1,000–2,000
● 2,000–5,000
◉ 5,000–10,000
◙ 10,000 or more

| 100 |

30,000 Number of Jews in community, 1941

1,600 in Drente

3,600 in Overijssel

5,200 in Gelderland

22,200 in Zuid Holland

1,600 in Nord-Brabant

Groningen
Westerbork
Enschede
Apeldoorn
Amsterdam 60,000
Haarlem
Hilversum
Utrecht
Arnhem
Hague 17,400
Rotterdam 13,000 (1940)
HOLLAND
Antwerp 55,000
Liège
Brussels 30,000
Charleroi
BELGIUM

Glasgow 15,000
Edinburgh
130
180
Belfast
NORTHERN IRELAND
Dublin
140
IRELAND
Newcastle
Sunderland
SCOTLAND
100
150
Leeds 30,000
Hull 200–500
100–200
Sheffield
Liverpool 7,500
Manchester 37,500
2,000
2,500
Birmingham 6,000
100–200
WALES
Cardiff 3,000
100
Bristol
300
Plymouth
230
ENGLAND
London 234,000
150
Southend
Chatham 200
Brighton
Portsmouth
300

In 1850, about 20,000 Jews, of whom about 3,500 were Spanish-Portuguese Jews from the older settlement

France

Rhine
Metz
Nancy
Strasbourg 2
Colmar 3
Mulhouse
Saône
Seine
Paris 148,000 (1941) 1
Loire 4
Rhone
Lyons
6
Bordeaux 5
Marseilles 8
FRANCE

Region	1897	1941
① Paris and suburbs	45,600	155,000
② North	3,200	400
③ East	42,200	33,700
④ Paris basin	*¹	27,700
⑤ West	*²	23,400
⑥ Southwest	4,800	22,300
⑦ Southeast	2,600	11,900
⑧ Mediterranean	5,300	43,200
Total	**103,700***	**317,600†**

*¹ Data from 1897 divided among regions 1, 2, 3, 5

*² Data from 1897 included in region 6

* Includes 32,500 Jews in Alsace-Lorraine, then part of Germany

† Includes 30,000 Jews in Alsace-Lorraine (1936 census)

FINLAND
Helsinki
ESTONIA
LATVIA
LITHUANIA
POLAND
SWEDEN 8,000
Stockholm
Göteborg
NORWAY 2,000
Oslo
Malmö
DENMARK 7,000
Copenhagen
111,900
GERMANY 504,000
CZECHOSLOVAKIA
91,000
Vienna 176,000
AUSTRIA Graz
HUNGARY
Zurich 20,000
SWITZ.
Basel
Lausanne
Geneva
Milan
Turin
Venice
Trieste
YUGOSLAVIA
Bologna
Florence
Genoa
Leghorn
ITALY 47,000
Rome 12,500
Ancona
85,000
BELGIUM
LUXEMBOURG 2,000
350,000
UNITED KINGDOM
150,000
IRELAND 4,000
Paris
FRANCE
Bordeaux
Marseilles
4,000
1,000
SPAIN
PORTUGAL 1,000

Number of Jews, 1930s
47,000 In country
12,500 In community

THE JEWS IN WESTERN EUROPE IN THE 1930S

Europe. Its development was similar in certain respects to that in Britain: the Spanish-Portuguese origins, the Ashkenazic newcomers in the late seventeenth and the eighteenth centuries, and the East European immigrants in the second half of the nineteenth century. In 1909, only 6,600 Sephardic Jews lived in Holland, 6 percent of the Jewish population. Dutch Jewry numbered 104,000 in 1899, a figure that remained stable until 1940.

In the interwar years, the internal life of most West European Jewish communities was marked by serious demographic problems. Whatever numerical increase there was in these communities resulted entirely from Jewish immigration, while the older segments of the Jewish populations showed a negative demographic balance, because of low birth rates, a growing rate of out-marriage, and conversion. In some countries (such as Switzerland, Italy, and Germany before 1933), not even the arrival of Jewish immigrants could compensate for the losses due to the other factors. Most of the West European Jewries were not organic Jewish communities in the sense of developing stable patterns of Jewish life accepted by most members. The extensive acculturation of the older element of Jewish society, and the differences between it and Jewish newcomers with very different characteristics, created a situation in which the diverse segments of Jewish society in each country had very little in common. Consequently, there was insufficient collaboration between the older Jewish strata and the newcomers, even problems that posed serious threats to all Jews, such as the growing menace of modern antisemitism.

THE JEWS IN GERMANY 1925

MORE than 500,000 Jews lived in Germany when the Second Reich was founded in 1871. German Jews, like all the country's inhabitants, became full citizens, but since the German states retained considerable internal autonomy, the status of the local Jewish communities varied from place to place. Between 1871 and 1933, German Jewry concentrated in larger cities, mostly in Prussia, Saxony, and Hamburg. In other German states, the number of Jews decreased. The urban and middle-class character of the Jewish population was reflected in its occupational structure: concentration in commerce, industry, and the professions.

Negative demographic tendencies began to characterize German Jewry in the 1880s: a falling birth rate, fewer marriages, aging, and more out-marriage. The arrival of Jewish immigrants from Posen province and from Eastern Europe (the *Ostjuden*) compensated somewhat for the losses among the older Jewish population. In 1900, 7 percent of all German Jews were foreign-born; by 1933, they had risen to 20 percent.

In spite of its demographic problems, German Jewry was one of the most active Jewries in modern times. German Jews had a high degree of self-awareness and defined themselves in a rich spectrum of ideological and religious positions. They were a good example of West European Jewry in general: socially and culturally integrated into the general society, many of them also wished to preserve some form of Jewish identity. In this respect, there were three main ideological options: the integrationist position, Zionism, and Orthodoxy. The integrationists, who usually belonged to the Liberal

Map labels:
DENMARK · SWEDEN · Baltic Sea · North Sea · HOLLAND · Königsberg · Altona · MECKLENBURG · HAMBURG · Bremen · Stettin · Elbe · P R U S · Hanover 5,500 · Berlin 172,700 · Magdeburg · Oder · Warsaw · Wisla · POLAND · Gelsenkirchen · Bochum · Essen · Dortmund · Duisburg · Elberfeld · Kassel · Halle · Leipzig 12,500 · Dresden · Breslau 23,240 · Krefeld · Düsseldorf · Cologne 16,100 · Bonn · Giessen · THURINGIA · Chemnitz · SAXONY · Hindenburg · Gleiwitz · Beuthen · HESSE · Fulda · Wiesbaden · Mainz · Offenbach · Frankfurt 29,400 · Worms · Darmstadt · Würzburg · Ludwigshafen · Heidelberg · Fürth · CZECHOSLOVAKIA · Karlsruhe · Nuremberg 8,600 · FRANCE · ALSACE-LORRAINE* · WÜRTTEMBERG · BAVARIA · Augsburg · Munich 10,100 · Danube · Vienna · Freiburg · BADEN · AUSTRIA · ITALY · SWITZERLAND · BRAUNSCHWEIG · ANHALT · OLDENBURG

Legend:
○ Community with 1,000–1,500 Jews
● Community with 1,500–2,500 Jews
◉ Community with 2,500–4,000 Jews
▣ Community with 4,000–5,000 Jews
■ Large community and number of Jews

Year 1871 | Year 1925 Jewish population by states (*Laender*) (in thousands)
* Assigned to France in 1919

Scale: 0 50 100 miles / 0 50 100 150 km

religious tendency, were the majority of German Jewry. They considered themselves German citizens in the political, national, and cultural senses, but stressed their religious particularism. Some defined Jewish religion very narrowly, favored far-reaching religious reforms, and sometimes adopted an extreme German nationalistic position. Others were more aware of the deeper meanings and implications of Judaism. The Zionists, especially many of their leaders, were as integrated into German life as the integrationists. Their integration, however, led them to a totally opposite conclusion: German Jews could not become completely German and were, in fact, a different people.

Among the Orthodox, the most articulate were the neo-Orthodox. They strove to be exemplary German citizens, blending full cultural integration into the general society with uncompromising observance of Jewish religious law, the *halakhah*. Although they were a small group, there was almost no assimilation among them. They kept apart from other German Jews, opposing both the Liberal religious trend and the Zionist position. In time, however, part of German Orthodoxy came to support religious Zionism.

Many German Jews were Socialists or Communists, some occupying leading positions in their parties. Since they believed that the solution to the problems of German Jewry was to be found in the economic and political change of German society as a whole, most of them remained aloof from the Jewish community. Finally, there were the foreign-born

East European Jews. Many continued to cling to their religious and cultural traditions, and their relations with the established part of German Jewry were often problematic.

The extreme self-consciousness of German Jewry and the elaborate formulations of German Jewish intellectuals in their efforts to explain their German and Jewish attachments were, in part, a reflection of the uncertain relationship between the Jews and the Germans. In the end, they achieved almost nothing. Most Germans neither understood nor cared about the hair-splitting distinctions drawn by German Jews between their German and their Jewish loyalties. The negative attitude of many Germans was not evoked by this or that interpretation of Judaism, but by Judaism per se. In this respect, too, German Jewry symbolized many of the tensions between Jews and non-Jews in other parts of Europe.

JEWISH EMIGRATION FROM GERMANY DURING THE NAZI PERIOD

THE appointment of Adolf Hitler as German chancellor in January 1933 marked the first step toward the ultimate disaster for not only the Jews of Germany, but also those of most of Europe. In the first part of the Nazi regime (1933–November 1938), the general aims of its Jewish policy were to strip the Jews of their civil rights (Nuremberg Laws, from September 1935) and remove them from German professional, social, and cultural life in order to force them to emigrate. In the next phase (November 1938–October 1941), the pressure on the Jews intensified and their institutions were closed. After October 1941, Jewish emigration from Germany was forbidden, and most German Jews were sent to concentration and extermination camps in Poland. About 500,000 Jews lived in Germany in 1933. By the end of 1937, about 130,000 had left the country. By October 1941, another 300,000 had escaped or were deported.

In 1933, the leaders of the major German Jewish organizations established a central institution, the Reichsvertretung der Juden in Deutschland (National Representation of the Jews in Germany), headed by Leo Baeck. Its aim was to assist German Jews under the Nazi regime. It provided information on emigration and vocational retraining, and organized social, educational, and cultural activities. After the *Kristallnacht* pogrom (November 9–10, 1938), the authorities closed the Reichsvertretung.

Annexation of Austria, March 13, 1938
Annexations, October 1938
German border, August 31, 1939

DENMARK
North Sea
Hamburg
HOLLAND
Berlin
Poznań
Münster
GERMANY
POLAND
Cologne
BELGIUM
From March 16, 1939: German protectorate
Prague
PROTECTORATE OF BOHEMIA-MORAVIA
Bamberg
Mannheim
Stuttgart
SLOVAKIA
FRANCE
Munich
Salzburg
Vienna
AUSTRIA
Innsbruck
SWITZERLAND
Graz
HUNGARY
ITALY

13.1%
14.4%
20.7%
4.9%
6.7%
18.1%
4.3%
8.2%
9.6%

To England
To other countries (2.6% to Europe)
To the Far East
To other countries
To Brazil
To Argentina
To rest of Americas
To Palestine
To France

0   50   100   150 miles
0   100   200 km

March 13, 1938: Austria annexed. 185,000 Jews (92% in Vienna)
August 1938: Central Bureau for Jewish Emigration established by Gestapo

F. EUROPEAN JEWRY **1940** FF.

THE HOLOCAUST 1939 TO 1945

Memorial at Yad Vashem, Jerusalem, to the victims of the concentration and extermination camps (sculptor Nandor Glid).

THE years 1939 to 1945 are inscribed in the chronicles of the Jewish people as the time of one of the worst calamities in its multimillennial history. More than one-third of the Jews of the world were exterminated by the Germans in Europe during World War II.

Beyond the horrors involved in the actual killing of the Jews, what made the Holocaust so uniquely terrible was its being based on the concept that it was necessary, for the good of the German nation and all mankind, to exterminate the Jewish people. As evil and perverted as this idea may seem, it gripped the minds and hearts of so advanced a people as the Germans, and directed their actions with terrifying consistency.

The resolution to exterminate the Jews had deep roots: the age-old tension between Christians and Jews in Europe, which was expressed over the centuries in Christian society's anti-Jewish hatred. In the ideological conditions of nineteenth-century Europe, that historical hatred developed into modern antisemitism. The more extreme antisemites began to preach the "removal" of Jews and Judaism from European culture and society. Against the background of Europe's (particularly, Germany's) interwar political and social troubles, political groups of the extreme right incorporated antisemitism into their platforms. In January 1933, the National Socialist Party came to power when its leader, Adolf Hitler, was nominated German chancellor. The way was now paved for the ultimate catastrophe of European Jewry.

Although there is much evidence that Nazi ideology considered the "solution" of the "Jewish problem" a major aim of its political program, the plans to implement it took time to mature. In the first period, from 1933 to 1939, Nazi policy aimed to exclude the Jews from German

THE HOLOCAUST
1939–1945

Extermination method	Number of Jewish victims (estimated)
Death camps	
Auschwitz (May 1940–January 1945)	1,800,000
Majdanek (November 1941–July 1944)	120,000
Chelmno (December 1941–January 1945)	310,000
Belzec (November 1941–June 1943)	600,000
Treblinka (June 1942–November 1943)	780,000
Sobibor (March 1942–November 1943)	250,000
Total	3,860,000
Major concentration camps	
(Bergen-Belsen, Mauthausen, Ravensbruck, Dachau, Sachsenhausen, Buchenwald, Stutthof, Gross-Rosen, Jasenovac, Jenowska)	400,000
Einsatzgruppen actions	1,200,000
Ghettos and transports	400,000
Camps and ghettos in Transnistria	90,000
Total	**5,950,000**

Extermination

Extermination camp

Ghetto

Concentration camp (transit, forced labor)

Mass-murder site

Areas conquered by Germany and other Axis countries

Date of German conquest

Countries that allied themselves with Germany in the war

May 1940   Date of German conquest

March 1941   Date of joining Germany in the war

The Allies

Neutral countries

January 20, 1942, Wannsee conference in Berlin of German government representatives. Plan "Final Solution" for the European Jews.

422

society and force them to emigrate. Jews were expelled from the public service (1933); they were stripped of their German citizenship and reduced to the status of German subjects (1935); they were gradually excluded from all cultural life and educational institutions; those with Polish citizenship were expelled to Poland (1938). After the annexation of Austria in March 1938, these measures and laws were immediately applied to the Jews in Vienna. During the *Kristallnacht* of November 9/10, 1938, all the synagogues in Germany were burned and Jewish businesses were damaged. But until September 1941, Jews could still emigrate from Germany or German-dominated countries—if they found a country willing to accept them.

The next phase started in September 1939 with the German conquest of Poland, which had a large Jewish population. At first the Jews were concentrated in several large ghettos. Many died or were killed during this phase. With the German invasion of the Soviet Union in June 1941, the large-scale killing of Jews began.

Einsatzgruppen

The *Einsatzgruppen* were German paramilitary units formed in preparation for the invasion of the Soviet Union. Their task was to deal with "dangerous" elements in the conquered territories, such as Communists and Jews. They were organized into 4 main groups of about 800 members each, each main group subdivided into smaller units that were assisted by Ukrainian and Lithuanian militiamen. Although they worked in coordination with and received logistical support from the German army, the *Einsatzgruppen* were under the command of the German Security Services (Sicherheitsdienst and SS). They entered a region as soon as it was occupied by the army, rounded up the Jews who had not managed to escape, and killed them, generally by shooting, alongside large burial pits, which in many instances had been dug by the victims themselves. The *Einsatzgruppen* were especially active from the middle of 1941 until the end of 1942. In that time, they killed between 900,000 and 1.3 million people, about 90 percent of whom were Jews.

Concentration and Extermination Camps

Concentration camps existed in Germany since the beginning of the Nazi regime, for political prisoners (Communists, socialists, liberals, and others), Jews, and, after the start of World War II, prisoners of war, political prisoners from the conquered countries, forced laborers, and Gypsies. During the war, there were hundreds of such camps throughout Europe. Conditions were, in general, very harsh, but there was a clear difference between the camps for Russian prisoners of war (which were terrible) and those for prisoners from the Western Allies. Many camps also served as transit points for Jews sent to Eastern Europe. On the way, many Jews perished from hunger, disease, and torture.

A unique type of camp—indeed, a uniquely modern creation—was the extermination camp, six of which functioned in Poland from 1941 until the beginning of 1945: Auschwitz, Treblinka, Majdanek, Chelmno, Belzec, and Sobibor. Auschwitz and Majdanek had non-Jewish inmates as well. Some of them were also used as workers' camps, serving nearby factories. Few Jewish prisoners were sent to work in the factories; in the end, those workers, too, were killed. Killing was done by gas poisoning, and the corpses were burned in huge crematoria especially devised for that purpose.

At the peak of its operation, the extermination process reached a horrifying level of "efficiency": a Jew who arrived in the morning would be dead by evening, his corpse burned and his belongings (clothes, as well as gold dental fillings and hair) sorted and prepared for shipment to Germany. In three and a half years, between 3 and 4 million Jews perished in the extermination camps.

The combined result of the operations of the *Einsatzgruppen*, the slaughter in the concentration and extermination camps, and the conditions in the ghettos in Eastern Europe was that 80 percent of the Jews in the German-dominated parts of Europe perished. The Jewish people survived, but decades later the Holocaust still defied evaluation. It destroyed some of the oldest and most vibrant centers of Jews and Judaism. It terminated a relationship between Jews and non-Jews that, for better or for worse, had existed for centuries. It created the need for new patterns of interaction between Jewish and general society. And it raised questions about the nature of man and civilization that seem unanswerable.

JEWISH REACTIONS AND RESISTANCE

THE Jews of Europe coped with the Nazi onslaught in various ways. In retrospect, the best solution would have been to leave Europe, but too few did so. At first, the Jews were oblivious to the looming dangers, and later the escape routes were closed. Once they fell under German domination, the Jews tried to conduct their private, family, social, and communal lives as normally as possible. In every

occupied community, the Germans forced the Jews to form a Jewish council (Judenrat), whose task was to govern Jewish communal life and carry out German orders. In principle, the councils were in keeping with the Jewish tradition of self-help, and up to a point they performed services that were both positive and necessary. But when their leaders were ordered to help organize the deportation of Jews to "the East" (the extermination camps)—which today we know meant collaborating in the killing of Jews rather than maintaining Jewish life—the councils found themselves in an impossible position. The behavior of some of their leaders later aroused fierce controversy. But even if some serious mistakes were committed, the outcome would have been no less tragic if the leaders had acted differently. Moreover, no Jewish council identified itself with Nazi ideology, supported German aims, or desired a German victory.

Resistance against the Germans erupted in several ghettos and concentration camps. In all instances, the Germans reacted swiftly and ruthlessly, executing the rebels who were caught. Those who escaped from the ghettos, the camps, or the *Einsatzgruppen* hid in the forests and swamps of Poland and western Russia. Some joined resistance groups. In Western Europe, Jews fought in the general resistance movement. In Eastern Europe, they fought alongside non-Jews or formed Jewish partisan units. Escaping Jews faced an additional handicap: having managed to elude the Germans, they now faced a hostile rural population in Eastern Europe. This hostility sometimes manifested itself also in the general resistance groups in which Jews participated. Nevertheless, here and there non-Jews—"Righteous Gentiles"—risked their lives to help Jews, even in Eastern Europe.

Tens of thousands of Jews participated in the resistance against the Germans in the occupied countries. In Poland and other East European countries, 15,000 to 20,000 Jews fought in general or in Jewish partisan units, or in resistance groups in ghettos and camps.

THE WARSAW GHETTO UPRISING

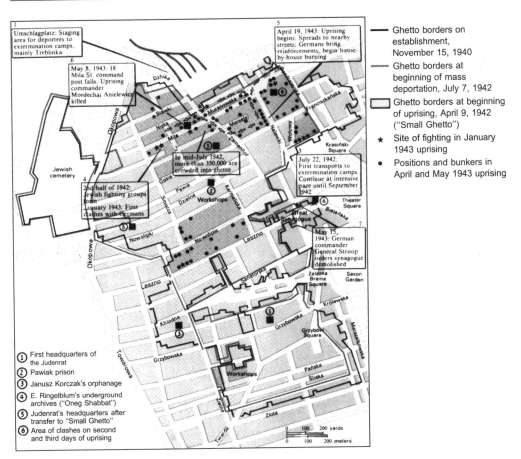

Umschlagplatz: Staging area for deportees to extermination camps, mainly Treblinka.

May 8, 1943: 18 Mila St. command post falls. Uprising commander Mordechai Anielewicz killed

April 19, 1943: Uprising begins. Spreads to nearby streets; Germans bring reinforcements, begin house-by-house burning

In mid-July 1942, more than 350,000 are crowded into ghetto

July 22, 1942: First transports to extermination camps. Continue at intensive pace until September 1942

2nd half of 1942: Jewish fighting groups form. January 1943: First clashes with Germans

May 15, 1943: German commander General Stroop orders synagogue demolished

Jewish cemetery

Ghetto borders on establishment, November 15, 1940

Ghetto borders at beginning of mass deportation, July 7, 1942

Ghetto borders at beginning of uprising, April 9, 1942 ("Small Ghetto")

★ Site of fighting in January 1943 uprising

● Positions and bunkers in April and May 1943 uprising

① First headquarters of the Judenrat
② Pawiak prison
③ Janusz Korczak's orphanage
④ E. Ringelblum's underground archives ("Oneg Shabbat")
⑤ Judenrat's headquarters after transfer to "Small Ghetto"
⑥ Area of clashes on second and third days of uprising

ABOUT 400,000 Jews lived in Warsaw on the eve of the German invasion of Poland in September 1939. In November 1940, the Germans declared the Jewish ghetto a closed area, concentrating all the Jews of the city and its suburbs there, and bringing in tens of thousands of Jews from outside. A Jewish council was founded.

In July 1942, the Germans began to send Jews from Warsaw to death camps. The head of the Jewish council, Adam Czerniakow, committed suicide, to avoid carrying out the German orders. About 300,000 Jews were sent from Warsaw to extermination camps, mainly Treblinka. Tens of thousands died or were killed in the ghetto itself. About 70,000 Jews remained in the ghetto in the autumn of 1942, and about 55,000 in the spring of 1943.

In the second half of 1942, resistance groups began to organize in the ghetto, affiliated with Zionist youth movements or Jewish political parties. With immense difficulty, arms were smuggled in and workshops were set up to make weapons and bombs. The first armed clashes with the Germans took place in January 1943. In the coming months, the Jewish resistance groups united to form the Jewish Fighting Organization (ZOB), headed by Mordechai Anielewicz. The revolt began on April 19, 1943. After suffering initial losses, the Germans brought in reinforcements and heavy guns, and started burning the ghetto, house by house. The fighting continued until the fall of the Jewish headquarters, at 18 Mila Street, on May 8, 1943, with Anielewicz among those killed. To mark the suppression of the uprising, the German commander, General Stroop, blew up the Warsaw Great Synagogue, which was located outside the ghetto. The ghetto itself was razed. About 50,000 Jews perished in the revolt.

AUSCHWITZ

AUSCHWITZ differed from the other extermination camps in size and in the sophistication of its death machinery. It began to function in May 1940, and was closed by the Germans in January 1945. About 1.8 million people were killed there in that period, close to 90 percent of them Jews. At the peak of its opera-

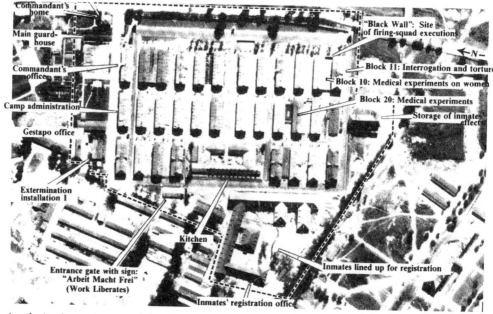

Auschwitz 1—main camp (photographed by the U.S. Army Air Force on August 25, 1944).

tions, in the summer of 1944, thousands of human beings were gassed every day and their bodies cremated.

Auschwitz was a complex of about forty camps, divided into three groups. *Auschwitz 1*: the main camp, containing the commandant's headquarters, the central administration of all the camps, and about 20,000 to 25,000 prisoners. *Auschwitz 2*, or *Birkenau*: the main extermination camp, more than a mile from Auschwitz 1. At its peak it contained about 146,000 prisoners, although planned for 250,000. *Auschwitz 3*, or *Buna*: a complex of labor camps for industrial production, built on the sites of villages close to Auschwitz 2. About 20 percent of the inmates of Auschwitz 2 worked in these factories. It is these inmates who had a number tattooed on their arms. Of the approximately 405,000 prisoners who worked in the factories at one time or another, about 30,000 survived.

THE ESCAPE FROM EUROPE (*BRIHA*)

ABOUT 250,000 Jews, survivors of the Holocaust and refugees, left Europe toward the end of and after the war (1944–1948). This movement, called *Briha* (Escape), was characterized by the fears and despair of the survivors. They wanted to leave Europe, that gigantic graveyard of their families and friends, and try to erase from their memory what they had seen and experienced. The anti-Jewish pogroms in Europe, even after the Holocaust (Kielce, Poland, in July 1946), strengthened their determination to flee the continent, and they went to various countries. Most wished to migrate to Palestine. The escape routes were strewn

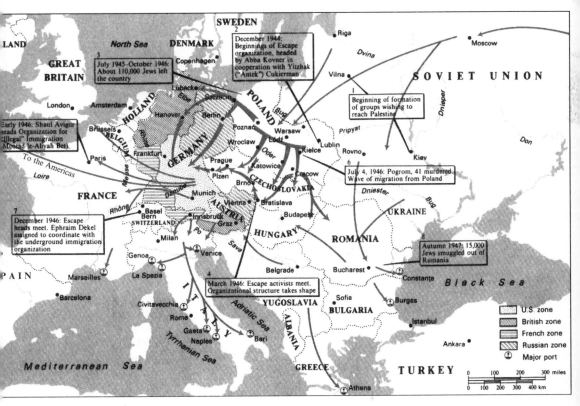

with obstacles: the frontiers were gradually sealed—not only between Eastern and Western Europe, but also between the occupied regions of Germany and Austria, and the passages to Italy, Romania, and Yugoslavia.

Emissaries from Palestine and representatives of American Jewish aid organizations prepared transit camps for the refugees in the American-occupied zone in southern Germany and Austria, from where they were sent to Mediterranean ports en route to Palestine. The Jewish refugee problem had worldwide repercussions, and various political groups, especially in the United States, sought to solve it.

THE OUTCOME OF THE HOLOCAUST 1951

THE Holocaust completely changed the demographic composition of the Jewish people. Sixty percent of all Jews lived in Europe in 1939, but only 30 percent in 1951. Worst hit were the large Jewish communities in Eastern Europe that had played such a significant role in the development of modern Jewry. Ninety percent of Polish Jewry—more than 3 million—perished; 90 percent of Lithuanian and Latvian Jewry; 85 percent of Czechoslovakian Jewry; 75 percent of Hungarian Jewry. In Western Europe, German Jewry disappeared, although not all the Jews were killed; many had left the country in the 1930s. More than 100,000 Dutch Jews, 75 percent of the total, were exterminated.

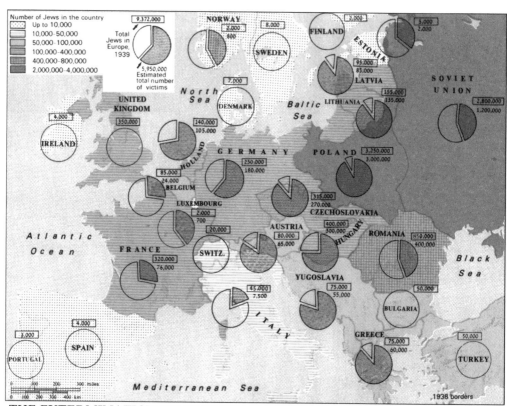

THE EXTERMINATION OF EUROPEAN JEWS, BY COUNTRIES

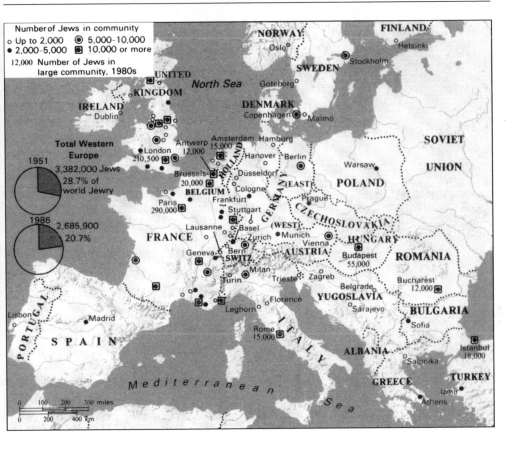

THE demographic configuration of European Jewry in the 1970s and 1980s was clearly a product of the Holocaust. Although some Jewish centers did not suffer directly under Hitler, and although Jewish life was rebuilt in all the communities on the continent, the Holocaust had a long-range destructive effect on the social and cultural structures of European Jewry, the full significance of which only gradually became evident. The demographic characteristics of European Jewry, which were problematic before World War II, deteriorated afterward, due to emigration as well as to the Holocaust. In the thirty years following the war, European Jewry gradually dwindled (especially in Eastern Europe), in spite of the influx, in the 1950s and 1960s, of hundreds of thousands of Jews, mainly from Muslim countries. Between 1951 and 1986, the Jewish population in Europe decreased by 20.6 percent; and its age composition indicated a decrease of 36.4 percent by the end of the century.

The Jews in France

France was the only European country whose Jewish population increased significantly in the second half of the twentieth century. Hundreds of thousands of Jews migrated from Algeria (where most Jews held French citizenship), Morocco, Tunisia, and Egypt. After Soviet Jewry, French Jewry was the largest in Europe (about 530,000 in the mid-1980s), but it was divided into very different communities. The Jews of

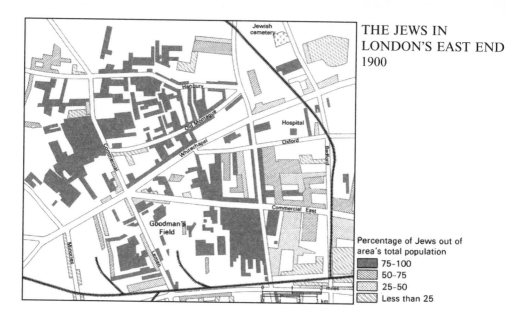

THE JEWS IN
LONDON'S EAST END
1900

Percentage of Jews out of
area's total population
■ 75-100
▤ 50-75
▦ 25-50
▨ Less than 25

North African origin adapted very rapidly to French demographic and cultural patterns.

The Jews in the United Kingdom
In the 1980s, Britain had the third largest Jewish community in Europe after the former Soviet Union and France, numbering 326,000 in 1986. In spite of some immigration (mainly from Commonwealth countries), British Jewry had decreased since the 1950s, when estimates (probably too high) had set the figure at 450,000 Jews. About 61 percent of British Jews lived in Greater London throughout the twentieth century.

THE JEWS IN THE SOVIET UNION LATE 20TH CENTURY

Two interrelated demographic trends characterized Soviet Jewry in the second half of the twentieth century: almost total urbanization and numerical decline. In 1979, the Soviet Union had 16 percent fewer Jews than it had had in 1959. Furthermore, estimates in the mid-1980s put the figure at only 1,515,000 Jews, or 13 percent fewer than in 1979. That year, about 75 percent of Soviet Jews lived in two republics: the Ukraine and the Russian Republic (R.S.F.S.R.).

Demographically, Soviet Jewry shared the traits and problems that characterized the Jews of Western Europe and America: concentration in large cities, out-marriage, and very low natural increase. The birth rate in the years 1959 to 1970 was 8.9 per 1,000, while the death rate was 15.5 per 1,000, meaning a negative population growth combined with an aging Jewish population. Although 98 percent of the Jews lived in cities, their proportion there, too, was declining: the Jews made up 4.7 percent of Moscow's population in 1959, and only 3.6 percent in 1970. The restrictions on Jewish cultural and religious self-expression certainly contributed to the growing assimilation of the Jewish population. Between 1959 and 1979, 236,000 Jews left the Soviet Union, the majority settling in Israel, and the rest in the United States and other countries.

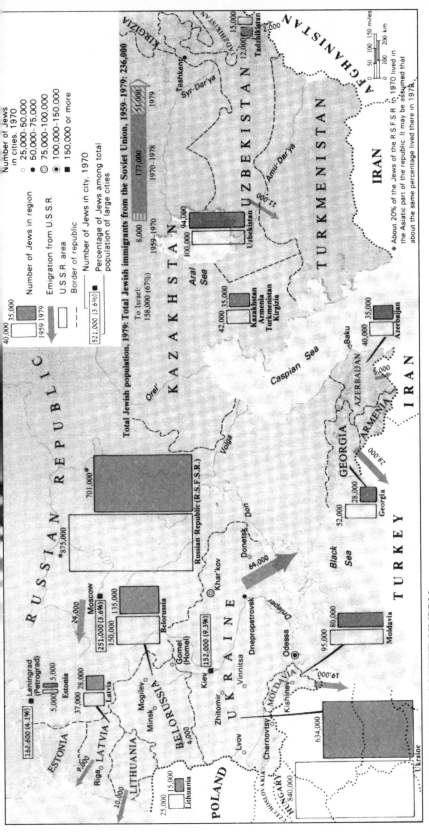

THE JEWS IN THE SOVIET UNION
LATE 20TH CENTURY

G. THE NEW CENTERS OF JEWRY

PALESTINE IN THE NINETEENTH CENTURY

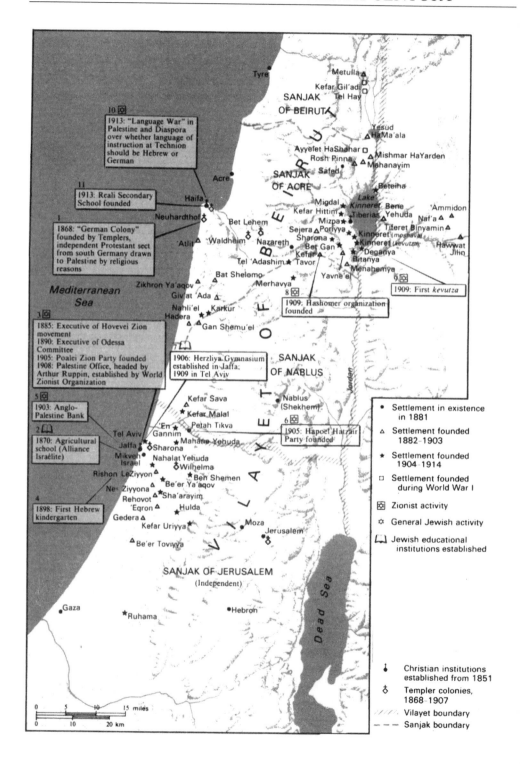

10 🔯
1913: "Language War" in Palestine and Diaspora over whether language of instruction at Technion should be Hebrew or German

11
1913: Reali Secondary School founded

I
1868: "German Colony" founded by Templers, independent Protestant sect from south Germany drawn to Palestine by religious reasons

3 🔯
1885: Executive of Hovevei Zion movement
1890: Executive of Odessa Committee
1905: Poalei Zion Party founded
1908: Palestine Office, headed by Arthur Ruppin, established by World Zionist Organization

9 📖
1906: Herzliya Gymnasium established in Jaffa; 1909 in Tel Aviv

5 🔯
1903: Anglo-Palestine Bank

2 📖
1870: Agricultural school (Alliance Israélite)

4
1898: First Hebrew kindergarten

8 🔯
1909: Hashomer organization founded

6 🔯
1909: First *kevutza*

6 🔯
1905: Hapoel Hatzair Party founded

7 📖

Tyre
Metulla
Kefar Gil'adi
Tel Hay
SANJAK OF BEIRUT
Yesud HaMa'ala
Ayyelet HaShahar
Rosh Pinna
Mishmar HaYarden
Safed
Mahanayim
Acre
SANJAK OF ACRE
Beteiha
Haifa
Lake Kinneret
Migdal
Bene
'Ammidon
Neuhardthof
Kefar Hittim
Tiberias
Yehuda
Naf'a
Bet Lehem
Mizpa
Tiferet Binyamin
Sejera
Poriyya
Kinneret *(moshava)*
'Atlit
Waldheim
Sharona
Kinneret *(kevutza)*
Hawwat Jihn
Nazareth
Bet Gan
Deganya
Kefar
Tel 'Adashim
Tavor
Bitanya
Tel 'Adashim
Menahemya
Bat Shelomo
Yavne'el
Zikhron Ya'aqov
Merhavya
Giv'at 'Ada
Nahli'el
Karkur
Hadera
Gan Shemu'el

Mediterranean Sea

SANJAK OF NABLUS

Kefar Sava
Kefar Malal
Petah Tikva
'En Gannim
Nablus (Shekhem)
Tel Aviv
Jaffa
Sharona
Mikveh Israel
Mahane Yehuda
Nahalat Yehuda
Wilhelma
Rishon LeZiyyon
Ben Shemen
Ne' Ziyyona
Be'er Ya'aqov
Rehovot
Sha'arayim
'Eqron
Hulda
Gedera
Kefar Uriyya
Moza
Jerusalem
Be'er Toviyya

SANJAK OF JERUSALEM
(Independent)

Gaza
Ruhama
Hebron

Dead Sea

Jordan

VILAYET OF

- Settlement in existence in 1881
△ Settlement founded 1882–1903
★ Settlement founded 1904–1914
□ Settlement founded during World War I
🔯 Zionist activity
☿ General Jewish activity
📖 Jewish educational institutions established

Christian institutions established from 1851
Templer colonies, 1868–1907
Vilayet boundary
Sanjak boundary

0   5   10   15 miles
0   10   20 km

432

IN Ottoman times, Palestine was not a separate administrative unit, but divided between different provinces. About 6,700 Jews lived in the country in the early nineteenth century, mostly in the four "Holy Cities": Jerusalem, Safed, Tiberias, and Hebron. The majority were Sephardim, although several groups of Ashkenazim had arrived in the eighteenth century: Rabbi Judah Hehasid and his followers in 1700, and groups of Hasidim in 1764 and 1777.

The Egyptian conquest (1832–1840) launched a new period. A combination of political and religious circumstances generated a growing interest in the Holy Land among Europeans. The powers opened consulates and extended protection to the increasing activities of the Christian churches, under the terms of the Capitulations. The country's economic development was much enhanced.

Among the Jews, too, there was a revival of interest in the country and its Jewish population, an expression of the traditional Jewish attachment to the Holy Land. Jewish individuals and institutions became active in Palestine, some before the founding of the Zionist movement. The most important of these did not even have nationalistic aspirations: the Alliance Israélite Universelle, Baron Edmond de Rothschild, the German-Jewish Hilfsverein, and the Jewish Colonization Association.

The Jewish population in Palestine grew rapidly, from about 27,000 in 1880 to between 85,000 and 90,000 in 1914. Between 1890 and 1914, the Jewish population grew by 104 percent, and the non-Jewish population by 22.2 percent. Although most Jews lived in cities before World War I (86.3 percent in 1914), there were already about 12,000 Jews in forty agricultural villages, most of them established after 1881.

The gradual development of the Zionist movement from the 1880s added a most important dimension to the Jewish community in Palestine. Although the movement's practical work was still very modest (until World War I, the non-Zionists did much more), it gave ideological meaning and purpose to the Jewish presence in Palestine and influenced its character. A Zionist school system was established, and children spoke Hebrew in Palestine even before 1914. In 1908, the Palestine Zionist Office, headed by Arthur Ruppin, was opened in Jaffa. Other Zionist institutions followed.

JEWISH IMMIGRATION TO PALESTINE/ISRAEL

ONE of the expressions of the historical bond between the Jewish people and the land of Israel was *aliyah*, immigration (in Hebrew, "ascension") to Palestine. The *aliyah* continued throughout the centuries of Jewish dispersion, although at times it was only a trickle. It gradually increased in the nineteenth century (especially in the second half), long before the development of the Zionist movement. Jewish settlers came from all parts of the Diaspora: Morocco, Yemen, Bukhara, Kurdistan, and, from the 1880s, Romania and Russia. Some of the historical *aliyah* routes were reopened in the twentieth century, during the development of the Zionist undertaking in Palestine.

The story of Jewish immigration to Israel after the foundation of the state had no parallel in modern history. No other human society doubled its population in only four years through immigration, as happened in Israel after 1948.

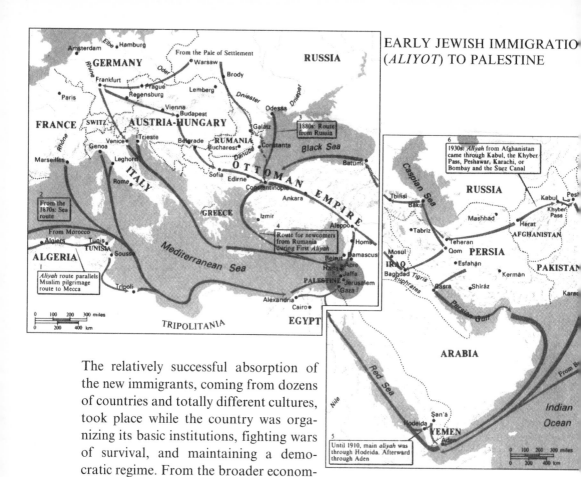

The relatively successful absorption of the new immigrants, coming from dozens of countries and totally different cultures, took place while the country was organizing its basic institutions, fighting wars of survival, and maintaining a democratic regime. From the broader economic perspective, as well, it seemed an impossible feat. Nevertheless, in a short time the Israeli population, veterans and newcomers alike, restored the economy to its prestate level and soon surpassed it.

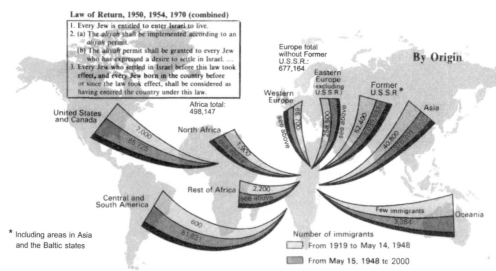

JEWISH IMMIGRATION (*ALIYAH*) TO ISRAEL AFTER 1948

The *aliyah* to Israel and the rapid absorption of the newcomers into the social fabric of Israeli society should be regarded as one of the great expressions of the constructive power of the Zionist idea.

THE BOUNDARIES OF PALESTINE

THE frontiers of Palestine were fixed only in the twentieth century. In 1906, a southern boundary was formed between Great Britain (Egypt) and the Ottoman Empire—from Rafah to Aqaba—giving the British administrative control over the Sinai Desert. The Sykes-Picot Agreement (May 1916) rather arbitrarily defined the territory of "Palestine." With some modifications, these lines became in 1920 the northern and northeastern frontiers of Palestine, although they included much less than the Zionists had hoped and asked for in 1919.

The British had intended to include the territory east of the Jordan River in an Arab state to be established under the Emir Faisal. After Faisal's expulsion from Damascus by the French in July 1921, the British decided to include the lands east of the Jordan in the Palestine Mandate, but not in the territory of the Jewish national home. Thus Transjordan was born, and the Palestinian frontier remained on the Jordan River, continuing south on that line to Aqaba.

Later, when plans were considered for the partition of the country between the Jews and Arabs, new boundary lines were drawn, first in 1937 (Peel Commission Report), and again in 1947 (United Nations Special Commission on Palestine [UNSCOP] Report).

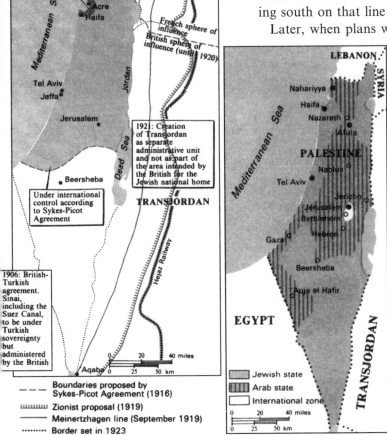

Boundaries proposed by Sykes-Picot Agreement (1916)
Zionist proposal (1919)
Meinertzhagen line (September 1919)
Border set in 1923

Jewish state
Arab state
International zone

UN DECISION
REGARDING
THE PARTITION
OF PALESTINE
29 NOVEMBER 1947

TOWARD THE ESTABLISHMENT OF THE JEWISH STATE IN PALESTINE 1940 TO 1948

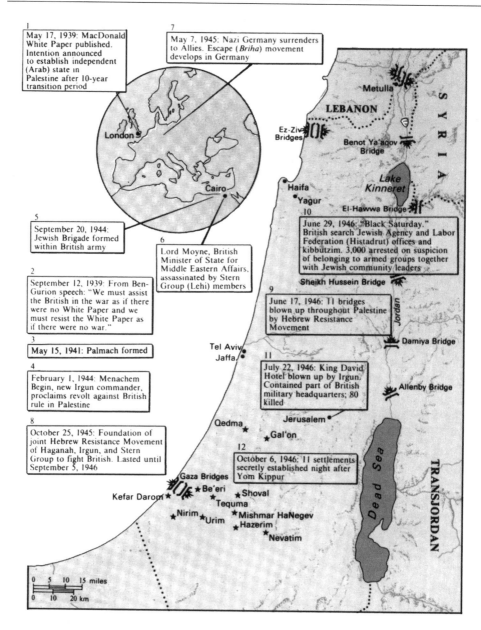

1
May 17, 1939: MacDonald White Paper published. Intention announced to establish independent (Arab) state in Palestine after 10-year transition period

7
May 7, 1945: Nazi Germany surrenders to Allies. Escape (Briha) movement develops in Germany

5
September 20, 1944: Jewish Brigade formed within British army

6
Lord Moyne, British Minister of State for Middle Eastern Affairs, assassinated by Stern Group (Lehi) members

2
September 12, 1939: From Ben-Gurion speech: "We must assist the British in the war as if there were no White Paper and we must resist the White Paper as if there were no war."

10
June 29, 1946: "Black Saturday." British search Jewish Agency and Labor Federation (Histadrut) offices and kibbutzim. 3,000 arrested on suspicion of belonging to armed groups together with Jewish community leaders

9
June 17, 1946: 11 bridges blown up throughout Palestine by Hebrew Resistance Movement

3
May 15, 1941: Palmach formed

4
February 1, 1944: Menachem Begin, new Irgun commander, proclaims revolt against British rule in Palestine

11
July 22, 1946: King David Hotel blown up by Irgun. Contained part of British military headquarters; 80 killed

8
October 25, 1945: Foundation of joint Hebrew Resistance Movement of Haganah, Irgun, and Stern Group to fight British. Lasted until September 5, 1946

12
October 6, 1946: 11 settlements secretly established night after Yom Kippur

London, Cairo

Metulla, LEBANON, SYRIA, Ez-Ziv Bridges, Benot Ya'aqov Bridge, Lake Kinneret, Haifa, Yagur, El-Hawwa Bridge, Sheikh Hussein Bridge, Jordan, Damiya Bridge, Tel Aviv, Jaffa, Allenby Bridge, Qedma, Jerusalem, Gal'on, Gaza Bridges, Be'eri, Shoval, Kefar Darom, Tequma, Mishmar HaNegev, Nirim, Urim, Hazerim, Nevatim, Dead Sea, TRANSJORDAN

0   5   10   15 miles
0   10   20 km

ZIONIST policy in the 1940s had two conflicting aims: helping Great Britain in the war against Germany, and fighting the British because of the MacDonald White Paper of 1939. The extermination of European Jewry added another factor to the political considerations of the Zionist leaders. During the war, there was a measure of collaboration between the British and the Zionists. After 1945, however, relations between the two gradually deteriorated.

Headline of May 14, 1948, Yom Hamedinah (Day of the State), issued jointly by all of Israel's newspapers.

The Biltmore Conference, held in New York in May 1942, proclaimed that the aim of the Zionist movement was to create a Jewish "commonwealth" in Palestine after the war. When the war was over, the Zionists organized a large-scale escape movement of Jews from Europe to Palestine.

In addition to the recognized resistance organizations—the Haganah and the Palmach—two anti-British resistance groups arose in Palestine, unconnected with the official institutions of the Yishuv: the Irgun and the Stern Group. A growing number of actions against the British by the Haganah, the Irgun, and the Stern Group, sometimes by all three together, triggered equally violent reactions by the British. The British refusal to comply with the recommendation of the Anglo-American Committee of Enquiry (April 1946) and admit 100,000 Jews into Palestine brought the tension in Palestine to new heights.

In February 1947, the British government presented the problem of Palestine to the United Nations. The United Nations Special Commission on Palestine (UNSCOP) was formed, and its recommendations were the basis of the United Nations decision of November 29, 1947, to partition Palestine between Jews and Arabs and create two states. The Zionists accepted the decision, and the Arabs rejected it, which is the main reason why an Arab state was not established in part of Palestine. Large-scale fighting between Arabs and Jews began shortly thereafter, developing into the War of Independence.

On May 14, 1948, the state of Israel was proclaimed.

THE WARS FOUGHT BY ISRAEL

AFTER its establishment in 1948 (and even before), Israel was repeatedly forced to defend its existence against Arab threats. The Arab world would not accept the existence of a Jewish state in the Middle East. The Arabs also thwarted the implementation of the United Nations proposal of November 1947 for the creation of an Arab state in part of Palestine. The Arab-Israeli conflict took political, economic, diplomatic, and, periodically, military forms. The most difficult of these wars was the War of Independence, which continued through 1948 and part of 1949. Six thousand Jews were killed (4,000 soldiers and 2,000 civilians). During the Six-Day War of June 1967, Israel seized the Sinai Peninsula and Gaza Strip from Egypt, the West Bank from Jordan, and the Golan Heights from Syria. In October 1973, Israel was surprised by an Egyptian-Syrian attack (the Yom Kippur War) but managed to repel it. After the peace treaty with Egypt (1979), Israel withdrew from Sinai.

437

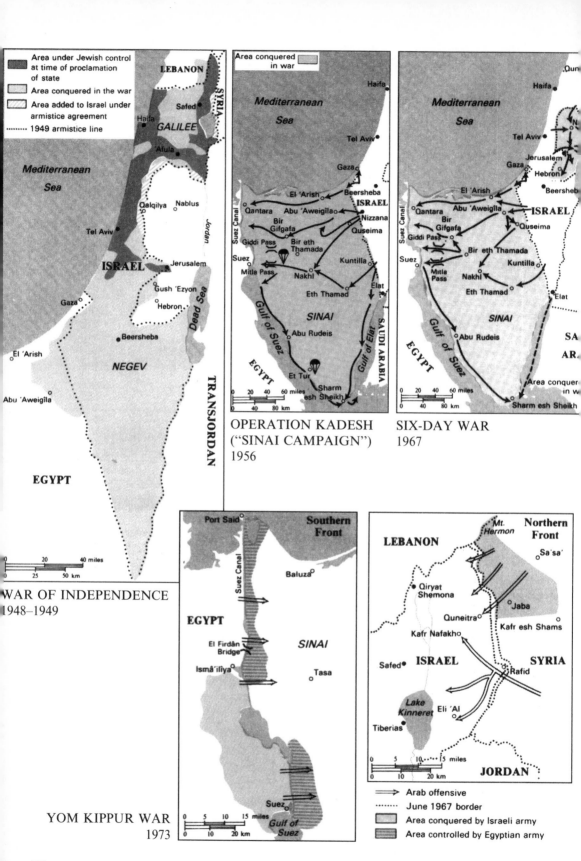

Legend (top-left map):
- Area under Jewish control at time of proclamation of state
- Area conquered in the war
- Area added to Israel under armistice agreement
- 1949 armistice line

LEBANON
SYRIA
Safed
Haifa
GALILEE
Afula
Mediterranean Sea
Qalqilya
Nablus
Tel Aviv
Jordan
ISRAEL
Jerusalem
Dead Sea
Gush 'Ezyon
Hebron
Gaza
TRANSJORDAN
Beersheba
El 'Arish
NEGEV
Abu 'Aweigîla
EGYPT

WAR OF INDEPENDENCE
1948–1949

Area conquered in war

Mediterranean Sea
Haifa
Tel Aviv
Gaza
Beersheba
El 'Arish
ISRAEL
Qantara
Abu 'Aweigîla
Nizzana
Quseima
Suez Canal
Bir Gifgafa
Giddi Pass
Bir eth Thamada
Suez
Kuntilla
Mitla Pass
Nakhl
Elat
Eth Thamad
Gulf of Suez
SINAI
Gulf of Elat
SAUDI ARABIA
Abu Rudeis
EGYPT
Et Tur
Sharm esh Sheikh

OPERATION KADESH
("SINAI CAMPAIGN")
1956

Mediterranean Sea
Haifa
Tel Aviv
Jerusalem
Gaza
Hebron
Beersheb
El 'Arish
ISRAEL
Qantara
Abu 'Aweigîla
Quseima
Suez Canal
Bir Gifgafa
Giddi Pass
Bir eth Thamada
Suez
Kuntilla
Mitla Pass
Nakhl
Elat
Eth Thamad
Gulf of Suez
SINAI
SA
AR
Abu Rudeis
EGYPT
Area conquered in w
Sharm esh Sheikh

SIX-DAY WAR
1967

Port Said
Southern Front
Baluza
Suez Canal
EGYPT
SINAI
El Firdân Bridge
Ismâ'ilîya
Tasa
Suez
Gulf of Suez

YOM KIPPUR WAR
1973

Mt. Hermon
Northern Front
LEBANON
Sa'sa'
Qiryat Shemona
Jaba
Quneitra
Kafr esh Shams
Kafr Nafakho
Safed
ISRAEL
SYRIA
Rafid
Lake Kinneret
Eli 'Al
Tiberias
JORDAN

Legend (bottom-right):
- → Arab offensive
- ······ June 1967 border
- Area conquered by Israeli army
- Area controlled by Egyptian army

438

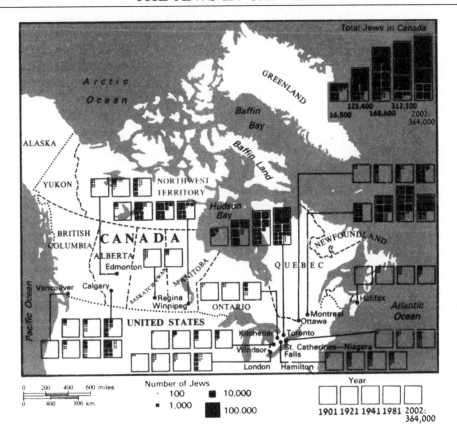

Total Jews in Canada

16,500 125,400 168,600 312,100 2002: 364,000

Number of Jews
· 100
· 1,000
■ 10,000
■ 100,000

Year
1901 1921 1941 1981 2002: 364,000

CANADIAN Jewry, one of the younger branches of the Jewish people, has its roots in the second part of the eighteenth century: the first Jewish congregation, Shearith Israel, was founded in Montreal in 1768. Although small, it was at the time one of the most important in the New World, and it remained the leading Canadian Jewish center until well into the twentieth century. The first Jews arrived from England (Spanish-Portuguese) and from the German lands in Central Europe. New communities were created during the nineteenth century, in Toronto and other cities. But it was only after the 1880s that a significant number of Jews began to arrive in Canada, part of the mass emigration from the Old World.

Although Canadian Jewry was connected with United States Jewry in many ways, it had distinct features. It shared with American Jewry the presence of three major religious trends (Reform, Conservative, and Orthodox) as well as many demographic characteristics. But Canadian Jewry defined itself differently vis-à-vis the general society. In principle, Canada was a binational country, with two officially recognized cultures and languages, English and French. This opened broad possibilities for the self-definition of other groups with a historical, cultural, or national identity, including the Jews. Combined with the fact that most Jews lived in the two major Jewish centers, Toronto and Montreal, this influenced the patterns of Jewish organi-

439

zation: Jewish institutions in Canada were more centralized than those in the United States.

In 1981, the Jews made up only about 1.4 percent of the population. Nevertheless, they were a noticeable element in Canadian life; about 75 percent of them lived in Toronto and Montreal (each with more than 100,000 Jews), concentrated in the middle and upper middle classes, and were prominent in the professions, commerce, and industry. Their proportion in several occupations far outstripped their proportion in the general population—a phenomenon found also among Jews in other countries.

THE DEVELOPMENT OF AMERICAN JEWRY 1878 FF.

AMERICAN Jewry as we know it emerged only in the second half of the nineteenth century. There were only 2,000 to 2,500 Jews in the United States at the beginning of the century, in about a dozen commu-nities. By mid-century, the number had risen to 50,000, and by 1880, to about 250,000. Many of the later characteristics of American Jewry were already evident in 1880. There were nearly 300 commu-

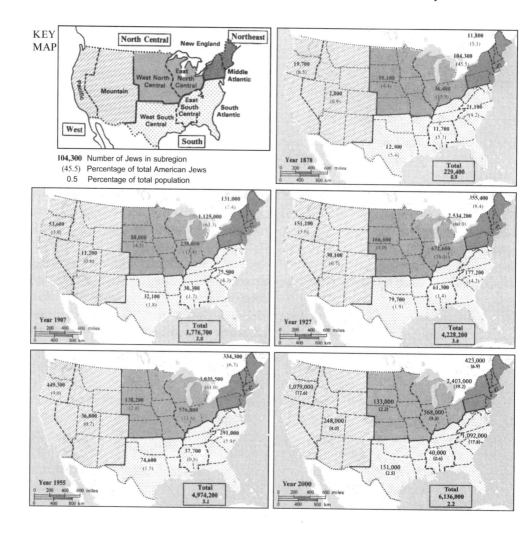

nities across the land; 50 percent of all American Jews lived in the Northeast; and 64 percent lived in 16 large cities, 30 percent in New York and Brooklyn (a separate city until 1898).

In the 1870s, American Jewry comprised two main types: a small stratum of Sephardim and a much larger group of Ashkenazim from German lands. Jews of Spanish-Portuguese origin had lived in the country since at least the eighteenth century; they were, in general, prosperous and well integrated. The nineteenth-century immigrants from Germany were on their way to prosperity and social adaptation. There was already a large number of East European Jews. Some integrated into "German" congregations; others formed their own synagogues.

In the 1880s, a new period began for American Jewry, with the mass immigration of the "Russians," the Jews from Eastern Europe.

JEWISH IMMIGRATION TO THE UNITED STATES
19TH AND 20TH CENTURIES

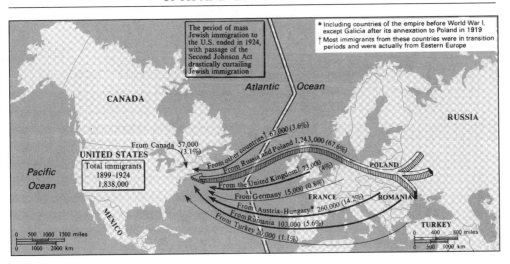

THE mass immigration of Jews to the United States, which started in the latter part of the nineteenth century, was one of the most important developments in modern Jewish history. The Jews were part of an enormous migratory movement, the largest in human history, which in the nineteenth and twentieth centuries brought tens of millions of Europeans to countries throughout the world, especially the United States. Its causes were the population growth in Europe in the nineteenth century, which exceeded the continent's economic capacity and forced people to look for homes in other countries; the development of large steamships, which made sea travel safer, cheaper, and quicker; and the attraction of America, that wide-open country, rich in resources and opportunities.

For the Jews, there were also the specific problems of East European Jewry, such as the oppressive policies of the Russian and Romanian governments. The semiurban character of the Jews made it easier for them to adapt to conditions in the growing cities of the industrializing countries of the Western world. The relative number of Jews emigrating from East European countries was much higher than that of non-Jews. They settled in Western Europe and in different countries in the Americas, primarily the United States.

From 1908 to 1924, the Jews were the second largest group of immigrants, after the Italians (whose number was twice as large). But for every 100 Italians who entered the United States in that period, 54.7 left; among the Jews, only 5.2 out of 100 left. This meant that the Jews were in fact the largest group of newcomers, since their net immigration (13.5 percent of the total) was slightly higher than that of the Italians. The Jewish immigration was also more balanced in its composition: 44 percent of immigrants were women (1889–1924), as compared with the overall immigration average of 31.7 percent; 24.4 percent of Jews were under fourteen years of age—the overall percentage of children (Jews included) was 12.4. Thus the data show that Jewish immigration was more family oriented and evenly distributed regarding sex and age than was the totality of immigration. It was also more "definitive": the Jews came to the United States to stay.

AMERICAN JEWRY IN THE 1920s

BY 1927, the Jewish population of the United States had grown to more than 4 million and had become the largest Jewish community in the world. In the 1920s, American Jewry comprised two major historical groups: the smaller "German" segment, descendants of nineteenth-century immigrants who had become fully Americanized and achieved comfortable social status and economic security; and the larger "Russian" group, immigrants from the various East European countries who had arrived mainly since the 1880s. Many were still newcomers, undergoing the difficult process of economic, social, and cultural adaptation to America. Another sector consisted of second-generation Americans. There were also smaller groups, such as the Jewish immigrants from Muslim countries. The oldest stratum of American Jewry, the Sephardim, had almost disappeared. The second Johnson Act (1924) practically shut the gates of the United States to Jewish immigration from Eastern Europe. About 120,000 Jews entered the United States in 1920 and 1921, only about 12,000 in 1925 and 1926.

In the 1920s, American Jewry underwent great organizational growth. The Jews had brought with them from Europe a rich tradition of communal organization, which developed unhindered in the free atmosphere of the New World. Every possible type of Jewish organization—religious, social, cultural, political—thrived in America. *Landsmannschaften* (associations of Jews from the same town or region in Europe), fraternal orders, Zionist associations, labor organizations, cultural enterprises, synagogues of every type—all could operate freely in the United States. The number of Jewish organizations ran into the thousands, some of them operating on a national scale, with tens of thousands of members, others on a smaller, local scale.

The synagogue gradually became the center of Jewish communal life, with all the other institutions—educational, social, or political—structured around it. In 1927, there were about 3,000 synagogues in the United States, belonging to three main religious trends: Reform, Conservative, and Orthodox.

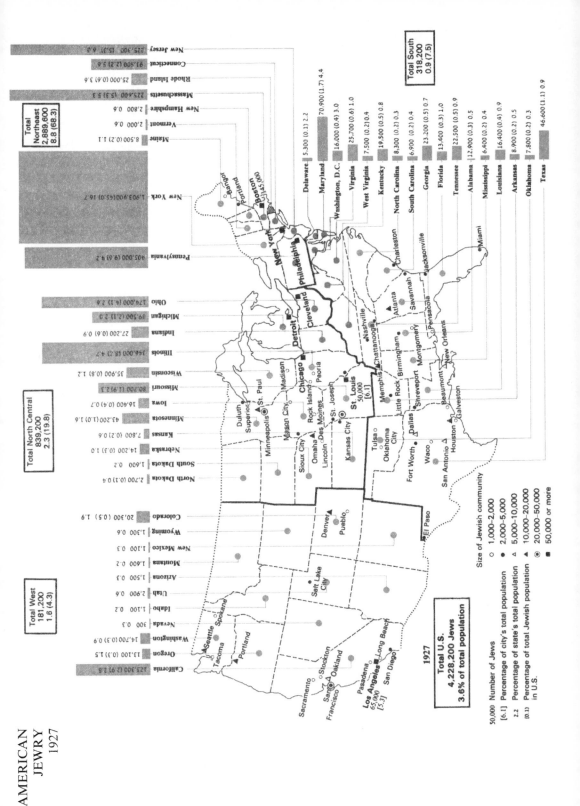

AMERICAN
JEWRY
1927

THE SOCIOECONOMIC DEVELOPMENT OF AMERICAN JEWRY

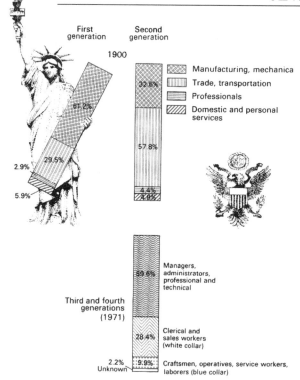

THE occupational structure and social status of American Jewry changed profoundly over the generations. Many first-generation American Jews (born in Europe and arrived in the United States as adults) worked as laborers (usually in the garment industry). Later, they or their children went into commerce, mostly small businesses. Some entered occupations requiring a higher education, such as school teaching. A typical figure among the first- or second-generation Jews (born in America, or born in Europe and arrived as small children) was the salesman. In the third and fourth generations, the outstanding phenomenon was the increase of Jews with a university education and prominent in the professions. Parallel to this, Jews developed from small shopkeepers to big businessmen, industrial entrepreneurs, and major providers of services.

The occupational structure of American Jewry differed considerably from that of the general American society, even of whites. Furthermore, their socioeconomic dynamics were unique: rapid development from a largely working- and lower-middle-class group to a predominantly middle- and upper-middle-class one.

THE JEWISH LABOR MOVEMENT IN THE UNITED STATES

MANY of the Jewish immigrants who arrived in the United States beginning in the 1880s began their life in the country as workers, mostly in the various branches of the garment industry. A Jewish working class, with a highly cultivated political and social consciousness, developed in the large cities, especially New York. The arrival in America of Jewish political activists, many associated with the Bund, who left Russia after the failure of the first Russian revolution (1904–1906), provided the American Jewish labor movement with a cadre of experienced political leaders.

The Jewish workers formed a sophisticated organizational network and participated in the establishment and development of the general American labor movement, in which they played an important part. Through negotiations and strikes, they improved working conditions. But they also created social and cultural frameworks that were Jewish in

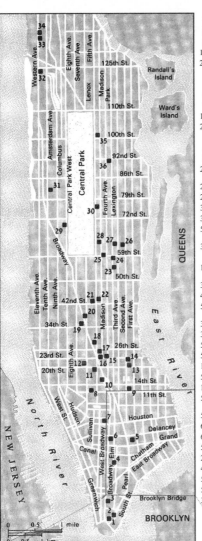

1. 1695: Beaver Street
2. 1729–1860: Mill Street
6. 1860–1883: Crosby Street
11. 1883–1897: Nineteenth Street
29. From 1897: Seventieth Street and
    Central Park West
} Shearith Israel Congregation (Sephardic)

4. 1827–1849: Elm Street
7. 1850–1865: Greene Street
19. 1865–1884: Thirty-fourth Street
28. 1885–1917: Madison Avenue
} B'nai Jeshurun Congregation (first Ashkenazic synagogue)

5. 1847–1854: Chrystie Street
9. 1854–1867: Twelfth Street
22. 1867–1929: Forty-third Street
} Temple Emanu-El

27. Rodeph Shalom Congregation (1847)
23. Central Synagogue (1872)
30. Temple Beth El
31. Sha'arei Tephillah Synagogue
59. Ohab Tzedek Synagogue

37. Chatham Square cemetery (1680s)
8. Eleventh Street cemetery
12. Twenty-first Street cemetery

35. Mount Sinai Hospital (1853)
45. Beth Israel Hospital (1890)
55. Jewish Maternity Hospital

34. Montefiore Home (1884)
33. Hebrew Benevolent and Orphan Asylum
55. Home for the Aged
55. Hebrew Sheltering House
13. Hebrew Charities Building
55. Hebrew Immigrant Aid Society (HIAS)
17. Federation of Jewish Philanthropies
56. Young Men's Benevolent Association

51. Educational Alliance (1893)
61. Educational Alliance, branch A
64. Hebrew Technical Institute for Boys
55. Hebrew Technical School for Girls
26. Baron de Hirsch Trade School
44. Rabbi Isaac Elchanan Yeshiva
53. Machzike Talmud Torah
57. Beth Hamidrash Hagadol
32. Jewish Theological Seminary of
    America (1902)

24. Independent Order B'nai B'rith (1843)
42. Independent Order B'nai B'rith, branch
62. Independent Order B'rith Abraham (1887)
36. Young Men's Hebrew Association (1901)
60. Independent Order B'rith Shalom (1905)
14. The Kehillah of New York (1909)
25. Intercollegiate Menorah Association (1913)
10. American Jewish Committee (1906)
18. Various Jewish social associations
21. Harmonie Club
63. Cooper Union
20. Federation of American Zionists (1898)
43. Federation of American Zionists (1914)

15. *American Hebrew* (1879)
3. *Hebrew Standard* (1883)
46. *Der Morgen Journal* (1901)
50. *Der Tog* (1914)
39. *Der Tegliche Herold* (1891)
47. *Die Yiddishe Welt* (1902)
48. *Forverts* (1897)
49. *Tageblat* (1885)

38. Windsor Theater
40. Yiddish Rialto (theater)
41. Grand Theater
58. People's Theater

54. Henry Street Settlement and Clinton Hall
16. Madison Square Garden

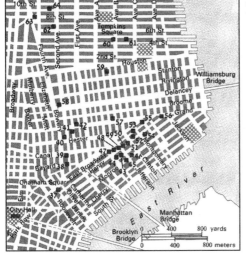

JEWISH INSTITUTIONS IN MANHATTAN UNTIL 1914

language (Yiddish) and content.

In the 1920s, the labor organizations, especially those with a strong Jewish membership, were racked by the struggle between socialists and Communists. On the whole, the socialists had the upper hand. These struggles, together with the gradual de-proletarianization of the Jewish immigrants after their entry into middle-class occupations, considerably diminished the importance of the working sector in American Jewry.

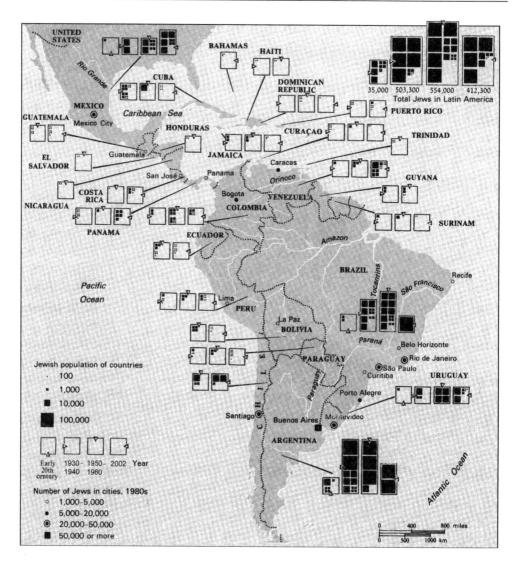

UNTIL the nineteenth century, the Inquisition laws forbade the presence of Jews in Spanish and Portuguese colonies. Jewish Sephardic communities were established in Recife, Brazil, during the short Dutch domination (1630–1654), and in the seventeenth and eighteenth centuries on the islands of the Caribbean Sea under Dutch, English, or French domination. Only in the late nineteenth century did Jews arrive in significant numbers in such countries as Uruguay,

Argentina, and Brazil, which had become independent. These republics, in spite of their Catholic character, adopted liberal constitutions, and almost without exception Jews could live there freely.

From the early twentieth century until the outbreak of World War II, the Latin American countries absorbed hundreds of thousands of Jewish immigrants, mostly from Eastern Europe, but also from the Muslim countries and, in the 1930s, from Germany. Most Jews adapted well, prospered, integrated socially and culturally into the general society, and organized Jewish institutions. But the social unrest and political problems in many Latin American nations during the second half of the twentieth century affected the Jews, who left some countries, such as Cuba, for good and others, such as Chile and Argentina, for extended periods. Some emigrated to more stable neighboring countries, such as Brazil, Venezuela, and Colombia.

Brazilian Jewry was the second largest in Latin America. Most Jews lived in São Paulo and Rio de Janeiro, well accepted by the general population and with relatively well-organized Jewish institutions. The small Jewish community of Belém, in northern Brazil, established by Moroccan Jews in the nineteenth century, had its own very distinct characteristics.

THE JEWS IN ARGENTINA

THE settlement of Jews in Argentina was stimulated by the activities of the Jewish Colonization Association (ICA), founded in 1891. ICA established agricultural colonies, mostly in the provinces of Entre Ríos and Santa Fé. Although in the 1930s, there were only 20,000 to 30,000 Jewish farmers, the ICA initiative brought many Jewish immigrants to Argentina; they settled in cities, especially in the capital, Buenos Aires. Gradually, Buenos Aires attracted most Argentinian Jews, including those living in the provincial cities or in the colonies. In the early twentieth century, two-thirds of Argentinian Jews lived in the provinces, especially Entre Ríos; by 1960, four-fifths lived in Greater Buenos Aires. In 1964, only about 800 Jewish families were engaged in agriculture, in the colonies.

Although in principle the Jews were citizens with full rights, in practice there was a strong antisemitic movement in Argentina, influenced by European traditions. There were anti-Jewish riots in 1919 and problems in later years as well, reflecting the country's internal tensions. The organization of Argentinian Jewry was strongly influenced (and dominated) by the Buenos Aires community. The Jews established two umbrella organizations. One was the Delegación de Aso-

ciaciones Israelitas Argentinas (DAIA), founded in 1933, whose purpose was to fight antisemitism and represent the community before the authorities. The other, Va'ad ha-Kehillot, organized in 1952, was based on the Ashkenazic community of Buenos Aires, the Asociación Mutual Israelita Argentina (AMIA). Va'ad ha-Kehillot became responsible for a broad spectrum of Jewish activities of a social, educational, religious, and cultural character. The Zionists had considerable influence in both bodies, and their representation was along the lines of the Zionist party structure.

From the 1960s, Argentina underwent much political and social unrest. This affected the Jewish community. The number of Jews in the country decreased significantly in the second half of the century, in part because of their low birth rate, and in part because of emigration.

The Jews in Buenos Aires
IN the second half of the twentieth century, Buenos Aires was the largest Jewish center in Latin America. Its development was similar to that of many other Jewish communities in the New World: beginnings in the nineteenth century, but real growth only toward the end of the century, with the immigration of a large number of Jews from Eastern Europe.

The way the united (Ashkenazic) Jewish community of Buenos Aires (AMIA) came into being, although it had precedents, was curious in twentieth-century conditions: it grew out of a burial society (*hevra kadisha*) formed in the mid-1890s that over the years assumed a wide range of other Jewish communal functions, to the point where it performed nearly all of them in the city. The result was a much tighter centralization of Jewish institutions under one umbrella than occurred in most other twentieth-century Jewish centers. Since in the 1960s, about 80 percent of all Argentinian Jews lived in Buenos Aires, AMIA influenced the Jewish life of the majority of the country's Jews. The Sephardic community of Buenos Aires had separate Jewish institutions.

Buenos Aires Jewry was known for its rich Jewish cultural life. Although the Zionists dominated AMIA, there was an important group of Yiddish intellectuals, many of whom were associated with the Bund.

The size of Buenos Aires Jewry reached its peak in 1960. Thereafter, the number decreased steadily.

THE JEWS IN SOUTH AFRICA

JEWS arrived in the land that became South Africa as early as the seventeenth century. But only in the nineteenth century did the country's economic development (after the discovery of gold and diamonds) attract a large number of Jews, mostly from Eastern Europe. They settled mainly in the Transvaal and the Cape, in the two main cities, Johannesburg and Cape Town. In 1980, over 95 percent of South African Jews lived in cities, about 57 percent in Johannesburg and 23 percent in Cape Town.

In the nineteenth century, the legal status of the Jews varied according to region; Jews living among the English were better off than those residing among the Dutch (Boers), for religious reasons. With the formation of the South African state (1902–1910), the Jews were granted full civil rights, but the rigid ethnic structure of the white population continued to leave its mark. In the larger cities, Jews tended to concentrate in certain neighborhoods, such as Glenhazel and Killarney in Johannesburg, where the Jews made up over half of the local population.

Compared with other modern Jewries, South African Jews were well organized

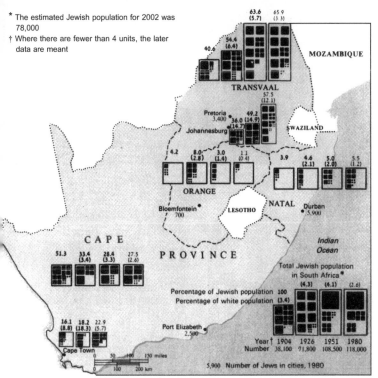

* The estimated Jewish population for 2002 was 78,000
† Where there are fewer than 4 units, the later data are meant

THE JEWS IN SOUTH AFRICA

MOZAMBIQUE

TRANSVAAL

Pretoria 3,400
Johannesburg

SWAZILAND

ORANGE

Bloemfontein 700

LESOTHO

NATAL

Durban 5,900

Indian Ocean

CAPE PROVINCE

Total Jewish population in South Africa*

Percentage of Jewish population 100
Percentage of white population (3.4)

Port Elizabeth 2,500

Cape Town

Year†	1904	1926	1951	1980
Number	38,100	71,800	108,500	118,000

5,900 Number of Jews in cities, 1980

0 50 100 150 miles
0 100 200 km

and had a well-developed Jewish consciousness. Zionist ideology and party organization were very influential. South African Jewry was headed by the South African Jewish Board of Deputies, formed in 1912, and modeled on the British pattern of Jewish organization.

THE JEWS IN AUSTRALIA AND NEW ZEALAND

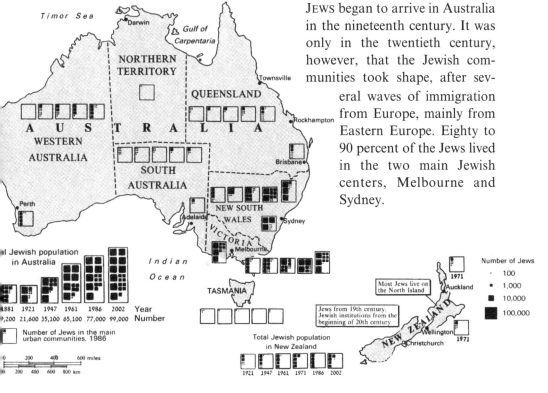

Timor Sea
Darwin
Gulf of Carpentaria

NORTHERN TERRITORY

Townsville

QUEENSLAND

Rockhampton

A U S T R A L I A

WESTERN AUSTRALIA

SOUTH AUSTRALIA

Brisbane

Perth

Adelaide

NEW SOUTH WALES
Sydney

VICTORIA
Melbourne

Indian Ocean

al Jewish population in Australia

1881	1921	1947	1961	1986	2002	Year
9,200	21,600	35,100	65,100	77,000	99,000	Number

Number of Jews in the main urban communities, 1986

0 200 400 600 miles
0 200 400 600 800 km

TASMANIA

Total Jewish population in New Zealand

1921 1947 1961 1971 1986 2002

Most Jews live on the North Island

Jews from 19th century. Jewish institutions from the beginning of 20th century

Auckland 1971

NEW ZEALAND

Wellington 1971
Christchurch

Number of Jews
· 100
• 1,000
■ 10,000
■ 100,000

JEWS began to arrive in Australia in the nineteenth century. It was only in the twentieth century, however, that the Jewish communities took shape, after several waves of immigration from Europe, mainly from Eastern Europe. Eighty to 90 percent of the Jews lived in the two main Jewish centers, Melbourne and Sydney.

H. A CHANGING WORLD JEWRY

LATE 20TH TO EARLY 21ST CENTURIES

THE transition from the second to the third millennium coincided with a time of significant change for the global societal system. The world's political equilibrium shifted from bipolar to more clearly dominated by one world power—the United States. Socioeconomic development and transactions reached a definitive stage of globalization, and new cultural patterns and technologies emerged. A short span of years witnessed the end of the Soviet Union as a major global power, the reunion of Germany, the revival of religious fundamentalism, particularly Islam, the return of "ethnic cleansing" in Europe and Africa, new waves of mass international migration, the beginning, and halt, of a peace process in the Middle East, the Catholic Church's improved attitude toward the Jewish people and its historic recognition of the State of Israel. A European monetary union, as well as the rise of the internet and other global and regional societal changes also emerged. Transformations of the global polity, economy and communications deeply affected the daily life, identity and boundary definition of nations, communities, and individuals. This was true of world society in general, and of world Jewry in particular.

Jewish history—as history in general—can be viewed as a sequence of sudden major events connected by longer or shorter periods in which politics, society and culture routinely unfold. The two crucial events that shaped much of Jewish history in the twentieth century were the *Shoah* (Holocaust) and the independence of the State of Israel. One major connecting process that because of its magnitude and global impact might actually be seen as a third founding factor, was intercontinental migration. The revolution brought about by these events and processes created new and lasting material and identificational terms of reference for Jewish life globally. The Six-Day War in 1967 and the fall of the Berlin wall in 1989 became further cardinal turning points for Jewish history and society. The Six-Day War brought about a dramatic arousal in Israel's centrality in the perceptions of world Jewry, and significantly enhanced the country's international standing that facilitated its economic and technological capabilities. Stemming from military conflict, the Israeli occupation of the West Bank and Gaza created the premises for a new and still unsolved stage of the Israeli-Arab conflict, but also generated powerful social and political consequences within Israeli society. The end of Soviet hegemony in Eastern and Central Europe and the ensuing dismemberment of the Former Soviet Union (FSU) and global geopolitical realignment made possible the major exodus from the FSU of which Israel absorbed a predominant share.

The pressures and dilemmas brought about by these global changes stimulated the emergence of conflicting visions of the present and future of world Jewry. In the Diaspora the quest for Jewish continuity was challenged by a growing pace of assimilation and alienation, while in Israel the once predominant paradigm of ingathering of the exiles, immigrant absorption, fusion of the Diasporas and nation building based on a Jewish majority was being challenged by alternative post- or non-Zionist views. These developments carried major consequences for Jewish demography.

JEWISH POPULATION SINCE WORLD WAR II

In 1945, following World War II, the world Jewish population was reduced to about 11 million. It then recovered somewhat during the 1950s and early 1960s, reaching over 12.6 million by 1970, and an estimated total of 12.9 million at the beginning of 2002. But while it took about thirteen years to add one million Jews to the post-Holocaust total, according to the most recent population estimates the subsequent forty-four years did not add a second million. Not only was world Jewry far from even approaching its pre-Holocaust size of 16.5 million, but its population increase was slowing down and by the end of the 1980s had reached zero or negative growth. Very modest increases during the 1990s reflected a temporary echo effect of the postwar baby-boom as well as re-identification, return or access to Judaism of people whose Jewish identification previously had been extremely marginal. This was connected with mass emigration from Eastern Europe.

World Jewry's overall increase since 1970 was less than 2 percent (0.06 percent a year), compared with over 70 percent in the total world population (about 1.7 percent yearly). Jewish zero population growth globally was the product of two distinct trends compensating one another—the State of Israel and the Diaspora. Each responds to two different sets of demographic determinants and consequences. The Israeli component, approaching 40 percent of the world total, operates as the majority of its own sovereign state. The Diaspora, about 60 percent of world Jewry, consists of many different-sized communities, each constituting a small to minuscule share of the total population of the respective country.

Since 1945, the respective size of these two Jewish population aggregates has tended to converge. The most notable change in Jewish demography since the late 1940s was the emergence of Palestine and later Israel as a large and viable center of Jewish life. Its Jewish population grew from approximately half a million in 1945 to over 5.1 million at the end of 2002, and its share of world Jewry grew from less than 5 percent to 39 percent. The total Jewish population outside Israel diminished from just under 10.5 million in 1945 to less than 8 million in 2002. Israel's Jewish population grew by more than 2 million between 1945 and 1970, and by nearly another 2.5 million between 1970 and 2002. Diaspora Jewry diminished by about 400,000 between 1945 and 1970, and declined by another 2.2 million between 1970 and 2002. Between 1945 and 2002 over 2.2 million Jews from the Diaspora immigrated to Israel, including about one million since 1970.

No. in thsds

World Jewish population, 1945–2002.

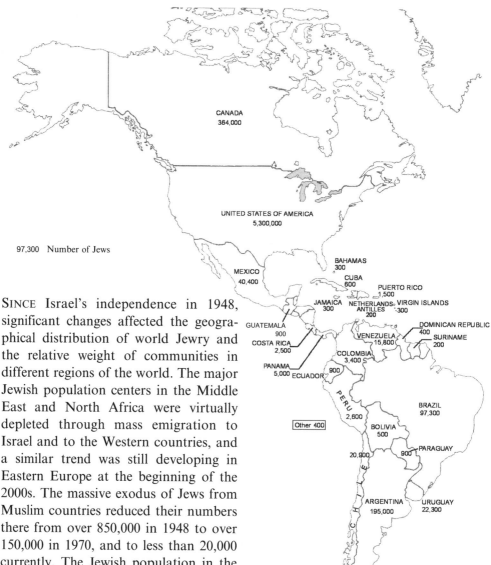

CANADA
364,000

UNITED STATES OF AMERICA
5,300,000

97,300   Number of Jews

BAHAMAS
300

MEXICO
40,400

CUBA
600

PUERTO RICO
1,500

JAMAICA
300

NETHERLANDS
ANTILLES
200

VIRGIN ISLANDS
300

GUATEMALA
900

COSTA RICA
2,500

PANAMA
5,000

ECUADOR
900

VENEZUELA
15,800

DOMINICAN REPUBLIC
400

SURINAME
200

COLOMBIA
3,400

PERU
2,600

Other 400

BRAZIL
97,300

BOLIVIA
500

20,900

PARAGUAY
900

ARGENTINA
195,000

URUGUAY
22,300

Since Israel's independence in 1948, significant changes affected the geographical distribution of world Jewry and the relative weight of communities in different regions of the world. The major Jewish population centers in the Middle East and North Africa were virtually depleted through mass emigration to Israel and to the Western countries, and a similar trend was still developing in Eastern Europe at the beginning of the 2000s. The massive exodus of Jews from Muslim countries reduced their numbers there from over 850,000 in 1948 to over 150,000 in 1970, and to less than 20,000 currently. The Jewish population in the former Soviet Union (FSU) declined from an estimated 2,375,000 in 1948 to 2,124,000 in 1970, and 438,000 in 2002; and in other East European and Balkan countries it declined from 850,000 in 1948 to 216,000 in 1970, and about 95,000 in 2002. The total in Latin America also diminished from 525,000 in 1948 to 514,000 in 1970, and to 412,000 in 2002; and in the African countries south of Sahara, mainly South Africa, it passed from 120,000 in 1948 and 125,000 in 1970, to 80,000 in 2002. On the other hand, the Jewish population in the main Western countries tended to be stable or increase. In the United States and Canada the estimated total passed from 5,235,000 in 1948 to 5,686,000 in 1970, and 5,664,000 in 2002; in Western Europe, from 850,000 in 1948 to 1,119,000 in

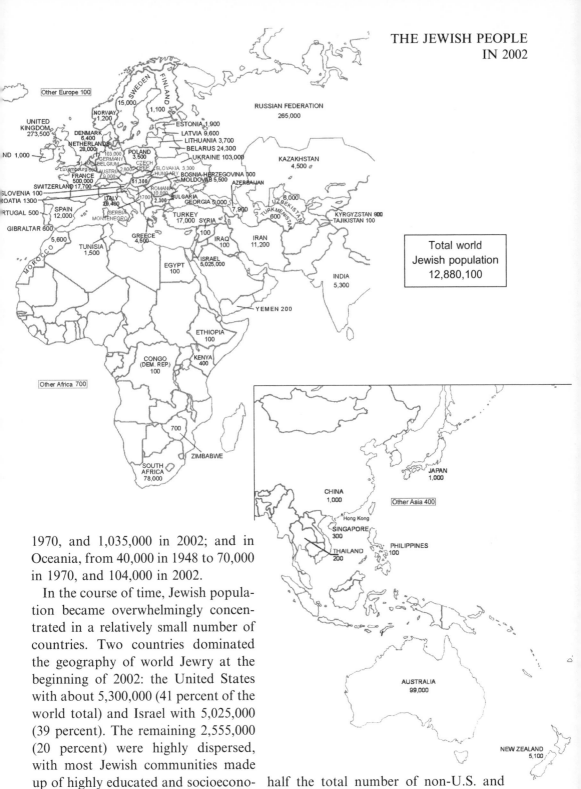

Other Europe 100

SWEDEN
15,000

FINLAND
1,100

NORWAY
1,200

RUSSIAN FEDERATION
265,000

UNITED
KINGDOM
273,500

DENMARK
6,400

NETHERLANDS
28,000

ESTONIA 1,900
LATVIA 9,600
LITHUANIA 3,700
BELARUS 24,300
UKRAINE 103,000

ND 1,000

GERMANY
103,000

POLAND
3,500

KAZAKHSTAN
4,500

Luxembourg 600
BELGIUM
31,400

FRANCE
500,000

AUSTRIA
9,000

CZECH
REP.

SLOVAKIA 3,300

HUNGARY
51,300

BOSNIA-HERZEGOVINA 300
MOLDOVA 5,500

AZERBAIJAN

SLOVENIA 100
CROATIA 1300

SWITZERLAND 17,700

ITALY
28,400

ROMANIA
10,800

BULGARIA
2,300

GEORGIA 5,000

6,000

UZBEKISTAN
7,900

PORTUGAL 500

SPAIN
12,000

SERBIA
MONTENEGRO

GREECE
4,500

TURKEY
17,000

SYRIA

TURKMENISTAN
600

KYRGYZSTAN 900
TAJIKISTAN 100

GIBRALTAR 600

5,600

TUNISIA
1,500

100

IRAQ
100

IRAN
11,200

EGYPT
100

ISRAEL
5,025,000

INDIA
5,300

MOROCCO

YEMEN 200

ETHIOPIA
100

CONGO
(DEM. REP.)
100

KENYA
400

Other Africa 700

700

ZIMBABWE

SOUTH
AFRICA
78,000

Total world
Jewish population
12,880,100

CHINA
1,000

JAPAN
1,000

Other Asia 400

Hong Kong

SINGAPORE
300

PHILIPPINES
100

THAILAND
200

AUSTRALIA
99,000

NEW ZEALAND
5,100

1970, and 1,035,000 in 2002; and in Oceania, from 40,000 in 1948 to 70,000 in 1970, and 104,000 in 2002.

In the course of time, Jewish population became overwhelmingly concentrated in a relatively small number of countries. Two countries dominated the geography of world Jewry at the beginning of 2002: the United States with about 5,300,000 (41 percent of the world total) and Israel with 5,025,000 (39 percent). The remaining 2,555,000 (20 percent) were highly dispersed, with most Jewish communities made up of highly educated and socioeconomically mobile populations. Four countries alone included more than half the total number of non-U.S. and non-Israeli Jews: France (500,000 Jews), followed by Canada (364,000), the Russian Republic (265,000), and the United Kingdom (273,000). Further important Jewish communities are found in Argentina, Germany, Ukraine, Australia, Brazil, and South Africa.

Trends to growth, stability or decline in the major Jewish communities were quite variable. The Jewish population in the United States increased by an estimated 100,000 between 1970 and 1990, from 5.4 to 5.5 million, less than might have been expected considering the total amount of known Jewish immigration to the United States. Between 1990 and 2000, there were 5.3 to 5.35 million Jews—150,000 to 200,000 less than in 1990. Substantial numbers of Jews did move to America, from the FSU, Israel, Latin America, South Africa, Iran and other countries, but the internal demographic, social and cultural forces balanced out much of the expected population increase and actually created a deficit.

Among other Western countries, France, Canada, the United Kingdom, Australia and Brazil had quite stable Jewish populations. But their recent size has in each case depended on the trends in international migration. All in all, the Jewish community with the fastest rate of growth since 1970 was Germany, whose Jewish population increased more than threefold, having attracted significant immigration from the FSU. Where, as in the case of Canada and Australia, an even modest inflow continued, the numbers increased, although by 2001 growth seemed to be over. Between 1970 and 2002 Canada's Jewry grew by 27 percent, and Australian Jewry by 52 percent. Jews in Brazil grew until the 1990s, but then probably began to diminish also due to growing rates of out-marriage. Where, as in the case of France, *aliyah* to Israel was quite visible, regularly ranging between 1,000 and over 2,000 a year, the numbers

diminished. French Jewry lost around 30,000 people between the late 1970s and 2002. Jews in the United Kingdom beginning with the 1970s, and possibly before, were in a mode of numerical decline due to a consistently higher number of recorded deaths over the estimated number of births, and lost 30 percent of their initial size between 1970 and 2002. Such a trend was shared with varying intensities by most other European and Latin American countries. An exception was Mexico and, at least until the 1990s, Venezuela, where the Jewish population tended to grow before stabilizing. On the other hand the estimate for Argentina fell from 282,000 in 1970 to 195,000 in 2002—not taking into account the sharp rise in emigration that took place in 2002 following the worsening of the economic crisis. South African Jewry, too, diminished by over one third from 118,000 in 1970 to 78,000 in 2002.

Republics of the FSU underwent a significant and still not yet completed process of Jewish population decline. The decrease of 1.7 million since 1970, or nearly 80 percent, was mostly explained by a great exodus whose first stage began shortly after the Six-Day War and peaked by the mid-1970s, followed by a period of repression and, since the end of 1989, a new unprecedented emigration spell. Some former Soviet republics, primarily Russia and to a much lesser extent the Baltics, were able to keep a substantial and today better organized Jewish presence. Other republics, like the Ukraine, Belarus, Moldova in Europe, and the republics in the Caucasus and Central Asia, experienced quicker and more massive Jewish population outflows and decline. Emigration was complemented by internal erosion produced by local demographic processes of aging and out-marriage.

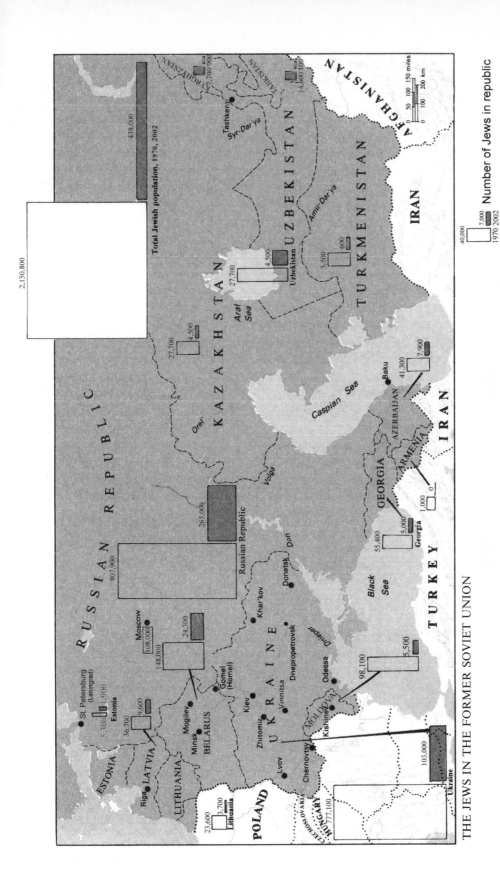

THE JEWS IN THE FORMER SOVIET UNION

Number of Jews in republic

1970 | 2002

Total Jewish population, 1970, 2002

2,150,800

The Jewish population in Israel increased by 96 percent between 1970 and 2002. While the leading catalyst behind Jewish population growth was a favorable net balance of immigration and emigration, natural increase accounted for about half of Israel's total Jewish population growth. In the course of time, Israel with all of its immigration had a growing majority of native-born Jews, who in 2001 accounted for about 63 percent of world Jewry.

CORE AND ENLARGED JEWISH POPULATIONS

No assessment of Jewish demographic trends is possible without explaining what the data mean, particularly the statistical definition of "who is a Jew." The figures here usually relate to the concept of *core Jewish population*, i.e., all those who, when asked, identify themselves as Jews; or, if the respondent is a different person in the same household, are identified by him/her as Jews. This is an intentionally comprehensive approach, reflecting both subjective feelings and community norms and bonds. The definition is admittedly looser in the Diaspora than in Israel where personal status is subject to the ruling of the Ministry of Internal Affairs. It broadly overlaps but does not necessarily coincide with the halakhic definition of a Jew as someone who is the child of a Jewish mother or converted by the apropriate religious and legal procedure. Inclusion in the core Jewish population does not depend on any measure of a person's Jewish commitment or behavior in terms of religiosity, beliefs, knowledge, communal affiliation, or otherwise. The core Jewish population includes all those who converted to Judaism, or decided to join the Jewish group informally and declare themselves Jewish. It excludes those of Jewish descent who have formally adopted another religion, as well as other individuals who did not convert out but currently refuse to recognize their Jewishness.

Concurrently, the concept of an *enlarged Jewish population* includes the sum of (a) the core Jewish population, (b) all other persons, Jewish by birth or parentage, who do not currently identify as Jews, and (c) all the respective non-Jewish household members (spouses, children, etc.). The enlarged Jewish population encompasses significantly more people than the core population.

The about 13 million Jews estimated worldwide at the dawn of the twenty-first century were intimately connected to several more millions of people. Some of the latter had Jewish origins or family connections but were not currently Jewish, whether because they changed their own identification, are the non-Jewish children of intermarried parents, or were non-Jewish members in intermarried households. These non-Jews shared the daily life experience, social and economic concerns, and cultural environment of

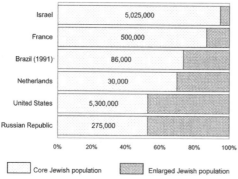

Core and enlarged Jewish populations of selected countries, 2000–2001.

their Jewish mates. The examples above indicate the extent of variation of *core* and *enlarged* Jewish populations in selected countries. Note that the criteria followed in the ensuing comparison were not the same in each place.

THE JEWS IN THE WORLD SYSTEM

To further understand the Jewish population change over the last several decades, the intensive and manifold relationships that exist between Jewish communities and contemporary society at large deserve closer scrutiny. One needs to relate the Jewish presence—as expressed in absolute numbers and as a percentage of the total population—to major social and economic indicators of the places where they live at the country, regional and provincial level. Did Jews simply move and redistribute at random, or did their mobility patterns reflect the pull and push of the main social forces in the larger market?

Three sets of data provide at least a partial answer. The geographical distribution of Jews is examined between 1990 and 2001 at the level of detail, respectively, of 190 countries globally, about 70 different economic regions within the European Union, and the United States. The Jewish and total populations of these countries, economic regions, and states were ranked in relation to the degree of economic development in each area. Geographical units were first sorted according to socioeconomic indicators, and then subdivided into five groups (quintiles), each with the same number of geographical units.

The different concentration of the Jewish presence out of the total population, by level of development of the environment, tended to be very consistent and statistically significant, passing from comparatively denser in the wealthier and more sophisticated areas to scantiest in the poorest and more back-

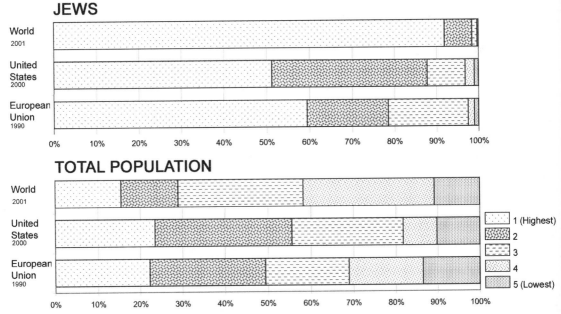

Total and Jewish population distribution, by socioeconomic development of regions of residence.

ward areas. In 2001, Jews represented about 2 per 1,000 of the total worldwide population, but they were six times as many in the top quintile of countries. Around 1990, Jews represented about 3 per 1,000 of the total population in the European Union, but more than two-and-a-half times more in the top quintile of its economic regions. In the United States in 2000, Jews represented 23 per 1,000 of the total population, but twice as many in the top quintile of states.

The concentration of Jews in the better locations, and Jewish-total population distribution differences were far greater among countries worldwide (76.4 percent) than among in the United States (32.2 percent). Over time, the more powerful locales were able to draw Jews from the weaker ones through international or internal migration. The inherent logic connecting the presence of Jews with the availability of certain basic socioeconomic and cultural conditions locally seemed to be quite the same, regardless of the geographical level chosen for analysis. A Jewish population that tended to be generally urban, highly educated, and quite specialized in its professional activities displayed awareness of the changing map of opportunities. But the data can also be interpreted as an indication of growing material and functional dependency of the Jewish presence on the general situation of society at large, whose major changes generally were far beyond the control of the Jewish community.

THE JEWS IN MAJOR URBAN AREAS

ANOTHER indicator of the sensitivity to global market forces of Jewish population distribution was the overwhelming concentration in major urban areas resulting from intensive international and internal migrations. Large urbanization of the Jews resulted in twenty metropolitan areas worldwide having an estimated population of 95,000 Jews or more and altogether comprising over 73 percent of the total world Jewish population in 2002. Over half of world Jewry

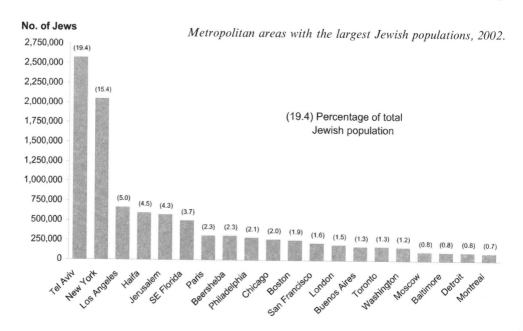

Metropolitan areas with the largest Jewish populations, 2002.

No. of Jews

(19.4) Percentage of total Jewish population

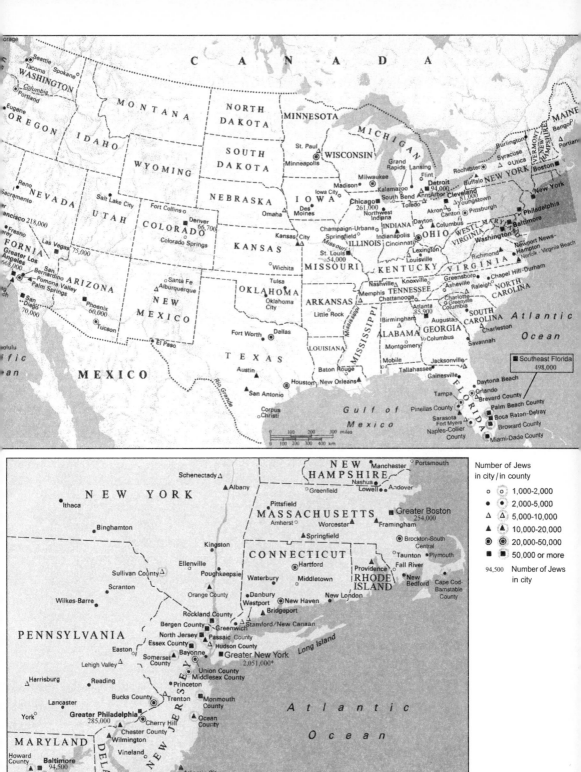

JEWISH CENTERS IN THE UNITED STATES 2002

(6,964,000, or 52 percent) lived in only six large metropolitan areas, each with half a million individuals or more: New York (including areas in New Jersey, Connecticut and Pennsylvania), Los Angeles (including Orange, Riverside and Ventura Counties), Miami–Fort Lauderdale–West Palm Beach–Boca Raton in the United States; and Tel Aviv, Haifa and Jerusalem in Israel.

In these and many other central places of world economic and cultural significance, large numbers of Jews enjoyed very favorable and perhaps unprecedented standards of living and were able to bring to fruition high levels of training and occupational skill. However, these were also the places where Jews faced the challenge of intensive competition with, and easy access to different cultures and social networks. At least in the Diaspora, Jewish cultural continuity tended to become a more difficult target precisely where Jews were physically more secure and where socioeconomic achievements were more easily attainable.

An unprecedented share of the global Jewish population was concentrated in the economically more developed and politically more stable parts of the world. While this augured well for the Jews, and set the scenario and expected rules for possible geographical changes in the future, it also portended a substantial amount of dependency of the Jewish minority upon the favorable conditions created by the majority. The emerging situation was radically different from the one that prevailed during most of modern Jewish history. In the past Jews were tolerated or discriminated against, and often nurtured hopes for societal changes that would benefit their political and social status. Under the more stable and attractive contemporary conditions, Jewish interests tended to increasingly coincide with the established societal order. At the end of a long transformation which brought with it political emancipation and economic achievement, the Jews found themselves in a more conservative mood in relation to society at large.

INTERNATIONAL MIGRATION OF THE JEWS

THE geographical configurations just described reflect to a large extent the effects of international migration. Historically, the Jews' great geographical mobility contributed to the anti-Jewish myth of the wandering Jew—supposedly a restless and rootless people. True, international migration was a factor of significant change in Jewish society, but attention should be paid to the political and socioeconomic context that stimulated frequent geographical mobility over time. A hostile environment, imbued with antisemitic prejudice and also rapid Jewish population growth, created at times highly unstable and risky conditions, the

response to which was, when feasible, mass and non-selective emigration.

Four million Jews migrated between 1881 and the eve of the establishment of the State of Israel in 1948. Since 1948 and up to the end of 2002, nearly 4.7 million Jews migrated from one continent to another. This overall estimate includes migration to and from Israel, but does not fully account for migration within continents, especially within Europe. Throughout the twentieth century, international migration of the Jews featured an uninterrupted series of major wavelike movements interspersed with minor ones. Each of these waves was prompted by

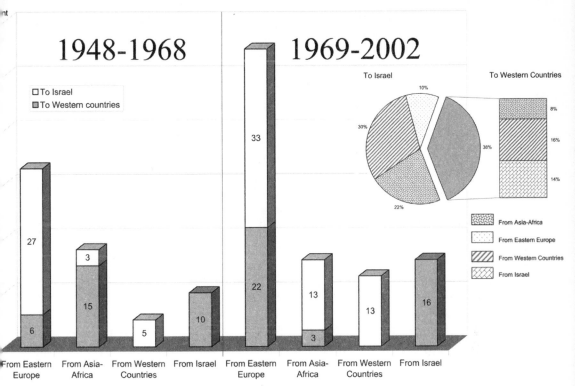

1948-1968

□ To Israel
▨ To Western countries

From Eastern Europe: 27 / 6
From Asia-Africa: 3 / 15
From Western Countries: 5
From Israel: 10

1969-2002

To Israel

10%
30%
38%
22%

To Western Countries

8%
16%
14%

From Asia-Africa
From Eastern Europe
From Western Countries
From Israel

From Eastern Europe: 33 / 22
From Asia-Africa: 13 / 3
From Western Countries: 13
From Israel: 16

INTERNATIONAL MIGRATION OF THE JEWS, BY MAJOR AREAS OF ORIGIN AND DESTINATION, 1948–2002

situations of political and economic crisis affecting Jewish communities in the respective regions of origin. What emerges is a general pattern of stable instability or unstable stability, dominated by negative (push) factors and by the variable availability of exit permits and ports of entry.

Since World War II, a first major wave involved mass migration following the establishment of the State of Israel and the unrestricted opening of its gates to Jewish immigration during the late 1940s and early 1950s, peaking in 1949–1951. A second wave was the great exodus from the FSU since the last months of 1989, peaking in 1990–1991. These major cyclical patterns resulted from a complex array of factors, and primarily periodical conflicts between major powers and sharp discontinuities in economic devel-

opment that affected the world geopolitical balance and the redistribution of areas of influence across the world system. The consequences of these global changes affected countries, communities, and individuals. Especially when Jews fulfilled a mediating role in rigidly stratified multi-ethnic countries, as in colonial North Africa or even under the Soviet regime, their position in society was deeply influenced by these major changes, and long-established mechanisms of interaction between Jews and other social, political and ethno-religious groups were disrupted. The periodic re-emergence of the urgent need to out-migrate clearly testified to the sensitivity and dependency of local Jewish communities on a much broader and complex international thread.

Of the total emigrants since 1948, 46

percent came from Eastern Europe, 30 percent from countries in Asia and Africa, 10 percent from Western countries, and 14 percent from Israel. Between 1948 and 1969 the majority of Jewish emigrants came from Muslim countries. Between 1969 and 2002 more than half came from Eastern Europe, especially the FSU. Thus, as already noted, Jewish geography worldwide ostensibly shifted from locations in semiperipheral and peripheral countries in Asia, Africa, Eastern Europe and Latin America, towards more attractive and stable societies in North America and Western Europe. Over the long term, Jewish migration constituted a very substantial volume of movement, both in absolute terms and in relation to the overall pool of Jewish population. On the average, every year 8 per 1,000 of all world Jews were on the move each year between 1948 and 1958, and 6 per 1,000 between 1969 and 2002. The respective yearly rates of emigration were 12 per 1,000 from Eastern Europe, and 83 per 1,000 from Asia and Africa during the earlier 20 years; and 51 per 1,000 from Eastern Europe and 97 per 1,000 from Asia and Africa during the later 34 years. In the process, Jewish communities in Muslim countries virtually ceased to be. The movement of Jews out of Slavic areas was quantitatively heavier, but did not reach the relative incidence of the exodus from North Africa and the Middle East. It is interesting to point to the stability over the last several years of the more recent Jewish migration wave from Eastern Europe. Some decline in the absolute frequency of immigration from the FSU to Israel since 1990 generated the impression that that massive flow was approaching an end. However, considering that the pool of potential immigrants was shrinking all the time—because of emigration and other demographic factors—the propensity to emigrate after the initial two-year peak was extremely stable and even periodically increased.

Choosing a country of destination reflected the Jewish emigrants' preference for economically more developed and politically more secure places. Since 1948, Israel became the main recipient of world Jewish migration, absorbing about 63 percent of the total: 69 percent of the nearly 2 million Jews migrated between 1948 and 1968, and 59 percent of the 2.7 million Jews who migrated between 1969 and 2002. The balance of Jewish migration went to Western countries, primarily the United States, but also France and to some extent, Canada, Australia and in more recent years Germany.

Western countries that absorbed significant numbers of Jewish immigrants also featured the lowest propensities for emigration. Overall, 1 per 1,000 of all Jewish residents in Western countries immigrated to Israel each year. Emigration propensities from Israel were quite low, too, and in fact were extremely low in comparison with other countries that absorbed a considerable number of immigrants. Israel emigration rates were on the average 5 per 1,000 from 1948 to 1968, and 4 per 1,000 from 1969 to 2002.

IDEOLOGICAL AND OTHER DETERMINANTS OF *ALIYAH*

ISRAEL'S role as a major country of Jewish immigration constituted, at first sight, an exception to the functional interpretation of Jewish migrations. In common wisdom, *aliyah* (the ascent to Zion) should be explained primarily on

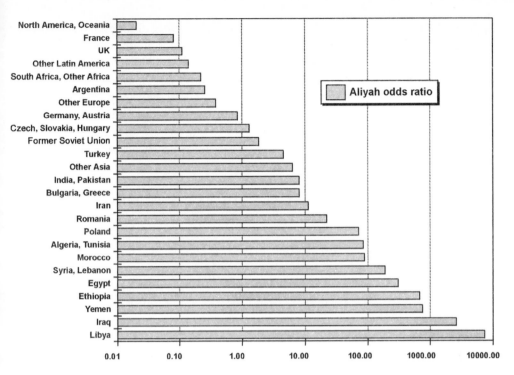

Countries of origin of the Jews in Israel compared with Diaspora Jewish population distribution, 2000.

ideological grounds. The two dominant factors in large-scale population transfer and resettlement may be expected to be, in this case, Israel's centrality in the perceptions of Diaspora Jews and the logistical support of international organizations led by the Jewish Agency. Detailed observation of the intensity of *aliyah* country by country, however, confirms the dependency of immigration on the varying incidence of negative, or push factors in the countries of origin. Thus Israel's central role in Jewish migrations was not inconsistent when viewed in a broader comparative framework. During the 1990s Israel joined the group of 20 to 25 more developed countries, and thus became an attractive location independently of ideological motives, at least for immigrants from less developed or less politically stable countries.

The table above presents an analysis of the relationship between the frequency of past migration to Israel and the growth of Jewish communities in the Diaspora. The countries and regions listed cover a wide cross-section of political regimes and economic standards of living. After relating *aliyah* levels to the size of each Jewish community of origin, a very significant variation appeared in the respective scales reflecting data on Jewish populations of a given origin in Israel, and in the same country of origin in 2000. The detailed ranking of countries featured the United States at the extreme with the lowest frequency of *aliyah*. Proceeding in the scale of intensity, we find France, the United Kingdom and other Western countries, followed by less stable Western countries such as Argentina and South Africa, central European and Balkan countries, the FSU, and—

with the highest frequencies of *aliyah*—countries mostly in North Africa and the Middle East. A more detailed description of *aliyah* from the FSU would show much higher propensities to migrate to Israel from the poorest and least stable parts of the FSU, such as Central Asia, the Caucasus, and Moldova, than from the better provinces of the Russian Republic (primarily the city of Moscow) and the Baltic states. *Aliyah* from the least attractive regions of the FSU was 1,000 times more frequent than from the United States. Even higher rates of *aliyah* were recorded for Ethiopia, one of the world's poorest countries, whose Jewish community was completely transferred to Israel.

JEWISH MARRIAGES, BIRTHS AND DEATHS

POPULATION changes reflect the natural facts of life: birth and death. Births, in turn, have long been largely governed by the mechanisms of family formation. Over the last quarter of the twentieth century, distinct erosion in conventional marriage patterns among Jews reflected similar general trends among developed Western societies. Propensities to marry significantly diminished. An increase in unmarried couples living together (overwhelmingly composed by one Jewish and one non-Jewish partner in the Diaspora), did not compensate for fewer and later marriages. Divorce rates increased and tended to approach the higher rates of non-Jews. In Israel such trends were more conservative, but they became more prominent too, as demonstrated by the presence of over one million unmarried individuals among the adult Jewish population.

During the 1990s between 40 and 50 percent of Jews who married in the United States, France and the United Kingdom had a non-Jewish partner, and higher percentages approaching 70 and 80 percent did in the FSU and other Eastern European countries. The differential frequency of out-marriages of Jewish men and women tended to disappear, equalling the higher levels previously recorded for men. The majority of children of out-marriages were not

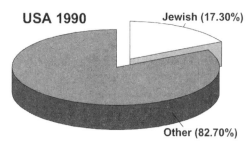

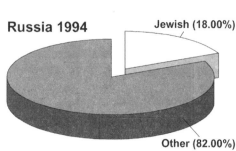

Children of mixed marriages.

identified as Jews. Similar relatively low proportions of children of out-marriages (about 20 percent) were identified by the respective parents as Jewish in Russia (with rather underdeveloped Jewish community resources), as in the United States (with highly developed Jewish resources). As a compound consequence, Jewish households were characterized by an increasing share of configurations different from the conventional nuclear family of Jewish parents living with their Jewish children. In the Diaspora this comprised an ever smaller minority of all Jewish households.

In a general context of low and declining death rates, fertility was quite stable among Jews in Israel, but eventually became about one half lower among the rest of Jewish communities worldwide. The latter reflected or even often anticipated the general decline of fertility in the more developed countries. Jews in Israel—increasingly part of the group of economically more developed societies—were an exception, becoming the group with the highest fertility among developed nations. Jews from similar places who migrated to Israel or to Europe adapted the social norms of their countries of absorption. In Israeli society, community was an important intervening factor in fertility trends resulting in larger families than could be found among Jews with similar backgrounds who moved to other countries. Cultural, religious and community related determinants of higher fertility in Israel led to a unique surplus of natural increase and helped to maintain a comparatively young age composition among the Jewish population. Jewish births in Israel were higher than the number of Jewish deaths by over 45,000 in 1990, and by over 58,000 in 2001.

In the Diaspora low fertility was the main determinant of rapid Jewish population aging. This in turn significantly contributed to a negative balance between Jewish births and deaths. Among the better documented examples, in the Russian Republic the number of Jewish deaths exceeded the number of Jewish births by over 10,000 in 1988, and by 7,600 in 2000 among a greatly diminished Jewish population. In Germany, the excess of Jewish deaths over Jewish births was over 300 in 1990, and had grown nearly threefold in 2001 while the Jewish population itself had grown threefold thanks to the steady inflow of immigrants

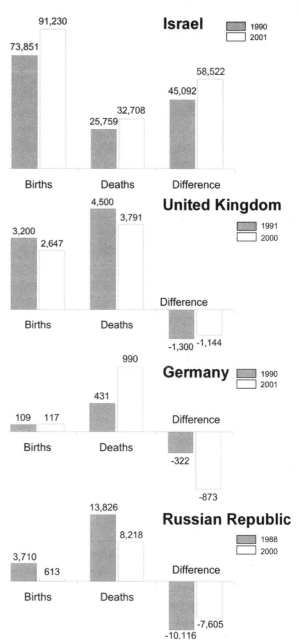

Vital statistics of the Jews in selected countries, 1990s.

from the FSU. In the United Kingdom, each year the number of Jewish deaths surpassed by over 1,000 the number of Jewish births. The spiral of low fertility, aging, and partial erosion of the younger generation through the non-affiliation with Judaism of a large portion of the children of out-marriage foreshadowed significant further changes in the demographic profile of world Jewry.

MAJOR BRANDS OF JEWISH IDENTIFICATION

PARTLY as the consequence, partly as the cause of the mobility and family trends described above—including the modes of socialization of the children of out-marriage—the spectrum of existing patterns of Jewish identification in Israel and in the Diaspora tended to widen. Viewed with extreme simplification, and ignoring for a moment the existence of specific cultural traits in each local community, contemporary Jewish identification coalesced into four major types. These four types can be determined by observing a combination of the Jewishness of individual beliefs and behaviors, and personal community connections. An attempt is presented here to associate some very rough quantitative estimates with the respective definitions.

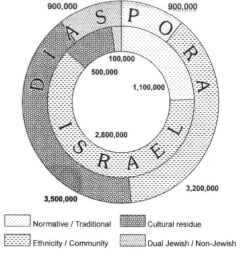

Main modes of Jewish identification, Israel and Diaspora Jewry, early 1990s.

(a) A *normative/traditional* type refers to people nearly exclusively adhering to a self-contained complex of Jewish beliefs, norms and values, and consistently performing Jewish traditional ritual practices. These mostly *religious* people were cohesively integrated in an exclusive Jewish community of reference and social network emphasizing religious leadership and enforcing negative sanction in case of deviance from the norm. This normative/traditional type, while characterized by deep internal political rivalries and even disagreements on fundamental issues of a religious nature, was sufficiently different from the others to retain meaning as an overall category. Their total number was estimated in the 1990s at two million worldwide, the majority living in Israel.

(b) An *ethnic-communal* type included people maintaining a cohesive community of reference through strictly or predominantly Jewish association networks, though in-group communication included large amounts of non-specifically Jewish cultural contents—for example, members in recreational organizations whose participants tended to be exclusively or mostly Jewish. Especially in the United States, many Jews whose main attachment to Judaism is through membership in a religious congregation actually sought for a sense of ethnic community—not necessarily religious exclusiveness. The total Jewish population thus defined approached six million, including about half in the Diaspora—mainly in Latin America, in the UK and other countries of the former Commonwealth, and among large sections of American Jewry. The other half lived in Israel, where indeed a blend of national Jewish identity with some traditionalism represents the predominant mode.

(c) A *cultural residue* type included

466

people for whom some attachment to Judaism could persist independently of any associative involvement in a Jewish community or a clearly recognizable personal Jewish behavior. Memory, curiosity, some notion of one's own Jewish historical past, tradition and culture, knowledge of a Jewish language, interest in Jewish scholarship, or even a sense of ancestral nostalgia, could be factors in such a form of sporadic, but nonetheless sincere belonging. Thus defined, culture provided a more ambiguous, less binding criterion for Jewish identification, as typical of the unaffiliated, and did not create an exclusively Jewish bond vis-à-vis general society. About four million Jews globally seemed to fit this definition, most of them in the Diaspora, typically in Eastern Europe, but also in large numbers in the United States, France and other West European countries.

(d) A *zero Jewish* or *dual Jewish/non-Jewish* type of identification could easily be documented in the Diaspora, having its counterpart among those non-Jews who for a variety of reasons kept some links with Jews and Judaism. These were people of Jewish origin whose cultural outlook and frame of reference are basically non-Jewish, but who nevertheless belonged within the definition of the core Jewish population. A declining intensity of Jewish identification tended to be substituted by increasing identification with other religious, ethnic, communal, or cultural contents—until the last remnants of Jewish identification became entirely marginal or faded away. Possibly one million Jews corresponded to such a definition, mostly outside Israel, typically including the most assimilated fringes of the Jewish population in Eastern Europe and in the Western countries.

Clearly, Jewish society cannot be divided into a few separate categories but rather consists of a highly dynamic and fluid continuum. Boundaries between the various identifications, and the degree of intensity within each were obviously very flexible and mutable. Historically, Jewish mobility across identificational sectors determined, on balance, a net flow from more religious to less religious. More recently, passages from one to any other type were easy and frequent, and did in fact occur all the time and often repeatedly among the same individuals' lifetime. Yet, a schematic representation of a cross-section of different modes of Jewish identification in the present generation could be useful when assessing the expected developments among a later generation. Different modes of family formation and Jewish family size, and different capacities to transmit Jewish identity to a younger generation evidently were associated with each major identificational type. Belonging to each type consequently implied different probabilities of remaining Jewish at a later time, both for the population directly involved (as an aggregate, not necessarily for each individual), and for their descendants in the next or subsequent generations.

JEWISH POPULATION PROJECTIONS

DEMOGRAPHIC projections have no claim to prophecy. Projected scenarios rather provide a better and more systematic understanding of the nature of current social forces, and of the possible implications of their future continuation. Following the overview of main recent and current trends shaping world Jewish population, the attempt to project current trends is based on an assumption of no major changes intervening at the global level. Such assumption does not in fact accurately reflect the main thrust of Jewish history during the twentieth century, but assuming major wars, revolutions, or catastrophes would extend the range of scenarios beyond control and would make the product even more easily equated to literary exercise than to social research. Stability or moderate change were posited in various alternative combinations of relevant variables, thus creating a range of more likely scenarios for the period between 2000 and the year 2050. High and low Jewish population scenarios were primarily obtained by assuming an increase or respectively a decrease by just 0.4 of a child in the currently recorded fertility rates. The lower range reflects a light increase in the current pace of emigration.

According to such conservative range of specifications, according to the medium scenario the Jewish population worldwide might slightly increase globally due to the natural increase in Israel surpassing the natural decrease in the Diaspora. From a baseline of about 13 million in 2000, world Jewry would be comprised in a range between 13 and 14.6 million by 2020. The total of Diaspora communities would be comprised between 7.2 and 8.1 million, and Jews in Israel would range between 5.6 and 6.6 million. Keeping in mind the high speculative character of the longer-run projections, the range in 2050 might be wider than 5 million, between a low of 12 million and a high of over 17 million.

In 2020, Israel would thus represent about 45 percent of the world's total Jewish population, against 37 percent in 2000. With little variation across the different assumptions, the two population curbs would cross after 2030. By then, and under the assumed circumstances, Israel would hold a majority of the total world's Jewish population. A shorter term, and quite realistic scenario would have Israel become the single largest Jewish community, getting ahead of the United States toward the end of the first or early during the second decade of the twenty-first century.

In spite of an expected moderate decline in numbers, North America with a medium projected population of about 6 million in 2020 would hold a larger share of the Diaspora than in 2000. Given its comparatively less aged composition and continuing positive international migration balance, it is only after the 2030s that more significant demographic erosion would possibly affect American Jewry. Moderate Jewish population declines can be expected in Canada and in the aggregate of the Australian and South African Jewish communities. On the other hand, continuing significant demographic decline is expected in Eastern Europe, while declining scenarios can also be

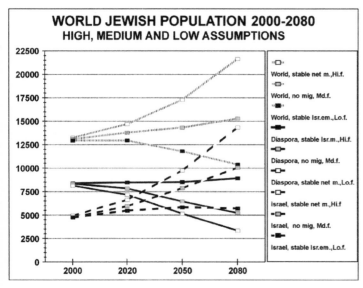

WORLD JEWISH POPULATION 2000-2080
HIGH, MEDIUM AND LOW ASSUMPTIONS

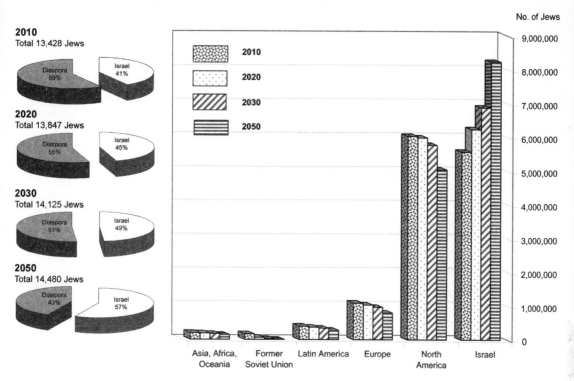

2010
Total 13,428 Jews

Diaspora 59%
Israel 41%

2020
Total 13,847 Jews

Diaspora 55%
Israel 45%

2030
Total 14,125 Jews

Diaspora 51%
Israel 49%

2050
Total 14,480 Jews

Diaspora 43%
Israel 57%

No. of Jews

9,000,000
8,000,000
7,000,000
6,000,000
5,000,000
4,000,000
3,000,000
2,000,000
1,000,000
0

2010
2020
2030
2050

Asia, Africa, Oceania | Former Soviet Union | Latin America | Europe | North America | Israel

THE JEWISH PEOPLE BY THE YEAR 2050: PROJECTIONS

expected for the aggregate of Western European communities and in Latin America. By 2050, there still would be 5 million Jews in North America, but barely 1 million in the rest of the world.

The leading demographic scenario for the future, therefore, points to a Jewish people increasingly concentrated in North America and in Israel, with Israel possibly becoming the largest Jewish community during the first decades of the twenty-first century. The sharp age-structural differences that developed between Israel and the Diaspora already made Israel the largest reservoir of Jewish youth and the principal target for Jewish education. On the other hand, in the course of the forthcoming decades the problem of ageing will become a crucial and problematic focus for Jewish community service in the Diaspora. Fewer economically productive individuals will be in charge to ensure satisfactory living conditions for a growing share of dependent elderly Jews.

These projections evinced the significant challenge to Jewish continuity that emerged during the last part of the twentieth century both from low levels of demographic reproduction and from the weak outcome of cultural reproduction among a large periphery of the Jewish population. An equally significant challenge of internal coherence and solidarity loomed large in the future of world Jewry in the guise of very different modes of Jewish identification, and of the tensions generated by those differences. These trends developed quite differently in Israel and in the majority of Jewish communities elsewhere, creating significant gaps in the prevailing paces of demographic growth and cultural attachment to Judaism into the twenty-first century.

INDEX

A

Aaron, Israel   317
Aaron ben Amram   158–159
Aaron ben Meir   159–160, 163, 165
Aaron ben Meshullam of Lunel   205
Aaron of Karlin   341
Abba (*amora*)   120
Abba Arikha, *see* Rav
Abba bar Abba (*amora*)   116
Abbahu (*amora*)   113
Abba Mari of Montpellier (ben Moses
    ben Joseph of Lunel)   206
Abbas I   395
Abbasids, Abbasid dynasty   137
— in Baghdad   167
— rule   156
Abbaye (*amora*)   119
'Abd al-Rahman II   168–169
'Abd al-Rahman III   172
Abdon son of Hillel   22
Abelard, Peter   198
Abenaes, Solomon (Ebn Yaish)   265
Abiathar ben Elijah   163, 165
Abijah (king of Judah)   30, 32
Abimelech (king of Gerar)   3–4
Aboab da Fonseca, Isaac   280
Abrabanel, Isaac   253, 256, 258, 276
Abrabanel, Samuel ben Isaac   273
Abraham (patriarch)   1–4, 108
Abraham ben Eliezer ha-Levi   269, 285
Abraham ben Samuel Zacuto, *see*
    Zacuto, Abraham ben Samuel
Abraham ben Solomon Treves ha-
    Zarfati   269
Abraham Joshua Heschel of Apta   341
Abraham of Saragossa   141
Abramowitsch, Shalom Jacob, *see*
    Mendele Mokher Sefarim
Abravalia family   196
Absalom   26–27
Abu Imran   153–154
Abu Isa, Isaac ben Jacob al-
    Isfahani   153–154
Abu Ishaq Jekuthiel ben Isaac ibn
    Hasan   170
Abu Jahl   135
Abulafia, Abraham   202
Abulafia, Meir ben Todros, of Toledo
    200
Academia de los Floridos   312
Academy of the Hebrew Language   362
Action Française   356
Adass Yeshurun   346
Adath Israel   345
Adath Yeshurun   346
Adiabenes   108
Adler, Marcus   346
Adolf (duke)   234
Adoni-bezek   11

Adoniram   28
Adret, Solomon ben Abraham
    (Rashba)   195, 205–206
Afonso III (of Portugal)   225
Afonso IV (of Portugal)   225
Afonso V (of Portugal)   241
Agobard (archbishop of Lyons)   143–
    144, 152
Agrarian League   356
Agrippa I   82–83
Agrippa II   83–85, 92
Agudat Israel   344, 347, 348, 395
Aguilar, Moses Raphael d'   280
Aha (*amora*)   114
Aha bar Jacob (*amora*)   117
Ahab (king of Israel)   32–33, 35, 44
Ahad Ha'am   365, 371
Ahavat Zion   336
Ahaz (king of Judah)   38–39
Ahdut Haavodah   376
Ahimaaz   153
Ahmad ibn Tulun   159
AJA, *see* Anglo-Jewish Association
Akiva, Rabbi   90, 96, 99–100, 109
Alantansi, Eliezer   270
Alashkar, Joseph ben Moses   269
Al-Bazak, Mazli'ah ben Elijah ibn   151
Albert III (elector of Brandenburg)   235
Albert V (duke of Austria)   235
Albotini, Judah ben Moses   269
Albinus (procurator)   83
Alconstantini, Bahya   195
Alconstantini, Moses   196
Alconstantini, Solomon   195
Alebrand (bishop)   176
Alexander I   322
Alexander II   322–323, 337, 358
Alexander III   323
Alexander III (pope)   193
Alexander VI (pope)   246–247, 273
Alexander Balas   62
Alexander Janneus   64–66, 76
Alexander Severus, *see* Severus
Alexander the Great   56–57
Alexandra (wife of Alexander
    Janneus)   66
Alexius I (emperor)   177
Alfasi, Isaac ben Jacob   166–167
Alfei Menashe   336
Alfonso (crown prince)   217
Alfonso III (of Aragón)   196
Alfonso III (of Asturias)   171
Alfonso V (of Aragón)   240
Alfonso VI (of Spain)   172–173
Alfonso X "the Wise"   196
Alfonso de Espina   240, 243
Alfonso de la Caballería   256
Al-Harizi, Judah   185, 189, 191
Alkabez, Solomon ben Moses ha-
    Levi   268, 270

Alkalai, David   367
Alkalai, Judah   366
*Allgemeine Zeitung des
    Judenthums*   346
Alliance Israélite Universelle   336, 382,
    384, 390, 392, 393, 394, 402–403,
    432–433
Almohads (Muwahhidun)   166, 168,
    171
Almoravids (al-Murabitun)   166, 168,
    171
Alroy, David (Menahem)   154
Ameimar (*amora*)   120
American Academy for Jewish
    Research   363
American Hebrew   445
American Israelite, The   352
American Jewish Archives   363
American Jewish Committee 403, 445
American Jewish Congress   402
American Jewish Historical
    Society   363
American Jewish History 0363
American Jewish Periodical Center   363
American Smelting and Refining
    Company   330
American Students for Israel   379
AMIA, *see* Asociación Mutual Israelita
    Argentina
Amittai family   152–153
Ammi (*amora*)   112–113
Ammonites   7
Amon (king of Judah)   46
Amorites   2, 6–8, 16, 18
Amos (prophet)   35–37
Amsterdam (partisan unit)   424
Amulo (archbishop of Lyons)   143–144
Anav, Jehiel   193
Anan ben David   153–155
Ananites   154–155
Andrade, Benjamin da Costa d'   280
Andreas (pupil of Abelard)   198
Andrew (apostle)   79
Andromachus   57
Andrusovo, Truce of   296
Angevin invasion of Italy   193
Anglo-American Committee of
    Enquiry   437
Anglo-American Corporation [of South
    Africa]   330
Anglo-Palestine Bank 374, 432
Anielewicz (partisan unit) 424
Anielewicz, Mordechai 425–426
Annenberg Research Institute 363
Anno (archibishop)   174
Anti-Defamation League   355
Antigonus II (Mattathias)   67, 69–70
Antiochus III   64
Antiochus IV   60, 62
Antiochus VI   63

Antiochus XII 65
Antipater (the Idumean) 66, 68–69
Antisemitic League 356
Antisemitic People's Party 356
Antoninus Pius 102–104
Aphes ha-Dromi (*amora*) 110–111
Apollonius 60–61
Arabians 44, 46, 50, 53
Arameans 32–33
Arba'a Turim 246, 270
Arcadeus 122
Archelaus (son of Herod) 73, 74, 82
Ardashir (Persian king) 115
Aretas (Nabatean king) 66
Aristobulus (son of Herod) 82
Aristobulus I 64
Aristobulus II 66–69
Armleder massacres 214–215
Arnstein (family) 330
Artaxerxes I 53–54
Artaxerxes II 55
Aruchas Bas Ami 366
Aryeh Leib of Polonnoye 341
Aryeh Leib of Shpola 341
Asa (king of Judah) 30–32
Asher, Asherites (tribe) 13, 15–20, 22
Asher ben Jehiel (Rosh) 199, 201, 205
Asher of Stolin 341
Ashi (*amora*) 120
Ashkenazi, Abraham Nathan ben
    Elisha Hayyim, *see* Nathan of Gaza
Asociación Mutual Israelita
    Argentina 447–448
Assembly of Jewish Notables 328–329
Asshurbanipal 44, 46, 48
Asshurnasirpal II 33
Assi (*amora*) 113, 116
Association for Jewish Studies 363
Association for the Culture and Science
    of Judaism, *see* Kulturverein
Assyrians 44–46
Astruc, *see* Abba Mari of Montpellier
Atatürk, *see* Kemal, Mustafa
Athias, Joseph 315
Atid 379
Atlas (partisan unit) 424
Aubriot, Hugues 219
Auerbach, Abraham Isaac 317
Augustine 124
Augustus (emperor) 70, 72
Aurangzeb (Moghul emperor) 281
Aurelian (emperor) 112
Austrian Reform Association 356
Autoemancipation 366, 371
Avelei Zion (Mourners of Zion) 154–
    155, 162
Avenger, The (partisan unit) 424
Avigur, Shaul 427
Avukah 379
Azariah (king of Judah) 37
Azikri, Eleazar ben Moses 268
Aziz, al- (caliph) 162
Aziz Mehmed Effendi, *see* Shabbetai
    Zevi
Azriel of Gerona 202
Azuri (king of Ashdod) 41

B

Baal (king of Tyre) 44–45
Baalis (Ammonite king) 51
Baasha (king of Israel) 30–32
Bacharach, Naphtali 269
Badis (king of Spain) 170
Baeck, Leo 420
Bahram V 119
Bakunin, Mikhail Aleksandrovich 354
Baldwin 177
Balfour, Arthur James; Balfour
    Declaration 373
Bamberger, Seligmann Baer 346
Bambus, Willy 366
Banet, Mordechai 349
Banu Hud dynasty 170
Banu Nadir (tribe) 133
Banu Tujib dynasty 170
Barak (son of Abinoam) 14, 22
Barasch, Julius 336
Barby, Meir 349
Bar Giora, Simeon, *see* Simon (son of
    Gioras)
Bar-Ilan University 362
Bar Kochba
    — (in Cologne) 378
    — (in Prague) 372
Bar Kokhba, Simeon 94, 96–99, 103–
    104
Baron, S. W. 250–251
Baron de Hirsch Trade School 445
Barrios, Daniel Levi De 279
Baruch of Tulchin 341
Barzapharnes (satrap) 69
Basel Program, *see* Zionist Program
Bashyazi, Elijah ben Moses 231
Basil I (the Macedonian) 145, 150
Basola, Moses ben Mordecai 266
Bathory, Stephen 292
Batis (eunuch) 57
Bauer, Bruno 354
Baybars 226
Bechar, Nissim 336
Begin, Menachem 436
Behrends, Leffmann 317
Beilis, Menahem Mendel 360
Bela IV (of Hungary) 289
Belisarius (Roman general) 126, 128
Belmont, August 331
Benderly, Samson 365
Benedict VIII (pope) 174
Benedict XIII (antipope) 238–239, 246
Bene Israel 398–400
Ben-Gurion, David 371, 436
Ben-Gurion University of the
    Negev 362
Ben-hadad I (king of Aram) 31
Ben Hananiah 336
Benjamin (tribe) 17, 18–20, 22, 28
Benjamin of Tudela 185–190, 250–251
Ben Meir family 165
Benveniste, Abraham 239–240
Benveniste, Emanuel 315
Ben-Yehuda, Eliezer 336, 365–367
Ben Ze'ev, Judah Leib 336

Beobachter 336
Berav, Jacob 265
Berber tribes 128, 165–166
Berdyczewski, Micha Josef 365
Berechiah (*amora*) 114
Beriah (clan) 10
Berlin, Naphtali Zvi Yehudah (the
    "Netziv") 349
Bernáldez, Andrés 253
Bernard of Clairvaux 180–181
Bernays, Isaac 346
Bertinoro, *see* Obadiah of Bertinoro
Besht, *see* Israel ben Eliezer Baal Shem
    Tov
Beta Esrael 391–392
    See also Falashas
Betar 377
Beth Elohim 313
Beth Hamidrash Hagadol 445
Beth Israel
    — (in Amsterdam) 312
    See also Talmud Torah
    — (in Hamburg) 312
Beth Israel Hospital 445
Beth Shalom 313
Beth Yaakov 312
    See also Talmud Torah
Beth Yaakov Hakatan 312
Bevis Marks 312
Bialik, Hayyim Nahman 359, 365
Bick, Jacob Samuel 336
Bikkurei ha-Ittim 336
Biltmore Conference 437
Bilu 372
Black Bureau 348
Black Death 215, 217–219, 222, 234–
    235, 238, 244, 251, 289
Black Hundred 356
Blau-Weiss 377–378
Bleichroeder, Gerson von 330
Bloch, Mattathias 299
Bloch, Samson (Simson) Halevi 336
Blood libels 180, 184, 193, 195, 210,
    212, 214–215, 219–220, 235, 237–238,
    263, 286, 289, 291, 297, 360–361
Bloomingdale's 331
B'nai B'rith 445
B'nai B'rith Hillel Foundation 379
B'nai Jeshurun Congregation 445
B'nei Akiva 376
B'nei Moshe 372
Boas, Tobias 317
Bodleian Library 362
Boeckel, Otto 356
Bohemond 177
Boleslav V (the Pious; of Kalisz) 220–
    221
Bonaparte, Napoleon, *see* Napoleon
    Bonaparte
Boniface VIII (pope) 193
Boniface IX (pope) 246
Borgia, Alfonso, *see* Calixtus III
Borgia, Rodrigo, *see* Alexander VI
Borochov, Ber 371
Boskowitz, Wolf 349
Brandeis University 363

Brenner, Joseph Hayyim 365
Briha movement, *see* Escape movement
B'rith Abraham 445
B'rith Shalom 445
British Museum 362
Brown University 363
Bucer, Martin 286
Buchner, Abraham 336
Bund 368–370, 379, 444
Bund juedischer Korporationen 378
Bund zionistischer Korporationen 378
Bureau of Jewish Education [of the *Kehillah*] 365
Busal, Hayyim ben Jacob Obadiah de 269

C

Cabron, Pedro 257
Cafman, Berakhiel ben Meshullam 269
Caleb, Calebites 10–11, 17, 21, 48
Caligula (emperor) 82, 84
Calixtus III (pope) 246
Canaan, Canaanites 2, 4, 10–19, 21, 23
Cansino, Jacob 279
Caracalla (emperor) 111
Cardozo, Abraham Michael 300
Caro, Joseph ben Ephraim 265, 268, 276
Carol, Georg 250
Cartel of Jewish Associations, *see* Kartell juedischer Verbindungen
Cartel of Zionist Associations, *see* Kartell zionistischer Verbindungen
Casimir III (the Great) 220–221
Casimir IV (Jagiellon) 221
Cassel, Ernest Joseph 330
Cassius (proconsul of Syria) 69
Castro, Abraham 275
Catherine II 319–320
Catholic Monarchs, *see* Ferdinand and Isabella
Cavalleria, Judah (ibn Lavi) de la 195
Central Archives for the History of the Jewish People 362
Central Bureau for Jewish Emigration 420
Central Conference of American Rabbis 352
Central Synagogue 445
Centralverein deutscher Staatsbuerger juedischen Glaubens (C.V.) 355
Central Zionist Archives 362
Central Zionist Office 373–374
Cestius Gallus (governor of Syria) 84–85
Chamberlain, Houston Stewart 353–354
Charlemagne 123, 141–144, 152, 170–171
Charles I (of England) 278
Charles I (of Spain), *see* Charles V (emperor)
Charles II (of England) 278
Charles IV (Holy Roman emperor) 217–218

Charles IV (of France) 248
Charles V (of France) 219–220
Charles V (Charles I of Spain; Holy Roman emperor) 237, 273–276, 286
Charles VI (of France) 219, 248
Charles VIII (of France) 219–220
Chatham Square cemetery 445
Chmielnicki, Bogdan 295–296, 298
— massacres 295, 298
Chorin, Aaron 347
Christian-Social Association 356
Christian-Social Workers Party 356
Church councils 210
— of 633 139
— of Buda 289
— of Constance 235
— of Elvira 126
— of Gerona 171
— of Szabolcs 288
— of Ticino 152
Cidellus, *see* Ferrizuel, Joseph ha-Nasi
Citizen's Club 356
City Library of New York 363
City University of New York 363
Class, H. [D. Frymann] 354–355
Claudius (emperor) 82–83, 92
Clement III (pope) 181
Clement VI (pope) 217
Clement VII (pope) 274–276
Clement VIII (pope) 273
Cleopatra (queen of Egypt) 70
Clermont-Tonnerre, Count Stanislas de 332
Clinton Hall 445
Clovis (king of Franks) 125
Cochin Jews 398–400
Cohen, E. 336
Collegiate Zionist League 379
Columbia Pictures 331
Columbia University 363
Comes Joseph 113
Committee of Jewish Delegations 402–403
Congregation Sinai 352
Conrad III (of Germany) 180–181
Consistory 328–329, 346, 383
Constantine the Great 113, 115, 124
Constantius II 115
Convention of German Jewish Student Fraternities, *see* Kartell-Convent der Verbindungen deutscher Studenten juedischen Glaubens
Conversos 224, 228–231, 239–241, 247, 253, 256, 259, 271– 283, 285–286, 299
Cooper Union 445
Cordovero, Moses ben Jacob 268
Coponius (prefect) 74–75
Cosmas (bishop) 176
Costa, Uriel da 279
Costa, da (family) 315, 317
Council of Ten 403
Council of the Lands (Council of Four Lands) 288, 292–295, 318
Crémieux, Adolphe; Crémieux Decree 334, 360, 383–384

Crescas, Hasdai 224
Cromwell, Oliver 278
Crypto-Jews 139, 282
Cum nimis absurdum (papal bull) 272
Cyrus the Great 53
Czerniakow, Adam 426

D

DAIA, *see* Delegación de Asociaciones Israelitas Argentinas
Damascus Affair 360, 387
Dan, Danites (tribe) 17–19, 22
Daniel ben Azariah (gaon) 165
Daniel ben Moses al-Qumisi 154–155
Daoud Pasha 393
Dari, Moses 154
Darius I (king of Persia) 53
Darwin, Charles; Darwinism 353–354
Dato, Mordecai 269
David (king of Israel) 11, 20–21, 23, 25–28, 122
David ben Abraham 206
David ben Daniel 163, 166
David ben Saul 206
David ben Solomon ibn Zimra (RaDBaZ) 266
David ben Zakkai 159–160, 165
David ben Zakkai II (exilarch) 190, 205
David of Lyons 141
David, Abraham 317
David, Alexander 317
Death to Fascism 424
De Beers (diamond firm) 330
Deborah (prophetess) 12–14, 21
Declaration of the Rights of Man and of the Citizen 328
Dekel, Ephraim 427
Delegación de Asociaciones Israelitas Argentinas 447
Delmedigo, Joseph Solomon 269
Dembo brothers 330
Demetrius I 62
Demetrius II 62–63
Demetrius III 65
Denikin, Anton Ivanovich 403
Derishat Zion 366
Der Israelit 346
Der Morgen Journal 445
Der Tegliche Herold 445
Der Zionswaechter 346
Deutschmann, Hayyim 349
De Vesoul, Manessier 219
Dhimmis 334, 380, 388
Dick, Isaac Meir 336
Dien 336, 338
Die Welt 374
Die Yiddishe Welt 445
Dimi (*amora*) 120
Dio Cassius 98
Diocletian 107, 113, 120–121
Disputations 124, 141, 198
— in Barcelona 190, 195
— in Paris 190, 201
— in Tortosa 238, 246

472

Divrei Shalom ve-Emet 336
Doenmeh (sect) 300, 389–390
Domatus of Lyons 141
Dominicans 195, 241
Donnolo, Shabbetai 150, 152–153
Dorshei Leshon Ever 336
Dostoyevsky, Feodor M. 353–354
Dov Baer of Mezhirech (the "Great Maggid") 340–341
Drach, Abraham 317
Dreyfus, Alfred; Dreyfus Affair 356
Dropsie College 363
Dror 376
Drumont, Edouard-Adolphe 353–354
Du'an Agreement 335
Dubno, Solomon 336
Dubnow, Simon 362, 366
Duehring, Karl Eugen 354–355
Duenner, Joseph Zvi 366
Dunash ben Labrat 169
Du Nuas (king of Himyar) 130–131, 134
Dvoretzky 424

E

East India Company 315
Edicts of expulsion 220, 235, 243, 254–255, 259
Edomites 38, 53
Educational Alliance 445
Edward I (of England) 209–210, 248
Eger, Akiva 347, 349
Eger, Meshullam 349
Egidio da Viterbo (cardinal) 275
Ehud (judge; son of Gera) 22
Eichel, Isaac 336
Eichenbaum, Jacob 336
Einsatzgruppen 410, 422–425
Eisenbaum, Anton 336
Eisenstadt, Meir 349
Eldad ha-Dani 154
Eleanor (queen mother of England) 209–210
Eleazar (son of Ananias) 84
Eleazar ben Arakh 90
Eleazar ben Hyrcanus 90
Eleazar ben Jacob (*tanna*) 109
Eleazar ben Pedat (*amora*) 112
Eleazar ben Simeon bar Yohai 109–110
Eleazar ben Yose (*tanna*) 109
Eleh Divrei Habrit 346
Eleventh Street cemetery 445
Eliezer ben Isaac 199–200
Eliezer ben Joel ha-Levi (Ravyah) 199–200
Eliezer ben Nathan of Mainz 199
Eliezer ben Solomon 199
Elijah (prophet) 278
Elijah ben Moses de Vidas 268
Elijah ben Solomon 163, 165
Elijah ben Solomon Zalman ("Gaon of Vilna") 340–341
Elijah of Ferrara 229
Elijah of Pesaro 266
Elijah the Tishbite 35

Elimelech of Lyzhansk 341
Elisha (prophet) 35
Ellissen (family) 330
Elon (judge) 22
El Tiempo 336
Emanuel (of Portugal), *see* Manuel I
Emden, Jacob 339
Emich (Emicho) of Leiningen 177
Ephraim, Ephraimites (tribe) 17–20, 22
Ephraim of Sudylkow 341
Eretz Hatsevi Academy, *see* Hatsevi Academy
Esarhaddon 44–45
Esau 4
Escapa, Joseph 297
Escape (*Briha*) movement 427, 436
Eshbaal (Ishbosheth) 21, 23
Eshmunazer (king of Sidon) 55
Eskeles, Berend 317
Esra (society) 366
Essenes 76
Estéban, Ines 278
Estéban, Juan 278
Estori ha-Parhi 190–191
Ethobaal (king of Sidon) 42
Ettinger, Solomon 336
Ettlinger, Jacob 346
Etz Haim Yeshiva (Amsterdam) 312–313
Etz Hayyim 397
Etz Hayyim (yeshiva, Volozhin) 349
Eugenius III (pope) 179–180
Eugenius IV (pope) 245
Eusebius Sophronius Hieronymus, *see* Jerome
Even Sappir 397
Eyebeschuetz, Jonathan 349
Ezekiel (prophet) 35, 393
Ezekiel, Solomon 393
Ezra 53–54
Ezra (youth movement) 376
Ezra of Gerona 202

F

Faisal, Emir 435
Falashas 391–392
See also Beta Esrael
Fano, Menahem Azariah da 269
Fatimids, Fatimid dynasty 151, 162, 165–167, 178
Federation of American Zionists 445
Federation of Jewish Philanthropies 445
Felix (procurator) 83
Ferdinand (of Portugal) 225
Ferdinand I (Holy Roman emperor) 287
Ferdinand I (of Castile and León) 171–172
Ferdinand II (Holy Roman emperor) 288
Ferdinand III "the Saint" 196
Ferdinand (V of Castile or II of Aragón) and Isabella 196, 237, 239, 241–243, 245, 247, 254, 259, 285

Ferorelli, Nicolo 251
Ferrer, Vincent, *see* Vincent Ferrer
Ferrizuel, Joseph ha-Nasi 172
Fettmilch, Vincent 286
Fichte, Johann Gottlieb 354
Filene's 331
Filosof, Joseph 300
Finkel, Nathan Zevi ben Moses 349
Finzi, Jacob Israel 269
First Amendment (American Constitution) 333
Firuz II (Sassanian king) 119
Flavius Silva 88
Florentin, Solomon 300
Foerster, Bernard 356
Folkspartei 368
Forverts 445
Forward (partisan unit) 424
Foscari, Marco 275
Four Lands (see Council of the Lands)
Fraenkel, David 346
Fraenkel-Teomim, Baruch 349
Fragosso (Genoese pirate) 257
Francis I (of France) 274
Francisco d'Aranda 224
Francos 390
Frank, Jacob 338–339
Frank, Leo 360
Frankel, Zacharias 344, 347, 361–362
Frederick (duke of Swabia) 183
Frederick I Barbarossa 181, 183
Frederick II 183–184, 191
Free Association for the Interests of Orthodox Judaism 346
Freigedank, K. [R. Wagner] 354
Freiheit, *see* Dror
French National Antisemitic League 356
French National Assembly 332
Friedlaender (family) 336
Friedlaender, David 336
Friedlaender, Israel 371
Friedrichsfeld, David 336
Fries, Jakob Friedrich 354
Frischmann, David 365
Frumkin, Israel Dov 336
Fuenn, Samuel Joseph 336

G

Gabai (family) 399
Gabbai, Meir ben Ezekiel ibn 269
Gabinius (proconsul of Syria) 67–68
Gabirol, Solomon ben Judah, Ibn 170
Gad (tribe) 17, 19, 22
Gallus (brother of Julian) 115
Gallus, Cestius, *see* Cestius Gallus
Gamaliel II, Rabban (of Jabneh; son of Simeon) 78, 89–90
Gamaliel III, Rabban (Gamaliel be-Rabbi, son of Judah ha-Nasi) 110–111
Gamaliel VI, Rabban 114, 128
Gaon of Vilna, *see* Elijah ben Solomon Zalman
Gautier de Brienne 179
Gedaliah (son of Ahikam) 51

Gegenwartsarbeit 371–372
Geiger, Abraham 343, 346–347, 361–362
General Federation of Jewish Workers, *see* Histadrut
General Jewish Congress 346
General Zionists 375
General Zionists (A), Union of 375–376
General Zionists (B), Federation of 375–376
Genghis Khan 226
German Antisemitic Alliance 356
German Antisemitic Congress 356
German Conservative Party 355–356
German-National Association 356
German National Commerce Clerks Association 356
German National Union 356
German People's Association 356
German-Populist Party 356
German Rural Party 356
German-Social Party 356
German-Social Reform Party 356
German Workers Party 356
Gershom, Rabbenu 173
Gesellschaft zur Foerderung der Wissenschaft des Judentums 357
Gessius Florus (procurator) 83–84
Gibeonites 10–11, 17, 28
Gideon (son of Joash) 21–22
Gimbel's 331
Gindelman 424
Ginsberg, Asher Hirsch, *see* Ahad Ha'am
Gobineau, Joseph Arthur, Count de 354
Godfrey of Bouillon 175, 177
Goldschmidt, Meyer (court jeweler) 184
Gómez, Maria (of Chillón) 278
Gompertz (family) 317
Gomperz (family) 317
González, Fernan (count of Castile) 172
Gordon, David 336, 366-367, 371
Gordon, Eliezer 349
Gordon, Judah Leib 336, 366
Gordonia 376
Gottlober, Abraham 336
Graetz, Heinrich 250, 362, 366-367
Grana 384
Grand Theater 445
Greater Actions Committee 373–374
"Great Maggid", *see* Dov Baer of Mezhirech
Great Synagogue
— (in Amsterdam) 312
— (in Warsaw) 425–426
Gregory I (pope) 139–141
Gregory VIII (pope) 181
Gregory IX (pope) 195, 211
Gregory X (pope) 184
Gregory XIII (pope) 272
Gregos, *see* Romaniots
Grodzinski, Hayyim Ozer 348
Gruber 424

Grynszpan 424
Guedemann, Moritz 336
Guenzburg (family) 330
Guenzburg, Horace 330
Guerin, Jules 356
Guggenheim (family) 331
Guide of the Perplexed 204–205
Gumpert (family) 317
Gumperts, Benedikt 317
Gutenberg, Johann 270

H

Ha-Ari (see Luria, Isaac ben Solomon)
Haavodah 378
Habbus (king) 169
Ha-Boker 336
Haboneh 378
Habonim 376
Habonim–Noar Halutzi 377
Hacarmel 336
Hacohen, A. 336
Hadad-ezer (of Damascus) 33
Hadassah 374
Hadrian (emperor) 94, 98–100, 102–103, 106–107
"Hafetz Hayyim", *see* Israel Meir Hacohen
Haganah 436–437
Haggai (*amora*) 114
Haidamacks 296
Haifa University 362
Hai Gaon (ben Sherira) 155, 158–160, 167, 170
Haim of Amdur 341
Haim, Joseph 393
Hakibbutz Haartzi 376–377
Hakibbutz Hadati 376
Hakibbutz Hameuhad 376
Hakim, al- (caliph) 162–163, 169, 174
Halevi, Abraham 387
Halevy, Joseph 392
Halfan, Elijah Menahem 269
Hama (*amora*) 120
Ha-Maggid 336, 338, 366
Ha-Meassef 335–336
Ha-Melitz 336, 338
Hameln, Haim 317
Ha-Mevasser 336
Hamnuna (*amora*) 117
Ha-Modia 348
Hamutal 46
Hananiah ben Teradyon 99
Hanina (*amora*) 114
Hanina bar Hama (*amora*) 110–111
Hanoar Haoved Hadati 376
Hanoar Haoved Haleumi 377
Hanoar Haoved Vehalomed 376
Hanoar Hatziyoni 377
Hanokem, *see* Avenger
Hanun (king of Gaza) 39
Ha-Olam 374
Haoved Hatziyoni 377
Ha-Peles 348
Hapoel Hamizrachi 344, 376
Hapoel Hatzair 432
Harkavy, Albert (Abraham Elijah) 336

Harmonie Club 445
Har Sinai Congregation 352
Harun al-Rashid (caliph) 141–142, 144
Harvard University 363
Hasdai Crescas, *see* Crescas, Hasdai
Ha-Shahar 336, 338, 365–366
Hashahar 377
Ha-Shelah ha-Kadosh, *see* Horowitz, Isaiah ben Abraham ha-Levi
Ha-Shiloah 365
Hashomer 432
Hashomer Hatzair 376–377
Hasmonaea 378
Hasmoneans, *see* Maccabees, Maccabeans
"Hatam Sofer", *see* Sofer, Moses
Hatikvah 378
Hatsevi Academy 165
Havatzelet 336
Hayom 365
Hayut, Zevi Hirsch 336
Hayyat, Judah ben Jacob 259–260
Hayyim and son Nissim (Spanish Jews) 151
Hayyim ben Isaac (Volozhiner) 349
Ha-Zefirah 336, 338
Ha-Zevi 336
Heber the Kenite 14, 16
Hebrew Benevolent and Orphan Asylum 445
Hebrew Charities Building 445
Hebrew Immigrant Aid Society 445
Hebrew Language Committee 362, 365
Hebrew Resistance Movement 436
Hebrew Sheltering House 445
Hebrew Standard 445
Hebrew Technical Institute for Boys 445
Hebrew Technical School for Girls 445
Hebrew Union College–Jewish Institute of Religion
— (in Cincinnati) 352, 363
— (in Jerusalem) 362
— (in Los Angeles) 363
— (in New York) 363
Hebrew University 362
Hechawer 378
He-Halutz 336
Hehalutz 374, 378
Heinrich (duke of Bavaria) 214
Heliogabalus 107, 111
Heller, Yom Tov Lipman 288
Heller, Zvi Hirsch 349
Helsingfors Conference 371–373
Henrici, Ernst 356
Henry I (of England) 180
Henry II (of England) 180
Henry II (of France) 328
Henry II (of Germany) 173
Henry III (of France) 291
Henry IV (of Germany) 173–174, 176
Henry IV (of Castile) 241
Henry of Albano (monk) 181
Henry of Trastámara 222–223
Henry Street Settlement 445
"Hep-Hep" disturbances 356–357

Heraclius (emperor) 132
Herman III (bishop) 175
Hermonia 378
Herod (the Great) 68–73, 77, 82, 84, 92, 100, 106–107
Herod Antipas 73–75, 79, 82
Herod of Chalcis 82
Herod Philip 73–75, 82–83
Herut 377
Herzl, Theodor 371–372
Herzliya Gymnasium 365, 432
Hess, Moses 366
Hezekiah 42–44, 48
HIAS, *see* Hebrew Immigrant Aid Society
Hibbat Zion 367, 372
Hildesheimer, Azriel 345–347, 349, 366, 392
"Hildesheimer's Seminary" 362
Hilfsverein 433
Hillel ben Samuel (of Verona) 206
Himyars 130–131
Hiram (king of Tyre) 27
Hirsch, Maurice de, Baron 330
Hirsch, Samson Raphael 345–346
Hirschel, Zacharias 317
Hisda (*amora*) 117
Hisdai ibn Shaprut 145, 147, 149, 168–169, 172
Histadrut 376, 436
Histadrut Haovdim Haleumit 377
Historical Society of Israel 362
Hitahdut 374, 376
Hitler, Adolf 354–355, 420–421, 429
Hiwi al-Balkhi 154–155
Hiyya bar Abba (*amora*) 113
Hiyya bar Joseph (*amora*) 117
Hobab (father-in-law of Moses) 16
Hochschule 346, 362
Hochschule für jüdische Studien 362
Holdheim, Samuel 343, 346–347
Holubek, Franz 356
Homberg, Naphtali Herz 336
Home for the Aged 445
Honorius (emperor) 122
Honorius IV (pope) 205
Horowitz, Isaiah ben Abraham ha-Levi 265
Horowitz, Joseph 349
Horowitz, S. 336
Horowitz, Shabbetai Sheftel 269
Hourwitz, Zalkind 336
Hosea (prophet) 35, 37
Hoshaya (*amora*) 110–112
Hoshaya bar Shammai (*amora*) 114
Hoshea (king of Israel) 39, 41–42
Hovevei Zion 432
Huna (*amora*) 117
Huna bar Hiyya (*amora*) 118
Huna bar Nathan (*amora*) 119
Huna Bereiah de-Rav Joshua (*amora*) 120
Hungarian Jewish Congress 347
Huss, Jan 235
Huzpit ha-Meturgeman 99
Hyrcanus I (Hasmonean king) 65

Hyrcanus II (Hasmonean king) 66–69

I

Iamani (king of Ashdod) 41
Ibn Aryeh 154
Ibn Gabirol (see Gabirol, Solomon ben Judah, Ibn)
Ibn Jau, Jacob 168
Ibn Jau Joseph 168
Ibn Khalfun, Isaac 170
Ibn Quraysh, Judah 165–166
Ibn Rustam 165
Ibn Shuaib, Samuel ben Joel 264
Ibn Verga, Solomon 256
Ibn Zur, Joseph 300
Ibzan (judge) 22
ICA, *see* Jewish Colonization Association
Iddi bar Avin (*amora*) 119
Idumeans 56, 61
Ihud Habonim 376
Ihud Hakevutzot veHakibbutzim 376
Il-Khan Ghazan 226
Il-Khan Hülegü 226
Independent Jewish Workers Party 369
Indiana University 363
Innocent III (pope) 183, 195
Innocent IV (pope) 184
Institute for Proletarian Jewish Culture 362
Intercollegiate Menorah Association 379, 445
Intercollegiate Zionist League 379
International Antisemitic Congress 356
International Territorial Organization 368
Irgun (Irgun Zva'i Leumi) 436–437
Irhuleni (of Hamath) 33
Isaac (patriarch) 3
Isaac (member of Charlemagne's delegation) 141–142
Isaac ben Abraham (Rizba) 199–200
Isaac ben Asher ha-Levi 199
Isaac ben Eleazar (*amora*) 114
Isaac ben Jacob, *see* Alfasi
Isaac ben Jacob ha-Lavan 199–200
Isaac ben Joseph 203
Isaac ben Meir 199–200
Isaac ben Moses of Vienna 199, 201
Isaac ben Samuel of Acre 192, 203
Isaac ben Samuel of Dampierre (Ha-Zaken) 200
Isaac Elchanan Yeshiva, *see* Rabbi Isaac Elchanan Yeshiva
Isaac ha-Levi Asir ha-Tikvah 229
Isaac Nappaha (*amora*) 113
Isaac the Blind 202
Isabella (daughter of Ferdinand and Isabella) 259
Isabella I (queen of Castile), *see* Ferdinand and Isabella
Isaiah (prophet) 35, 39, 43
Isanians (Jewish sect) 153
Isfahani, Isaac ben Jacob al-, *see* Abu Isa
Ishbosheth, *see* Eshbaal

Ishmael (son of Nethaniah) 51
Ishmael ben Elisha 90, 99
Ishmaelites 4, 175
    See also Midianites
Israel (family) 317
Israel (family) 387
Israel Academy of Sciences and Humanities 362
Israel ben Eliezer Baal Shem Tov (the "Besht") 339, 341
Israel Exploration Society 362
Israeli, Isaac ben Solomon 161
Israelites 8–19, 28, 30, 32
Israel Meir Hacohen ("Hafetz Hayyim") 349
Israel of Kozienice (the "Maggid") 341
Israel of Ruzhin 341
Israel State Archives 362
Issachar (tribe) 13–15, 17, 19, 22–23
ITO, *see* International Territorial Organization
Itureans 67
Ivan the Terrible 290–291
Ivri Anochi 336
Ivriyah 378
Izhak Ben-Zvi Institute 362
Izraelita 336

J

Jabin (king of Hazor) 12
Jacob (patriarch) 4–5
Jacob ben Asher 246, 270
Jacob ben Jekuthiel 174
Jacob ben Meir Tam, *see* Tam, Jacob ben Meir
Jacob ben Nissim ibn Shahin 160–161
Jacob Isaac of Lublin 341
Jacob Isaac of Przysucha 341
Jacob Joseph of Polonnoye 341
Jacobson, Israel 346
Jaddua (high priest) 57
Jael (wife of Heber the Kenite) 14, 16
Jagiellon, Alexander 290–291
Jair the Gileadite 22
James I (king of Aragón) 190, 193, 196
James II (king of Aragón) 217
Janneus, Alexander, *see* Alexander Janneus
Jastrow, Marcus (Mordecai) 336
Jawhar (Fatimid general) 162
Jehiel ben Isaac ha-Zarefati 191
Jehiel ben Solomon 336
Jehiel Michel of Zloczów 341, 351
Jehiel of Paris 190–191, 199, 201, 212, 249
Jehoahaz (king of Judah) 46
Jehoiachin (king of Judah) 50
Jehoiakim (king of Judah) 46, 50–51
Jehoram (king of Judah) 33
Jehoseph ha-Nagid 170
Jehoshaphat (king of Judah) 33, 48
Jeiteles (family) 336
Jellinek, Adolf 336
Jephtah the Gileadite 22
Jerachmeelites 21
Jeremiah (*amora*) 114

Jeremiah (prophet) ·35, 48
Jeremias, Bendix 317
Jeroboam (king of Israel) 28–30
Jeroboam II (king of Israel) 35–37
Jerome 126
Jerónimo de Santa Fé (Joshua ha-
Lorki) 238–239
Jerusalem 336, 345
Jeschurun 346
Jesus 75, 77–81, 124, 176
Jewish Agency 375, 392, 436
Jewish Brigade 436
Jewish Colonial Trust 374
Jewish Colonization Association
(ICA) 433, 447
Jewish Ethnographic and Historical
Society 362
Jewish Fighting Organization
(ZOB) 426
Jewish Historical Society of England
362
Jewish Humanitarian Society, *see*
Juedische Humanitaetsgesellschaft
Jewish Institute of Religion 363
See also Hebrew Union College
Jewish Maternity Hospital 445
Jewish National and University
Library 362
Jewish National Fund 374–375
Jewish People's Party, *see* Folkspartei
Jewish Publication Society of
America 363
Jewish Relief Act 333
Jewish State Party 375
Jewish Statute 322
Jewish Theological Seminary 347, 362
Jewish Theological Seminary of
America 352, 363, 445
Jews' College 362
Joachim of Fiore (monk) 181
Joana (daughter of Henry IV of
Castile) 241
Joel ben Isaac ha-Levi 199–200
Johanan (*amora*) 108, 111–113
Johanan ben Nuri (*tanna*) 109
Johanan ben Zakkai 89–90
Johanan ha-Sandlar 109–110
Johann (bishop) 174–176
John (king of England) 183
John I (of Aragón) 224
John II (of Castile) 240, 257
John II Casimir Vasa (of Poland) 295
John III (of Portugal) 274
John III Sobieski (of Poland) 297
John XXII (pope) 217
John Chrysostom 124
John Frederick 286
John of Austria 263
John of Brienne 191
John of Capistrano 234–235
John of Gischala 86–87
John the Baptist 77
Johnson Act 441–442
Joint Foreign Committee 402
Jonah (*amora*) 114
Jonah (prophet) 35, 393

Jonah ben Abraham Gerondi 206
Jonathan ben David ha-Kohen of
Lunel 190, 200
Jonathan the Hasmonean 62–64
Jordania 378
Joseph (brother of Herod) 70
Joseph (king of Khazars) 145, 147, 149
Joseph (son of Jacob) 4
—, House of 28
Joseph (son of Mattathias), *see*
Josephus Flavius
Joseph II 324–326, 336
Joseph bar Hiyya (*amora*) 118–119
Joseph ben Baruch of Clisson 190, 199
Joseph ben Gershon of Rosheim 237,
275, 286
Joseph ben Phineas 158–159
Joseph de Montagna 229
Joseph ibn Abitur 164, 169
Joseph of Arimathaea 78
Joseph of Lyons 141
Joseph of Nazareth 77
Josephus Flavius 5, 47, 51, 57, 76, 88,
96
Joshua ben Korha (*tanna*) 109
Joshua ben Levi (*amora*) 110–111
Joshua of Belz 348
Joshua son of Nun 8, 10–12, 16, 105
Josiah (king of Judah) 46–48, 50
Jost, Marcus 336
Jotham (king of Judah) 37-39
Jovian (emperor) 115
Juan de San Martín 241–242
Judah (*amora*) 118
Judah (*tanna*) 108–110
Judah (tribe) 4, 10–12, 17–22, 48
Judah bar Ezekiel (*amora*) 117
Judah bar Simon (*amora*) 113
Judah ben Bathyra (*amora*) 116
Judah ben Bava 99–100
Judah ben Isaac (Sir Leon of
Paris) 199–200
Judah ben Nathan (Rivan) 200
Judah ben Samuel he-Hasid of
Regensburg 201
Judah Halevi 164, 189
Judah ha-Nasi 101, 106, 110, 116
Judah Hehasid 433
Judah ibn Quraysh, *see* Ibn Quraysh,
Judah
Judah Nesiah (*amora*) 101, 112-113
Judas Maccabeus 61, 64
Juedische Humanitaetsgesellschaft 378
Juedisch-Theologisches Seminar 344
Julian (the Apostate) 114–115, 119,
122
Julius II (pope) 272–273
Julius III (pope) 272–273
Julius Caesar 68–69, 81
Julius Severus, *see* Severus
Jung Israel 378
Jung-juedischer Wanderbund 377
Junior Hadassah 377
Justinian I (emperor) 122, 127–129
Jutrzenka 336

K

Kadimah (movement)
— (in Germany) 378
— (in Vienna) 372, 378
Kadimah (partisan unit), *see* Forward
Kaf ha-Ketoret 268
Kahana (*amora*) 120
Kahinan (Jewish tribe) 134
Kalischer, Zvi Hirsch 366–367
Kálman (king of Hungary) 288
Kalonymus 151, 173–174, 176
Kameraden 377
Kann, Isaac (Baer Loew) 317
Kaplan, Mordecai Menahem 352, 371
Kaplinsky 424
Karaimskaya Zhizn 391
Karaimskoye Slovo 391
Karaites 154–155, 160, 162–164, 173,
187–188, 221, 230–231, 291, 385, 387,
390–391
Karna (*amora*) 116
Kartell-Convent der Verbindungen
deutscher Studenten juedischen
Glaubens (KC) 378
Kartell juedischer Verbindungen
(KJV) 378
Kartell zionistischer Verbindungen
(KZV) 378
Katzenellenbogen, Abraham 341
Katzenellenbogen, Zevi Hirsch 336
Kavadh (Sassanian king) 120
Kenaz, Kenazzites 10–11, 21
Kedoorie (family) 399–400
Kehillah of New York 365, 445
Kemal, Mustafa (Atatürk) 388
Keneseth Israel 352
Kenites 11, 16, 21
Kerem Hemed 336
Keren Hayesod, *see* Palestine
Foundation Fund
Keren Kayemet le-Israel, *see* Jewish
National Fund
Khaybar, Jews of 135–136
Khazars 144–147, 149
Khosrau II (king of Persia) 132–133
Khwarizmian Turks 191
Kilkis, Nathan ben Moses 203
Kimhi, David 206
King David Hotel 436
Kirkisani, Jacob al- 154–155
Klatzkin, Jacob 371
Kley, Eduard 346
Knesset Beit Yitzhak 349
Knesset Israel 349
Kol Mevasser 336
Korczak, Janusz 425
Koreish, *see* Ibn Quraysh, Judah
Kornfeld, Aaron 349
Kovner, Abba 427
Kozienice, Maggid of, *see* Israel of
Kozienice
Kristallnacht 420, 423
Krochmal, Nahman 336, 366
Kuh, Moses Daniel 317
Kuhn and Loeb 331

See also Schiff, Jacob H.
Kulturverein 337

L

Labor Movement Archives 362
Ladislaus II Jagiellon (king of
    Poland) 220
Laemel School 336
La Epoca 336
Lagarde, Paul Anton de 354
Landau, Ezekiel 349
Landau, Moses 336
Landsmannschaften 442
Lapouge, George Vacher de 354
Lateran Councils (III, IV) 193
Latif, Isaac ben Meir 229
Lavi, Simeon 269
Lazard Brothers 330
Lazarus 80
League of Antisemites 356
League of Nations 373
Leeser, Isaac 352
Leff, Leopold 336
Lefin, Mendel 336
Left Poalei Zion 375–376
Lehi, see Stern Group
Lehman Brothers 331
Lehmann, Behrend 317
Lehren, Zevi Hirsch 346
Lenin, Vladimir Ilyich 370
Lenin State Library 362
Leo III (emperor) 145
Leo X (Giovanni de' Medici; pope) 272
Leo Baeck Institute
    — (in Jerusalem) 362
    — (in London) 362
    — (in New York) 363
Leon of Paris, Sir, see Judah ben Isaac
Leopold I 316–317
Letteris, Meir 336
Levanda, Lev 366
Levi 4
Levi, Behrend 317
Levi, Gerd 317
Levinsohn, Isaac Baer 336
Levi Yitzhak of Berdichev 341
Levita, Elijah (Bahur) 272
Levy, Anschel 317
Lewis (department-store chain) 330
Library of Congress 363
Licet Judaeis (papal bull) 184
Liebmann (family) 317
Lilienblum, Moses Leib 336, 365–366,
    371
Lilienthal, Max (Menahem) 336
Lipkin (Salanter), Israel 349–350
Lipschitz, Jacob Halevi 348
Livia (wife of Augustus) 74–75
Loew, Leopold 347
López de Ayala, Pedro 222
Lorki, Joshua, see Jerónimo de Santa Fé
Louis I (the Pious; Holy Roman
    emperor) 141, 143
Louis II (of Germany) 150, 152
Louis II (of Hungary) 289–290
Louis VII (of France) 180–181

Louis IX (of France) 180, 183, 212
Louis X (of France) 219, 248
Louis XIV (of France) 280
Lucuas (Jewish rebel leader) 93
Ludwig IV (of Bavaria) 214
Lueger, Karl 356
Luli (Elulaios) of Sidon 42
Luncz, Abraham Moses 336
Luria, David 367
Luria, Isaac ben Solomon (Ha-
    Ari) 268–270
Luther, Martin 286
Luzzatto, Samuel David 336, 361–362,
    366-367
Lysias (governor under Antiochus
    IV) 61

M

Maccabees, Maccabeans 60, 63–64, 68
Maccabi 377–378
Maccabi Hatzair 377
MacDonald White Paper 436
Macedonians 56–57
McGill University 363
Machir 13–15
Machzike Talmud Torah 445
Macy's 331
Madison Square Garden 445
Magen Avraham 313
Magis 115, 117, 119
Magnus, Marcus 317
Mahalalel Halleluyah 299
Mahanot Haolim 376
Maharam, see Meir ben Baruch of
    Rothenburg
Mahzike Hadas 348
Mahzike Hadath 346
Maimon, Solomon 336
Maimonides (Rambam) 166, 190–191,
    195, 200, 204–206
Malchus II (Arabian king) 70
Malkah, Judah ben Nissim ibn 202
Mamluks 226, 228–229, 234, 265
Mana (amora) 114
Manasseh
    — king of Judah 44–46
    — tribe 14, 17, 19–20, 22
Manasseh ben Israel 269–270, 275,
    277–279, 312, 315
Mannheimer, Isaac Noah 346
Mansur, al- (caliph) 155
Manuel I (of Portugal) 256, 259
Mapu, Abraham 336
Marcus (family) 317
Marcus Aurelius (emperor) 103
Margarita, Antonius 286
Mariamme the Hasmonean 70, 82
Mark Antony 72
Markov, N. E. 356
Marks and Spencer 330
Marr, Wilhelm 353–354, 356
Marranos 312
Martha (sister of Lazarus) 80
Martin V (pope) 245–246
Martinez, Ferrant (archdeacon of
    Écija) 222–223

Mar Ukba, see Ukba, Mar
Marx, Karl 354
Mary (mother of Jesus) 77
Mary (sister of Lazarus) 80
Mary Magdalene 79–80
Mar Zutra, see Zutra, Mar
Maskilim 335–338
Mas'udi (Arab historian) 144
Mattathias 60–61
    See also Antigonus II
Matthias Corvinus (king of
    Hungary) 289
Mattnah (amora) 117
Maurras, Charles 356
Maximilian I (Holy Roman
    emperor) 235
Maximilian II 287
May Laws (Temporary Laws) 322,
    355
Mazdak 120
Medes 108
Medici, Giovanni de', see Leo X
Megabyzus (satrap) 54
Megaleh Temirin 336
Mehmed III (sultan) 289
Mein Kampf 354
Meir (brother of Joseph ben Baruch of
    Clisson) 190
Meir (tanna) 100, 109–110
Meir ben Baruch of Rothenburg
    (Maharam) 190, 199
Meir ben Samuel of Ramerupt 200
Menahem
    — king of Israel 37–38
    — son of Judas the Galilean 84–85
Menahem ibn Saruk 169
Menahem Mendel of Kotsk 341
Menahem Mendel of Rymanov 341
Menahem Mendel of Vitebsk 341
Menashe of Ilija 336
Mendele, Abraham 317
Mendele Mokher Sefarim 336, 365
Mendelsohn, Eric 331
Mendelssohn (family) 330
Mendelssohn, Joseph 330
Mendelssohn, Moses 335–336, 345
Mendes (family) 315, 317
Mendes, David Frank 336
Mendes-Nasi, Gracia, see Nasi, Gracia
Meshullam of Volterra 228–229
Meshullam Feibish of Zbarazh 341
Metro-Goldwyn-Mayer 331
Meunites 39
Micah (prophet) 35, 43
Michalovce Orthodox convention 346
Midianites 2, 8
    See also Ishmaelites
Midreshet Sede Boqer 362
Miguel de Morillo 241–242
Mikveh Israel (agricultural school) 366
Mikveh Israel
    — (in Curaçao) 313
    — (in Philadelphia) 313
    — (in Savannah) 313
Milano, Attilio 251
Mislawi Jews 394

Mithradates (king of Pontus) 66–68
Mitnagdim 337, 340, 344, 407
Mitrani, B. 336
Mizrachi 344, 348, 374–376
Mohammed (prophet) 334, 380
Mohammed Ali 385
Mohr, Abraham 336
Molcho, Solomon 268, 275–276
Mommsen, Theodor 354
Mongols 226–228, 289
Montagu, Samuel 330
Montefiore, Moses 360, 366–367, 382, 387
Montefiore Home 445
Morais, Sabato 352
Mordecai and Esther 395
Mordecai ben Hayyim 300
Mordecai ben Hillel 199, 213
Mordechai of Lachowicze 341
Mordechai of Nezchies 341
Moreh Nevukhei Ha-Zeman 336, 366
Morpugo (family) 336
Moses 8
Moses (Spanish court Jew) 151
Moses ben Hanokh 169
Moses ben Jacob of Coucy 200
Moses ben Judah of Kiev 269
Moses ben Maimon, *see* Maimonides
Moses de León 202–203
Moses Haparsi, *see* Abu Imran
Moses of Burgos 202
Moses of Zurich 238
Moshe Gaon 157
Moshe Leib of Sasov 341
Mossad le-Aliyah Bet, *see* Organization for "Illegal" Immigration
Mount Sinai Hospital 445
Moyne, Lord 436
Mstislav (prince of Cracow) 221
Mstislav the Brave 147
Muhammad 133–137
    See also Mohammed
Muhammad II 230, 262
Muhammad ibn Abdullah ibn Yahya (vizier) 158
Mu'izz, al- (caliph) 150, 162
Mundhir II (king) 170
Munk, Solomon 336
Muqtadir, al- (caliph) 158
Murabitun, al-, *see* Almoravids
Musar movement 344, 348–350
Mushka, Mushkanites 153
Muwahhidun, *see* Almohads
Myśl Karaimska 391

N

Nabateans 56–57, 65, 67, 70–71, 108
Nabonidus (king of Babylon) 53
Nabopolassar (king of Babylon) 48
Nadab (king of Israel) 30
Naftali of Ropczyce 341
Naharay ben Nissim 149
Nahawendi, Benjamin ben Moses al- 154–155
Nahman bar Isaac (*amora*) 119
Nahman bar Jacob (*amora*) 117, 119

Nahmanides (Ramban) 185, 188, 190–191, 204–206, 229, 249
Nahmanides of Gerona 195
Nahman of Bratslav 341
Nahman of Horodenka 341
Nahman of Kosov 341
Nahmias, David ibn 270
Nahmias, Samuel ibn 270
Nahum 394
Nahum of Chernobyl 341
Najara, Israel ben Moses 268
Najara, Jacob 299
Naphtali (tribe) 13–17, 19–20, 22
Napoleon Bonaparte 328–329, 333
Nasi, Gracia 265–266, 274
Nasi, Joseph 263, 265, 274
Nathan ben Jehiel 151, 193
Nathan Brothers 317
Nathan ha-Bavli (*tanna*) 109-110
Nathan of Gaza 298–300
National Anti-Jewish Party 356
National Library 362
National Religious Party 376
National Representation of the Jews in Germany, *see* Reichsvertretung der Juden in Deutschland
National Socialist German Workers Party (NSDAP) 421
Natonek, Joseph 366
Natorei Karta 344, 347
Navarro, Abraham 281
Nebuchadnezzar (Nebuchadrezzar) 50–51
Nebuzaradan 51
Neco II (king of Egypt) 48
Nefutseh Israel 313
Nefutzot Yehuda 312
Nehemiah 53–55, 64
Nehemiah (*tanna*) 109
Nehemiah ha-Kohen 298–299
Nehushta 50
Neiman-Marcus 331
Neologists; Neology 343, 346–347
Nero (emperor) 83, 92
Nerva (emperor) 103
Netira 158
Netter, Charles 366
Nevakhovich, Judah Leib 336
Neveh Shalom
    — (in Amsterdam) 312
    See also Talmud Torah
    — (in Surinam) 313
"New Christians" 312–313, 327
New York Public Library 363
New Zionist Organization 376
Nicholas I 322–323
Nicholas II 323
Nidhe Israel 313
Nietzsche, Friedrich 354
Nifoci, Isaac 228–229
Nissim of Kairouan 170
Normans, invasions of 144, 152, 168
North American Jewish Students Network 379
Notkin, Nata N. 336
Nuremberg Laws 420

O

Obadiah, *see* Abu Isa
Obadiah of Bertinoro 228–229, 245, 249
Occident, The 352
Octavian, *see* Augustus
Odessa Committee 372, 432
Ohab Tzedek synagogue 445
Ohel Leah synagogue 400
Ohio State University 363
Oleg 147
Omar 135–136
Omar II 334, 380
Onias (high priest) 58
"Operation Ezra and Nehemiah" 393–394
"Operation on Eagles' Wings" 397
Oppenheim, Abraham 330
Oppenheimer, Emanuel 317
Oppenheimer, Ernest 330
Oppenheimer, Joseph Suesskind 317
Oppenheimer, Samuel 316–317
Oppenheimer, Wolf 317
Ordoño I (king of Asturias) 171
Organization for "Illegal" Immigration 427
Organization of Teheran Jews 396
Orobio de Castro, Isaac 279, 312
ORT 395
Osorkon IV (king of Egypt) 41
Ostjuden 418
Othniel (son of Kenaz) 22
Otto I (the Great; Holy Roman emperor) 173
Otto II (Holy Roman emperor) 173
Otzar ha-Hochmah 336
Otzar Hatorah 395
Oxford Centre for Postgraduate Hebrew Studies 362

P

Pablo de Santa María 238–239
Pacorus (son of Ordes) 69
Pahlevi dynasty 335
Pahlevi, Reza Shah 395
Palaestina-Verein 366
Palestine Foundation Fund 374–375
Palestine Jewish Colonization Association, *see* PICA
Palestine Land Development Company 374
Palestine Zionist Office 373, 432–433
Palmach 436–437
Paltiel (10th cent. physician) 150, 152–153, 162
Pan-German League 356
Papa (*amora*) 120
Papa ben Nazer 117
Papa Saba (*amora*) 116
Paradesi synagogue 399
Paramount Pictures 331
Paris Peace Conference 402–404, 414
Parthians 69–70, 81, 115
Paul (apostle) 81
Paul III (pope) 184

Paul IV (pope)   272–273
Paul VI (pope)   184
Paz, Samuel de   300
Pedro (king of Portugal)   225
Peel Commission   435
Pekah (king of Israel)   37–39
Pekahiah (king of Israel)   37–38
"Pekidim and Amarkalim"   346
Penso de la Vega, Joseph   312
People's Theater   445
Perdiccas   57
Péreire Brothers   330
Peretz, Isaac Leib   336
Perl, Joseph   336
Perles, Isaac Meir   349
Perles, Meir   349
Perles, Moshe   349
Peter (apostle)   79
Peter III (of Aragón)   195
Peter IV (of Aragón)   217
Peter the Cruel (king of Castile)   222–223
Peter the Hermit   174–175, 177
Peter the Venerable)   181
Pethahiah of Regensburg   189, 200
Petter ben Joseph of Carinthia   200
Petlyura, Simon   403–404
Pfefferkorn, Johannes   286, 288
Pharisees   65, 76, 84, 89
Phasael (brother of Herod)   68–69
Philip II (Philip Augustus; king of France)   180–181, 201, 213
Philip II (king of Spain)   263–264, 272
Philip III (king of Spain)   275
Philip IV (the Fair; king of France)   211, 248, 250, 279
Philippson, Ludwig   346
Philistines   2, 6, 14, 16–18, 20, 23, 30–31, 38, 45
Philo (of Alexandria)   83
Phinehas bar Hama (amora)   114
Phoenicians   18, 44
   See also Sidonians
PICA   419
Pico della Mirandola, Giovanni   202
Pineles, Hirsch Mendel ben Solomon   336
Pinelo, Francisco   256
Pines, Yehiel Michel   336, 365–366, 371
Pinhas of Korets   341
Pinheiro, Moses   300
Pinsker, Leon (Judah Leib)   336, 366, 371
Pinsker, Simhah   336
Pires, Diogo, see Molcho, Solomon
Pirhei Zafon   336
Pittsburgh Convention; Pittsburgh Platform   343, 351–352
Plantation Act   333–334
Poalei Agudat Israel   344, 376
Poalei Zion   368–369, 374–376, 432
Pollack, Jacob ben Joseph   290
Polyakov, Eliezer   330
Polyakov, Samuel   330
Pompey   66–68, 81, 106
Pontius Pilate   74–75, 78

Poppers, Meir   269
Poryat, Moses   266
Prado, Juan de   279, 312
Priluk, Aryeh Loeb   269
Primo, Samuel   299
"Pro-Falasha Committees"   392
Protocols of the Elders of Zion   353–354
Proudhon, Pierre Joseph   354
Psammeticus II (king of Egypt)   50
Ptolemies   58–59
Ptolemy Lathyrus (king of Cyprus)   64–65
Ptolemy VI   62

Q, R

Quietus, Lusius   94
Ra'aya Meheimna (The Faithful Shepherd)   203
Raban, see Eliezer ben Nathan of Mainz
Rabbah bar Avuha (amora)   117
Rabbah bar Bar Hana (amora)   118
Rabbah bar Huna (amora)   118
Rabbah bar Nahmani (amora)   118–119
Rabbenu Tam (see Tam, Jacob ben Meir)
Rabbi Isaac Elchanan Yeshiva   352, 445
Rabbi Kook Institute   362
Rabbinical Assembly   352
Rabinovich, Osip Aronovich   336
Rabinowitz, A. E.   348
Rabshakeh (Assyrian officer)   43
Rachel (matriarch)   4
RaDBaZ, see David ben Solomon ibn Zimra
Radhanites   147–149, 234
Radicals Party   375
Rambam, see Maimonides
Ramban, see Nahmanides
Rameses II   18
Rameses III   2, 12, 23
Ramiro III (of Castile)   172
Raphael Joseph   298
Rapoport, Solomon Judah Leib   336, 361–362
Rappaport, Abraham Kohen   269
Rashba, see Adret, Solomon ben Abraham
Rashbam, see Samuel ben Meir
Rashi (Solomon ben Isaac)   173, 198–201, 250
Ratherius (bishop of Verona)   150, 152
Rav (amora)   116–117
Rava bar Joseph (amora)   119–120
Ravina (amora)   120
Ravyah, see Eliezer ben Joel ha-Levi
Raymond de Saint-Gilles   179
Raymond of Toulouse   177
Razsvet   336
Reali Secondary School   432
Rebekah (matriarch)   3
Reccared (king of Visigoths)   138–139
Reconstructionism   344, 352
Reconstructionist Rabbinical College   363

Reggio, Isacco Samuel   336
Rehoboam (king of Judah)   28, 30
Reichsvertretung der Juden in Deutschland   420
Reifmann, Jacob   336
Reines, Isaac Jacob   349, 371
Renan, Ernest   354
Reshit Hokhmah   268
Resh Lakish (amora)   111–113
Re'u (Egyptian general)   41
Reuben (tribe)   17, 19, 22
Reuchlin, Johannes   286
Reuveni, David   274–276
Reuwich, Erhard   228
Revenge (partisan unit)   424
Revisionists   375–376
   See also Union of Zionist Revisionists
Rezin (king of Damascus)   37–38
Riba, see Isaac ben Asher ha-Levi
Ricci, Matteo   282
Richard I (the Lion Hearted; king of England)   178, 180, 183
Rif, see Alfasi, Isaac ben Jacob
Rindfleisch massacres   213–215, 251
Ringelblum, Emanuel   425
Rivan, see Judah ben Nathan
Rizba, see Isaac ben Abraham
Robert (king of France)   250
Robert of Flanders   179
Robert of Normandy   177, 179
Rodeph Shalom Congregation   445
Rofe, Meir   300
Romaniots   230, 232, 291, 380, 387, 389
Romanus I Lecapenus   144–146
Rome and Jerusalem   366
Rosenberg, Samuel   349
Rosenheim, Jacob   348
Rosenthal, Naphtali   336
Rosh, see Asher ben Jehiel
Rothard (archbishop)   177
Rothschild (family)   331
   —, Baron Edmond de   366, 433
   —, James   330
   —, Karl Mayer   330
   —, Mayer Amschel   317
   —, Nathan   330
   —, Salomon Mayer   330
Rovigo, Abraham ben Michael   300
Rudolf I (of Hapsburg, king of Germany)   190
Rudolf II   289
Rudolph (Cistercian monk)   181
Ruediger (bishop)   173–174
Ruelf, Isaac   366
Rufus, Tinneius   96–97, 100
Ruppin, Arthur   432–433
Russian Social Democratic Party   370
Russischer juedischer wissenschaftlicher Verein (Russian-Jewish Scientific Society)   372, 378
Russkiy Yevrey   336

S

Saadiah Gaon   158–159, 161, 163

Saba, Abraham ben Jacob   269
Sachs, Michael   336
Sadducees   65, 76, 90
Safawid dynasty   394
Sahl ben Mazliah   164
Sahula, Isaac ben Solomon Abi   202
Saladin   181, 188, 191
Salih, Yahya   397
Salmon ben Jeroham   155
Salome (sister of Herod)   73, 75
Salomons, David   330
Samaritans   56–57, 67, 80, 96, 187–188
Samson (judge)   22
Samson ben Abraham of Sens   189,
   199–200
Samson ben Joseph of Falaise   200
Samuel (*amora*)   116-117
Samuel bar Judah (*amora*)   118
Samuel ben Adaya   136
Samuel ben Hofni   158, 167
Samuel ben Kalonymus he-Hasid of
   Speyer   201
Samuel ben Meir (Rashbam)   199–200
Samuel ben Nahman (*amora*)   112
Samuel ben Samson   190
Samuel d'Ortas   270
Samuel ha-Nagid (Samuel ben Joseph
   Halevi ibn Nagrela)   169–170
Samuel, Herbert   373
Sanballat (satrap)   56
Sancho III (the Great; king of
   Castile)   172
Sanhedrin   101–102, 104, 108, 110,
   113–115, 160, 329
San Remo Conference   373
Santangel, Luis de   256
Saphir, Jacob   397
Saracens   108
Sargon II (king of Assyria)   28, 41–42
Sarmiento, Pedro   240
Saronia   378
Sarug, Israel   269
Sasportas, Jacob   299
Sassanid dynasty/kingdom   115, 122,
   128
Sassoon (family)   399–400
Satanow, Isaac   336
Satmar Rebbe, *see* Teitelbaum, Joel
Saul (king of Israel)   8, 21, 23–24
Saul of Tarsus, *see* Paul (apostle)
Saxons   141
Scaurus (Roman commander)   66
Schechter, Solomon   352
Schick, Moses   349
Schiff, Jacob H.   331
   See also Kuhn and Loeb
Schocken department store   331
Schoenerer, Georg von   356
Schola peregrinorum (sect of
   foreigners)   141
Schorr, Joshua Heschel   336
Schreiner, Abraham   330
Schulman, Kalman   336
Schwartz, Abraham   349
Schwarz, Yehoseph   336
"Science of Judaism"   303, 337, 361, 363

Scouts movement   377
SD, *see* Sicherheitsdienst
Sears Roebuck   331
Secession Laws   345
Seckel, Moses   317
Sefer Dinim   155
Sefer Gezerot   131, 176
Sefer ha-Madda   204
Sefer ha-Massa'ot   185
Sefer ha-Meshiv   268
Sefer Haredim   268
Sefer Hasidim   201
Sefer ha-Yashar   200
Sefer ha-Zohar   202–203
Sefer Mitzvot   155
Sefer Mitzvot Gadol (*Se Ma G*)   200
Sefer Mitzvot Katan (*Semak*)   238
Seleucids   58, 61–62, 65–66
Seligman (family)   331
Selim I (sultan)   265, 274
Selim II (sultan)   263
Seljuks   164, 177
Sennacherib (Assyrian king)   42–45
Sephardic Jews (Sephardim)   230, 279,
   299
   See also Spanish-Portuguese Jews
Severus (bishop)   124–125
Severus (Roman emperor)
   —, Alexander   111
   —, Julius   96–98
   —, Septimius   106–107, 111
Sha'arei Kedushah   268
Sha'arei Tephillah Synagogue   445
Shabbetai Zevi; Shabbateanism   295,
   297–300, 338–339, 389, 397
Shallum (king of Israel)   37
Shalmaneser III   33, 35
Shalmaneser V   41–42
Shalom Shakhna ben Joseph   290
Shamash-shum-ukin   44
Shamgar (son of Anath)   13–14, 22
Shani, Isaac   269
Shapira (Hasidic dynasty)   349
Shapira, Nathan   269
Shapur I (Sassanian king)   115–117
Shapur II (Sassanian king)   118–119
Sharaf, Judah   299–300
Shearith Israel
   — (in Montreal)   313, 439
   — (in New York [New
      Amsterdam])   313, 445
Shemaiah (prophet)   28
Shemaiah of Troyes   200
Shenazzar (Sheshbazzar; son of
   Jehoiakim)   53
Shephatiah ben Shabbetai   150, 152–153
Sherira ben Hanina Gaon   159–161,
   167
Sheshet (*amora*)   117
Shilkanni, *see* Osorkon IV
Shimshon of Slonim   336
Shishak (king of Egypt)   30
Shivhei Habesht   339
Shneur Zalman of Lyady   341
Shobi (son of Nahash)   26
Sholal, Isaac ha-Kohen   265

Shomer Israel   336
Shulhan Arukh   268
Sicherheitsdienst   423
Sicut Judaeis (papal bull)
   — of Gregory I   139–140
   — of Gregory X   184
Sidonians   17–18, 61
   See also Phoenicians
Sidqia (of Ashkelon)   42–43
Sigismund (of Germany)   234
Sigismund II Augustus (king of
   Poland)   290–291
Sigismund III Vasa (king of
   Poland)   292
Silbermann, Eliezer Lipmann   336
Silva (family)   315, 317
Simeon, Simeonites (tribe)   4, 11, 17,
   19, 21–22, 48
Simeon Bar Giora, *see* Simon (son of
   Gioras)
Simeon bar Yohai   100, 109–110
Simeon ben Gamaliel (*tanna*)   109–110
Simeon ben Judah ha-Nasi   110
Simeon ben Lakish, *see* Resh Lakish
Simeon ben Pazzi (*amora*)   112
Simha Bunim of Przysucha   341
Simhah ben Samuel of Vitry   200
Simlai (*amora*)   112
Simon (son of Gioras)   85–87
Simon, James   330
Simon Maccabeus   64
Simon of Sens   190, 192
Simon of Trent   184
Simon the Just   57
Sinzheim, Joseph David   328
Sinzheim, Loew   317
Sisebut (king of Spain)   138–139
Sisenand (king of Spain)   139
Sisera   12, 14–16
Sivan   336
Sixtus IV (pope)   235, 241–242, 246
Slobodka yeshiva   349
Slonimsky, Hayyim Selig   336
Small Congress   374
Smolenskin, Peretz   336, 365–366
Social Darwinism   353–354
Social Reich Party   356
Society for Jewish Statistics   362
Society for Jewish Studies (S.E.J.)   362
Society for the Advancement of Jewish
   Scholarship, *see* Gesellschaft zur
   Foerderung der Wissenschaft des
   Judentums
Society for the Promotion of Culture
   Among the Jews of Russia   336
Society for the Support of Jewish
   Farmers and Artisans in Syria and
   Palestine   372
Society of the Friends of Reform   346
Sofer, Moses ("Hatam Sofer")   345,
   347, 349–350
Sofer, Simon   348
Sokolow, Nahum   336
Solal, *see* Sholal, Isaac ha-Kohen
Solomon (grandson of Simon of
   Sens)   192

Solomon (king of Israel) 19, 21, 26–28
Solomon ben Abraham Adret, *see*
  Adret, Solomon ben Abraham
Solomon ben Abraham of
  Montpellier 205–206
Solomon ben Isaac, *see* Rashi
Solomon ben Judah (gaon) 165
Solomon ben Samson 175
Solomon ben Samuel (Petit) 205–206
Solomon ha-Levi, *see* Pablo de Santa
  María
Soloveichik, Hayyim 348–349
Soncino, Gershom ben Moses 271
Sonnenberg, Libermann von 356
South African Jewish Board of
  Deputies 449
Soviet Communist Party 368, 370
  See also Yevsektsia
Spanish-Portuguese Jews 302, 312–
  315, 331, 340, 381, 383–384, 387, 389,
  399, 402, 415–418, 439, 441, 442, 446
  See also Sephardic Jews (Sephardim)
Spencer, Herbert 354
Spertus College of Jewish Studies 363
Speyer (family) 331
Spinoza, Baruch 279
Spior, Nathan ben Reuben 269
SS 423
Status Quo Ante 346
Statutum de Judaismo 210
Steinschneider, Moritz 362
Stephen (king of England) 181
Stern, Bezalel 336
Stern, Max Emanuel (Mendel) 336
Stern Group 436–437
Stieglitz, E. 330
Stoecker, Adolf 356
Stroop, Juergen (Josef) 425–426
Students' Antisemitic League 356
Suess, Jud, *see* Oppenheimer, Joseph
  Suesskind
Sulamith 336, 346
Suleiman I (the Magnificent) 169, 262–
  263, 289
Sviatoslav (prince of Kiev) 145, 147
Sykes-Picot Agreement 435
"Synthetic Zionism" 371, 373
Syrkin, Nachman 371

T

Tabal (Tabel) 38
Tageblat 445
Taharka, *see* Tirhaka
Taitazak, Joseph 268–269
Talmud Torah 312
Tam, Jacob ben Meir (Rabbenu
  Tam) 181, 199–200
Tamar (daughter-in-law of Judah) 4
Tamerlane, *see* Timur
Tancred 179
Tanhuma bar Abba (*amora*) 114
"Tarbut" (school network) 365
Tarfon (*tanna*) 90, 99, 102
Tarta, Isaac de Castro 282
Tefnakhte, *see* Osorkon IV
Teitelbaum, Joel 347

Teitelbaum, Moshe 341
Teixeira, Diego Abraham 315, 317
Tel Aviv University 362
Temple Beth El 445
Temple Emanu-El 352, 445
Temple Society 346
Temple University 363
Temporary Laws, *see* May Laws
Ten Lost Tribes 228, 277
Teudah Be-Yisrael 336
Theodoric (king of the
  Ostrogoths) 139
Theodosius I (emperor) 122
Theodosius II (emperor) 114, 122
Thutmose III 4, 14, 47
Thutmose IV 13
Tiberius (emperor) 74–75, 82, 103
Tiberius Alexander (Roman
  procurator) 83
Tiflisites (religious sect) 153
Tiglath-pileser I 33
Tiglath-pileser III 37–41
Tikkunei ha-Zohar 203
Timur (Tamerlane) 226
Tirhaka (Taharka) 43–44
Titus (emperor) 86–87, 124
Toi (king of Hamath) 27
Tola (son of Puah) 22
Toldot Yaacov Yoseph 341
Toledano, Eliezer 270
Toleranzpatenten 324–325
Tomer Devorah 268
Torah Vaavodah 376
Torquemada, Tomás de 184, 241
Tosafists 199
Tota (queen of Navarre) 172
Touansa 384
Toussenel, Alphonse 354
Trajan (emperor) 93–94, 103–104,
  106–107
Trani, Moses 265
Treitschke, Heinrich von 353–355
Tryphon (regent) 63
Tsamtsam a-Dullah 151
Tugendhold, Jacob 336
Tunisian Jewish Welfare Fund 384
Turbo (Roman commander) 93
Twentieth-century Fox 331
Twenty-first Street cemetery 445
Tyrians 46
Tzeirei Zion 403
Tzur Israel 313

U

Uganda Scheme 371, 373
Ukba, Mar (exilarch) 116
Ullman, Samuel 317
Union for Liberal Judaism in
  Germany 346
Union of American Hebrew
  Congregations 352
Union of Jewish Students, *see* Verein
  juedischer Studenten
Union of Orthodox Hebrew
  Congregations 346
Union of Orthodox Jewish

Congregations of America 352
Union of Radical Zionists 374
Union of the Russian People 356
Union of Zionist Revisionists 374
  See also Revisionists
United Christians 356
United Nations Special Commission on
  Palestine 435, 437
United Nobility 356
United Synagogue 346
United Synagogue of America 352
University Library
  — (in Amsterdam) 362
  — (in Cambridge) 362
University of Arizona 363
University of California, Berkeley 363
University of California, Los Angeles
  363
University of Denver 363
University of Florida 363
University of Judaism 363
University of Maryland 363
University of Pennsylvania 363
University of Toronto 363
University of Washington 363
University of Wisconsin 363
UNSCOP, *see* United Nations Special
  Commission on Palestine
Urban II (pope) 177
Urban V (pope) 244
Uri of Strelisk 341
Usatges, Book of (Book of Usages) 171
Uzziah (king of Judah) 35–36

V

Vaad Haaratzot, *see* Council of the
  Lands
Va'ad ha-Kehillot 447–448
Vaballathus (Palmyrene ruler) 112
Valerian (emperor) 112
Valerius Gratus (prefect) 75
Verein juedischer Studenten
  (VJSt) 378
Vespasian (emperor) 90, 92, 104, 107,
  124
Viadrina 378
Villena, marquis of 241
Vincent Ferrer (friar) 224, 240
Visigoths 128, 138–139
Vital, Hayyim ben Joseph 268
Vitold (grand duke of Lithuania) 220–
  221
Vladislav II (king of Bohemia) 287
Vogelsang, Karl von 356
Volkmar 175–176
Voltaire 354
Voskhod 336, 338
Vratislav II (king of Bohemia) 173, 176

W

Wagner, Richard 354
Wandervogel 377
Wannsee Conference 422
Warburg (family) 330
Warner Brothers 331

Wecelinus 174
Weizmann, Chaim 373, 376, 403
Weizmann Archives 362
Wertheimer (family) 317
Wessely, Naphtali Herz 336
West India Company 315
West London synagogue 346
Westphalia, Treaty of 327
William (Christian child) 184
William Carpenter (viscount of
  Melun) 175–176
William of Blois (bishop of
  Worcester) 210
Windsor Theater 445
Wise, Isaac Mayer 343, 352
Wissenschaft des Judenthums, see
  "Science of Judaism"
Wolf, Joseph 346
Wolf of Zbarazh, Rabbi 341
Wolfson, Isaac 330
Women's International Zionist
  Organization (WIZO) 374
World Union of Jewish Studies 362
World Union of Progressive Judaism
  346
World Zionist Organization 348, 368,
  372–376, 397, 432
Wulf, Moses Benjamin 317
Wulff (family) 317

Y

Yad Vashem Institute 362
Yahya, Imam 398
Yakhini, Abraham 300
Yale University 363
Yannai (amora) 111
Yaqub ibn Killis 162
Yaroslav the Wise 147

YaSHaR of Candia, see Delmedigo,
  Joseph Solomon
Yavneh 379
Yavnieli, Shmuel 397
Yeger 424
Yehuda (family) 399
Yellin, David 365
Yeshevav the Scribe 99
Yeshiva University 352, 363
Yeshuat Israel 313
Yevsektsia 368, 370
  See also Soviet Communist Party
Yezdegerd I 119
Yezdegerd II 119
Yiddish Rialto 445
Yitshaki, David 299
YIVO Institute for Jewish Research
  — (in New York) 363
  — (in Vilna) 362
Yose (amora) 114
Yose (tanna) 100, 109–110
Yose bar Hanina (amora) 112
Yose ben Avin (amora) 114
Yose ben Halafta (tanna) 109
Yose ben Joezer 60
Young Judea 377
Young Men's Benevolent Association
  445
Young Men's Hebrew Association 445
"Young Turks" 335, 390
Yudghan 153–154
Yusuf ibn Tashfin 166, 168
Yusuf ibn Ziri 165

Z

Zacchaeus 80
Zacuto, Abraham ben Samuel 259
Zahir, al- (caliph) 162

Zalman Shazar Center for Jewish
  History 362
Zamosc, Israel 336
Zayyah, Joseph ben Abraham ibn 269
Zealots 76, 84, 87, 89
Zebidah 46
Zebulun (tribe) 13, 14–15, 17, 19–20, 22
Zechariah (king of Israel) 37
Zedekiah (king of Judah) 50
Zederbaum, Alexander 336
Ze'eira (amora) 108, 113, 119
Zeitlin, Joshua 336
Zemah, Jacob 269
Zeno (Byzantine emperor) 129
Zenobia (Palmyrene ruler) 112, 117
Zephira 378
Zerah the Cushite 31
Zerubbabel 53
Zeta Beta Tau Fraternity 379
Zevi, Mordecai 297
Zevi, Sarah 297
Zevi, Shabbetai, see Shabbetai Zevi
Zevid (amora) 120
Zev Wolf of Zhitomir 341
Zimberlin, John 215
Zionist (Basel) Program 372
Zionist Commission 373
Zionist Congress 372–376
Zionist Executive 374
Zionist Organization of America
  (ZOA) 378
Zizat Novel Zevi 299
ZOB, see Jewish Fighting Organization
Zoref, Joshua Heshel ben Joseph 300
Zoroastrian priesthood, see Magis
Zunz, Leopold 361–362
Zutra I, Mar (exilarch) 119–120
Zutra II, Mar (exilarch) 120